DATE DUE

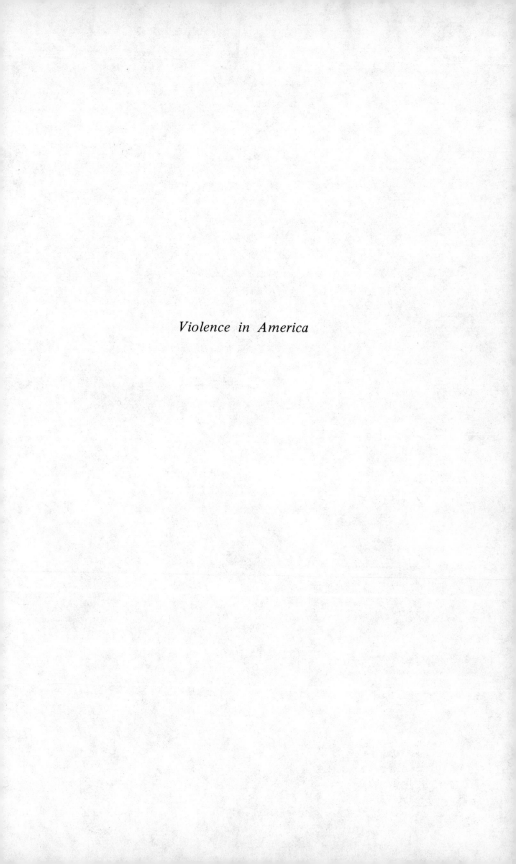

Violence in America

VIOLENCE IN AMERICA

Historical & Comparative Perspectives

revised edition

Hugh Davis Graham
Ted Robert Gurr
Editors

Preface by
Milton S. Eisenhower

 **SAGE PUBLICATIONS** Beverly Hills London

To Janet and Erika

For information address:

SAGE PUBLICATIONS, INC.
275 South Beverly Drive
Beverly Hills, California 90212

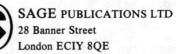

SAGE PUBLICATIONS LTD
28 Banner Street
London ECIY 8QE

Printed in the United States of America

Library of Congress Cataloging in Publication Data
Graham, Hugh Davis
  Violence in America.

  Report of the Task Force on Historical and
Comparative Perspectives to the National Commission
on the Causes and Prevention of Violence.
  Includes bibliographies and index.
  1. Violence – United States.   I. Gurr, Ted Robert, 1936-
joint author.   II. United States. National Commission on the Causes
and Prevention of Violence. Task Force on Historical and Comparative
Perspectives.   III. United States. National Commission on the
Causes and Prevention of Violence. IV. Title. V. Title: Violence in
America.
HN90.V5G7 1979   301.6'33'0973   78-21934
ISBN 0-8039-9063-2
ISBN 0-8039-0964-0 pbk.

FIRST PRINTING

CONTENTS

ABOUT THE EDITORS

HUGH DAVIS GRAHAM is professor of history at the University of Maryland Baltimore County. He has specialized in the study of politics in the American South and the role of violent conflict in American history. He received the Ph.D. from Stanford University in 1964 and taught at San Jose State College, Stanford, and Johns Hopkins University. From 1972 to 1977 he was dean of the division of social sciences at the University of Maryland Baltimore County. Among his writings are *Crisis in Print* (Vanderbilt University Press, 1967); *Violence* (Johns Hopkins University Press, 1971); *Desegregation* (Harper and Row, 1972); and *Southern Politics and the Second Reconstruction,* coauthored with Numan V. Bartley (Johns Hopkins University Press, 1975), which won the Chastain Award of the Southern Political Science Association as the best book on Southern politics in 1975. In 1968-1969 he was codirector, with Ted Robert Gurr, of the Historical and Comparative Task Force of the National Commission on the Causes and Prevention of Violence, and coeditor with Gurr of the first edition of *Violence in America* (U.S. Government Printing Office, 1969). In 1970-71 he held a Guggenheim Fellowship and also has received research grants from the Social Science Research Council and the National Endowment for the Humanities.

TED ROBERT GURR is Payson S. Wild Professor of political science at Northwestern University and began a three-year term as chairperson of the department in 1977. His research has focused on political conflict, authority, and institutional change since 1965, when he received his Ph.D. from New York University. He was a research associate of the Center of International Affairs at Princeton University and taught at Princeton and New York University before joining the Northwestern faculty in 1970. His 1970 book, *Why Men Rebel* (Princeton University Press), received the American Political Science Association's Woodrow Wilson Prize as the year's best book in political science. He is author or editor of a dozen other books and monographs, among them *Politimetrics* (Prentice-Hall, 1972); *Patterns of Authority,* coauthored with Harry Eckstein (Wiley-Interscience, 1975); *Rogues, Rebels, and Reformers* (Sage Publications, 1976); and The *Politics of Crime and Conflict,* coauthored with Peter N. Grabosky and Richard C. Hula (Sage Publications, 1977). In 1968-1969 he codirected the Historical and Comparative Task Force of the National Commission on the Causes and Prevention of Violence. In 1970 he was a visiting fellow of the Richardson Institute of Peace and Conflict Research (London), and in 1976 was a visiting fellow at the Institute of Criminology, University of Cambridge. He has held a Ford Faculty Fellowship, a Guggenheim Fellowship, and a Senior Fellowship from the German Marshall Fund of the United States.

PREFACE
Milton S. Eisenhower

Ten years ago, when the National Commission of the Causes and Prevention of violence decided to publish the reports of our research task forces, we had no idea that our report, *Violence in America*, would quickly become a nationwide best seller. In the spring of 1968 our nation was torn by racial violence in the cities, antiwar protest and rebellion on many campuses, and anguish and rage over the assassinations of Robert Kennedy and Dr. Martin Luther King, Jr. In June, President Lyndon Johnson asked me to serve as chairman of the Commission, whose mission was to "go as far as man's knowledge takes it" in searching out the causes of violence and the means of preventing it. We in turn sought out the best minds to staff our research task forces, customarily pairing a laywer and a social scientist to direct research and recommend policy alternatives on such broad subjects as violent crime and criminal justice, firearms control, the role of the mass media, political assassinations, and racial and student protest, and also to investigate violent episodes that had occurred in Chicago, Miami, and Cleveland. Hence our executive director was a prominent lawyer, Lloyd N. Cutler, and our codirectors of research were distinguished sociologists, Marvin E. Wolfgang and James F. Short, Jr. They directed an ambitious research program involving two hundred scholars, supplemented by important contributions of an advisory panel, academic and youth conferences, and 19 days of public hearings. The capstone of 18 months' effort was the commission's final report, *To Establish Justice, To Insure Domestic Tranquility*, issued in December 1969.

We decided at the outset that our analysis should be informed by an understanding of the historical roots of violent conflict in America, interpreted in the light of the experience of other nations, whose past and present so often seemed less turbulent than ours. So our first task force was asked to survey the historical and comparative evidence; we appointed as its codirectors a Princeton political scientist, Ted Robert Gurr, and a Johns Hopkins historian, Hugh Davis Graham. They faced formidable problems. Studies of violence in American history were usually episodic and anecdotal, and rarely offered generalizations that might help interpret the present. Comparative studies, on the other hand, were quick to generalize but were often suspect because of unresolved disputes about theory, methods, and evidence. Nonetheless, Graham and Gurr were able to enlist 29 scholars, who surveyed the best historical and comparative evidence about violence to be found in the fields of history, law, and the social and behavioral sciences. They did so in a remarkably short time. Their report, *Violence in America: Historical and Comparative Perspectives*, was released on June 5, 1969, the anniversary of Robert Kennedy's assassination. It offered an uncompromising portrait of a nation whose past was often marred by violence, but it showed by comparison with other nations that the American experience, though more extensive and voluminous, was neither unique nor beyond explanation and remedy.

Violence in America was issued as Volumes 1 and 2 of an eventual total of 13 research reports to the Commission. The Government Printing Office edition was shortly followed by paperback editions from Bantam and New American Library (Signet), and a clothbound edition by Frederick Praeger. Widespread attention was focused on the report by the mass media and, as a result, *Violence in America* not only found an immediate mass market but subsequently became a standard text in college classrooms throughout the nation, with several hundred thousand copies in use. It has been in the public domain from first publication, and many of its contributions have been reprinted elsewhere.

The tumult of the 1960s which inspired the commission to look for historical insights has itself become history. Many Americans wish to blot out the memory of the Vietnam War and resistance to it; the exploding campuses and burning cities; the contagion of political assassinations. But not even the most sanguine among us can believe that the sources of violence in American society have vanished or diminished. The dark side of American tradition in which some find a rationale for violence still broods on the edge of memory. Demonstrations may have gone temporarily out of fashion, but invidious distinctions continue to be made among racial and ethnic groups, and between the sexes. Added to them are higher rates of inflation and unemployment and a chronic energy crisis, all of which threaten economic well-being and social peace. So crime rates have soared even higher than their levels in the 1960s. Riots are rare now, but there is a horrifying escalation of hostage-taking and terrorism for innumerable private and political motives, as well as for all other categories of violent crime. Self-styled revolutionaries are mostly silent, but extremist groups like the Ku Klux Klan and American Nazi Party are noisily active.

In response to the persistence of old issues and the emergence of new ones, Professors Gurr and Graham have thoroughly revised *Violence in America*. Many of the original chapters have been retained and updated to take into account a decade of events that have altered trends and changed perspectives. They ask, for example, what happened to race riots and student protest. Are they as much a closed chapter as the violent labor-management struggles of an earlier era? Ten other chapters have been omitted to make way for treatments of new topics, such as the new militance of native Americans, the cross-national rise in common crime, and the international spate of terrorism. Other new chapters, including several by the editors, offer new interpretations of the social and political origins and the limits of democratic tolerance of dissent and disorder.

Americans can take legitimate pride in the recent progress we have made— movement toward racial equality, an end to the brutal Vietnam War and the inequitable draft, a peaceful resolution of a severe constitutional crisis, and overall the maintenance of common faith in the fairness and responsiveness of our basic American institutions. We know too that many of our most persistent problems are international in scope, and indeed some are often more severe in other societies. Yet we must also be aware that others, such as the legacy of slavery and our historic devotion to firearms, are peculiar to our past. Worst of all, violent crime in our country is 50 percent greater now than when the Commission made its report to the President. The situation is so bad that it threatens the quality of American life. In our final report to the President in 1969, the Commission observed that the United States has shown a remarkable capacity for responding to crises and moving on to higher pinnacles of power and achievement, especially in the face of external challenges. But we also observed that when in mankind's long history other great civilizations fell, it was less often from external assault than from internal decay. Our conclusion then is no less apt today: "The greatness and durability of most civilizations has been finally determined by how they have responded to these challenges from within. Ours will be no exception."

EDITORS' INTRODUCTION

Hugh Davis Graham and Ted Robert Gurr

A decade has passed since the original publication of *Violence in America* in 1969. As Milton Eisenhower observes in the preface to this revised edition, the original edition, which was published by the U.S. Government Printing Office, was promptly reprinted by three major trade publishers (Bantan, Praeger, and Signet) for a combined circulation in excess of 300,000, and the volume quickly became a classroom standard. All editions are now out of print, and the classroom vacuum thus created might have been filled easily and relatively inexpensively by reprinting a minimally revised edition (since virtually all of the original contributions were in the public domain). But we as coeditors, and Sage Publications, have chosen not to do so for several substantial reasons.

First, the decade of the 1970s has produced an altered perspective that could not have been anticipated from the mood of the late 1960s, when antiwar violence, campus turmoil, ghetto riots, and a contagion of political assassinations generated a kind of apocalyptic perception that the seams of American society were coming apart. Yet today, a decade hence, the Vietnam War and military conscription are curiously dim recollections; the campuses are calm and underpopulated; the ghettos rot quietly in the aftermath of their explosive destruction; and political assassinations seem to prompt more reinvestigation than fear. In hindsight, our original if understandable concentration in *Violence in America* on why violence flared seems inadequately balanced by attention to why and how it recedes or changes its form.

A second endowment of the 1970s is the emergence of new issues and forms of violence, such as those involving the rights of American Indians and the demands of revolutionary groups given to bombing, hijacking, and kidnapping. These, together with a sharpened debate over the origins and dimensions of crime—ranging from the street corner, through corporate boardrooms, to the sanctuaries of high public office—require new description and analysis, just as the recession of the antiwar, student, and racial forms of collective violence require reassessment.

Yet a third reason for a thoroughgoing revision is the decade's accumulation of interdisciplinary research that should be taken into account in new and revised analyses alike—more on that in a moment. Add to this the opportunity posed by a revision to cull elements of redundancy and shopworn views from the rather massive original edition, and the result is both a more timely and lean analysis that omits half of the first edition's 22 chapters. Furthermore, of those retained only four have kept their original form, i.e., Louis Hartz's comparative analysis of fragment cultures in

13

Chapter 4, Kenneth Lynn's literary study in Chapter 5, Sheldon Hackney's classic essay on Southern violence in Chapter 15, and Bernard Siegel's theoretical analysis of American groups that have responded defensively to threatening circumstances in Chapter 18. The remaining seven of the original chapters have been revised for the new edition, primarily to take into account subsequent events, but also to reflect subsequent research, and their reference notes represent a unique bibliographical resource. Finally, nine of the revised edition's 20 chapters are new. These include four by the editors (one by Graham and three by Gurr), and five especially commissioned essays by newcomers to the anthology: G. David Garson and Gail O'Brien on the Reconstruction South in Chapter 8; Jeanne Guillemin on American Indians in Chapter 10; J. Bowyer Bell (together with Ted Robert Gurr) on revolutionary terrorism in Chapter 12; Wesley Skogan on contemporary American crime in Chapter 14; and Richard Libman-Rubenstein on political group violence in Chapter 17.

What is not new is the conceptual approach to the study, which reflects our original commitment to combining the vertical dimension of historical analysis with the horizontal or comparative dimension that is implicit in the social and behavioral disciplines, and is most explicit in cross-national research, where American patterns of violence are compared with those thoroughout the world. Yet when our original study was published, the behavioralism that dominated the social sciences had blunted their historical awareness; and history, for its part, had retained too much of its national parochialness. Hence the original *Violence in America* combined the historical and comparative perspectives (as the subtitle attests), but too often in a somewhat compartmentalized fashion, with separate parts devoted to historical background and cross-national comparison. They alternated more than combined historical and social scientific analyses of such specific issues as the frontier, labor, race, revolution, and the like. Today many behavioral scientists have rediscovered both their modesty and their need for historical analysis, and historians are becoming increasingly sophisticated about the concepts and methods of rigorous social research. Hence, also, this revised study combines the historical and comparative perspectives in a more integrated fashion, beginning in Part I with an overview of American patterns of violence by historian Richard Maxwell Brown, and political scientist Ted Robert Gurr's comparison of the United States and worldwide patterns of political protest and rebellion during the 1960s. Part II is further testimony to the interdisciplinary blending of history and social scientific comparison, as the historical roots of modern collective violence are explored by sociologist Charles Tilly, political scientist Louis Hartz, and literary and intellectual historian Kenneth Lynn.

Six specific issues which have given rise to violent conflict in America are addressed in Part III: public order on the frontier, workers' rights, race relations, opposition to war, the rights of American Indians, and revolutionary change. A separate section, Part IV, is devoted to the persistent and volatile issue of violent crime, and advances striking and highly controversial interpretations of common historical crime waves in Western society, the causes of the apparent decline of serious crime in the United States in the late 1970s, and cultural as opposed to strictly sociological explanations of murder and suicide. Part V offers some alternative (and not necessarily congenial) explanations of the processes of rebellion and adjustment, and in Part VI the editors offer some conclusions on the apparent paradox of coexisting violence and institutional stability in the United States and Western Europe, and on alternative strategies of response to poltical violence in democratic societies.

But if we claim a common commitment to interdisciplinary research that is self-consciously both historical and comparative, it should be understood that this book is not organized around a single, general theory about the nature or causes of social violence. On the contrary, the contributors take account of a number of theoretical approaches. The importance of frustrated expectations is emphasized by James C. Davies in Chapter 16, while Louis Hartz highlights the importance of cultural and ideological factors in Chapter 4. For Charles Tilly, in Chapter 3, popular frustrations and beliefs are less important than the ways in which people are organized for collective action. All of the contributors recognize that the structure of a society ultimately determines the shifting pattern of challenge and response among groups. A Marxist interpretation of American society is used by Libman-Rubenstein in Chapter 17, while Tilly takes the less deterministic position that the form and content of violent conflict depends on whether the groups involved are seeking, maintaining, or losing their grip on power. Bernard Siegel complements Tilly's analysis by asking in Chapter 18 about the strategy and fate of powerless minorities. Historical analysis itself is put to different purposes. In Chapter 7 Philip Taft and Philip Ross treat labor-management violence as a closed episode in American history, one which offers few lessons for the future. Robin Brooks emphasizes the limitations of historical analysis for understanding Americans' opposition to the Vietnam War in Chapter 10, but also criticizes our dangerous and willful blindness to the historical precedents. And in Chapter 9, Morris Janowitz identifies historical stages in the shape of racial violence, which he interprets as reflections of developmental changes in American society and culture.

In short, many theoretical positions are represented in this book. But there are two views that will not be found here. None of the contributors supposes that violence in America is mainly the result of the willful malevolence of conspirators or the irrational behavior of the dregs of society. Conspirators, madmen, and social outcasts have played some small dramatic parts in American violence, but to give them larger credit or blame is a fundamental misunderstanding of the real social and political meanings of the history of violence in America.

Part I
Historical and Comparative Perspectives
An Overview

Preliminary to any analysis of the role of violence in America, whether historical or comparative, is the task of surveying its historical occurrence. In Chapter 1 historian Richard Maxwell Brown describes the forms, extent, and transformations of American violence in a survey that is ever mindful of its Janus-faced quality, endowing us with a legacy of violent means that is richly associated both with good and evil ends. Collective violence attended both our national birth in the Revolution and our national preservation and the expurgation of slavery in the Civil War. But the legacy of both those noble conflagrations included class and racial warfare, lethal family and clan feuds, political assassination, and the haunting notion that might makes right for the winners. The forces of law and order were necessarily brought to bear on rural and frontier social bandits and modern urban criminals, but often for the socially conservative purposes of protecting the class distinctions and property distributions of the status quo. Vigilante justice was dominated by community elites more often than by spontaneous mobs, and the intense group competition encouraged by American pluralism itself invited scapegoating against unpopular minorities. Brown's extensive documentation constitutes a uniquely comprehensive bibliographical guide to the historical literature on American violence. Although his essay is primarily descriptive, he has prepared in Chapter 6 a theoretical analysis of the American vigilante tradition.

But the historical dimension demands its comparative complement, for how else can we make judgments about whether American patterns of violence differ in meaningful degrees and ways from those of other societies? In Chapter 2 political scientist Ted Robert Gurr provides this dimension of cross-national analysis by comparing patterns of collective violence during the tumultous 1960s. Specifically, Gurr analyzes patterns of protest and rebellion (while carefully defining the difference between the two) in 87 of the larger countries of the world (which contain 73 percent of its people—or 95 percent of those outside China) where reasonably accurate data were available. Gurr's data base, which includes more than 2200 episodes of civil strife, enables him to show how nations of different political characteristics and varying levels of economic development compare in severity of conflict, types of social groups and organizations involved, and issues of conflict.

From these comparisons emerge a basic pattern. Protest and rebellion in the United States in the 1960s were more widespread and intense (proportional to population) that in all but the largest countries of Western Europe and the British Commonwealth. On the other hand, it was far less widespread and lethal than in many nations of Latin America, Africa, and Asia. Although some six million Americans participated in the civil rights, antiwar, and campus turmoil of the 1960s, 80 percent of these were involved in peaceful and legal demonstrations. In a world in which the gun and not the ballot is the predominant arbiter of public affairs, and dissent from official orthodoxy has either taken the form of bloody revolt or brutal repression, most dissident citizens of the United States, and of the Western democracies generally, were protesting rather than rebelling, and did so far more often peacefully than violently.

The historical and comparative evidence of this part suggests a paradoxical relationship, one in which Western-style democracy encourages citizen participation and demands that include protest and occasionally violent civil strife, but which rarely strike rebelliously at the heart of democratic institutions.

Chapter 1
Historical Patterns of
American Violence

RICHARD MAXWELL BROWN

Violence has accompanied virtually every stage and aspect of our national existence. Our most heroic episode, the Revolution, was shot through with domestic violence in both its origins and its progress. During the Civil War, when the slave gained freedom and the unity of our country was preserved, internal violence flared behind the lines of the bloodily contending Northern and Southern armies. Nor did the violence pale in the postwar period, which turned out to be one of the most turbulent epochs in American history.

One significant feature of the Revolution is that the example of violent resistance to the mother country, and all the acts of violence associated with that great event, served as a grand model for later violent actions by Americans in behalf of any cause—law and order, for example—deemed good and proper, for a salient fact of American violence is that, time and again, it has been the instrument not merely of the criminal and disorderly but of the most upright and honorable. Thus, in our two great national crises—the Revolution and the Civil War—we called on violence to found and to preserve the nation.

Apart from its role in the formation and preservation of the nation, violence has been a determinant of both the form and the substance of American life. The threat to the structure of society mounted by the criminal and the disorderly has been met energetically by the official and unofficial violence of the forces of law and order. Often perceiving a grave menace to social stability in the unsettled conditions of frontier life and racial, ethnic, urban, and industrial unrest, solid citizens rallied to

AUTHOR'S NOTE: *Richard Maxwell Brown is Beekman Professor of Northwest and Pacific history at the University of Oregon. Formerly he taught at Rutgers University and the College of William and Mary. He is author of* The South Carolina Regulators *(Harvard University Press, 1963) and* Strain of Violence: Historical Studies of American Violence and Vigilantism *(Oxford University Press, 1975). He has edited several other volumes, the most recent of which is* Tradition, Conflict, and Modernization: Perspectives on the American Revolution, *coedited with D.E. Fehrenbacher (Academic Press, 1977). He is continuing his research on American vigilantism and is also at work on a book on the Mussel Slough conflict, upon which Frank Norris based his novel,* The Octopus.

This chapter is from *Strain of Violence: Historical Studies of American Violence and* Vigilantism, *by Richard Maxwell Brown. Copyright© 1975 by Oxford University Press, Inc. Reprinted by permission.*

the cause of community order. They did this indirectly by granting to the police and other duly constituted agents of the community the power to commit violence to preserve order. Not confining themselves to passive approval of police action, these upright citizens revealed their deep commitment to community order by their own violent participation in lynch mobs and vigilante movements and related extralegal bodies. Violence, thus employed, has been socially conservative. Whether employed legally or extralegally, it has been used to support the cohesive, three-tiered structure of the American community with its upper, middle, and lower classes and its underlying social values of law and order and the sanctity of property. The second part of this overview, then, deals broadly with the challenge to the respectable community posed by the criminal, murderous, turbulent, depressed elements of American life and the violent response to this challenge by the established order.

Much American violence has related not only to the structure of the community but to the substance of the American experience—the nature and content of our society. In this connection, violence has characterized the struggle of American groups in conflict from the colonial period to the present. Group hostility has often escalated to the level of violence in white-Indian wars, white-black confrontations, ethnic rivalries, religious vendettas, agrarian uprisings, and the struggles of laborers against industrialists. Here, too, the violence has been tinctured with social conservatism. Established groups have been quick to resort to violence in defense of the status quo they dominate.

In one way or another, much of our nineteenth- and twentieth-century violence has represented the attempt of established Americans to preserve their favored position in the social, economic, and political order. This seems to be the true significance of much of the urban rioting of the nineteenth century, of the industrial violence down to the 1930s, and of the twentieth-century race riots. Conversely, the unsympathetic and unyielding stance of established power in the face of rightly aggrieved groups has frequently incited insurgent violence that stretches from the afflicted yeomanry and lower gentry, who enlisted in Bacon's Rebellion in late seventeenth-century Virginia, to the distressed urban black rioters of our own generation.[1]

I

Our nation was conceived and born in violence—in the violence of the Sons of Liberty and the patriots of the American port cities of the 1760s and 1770s. Such was the Boston Massacre of 1770, in which five defiant Americans were killed by British officers and troops who were goaded by patriotic roughnecks. The whole episode was a natural continuation of nearly a century of organized mob violence in Boston. The same was true of the Boston Tea Party, wherein the ancient, organized South End Mob of Boston was enlisted in the tea-dumping work. During the long years of resistance to British policy in the 1760s and 1770s, the North End and South End Mobs, under the leadership of Henry Swift and Ebenezer Mackintosh, had been more or less at the beck and call of Samuel Adams, the mastermind of patriot agitation, and of the middle-class partriots who made up the "Loyal Nine."

With the decision in 1774 to resist the British by military means, the second round of revolutionary violence began. The main goal of revolutionary violence, in the transitional period from 1774 to 1777, was to intimidate the Tories who lived in fairly large numbers in seaport cities and the hinterland. The countrywide Continental Association of 1774 was drawn up to interrupt all trade between the colonies and the mother country, but a related purpose was to ferret out Tories, expose them to public contumely and intimidation, and bring them to heel or to silence.[2] When exposure in the newspapers was not enough, strong-arm tactics were used against the Tories. The old American custom of tarring and feathering was mainly a product of the patriotic campaign to root out Toryism.

Aside from the regular clash of the Continental and British armies, the third and final phase of revolutionary violence was the guerrilla activity all the way from the Hudson to the Savannah. Wherever strong British occupying forces were to be found—as in New York City, Philadelphia, and Charleston—in opposition to an American-dominated hinterland, the result was the polarization of the population and the outbreak of savage guerrilla warfare, desperate hit-and-run forays, and the thrust and counterthrust of pillage and mayhem. Thus, the lower Hudson Valley of New York was the theater of rival bushwhacking parties of Whigs and Tories. The Hackensack Valley of North Jersey, opposite the British bastion on Manhattan Island, was a sort of no man's land across which bands of Whigs and Tories fought and ravaged.[3] South Jersey's bleak and trackless pine barrens furnished ideal cover for the "land pirates" of both Whig and Tory persuasion, who appeared as the result of the British and American competition for the allegiance of New Jersey and the Philadelphia area.[4]

South Carolina emerged as the great battlefield of the war after 1780. North Carolina and Georgia suffered at the same time from the scourge of guerrilla warfare, but casualties were light compared to those incurred as a result of the dreadful cut-and-thrust of the Whig and Tory forces in the Palmetto state, where Andrew Pickens, Thomas Sumter, and Francis Marion led Whig-partisan bands in their own sectors of the Back Country. Negro slaves were stolen back and forth, and baleful figures, like the half-crazed Tory leader Bloody Bill Cunningham, emerged from the shadows to wreak their special brand of murder and massacre. Neither side showed any mercy. Prisoners were tortured and hanged. Virginians felt the destruction of Benedict Arnold's vengeful campaign in 1781 but experienced nothing like the sufferings in South Carolina. Still, it was characteristic of the rising passions of the time that strife among Whigs and Tories in the Virginia Piedmont gave rise to an early manifestation of lynch law.

Two things stand out about the Revolution. The first, of course, is that it was successful and immediately became enshrined in our tradition and history. The second is that the meanest and most squalid sort of violence was from the very beginning to the very end put to the service of revolutionary ideals and objectives. The operational philosophy that the end justifies the means became the keynote of revolutionary violence. Thus, given sanctification by the Revolution, Americans have never been loath to employ the most unremitting violence in the interest of any cause deemed a good one.

Violence was interwoven with the creation of the American nation. By the same token, it became the handmaiden of American salvation in the era of Civil War and Reconstruction, for the Civil War was not only a time of pervasive violence in its own right but had an almost incalculable effect in the following decades. The latter part of the nineteenth century was one of the most violent periods of American history—an era of Ku Kluxers, lynch mobs, White Caps, Bald Knobbers, night riders, feudists, and outlaws—and much of that violence is traceable to the Civil War and to the earlier legitimizing effect of the revolutionary war.

The years before the Civil War were years of mounting violence in both North and South. Feeling against the Fugitive Slave Law in the North gave rise to vigilance committees concerned with protecting runaway slaves and to increasingly fervent abolitionism. Below the Mason-Dixon Line, abolitionists had long since ceased to exist in anything save the minds of slaveholders and Southern nationalists, but from this delusion were formed vigilante movements to deal with nonexistent abolitionists. Violence of the most tangible sort was far from absent. Bleeding Kansas was truly just that as marauding bands of slaveholder and antislaveholder sympathizers surged through the territory.

In the East, John Brown's raid on Harper's Ferry sent a tremor of fear through those who genuinely wished to forestall a bloody civil war. For the more sanguinary in the North, John Brown was an inspiration for holy war against slavery; to the war-minded in the South, the John Brown raid was seen as proof that the South could never rest easy in a union that included free states and harbored abolitionists. The nation sensed that it was on the verge of a grand Armageddon.[5] The general nervousness came to a height in the South in the summer of 1860 as Southerners gloomily awaited the almost certain election of Lincoln. Forebodings of violence, never far from the surface, were suddenly realized in the Great Fear that swept across the South in the summer of 1860. From the Rio Grande to the Atlantic plot after plot by secret abolitionists and unionists for the raising-up of slaves in bloody rebellion were exposed.[6] At this distance it seems that the fears of slave uprisings were groundless, but parts of the South were in the grips of a hysteria that was real enough. Vigilante groups and self-styled committees of safety sprung up. The Great Fear of the South in the summer of 1860 seems to have been as baseless in fact as the remarkably similar *grande peur* (Grand Fear) that gripped the French peasantry in the first year of the French Revolution. Both the Great Fear in the American South and the *grande peur* in France revealed the profound anxieties that lacerated the white Southerners and the French peasants in the summers of 1860 and 1789, respectively.

Symbolically, the Great Fear on the eve of the Civil War was altogether fitting as a prelude to the decade and more of violence and mischief that would follow. The struggle between the armies of the North and the South still stands as the most massive military bloodletting in American history, but almost forgotten is the irregular underwar of violence and guerrilla conflict that paralleled military action by the regulars. In numerous localities throughout the North, resistance to the military draft was continuous and violent. The apogee of resistance to the draft occurred in New York City with the massive riots of 1863, when the city suffered through three days of fierce rioting.[7] Related troubles occurred throughout the war years in southern Indiana, southern Illinois, and southern Iowa, where widespread Copperhead feeling caused large-scale disaffection, antidraft riots, and guerrilla fighting between Union soldiers and deserters and Copperhead sympathizers.[8] The guerrilla war along the Kansas-Missouri border has seldom been equaled for unmitigated savagery. The Kansas Jayhawkers traded brutal blows with Missouri's Confederate guerrillas, headed by William Quantrill's band, which also included Frank and Jesse James and the Younger boys.[9] Kentucky, too, was the scene of frequent ambushes and affrays.[10]

The Confederate South was bedeviled by pockets of resistance to official policy. The mountain regions of north Arkansas, north Alabama, and eastern Tennessee contained important centers of Unionist sentiment, where the people had never become reconciled to the war effort. Even Mississippi had one county (Jones) where there was widespread disloyalty to the Confederate cause—as did Alabama (Winston). The frontier areas of northern and central Texas were liberally dotted with Unionist sympathizers and antislavery Germans. At best the German-Americans never gave more than grudging support to the war and sometimes resorted to sabotage. The result was brutal retaliation by the "Heel Flies" (Confederate home guards) who were often quite careless of whom they injured.[11]

Among legacies of the Civil War was a surge of domestic violence. Racial strife and Ku Klux Klan activity became routine in the old Confederate states. Regulator troubles broke out in central Kentucky and the Blue Grass region. Outlaw and vigilante activity blazed up in Texas, Kansas, and Missouri. As late as the closing years of the century, white capping, bald knobbing, and night riding, while spurred by particular social and economic conditions, remained as legacies of the violent emotions and methods bred by the Civil War. Especially prominent, too, in the violent heritage of the Civil War was the surge of local feuding in southern Appalachia and in Texas during the postwar period.

The family blood feud was virtually nonexistent in this country before the Civil War. The feud appears on the scene quite dramatically in the decades following the war. The era between the Civil War and World War I is the great era of the southern mountain feud in Kentucky, West Virginia, and Virginia. This is the period that produced the Hatfield-McCoy feud (1873-1888) of the Kentucky-West Virginia border, the Martin-Tolliver (1884-1887) and Hargis-Cockrell (1902-1903) feuds of eastern Kentucky, and the Allen family outburst at Hillsville in the Virginia Blue Ridge in 1912.[12]

The evidence is convincing that southern mountain feuding was triggered by animosities generated by the Civil War. The mountains were divided country, where Confederate and Union sympathizers fought in rival armies and slew each other in marauding guerrilla bands. After the war, old hatreds did not die out but, fueled anew by political partisanship and moonshine whiskey in a region bedeviled by isolation, poverty, and minimal education, burned on as never before. The formal law barely operated; its power was manipulated for selfish purposes by close-knit political and family factions. Since regular law and order was such a frail reed, families and individuals came increasingly to depend upon their own strong arms. Each feuding family, in self-defense, had its own clan leader: a man who best combined in the highest degree the qualities of physical strength, bravery, wealth, and family leadership. Such men were "Devil Anse" Hatfield and Judge James Hargis. In the absence of an effective system of law and order, these men functioned as family "enforcers," around whom the feuding families rallied for protection.

The great feuds of Texas and the Southwest were strikingly similar to those of the southern Appalachians, were about as well known in their own day, and had similar origins. As in the Appalachians, the main era of feuds in Texas was between the Civil War and World War I. The Texas feuds took place principally in the central portion of the state, which, like the southern mountains, was a region of conflicting Civil War loyalties and mordant Reconstruction hatreds. The war-spawned turbulence of central Texas was heightened by a combination of other factors: the extremely rapid development of the cattle industry with its accompanying frantic competition, rustling, and disorder; the fact that the western margins of the central Texas region were seared repeatedly by one of the cruelest of all American-Indian wars, that of the Comanches and Kiowas with the white settlers; and, finally, by the ethnic hostility between antislavery, pro-Union German settlers and native Southern inhabitants. The result was a series of deadly feuds that were every bit as terrible as their Appalachian counterparts.[13] Not even the Hatfield-McCoy feud exceeded for length, casualties, and bitterness the great Sutton-Taylor feud (1869-1877) of DeWitt and other counties in Texas. Among the major feuds of central Texas were the Horrell-Higgins feud of Lampasas County (1876-1877), the Jaybird-Woodpecker feud of Fort Bend County (1888-1890), and the Townsend-Stafford/Reese feuds of Colorado County (1890-1906).

In New Mexico Territory, the family and factional feud was built into the political system.[14] New Mexico before the First World War was probably the only American state where assassination became a routine political tactic. The most deadly of all American feuds was fought in neighboring Arizona from 1886 to 1892. This was the "Pleasant Valley War" between the Graham and Tewksbury families, a conflict that was exacerbated by the Grahams being cattlemen and the Tewksburys sheepmen. The bitter feud was fought, like the title phrase of Zane Grey's novel of the vendetta, "to the last man." Only with the lone survivor of the two families did it come to an end.[15]

As in so many other instances of American violence, the Civil War forms the "great divide" in regard to the phenomenon of political assassination. Not one important American assassination occurred before the Civil War (an 1835 attempt on Andrew Jackson's life by a crazed individual failed). The role of the Civil War vis-à-vis political assassination is partly cause and partly coincidence. Some of the assassinations noted below are traceable directly to the Civil War (Lincoln by John Wilkes Booth and his accomplices; John W. Stephens and others, who were felled in Reconstruction-era assassinations), or indirectly (President Garfield by a deluded stalwart Republican factionist; John M. Clayton of Arkansas, undoubtedly a victim of unreconstructed Democrats; William Goebel of Kentucky, almost certainly killed by hotheaded mountain Republicans from eastern Kentucky's feud region, and there were the series of New Mexican assassination plots, in which Republicans and Democrats, inflamed partly by old Civil War animosities, killed or sought to kill each other). But our twentieth-century assassinations clearly spring from the problems of modern America. Even the assassinations of our time refer back, ultimately, to the example of the acts of assassination so prevalent in the post-Civil War era.

The Civil War marked the replacement of the two-man personal duel by assassination as the main mortal hazard to the American politician and statesman.

The duel, involving nonpolitical as well as political gentlemen, was common before the Civil War. Most famous of all was Alexander Hamilton's death in a duel with Aaron Burr but, among other leading instances of noted politicos who fought duels, were Andrew Jackson (who in two prepresidential duels killed one man); Senator Thomas Hart Benton of Missouri, one of the political giants of the ante-bellum period, who killed a man in a duel early in his career; the eminent Virginia political journalist, Thomas Ritchie, Jr., who slew a rival editor in an 1845 duel; and, in 1857, on the eve of the Civil War, Judge David S. Terry of California, who killed Senator David C. Broderick of the same state in a duel. Dueling faded after the Civil War, as state antidueling laws began to be obeyed rather than ignored and as leading men came to see no dishonor in rejecting challenges to participate in what public opinion had come to view as an outmoded, barbarous practice.[16]

With the lapse of dueling, political assassination came to the fore. In quantitative terms, assassination has not been conspicuous in the history of American violence, but, at the highest level of our political system, the presidency, it has had a heavy impact. In a hundred-year span (1865-1965) four presidents (Lincoln, Garfield, McKinley, and Kennedy) fell to assassins' bullets, and others were the intended objects of assassination. One of the victims, Lincoln, was the target of an assassination conspiracy. The other three victims—Garfield, McKinley, and Kennedy—were the prey of freelance assassins in varying states of mental instability. Charles Guiteau, the slayer of Garfield, was a disappointed office seeker, but mental derangement seems to have been at the bottom of his action.[17] Both Leon Czolgosz, the assassin of McKinley, and Lee Harvey Oswald, Kennedy's assassin, appear to have had strong ideological commitments. Czolgosz was an anarchist, and Oswald was a self-styled Marxist. Both, however, were independent operatives. Czolgosz was rejected by the organized anarchist movement of his day, and Oswald was not a member of the Communist organization in America or of any of the American-Marxist splinter groups. Czolgosz seems to have been in the early stages of insanity.[18] Evidence amassed by the Warren Commission strongly suggests that Oswald was psychotic, but the Commission itself cautiously refrained from reaching that conclusion—saying only that Oswald was "profoundly alienated from the world in which he lived."[19]

Although the mortality rate of American presidents in the last century has been a high one at the hands of assassins, some comfort can be taken in the fact that assassination has not become a part of the American political system as it has elsewhere in the world, in the Middle East, for example.[20] None of the major political parties have resorted—even indirectly—to assassination at the national level. Notable, also, is the immunity other high political officials—vice-presidents, Supreme Court justices, and cabinet officers—have enjoyed from assassination.

Despite some prominent cases, assassinations at the state and local level have, on the whole, been few and far between with the exceptions of the New Mexico Territory (discussed below) and the South during Reconstruction. In the often chaotic Reconstruction period in the South, the assassination of John W. Stephens was typical. Stephens, a native white Southerner and a rising radical Republican politician of Caswell County, North Carolina, was in 1870 the victim of an assassination plot by a local faction of the Ku Klux Klan-oriented conservative political opposition.[21] Stephens's killers certainly wanted him out of the way because of his political effectiveness, and the killing was just one of many, many examples of the terrorist impulse of the Klan movement throughout vast areas of the South. Similar to the assassination of Stephens was the killing—years later—of John M. Clayton, Republican congressional candidate in Arkansas, by "parties unknown." Although defeated in the fall election of 1888, Clayton was contesting the result when he was killed in January 1889 while visiting Plummerville, Arkansas.[22]

In our own time, two notable political assassination attempts below the presidential level were successfully aimed at Senator Robert F. Kennedy of New York in 1968, and unsuccessfully at Governor George C. Wallace of Alabama in 1972. In the 1960s, three outstanding black leaders—Martin Luther King, Malcolm X, and Medgar Evers—perished at the hands of assassins as did the white leader of the American Nazi Party, George Lincoln Rockwell. More recently, Joseph Yablonski, insurgent leader, was assassinated in the course of a struggle for the control of the United Mine Workers union. Much earlier, one of the most famous assassinations in American history took the life of Senator Huey Long of Louisiana at the height of his flourishing national political career on September 8, 1935. Long's assassin was slain on the spot, and, to this day, considerable mystery surrounds his motives. Authorities differ, and it is not clear whether Long's killer acted from strictly personal emotion and grievance or whether he was part of an assassination conspiracy.[23] An earlier famous (but now forgotten) assassination of a leading state figure definitely stemmed from the context of a political conflict. This was the fatal wounding of the governor-elect of Kentucky, William Goebel, at Frankfort on January 30, 1900. The charismatic leader of the Democratic party in Kentucky, Goebel had been waging a hot battle against the Republicans and the railroad interests of his state at the time of his death. His assassination occurred during an infusion into Frankfort of thousands of anti-Goebel Republicans from the hot-blooded mountain region of eastern Kentucky. Mortal feuds had often been linked with local political rivalries in the Kentucky mountains in previous decades (see the section above on feud violence), and it is not surprising that Goebel's assassins seem to have sprung from that background.[24]

Apparently the only place in America where assassination became an integral part of the political system was the New Mexico Territory from the end of the Civil War down to about 1900. Many assassinations occurred there, among the most prominent being that of Colonel Albert J. Fountain, a leading Republican of southern New Mexico, in 1896. Other leading New Mexican politicians narrowly missed being killed, and many New Mexicans were convinced that the two chieftains of the Republican and Democratic parties, respectively, had been involved in assassination plots. Thomas B. Catron, the autocratic Republican boss, was thought by many to have been a party to one of the notable assassinations of the era; Catron himself seems to have been the target of an unsuccessful assassination attempt. The recent biographer of Colonel Fountain has brought forth strong evidence to support his charge that Albert Bacon Fall, the incisive Democratic leader, was guilty of leading complicity in the plot against Fountain. The most important point is that virtually all political factions in New Mexico accepted and used assassination as a way of eliminating troublesome opponents.[25]

The frightening phenomenon of assassination in territorial New Mexico still awaits searching study by the historian. In the absence of such a study, it is hard to say just why assassination became such a prominent political feature only in New Mexico. The territory was indeed a violent one at the time; it was scarred by a savage Indian war (with the Apaches), numerous vigilante movements and lynch mobs, a host of criminal outlaws (Billy the Kid, Clay Allison, and others), and such mordant local conflicts as the Lincoln County War and the Maxwell Land Grant troubles. This high level of violence might well have had the effect of skewing the political system in the direction of assassination as a tactic, although this did not happen in neighboring Texas, which, at the time, was every bit as violent as New Mexico. Nor does the large Latin element of the population seem to have added a measure of volatility to the political climate of New Mexico Territory, for Anglo-American politicians, such as Catron (from Missouri) and Fall (from Kentucky), were leaders in a political system that was often characterized by assassination.

A third explanation for the prevalence of political assassination in New Mexico is suggested by social scientists, who have recently posited a "contagion phenomenon" in regard to such "highly publicized and dramatic acts of deviant behavior" as prison riots, bomb scares, slum uprisings, mass murder, and psychopathic sexual acts.[26] Beginning with the first assassination in New Mexico (that of the territorial chief justice, John P. Slough, in 1867), it is possible that something like a "contagion phenomenon" set in to perpetuate assassination until it became a part of the political system itself. After 1900 the level of general turbulence in New Mexico life subsided. It may have been no coincidence that the politics of assassination faded, too. Students of the "contagion phenomenon" have seen it as a short-run phenomenon characterized by an accelerating pace followed by an abrupt end, which might, in long-run terms, be analogous to the experience in New Mexico and in America from 1963 to 1968 when John F. Kennedy, Robert F. Kennedy, Martin Luther King, Medgar Evers, and Malcolm X were all cut down by assassins.

II

An examination of American criminal violence reveals four noteworthy facts: (1) Organized interstate (or, earlier, intercolonial) gangs of criminals are an old story, going well back into the eighteenth century. (2) Before the Civil War, the most prevalent type of criminal activity—especially in frontier areas—was horse theft and the counterfeiting of the myriad number of private banknotes then in circulation. (3) After the Civil War, a new era of crime began with the popularization of train robbery by the Reno brothers of Indiana and bank robbery by the James-Younger gang of Missouri. (4) The modern era of big-city organized crime with its police and political connections began to emerge in the early twentieth century.

America has long been ambiguous about crime. Official condemnation of the outlaw has been matched by social adulation. The ambiguity is not restricted to America, for the British historian, E.J. Hobsbawm, has shown the existence in European history of the "social bandit." By social bandit, Hobsbawm means largely what we have come to denote by a "Robin Hood," i.e., an outlaw whom society views as its hero rather than its enemy, an outlook that reflects widespread social alienation.[27]

There have indeed been American social bandits. Jesse and Frank James gained a strong popular following in Mid-America after the Civil War. To the many Southern sympathizers in Missouri, the James brothers, who were former Confederate guerrillas, could do no wrong, and, to many Grange-minded farmers, the Jameses' repeated robberies of banks and railroads were no more than these unpopular economic institutions deserved.[28] Other social bandits have been Henry Berry Lowry (a hero to his people—the Lumber River Indians of southeast North Carolina—during a period of harassment by the dominant white faction during the Reconstruction era), Billy the Kid (the idol of the poor Mexican herdsmen and villagers of the Southwest). Pretty Boy Floyd (Public Enemy No. 1 of the 1930s, who retained the admiration of the sharecroppers of eastern Oklahoma from which stock he sprang), and John Dillinger (the premier bank robber of the Depression Era).[29] Modeling himself on an earlier social bandit, Jesse James, John Dillinger by freehanded generosity cultivated the Robin Hood image while robbing a series of Midwestern banks. The rural-small-town era of American crime came largely to an end with the demise of John Dillinger, Pretty Boy Floyd, Clyde Barrow and Bonnie Parker, and other "public enemies" of the 1930s. With them the American tradition of the social bandit declined.

While the tradition of the rural American social bandit was waxing and waning, urban crime was increasing in importance. The first urban criminal gangs arose in New York and other cities in the pre-Civil War decades, but these gangs were limited in significance and restricted to such ethnic "slum" neighborhoods as Five Points and the Bowery in New York City.[30] Murder, mayhem, and gang vendettas were a feature of the proliferation of these gangs. Meanwhile, in the early decades of the twentieth century the present pattern of centralized, citywide criminal operations under the control of a single "syndicate" or "organization" began to take shape in New York under Arnold Rothstein.[31] Converging with this trend was, apparently, the Mafia tradition of criminal organization, which Sicilian immigrants seem to have brought into East Coast port cities in the decades around 1900.[32] During the 1920s and 1930s, the two trends merged into the predominant pattern of centralized operations under Mafia control, which the Kefauver crime investigation highlighted in 1951.[33] Systematic killing to settle internal feuds and the use of investment capital (gained from illicit activities), threats, and extortion to infiltrate the world of legitimate business have been the characteristics of contemporary urban organized crime.[34]

In contrast to the relatively impersonal, well-organized criminal gangs and the widely admired exploits of the American social bandits has been a type of personalized violence, historically, that has aroused deep emotions of horror in the populace: freelance multiple murder. The vendettas of criminal combines have produced some notable killings (for example, the St. Valentine's Day massacre of Chicago, 1929, and New York City's so-called Castellammarese War, 1930-1931, involving competing Italian-American crime factions), but to be considered here is the murder of many persons by one or two individuals—freelance multiple murders—unconnected with any gang. It was the summer of 1966 that made Americans wonder whether the freelance multiple murder was becoming the characteristic American crime, for, in the space of a few weeks, two shocking mass murders occurred. First, in Chicago, Richard F. Speck murdered, one by one, eight student nurses. Then, less than a month later, Charles Whitman ascended to the top of the tower of the University of Texas library in Austin and left tower and campus strewn with 13 dead or dying and 31 wounded as a result of his unerring marksmanship. The utter horror of these two killing rampages attracted worldwide attention, but not a year goes by without the appearance of one or more multiple murders. Speck, the hapless product of a blighted personal background, saw himself as "Born to Raise Hell." Whitman came from an upright and respectable middle-class background that was allegedly, on closer examination, a veritable witches' cauldron of tensions and hatreds.[35]

Neither Speck nor Whitman were normal in the usual sense of the word, and the freelance multiple murderer is often a fit subject for the abnormal psychologist. (Recently it has been suggested that male killers, such as Speck, have a genetic abnormality arising from a doubling of the male sex chromosome.) But some observers have wondered whether the anxieties and neuroses of contemporary life in American have not led to a rise in the abnormal behavior exemplified by multiple (or mass) murder.[36] Crime statistics are not sufficiently available to answer the question, but there have been many examples of freelance multiple murderers in American history. The annals of crime in the United States abound with them. Among the earliest were the brutal Harpe brothers, Micajah (Big Harpe) and Wiley (Little Harpe), who during the years 1798 and 1799 accounted for anywhere from about 20 to 38 victims in the frontier states of Kentucky and Tennessee. Dashing out babies' brains against tree trunks in sudden frenzies was a practice that they may have learned from the Indians. Finally, in August 1798, a party of Kentucky settlers ended the career of Micajah. Wiley escaped but was captured, tried, and hanged in Mississippi in 1804. So feared and hated were the Harpes that, following death, the head of each was cut off and displayed as a trophy of triumphant pioneer justice.[37]

Numerous freelance multiple murderers crop up in the nineteenth century. Among them was the evil Bender family of southeastern Kansas. The Benders, from 1871 to 1873, did away with at least twelve unwary travelers who had the bad judgment to choose the Bender roadside house for a meal or lodging. Eventually the Benders were detected, but they seem to have escaped into anonymity one jump ahead of a posse.[38] Another mass murderer was H.H. Holmes (the alias of Hermann Webster Mudgett) of Englewood (near Chicago), Illinois. He confessed to killing 27 people from about 1890 to 1894—many of whom he had lured to their death in his bizarre castlelike house while they were attending the Chicago World's Fair in the summer of 1893.[39] Although example after example can be named, such questions as the actual number of multiple murderers and their relationship to social conditions still await the deeper study of the historian.[40]

The threatening presence of the criminal and disorderly in American life has incurred the violent riposte of the forces of law and order, ranging from the police and associated legal bodies to lynch mobs, vigilantes, and related extralegal groups.

Law enforcement in colonial America was quite simple, consisting mainly of sheriffs for the counties and constables for the cities and towns. With the tremendous expansion of population and territory in the nineteenth century, the system took on a much greater complexity. Added to the county sheriffs and local constables were municipal police organizations, state police (including such special and elite forces as the rangers of Texas and Arizona) and federal marshals and Treasury agents.[41] The most important development of the century was the rise of the modern urban police system in the midcentury years from 1844 to 1877. The new system was a direct response to the great urban riots of the 1830s, 1840s, and 1850s. The antiquated watch-and-ward system (daytime constables and nighttime watchmen) was simply inadequate to cope with large-scale rioting and increasing urban disorder. The reform in the police system came first in New York, Philadelphia, Boston, and other cities that had acute problems of criminal violence and rioting.[42] (Thus, the Riot Era, from the 1830s through the 1850s, produced the present urban police system. The riots of the 1960s have, similarly, spurred a trend toward the professionalization of the police as the obverse of another result of the 1960s riots: increasing hostility between the predominantly white police and black ghetto militants.)

Scarcely less important than the development of the urban police system was the creation of the National Guard to replace the obsolete state militia system that dated back to the eighteenth century. The rapid development of the National Guard system in the 1880s was largely a response to the great urban labor riots of 1877. The National Guard was established first and most rapidly in the industrial states of the North that were highly vulnerable to labor unrest: Massachusetts, Connecticut, New York, Pennsylvania, Ohio, and Illinois. By 1892, the system was complete throughout the nation.[43] Officered primarily by businessmen and professionals, and sometimes the recipients of large subsidies from wealthy industrialists, National Guard contingents were often called out to suppress labor violence from the late nineteenth century down to the time of the Second World War.

In the latter half of the nineteenth century there also grew up a sort of parapolice system with the founding of numerous private detective agencies (headed by the famed Pinkerton National Detective Agency) and the burgeoning of thousands of local anti-horse thief associations or detecting societies, which were often authorized by state laws and invested with limited law enforcement powers.[44] After the Civil War, industrial corporations frequently set up their own police forces. Most notable in this category were the private coal and iron police that the state of Pennsylvania authorized to deal with labor unrest in mines and mills.[45] It was during the nineteenth century, as well, that the science of crime detection was inaugurated.[46]

Undue violence in the course of enforcing the law has long been a matter of concern. In an earlier generation, the public worried about the employment of the "third degree" to obtain criminal confessions. In our own time, the concern is with "police brutality," often against blacks.[47] The use of violence by police in the pursuit of their regular duties has been related to the large measure of violence associated with the incarceration of prisoners in jails and prisons. For over a century and a half we have gone through bursts of prison reform only to have the system as a whole lapse back into (if indeed it every really transcended) its normal brutality and sadism. As time has passed, many of the most well-meaning reforms (such as the early-nineteenth-century system of solitary confinement) have proved to be ill-conceived.[48] Even as our knowledge and expertise have increased, prison reform has foundered again and again on the rock of inadequate financial support from an uncaring society.

Police brutality, police riots (in which large numbers of police rage out of control in a law-enforcement situation, as happened in Chicago at the 1968 Democratic National Convention), and the violence in penal institutions all illustrate the paradoxical but intimate and all too common connection between lawfulness and lawlessness. Heightening the paradox is the contradictory coupling of lawlessness in behalf of lawfulness to be found, historically, in lynch law and vigilantism.[49]

Lynch law has been defined as "the practice or custom by which persons are punished for real or alleged crimes without due process of law." The first organized movement of lynch law in America occurred in the South Carolina back country in 1767-1769.[50] It appeared again in the Virginia Piedmont near the present city of Lynchburg during the latter years of the Revolution. The Virginia movement was initiated by Colonel Charles Lynch (from whom "lynch law" gained its name) and was employed against Tory miscreants. Well into the nineteenth century, lynch law meant merely the infliction of corporal punishment—usually 39 lashes or more well laid on with hickory withes, whips, or any readily available frontier instrument. By the middle of the nineteenth century, lynch law had come to be synonymous, mainly, with hanging or killing by illegal group action. The term lynch mob refers to an organized, spontaneous, ephemeral mob that comes together briefly to do its work and then breaks up. The more regular vigilante (or regulator) movements engaged in a systematic usurpation of the functions of law and order.[51]

Lynch-mob violence (in contrast to vigilante violence) was often resorted to in trans-Appalachian frontier areas before the Civil War, but it became even more common after the Civil War. In the postwar period (down to the first World War), lynch-mob violence was employed frequently in all sections of the country and against whites as well as against blacks, but in this period it was preeminently directed against the Southern black. From 1882 to 1903 the staggering total of 1,985 blacks were killed by Southern lynch mobs. Supposedly the lynch-mob hanging (or, too often, a ghastly burning alive) was saved for the black murderer or rapist, but statistics show that blacks were frequently lynched for lesser crimes or in cases where there was no offense at all or the mere suspicion of one. Lynch-mob violence became an integral part of the post-Reconstruction system of white supremacy.[52]

Although predominant in the South, lynch-mob violence was far from being restricted to that section. In the West, the ephemeral "necktie party" was often foregathered for the summary disposal of thief, rapist, rustler, murderer, or all-around desperado. Frenzied mobs also worked their will in the North and East, where (as in the West) villainous white men were the usual victims.

The phenomenon of vigilantism appears to be native to America. The British Isles—especially Scotland and Ireland—were violent enough in the seventeenth and eighteenth centuries, but a tradition of vigilantism was unknown there. The taking of the law into one's own hands, the classic definition of vigilantism, was repugnant to the British approach to law and order. Vigilantism arose in response to a typical American problem: the absence of effective law and order in a frontier region. It was a problem that occurred again and again beyond the Appalachian Mountains. It stimulated the formation of hundreds of frontier vigilante movements.[53]

The first phase of American vigilantism occurred mainly before the Civil War and dealt largely with the threat of frontier horse thieves and counterfeiters. Virtually every state or territory west of the Appalachians possessed well-organized, relentless vigilante movements. We have tended to think of the vigilante movement as being typical of the Western plains and mountains, but, in actuality, there was much vigilantism east of the Missouri and Mississippi rivers. The main thrust of vigilantism was to reestablish in each newly settled frontier area the community structure of the old settled areas along with the values of the sanctity of property and law and order. Vigilante movements were characteristically in the control of the frontier elite and represented the elite's social values and preferences. This was true of the first vigilante movement, which was in South Carolina during 1767-1769, with members known as "Regulators"—the original, but now obsolete term for vigilantes, and it was also true of the greatest of all American vigilante movements, that of San Francisco in 1856. The San Francisco vigilance committee of 1856 was dominated lock, stock, and barrel by the leading merchants of the city, who organized to stamp out crime and political corruption.

Although the typical vigilante movements were dominated by social conservatives who desired to establish order and stability in newly settled areas, there were disconcertingly numerous departures from the norm. Many vigilante movements led not to order but to increasing disorder and anarchy. In such cases, vigilantism left things in a worse condition than had existed before. Frequently the strife between vigilantes and their opponents (exacerbated by individual, family, and political hatreds) became so bitter and untrammeled that order could be restored only by the governor calling out the militia. Such was the case when the Bald Knobbers of the Missouri Ozarks rose in 1885-1886 to curb the evils of theft, liquor, gambling, and prostitution in Taney and Christian counties. Intervention by outside authorities was finally needed.[54]

The elite nature of nineteenth-century vigilante leadership is revealed by the prominent men who figured in vigilante movements; they included U.S. senators and congressmen, governors, lawyers, and capitalists.[55] Even presidents of the United States were attracted to vigilantism. President Andrew Jackson once approved the resort of Iowa pioneers to vigilante methods pending the clarification of their territorial status.[56] As a young cattle rancher in North Dakota, Theodore Roosevelt begged to be admitted to a vigilante band that was being formed to deal with rustlers and horse thieves. The cattlemen rebuffed the impetuous young Harvard blueblood and went on with their vigilante movement.[57] Today, among educated men of standing, vigilantism is viewed with disapproval, but it was not always so in the nineteenth century. In those days, the leaders of the community were often prominent members of vigilante movements and proud of it.

America changed from the basically rural nation it had been in the ante-bellum era to an urban, industrial nation after the Civil War. The institution of vigilantism changed to match the altering character of the nation. From a generally narrow concern with the classic frontier problems of horse thieves and counterfeiters, vigilantism broadened its scope to include a variety of targets connected with the tensions of the new America: Catholics, Jews, blacks, immigrants, laboring men and labor leaders, political radicals, advocates of civil liberties, and nonconformists in general. This new vigilantism, or neovigilantism, flourished as a symptom of the growing pains of post-Civil War industrial and urban America but utterly failed to solve the complex social problems of the era.[58]

The post-Civil War era also saw the climax of two movements that had strong affinities with vigilantism. One was the anti-horse thief association, which had its greatest growth in the rural Midwest and Southwest after the Civil War, although its roots were to be found in the Northeastern United States as early as the 1790s. The anti-horse thief association pattern involved state charter of local associations that were often vested with constabulary power. By 1900, the movement's associations numbered hundreds of thousands of members in its belt of greatest strength, which stretched from the Great Lakes to the Rio Grande. Forming a flexible and inexpensive (the members shared costs whenever they arose) supplement to immobile, expensive, and inefficient local law enforcement, the associations afforded the farmer insurance against the threat of horse and other types of theft. With the rapid development of the automobile around the time of the First World War the anti-horse thief associations lost their raison d'être.

Quite different in character was the White Cap movement. White Caps first appeared in southern Indiana in 1887,[59] but, in short order, the phenomenon had spread to the four corners of the nation. The White Cap movement copied the vigilante movements of the late eighteenth and early nineteenth centuries in its preference for flogging as a mode of punishment. White capping varied greatly from locality to locality and region to region. In northern Texas and southern Mississippi the White Caps were anti-black,[60] in southern Texas they were anti-Mexican,[61] and in northern New Mexico the White Caps were a movement of poor Mexican herders and ranchers against land-enclosing rich Mexicans and Americans. In the late 1960s, Reies Tijerina's sometimes violent *Alianza* movement to regain land (originally held in ancient ancestral Spanish land grants) for the poor Mexican-Americans of New Mexico and the Southwest was in some respects a revival of the late nineteenth-century White Cap movement of New Mexico.[62]

In general, however, white capping was most prevalent as a sort of spontaneous movement for the moral regulation of the poor whites and ne'er-do-wells of the rural American countryside. Thus, drunken, shiftless whites who often abused their families were typical targets of White Cap violence, and loose women frequently became the victims of White Caps.[63] Vigilantism as far back as the South Carolina Regulators of 1767-1769 had often been concerned with the moral regulation of incorrigible whites, hence white capping was, in part, a throwback to the early era of frontier vigilantism. At the same time, white capping seems to have been an important link between the first and second Ku Klux Klans. White Cap methods, in regard to punishment and costume, seem to have been influenced by the first Klan, whereas White Cap attacks on immoral and shiftless whites foreshadowed the main thrust of the second Klan of the 1920s. Chronologically, white capping began in the 1880s, about two decades after the first Klan, and, by the turn of the century, it had become such a generic term for local American violence that Booth Tarkington made White Cap violence the pivot of his popular novel *The Gentleman from Indiana* (1899). At the time of the First World War, white capping was fading from view; shortly thereafter the second Ku Klux Klan rose to take its place.

III

Unquestionably the longest and most remorseless war in American history was the one between whites and Indians that began in tidewater Virginia in 1607 and continued, with intermittent truces, for nearly 300 years down to the final event, the massacre of the Sioux by U.S. troops at Wounded Knee, South Dakota, in 1890. Nor has white-Indian conflict disappeared. Such conflict is ordinarily nonviolent, but that was not the case in early 1973 when a violent confrontation between militant members of the American Indian Movement (AIM) and white federal agents, which took place, again, at Wounded Knee, led to fatalities.

Bitter, implacable white-Indian hostility was by no means inevitable. The small Indian population that existed in the continental United States allowed plenty of room for white settlement. The economic resources of the white settlers were such that the Indians could have been easily and fairly reimbursed for the land needed for occupation by the whites. In fact, a model of peaceful white-Indian relations was developed in seventeenth-century New England by John Eliot, Roger Williams, and other Puritan statesmen. The same was true in eighteenth-century Pennsylvania where William Penn's humane and equitable policy toward the Indians brought that colony decades of white-Indian amity.[64] Racial prejudice and greed in the mass of New England whites finally reaped the whirlwind in King Philip's War of 1675-1676, which shattered the peaceful New England model.[65] The same sort of thing happened in Pennsylvania in 1763, when Pontiac's Rebellion (preceded by increasing tensions) ended an era of amicable white-Indian relations in the Keystone colony.

Other Indian wars proliferated during the seventeenth and eighteenth centuries, nor did the pace of the conflict slacken in the nineteenth century. It is possible that no other factor has exercised a more brutalizing influence on the American character than the Indian wars. The struggles with the Indians have sometimes been represented as being "just" wars in the interest of promoting superior Western civilization at the expense of the crude stone-age culture of the Indians. The recent ethnohistorical approach to the interpretation of white-Indian relations has given us a more balanced understanding of the relative merits of white and Indian civilizations. The norms of Indian warfare were, however, more barbaric than those of early modern Western Europe. Among the Indians of eastern America, torture was an accepted and customary part of war-making. In their violent encounters with Indians, the white settlers adopted the cruel practices of Indian conflict. Scalping had not been prevalent in Europe since the Dark Ages, but in the new world white men— responding to the Indians' widely (but not universally) practiced habit of scalping— reverted to this savage form of warfare. Down to the battle at Wounded Knee, lifting the hair of an Indian opponent was the usual tactic among experienced white fighters. Broken treaties, unkept promises, and the slaughter of defenseless women and children all, along with brutal warfare, continued to characterize the white American's dealings with the Indian.[66] The effect on our national character has not been a healthy one; it has done much to further our proclivity to violence.

In the realm of intergroup conflict, racial violence between whites and blacks, extending far back into the eighteenth century, is unequaled in persistence as a factor in the history of American violence. The first slave uprising occurred in New York

City in 1712 and was put down with great ruthlessness. In 1739, there was the Stono Rebellion in South Carolina, and, in 1741, New York City was again wracked with fears (apparently justified) of a slave conspiracy. The result was that New York white men went on a hysterical rampage in which scores of blacks were burned, hanged, or expelled. The demographic situation in what is now the United States (in contrast to that of the West Indies and South America where the black-white population ratio, more favorable to blacks, enhanced slave insurgency) was such as to inhibit slave rebellions. There were, however, two major aborted plots for slave uprisings by Gabriel Prosser in Richmond, 1800, and by Denmark Vesey in Charleston, 1822, as well as two major actual rebellions by Louisiana slaves in St. Charles and St. John the Baptist parishes in 1811 and by slaves in Southhampton County, Virginia, in 1831 under the leadership of Nat Turner. The rebellion of Nat Turner, although a failure, is better known than the single successful instance of large-scale violent resistance to slavery by American blacks: the case of the Florida Maroons, who, in coalition with the Seminole Indians, successfully fought down to 1838 to maintain their status as freed men or escapees from white servitude. Lesser instances of maroon resistance to slavery abounded in the South during the nineteenth century, while countless blacks resisted slavery, too, by such acts of low-level violence as assault, murder, arson, and running away.[67]

With the end of slavery and its conjoined slave patrols and black codes, the white people of the South developed a special organization for dealing with the blacks: the Ku Klux Klan. The latter has been one of the most consistent features in the last 100 years of American violence. There have been three Ku Klux Klans: the first Ku Klux Klan of Reconstruction times, the second Ku Klux Klan of the 1920s, and the third, current, Ku Klux Klan of the 1950s to 1970s. The first Ku Klux Klan was employed to intimidate the Radical Republicans of the Reconstruction Era and, by violence and threats, to force the freedman to accept the renewed rule of Southern whites.[68] The second Ku Klux Klan differed significantly from both its predecessor and successor. Although the second Ku Klux Klan was founded in Atlanta in 1915, its greatest growth and strength actually took place beyond the borders of the old Confederacy. During the early 1920s it became a truly national organization. For a time it enjoyed great strength in the Southwest, West, North, and East. The strongest state Klan was in Indiana, and such wholly un-Southern states as Oregon and Colorado felt its vigor. The second Ku Klux Klan surely belongs to the violent history of America, but, unlike either the first or the third Klans, blacks were only a secondary target for it. Although denunciation of Catholics and Jews ranked one-two in the rhetoric of the second Klan, recent students of the movement have shown that Klan violence—whippings, torture, and murder—were directed less against Catholics, Jews, and blacks than against ne'er-do-wells and the allegedly immoral of the very same background as the Klansmen: white, Anglo-Saxon Protestant. The Klan, thus, attacked Americans of similar background and extraction who refused to conform to the Bible Belt morality that was the deepest passion of the Klan movement of the 1920s.[69] The Ku Klux Klan resurgence of the last 15 years has been largely restricted to the South; it is only too well known for acts of violence against the civil rights movement and against desegregation.

Paralleling the Ku Klux Klan has been a host of other movements of racial, ethnic, and religious malice. Before the Civil War, the Northeastern United States was marked by convent burnings and anti-Catholic riots.[70] This "Protestant Crusade" eventually bred the political Know Nothing movement. Anti-Chinese agitation that often burst into violence became a familiar feature in California and the West as the nineteenth century wore on.[71] In 1891, eleven Italian immigrants were the victims of a murderous mob in New Orleans. The fear and loathing of Catholics (especially Irish and Italians), which often took a violent form, was organized in the nonviolent but bigoted American Protective Association (A.P.A.) of 1887.[72] Labor clashes of the late nineteenth century and early twentieth century were in reality, often, ethnic clashes with native, old stock Americans ranged on one side as owners, foremen, and skilled workers against growing numbers of unskilled immigrants—chiefly Jews, Slavs, Italians, and others from southern and eastern Europe.[73]

The arena of violent racial, ethnic, religious, political, economic, and industrial group conflict in American history has frequently been the urban riot. The situation seemed at its worst in the late 1960s when the country was widely believed to be on the verge of some sort of urban apocalypse, but the fact is that our cities have been in a state of more or less continuous turmoil since the colonial period.[74] As early as the latter part of the seventeenth century the cores of the organized North End and South End Mobs that dominated Boston in the eighteenth century had already formed. Maritime riots occurred in Boston during the middle eighteenth century and were frequent in the colonies in the 1760s.[75] Leading colonial cities of the revolutionary era—Charleston, New York, Boston, and Newport, Rhode Island—were all rocked by the Liberty Boy troubles, which embodied an alliance of unskilled maritime workers, skilled artisans, and middle-class businessmen and professionals in riotous dissent against toughening British colonial policy as exemplified by the Stamp Act and Townshend Acts.

Economic and political conditions brought more urban turmoil in the post-revolutionary period of the 1780s and 1790s, and, by the midnineteenth century, with industrial and urban expansion occurring by leaps and bounds, the cities of America found themselves in the grips of a new era of violence. The pattern of the urban immigrant slum as a matrix of poverty, vice, crime, and violence was set by Five Points in lower Manhattan before the Civil War. Ulcerating slums along the lines of Five Points and severe ethnic and religious strife stemming from the confrontation between burgeoning immigrant groups and the native American element made the 1830s, 1840s, and 1850s decades of sustained urban rioting, particularly in the great cities of the Northeast. It may have been the era of the greatest urban violence America has ever experienced. During this period, at least 35 major riots occurred in Baltimore, Philadelphia, New York, and Boston.[76] Baltimore had twelve, Philadelphia eleven, New York eight, and Boston four. The violence also extended into the growing cities of the Midwest and the lower Mississippi Valley; Cincinnati had four major riots during this period. But the urban violence of the 1830s to 1850s was not restricted to the greatest and best-known cities. In a recent thorough study, John C. Schneider announced that "at least seventy percent of American cities with a population of twenty thousand or more by 1850 experienced some degree of major disorder in the 1830-1865 period." Specifically, Schneider found that the American cities of 20,000 or more in size suffered eighty major riots from 1830 to 1865.[77] Among the most important types of riots were labor riots, election riots, antiabolitionist riots, antiblack riots, anti-Catholic riots, and riots of various sorts involving the turbulent volunteer firemen's units.

Except for Civil War draft riots, the urban violence subsided in the 1860s and 1870s until the year of 1877 produced a tremendous nationwide railroad strike that began along the Baltimore and Ohio Railroad and spread to the Far West. Violent rioting shook Baltimore, and great stretches of Pittsburgh were left in smoking ruins.[78] (The similarity of what befell Baltimore and Pittsburgh in 1877 and what befell Los Angeles, Chicago, Newark, Detroit, Washington, and other cities from 1965 to 1968 is striking.) Many other cities suffered less serious damage.

The forces of law and order responded strongly to the nineteenth-century urban violence. The modern urban police system was created in response to the riots of the 1830s, 1840s, and 1850s, and the present National Guard system to the uprisings of 1877. To deal with urban tumult, vigilantism was also used frequently in the nineteenth century. The greatest of all American vigilante movements occurred in the newly settled (by Americans) but thoroughly urban and up-to-date San Francisco of 1856; other nineteenth-century urban vigilante movements occurred in Los Angeles, New Orleans, San Antonio, St. Louis, Cincinnati, Rochester, and Natchez.[79]

The prototype of the antiblack urban race riot was established in the North as far back as the 1820s and 1830s, and after the Civil War it was replicated in such major Southern outbreaks as the riots in Wilmington, North Carolina (1898) and Atlanta (1906). These earliest riots were, in effect, pogroms—one-sided attacks on urban blacks by whites. By the era of the First World War, however, the pogrom-type race riot was eclipsed by the appearance of the "communal" riot, in which, with whites still usually dominant, mobs of counterrioting blacks and whites raged through city streets. Among a number of communal riots from 1917 to the 1940s, the greatest were those of Washington, D.C. and Chicago in 1919 and Detroit in 1943. In the 1960s, two long-term trends combined to reverse the typical pattern of white primacy in rioting: one was a demographic revolution, in which, during the course of the twentieth century, American blacks made the transition from being a predominantly rural, Southern people to a predominantly urban people heavily concentrated in black ghetto areas of Northern and Western cities; the other was a comparable revolution in black consciousness, resulting in a mood of black pride and aggressiveness that became stunningly evident in Los Angeles's Watts riot of 1964, the first of the black superriots of the 1960s.[80]

Violent American group conflict has by no means been restricted to the urban sector with its manifold racial, ethnic, and economic antagonisms. The countryside, too, has been the domain of relentless violence growing out of our agrarian history. The tree of liberty in America has been nurtured by a series of movements in behalf of the ever-suffering farmer or yeoman. Often these movements—generally considered to be liberal in their political character—have been formed for the purpose of redressing the economic grievances of the farmer; at times they have been land-reform movements. The dissident farmer movements have been deemed among the most heroic of all American movements of political insurgence; they have been the especial favorites of historians who, with love and sympathy, have chronicled their ups and downs. There have been many agrarian uprisings and they have been equally prevalent in both the colonial and national periods of our history. The initial agrarian uprising was that led by Nathaniel Bacon in late-seventeenth-century Virginia, followed by the New Jersey land rioters of the eighteenth century. Similarly, in the 1760s, were the Paxton Boy's movement of Pennsylvania,[81] the North Carolina Regulators (not a vigilante movement but one for reform of local government),[82] and the New York antirent movement (which stretched on into the nineteenth century).[83] With independence, there appeared Shays's Rebellion in Massachusetts (1786-1787), the Whiskey Rebellion in western Pennsylvania (1794), and Fries' Rebellion in eastern Pennsylvania (1798-1799).[84] Further west—in the Mississippi Valley before the Civil War—there appeared the Claim Clubs to defend the land occupancy of squatters.[85]

After the Civil War, a plethora of economic problems for the farmer gave rise to the Grangers, the Greenbackers, the Farmers' Alliance (which originally began in central Texas as a quasi-vigilante movement), and the Populist party.[86] About the same time there appeared a land reform movement in California against the monopolistic landholdings of the Southern Pacific Railroad,[87] and, in New Mexico, there appeared a White Cap movement of poor Mexicans against the land-enclosing tactics of well-to-do Mexicans and Americans, as mentioned earlier. Western Kentucky, and the Ohio-Mississippi Valley area, generally, was the scene in the early 1900s of a tobacco farmers' cooperative movement to end the control of the American Tobacco Company and foreign companies over the marketing system.[88] Farmers became increasingly attracted to the Socialist party, and the nonindustrial state of Oklahoma soon led the nation in Socialist party members. Connected with the rise of socialism among Oklahoma farmers was the appearance there during the First World War of the Working Class Union, which developed into a pacifist, antidraft movement of sharecroppers and small farmers.[89] In the upper Great Plains of North Dakota during 1915 there rose the radical Nonpartisan League, which enacted many reforms in that state and inspired similar progressive farm movements in other states of the Northwest.[90] The Farm Bloc emerged in Congress in the 1920s to promote legislation for easing the agricultural depression. When conditions worsened in the 1930s, the Farmers' Holiday Association, formed in the Midwest, led farmer strikes and boycotts in protest against the economic system.[91] In the 1960s, the National Farmers' Organization adopted similar tactics.

The insurgent farmer movements have thus formed one of the longest and most enduring chronicles in the history of American reform but one that has been blighted again and again with violence. Nathaniel Bacon's movement became a full-fledged rebellion that resulted in the burning of Jamestown. The New Jersey land rioters used violence to press their claims against Jersey land companies. The New York antirent movement frequently used force against dominant landlords. The North Carolina Regulators rioted against the courthouse rings that ground them down under the burden of heavy taxes and rapacious fees. The Paxton Boys of Pennsylvania followed their massacre of Indians with a march on Philadelphia. The followers of Daniel Shays in Massachusetts broke up court sessions in order to forestall land foreclosures. The farmers of Pennsylvania rebelled against taxes on liquor and land in the Whiskey and Fries uprisings. The Western Claim Clubs (which, paradoxically, were sometimes dominated by land speculators pursuing their own interests) used intimidation to protect "squatters' rights." The land reform movement in California spawned a night-rider league in Tulare County (1878-1880) to resist railroad land agents. The tobacco farmer cooperative movement in Kentucky did not succeed in breaking monopoly domination of the marketing system until it utilized a night-rider organization and raided several western Kentucky towns, destroyed tobacco warehouses, and abused noncooperating farmers. The New Mexican White Caps fought the land-enclosure movement with a reign of terror. The Working Class Union of Oklahoma fomented the Green Corn Rebellion; the "rebels" contemplated only a peaceful march on Washington but did arm themselves and commit a few acts of violence before being rooted out of the hills and breaks along the South Canadian River by sheriffs and posses. The Farmers' Holiday Association dumped milk cans, blocked roads, and roughed up opponents. Farmer grievances were serious, and, repeatedly, farmers used a higher law—the need to right insufferable wrongs, the very justification of the American Revolution—to justify the use of violence in uprising after uprising.

The labor movement in American history—like the farmers'—has been bathed in the same sort of glory that anointed the agrarian uprisings. Most would agree that by raising the health and living standards of the working man the American labor movement has been a significant factor in advancing the social well-being of the nation. But the labor movement reveals the same mixture of glorious ends with inglorious means—violence—that has characterized the agrarian movement. (Ironically, the white backlash against the black uprisings in the cities of our time has been strongest in the rural countryside and the blue-color metropolitan wards, i.e., among the inheritors of the violent agrarian and labor movements.)

A rudimentary labor movement was to be found in the port cities of the colonial period. Although there was no organization of laborers as such, sailors, longshoremen, and other workers of the maritime industry occasionally rioted—stirred up by impressment gangs and sporadic economic stringency. The unskilled workers and skilled artisans who contributed the force to the violent Liberty Boy movement of the 1760s were made especially restless by the economic depression that followed the end of the Great War for the Empire.

It is with the coming of the Industrial Revolution to America in the nineteenth century that the labor movement really gets underway, concomitantly with the tremendous growth of American industry after the Civil War. Various labor organizations mushroomed: the Knights of Labor, American Railway Union, American Federation of Labor, Western Federation of Miners (W.F.M.), and the Industrial Workers of the World (I.W.W.). All made the strike a major weapon, and, in case after case, violence broke out during the strike. The blame was certainly not on the side of labor alone. The unyielding attitude of capitalists in regard to wages, hours, and working conditions gave impetus to the desire to unionize that led to the calling of strikes. The violent attempts by capital to suppress unions and break up strikes frequently incited the workers to violence. But laborers, too, were often more than ready to resort to violence, as many of the great upheavals after the Civil War indicate. The great railroad strike of 1877 triggered massive riots, which, in Pittsburgh, reached the level of insurrection. About the same time, the decade-long Molly Maguire troubles in the hard-coal field of eastern Pennsylvania came to a climax. The Molly Maguires were a secret organization of Irish miners who fought their employers with assassination and mayhem.[92] Such events as the Haymarket Riot in Chicago (1886),[93] the Homestead strike (1892),[94] the Coeur d'Alene, Idaho, silver mining troubles (1892 and after), and the 1910 dynamiting of the Los Angeles *Times* building (by the McNamara brothers of the supposedly conservative American Federation of Labor) led Louis Adamic correctly to label the period from the late 1800s to the early 1900s as the "dynamite era" in American labor relations.[95]

The Western mining state of Colorado affords a paradigm of the dynamite era of labor violence. From 1884 to 1914, Colorado had its own "Thirty Years' War" of strikes and violence, which typified the economic, class, and ethnic tensions of the period.[96] Colorado's 30-year period of acute labor violence came to a climax with what may have been the most violent upheaval in American labor history: the coal miners' strike against the Colorado Fuel and Iron Company (1913-1914). During the first five weeks of the strike (which took place in southern Colorado) there were 38 armed skirmishes in which 18 persons were killed. The final horror took place on April 20, 1914, at Ludlow, Colorado. A 15-hour battle between strikers and militiamen ended in the burning of the strikers' tent city during which two mothers and eleven children suffocated to death in the "Black Hole of Ludlow." Following this tragedy, maddened miners erupted in a ten-day rebellion that brought anarchy and unrestrained class warfare to a 250-mile area of southern Colorado before federal troops ended the violence. The Ludlow conflict was, in truth, an actualization of the apocalyptic visions of class warfare of Jack London in *The Iron Heel* (1907) and other writers of the period.

The last great spasm of violence in the history of American labor, to date, came in the 1930s, with the sit-down strike movement that accompanied the successful drive to unionize the automobile and other great mass production industries. A tendency to labor violence survives, however, as the case of the national strike of independent truck drivers in early 1974 shows. The strikers had been a part of the so-called "middle American" element that had most strongly opposed black riots and campus violence in the 1960s and had responded positively to Governor George Wallace's national political campaigns in behalf of law and order, but when the independent truckers found themselves fighting for economic survival against a combination of fuel shortages and high fuel prices, they did not hesitate to use violence against nonstriking truck drivers in their effort to make their strike effective and bring about a change in the federal government's policy on the allocation and pricing of diesel truck fuel. As a result of the strikers' violence, men were killed and injured and in eight states, it was necessary to call out the National Guard to keep the main highways open until the strike ended.[97]

IV

By now it is evident that, historically, American life has been characterized by continuous and often intense violence. It is not merely that violence has accompanied such negative aspects of our history as criminal activity, political assassination, and racial conflict. On the contrary, violence has formed a seamless web with some of the most positive events of U.S. history: independence (revolutionary violence), the freeing of the slaves and the preservation of the Union (Civil War violence), the occupation of the land (Indian wars), the stabilization of frontier society (vigilante violence), the elevation of the farmer and the laborer (agrarian and labor violence), and the preservation of law and order (police violence). The patriot, the humanitarian, the nationalist, the pioneer, the landholder, the farmer, and the laborer (and the capitalist) have used violence as a means to a higher end.

All too often unyielding and unsympathetic, established political and economic power has incited violence by its refusal to heed and appease just grievances. Thus, Governor Berkeley of Virginia ignored the pleas of Virginia planters, and the result was Bacon's Rebellion. The British government in 1774-1776 remained adamant in the face of patriot pleas, and the result was the American Revolution. The tobacco trust scoffed at the grievances of farmers, and the result was the Kentucky Night Rider movement. American capitalists ground workers into the dust, and the result was the violent labor movement. The possessors of power and wealth have often been arrogant in their refusal to share their advantages until it has been too late. Arrogance is indeed a quality that comes to unchecked power more readily than sympathy and forbearance.

By the same token, one can argue that the aggrieved in American history have been too quick to revolt, too hastily violent. We have resorted so often to violence that we have long since become a trigger-happy people. Violence is clearly rejected by us as a part of the American value system, but so great has been our involvement with violence over the long sweep of our history that violence has truly become part of our unacknowledged (or underground) value structure.[98]

NOTES

1. Among general works on American violence are the following: Richard Maxwell Brown, ed., *American Violence* (Englewood Cliffs, N.J., 1970); Richard Hofstadter and Michael Wallaces, eds., *American Violence: A Documentary History* (New York, 1970); and Thomas Rose, ed., *Violence in America: A Historical and Contemporary Reader* (New York, 1970), are three documentary collections. A notable interdisciplinary volume is by Hugh Davis Graham and Ted Robert Gurr, eds., *The History of Violence in America* (New York, 1969), originally published (Washington, 1969) under the title of *Violence in America: Historical and Comparative Perspectives* as a task force report of the National Commission on the Causes and Prevention of Violence; see also James F. Short, Jr., and Marvin E. Wolfgang, eds., *Collective Violence* (Chicago, 1972). Two studies of American protest and violence are Jerome H. Skolnick, *The Politics of Protest* (New York, 1969), and Richard Rubenstein, *Rebels in Eden: Mass Political Violence in the United States* (Boston, 1970); two treatments of political violence are by H. L. Nieburg, *Political Violence: The Behavioral Process* (New York, 1969), and Ted Robert Gurr, *Why Men Rebel* (Princeton, 1970). Hugh Davis Graham et al., *Violence: The Crisis of American Confidence* (Baltimore, 1971), presented a spectrum of recent American opinion on violence. This essay is drawn from my *Strain of Violence* (New York, 1975), Ch. 1, which, in turn, represented a revision of my similar essay in Graham and Gurr, eds., *Violence in America*, Ch. 2.

2. See, for example, Ivor Noël Hume, *1775: Another Part of the Field* (New York, 1966), 32-34, 125-30, 284-88.

3. Adrian C. Leiby, *The Revolutionary War in the Hackensack Valley* (New Brunswick, 1962).

4. Miles R. Feinstein, "The Origins of the Pineys of New Jersey" (B. A. thesis, Rutgers University, 1963), 56-73.

5. On the sense of foreboding, see Francis Grierson's *Valley of the Shadows,* ed. Bernard De Voto (New York, 1966). Of the many writings on John Brown, see Stephen B. Oates's *To Purge This Land with Blood: A Biography of John Brown* (New York, 1970).

6. Allan Nevins, *The Emergence of Lincoln,* Vol. 2, *Prologue to Civil War, 1859-1861* (New York, 1950), 306-8.

7. The newest treatment is by Adrian Cook, *The Armies of the Streets: The New York Draft Riots of 1863* (Lexington, 1974), the first extended scholarly study.

8. Frank L. Klement, *The Copperheads in the Middle West* (Chicago, 1960).

9. Richard S. Brownlee, *Gray Ghosts of the Confederacy: Guerrilla Warfare in the West, 1861-1865* (Baton Rouge, 1958).

10. E. Merton Coulter, *The Civil War and Readjustment in Kentucky* (Chapel Hill, 1926).

11. Georgia L. Tatum, *Disloyalty in the Confederacy* (Chapel Hill, 1934), 36-44, 54-72, 143-55.

12. Virgil C. Jones, *The Hatfields and the McCoys* (Chapel Hill, 1948); Meriel D. Harris, "Two Famous Kentucky Feuds and Their Causes" (M.A. thesis, University of Kentucky, 1940); Rufus L. Gardner, *The Courthouse Tragedy, Hillsville, Va.* (Mt. Airy, N. C., 1962).

13. C.L. Sonnichsen, *I'll Die before I'll Run: The Story of the Great Feuds of Texas* (New York, 1962) and *Ten Texas Feuds* (Albuquerque, 1957).

14. One of the most spectacular of the family-factional feuds in New Mexico was the Lincoln County War, 1878 and later, from which Billy the Kid emerged to fame. See Maurice G. Fulton, *History of the Lincoln County War,* ed. Robert N. Mullin (Tucson, 1968).

15. Earle R. Forrest, *Arizona's Dark and Bloody Ground* (Caldwell, Idaho, 1936); Zane Grey, *To the Last Man* (New York, 1922).

16. William O. Stevens, *Pistols at Ten Paces: The Story of the Code of Honor in America* (Boston, 1940), 84-86, 147-85, 228-44, 260-61, 280-81.

17. Charles E. Rosenberg, *The Trial of the Assassin Guiteau* (Chicago, 1968).

18. Walter Channing, "The Mental Status of Czolgosz, the Assassin of President McKinley," *American Journal of Insanity,* 49 (1902-1903): 233-78.

19. *Report of the Warren Commission on the Assassination of President Kennedy* (New York, 1964), 350-99, 596-659. For studies of the psychology of the assassins of leading public figures, with emphasis upon presidental assassins, that stress the factor of individual abnormality, see the articles by Lawrence Z. Freedman, David A. Rothstein, and Thomas Greening in William J. Crotty ed., *Assassinations and the Political Order* (New York, 1971). Also emphasizing the factor of individual abnormality is the book by James F. Kirkham, Sheldon G. Levy, and William J. Crotty, *Assassination and Political Violence: A Report to the National Commission on the Causes and Prevention of Violence* (Washington, 1969), 62-69, which also contains the most complete quantitative data on assassinations in America to date.

20. This is a generally held view supported by, among others, William J. Crotty, 3, and Lawrence Z. Freedman, 144, in Crotty, *Assassinations and the Political Order,* and by Kirkham, Levy, and Crotty in *Assassination and Political Violence,* xvii-xviii, 110. A dissent is registered by Richard E. Rubenstein, 415-17, in Crotty, *Assassinations and the Political Order.*

21. Allen W. Trelease, *White Terror: The Ku Klux Klan Conspiracy and Southern Reconstruction* (New York, 1971), 212-15. Albion W. Tourgee incorporated Stephens's assassination into his best-selling novel, *A Fool's Errand* (New York, 1969).

22. Daniel W. Crofts, "The Blair Bill and the Elections Bill: The Congressional Aftermath to Reconstruction" (Ph.D dissertation, Yale University, 1968), 244-45.

23. On Kennedy: Robert B. Kaiser, *"R. F. K. Must Die"* (New York, 1970), and Thomas C. Greening in Crotty, *Assassinations and the Political Order.* On Wallace: Arthur H. Bremer, *An Assassin's Diary* (New York, 1973), which reveals that Wallace was a surrogate for Bremer's original intended victim, President Richard M. Nixon, whose shooting Bremer failed to carry out. The assassinations of King, Malcolm X, Evers, Rockwell, and Yablonski await further study. On the Long assassination: T. Harry Williams, *Huey Long* (New York, 1969), and "Louisiana Mystery—An Essay Review" in *Louisiana History,* 6 (1965), which surveys the numerous works on the event, including books by Hermann R. Deutsch and David Zinman.

24. Thomas D. Clark, "The People, William Goebel, and the Kentucky Railroads," *Journal of Southern History,* 5 (1939): 34-48. See, also, Woodson Urey, *The First New Dealer* (Louisville, 1939), a biography of Goebel.

25. Howard R. Lamar, *The Far Southwest, 1846-1912: A Territorial History* (New Haven, 1966), 192-95. In the 1890s Fall was still a Democrat. He did not switch to the Republican party until after the turn of the century. Today Fall is chiefly remembered for his connection with the unsavory Teapot Dome scandal as Harding's Secretary of the Interior, but Arrell M. Gibson in *The Life and Death of Colonel Albert Jennings Fountain* (Norman, 1965) branded Fall as the leading plotter against Fountain. A milder treatment of Fall's role in the Fountain case appears in C. L. Sonnichsen, *Tularosa: Last of the Frontier West* (New York, 1960). Two leading authorities attest assassination as a political weapon in territorial New Mexico: Lamar, *Far Southwest,* 192-95; and Warren A. Beck, *New Mexico: A History of Four Centuries* (Norman, 1962). See also Crotty, *Assassinations and the Political Order,* 25-26.

26. See statements by Joseph Satten, Amitai Etzioni, and other social scientists reported in the New York *Times,* June 9, 1968, Sec. I, p. 64, cols. 1-3; and see also Ladd Wheeler's "Toward a Theory of Behavioral Contagion," *Psychological Review,* 73 (1966): 179-92; and Ladd Wheeler and Anthony R. Caggiula's "The Contagion of Aggression," *Journal of Experimental Social Psychology,* 2 (1966): 1-10.

27. Eric J. Hobsbawm, *Social Bandits and Primitive Rebels* (Glencoe, 1959).

28. William A. Settle, *Jesse James Was His Name or Fact and Fiction Concerning the Careers of the Notorious James Brothers of Missouri* (Columbia, Mo., 1966). A recent novel that gives a social-bandit image to certain fictional Mafia leaders is Mario Puzo's *The Godfather* (New York, 1969), and the later film version of the book conveys the same image.

29. W. McKee Evans, *To Die Game: The Story of the Lowry Band, Indian Guerrillas of Reconstruction* (Baton Rouge, 1971). For the enormous literature on Billy the Kid, see Ramon F. Adams's *A Fitting Death for Billy the Kid* (Norman, 1960). Paul I. Wellman, *A Dynasty of Western Outlaws* (New York, 1961), Ch. 12. This provocative book traces a Southwestern criminal dynasty from Civil War guerrilla William C. Quantrill through the Jameses to Pretty Boy Floyd. John Toland, *The Dillinger Days* (New York, 1963), and William Schnurr, *Johnnie Death* (New York, 1974), a novel based on Dillinger's career. The popular movie, *Bonnie and Clyde,* depicts Clyde Barrow and Bonnie Parker as social bandits as does, more realistically, Jan I. Fortune, *The True Story of Bonnie & Clyde: As Told by Bonnie's Mother and Clyde's Sister* (New York, 1968).

30. Herbert Asbury, *The Gangs of New York: An Informal History of the Underworld* (New York, 1928). A significant study of the general level of urban criminal violence is Roger Lane's "Urbanization and Criminal Violence in the Nineteenth Century: Massachusetts as a Test Case," in Graham and Gurr, *History of Violence in America,* 468-84.

31. Leo Katcher, *The Big Bankroll: The Life and Times of Arnold Rothstein* (New York, 1959).

32. Donald R. Cressey, *Theft of the Nation: The Structure and Operations of Organized Crime in America* (New York, 1969), 8ff.

33. Estes Kefauver, *Crime in America,* ed. Sidney Shalett (Garden City, N. Y., 1951). See also John Kobler, *Capone* (New York, 1971). An important new study is William H. Moore, "The Kefauver Committee and the Politics of Crime, 1950-1952" (Ph.D dissertation, University of Texas at Austin, 1971).

34. *The Challenge of Crime in a Free Society: A Report of the President's Commission on Law Enforcement and Administration of Justice* (Washington, 1967), 187-200. See also President's Commission on Law Enforcement and Administration of Justice, *Task Force Report: Organized Crime* (Washington, 1967); Peter Maas, *The Valachi Papers* (New York, 1968); Hank Messick, *Lansky* (New York, 1971); and on the Bonanno family, Gay Talese, *Honor Thy Father* (New York, 1971). The leading scholarly studies are Cressey's *Theft of the Nation* and two books that ably attack many standard conceptions about the Mafia: Joseph L. Albini, *The American Mafia: Genesis of a Legend* (New York, 1971), and Francis A.J. Ianni, *A Family Business: Kinship and Social Control in Organized Crime* (New York, 1972). See also Jay R. Nash, *Bloodletters and Badmen: An Encyclopedia of American Criminals from the Pilgrims to the Present* (New York, 1973).

35. On Speck, see Jack Altman and Marvin C. Ziporyn, *Born to Raise Hell* (New York, 1967). On Whitman: *Time,* Aug. 12, 1966, pp 19ff. Another alleged freelance mass murderer, most recently, is Dean Allen Corll. For some other noted freelance mass murderers, see Nash, *Bloodletters and Badmen.*

36. On the biological factor: Donald J. Mulvihill and Melvin M. Tumin with Lynn A. Curtis, *Crimes of Violence: A Staff Report to the National Commission on the Causes and Prevention of Violence* (Washington, 1969), Vol. 2, 420-23; Gerald E. McClearn, "Biological Bases of Social Behavior with Specific Reference to Violent Behavior," ibid, Vol. 3, 997-1003; Frank Ervin, "The Biology of Individual Violence: An Overview," ibid, Vol.3, 1020-21, 1032-33. A study that examines the relationship between the anxieties and neuroses of the 1890's and local violence and disorder is Michael Lesy's *Wisconsin Death Trip* (New York, 1973).

37. Otto A. Rothert, *The Outlaws of Cave-In-Rock* (Cleveland, 1924), 55-156, 241-66. See also Robert M. Coates, *The Outlaw Years . . .* (New York, 1930).

38. John T. James, *The Benders of Kansas* (Wichita, 1913).

39. Frank P. Geyer, *The Holmes-Pitezel Case . . .* (Philadelphia, 1896). Colin Wilson and Patricia Pitman, *Encyclopedia of Murder* (New York, 1962), 286-89. For other freelance multiple murderers see also Nash, *Bloodletters and Badmen.*

40. Pioneering treatments in this direction are Lesy's *Wisconsin Death Trip* and Sheldon Hackney's "Southern Violence," in this volume, Ch. 15. Useful to the study of murder in American history is Thomas McDade's *The Annals of Murder: A Bibliography of Books and Pamphlets on American Murders from Colonial Times to 1900* (Norman, 1961), in which the 1,126 bibliographical entries are heavily annotated. A relevant literary study is by David B. Davis, *Homicide in American Fiction, 1798-1860: A Study in Social Values* (Ithaca, 1957).

41. Walter Prescott Webb, *The Texas Rangers* (Austin,1965); Ben H. Procter, "The Modern Texas Rangers: A Law Enforcement Dilemma in the Rio Grande Valley," in John A. Carroll, ed., *Reflections of Western Historians* (Tucson, 1969); Frank R. Prassel, *The Western Peace Officer: A Legacy of Law and Order* (Norman, 1972). Philip D. Jordan deals primarily with the Mississippi Valley in *Frontier Law and Order* (Lincoln, 1970).

42. George A. Ketcham, "Municipal Police Reform: A Comparative Study of Law Enforcement in Cincinnati, Chicago, New Orleans, New York, and St. Louis, 1844-1877" (Ph.D. dissertation, University of Missouri, Columbia, 1967); Selden D. Bacon, "The Early Development of American Municipal Police: A Study of the Evolution of Formal Controls in a

Changing Society" (Ph.D. dissertation, Yale University, 1939). James F. Richardson, *The New York Police: Colonial Times to 1901* (New York, 1970). William R. Miller, "The Legitimation of the London and New York City Police, 1830-1870" (Ph.D. dissertation, Columbia University, 1973). Roger Lane, *Policing the City: Boston, 1822-1885* (Cambridge, Mass., 1967).

43. Martha Derthick, *The National Guard in Politics* (Cambridge, Mass., 1965), 16-17. Joseph L. Holmes. "The National Guard of Pennsylvania: Policeman of Industry, 1865-1905" (Ph.D. dissertation, University of Connecticut, 1971).

44. James D. Horan, *The Pinkertons: The Detective Dynasty that Made History* (New York, 1968). Anthony S. Nicolosi, "The Rise and Fall of the New Jersey Vigilant Societies," *New Jersey History,* 86 (1968): 29-32; Hugh C. Gresham, *The Story of Major David McKee, Founder of the Anti-Horse Thief Association* (Cheney, Kan., 1937); Patrick B. Nolan, "Vigilantes on the Middle Border: A Study of Self-Appointed Law Enforcement in the States of the Upper Mississippi from 1840 to 1880" (Ph.D. dissertation, University of Minnesota, 1971).

45. J. P. Shalloo, *Private Police: With Special Reference to Pennsylvania* (Philadelphia, 1933), 58-134.

46. Jurgen Thorwald, *The Century of the Detective,* trans. Richard and Clara Winston (New York, 1965).

47. On the third-degree problem, see the study by the Wickersham Commission: National Commission on Law Observance and Enforcement, *Report on Lawlessness in Law Enforcement* (Washington, 1931), 13-261. On police brutality since the Second World War, see, for example, Albert J. Reiss, "Police Brutality—Answers to Key Questions." *Trans-Action,* 5 (1968): 10-19; and William A. Westley, *Violence and the Police: A Sociological Study of Law, Custom, and Morality* (Cambridge, Mass., 1970).

48. Two older historical studies are Harry E. Barnes's *The Story of Punishment* (Boston, 1930), and Blake McKelvey's *American Prisons* (Chicago, 1936). Recent studies are W. David Lewis, *From Newgate to Dannemora: The Rise of the Penitentiary, 1796-1848* (Ithaca, 1965); Karl A. Menninger, *The Crime of Punishment* (New York, 1968); Norman Johnston, Leonard Savitz, and Marvin E. Wolfgang, *The Sociology of Punishment and Correction* (New York, 1970).

49. Rodney Stark, *Police Riots: Collective Violence and Law Enforcement* (Belmont, Calif., 1972); Daniel Walker, *Rights in Conflict: The Violent Confrontation of Demonstrators and Police in the Parks and Streets of Chicago during the Week of the Democratic National Convention of 1968* (New York, 1968).

50. Mitford M. Mathews, ed., *A Dictionary of Americanisms on Historical Principles* (Chicago, 1956), 1010; Richard Maxwell Brown, *The South Carolina Regulators* (Cambridge, Mass., 1963), 38-39ff.

51. James E. Cutler, *Lynch-Law: An Investigation into the History of Lynching in the United States* (New York, 1905), 24-31.

52. In addition to Cutler, *Lynch-Law,* see Walter White, *Rope & Faggot: A Biography of Judge Lynch* (New York, 1929); and Arthur F. Raper, *The Tragedy of Lynching* (Chapel Hill, 1938).

53. For a fuller treatment of vigilantism, see Ch. 6.

54. Lucile Morris, *Bald Knobbers* (Caldwell, Idaho, 1939).

55. For an expanded treatment of elite participation in vigilantism, see Ch. 6 of my *Strain of Violence.*

56. Eliphalet Price, "The Trial and Execution of Patrick O'Conner," *Palimpsest,* 1 (1920): 86-97.

57. Granville Stuart, *Forty Years on the Frontier,* ed., Paul C. Phillips (Cleveland, 1925), Vol. 2, 196-97.

58. Episodes of neovigilantism appear in John W. Caughey, ed., *Their Majesties the Mob* (Chicago, 1960).

59. The Chicago *Tribune*, Jan. 23, 1887, p. 3, col. 7, and the New York *Times*, Oct. 12, 1887, p. 2, col. 1, record the outbreak of white capping in Crawford, Orange, and Harrison counties of southern Indiana in 1887. It is possible, however, that white capping occurred earlier, in late 1886. Within the year White Cap activity had spread to Ohio; it is described in the *Ohio State Journal* (Columbus), Nov. 26, 29, Dec. 1, 3, 5-7, 10, 12, 21, 1888. The New York *Times* story of Oct. 12, 1887, is reprinted in Brown, *American Violence*, 96-99. On the Indiana origins of white capping, see Madeleine M. Noble, "The White Caps of Harrison and Crawford County, Indiana: A Study in the Violent Enforcement of Morality" (Ph.D. dissertation, University of Michigan, 1973). Sally L. James, "American Violent Moral Regulation and the White Caps" (senior honors essay, College of William and Mary, 1969), treats the movement nationally as well as in its Indiana beginnings.

60. Samuel L. Evans, "Texas Agriculture, 1880-1930" (Ph.D. dissertation, University of Texas, 1960), 320-21. *Texas Farm and Ranch* (Dallas), Oct. 1, 8, 1898. William F. Holmes, "Whitecapping: Agrarian Violence in Mississippi, 1902-1906," *Journal of Southern History*, 35 (1969): 165-85.

61. Sheriff A. M. Avant, Atascosa County, Sept. 20, 1898, to Governor C. A. Culberson in Letters to Governor C. A. Culberson (manuscripts in Texas State Archives, Austin).

62. "The 'White Caps,' 1890-1893" (file of manuscripts and clippings in L. Bradford Prince papers in the New Mexico State Records Center, Santa Fe). See especially the August 12, 1890, memorandum of Governor Prince to John W. Noble, federal Secretary of the Interior. Secondary sources on the White Caps include Andrew Bancroft Schlesinger's "Las Gorras Blancas, 1889-1891," *Journal of Mexican-American History*, 1 (1971); and Robert W. Larsen's "The 'White Caps' of New Mexico: The Political and Ethnic Origins of Western Violence" (unpublished paper, Organization of American Historians, Washington, 1972). On Tijerina's *Alianza* movement and its violent activities, see Peter Nabokov, *Tijerina & the Courthouse Raid* (Albuquerque, 1969); Michael Jenkinson, *Tijerina* (Albuquerque, 1968); and Richard Gardner, *Grito!: Reies Tijerina and the New Mexico Land Grant War of 1967* (Indianapolis, 1972).

63. For example, Robert E. Cunningham, *Trial by Mob* (Stillwater, 1957), 12-13; Ethelred W. Crozier, *The White-Caps: A History of the Organization in Sevier County* (Knoxville, 1899), 10-11, 87ff., 180ff.

64. Douglas E. Leach, *The Northern Colonial Frontier, 1607-1763* (New York, 1966). See also Alden T. Vaughan, *New England Frontier: Puritans and Indians, 1620-1675* (Boston, 1965).

65. Douglas E. Leach, *Flintlock and Tomahawk: New England in King Philip's War* (New York, 1966).

66. *Encyclopaedia Britannica* (11th edition; New York, 1910-1911), Vol. 24, 286-87. Leach, *Northern Colonial Frontier*, 112. Major Indian wars are treated in William T. Hagan, *American Indians* (Chicago, 1961); William Brandon, *The American Heritage Book of Indians* (New York, 1961); and Dee Brown, *Bury My Heart at Wounded Knee: An Indian History of the American West* (New York, 1970). See also Wilbur R. Jacobs, *Dispossessing the American Indian: Indians and Whites on the Colonial Frontier* (New York, 1972).

67. See *Strain of Violence*, Ch. 7.

68. Trelease, *White Terror*.

69. On violent aspects of the second Ku Klux Klan, see David M. Chalmers, *Hooded Americanism: The First Century of the Ku Klux Klan, 1865-1965* (Garden City, N.Y., 1965); and Charles C. Alexander, *The Ku Klux Klan in the Southwest* (Lexington, 1965).

70. Ray A. Billington, *The Protestant Crusade, 1800-1860: A Study of the Origins of American Nativism* (New York, 1938).

71. Robert E. Wynne, "Reaction to the Chinese in the Pacific Northwest and British Columbia: 1850 to 1910" (Ph.D. dissertation, University of Washington, 1964).

72. See *Strain of Violence*, Ch. 6; Donald L. Kinzer, *An Episode in Anti-Catholicism: The American Protective Association* (Seattle, 1964).

73. See, for example, David Brody, *Steelworkers in America: The Nonunion Era* (Cambridge, Mass., 1960).

74. Important comparative studies of violence in eighteenth-century America and Great Britain are Lloyd I. Rudolph's "The Eighteenth-Century Mob in America and Europe," *American Quarterly*, 11 (1959): 447-69; William Ander Smith's "Anglo-Colonial Society and the Mob, 1740-1775" (Ph.D. dissertation, Claremont Graduate School, 1965); and Pauline Maier's "Popular Uprisings and Civil Authority in Eighteenth-Century America," *William and Mary Quarterly*, 3d Ser., 27 (1970): 3-35.

75. Jesse Lemisch, "Jack Tar in the Streets: Merchant Seamen in the Politics of Revolutionary America," *William and Mary Quarterly*, 3d Ser., 25 (1968): 387-93.

76. For source citations and a taxonomy of the major riots in Baltimore, Philadelphia, New York, Boston, and Cincinnati, see *Strain of Violence*, 334-36, notes 116-25.

77. John C. Schneider, "Mob Violence and Public Order in the American City" (Ph.D. dissertation, University of Minnesota, 1971). A perceptive study dealing with rural as well as urban rioting is David Grimsted, "Rioting in Its Jacksonian Setting," *American Historical Review*, 77 (1972): 361-97. Also see Leanoard L. Richards, *"Gentlemen of Property and Standing": Anti-Abolition Mobs in Jacksonian America (New York, 1970)*.

78. Robert V. Bruce, *1877: Year of Violence* (Indianapolis, 1959), a most important study.

79. See *Strain of Violence*, Chs. 4-5.

80. Ibid., Ch. 7.

81. On Bacon's Rebellion: Wilcomb E. Washburn, *The Governor and the Rebel: A History of Bacon's Rebellion in Virginia* (Chapel Hill, 1957); Thomas J. Wertenbaker, *Torchbearer of the Revolution: The Story of Bacon's Rebellion and Its Leader* (Princeton, 1940). On the New Jersey land rioters: Gary S. Horowitz, "New Jersey Land Riots, 1745-1755" (Ph.D. dissertation, Ohio State University, 1966). On the Paxton Boys: Brooke Hindle, "The March of the Paxton Boys," *William and Mary Quarterly*, 3d Ser., 3 (1946): 461-86; Wilbur R. Jacobs, ed., *The Paxton Riots and the Frontier Theory* (Chicago, 1967); and David Sloan, "The Paxton Riots" (Ph.D. dissertation, University of California at Santa Barbara, 1968).

82. John S. Bassett, "The Regulators of North Carolina (1765-1771)," American Historical Association, *Annual Report for the year 1894*, 141-212. On the background of the North Carolina Regulators: Marvin L. M. Kay, "The Payment of Provincial and Local Texas in North Carolina, 1748-1771." *William and Mary Quarterly*, 3d Ser., 26 (1969): 218-40. A collection of historical sources is William S. Powell, James K. Huhta, and Thomas J. Farnham, eds., *The Regulators in North Carolina: A Documentary History, 1759-1776* (Raleigh, 1971). The best general study remains Elmer Douglas Johnson's "The War of the Regulation: Its Place in History" (M.A. thesis, University of North Carolina at Chapel Hill, 1942).

83. Irving Mark, *Agrarian Conflicts in Colonial New York, 1711-1775* (New York, 1940); Patricia U. Bonomi, *A Factious People: Politics and Society in Colonial New York* (New York, 1971); David M. Ellis, *Landlords and Farmers in the Hudson-Mohawk Region, 1790-1850* (Ithaca, 1946); Henry Christman, *Tin Horns and Calico* (New York, 1945); Sung Bok Kim, "The Manor of Cortlandt and Its Tenants: New York, 1697-1783" (Ph.D. dissertation, Michigan State University, 1966).

84. Marion L. Starkey, *A Little Rebellion* (New York, 1955); Robert A. Feer, "Shays's Rebellion" (Ph.D. dissertation, Harvard University, 1958); Van Beck Hall, *Politics without Parties, 1780-1791* (Pittsburgh, 1972); Leland D. Baldwin, *Whiskey Rebels* (Pittsburgh, 1939); William W. H. Davis, *The Fries Rebillion, 1798-1799* ... (Doylestown, Pa., 1899);

Peter Levine, "The Fries Rebellion: Social Violence and the Politics of the New Nation," *Pennsylvania History,* 15 (1973): 241-58.

85. Allan G. Bogue, "The Iowa Claim Clubs: Symbol and Substance," *Mississippi Valley Historical Review,* 45 (1958): 231-53.

86. Robert Lee Hunt, *A History of Farmer Movements in the Southwest: 1873-1925* (n.p., n.d.), 28-29. Still the most complete account of the Populist movement is John D. Hicks's *The Populist Revolt* (Minneapolis, 1931). For the violent suppression of a local interracial white-black Populist movement: Lawrence C. Goodwyn, "Populist Dreams and Negro Rights: East Texas as a Case Study," *American Historical Review,* 76 (1971): 1435-56.

87. James L. Brown, in *The Mussel Slough Tragedy* (n.p., 1958), deals with the settlers' land league in the Hanford vicinity and its night-riding activities, which came to a climax in the Mussel Slough gun battle, an episode that Frank Norris used as the basis of his novel, *The Octopus: A Story of California* (New York, 1901).

88. James O. Nall, *The Tobacco Night Riders of Kentucky and Tennessee, 1905-1909* (Louisville, 1939). See also Robert Penn Warren's brilliant novel, *Night Rider* (Boston, 1939). Paul J. Vanderwood, in *Night Riders of Reelfoot Lake* (Memphis, 1969) studies another night-rider movement—that along Reelfoot Lake in northwest Tennessee in 1908.

89. John Womack, Jr., "Oklahoma's Green Corn Rebellion" (B.A. thesis, Harvard College, 1959); H. C. Peterson and Gilbert C. Fite, *Opponents of War, 1917-1918* (Madison, 1957), 40-42, 171-76.

90. Robert L. Morlan, *Political Prairie Fire: The Nonpartisan League, 1915-1922* (Minneapolis, 1955).

91. John L. Shover, *Cornbelt Rebellion: The Farmers' Holiday Association* (Urbana, 1965).

92. "Molly Maguire" was an anti-British persona in Irish folklore whom the Irish miners of Pennsylvania adopted as a symbol of their resistance to the authority of the mine owners and bosses. Wayne G. Broehl, Jr., *The Molly Maguires* (Cambridge, Mass., 1964) is an outstanding study that treats in depth the European roots, as well as the American substance, of a violent movement.

93. Henry David, *The History of the Haymarket Affair* (New York, 1936).

94. Leon Wolff, *Lockout . . .* (New York, 1965).

95. Louis Adamic, *Dynamite: The Story of Class Violence in America* (New York, 1934), 179-253. Another old but still useful work is by Samuel Yellen, *American Labor Struggles* (New York, 1936). An excellent newer study is by Graham Adams, Jr., *Age of Industrial Violence, 1910-1915: The Activities and Findings of the United States Commission on Industrial Relations* (New York, 1966). The most systematic and comprehensive treatment is by Philip Taft and Philip Ross, "American Labor Violence: Its Causes, Character, and Outcome," in Graham and Gurr, *History of Violence in America,* 281-395.

96. George S. McGovern, "The Colorado Coal Strike, 1913-1914" (Ph.D. dissertation, Northwestern University, 1953), 81-111. A revised and expanded version of Senator McGovern's dissertation is George S. McGovern and Leonard F. Guttridge, *The Great Coalfield War* (Boston, 1972).

97. *Newsweek,* Feb. 18, 1974, 19-22. See Roger Lane, "The Squeaky Wheel Gets the Oil: Independent Truckers and the OPEC Embargo of 1973-74," in Roger Lane and John J. Turner, Jr., eds., *Riot, Rout, and Tumult* (Westport, Conn., 1978), 364-73.

98. This is the import of a meticulous quantitative study—Monica D. Blumenthal, Robert C. Kahn, Frank M. Andrews, and Kendra B. Head, *Justifying Violence: Attitudes of American Men* (Ann Arbor, 1972)—that, on the basis of in-depth interviews in 1969 with 1,374 men, found "that half to two-thirds of American men . . . justify shooting in the situations described as requiring social control" (243). A powerful study that explicates the early relationship between violence and consciousness is Richard Slotkin, *Regeneration through Violence: The Mythology of the American Frontier, 1600-1860* (Middletown, 1973).

Chapter 2

Political Protest and Rebellion in the 1960s

The United States in World Perspective

TED ROBERT GURR

Episodes of antigovernment protest and rebellion are not spontaneous or random occurrences. Most of them are dramatic manifestations of underlying conflict between groups contending over questions of power and policy. Since political conflict is common in all societies, it ought not to be surprising that protest and rebellion are and have been recurring counterparts to conventional politics in most countries throughout recorded history. Sorokin analyzed the histories of eleven European states and empires over 2500 years and found that they averaged only four peaceful years for each year in which major disturbances were in progress.[2] In most regions of the contemporary world, governments change hands more often at gunpoint than as a result of national elections. Calvert has determined that 363 governments were altered by forceful intervention (revolution, in the narrow sense of the word) between 1901 and 1960, an average of six per year. Between 1960 and 1969 the average increased to nine per year.[3] In some countries, especially in Western Europe but also in some Asian and Latin American countries, demonstrations and political strikes have become a normal part of the political process.[4] Taylor and Hudson have documented the occurrence of some 5400 political demonstrations worldwide between 1948 and 1967.[5] In general, none but the smallest contemporary countries can expect to be free of open political conflict for more than a decade.

Open conflict between governments and citizens takes diverse forms, some of them much more intense than others. Moreover, there are vast differences among countries and regions in the typical forms, extent, and intensity of civil conflict. This chapter surveys the most precise evidence available about the characteristics of political protest and rebellion in 87 of the world's larger countries during the 1960s with special attention to the United States. The United States proves to have had more widespread and intense civil conflict than most other Western democracies

AUTHOR'S NOTE: *The author is Payson S. Wild Professor of political science at Northwestern University. His many books and monographs include* Why Men Rebel, *which won the Woodrow Wilson Prize as the best book in political science of 1970, and* Rogues, Rebels, and Reformers: A Political History of Urban Crime and Conflict *(1976).*

during that turbulent decade, but far less than many countries in Latin America, Africa, and Asia.

No general explanation or moral judgments are offered about protest and rebellion in this chapter, but a few general comments are in order. It is obvious that most open conflict in contemporary societies pits weak dissidents against powerful governments. Only in the Third World is it at all common to find dissidents whose numbers and military force of arms are a match for those of the state. The frequency of protest and rebellion despite these disparities of power is a testament to both the despair and unquenchable hopes of dissidents. The desire for change inspires protest in the hope that groups in power will respond favorably, while despair about resistance to change is often translated into rebellion. Of course protest and rebellion both can be powerful agents of social change, but only in limited circumstances: protest is effective if those in power accept the desirability of reform, while rebellion can be effective in those uncommon circumstances where a government's will and capacity to resist can be broken.[6] There is a tendency in much contemporary scholarship on protest and revolution to emphasize the ways in which calculating leaders can manipulate people and circumstances to build the conditions of successful challenges against governments. There is too little attention to the grievances, hopes, and fears of ordinary people which ultimately determine whether they are willing to be mobilized by ambitious leaders in risky and often deadly challenges to the status quo.[7]

TYPES OF POLITICAL CONFLICT AMONG CONTEMPORARY NATIONS

The subject of this survey is "open political conflict," which includes all overt, collective confrontations between groups contending over political issues. The most common political confrontations are those between private groups and governments; but private groups also clash among themselves in disputes over elections and government policies. Open political conflict includes symbolic confrontations, such as peaceful demonstrations and political strikes, as well as violent events like rioting, terrorism, and guerrilla warfare. All these forms of open conflict are sometimes given the inappropriate label "political violence." In fact not all of them are violent; political strikes and demonstrations usually are nonviolent, unless authorities try to suppress them, and in many countries they are entirely legal. Two other phrases are used in this survey as synonyms of open political conflict: they are "civil conflict" and "political protest and rebellion."

It matters greatly for the political life of a nation, and the well-being of its citizens, whether civil conflict takes the form of terrorism or demonstrations, coups d' état or revolutionary warfare. The simplest distinction that can be made between the manifestations of civil conflict is between *protest* and *rebellion*. The essence of the distinction is the issue of conflict. *Protest* arises from conflict over limited issues, such as opposition to particular policies or personnel of a government, or antagonisms between groups competing for political influence. *Rebellion* centers on more fundamental issues, especially struggles over who shall govern and by what means.

Other differences in civil conflict follow from the basic distinction between protest and rebellion. The typical forms of protest are political strikes, demonstrations, riots, and clashes. Many people usually take part in them, but ordinarily they are short-lived and confined to small areas of the cities in which they occur. Only large-scale riots are likely to result in extensive violence. Many of the casualties of protest are inflicted by the police and military when trying to stop protest. The typical forms of rebellion are coups and plots, terrorist campaigns, and guerrilla, civil, and revolutionary warfare. The planning and execution of coups and terrorist campaigns involve a conspiratorial strategy, which is most likely to be chosen by rebels who are few in number and face a powerful opponent. If rebels are more numerous, or if they calculate that their opponents are weak or irresolute, they are more likely to chose protracted, open warfare. *Conspiracy* and *internal war* are terms for these two kinds of rebellion.[8] Both are likely to require dedicated, persistent effort and involve great risks for those who initiate them. The costs of internal war, in destruction and human suffering, are especially great, a fact which the American Revolution and Civil War proved to past generations of Americans, and the Vietnam War recently demonstrated.

For the survey reported here, information was collected on all the kinds of open political conflict cited above for 87 of the world's largest nations and colonies from 1961 through 1970. The People's Republic of China and a number of small African and Asian countries were not included because of inadequate information; the 87 countries nonetheless include 73 percent of the world's people; and 95 percent of its population outside of China. The information was gathered mainly from the New York *Times* and supplemented by information from specialized regional news sources, such as *Asian Recorder* and *African Recorder*. More than 2,200 episodes of conflict were identified, counting campaigns of demonstrations, riots, or terrorism over related issues as single "episodes." For each episode, information was systematically recorded on the kinds of dissident groups involved, the approximate number of people who took part, their grievances, whom they acted against, how long the episode lasted, the severity of governmental response, and indicators of the intensity of conflict, such as numbers of casualties and arrests.[9]

Some summary information on the 2,200 episodes of conflict is shown in Table 2.1. Protest was far more common than rebellions, and far less deadly. Most of the 10,000 victims of the 1,525 campaigns and episodes of protest died not in confrontations with officials but in clashes with competing private groups. By contrast, more than three million people died in less than 200 internal wars. Over a million of them were killed in the Vietnam War between 1961 and 1970, a conflict counted here as a guerrilla war.[10] Most guerrilla wars are much more localized and less deadly than the Vietnam War, as can be seen from the median numbers of dissidents (2,600) and deaths (48 per year). These conflicts often sputter on for many years in the hinterlands of poor countries, where they represent more of a nuisance than a serious revolutionary threat.

Civil wars, in which one region of a country attempts to secede from the others, can be equally deadly. More Americans died in the American Civil War than in any international war in which the United States ever fought, for example. The attempted secession of Biafra from Nigeria from 1967 to January 1970 was crushed at a cost estimated as high as two million lives, some 100,000 of whom were military casualties; the others were victims of starvation and disease. (From the North

Table 2.1: Episodes of Political Conflict in the 1960s in 87 Countries

	Number Recorded[a]		Median Number[b] of Dissidents	Median[b] Days Duration	Median Number[b] of Deaths	Estimated Total Deaths[c]
	Western Democracies	Other Countries				
PROTEST						
Political strikes	35	72	40,000	1.1	.12	630
Demonstrations	185	424	1,300	½	less than .01	60
Riots	161	466	1,300	½	.14	3,500
Political clashes	61	121	400	½	.20	5,400
CONSPIRACY						
Antiregime plots	7	112	30	12	.04	300
Coups and attempts	2	97	400	1.2	.57	2,700
Small-scale terrorism[d]	94	213	30	½	.15	1,900
INTERNAL WAR						
Guerrilla wars[d]	12	120	2,600	365[e]	48[e]	1,300,000 +
Civil wars	0	33	10,000	365[e]	200[e]	1,500,000 +
Local rebellions	2	26	4,000	3	12	3,000
Revolts, private wars	0	11	40,000	100	4,000	300,000 +

a. Data on protests include both episodes or campaigns (for example, all antiwar demonstrations in the United States in 1966 are counted as a single campaign, all those in 1967 as another campaign, and so forth) and isolated events that were not part of larger campaigns. Data on internal wars register each year of a war as a separate case.

b. The median number is the midpoint. For example, half of all political strikes had more than 40,000 participants and half had fewer. Median numbers of deaths less than 1 signify that the majority of episodes had no deaths. The closer the median to 0, the fewer the number of events which had deaths.

c. Including dissidents, government personnel, foreign troops and advisors, and people killed accidentally or incidentally. People executed by governments for taking part in civil conflict also are counted.

d. Large-scale campaigns of terrorism are counted as guerilla wars.

e. Since each year of guerrilla and civil wars are tabulated separately in this analysis, the median duration and deaths for these events are annual figures.

Vietnamese point of view, the Vietnam War was a civil war, even though the strategy during the 1960s was to rely mainly on guerrilla warfare and terrorism.) "Revolts" are countrywide, urban and rural uprisings which aim at sweeping political change. A major example in the 1960s was the 1965 revolt of the people of the Dominican Republic against an attempt to reimpose military-oligarchic rule, a conflict which precipitated military intervention by the United States. "Private wars" are campaigns of terror and murder between rival political or communal groups. They are most likely to occur in Third World countries where governments are either too weak to impose order or tacitly favor one group over the other. The most deadly private war during the 1960s occurred in Indonesia in 1965-1966, when conservative religious and political groups throughout the country carried out a murderous pogrom of Communists in retaliation for an attempted coup. Estimates of deaths range from the government's figure of 87,000 to 500,000.[11]

THE TURBULENT 1960s: THE UNITED STATES IN COMPARATIVE PERSPECTIVE

Civil Conflict in the United States

More than six million Americans resorted to demonstrations, riots, or terrorism to express their political demands and private antagonisms during the 1960s. The great majority of them, over 80 percent, took part in protest activities that were both legal and peaceful. In the minority of events that were violent, an estimted 350 people died and more than 12,000 were reported injured. Nearly 100,000 people were arrested, most of them for rioting or looting, but many others for protest activity that exceeded the varying limits of official tolerance. The best available information on group protest and violence during the most turbulent part of the 1960s has been compiled and summarized in Table 2.2. The data are listed for three successive 30-month periods, begining in mid-1963. Some of this information was gathered by officials and other scholars, as shown in the notes. Most of it was collected especially for this survey, mainly from the New York *Times* and checked, where possible, against other sources. Many small nonviolent episodes of conflict are never reported in the national press and many estimates and plain guesses have been incorporated in the data summarized here. But this is the most comprehensive survey yet published, and while more detailed studies of particular campaigns will suggest some corrections, the general picture presented here is not likely to change significantly. It should be noted that the totals cited at the beginning of this paragraph, and in other tables and discussions, include data on civil conflict in the first quarter of the 1960s as well as conflict over issues not listed in Table 2.2.[12]

At the beginning of the 1960s the only significant issue of political protest was civil rights, which mobilized hundreds of thousands of civil rights demonstrators each year and a few tens of thousands of opponents. Civil rights protest lost its capacity to attract marchers and public attention after 1965 as opposition to the Vietnam War escalated. War protest reached a peak during the coordinated Moratorium campaigns of 1969, which were the largest protests ever organized in the United States for any purpose up to that time. This period also saw the rise of protest on university

Table 2.2: Characteristics of Major Types of Protest and Political Violence in the United States, June 1963-December 1970[a]

Type of Event and Period:
Period I: 6/63-12/65
Period II: 1/66-6/68
Period III: 7/68-12/70

	Number of Events Identified[b]	Estimated Number of Participants[c]	Reported Deaths[d]	Reported Injuries[e]	Reported Arrests[f]
Civil Rights and School Integration Demonstrations[g]					
Period I	243	1,000,000	0	263	14,313
Period II	120	254,000	0	87	1,388
Period III	60	202,000	0	10	1,200
Anti-Civil Rights and Anti-School Integration Demonstrations and Attacks[h]					
Period I	47	45,000	2	50	634
Period II	33	63,000	0	197	272
Period III	10	3,000	0	0	457
Ghetto Riots and Interracial Clashes[i]					
Period I	48	(100,000)	56	1,800	12,500
Period II	200	(150,000)	140	6,156	37,362
Period III	256	(100,000)	42	1,050	4,632
Terrorist Attacks against Minorities and Civil Rights Activists[j]					
Period I	160	no data	19	54	56
Period II	77	no data	11	34	62
Period III	31	no data	6	20	43
Black Activists' Attacks on Whites and Shoot-outs with Police[k]					
Period I	4	no data	0	0	3
Period II	28	no data	3	5	40
Period III	60	no data	49	127	217

Table 2.2: Characteristics of Major Types of Protest and Political Violence in the United States, June 1963-December 1970[a] (cont)

Type of Event and Period:
Period I: 6/63-12/65
Period II: 1/66-6/68
Period III: 7/68-12/70

	Number of Events Identified[b]	Estimated Number of Participants[c]	Reported Deaths[d]	Reported Injuries[e]	Reported Arrests[f]
Antiwar Demonstrations, on and off Campus[l]					
Period I	no data	161,000	0	1	443
Period II	no data	591,000	0	400	2,815
Period III	no data	2,233,000	5	1,250	4,050
Student Protests and Rebellions over Campus Issues[m]					
Period I	22	11,000	0	0	815
Period II	69	65,000	0	251	1,229
Period III	156	137,000	1	428	6,140
Antiestablishment Bombings and Arson[n]					
Periods I and II	no significant incidents				
Period III	125	no data	4	61	22

a. The data in this table include many estimates, especially for numbers of participants. A number of more limited forms of civil conflict are not shown here, including the assasination of political leaders; factional terrorism within the Black Muslim and Black Panther movements; attacks on white radicals and counterculture groups; the local rebellion of Mexican-Americans in New Mexico in June 1967; labor violence; and protests over environmental issues and women's rights, which began near the end of the period.

b. As reported in news sources, with the inclusions and exclusions listed in footnotes g to n. Demonstrations and riots that lasted for more than one day are counted only once. Simultaneous demonstrations in several neighborhoods or cities are counted separately. The primary source for most of the data is the New York *Times*, whose coverage other studies have shown to be comprehensive but not absolutely complete. Events which are small in scale, nonviolent, and occur in small communities are less likely than others to be reported in the *Times*.

c. Only private participants are counted here, not the police, National Guardsmen, and other officials involved in suppressing or containing protest and violence. The estimates of participants for many events are rough estimates and in some instances—especially for smaller events—are "guessestimates" assigned by coders. Figures in parentheses are especially tentative.

d. These date are more accurate than others in this table but cannot be assumed to be absolutely precise. They probably understate the actual totals because not all conflict deaths are accurately reported in the press and not all reported deaths have assuredly been identified by the compilers of the data.

e. Reports of injuries are of questionable reliability, whatever their source, since there are no standard reporting practices for them, either by officials or the press. Minor injuries to private citizens usually go unreported in any case.

Table 2.2: Characteristics of Major Types of Protest and Political Violence in the United States, June 1963-December 1970ᵃ (cont)

f. For riots and demonstrations these figures can be assumed to be roughly accurate; for terrorist attacks they are understated because most subsequent arrests are not included.

g. As reported in the New York *Times Index*. Excluded are events involving less than 100 people; indoor rallies and meetings; boycotts; and demonstrations that become riots or clashes with segregationists.

Also see note m, below.

h. Demonstrations opposing forced busing, school integration, and local control of school by blacks; counterdemonstrations against civil rights marchers; and group attacks by segregationists on civil rights demonstrators, all as reported in the New York *Times Index*. Excluded are events involving less than 100 people, indoor rallies and meetings, boycotts, strikes, and walkouts.

i. Data on ghetto riots for periods I and II are from Bryan T. Downes with Stephen W. Burke, "The Black Protest Movement and Urban Violence," paper read at the annual meeting of the American Political Science Association, Washington, D.C., September 1968, pp. 12-15. They define their subject as "hostile outbursts" initiated by blacks. We have added to their data information on ghetto riots for period III, from the New York *Times Index*, plus data on other black-white clashes for all three periods, from the same source (except those centering around civil rights demonstrations, included under the previous heading).

Most of these interracial clashes, as distinct from ghetto riots, involved high school students and were small.

j. Clandestine acts of terror and violence, including bombings, arson, shootings, beatings, and major cross-burning incidents, as reported in the New York *Times Index*. Most occurred in the Southern states and were the work of the KKK. Numbers of participants are rarely given. The total strength of the Klan organizations in the South in 1967 was about 16,000, according to the U.S. House Un-American Activities Committee (*The Present-Day Ku Klux Klan Movement*, Washington, D.C.: U.S. Government Printing Office, 1967, 3-5), but only a fraction were thought to be involved in violence against civil rights activists.

k. Isolated fire-bombings and sniping attacks by blacks against private citizens and their property, and against police, plus shoot-outs between black activists—mainly Black Panthers—and the police, as reported in the New York *Times Index*. Arson and shoot-outs during ghetto riots are included under that heading, not here. Numbers of participants rarely are known or reported.

l. For periods I and II, from data reported by Irving Louis Horowitz, "The Struggle is the Message," paper prepared for the Task Force on Group Protest and Violence, National Commission on the Causes and Prevention of Violence, September 1968, Tables 1, 2, and 3. For period III, from the New York *Times Index*. Comparable information on numbers of events cannot be reported because the war protest movement included both isolated demonstrations and coordinated nationwide campaigns of demonstrations; news reports of the latter usually identify only a few demonstrations in the larger locales.

m. High school and college demonstrations, sit-ins, and rebellions concerned primarily with campus issues, as reported in the New York *Times Index*. Campus civil rights protests are included under civil rights demonstrations; student antiwar protests are included under antiwar demonstrations. The most tumultuous campus rebellions are included here, including the 1968 episodes at Columbia University and San Francisco State. Minority rights and the war were among the issues of these rebellions, and others included here, but they were distinguished by their general antiestablishment and antiuniversity character.

n. Terrorist acts attributed to radical groups, occurring at high schools, colleges, businesses and banks, public buildings, etc., as reported in the New York *Times Index*. The Weather Underground claimed responsibility for many of them. Such acts which occurred during antiwar demonstrations and campus protests are included under those headings, not here.

and college campuses over a multitude of issues not directly related to the war. The real beginning of this kind of protest was the Free Speech Movement at the University of California's Berkeley campus in 1963. The ugliest episodes, at San Francisco State in 1968-1969, Columbia University in spring 1969, and Kent State University (Ohio) in May 1970, resembled mini-civil wars more than the peaceful demonstrations of the mid-1960s. By the end of the decade new issues of protest had begun to emerge, including environmental causes and the rights of women, Indians, and Hispanic-Americans. Widespread antiwar protest continued until the conclusion of the peace treaty in 1972, which paved the way for American troop withdrawal. Lesser protests sputtered on against American military assistance to the Thieu regime until spring 1975, when the Communist forces seized Saigon.

There was a dark, violent underside to each of the major conflicts which generated peaceful protest in the 1960s. Beginning late in the 1950s, white terrorists in the South carried out localized but deadly campaigns of terror against civil rights activists. These manifestations of white supremacy wilted as public opinion shifted against die-hard segregationists and as the federal government demonstrated its willingness to intervene. The first serious black ghetto riots in the North began while violent Southern resistance to integration was near its peak, in the summer of 1964. In the next five years virtually every Northern city with a sizeable black population had serious episodes of racial violence—the rare exceptions include Indianapolis, St. Louis, and Philadelphia—and some had several. Some people called them rebellions, and by whatever name they were the most deadly and destructive events of the decade.[13] Nearly 250 people died in them, most of them shot by police and National Guardsmen, and many blocks of cityscape were burnt out, some of them still not rebuilt a decade later. But each city's serious riot seemed to inoculate it against others, so by 1970 violent ghetto protests were declining sharply in numbers and even more sharply in size. A new form of black dissidence emerged as ghetto rioting declined: terrorist attacks on whites, especially white police. In the public view the Black Panthers were responsible for the new wave of black-on-white terrorism, for they preached virulent hatred of the "pigs." Most terrorist attacks on whites seem to have been carried out by free-lancers, though, and the Panthers, out-numbered and out-gunned, lost their handful of dramatic confrontations with the police.[14] So by 1970 black-on-white terrorism already had reached and passed its peak. Not so the revolutionary off-shoots of the antiwar movement and Students for a Democratic Society. A variety of clandestine radical groups were established after 1968, their purpose to work for revolution in capitalistic "Amerika," their favored tactic the symbolic bombing of public buildings and corporate headquarters. This mode of violent dissidence continued unabated into the early 1970s before it began to subside.

We cannot say whether these ten years were the most tumultuous in American history,[15] but quantitative comparisons can be made with other contemporary nations. The basic measures used are man-days of participation in conflict (the number of participants in each episode times the number of days it lasted, summed for all episodes) and deaths from conflict. Since countries vary greatly in population, direct comparison is possible only if these measures are weighted by population. Some essential findings are reported in Table 2.3. During the 1960s Americans

Table 2.3: Some General Characteristics of Civil Conflict in the United States, 1961-1970, Compared with Other Nations

	United States	Median for 18 Western Democracies[a]	Median for 87 Countries[b]
Extent of Political Protest			
Man-days of participation	5,400 per 100,000 population	700 per 100,000	900 per 100,000
Rank of the U.S. compared with		4th of 18	19th of 87
Extent of Rebellion			
Man-days of participation	250 per 100,000 population	9 per 100,000	130 per 100,000
Rank of the U.S. compared with		4th of 18	39th of 87
Intensity of Civil Conflict			
Conflict deaths	18 per 10 million population	0[c]	21 per 10 million
Rank of the U.S. compared with		1st of 18	45th of 87
Rank of Total Magnitude of Civil Conflict in the United States Compared with[d]			
In 1961-1965		5th of 18	43rd of 87
In 1966-1970		2nd of 18	23rd of 87

a. Nations used in this comparison are Australia, Austria, Belgium, Britain (excluding Northern Ireland), Canada, Denmark, Federal Republic of Germany, Finland, France, the Republic of Ireland, Israel, Italy, the Netherlands, New Zealand, Norway, Sweden, Switzerland, and the United States. The median is the middle value: in each comparison, half the countries have values above the figure shown and half have lower values.

b. All the world's larger countries except China are included in the 87. China, North Korea, North Vietnam, and a number of small African, Asian, and Caribbean nations are excluded for lack of reliable information. The 87 countries include three dependent territories: Hong Kong, Northern Ireland, and Puerto Rico. All together the 87 countries and dependencies had 73 percent of the world's population in 1965, or 95 percent of its population aside from China.

c. Ten of the 18 Western democracies had no reported deaths from conflict during the 1960s.

d. The total magnitude of conflict is a composite indicator which takes into account the extent and intensity of both protest and rebellion. The procedures used to construct the measure are described in Ted Robert Gurr and Raymond Duvall, "Civil Conflict in the 1960s: A Reciprocal Theoretical System with Parameter Estimates" *Comparative Political Studies,* 6 (July 1973): 142-43 and 167, note 2.

averaged 5,400 man-days of participation in protest (demonstrations and riots) per 100,000 population. This figure is about eight times the median (midpoint) value for other Western democracies and six times the median value for all 87 countries in the survey. But there were 18 countries, including three other Western democracies, which had even higher rates of participation in protest than the United States. Similar results are obtained when we compare man-days of rebellion (counting all terrorist activities in the United States as rebellion, and using rough estimates of the number of people involved). There was much less rebellion than protest in the United States but the same was true of other Western societies, among which the United States again ranked fourth. Compared against all countries, the United States was about "average."

When intensities of conflict are compared, using deaths per 10 million population, the United States had the sad distinction of leading all other Western societies during the 1960s, with 18 per 10 million. But conflict in non-Western societies is far more deadly than in the West, so the United States ranked below the midpoint of all 87 countries—most of which are in Latin America, Asia, and Africa. It also should be pointed out that political violence was not a demographically significant cause of death during the 1960s in the United States. Americans were 1,500 times more likely to die in auto accidents than in civil strife (based on an annual traffic fatality rate of about 2,700 per 10 million people) and 320 times more likely to be murdered (based on an average annual murder rate of 580 per 10 million people). The most serious social costs of violent conflict are disruption, intensified fear and hatred between social groups, and the risk of political reprisals and erosion of political rights in the name of security.

All these above comparisons take into account the entire decade of the 1960s. The last two lines of the table compare total magnitudes of conflict (a composite indicator that takes into account both man-days and deaths) for the two halves of the decade. We know from other data (not reported here) that civil conflict intensified in most Western democracies during the second half of the 1960s.[16] What the comparison shows is that it increased even more in the United States than elsewhere: The United States "improved" its relative ranking by both international standards of comparison.

Civil Conflict in Other Countries

Most countries of the world are far smaller than the United States and lack its ethnic and regional diversity. So it is instructive to compare civil conflict in the United States with specific countries, as is done in Table 2.4. The most meaningful standard of comparison is provided by the other democratic nations of Western Europe and the British Commonwealth, for these are the nations against which Americans typically judge their cultural, political, and economic progress.

All four large European democracies—Germany, Britain, Italy, and France—had substantial conflict in the 1960s, the latter two far exceeding the United States in the extent of protest and rebellion, though not in deaths. Most smaller Western democracies had lesser magnitudes of conflict, with the single bloody exception of Northern Ireland—where a root cause of rebellion was the very imperfect nature of "democracy" as applied to the Catholic minority. The effectiveness of small, modern democracies in minimizing open conflict is illustrated by the fact that ten of the 17 nations (out of 87) which recorded no deadly political conflict during the 1960s were of this type. They are Australia, Austria, Denmark, the Republic of Ireland, the Netherlands, New Zealand, Norway, Sweden, and Switzerland. The small democracies which *did* have deadly internal conflicts during the decade were those with sharp communal cleavages: between Catholics and Protestants in Northern Ireland, between the Flemish and Walloons in Belgium, between French- and English-speaking Canadians, between Jews and Arabs in Israel.

Conflict in the world's other large nations—listed in the lower half of Table 2.4— provides important contrasts to the Western experience. First, the data show how

Table 2.4: Characteristics and Magnitude of Civil Conflict in Selected Countries 1961-1970, Compared with the United States[a]

	Man-Days of Protest per 100,000	Man-Days of Rebellion per 100,000	Conflict Deaths per 10 million
Large Western Democracies (1970 population 50 million +)			
United States	5,400	250	18.3
West Germany	3,100	0	0.3
Britain	400	20	0.5
Italy	22,100	1,300	8.0
France	130,000	15,000	17.1
Some Small Western Democracies			
Canada	40	700	1.5
Australia	500	0.1	0
Sweden	950	0	0
Israel	1,500	70	11.8
Republic of Ireland	100	70	0
Northern Ireland	1,400	40,000	129.3
Other Major Nations of the World			
Europe: USSR	10	0.3	18
Poland	800	0	118
Spain	550	1,900	13
Middle East: Turkey	100	50	14
Egypt	10	40	9
Iran	950	10	76
Asia: India	3,300	4,700	42
Indonesia	500	100,000+	30,000+
Japan	450	0.5	0.1
Africa: Nigeria	20,000+	150,000+	250,000+
South Africa	350	200	16
Latin America: Brazil	300	150	7
Mexico	430,000	9,000	26
Argentina	100,000	35,000	31

a. Within each group countries are listed by descending population rank. The data are rounded to reflect their imprecision. Estimates of death are more accurate than estimated of man-days. Estimates for Western countries are more accurate than those for Communist and Third World countries.

effective autocratic regimes are in suppressing opposition. Five of the countries had authoritarian regimes during the 1960s, which prohibited most kinds of dissent: the USSR, Poland, Spain, Iran, and South Africa. Their success is evident from their low levels of protest and rebellion (except for rebellion in Spain); the cost is apparent in their relatively high conflict fatalities, which are principally the result of deadly government responses to open opposition. The second observation concerns the "new nations" which gained independence after 1945: India, Indonesia, and Nigeria. The new nations have been especially prone to devastating internal wars.

These have arisen out of political, regional, and communal conflicts, such as those which proved so deadly in Indonesia and Nigeria—as well as the Congo, Pakistan, Vietnam, and many others not shown here. India has avoided the most serious of such conflicts, perhaps because of the flexibility of her democratic institutions. The two other large non-Western democracies shown on Table 2.4 are Turkey and Japan. Their record for avoiding open conflict during the 1960s was as good as or better than those of the large Western democracies. Then there are the nations of Latin America, whose chronic "instability" is illustrated by very high levels of protest and rebellion in Mexico (most significantly, a prolonged campus take-over by many thousands of students) and in Argentina (most importantly, frequent political strikes and demonstrations by Peronists). But these and most other Latin countries have fewer reported conflict deaths than might be expected from the wide extent of conflict.

The comparison of specific countries in Table 2.4 provides an introduction to a more thorough examination of the ways in which civil conflict varies among types of countries. A nation's political institutions evidently affect the shape and extent of conflict. The poorer countries have more deadly conflict than wealthier countries. And some world regions are more conflict-ridden than others. To measure the extent of these differences, the 87 countries were divided into similar groups and their median rates of conflict participation and conflict deaths were determined. Some results are summarized in Table 2.5, with the world medians at the top, then the medians for countries grouped according to their political system, level of economic development, and world region.

The sharpest differences in typical levels of conflict are associated with the type of political system. The "elitist" regimes are characteristically ruled by small and often factional elites, many of whom depend on foreign economic and political support to remain in power. They lack both the comprehensive political institutions which characterize democracies and the comprehensive agencies of political control which characterize the Communist states and other autocracies. In the typical elitist country, civil conflict was 20 times more widespread than in the typical democracy, and 40 times as deadly as in the typical autocracy. Overt and covert intervention in conflict situations is all too common in these countries. The foreign encouragement and military support received by both regimes and dissidents in these countries bear much of the responsibility for the deadly and protracted character of their internal disputes. Elitist nations are not inevitably turbulent. Some of the smaller ones enjoyed levels of civil peace in the 1960s comparable to those of the typical democracy, among them El Salvador, Malagasy, Paraguay, and Tanzania. But these are very much the exceptions, and for the first two of them, the 1970s have already proven civil peace to be ephemeral.

The democracies and autocracies differ distinctly in patterns of conflict, as was suggested above. The typical democracy in the 1960s had approximately twice the extent of conflict as the typical autocracy, but only half the rate of conflict deaths. The crux of the matter is that peaceful protest is tolerated in democracies and serious rebellion is uncommon. In the autocracies, conflict is more likely to be manifest in violent forms, including rebellion, and the authorities use greater force to suppress it.

A country's level of economic development is almost as important for its magnitude of civil conflict as its form of government. The relationship shown in

Table 2.5: The Extent and Intensity of Civil Conflict, 1961-1970, by Type of Country

	Man-Days of Protest and Rebellion per 100,000 Population[a]		Conflict Deaths per 10 Million Population	
	Median[b]	Extreme Cases[c]	Median[b]	Extreme Cases[c]
All 87 countries[b]	1,030	South Vietnam Congo (Zaire)	21	South Vietnam Nigeria
Countries Grouped by Type of Political System				
Democracies (37)	1,260	Mexico N. Ireland	8	Venezuela Colombia
Autocracies (19)	510	Algeria Cuba	14	Jordan Algeria
Elitist (31)	32,700	South Vietnam Congo (Zaire)	550	South Vietnam Nigeria
Countries Grouped by Level of Economic Development				
High (28)	680	N. Ireland France	0.4	Venezuela N. Ireland
Medium (29)	2,500	Dominican Rep. Mexico	31	Dominican Rep. Colombia
Low (30)	22,500	South Vietnam Congo (Zaire)	400	South Vietnam Nigeria
Countries Grouped by World Region				
European (30)	490	N. Ireland France	0.6	S. Rhodesia N. Ireland
Latin (22)	5,700	Dominican Rep. Mexico	32	Dominican Rep. Colombia
Afro-Asian (35)	9,800	South Vietnam Congo (Zaire)	200	South Vietnam Nigeria

a. These figures do not include estimates of participation by police and military personnel in conflict situations.

b. The median is the middle value for each group of nations. Averages are much higher because of a few extreme cases. For example the *average* man-days for all 87 countries are 164,000, though only eight countries have a higher rate; while the average conflict death rate is 14,000, a rate exceeded by only six countries.

c. The two countries in each group which have the highest rates.

Table 2.5 appears to be linear: the higher the economic development, measured by per capita gross national product (GNP), the less extensive and the less deadly is civil conflict. Correlation analysis specifies exactly how strong the relationship is. GNP per capita in the early 1960s correlates $-.55$ with conflict deaths per 10 million in 1961-1965, showing that the wealthier a nation, the less intense conflict is likely to be. Per capita GNP has a weaker $-.42$ correlation with man-days of conflict, which is consistent with our observation that wealth helps transform civil conflict—by making it less deadly—but is not so likely to reduce its extent. These relationships are far short of a perfect -1.00, though, because some economically advanced nations, like the United States, France, and Venezuela, had very disruptive conflicts in the 1960s, while some of the poorer countries, like Ceylon (now Sri Lanka), Malagasy, and Egypt had little conflict.

The differences among the world regions, shown at the bottom of Table 2.5, seem explained largely by differences in economic development and political system. Conflict is lowest in Europe and North America because, first, these regions are the world's richest and, second, because they have institutionalized systems of government of either the democratic or authoritarian types. The Afro-Asian countries are most likely to be poor and to have unstable, elitist rule, hence conflict there is typically greatest. (When the Asian and African countries are compared separately, their levels of conflict are similar.) The Latin countries (a group in which we include Spain and Portugal) are in between. Most are at an intermediate level of economic development. Politically they include democracies (nine in the early 1960s), autocracies (three), and elitist systems (ten). As a result their typical levels of conflict fall midway between the European countries and the Afro-Asian ones.

These comparisons do not imply a necessary connection between economic development, type of political system, and level of civil conflict. It could be argued, for example, that democratic nations are able to maintain democratic processes and institutions precisely because they are free of intensely violent conflict. It is even more likely that violent conflicts within elites and their foreign supporters in unstable Third World countries explain the failure to establish the institutions—democratic or authoritarian—that might restrain conflict. The shape of political institutions is precisely the issue of internal wars in most of these countries: dissidents seek to establish a new political order, usually of a socialist kind, that will lay the foundations for social and economic progress. And of course the lack of political order and the pattern of dependency on foreign countries contribute to the continuing poverty of these countries. In the more developed countries material wealth makes it possible to satisfy many popular demands without violent conflict, so wealth may be said to be a cause of civil peace. Historically, however, industrial development was limited in many now prosperous societies until basic political conflicts were resolved and imperial dependencies broken. It is clear that the connections between political system, economic development, and patterns of conflict are very different from one country and regime to another. Still, the results of the comparisons do make it possible to anticipate how much civil conflict various kinds of countries are likely to experience, even if one cannot make forecasts for specific countries.

DISSIDENTS AND THEIR OBJECTIVES

In this section we venture below the surface of general comparisons to seek a better understanding of what kinds of people are most likely to take part in civil conflict and what kinds of objectives they seek.

Who Are the Dissidents?

Many Americans believe that protest and rebellion are mainly the work of radicals and riff-raff, not "ordinary people." The belief is not a new one: the British officials of colonial America dismissed our revolutionary forefathers as "rabble" despite the fact that people from every walk of life supported the cause of independence. Much the same was true of civil conflict during the 1960s. Almost every class and group of Americans took part in protest. Civil rights and peace demonstrations included not only political activists and students but tens of thousands of blue- and white-collar workers and professionals. Ghetto rioters included relatively large numbers of unemployed youth, but also many skilled and unskilled workers.[17] "Backlash" protest mobilized both working- and middle-class whites. The ecology and women's rights movements drew their supporters and marchers mainly from the urban and suburban middle classes. The terrorists and rebels of the 1960s were almost equally diverse. They included small-town blue-collar workers and small businessmen, who formed the backbone of the Ku Klux Klan; militant young blacks, most of them well-educated; and white student radicals, most of whom came from upper-middle-class families. Only farmers and public employees—civil servants, the police, military personnel—did not often join in protest or rebellion, and their absence from the ranks of protesters was only temporary, as events of the 1970s have demonstrated.

In the United States, almost every group with a serious grievance has been willing to participate in protest, and where anger and ambition were greatest, they have been willing to use violence. Comparative evidence suggests that this portrait is not exceptional; it is the norm. Table 2.6 summarizes some of the evidence. An examination of our coded descriptions of 1,398 episodes of protest shows that members of working-class groups reportedly played a significant part in nearly 60 percent of them.[18] The proportions are somewhat higher in European countries than in the Third World and still higher in the United States. (Note that the United States is included in the European group in this comparison and all those that follow.) Members of the middle classes played an even greater role in protest; 77 percent of all episodes around the world involved people of middle-class background, and 83 percent in the United States. These figures count students, who took part in more than half of all protest events, as a middle-class group. When student protests are set aside, we find that 59 percent of the remaining protests in European societies in the 1960s involved significant participation by other middle-class groups. For the United States the comparable figure is 64 percent.

Another important feature of protest in Western societies is that it often cuts across classes. Between 1961 and 1965, for example, the data show that just under 50 percent of all episodes of protest in European countries involved both middle-class and working-class participants. These comparison do not take into account the relative or absolute numbers of people from different classes who participate in protest. They do strongly suggest, however, that protest in the contemporary world is not solely or primarily a lower-class phenomenon. Public protest cuts across class lines to mobilize discontented people whatever their social status.

Class participation in rebellions presents a somewhat different picture than participation in protest. In European countries, the lower and middle classes are about equally likely to participate, and the percentages (shown in Table 2.7) are similar to those for participation in protest. (There are too few American cases with reliable data to list them separately.) It is participation by the political classes—the military, police, and public officials—that distinguishes rebellion from protest. The

Table 2.6: Classes of Dissidents in Protest Episodes, 1961-1970, by Type of Country

| | Percentages of Episodes in which Specified Classes Reportedly Participated[a] | | |
	USA	Europe[b]	Third world[c]
Number of episodes[d]	53	468	930
Laboring Classes			
Peasants, farmers	2%	4%	5%
Urban workers, unemployed	11	23	17
Any laboring-class group[e]	83	60	57
Middle Classes			
Students	47	53	51
White-collar workers, professionals, businessmen	21	13	8
Any middle-class group[e]	83	75	77
Political classes[f]	4	5	6

a. Percentages add to more than 100 because most events involved dissidents of several classes. See note 18 on how "participation" was determined.

b. Including the United States, European and other Western democracies, and the European Communist states.

c. The 57 countries of Latin America, Africa, and Asia included in this study.

d. For 1,398 episodes of protest whose major participants could be identified from news accounts. "Episodes" include protest campaigns (some of which include dozens, even hundreds of separate actions) and single events not part of campaigns.

e. Including episodes with mixed or undifferentiable participation from this general class.

f. Dissident officials and civil servants of all ranks; dissident police and military personnel. Soldiers and police who clash with dissidents in the course of carrying out their duties are *not* counted here.

percentages in European countries are relatively small: 27 percent of rebellions in the 1960s involved dissident members of the "political establishment" compared with 5 percent of protests. In the Third World the importance of the political classes in rebellion is more pronounced. In fact, they were at least as likely to play a major role in rebellions as either the lower or the middle classes. Sometimes they acted alone, as in most coups d'état; more often they formed alliances with private groups. But the important point is that disaffected members of the political establishment are the principal agents of rebellion in the modern world. It is their presence, usually as leading participants, that typically marks the difference between dissidence which takes the form of protest and outright rebellion.

Organizations

Most dissidents have some common bond that unites them in conflict situations. Even the members of a leaderless crowd of looters are likely to have some sense of shared identity. This raises a comparative question: How important are different kinds of organizations in providing the cohesion that is necessary for collective action? Group cohesion may be provided by communal organizations, or simply by people's awareness that they belong to the same ethnic, religious, or territorial community. Most scholars would expect these communal sources of cohesion to be

Table 2.7: Classes of Dissidents in Rebellions, 1961-1970, by Type of Country

| | Percentages of Episodes in Which Specified Classes Reportedly Participated[a] | |
	Europe[b]	Third World[c]
Number of rebellions[d]	67	401
Laboring classes, any	60%	53%
Middle classes, any	53	49
Political classes		
Military or police only	18 ⎤	28 ⎤
	⎬27	⎬53
All others[e]	9 ⎦	25 ⎦

a. See Table 2.6, note a.
b. See Table 2.6, note b.
c. See Table 2.6, note c.
d. For 468 rebellions whose major participants could be identified from news accounts and other sources. Each distinguishable terrorist campaign was counted as a single rebellion. Each year of a rebellion that lasted two years or more was counted as a separate episode.
e. Including rebellions in which the military or police collaborated with dissident civilian political figures.

most important in "traditional" societies, whereas specialized economic and political associations are more important in modern societies. Important associational groups involved in conflict in modern societies are trade unions, legal political parties and issue-oriented groups like ecology and civil rights organizations, and student action groups. We might expect these kinds of associations to be especially important as sources of dissidence in open, democratic societies. In authoritarian political systems, dissidents more likely will find it necessary to establish secret organizations, or to subvert part of the government apparatus.

To test our suppositions, we recorded the type of group which mobilized dissidents in each episode of conflict. Then the man-days of participation by dissidents were estimated for each episode and totaled, by type of mobilizing group, for each country. This information provides a "profile of mobilization," showing what proportions of man-days of dissidence in each country were organized by communal groups, by open political groups, and so forth. When these figures are averaged by type of country, as they are in Table 2.8, we can see the effects of economic development and type of political rule on mobilization for conflict. The number of comparisons to be made has been simplified by combining protest and rebellion.

Taking all 87 countries together, associational political groups of all kinds were responsible for just over 50 percent of all man-days of dissidence in the 1960s. Among these, open political parties and interest groups were more important than clandestine ones by a ratio of about four to three. Next most important were communal and territorial groups (including political organizations representing the interests of a particular community): they accounted for just less than one-fifth of all

Table 2.8: Proportional Man-Days of Dissidence by Type of Mobilizing Group, 1961-1970, by Type of Country[a]

	Open Political Groups	Clandestine Political Groups	Communal and Territorial Groups	Economic Groups	Nonpolitical Student Groups	Governmental Factions	No Data
Average for 87 countries	.29	.22	.19	.13	.07	.03	.10
Countries Grouped By Type of Political System							
Democratic (37)	.28	.20	.21	.17	.06	.01	.10
Autocratic (19)	.33	.25	.12	.07	.10	.02	.15
Elitist (31)	.27	.23	.22	.12	.05	.07	.05
Countries Grouped by Level of Economic Development							
High (28)	.34	.18	.18	.17	.04	.00	.10
Medium (29)	.31	.24	.09	.12	.10	.03	.12
Low (30)	.21	.23	.30	.09	.05	.07	.07

a. Proportions add to slightly more than 1.00 because in instances of clashes between two private groups, the man-days for the event were double-counted, once for each type of mobilizing group. The groups most often involved in clashes were communal, economic, and open political ones.

b. Groups organized to represent people of a distinctive territory, religion, language, ethnic identity, or some combination of these properties. Political groups created to represent the interests of a distinctive territorial or communal group are also included here.

dissident action. Third most important were trade unions and other economic groups, accounting for 13 percent. Nonpolitical campus groups accounted for 7 percent; student participation in political groups was registered under the political categories. Only 3 percent of dissident activity was estimated to take place within the governmental hierarchy itself; this reflects mainly the activities of military men organizing plots and coups, though it also includes some general strikes by civil servants.

The supposition that communal groups are the major source of dissidence in the poorer countries while associational groups are most important in developed countries proves accurate, to a degree. The archtypical associational groups— economic and open political organizations—were distinctly more important in the most-developed countries, where they mobilized just over 50 percent of all political dissidence compared with only 30 percent in the least-developed countries. Dissidence in the least-developed countries was relatively more likely to originate with communal and clandestine groups, and more likely than in any other group of countries to show up within the government itself. The one anomalous result is that communal and territorial groups were a significant source of dissidence in the wealthiest countries. This reflects the activities of communal and regional dissidents throughout Western Europe and North America in the 1960s, including minority groups in the United States, the Quebecois in Canada, Catholics in Northern Ireland, Scottish and Welsh nationalists in Britain, the German-speaking people of Northern Italy, Bretons in France, and even advocates of autonomy for Switzerland's Jura region.

A country's type of political system had less effect on the sources of organized dissidence in the 1960s than its level of economic development. There was very little difference in profiles of group mobilization between the democratic and elitist nations, for example, except that dissident government factions almost never played a role in conflict in the democratic nations. The authoritarian regimes were much more successful than others in limiting dissidence by both communal and economic groups. Organized labor in these countries, for example, is under much tighter reign than in democratic nations. As expected, clandestine groups were more important sources of dissidence in autocratic countries than others, but only slightly so. What seems most surprising is that the autocratic regimes were no better able to control dissidence by students and open political groups. On the contrary, proportionally more dissidence originated from these groups in authoritarian countries than in countries with other political forms. Autocratic regimes which faced particularly high levels of dissidence from student and political groups during the 1960s were Czechoslovakia, Jordan, Portugal, and Rhodesia. We saw above that autocratic governments are both more successful and harsher than others in keeping dissent under control. The present comparisons shows that when they do face open resistance, it is likely to come from the kinds of organizations—universities and open political groups—that the state most strenuously attempts to control.

Dissidents' Objectives

The most basic distinction among motives for dissidence is between the desire for limited political change ("reform") and for fundamental revision in the rules of the political game ("revolution"). Most dissidents in the United States during the 1960s had limited aims. Civil rights demonstrators asked for integration and remedial public action to alleviate the consequences of discrimination; they did not agitate for class or racial warfare. Peace marchers vehemently opposed U.S. foreign policy and some of the men who conducted it; those who wanted to go beyond the reversal of policy and bring about violent revolution could muster so few followers that they had to go underground. Some black militants talked of revolutionary warfare; such sentiments were rarely voiced by ghetto rioters. By the testimony of most of their words and actions, the rioters were retaliating against the accumulated burden of specific grievances: inconsistent and abusive police control, economic privation, and social degradation. Southern Klansmen, Northern foes of integration, and white vigilantes did not oppose the existing socioeconomic or political system per se; rather, they tried to protect their conception of it, and their imperiled position in it, from blacks, Jews, criminals, subversives, hippies, and a host of other perceived enemies of "the American way of life."

The comparative evidence summarized in Table 2.9 shows that in the "average" nation half of all dissidence was centered on specific, limited political issues: demands for increased political participation ("freedom now!"); changes in substantive government policies ("stop the bombing now!", "equal rights for women!"); or the personality of particular public figures ("dump the Hump!" "Nixon must go!"). Only a third as much dissidence (17 percent) had the revolutionary objective of seizing political power or escaping from it by secession. A much smaller proportion —an average of 5 percent of all man-days of dissidence—was expended in violent clashes between rival political groups. The last political category of motives is an important one. It consists mainly of inarticulate (or poorly reported) dissidence that was aimed partly at people in authority, but, like ghetto riots in American cities, did not express a clear set of political demands. Another component, significant in some countries, was antiforeign protest—much of it aimed by Europeans against U.S. intervention in Vietnam.[19]

Countries differed significantly in the relative importance of different kinds of motives. In democratic countries, dissidents very rarely had revolutionary objectives; reformist demands were ten times more common. Autocratic governments faced proportionally three times as much revolutionary opposition, but were less likely to hear reformist demands than the democratic governments. Even so, the rulers of authoritarian countries confronted far less revolutionary opposition than the rulers of the elitist countries, where revolutionary objectives accounted for almost as much dissident activity (32 percent) as reformist ones (38 percent).

Economic development also affects the pattern of dissidence. The less developed a country, the more likely was conflict waged over the revolutionary issues of who should rule and how, and the less likely it was to be limited to questions of policies and personnel. Conflict was also more likely, in poorer countries, to involve combat with rival groups over whose political views or influence should prevail.

There is a straightforward explanation of why revolutionary dissidence should be more common in poor and elitist nations and reformist dissidence more common in the wealthy democratic nations—and to a lesser extent in the autocratic nations. Wealthy nations have the resources that can be used to help satisfy many kinds of demands. The leaders of democratic nations usually believe that they *should* make

Table 2.9: Proportional Man-Days of Political Dissidence, 1961-1970, by Type of Motive

	To Seize Political Power	To Change Political Policies or Personnel[a]	To Suppress Rival Political Group	Other Political Motives[b]	Economic Motives[c]	Social Motives[c]
Average for 87 countries[d]	.17	.49	.05	.27	.24	.32
Countries Grouped by Type of Political System						
Democratic (37)	.06	.59	.05	.35	.26	.33
Autocratic (19)	.17	.44	.06	.31	.08	.23
Elitist (31)	.32	.38	.03	.14	.30	.36
Countries Grouped by Level of Economic Development						
High (28)	.03	.53	.01	.40	.21	.27
Medium (29)	.18	.49	.04	.20	.14	.22
Low (30)	.30	.43	.08	.21	.35	.46

a. Episodes of conflict whose coded political motives were to increase political participation; promote or oppose a specific domestic policy; or to promote or oppose a specific domestic political figure.

b. Episodes of conflict whose coded political motives were retaliation; opposition to a foreign nation's policies or leaders; or diffuse political motives. The last is the most common of the three codings combined here and usually signifies episodes which had political targets but no clearly articulated (or clearly reported) specific motives.

c. Economic and social motives expressly articulated in episodes which had some political motives and targets as well. Strikes against private employers and racial clashes without political overtones would not be included here.

d. Totals add to more than 100 because many episodes had several different kinds of motives.

some kind of favorable response to popular protest, and fear losing their positions if they do not. Both democratic and autocratic governments have the institutional means to "deliver" reforms, if and when they make the commitment to do so. None of these conditions is likely to be found in the typical underdeveloped, elitist country. Their rulers have few administrative or economic resources and are likely to fear that any gains for dissidents will occur at their own expense. As a result, both rulers and dissidents often see conflict as a zero-sum game in which the only victory is total political victory.

The motives for dissidence are often mixed and seldom limited to political issues alone. A demand for voting rights is, on the face of it, an exclusively political one. So is a protest against an unpopular official. A general strike to protest a government's inability to deal with inflation, by contrast, directly involves both political issues (a demand for change in government economic policies) and economic ones (a demand for secure income). By the same token, when an ethnic minority rebels for regional autonomy, it both challenges the political formula of the state and aims to improve the minority's communal well-being. Our data show the extent to which political dissidence involved these and other kinds of explicit economic or social objectives as well. The last two columns of Table 2.9 show that social motives were articulated in about a third of all political dissidence and economic motives in about a quarter. Economic and social motives were most common in the poorest and elitist countries, which is one more element of these countries' revolutionary syndrome. Economic grievances in poor countries tend to be intense and widespread and are often reinforced by communal conflict in which one ethnic group or region demands a fairer share of power and resources. Such a multiplicity of motives is a hallmark of revolutionary movements and internal wars in general. We also find, though, that economic and social motives are fairly common in the most developed and especially the democratic nations. Here the explanation is not "revolution" but (a) the political activism of labor unions, which are large enough, and free enough, to give political expression to economic demands, and (b) the demands of minorities for a larger share of the national pie. By contrast, in the autocratic countries the amount of dissidence over economic issues was minimized by some combination of equitable policies of distribution (in Communist states) and government coercion. Social motives for dissidence were also uncommon in these countries, presumably for the same combination of reasons.

A COMPARATIVE INTERPRETATION OF CIVIL CONFLICT IN THE UNITED STATES

The United States unquestionably experienced more widespread and intense civil conflict during the 1960s than all but a very few other Western democracies. It is equally certain that political violence in America was far less extensive and less disruptive than violence in a substantial number of non-Western nations. Not since the Civil War have Americans experienced any strife whose scale or threat to political order approached the internal wars of the 1960s in countries like Venezuela, Colombia, the Sudan, or Iraq, much less the grim, nationwide bloodletting of

Nigeria, the Congo (now renamed Zaire), Indonesia, or South Vietnam. Americans have also been spared all but a hint of the chronic revolutionary conspiracy and terrorism that has recently plagued such countries as Argentina and Uruguay, Northern Ireland and Italy, Iran and Iraq. But this is merely to say that conditions in the United States could be worse. They do not provide much comfort when the tumult of the United States is contrasted with the domestic tranquility of smaller democratic nations like Australia, Sweden, and Austria, or with the civil order—however maintained—of countries as different as the Soviet Union and Tanzania, Sri Lanka and Paraguay.

Probably the most important general conclusion suggested by the evidence reviewed above is that civil strife in the United States is different in degree but not in kind from strife in other Western nations. Peaceful protest is by far the most common manifestation of civil conflict in the United States and in the nations with which Americans identify in political, economic, and cultural terms. When violent civil conflict does occur in these countries, it usually takes the form of demonstrations-become-riots, political and ethnic clashes, and small-scale terrorism. What the United States has avoided, along with most other Western countries, are serious conspiratorial and revolutionary movements. Many people committed to social change in Western societies used revolutionary rhetoric during the 1960s and early 1970s. Few had the dedication, skills, or calculated willingness to kill that are necessary to organize and sustain an armed revolutionary movement. The fact of the matter is that their revolutionary rhetoric was seldom more than a dramatic way of calling attention to reformist demands for social justice and more responsible government.

Another index of similarity between dissidence in Europe and the United States is the similarity of the classes and groups of people involved. Civil conflict in all Western democracies is a cross-class phenomenon in the sense that it typically cuts across the social spectrum from blue-collar workers to students to professionals, but almost never enlists dissident members of the political elite or the military. Civil conflict in Western societies is also likely to occur within or on the periphery of the conventional political process. That is, it involves political parties, unions, and particularly special interest groups, but not clandestine revolutionary organizations or cells of plotters embedded in the government hierarchy. All historical and contemporary evidence suggests that some open conflict is inevitable in large societies. If so, surely it is preferable, for those who think that social order and change both ought to be achieved by peaceful means, that civil conflict take the form of open protest, even violent protest, rather than armed revolutionary movements. Other members of society at least have warning and time to ward off the more destructive manifestations of discontent, if they can and will treat its causes rather than its symptoms.

In two dismal respects American protest and rebellion in the 1960s differed from its counterparts in other Western societies. One was the resort of right-wing groups to murderous violence in political causes. White supremacists in the South were the most prominent examples; if the assassinations of John F. Kennedy and Dr. Martin Luther King are ever traced definitively to conspiracy, they too will fit the pattern. The one Western parallel in the 1960s was the Secret Army of displaced Algerian settlers who, with far greater grievance than white American Southerners, conducted a brief terrorist campaign in France early in the decade. Since then Protestant murder squads in Northern Ireland have added another example. But these two episodes spun off from internal wars. The United States is unique among contemporary Western democracies in nurturing an enduring tradition of private political murder in resistance to change. The other side to this example of American exceptionalism is the violence with which authorities respond to some kinds of protest. The contrast is highlighted by two examples: in Detroit in the summer of 1967 authorities quelled a ghetto riot at the cost of some 40 lives; in France in May and June 1968 a nationwide attempt of students and workers to overthrow the Gaullist government was put down at the cost of a single, accidental death. Statistics bear out the contrast of these two episodes: of the 350 people who died in episodes of protest in Western democracies during the 1960s, all but 86 of them were American, mainly victims of police and National Guard gunfire. It was all too clear in the 1960s that the nonviolent response to protest which characterizes other Western democracies had not taken root in the United States. Police and National Guard policies changed as a result of the shock of the 1960s, but there have been few comparable challenges in the 1970s to put them to the test.

We have not proposed a general answer for why the United States had more protest and rebellion in the 1960s than most other Western societies, but some of the elements of explanation can be mentioned in conclusion. The essence of political democracy is that it has established means for translating popular grievances into political demands to which government is expected to be responsive. The American government insisted on fighting a foreign war despite the obvious anger and resistance of precisely those young people whom it expected to do the fighting. So it is not farfetched at all to say that antiwar protest and its revolutionary offshoots were the results of the temporary unresponsiveness of a democratic government to some citizens' demands. Civil rights protest, as well as demonstrations over a number of other issues, had one cause in common with war resistance: street protest was chosen because people with a grievance had concluded that the conventional paths of political influence were closed to them.

The sheer size and, especially, the ethnic diversity of the United States also contributed to the shape and extent of conflict in the 1960s. We have shown that the unsatisfied demands of regional, ethnic, and linguistic minorities for socioeconomic benefits and greater political rights are a particularly common source of open conflict in other Western nations. The partial or discriminatory distribution of rights and benefits to minority groups, and the grudging national response to their desires for establishing their own satisfying ways of life, is a serious unresolved problem in many modern nations. It is a set of problems that has persisted in some Western countries long beyond the solution of fundamental questions about the nature of the state, the terms of political power and who should hold it, and economic growth. Such problems also are found in less-developed countries of the Third World, where they often lead to intense and protracted civil wars or to massive communal rioting. Their manifestations in the West are usually less severe and in some countries they have stimulated significant reforms—for Scottish nationalists in Britain, French-speaking Canadians, and blacks in the United States, among others. It is nonetheless ironic that nations that have been missionaries of technology and political organization to the rest of the world, nations that can reasonably claim to provide more satisfying lives for most citizens than any others in human history, have found it so difficult to provide satisfactory conditions of life for *all* their citizens.

NOTES

1. The initial phase of research reported in this chapter was carried out at the Center of International Studies, Princeton University, with support from the Center for Research in Social Systems of the American University and the Advanced Research Projects Agency of the Department of Defense. Since 1970 the research has been conducted at Northwestern University with support from the National Science Foundation. The analyses reported here were made while the author held a Common Problems Senior Fellowship awarded by the German Marshall Fund of the United States. The data on civil conflict were gathered under the supervision of Charles Ruttenberg (1965-1967) and Jean Hardisty (1971-1974). Vaughn Bishop prepared the data for analysis, Robin Gillies carried out the statistical analyses.

2. Pitirim A. Sorokin, *Social and Cultural Dynamics, Vol. III: Fluctuation of Social Relationships, War, and Revolution* (New York: American Book Co., 1937), 504 and passim.

3. Peter A.R. Calvert, *A Study of Revolution* (Oxford: Clarendon, 1970).

4. There is convincing opinion-survey evidence that substantial majorities in a number of Western countries regard protest activities as conventional and effective means of political action; see Samuel Barnes, Max Kaase, and collaborators, *Political Action* (Beverly Hills: Sage Publications, 1980).

5. Charles Lewis Taylor and Michael C. Hudson, eds., *World Handbook of Political and Social Indicators* (New Haven, Conn.: Yale University Press, 1972), 62-77, 88-101.

6. Conditions for successful protest and revolution are specified in Ted Robert Gurr, "The Revolution-Social Change Nexus: Some Old Theories and New Hypotheses," *Comparative Politics*, 5 (April 1973), 382-392.

7. The mechanistic, organizational approach to explaining group conflict is emphasized by William A. Gamson, *The Strategy of Social Protest* (Homewood, Ill.: Dorsey Press, 1975); and Charles Tilly, *From Mobilization to Revolution* (Reading, Mass.: Addison-Wesley, 1978). Studies which emphasize psychological factors, such as alienation, discontent, and ideology are Ted Robert Gurr, *Why Men Rebel* (Princeton, N.J.: Princeton University Press, 1970); David C. Schwartz, *Political Alienation and Politial Behavior* (Chicago: Aldine, 1973); and Mostafa Rejai, *Leaders of Revolution* (Beverly Hills: Sage Publications, 1979).

8. There is no scholarly agreement on the best ways of distinguishing among the forms of civil conflict. The basic distinction made here between protest and rebellion has many parallels in the literature. One example is Daniel V.J. Bell's distinction between "resistance behavior" aimed at specific policies or persons vs. resistance to the political system itself, in *Resistance and Revolution* (Boston: Houghton Mifflin, 1973), Ch. 4. Another is Douglas A. Hibbs, Jr.'s distinction between collective protest and internal war, in *Mass Political Violence: A Cross-National Causal Analysis* (New York: Wiley-Interscience, 1973), Ch. 2. The distinction used here between conspiracy and internal war as two subtypes of rebellion is drawn from Gurr, *Why Mean Rebel*, Ch. 10. The term "revolution' is not used in this survey because it refers to one possible result of political violence; it is not a form of conflict per se.

9. The detailed instructions for coders and the coding sheet on which information was recorded are reproduced in Ted Robert Gurr and associates, *Comparative Studies of Political Conflict and Change: Cross National Datasets* (Ann Arbor, Mich.: Inter-university Consortium for Political and Social Research, 1978). The coded data on 2,200 events also are available from the Consortium. For a detailed description of the process of data collection and

its problems see Jean Hardisty, "Coding Data on Conflict and Its Reliability," Ch. II.2 in Ted Robert Gurr et al., *World Patterns of Conflict* (Beverly Hills: Sage Publications, 1980).

10. Despite the notorious reliance on "body counts" in the Vietnam War, which helped make it the best-documented internal war in history, no precisely accurate estimate of the death toll could ever be established: estimates of Communist losses were inflated, civilian deaths often went unrecorded. Our data, which come mainly from year-end summaries in the American press, show 1,340,000 deaths during the 1961-1970 decade including a rough estimate of 300,000 civilian fatalities between 1966 and 1970.

11. Reports of deaths from internal wars always include some guesswork and different sources report different estimates, often for political reasons. We used the estimates of outside observers where possible, and when there were several equally believable estimates—as in the Indonesia case—we averaged the highest and lowest. The high and low figures cited for Indonesia are both from Stephen Sloan, *A Study in Political Violence: The Indonesian Experience* (Chicago: Rand McNally, 1971), p. 4. The figures for the Biafran civil war are from Donald G. Morrison et al., *Black Africa: A Comparative Handbook* (New York: Free Press, 1972), 317.

12. There are few general studies or surveys of violent conflict during the 1960s and most of them offer distinctive radical, liberal, or conservative interpretations. Examples are Lynn B. Iglitzin, *Violent Conflict in American Society* (San Francisco: Chandler, 1972); Jerome H. Skolnick, *The Politics of Protest* (New York: Ballantine, 1969), a report prepared for the National Commission on the Causes and Prevention of Violence; and Robert Brent Toplin, *Unchallenged Violence, an American Ordeal* (Westport, Conn.: Greenwood Press, 1975). An excellent general study of student protest is Seymour Martin Lipset, *Rebellion in the University* (Boston: Little, Brown, 1971). The best retrospective view of ghetto riots is Joe R. Feagin and Harlan Hahn, *Ghetto Revolts: The Politics of Violence in American Cities* (New York: Macmillan, 1973). Important sources of factual material are the reports of presidential commissions, especially the National Advisory on Civil Disorders (1967-1968), the National Commission on the Causes and Prevention of Violence (1968-1969), and the President's Commission on Campus Unrest (1970). Useful news chronologies have been prepared by Facts on File, Inc., including Lester A. Sobel, ed., *Civil Rights 1960-1966* (New York, 1967); and Thomas F. Parker, ed., *Violence in the U.S., Vol. 1: 1956-1967*, and *Vol. 2., 1968-1971* (New York, 1974). A commentary on the subsidence of protest since the late 1960s is Anthony Oberschall, "The Decline of the 1960s Social Movements," in Louis Kriesberg, ed., *Research in Social Movements, Conflict, and Change* (forthcoming).

13. There is dispute over whether to categorize the ghetto uprisings as "riots" or "revolts." By almost all conventional definitions, both journalistic and academic ones, they were riots: the participants were unorganized, had no revolutionary programs or slogans, in fact rarely did more than defy local authorities for a few hours or days while venting their anger against abusive local police and white merchants, often in a carnival atmosphere accompanied by looting (hence the sometimes-used term "welfare riot"). On the other hand some scholars point to the political alienation and hostility toward white government and society that were common among ghetto rioters, as determined in after-the-fact opinion surveys, as evidence that the riots were revolts or even proto-revolutionary actions. A strong but not convincing case to this effect is made by Feagin and Hanh in *Ghetto Revolts*.

14. The clandestine Black Liberation Army, described by Bell and Gurr in Chapter 12 below, was responsible for some unprovoked murders of police officers. The Panthers, by contrast, were a public group and, though armed, followed a defensive policy of using violence only when attacked. Most shoot-outs between Panthers and police were initiated by police action.

15. The only published quantitative study which traces the history of political violence in the United States is Sheldon G. Levy, "A 150-year Study of Political Violence in the United

States," Appendix to Part I of the first edition of this book. The study is flawed by serious methodological problems and its results are not directly comparable with the data reported here. One general conclusion is that the number of politically violent events in the 1960s had no historical precedent, but deaths from political violence were proportionally much more numerous in the last half of the nineteenth century.

16. For a more comprehensive survey of civil conflict in the 1960s see Part II, "World Patterns of Conflict," in Gurr et al., *World Patterns of Conflict*.

17. Important studies of who participated in the ghetto riots are *Report of the National Advisory Commission on Civil Disorders* (New York: Bantam Books, 1968), 127-135; Robert M. Fogelson and Robert B. Hill, "Who Riots? A Study of Participation in the 1967 Riots," *Supplemental Studies for the National Advisory Commission on Civil Disorders* (Washington, D.C. National Advisory Commission on Civil Disorders, 1968), pp. 217-248; Nathan S. Caplan and Jeffrey M. Paige, "A Study of Ghetto Rioters," *Scientific American*, 219 (August 1968); and David O. Sears and John B. McConahay, *The Politics of Violence: The New Urban Blacks and the Watts Riot* (Boston: Houghton Mifflin, 1973),esp. Ch. 2.

18. The "episodes" counted here range from small, single events to year-long campaigns consisting of dozens, even hundreds of events. Moreover, when an episode involved several groups, it was seldom possible to find out what proportions came from what groups. Our formal rule was to record a socioeconomic class as having participated in an episode if it reportedly made up at least a tenth of the rank-and-file or a third of the leadership. In practice, we usually had to rely on statements which merely identified a group as being present and active. So these figures cannot be interpreted as saying that "60 percent of the participants" were members of the laboring classes.

19. There is an unusually large proportion of "other and diffuse" political motives for dissidence in the most developed and democratic groups of countries. This is due in part to the inclusion of antiforeign protest in this category, which was more common in these countries than others. More important, it is an index of the extent of general "antiestablishment" sentiment in motivating general strikes, riots, and demonstrations in some Western countries —sentiments too complex or vaguely articulated to be categorized more precisely.

Part 2
The Historical Roots

Gurr's comparative survey of collective protest and violence in America and Europe emphasized similarities as well as differences, since America's cultural antecedents are predominantly European, and since Europe has shared with the United States the experience of modern industrial transformation. So much of our subsequent historical and comparative analysis contrasts the American tradition of violence to that of Europe, and Part II begins with an analysis of collective violence from a European perspective by a historical sociologist, Charles Tilly. This is followed by political scientist Louis Hartz's comparative analysis of "fragment cultures"—societies arising from the massive migrations of European populations, especially to the United States, Latin America, Canada, South Africa, and Australia. The concluding chapter in Part II, by intellectual and literary historian Kenneth Lynn, probes the historical roots of violence as revealed in American literature and folklore.

In Chapter 3, Charles Tilly confronts the traditional view that the fundamentally transforming processes of industrialization and urbanization in Western society have evolved through a standard life cycle: "an early stage consisting of chaotic responses to the displacements and disruptions caused by the initial development of urban industry, a middle stage consisting of the growth of a militant and often violent working class, [and] a late stage consisting of the peaceful integration of that working class into economic and political life." According to this conventional model, collective violence should decline as the modern nation-state matures; collective violence becomes increasingly anachronistic and abnormal.

On the contrary, Tilly's political analysis in Chapter 3 reveals a commonality of collective protest and violence that suggests that it has historically functioned as an integral part of the political process, and as such has been quite normal in most European societies. The American belief that it is abnormal, shared by many Europeans, is a consequence of selective historical recollection. Tilly's sociological and historical studies of collective violence in France, the most extensive and systematic such studies ever made, provide precise documentation of these assertions. They are substantiated by comparative evidence from other European nations.

The European evidence demonstrates that the growth of the nation-state and industrialization do not in the long run minimize collective violence but lead to changes in its form, and especially to its politicization. Preindustrial societies are characterized by such "primitive" collective violence as brawls and communal clashes, usually with diffuse and unpolitical objectives. As the scope and power of the European state expanded, "reactionary" disturbances began to supplant primitive violence: revolts against tax collectors and food riots pitted either communal groups or loosely organized common people against the representatives of government, in retaliation for their infringement on or failure to protect old life ways. The third form of collective violence, the "modern," has almost entirely supplanted reactionary violence in Europe, under the impetus of industrialization, urbanization, and the development of enduring economic and political associations. The demonstration and the violent strike are the clearest examples. They involve specialized associations with relatively well-defined objectives, organized for political or economic actions, and opposed by employers and authorities, whose decision on whether, when, and how to intervene weighed heavily in determining whether and to what degree violence occurred. These forms of action are "modern," not only in their organizational complexity but because their participants are forward looking: they are striking for rights due them but not yet enjoyed.

The periods of transition from primitive to reactionary to modern collective violence are clearly discernible in the histories of most European nations. Industrialization and urbanization are profoundly but indirectly linked with the transition. In France, urbanization damped collective violence in the short run. As in the ghetto riots of the United States, it was the long-resident urban Frenchman who was most likely to have both the sense of grievance and the associational means on the basis of which he forcefully demanded his rights. In a fundamental sense, Tilly's three categories refer less to types of violence than to types of groups, who are either acquiring, maintaining, or losing position in relation to the structure of power, and whose organizational base historically has been shifting from local-communal to larger associational forms. The most consequential point is that collective violence appears as essentially a by-product of political processes—"as a by-product of struggles for power, of contention over the authoritative allocation of collective costs and benefits, of efforts to defend or augment collective rights"—in a world revolutionarily transformed by the expansion of capitalism and the rise of the national state.

While Tilly deals primarily with the internal consequences of Europe's industrial and urban transformation and its attendant dislocations and migrations, the vast outmigration of the seventeenth, eighteenth, and nineteenth centuries was an international phenomenon of unprecedented magnitude, which in addition to the United States created immigrant societies in Canada, Latin America, South Africa, and Australasia. These emergent societies have shared the common experiences of frontier expansion and the necessities of dealing with native populations, relaxing or severing colonial bonds, and forging a cohesive and distinct if hybrid culture. A comparison of their similarities is necessary in order to balance the ethnocentricity that has characterized too much of American introspection.

But such a comparison, while properly emphasizing the degree to which the Statue of Liberty was not the only beacon tempting men to uproot themselves in search of a better life, also reveals important dissimilarities. Chief among them is the remarkable extent of ethnic diversity that has characterized the American experiment in cultural assimilation. Most other immigrant societies have tended to draw disproportionately from only a few favored ethnic stocks. The British have been predominant in Australia and New Zealand. Together with the French, they have dominated Canada; with the Dutch, South Africa. In a century of immigration, Argentina received 40 percent of its newcomers from Italy and another 27 percent from Spain. Italians and Spaniards, together with a large Portuguese contingent, constituted 76 percent of Brazil's immigration. Contrast this to the United States, which during the period 1820 to 1945 recruited the following ethnically diverse European proportions: the British Isles, 33 percent; Germany, 16 percent; Austria-Hungary, 13 percent; Italy, 12 percent; Russia and Poland, 10 percent; Scandinavia, 6 percent; and in addition we of course received myriad smaller injections of ethnic pluralism to join the native Indians, the Africans, Asians, and Hispanics.

Indeed, it is probable that this very ethnic diversity and the protracted and diffuse nature of its infusion combined to limit its impact in America. John Higham, historian of American nativism, argues that we must exclude the founders of a society from the category of immigrant because as original settlers they (in the American case, the English—who in 1790 comprised approximately 60 percent of the white population) firmly established "the polity, the language, the pattern of work and settlement, and many of the mental habits to which the immigrants would have to adjust." Given this preemption of the levers of power by the dominant Anglo-Americans, subsequent immigrant groups have been cast into fierce competition with one another in their collective quest for economic security and for acceptance as legitimate Americans. This scramble for material advantage and for status has produced violent confrontations, both between the newcomers and the often nativist Anglo-American estalishment, and between the economically competing and status-conscious ethnic minorities themselves. The search for respectability has reinforced that exaggerated sense of "Americanism" which has been so deeply enshrined in the mythology of the revolutionary new nation. The stakes were high, and the quest was often explosive.

The American character, then, was forged through an extraordinary 300-year process of settlement during which the Indians were driven back, the British, Spanish, and French were driven off, the Africans were involuntarily driven over, the Mexicans involuntarily annexed, and the immigrant minorities were thrust irrevocably into a vibrant competition both with a raw physical environment and with one another. That Americans often resorted to violence under such trying circumstances is no surprise. But more important today is the question of the pervasiveness of the legacy of nativism, vigilantism, and ethnic aggression that was an inevitable by-product of the interaction of immigrant and open continent. How deeply has the immigrant and frontier experience embedded a proclivity for violence in our national character, and how does a comparison with similar societies enlighten our experience?

In comparing in Chapter 4 the cultural evolutions of the immigrant societies of Latin America, the United States, Canada, South Africa, and Australasia, Louis Hartz speaks of them as "fragment cultures" in which migrating European populations imposed their cultural values upon their new overseas societies. All have shared certain fundamental problems, such as the relationship with the mother country and with the native non-Western population, and all have experienced a tightening consensus through the shrinking of their social world. But crucial in determining their sharply varying forms of adjustment has been, first, the nature of their imported values—i.e., whether they were primarily feudal, as in the case of Spanish migrations, or liberal-enlightenment, as in the English. The second major determinant has been the mixture of the cultural fragmentation. In some a single fragment has been predominant, as in the case of the English in Australia and New Zealand or the Spanish in much of Latin America. In others, the fragmentation has been dual, as with the English and French in Canada and the English and Dutch in South Africa. In the latter case, both cultural fragments have inherited the values of bourgeois liberalism, whereas in Canada the two fragments have not only differed ethnically and linguistically, but also their values have derived from conflicting traditions. But in the unprecedentedly fragmented United States, the bourgeois-liberal ethic, in combination with ethnic pluralism, has produced in the cult of "Americanism" a nationalistic impulse toward an iron conformity that has nurtured a particularly virulent strain of moral vigilantism. To Hartz, this common process of heightened consensus fortified by nationalism can be terrifying and violent, as when an excess of national emotion sends militants off in pursuit of phantom subversives. Yet these convulsions always take the form of "law and order" movements, because "such patriotic crusades do express, in pathological form, the normal spirit of legalism in the fragment world."

Finally, students of national character rightly assume that a close scrutiny of the folklore and creative literature of a culture will isolate certain fundamental themes and images that are far more revealing of its cultural values than are opinion polls or official rhetoric. If one pursues the theme of violence in the American folk and literary tradition, one will find it in abundance. Yet it is striking how America's historians, unlike her literary giants, have been so long insensitive to the white man's explosive encounter with Indian and African. The remarkably tenacious appeal of the Leather-stocking saga and the wild western surely reflect an abiding romantic fascination with our violence-prone frontier origins. Yet so rich is the lode of American literature that, like the Bible, one can "prove" almost any hypothesis by citing it. Are we a people peculiarly and morbidly fascinated by violence? In support of this contention, one might cite the savage humor and the blood-thirsty tall tale of frontier folklore, or the searing urban and industrial chaos and class animosity reflected in the utopian novels of Ignatius Donnelly and Jack London, the fascination with war of Stephen Crane, Ernest Hemingway, and John Dos Passos, and especially the racial agony mirrored in Mark Twain, Herman Melville, and Richard Wright.

The trouble with citing these persistent themes as conclusive testimony to the sickness of American society has been, as Kenneth Lynn observes in Chapter 5, that "they tend to extrapolate violent incidents in American writing out of their literary context, without regard to the curse-lifting effect of self-parody and other forms of humor, or to the ways in which fictional conventions and authorial prejudice affect representations of reality, or to the dreams of peace which render ambivalent even the most violent of our writer's nightmares." But while Lynn sharply challenges both social scientists who assume that our violent literature is but a mirror image of society, and radical literary critics who seek a revolution in American values, he acknowledges the profound uniqueness of our racial chasm. He sees in the representative work of Melville, Twain, and Wright little hope that "the violence and the hatred, the fear and the guilt that separate black and white Americans from each other will ever end."

Chapter 3
Collective Violence in European Perspective

CHARLES TILLY

As comforting as it is for civilized people to think of barbarians as violent and of violence as barbarian, western civilization and various forms of collective violence have always clung to each other. We do not need a stifled universal instinct of aggression to account for the bursting out of violent conflicts in our past, or in our present. Nor need we go to the opposite extreme and search for pathological moments and sick people in order to explain collective acts of protest and destruction. Historically, collective violence has flowed regularly out of the central political processes of Western countries. People seeking to seize, hold, or realign the levers of power have continually engaged in collective violence as part of their struggles. The oppressed have struck in the name of justice, the privileged in the name of order, those in between in the name of fear. Great shifts in the arrangements of power have ordinarily produced—and have often depended on—exceptional moments of collective violence.

Yet the basic forms of collective violence vary according to who is involved and what is at issue. They have changed profoundly in Western countries over the last few centuries, as those countries have built big cities and modern industries. For these reasons, the character of collective violence at a given time is one of the best signs we have of what is going on in a country's political life. The nature of violence and the nature of the society are intimately related.

Collective violence is normal. That does not mean it is intrinsically desirable, or inevitable. For century after century, the inhabitants of southern Italy endured malaria as a normal fact of life; today, American city-dwellers endure smog and

AUTHOR'S NOTE: *Charles Tilly is professor of sociology and professor of history at the University of Michigan and director of the university's Center for Research on Social Organization, as well as an associate director of studies at the Ecole des Hautes Etudes en Sciences sociales at the Sorbonne in Paris. He is well known for his many contributions to the study of European social and political history, including* The Vendée *(Harvard University Press, 1964);* Strikes in France, 1830 to 1968, *coauthored with Edward Shorter (Cambridge University Press, 1974);* The Formation of National States in Western Europe, *as editor and contributor (Princeton University Press, 1975);* The Rebellious Century 1830-1930, *coauthored with Louise Tilly and Richard Tilly (Harvard University Press, 1975); and* From Mobilization to Revolution *(Addison-Wesley, 1978).*

nerve-rending traffic as normal facts of life; few people hail malaria, smog, or traffic jams. Europeans of other centuries often destroyed children they could not provide for. Now infanticide has become rare. Few of us mourn its passing. But the fact that infanticide persisted so long in the face of persuasive teachings and fearsome penalties tells us something about the poverty and population presssure under which people used to live in Western countries. It may even help us understand some apparently barbaric practices of people outside the West today. In a similar way, both the persistence of the phenomenon of collective violence and the change in its form within European countries over the last few centuries have something to teach us about their political life, and even about contemporary forms of protest.

OURS IS VIOLENT HISTORY

Long before our own time, Europeans were airing and settling their grievances in violent ways. "To the historian's eyes," says Marc Bloch, the great historian of feudal Europe, "the agrarian rebellion is as inseparable from the seigniorial regime as the strike from the great capitalist enterprise."[1] The chief moments at which ordinary people appeared unmistakably on the European historical scene before the industrial age were moments of revolt: the Jacquerie of 1358, which lent its name to many later peasant rebellions; Wat Tyler's popular rebellion of 1381; the German peasant wars of 1525; the astonishing provincial insurrection against Henry VIII in 1536 and 1537, which came to be known as the Pilgrimage of Grace; the bloody revolt of the Don Cossacks in the 1660s. Much of the time the peasant suffered in silence. Now and then he found his tongue, and his voice was violent.

Collective violence as voice is a metaphor which occurs in almost all historians of popular movements before our own time. In their discussion of the English agricultural laborer, J.L. and Barbara Hammond summed it up for all their colleagues:

> The feelings of this sinking class, the anger, dismay, and despair with which it watched the going out of all the warm comfort and light of life, scarcely stir the surface of history. The upper classes have told us what the poor ought to have thought of these vicissitudes; religion, philosophy, and political economy were ready with alleviations and explanations which seemed singularly helpful and convincing to the rich. The voice of the poor themselves does not come to our ears. This great population seems to resemble nature, and to bear all the storms that beat upon it with a strange silence and resignation. But just as nature has her own power of protest in some sudden upheaval, so this world of men and women—an underground world as we trace the distances that its voices have to travel to reach us—has a volcanic character of its own, and it is only by some volcanic surprise that it can speak the language of remonstrance or menace or prayer, or place on record its consciousness of wrong.[2]

And then the Hammonds proceed to read the rebellion of 1830 for signs of what was happening to the agrarian population of England.

Even with the growth of representative political institutions ordinary people continued to state their demands through violence. The French historian of England, Elie Halévy, stated the matter clearly:

Throughout the eighteenth century England, the sole European country where the reigning dynasty had been set up as the result of a successful rebellion, had been the home of insurrection. There had been an outbreak of anti-Jewish rioting in 1753, when the Government had decided to grant the right of naturalization to the Jews domiciled in England. The Cabinet had yielded and repealed the statute. . . . In 1768 there were riots against the Government. The popular hero Wilkes triumphed in the end over the opposition of court and Cabinet. In 1780 an anti-Catholic riot broke out; during four entire days the centre of London was given up to pillage. A Government without a police force was powerless either to prevent these outrages or repress them promptly. The right to riot or, as it was termed by the lawyers, "the right to resistance," was an integral part of the national traditions.[3]

That "right of resistance" was, in fact, a part of the English legal tradition the American colonists insisted on in the very act of separating themselves from the mother country, and emphasized in their writings about the new state they were bringing into being.

Nor did collective violence fade out with the American Revolution, or the French Revolution, or the multiple revolutions of 1848, or the American Civil War. Western history since 1800 is violent history, full enough of revolutions, coups, and civil wars, but absolutely stuffed with conflict on a smaller scale.

The odd thing is how fast we forget. When Lincoln Steffens visited London in 1910, he found distinguished members of Parliament convinced that England was on the brink of revolution as a result of the angry strikes of that time. The strikes and the talk of revolution spread through Great Britain during the next few years. In prickly Ireland—still part of the United Kingdom, but barely—a real revolution was shaping up. Now we look back to England as a country which solved its internal problems peacefully.

During the American rail strike of 1911,

In New Orleans railroad workers stole company records, switched or destroyed identification cards on freight cars, and cut the air hoses of as many as fifteen to twenty cars a day. Mobs of varying size constantly bombarded nonstrikers with stones and gunfire. . . . In Illinois periodic incursions damaged or destroyed company property. On one occasion, strike sympathizers in Carbondale turned loose a switch engine, which rammed into a freight train on the main line. . . . Turbulence and bloodshed led to a complete breakdown of civil government in sections of Mississippi. . . . For two successive nights hordes swarmed through the streets of Central City, Kentucky. They set upon men in railroad cars and fired at employees lodged in temporary sleeping quarters. . . . In the neighboring state of Tennessee the strike bred a rash of mobbings, stonings, gun battles, and killings.[4]

Following the sacred ritual of such conflicts, the governor of Mississippi declared martial law and blamed his state's troubles on "foreign agitators." Then it was the Americans' turn to speak of revolution. Only comfortable hindsight permits us to congratulate ourselves on our peaceful resolutions of violence.

Few French people recall that as recently as the end of 1949 revolutionary committees blew up trains and seized control of railroad stations, post offices, city halls, and other public buildings in a dozen major French cities, including Marseille,

Grenoble, Nice, and St. Etienne. Then the newspapers screamed "revolution" in fear or jubilation. Now November and December, 1947, look like little more than an exceptional period of strike activity—so much so that French and American newspapers alike commonly treated the momentous but essentially nonviolent student protests of May 1968, as "the largest French movement of protest since the war." The memory machine has a tremendous capacity for destruction of the facts.

There are many reasons for historical forgetfulness, besides the simple desire to ignore unpleasant events. The record itself tends to cover the rebel's tracks. The most detailed and bulkiest historical records concerning collective violence come from the proceedings of courts, police departments, military units, or other agencies of government working to apprehend and punish their adversaries. The records therefore lean toward the views of those who hold power. Protesters who escape arrest also escape history.

Yet the most important reason is probably that so long as historians concentrate on political history as seen from the top, the only protests which matter are those which produce some rearrangement of power. The Hammonds again make the essential point when discussing the rebellion of 1830:

> This chapter of social history has been overshadowed by the riots that followed the rejection of the Reform Bill. Everyone knows about the destruction of the Mansion House at Bristol, and the burning of Nottingham Castle; few know of the destruction of the hated workhouses at Selborne and Headley. The riots at Nottingham and Bristol were a prelude to victory; they were the wild shout of power. If the rising of 1830 had succeeded, and won back for the labourer his lost livelihood, the day when the Headley workhouse was thrown down would be remembered by the poor as the day of the taking of the Bastille. But this rebellion failed, and the men who led the last struggle for the labourer passed into the forgetfulness of death and exile.[5]

This selective memory even operates at an international scale. Modern Spain and modern France have acquired the reputation of violent nations, while Sweden and England pass for areas of domestic tranquility. Such differences are hard to measure objectively. But if numbers of participants or casualties or damage done are the standards, then the actual differences are far smaller than the differences in reputation. One international estimate of "deaths from domestic group violence per million population" from 1950 through 1962 rates Sweden and England at 0, Spain at 0.2, and France at 0.3, as compared with 2 for Greece, 10 for Ethiopia, 49 for South Korea, or 1,335 for Hungary.[6] Of course Spain and France acquired their disorderly reputations well before the 1950s. Yet during the very period of these statistics, France experienced the great riots brought on by the Algerian war and the series of insurrections which brought down the Fourth Republic. Obviously the amount of bloodshed is not what matters most.

The day-by-day record of these countries over a longer period likewise reveals much more collective violence in Sweden or England than their peaceable reputations suggest. The large difference in notoriety most likely comes from the fact that in Spain and France the protesters sometimes succeeded in toppling the regime. There *is* a real difference, an important puzzle: how did the British political system survive protest and yet change in fundamental ways, while Spanish regimes snapped and crumbled? But the secret is by no means simply the contrast between anarchic peoples and law-abiding ones.

The record so far available suggests that the histories of collective violence as such in Western European countries over the modern period have had a good deal in common. There have been large differences in the ways the rulers of different states have responded to collective violence, or initiated it, and consequently in its impact on the structure of power. There have been fewer differences in the evolution of the basic forms and conditions of collective violence.

In these circumstances, it is tempting to turn away from reflections on national politics or national character toward ideas about the impact of industrialization. A number of theories proposed to account for various forms of protest in contemporary nations as well as in the Western historical experience suggest a standard cycle: a relatively integrated traditional society breaks up under the stress and movement of industrialization, the stress and movement stimulate a wide variety of violent reactions—at first chaotic, but gradually acquiring a measure of coherence. New means of control and ways of reintegrating the displaced segments of the population into orderly social life eventually develop, and finally a mature industrial society held together by widespread, generally pacific political participation emerges. In such a theory, the stimulus to collective violence comes largely from the anxieties people experience when established institutions fall apart.

Not only scholars hold such a theory. It is our principal folk theory of social change. It reappears almost every time ordinary Americans (and, for that matter, government commissions and well-informed journalists) discuss riots, or crime, or family disorganization. It encourages, for example, the general illusion that highly mobile people and recent migrants to the city have greater inclinations to rioting, crime, or family instability than the general population. It encourages the dubious notion that if poor nations only become rich fast enough, they will also become politically stable. But the theory runs into trouble when it turns out that recent migrants are not more disorganized than the rest of the population, that murder is about as common (proportionately speaking) in the country as it is in the city, or that the world's wealthiest nations are quite capable of domestic turmoil.

POLITICS AND VIOLENCE

My own explorations of Western Europe, especially France, over the last few centuries suggest a more *political* interpretation of collective violence. Far from being mere side-effects of urbanization, industrialization, and other large structural changes, violent protests grow most directly from the struggle for established places in the structure of power. Even presumably nonpolitical forms of collective violence like the antitax revolt are normally directed against the authorities, accompanied by a critique of the authorities' meeting of their responsibilities, and informed by a sense of justice denied to the participants in the protest. Furthermore, instead of constituting a sharp break from "normal" political life, violent protests tend to accompany, complement, and extend organized, peaceful attempts by the same people to accomplish their objectives.

Over the long run, the processes most regularly producing collective violence are those by which groups acquire or lose membership in the political community. The form and locus of collective violence therefore vary greatly depending on whether the major political change going on is a group's acquisition of the prerequisites of membership, its loss of those prerequisites, or a shift in the organization of the entire political system.

The impact of large structural changes, such as urbanization, industrialization, and population growth, it seems to me, comes through their creation or destruction of groups contending for power and through their shaping of the available means of coercion. In the short run, the growth of large cities and rapid migration from rural to urban areas in Western Europe probably acted as a damper on violent protest, rather than a spur to it. That is so for two reasons:

(1)   The process withdrew discontented people from communities in which they already had the means for collective action and placed them in communities where they had neither the collective identity nor the means necessary to strike together.

(2)   It took considerable time and effort both for the individual migrant to assimilate to the large city, and thus to join the political strivings of his fellows, and for the new forms of organization for collective action to grow up in the cities.

If so, the European experience resembles the American experience. In the United States, despite enduring myths to the contrary, poor, uprooted newcomers to big cities generally take a long time to get involved in anything—crime, delinquency, politics, associations, protest, rioting—requiring contacts and experiences outside a small world of friends and relatives. These things are at least as true of European cities.

In the long run, however, urbanization deeply shaped the conditions under which the new groups fought for political membership, and urbanization's secondary effects in the countryside stirred a variety of protests. The move to the city helped transform the character of collective violence in at least three ways:

(1)   by grouping people in larger homogeneous blocs (especially via the factory and the working-class neighborhood) than ever before;

(2)   by facilitating the formation of special-interest associations (notably the union and the party) incorporating many people and capable of informing, mobilizing and deploying them relatively fast and efficiently;

(3)   by massing the people posing the greatest threat to the authorities near the urban seats of power, and thus encouraging the authorities to adopt new strategies and tactics for controlling dissidence.

For the people who remained in the country, the rise of the cities meant increasingly insistent demands for crops and taxes to support the urban establishment, increasingly visible impact on individual farmers of tariff and pricing policies set in the cities, and increasingly efficient means of exacting obedience from those in the country. All of these, in their time, incited violent protest throughout Europe.

Of course, definitive evidence on such large and tangled questions is terribly hard to come by. Up until very recent times, few historians have taken the study of collective violence as such very seriously. As Antonio Gramsci, the Italian socialist philosopher-historian, put it:

This is the custom of our time: instead of studying the origins of a collective event, and the reasons for its spread . . . they isolate the protagonist and limit themselves to doing a biography of pathology, too often concerning themselves with unascertained motives, or interpreting them in the wrong way; for a social elite the features of subordinate groups always displaying something barbaric and pathological.[7]

Since the Second World War, however, a considerable number of French and English historians, and a much smaller number of Americans, have begun to study and write history "from below"—actually trying to trace the experiences and actions of large numbers of ordinary men from their own point of view. This approach has had a special impact on the study of protests and rebellions. As a result, we are beginning to get a richer, rearranged picture of the political life of plain people in France and England (and, to a lesser extent, other European countries) over the last few centuries.

The new variety of evidence makes it possible to identify some major shifts in the predominant forms of collective violence in those countries over the modern period. Without too much shoving, we can place the forms of collective violence which have prevailed during that long period in three broad categories: primitive, reactionary, and modern.[8] The primitive varieties once predominated, until centralized states began dragging Europeans into political life on a larger than local scale. As Thorstein Veblen put it in his sardonic *Imperial Germany and the Industrial Revolution*, "so soon as the king's dominions increased to such a size as to take him personally out of range of an effectual surveillance by neighborly sentiment . . . the crown would be able to use the loyalty of one neighborhood in enforcing exactions from another, and the royal power would then presently find no other obstacle to its continued growth than the limit placed upon it by the state of the industrial arts."[9] In the process, the king's retinue produced the apparatus of the state, which then acquired momentum of its own. That transformation accelerated through much of Western Europe after 1600. Since then, the primitive forms of collective violence have dwindled very slowly, but very steadily. Now they occur only rarely, only at the margins of organized politics.

The reactionary forms, by contrast, burgeoned as the national state began to grow. That was far from coincidence; they most often developed as part of the resistance of various communal groups to incorporation into the national state and the national economy. But the state won the contest; in most countries of Western Europe the reactionary forms of collective violence peaked and then faded away in their turn during the nineteenth century. They gave way to modern forms of collective violence, characterized by larger-scale, more complex organization, and bids for changes in the operation or control of the state apparatus, rather than resistance to its demands. Although during very recent years we have seen what might be signs of another large shift in the form and locus of collective violence, for the last century the modern forms have pushed all others aside.

PRIMITIVE COLLECTIVE VIOLENCE

Primitive varieties of collective violence include the feud, the brawl among members of rival gilds or communes, and the mutual attacks of hostile religious groups. (Banditry, as E.J. Hobsbawm has said, stands at the edge of this category by virtue of its frequent action against the existing distribution of power and wealth, and its frequent origin in the state's creation of outlaws as part of the attempt to extend legal authority to formerly ungoverned areas.) Primitive forms of collective violence share several features: small scale, local scope, participation by members of communal groups as such, inexplicit and unpolitical objectives. Almost regardless of the questions at issue, for example, Frenchmen could count on a national political crisis to produce battles between Protestants and Catholics in Nimes and Albi. Attacks on the persons and properties of Jews accompanied eighteenth-century rebellions in England and nineteenth-century rebellions in France. The vendetta and the bandit raid, too, took on a degree of political significance in times of national crisis.

The *rixe de compagnonnages*—the battle royal between members of rival craft corporations—often left blood in the streets. In 1830, a characteristic *rixe* in Bordeaux involved 300 artisans; two were reported dead, many were wounded, and the local inns were left a shambles. In 1835, the newspaper *Le Constitutionnel* carried the following story from Châlons-sur-Saône:

> The *compagnons du Devoir*, called *Dévorans*, following an altercation on the previous day and a challenge by letter to fight the *compagnons de Liberté*, called *Gavots,* in the open country, attacked the mother house of the latter in the rue St. Antoine. Huge stones, big enough to kill an ox, were thrown through the windows.[10]

The very prevalence of such fracases gave the inhabitants of nineteenth-century French cities a wide acquaintance with collective violence. In London, likewise, "It was usual for the boys of St. Anne's parish to fight those of St. Giles armed with sticks for 'a week or two before the holidays.' This fact survives, because in 1722 the captain of the boys of St. Giles, a chimney sweep aged 21, was killed by another boy, aged 16. Earlier still, 'prentice riots were serious and frequent disturbances to the peace of London'."[11] The prevalence of the *rixe* in Europe before modern times simply expressed the intense solidarity of each group of urban crafts men, for (as been said of German artisans) "Their group spirit turned against other groups and took an insult to an individual as an affront to the whole association."[12] Something like that solidarity lies close to the core of most of the primitive forms of collective violence.

This does not mean the fighting was always in rage and deadly earnest. Just as today's lumbermen or sailors on a weekend will now and then tear up a bar out of sheer boredom, frustration, or high spirits, the workmen of Berlin or Turin sometimes brawled for the fun of it. On such occasions, the traditional enmities provided no more than the pretext. In the European city of the preindustrial age, funerals, feasts, and fairs provided public occasions out of which flowed collective violence offering diversion to the young as well as expressing deeply rooted communal rivalries.

Students, and even schoolboys, displayed some of the same violent propensities. At the Jesuit college of La Flèche, during the carnival days of 1646, the boys declared they had been dishonored by the public flogging of some of their number, and staged an armed mutiny. "The rebels . . . stood in the avenues, armed with swords, sticks, blackjacks, and stones, driving back the pupils who came out when the bell rang to go to the classrooms."[13] In England,

> There was indiscipline and rebellion everywhere. At Winchester, in the late eighteenth century, the boys occupied the school for two days and hoisted the red flag. In 1818 two companies of troops with fixed bayonets had to be called in to suppress a rising of the pupils. At Rugby, the pupils set fire to their books and desks and withdrew to an island which had to be taken by assault by the army. There were similar incidents at Eton.[14]

Again, the intense solidarity of the students—a kind of brotherhood in league against their masters—facilitated their indignation and their common action.

A number of the other common primitive forms of collective violence had this curious combination of *esprit de corps*, recreation, and grim determination, a combination which the English somehow managed to transmute into the sporting spirit. The free-for-all among men from different towns (from which it is said, in fact, that various forms of football developed) has some of this character. So does the rag, charade, or charivari. Yet it would be quite wrong to consider the primitive varieties of collective violence as nothing but early versions of soccer. The deadly vendetta, the endemic banditry of the European highlands, the pervasive Sicilian scourge called Mafia, and the occasional millenarian movements which have racked southern Europe share many traits with the apparently trivial kinds of collective violence. What sets the primitive forms of violence off from the others is not a lack of seriousness, but their activation of local communal groups as such, and usually in opposition to other communal groups.

REACTIONARY COLLECTIVE VIOLENCE

Reactionary disturbances are also usually small in scale, but they pit either communal groups or loosely organized members of the general population against representatives of those who hold power, and tend to include a critique of the way power is being wielded. The forcible occupation of fields and forests by the landless, the revolt against the tax collector, the anticonscription rebellion, the food riot, and the attack on machines were western Europe's most frequent forms of reactionary collective violence. The risky term "reactionary" applies to these forms of collective violence because their participants were commonly reacting to some change which they regarded as depriving them of rights they had once enjoyed; they were backward-looking. They were not, however, simple flights from reality. On the contrary, they had a close connection with routine, peaceful political life.

For ordinary Europeans of a few centuries ago, the most persistent political issues were the demands of the nation-state and of the national economy. And the food riot, as unlikely as it seems, illustrates the pressing nature of these demands very well. Seemingly born of hunger and doomed to futility, the food riot actually expressed the indignation of men and women who felt they were being deprived of their rights and who, by rioting, were often able to restore a semblance of those rights—if only temporarily.

The west European food riot had a classic form: seizure of grain being stored or transported in a town, demonstrations (and sometimes bodily harm) directed against those presumed to be profiteering through the shipment or hoarding of grain, and sale of the grain at a publicly proclaimed just price, the proceeds going to the owner of the grain. Such food riots occurred throughout the eighteenth century in England, and during the first third of the nineteenth century. They were, indeed, one of the chief components of England's large agrarian rebellion of 1816. A.J. Peacock describes the beginning of one of the principal incidents of that rebellion:

> A crowd has started assembling in the market place at about nine o'clock that morning. About an hour later some women came along who announced that their men were following them but had stopped along the Thetford road to collect sticks. Eventually fifty or more, all armed, and led by William Peverett, a labourer, marched into the square carrying white and red flags. Willett, the butcher, who was amongst the crowd, told Peverett that the parish would let them have the flour at 2s. 6d. if they would disperse, and asked for a deputation to go along with him to meet the magistrates. Helen Dyer, a married woman, had earlier told Willett that, although she could not read, she had a paper containing the crowd's demands, which she wanted shown to the magistrates. On it was written, "Bread or Blood in Brandon this day."[15]

Finally, after several days of milling, grumbling, stoning of windows, and pulling down of buildings, the magistrates

> guaranteed the price of flour at 2s. 6d, per stone, with an advance of wages to 2s. per head for a fortnight, and unless the millers reduce their prices by that time, the officers of the parish will purchase their grain at the cheapest rate, and furnish the poor with provisions at prime cost.[16]

To modern eyes, the curious feature of this event is that the rioters did not loot, did not steal, but demanded to *buy* food at a price they could afford. Furthermore, it is clear that the crowd directed their anger at the authorities, expected them to act, and, indeed, bargained with them.

In fact, the food riot was an attempt to make the merchants and the municipal authorities meet their traditional responsibilities: holding grain within the town to meet local needs before permitting it to enter the national market, and assuring the town poor of a supply of grain at a price properly adjusted to the local level of wages. As great cities grew up in western Europe during the seventeenth and eighteenth centuries, and national markets in grain developed to feed them, it became harder and less profitable for merchants and officials to give priority to local needs. And so men rioted to hold them to the bargain. The geography of the food riot (at least in France, where it has been best mapped) suggests as much: not in the areas of greatest famine and poverty, but in the hinterlands of big cities and grain-shipping ports.

The case of Italy points up the importance of the control (as opposed to the sheer quantity) of the food supply.[17] In England, the classic food riot virtually disappeared after 1830; in France, after 1848; in Italy, toward the end of the nineteenth century. The timing of that disappearance corresponds approximately to the pace of technical improvements in the production and distribution of grain. It also follows the destruction of traditional controls over the grain trade, but at a significant distance.

The bad harvests of 1853, for example, brought food riots through much of western Europe. In the Italian peninsula, the riots of that year concentrated in the prosperous

North—Piedmont, Parma, Tuscany—although shortage was at least equally acute in the silent South. The northern authorities had generally adopted policies favoring free trade in grains; in the southern Kingdom of the Two Sicilies, paternalism reigned.

In 1859, however, the new, progressive King Francesco of the Two Sicilies began to liberalize the grain trade. In 1860 he faced widespread food riots of the South. At the time of the October, 1860, plebiscite on the unification of Italy there were rebellions in the South, to the theme "The old king fed us." The old king was Francesco's father, who had maintained the traditional controls.

All this may appear unduly complicated for anything so simple as a food riot. That is the point: the extent to which these recurrent, apparently spontaneous events rested on and grew from the local structure of politics, and the extent to which the crises of local politics were responses to pressures from the center. Far from being a momentary, rural, local reaction to misery, the food riot recorded the urbanization and centralization of European nation-states.

The food riot had companions. The anticonscription rebellion, the resistance to the tax collector, the violent occupation of fields and forests, the breaking of reapers or power looms all had many of the same characteristics. Although they often appeared in bunches, each of the events was more or less local and self-contained. Instead of pitting one communal group against another, they stood a significant segment of the population against the local elite or the representatives of the central power. ("When the French peasant paints the devil," said Karl Marx in 1850, "he paints him in the guise of the tax collector.")[18] The organization of the formations taking part was rudimentary. It was essentially the organization of everyday life: users of a common market, artisans of the same shop, a single commune's draft-age boys, and so on. Because of this tie with everyday groupings, those who took part often included women, children, and old people. The participants were either resisting some new demand (taxes, conscription) laid on them by outsiders, protesting against what they viewed as a deprivation of their traditional rights (the prohibition of gleaning in fields and forests, the introduction of machinery), or both. All of them, in one way or another, amounted to action against the forcible integration of local groupings into the national economy and the national state. I believe—but this is a hunch for which little evidence is yet available—that all the reactionary forms of collective violence will turn out to have had an extraordinary appeal for just those segments of the European population whose political and economic identities these changes were dissolving. The large numbers of rural artisans whose livelihoods disappeared with the expansion of urban industry during the nineteenth century are the most important case, but agricultural day-laborers and petty nobles faced some of the same problems.

The rural unrest of England during the early nineteenth century falls into this general pattern. In addition to recurrent food riots, the English countryside produced movements of protest in 1816, 1822, 1830, 1834-1835, and 1843-1844, with the 1830 rebellion covering much of southeastern England. During the events of 1830, the village rebels concentrated on three sorts of action: (1) levying a once-traditional contribution of beer or money on the local rich; (2) imposing a wage agreement on the employers of day-laborers; (3) destroying new farm machinery, especially threshers. For those who resisted, the crowds reserved personal attacks, the tearing down of buildings, and the burning of hayricks. During one of the larger outbreaks, in Wiltshire,

> The mob destroyed various threshing machines of Mr. Bennett's farms, and refused to disperse; at last, after a good deal of sharp language from Mr. Bennett, they threw stones at him. At the same time a troop of yeomanry from Hindon came up and received orders to fire blank cartridges above the heads of the mob. This only produced laughter; the yeomanry then began to charge; the mob took shelter in the plantations round Pyt House and stoned the yeomanry, who replied by a fierce onslaught, shooting one man dead on the spot, wounding six by cutting off fingers and opening skulls, and taking a great number of prisoners.[19]

As hopeless as this sort of popular agitation may seem, it actually had a measure of success. As E.J. Hobsbawm states it, "The day-laborers succeeded to a large degree in destroying the machines and achieving wage raises and other improvements, and they held onto their gains for some years, mostly because the unexpected sight of their massive force . . . instilled a salutary fear in the rural gentry and farm owners."[20] Of course, this was only a delaying action; the reactionary forms of rural protest did not last much longer, mechanized farming did win out, and millions of agricultural workers eventually left the land. Nevertheless, in the context the actions of 1830 had a logic poorly conveyed by words like "riot" and "protest."

The same may be said of the handloom weavers, whose nineteenth-century rebellions stirred the countryside in most sections of Europe. What we loosely call Luddism took the form of a well-concerted avenging action. Ned Ludd, the mythical enemy of shearing-frames and power-looms, who in 1811 and 1812 issued threats and manifestos from his retreat in Sherwood Forest, had much in common with Captain Swing, the equally mythical leader in whose name the agrarian rebels of 1830 wrote their warnings. Here is a Luddite letter:

> We will never lay down Arms [till] The House of Commons passes an Act to put down all Machinery hurtful to Commonality, and repeal that to hang Frame Breakers. But We. We petition no more—that won't do—fighting must.
>
> Signed by the General of the Army of Redressers
>
> Ned Ludd   Clerk
>
> Redressers for ever Amen.[21]

The Army of Redressers, they called themselves. Their pseudonym epitomizes the defensive, indignant, focused, rule-bound character of their rebellion. "Luddism," says E.P. Thompson, "must be seen as arising at the crisis-point in the abrogation of parternalist legislation, and in the imposition of the political economy of *laissez faire* upon, and against the will and conscience of, the working people."[22] Far from reacting in aimless confusion, the Luddites, and most of the European machine-breakers, knew what they were doing. While the food riot and machine-breaking were quite distinct in form and content, they shared the same sort of crude rationality.

Much of the popular protest which took place during the Italian *Risorgimento* has this reactionary character. During the 1850s there were scattered strikes in the industrial centers and a few revolts of a fairly modern variety in cities like Milan, Livorno, and Genoa. But most of the disturbances took the familiar form of the food riot, or consisted of *occupazioni delle terre*—mass squatting on lands formerly held in common as a means of demanding their distribution in compensation for lost rights in the commons. Even as Garibaldi marched up the peninsula on his way to unifying Italy, Sicilians were attacking tax collectors and occupying the commons. At times, villagers in the South shouted "Down with the Constitution," "Down with the Nation," "Long live the King"—a set of cries which recalls the much older motif of French tax rebellions, *"Vive le roy et sans gabelle."*

By this time, a rather different (and, to us, more familiar) kind of collective violence had been taking shape in the cities of Italy, as it had been in most cities of Europe. There, political clubs, secret societies, and workers' organizations were organizing collective action through strikes, demonstrations, banquets, meetings, and military coups. The most advanced sections of the countryside were also being drawn into these newer forms of action. Although they were not intrinsically violent in themselves, the new political and economic forms became increasingly important contexts for collective violence.

When and how fast this happened varied from country to country. But it happened almost everywhere. The numerous disturbances which occurred in France at the middle of the nineteenth century were mixed in character. The great bulk of them fit the standard reactionary models: tax rebellions, food riots, machine-breaking, and so on. The 1848 Revolution notwithstanding, strikes, demonstrations, and revolutionary movements produced only a small share of the collective violence. The violent disturbances of the 1930s, by contrast, grew almost entirely out of organized strikes and demonstrations; with the important exception of the Resistance during the Second World War, the 1940s and 1950s brought little change in this respect. In between the 1840s and the 1940s a profound transformation of the character of collective violence took place. Even in the midnineteenth century, a growing minority of conflicts involved more complex and durable organization, more explicit and far-reaching objectives, a forward-looking perspective. After 1848, these very rapidly became the prevailing characteristics of the events producing collective violence.

In the process, solid citizens and national leaders developed an acute fear of the masses and organized a whole set of new means for maintaining public order. The elite feared the ordinary people of country and city alike, although they concentrated their efforts at crowd control in the cities, where they themselves spent most of their time. It was true in England. Looking back from the 1860s, novelist and pamphleteer Charles Kingsley wrote:

From the middle ages, up to the latter years of the French war, the relation between the English gentry and the labourers seems to have been more cordial and wholesome than in any other country of Europe. But with the French Revolution came a change for the worse. The Revolution terrified too many of the upper, and excited too many of the lower classes; and the stern Tory system of repression, with its bad habit of talking and acting as if "the government" and "the people" were necessarily in antagonism, caused ever-increasing bad blood. Besides, the old feudal ties between class and class, employer and employed, had been severed. Large masses of working people had gathered in the manufacturing districts in savage independence. The agricultural labourers had been debased by the abuses of the old Poor-law into a condition upon which one looks back now with half-incredulous horror. Meanwhile, the distress of the labourers became more and more severe. Then arose Luddite mobs, meal mobs, farm riots, riots everywhere; Captain Swing and his rickburners, Peterloo "massacres," Bristol conflagrations, and all the ugly sights and rumours which made young lads, thirty or forty years ago, believe (and not so wrongly) that "the masses" were their natural enemies, and that they might have to fight, any year, or any day, for the safety of their property and the honour of their sisters.[23]

Kingsley's pronouncement is bad history and worse explanation. But it states a popular theory with extraordinary force. Englishmen and other Europeans of the time developed a set of beliefs which are still widespread today; the beliefs equate the "working classes" with the "dangerous classes" and argue that misery, crime, personal disorganization, and rebellion sprang from approximately the same causes and occurred in approximately the same segments of the population. The causes were the breakdown of traditional social arrangements, the desperation brought on by extreme poverty, and the demoralizing overpopulation of the great cities.

A unique essay contest run by King Maximilian of Bavaria in 1848 produced hundreds of fearful statements from middle-class Germans concerning the rise of overpopulation, mechanization, and immorality.[24] It matters little that many of the analyses (for example, those attributing the growth of the urban population to the increase in illegitimacy) were wildly mistaken. The fear was there. And in France:

On the bourgeois opinion of the time, we can take the work of Balzac as the most remarkable piece of evidence, above all because it bears the marks of these two facts: on the one hand the blending of the working classes and the dangerous classes, the proletariat and the underworld, misery and crime; on the other hand, the division between two categories of the population, that daily settlement of differences of which criminality is an expression, and that sporadic settlement of differences of which riots and revolution are the expression.[25]

In response, some French, Germans, and English organized inquiries into poverty; others organized police forces.

For several centuries before this time, the central task of the European police had been control of the grain trade, markets, and, by extension, public assemblies. The notion of a professional organization devoted mainly to the detection and apprehension of criminals took hold in the nineteenth century. But before that professionalism developed, the European states were expanding and reorganizing their police forces very largely as a means of dealing with the new threats from "the masses." The new police began to replace both the army and those older repressive forces which had been fairly well matched to the primitive and reactionary forms of collective violence: the local militias, part-time constabularies, the personal employees of justices of the peace. Sir Robert Peel's organization of the London metropolitan police in 1829 (which immortalized him by transferring his nickname "Bobby" to the police officers themselves) had the well-recognized dual purpose of putting aside thugs and putting down rebellions. It is even clearer that the setting up of a nationwide provincial police by the Rural Police Act of 1839 "was precipitated by the Chartist disturbances of that year and, in particular, by the desire to relieve the military of a pressure which was in the highest degree inconvenient and injurious."[26]

European police forces of the period acquired great political importance, not only as agents of crowd control, but also as the organizers of political espionage via networks of spies and informers. Their reorganization throughout Europe in the early nineteenth century marked a victory of the national over the local, a nationalization of repressive forces. As Allan Silver says, "The police penetration of civil society . . . lay not only in its narrow application to crime and violence. In a broader sense, it represented the penetration and continual presence of central political authority throughout daily life."[27] Although the new police forces by no means succeeded in eliminating collective or individual violence from everyday life, they did speed the decline of the older forms of protest. By matching more complex and specialized organization of repression to the more complex and specialized organization of the newer forms of protest, they probably even earned some of their reputation for staving off revolution.

MODERN COLLECTIVE VIOLENCE

The *modern* varieties of political disturbance (to use another tendentious term) involve specialized associations with relatively well-defined objectives, organized for political or economic action. Such disturbances can easily reach a large scale. Even more clearly than in the case of reactionary collective violence, they have a tendency to develop from collective actions which offer a show of force but are not intrinsically violent. The demonstration and the violent strike are the two clearest examples, but the coup and most forms of guerrilla also qualify. These forms deserve to be called "modern" not only because of their organizational complexity but also because the participants commonly regard themselves as striking for rights due them, but not yet enjoyed. They are, that is, forward-looking.

In England, the modern varieties of collective violence came into their own fairly early. Joseph Hamburger, whose general purpose is to refute the notion that England came close to revolution before the 1832 Reform Bill, nevertheless describes some good-sized disturbances in 1831:

> There were also disturbances in London during the days immediately after the Lords' rejection of the Bill. They mainly occurred in connection with a procession that was organized, with Place's help, by two London Radicals, Bowyer and Powell. Organized by parishes, people were to march to the palace and present an address in support of the Bill to the King. When it took place on October 12, 300,000 persons were said to have taken part. The Home Secretary informed the deputations that the King could not receive their petitions, but they could present them through County Members. Hume received some of them in St. James Square and later left them at the palace. The procession than marched past the palace as a demonstration of its size and resolution. It consisted of "shopkeepers and superior artisans"; nevertheless, during the day there were attacks on some Tory peers as well as the usual broken windows.[28]

Obviously, the violence in this case was minor, but the order and size of the demonstration was impressive. Much more so than in the case of reactionary disturbances, the extent of violence in this sort of event depends heavily on the reactions of the demonstrators' opponents.

During the widespread Chartist agitation of the following two decades the standard routine involved a fire-eating speech by a Chartist leader followed by a procession through the streets, spewing threats and displaying weapons. The threats, however, rarely come to anything except when they confronted the Queen's soldiers. While once in a great while a member of the crowd fired at the troops, their usual tactic was to stone them: "At Preston, during the Plug-Plot disturbances, a mob which had belaboured the soldiers with stones stood its ground for a while when the order to fire was given and several of its members were struck, but the shooting of a ring-leader, who had stepped out in front of the mob to encourage his followers to continue the assault, put a damper on the proceedings, and caused the crowd to disperse."[29] The British army and police soon developed effective, and largely nonviolent, methods of crowd control.

Despite the development of effective policing, England still witnessed plenty of collective violence later in the century. There was a wave of "riots" in London in 1866, another in 1886 and 1887: most of these events consisted of demonstrations which got out of hand. But the real resurgence of this form of violence came early in the twentieth century, as the movements for temperance and (more importantly) for woman's suffrage began to mount demonstrations in the course of which the women showed unwonted determination: "they smashed windows, fired pillar-boxes, slashed pictures, threw things at M.P.s, and even burned down churches and houses; in reply they were treated with great roughness by policemen and worse by crowds. They were kicked and beaten; their hair was pulled and their clothes half-torn off; hatpins were pushed into them; they were knocked down and trampled upon."[30]

It was about this time that Lincoln Steffens heard English leaders talking about the possibility of revolution. For three different movements were swelling and coalescing in the years just before the First World War: the demand for woman's suffrage, huge (and sometimes insurrectionary) strikes, and opposition to war. A famous leaflet of the time communicates some of what was happening:

> You are Workingmen's Sons.
> When we go on Strike to better Our lot which is the lot also of Your Fathers, Mothers, Brothers and Sisters, *You* are called upon by your Officers to *Murder Us.*
> Don't do it. . . .
> Don't you know that when you are out of the colours, and become a "Civy" again, that You, like Us, may be on strike, and You, like Us, be liable to be Murdered by other soldiers.
> Boys, Dont't Do It.
> "Thou shalt not kill," says the Book.
> Don't forget that!
> It does not say, "unless you have a uniform on."
> No! *Murder is Murder.*
> Think things out and refuse any longer to Murder Your Kindred. Help Us to win back Britain for the British and the World for the Workers.[31]

Some of these movements (like the drive for women's suffrage) succeeded; some (like the various demands of organized labor) met a mixture of success and failure; and some (like pacifism) failed utterly. England survived. But the essential point is that the characteristic forms of collective violence accompanying those movements differed fundamentally from those which had prevailed a century before.

The rise of the strike as a context for collective violence followed a similar rhythm. Although they often reimpose one restriction on another, most European states legalized the strike some time during the nineteenth century: England in 1824, Saxony in 1861, France in 1864, Belgium in 1866, Prussia in 1869, Austria in 1870, the Netherlands in 1872. That did not, however, make all subsequent strikes peaceful. Occasionally the violence began when the workers themselves attacked a factory, mine, or manager's home. Sometimes the workers demonstrated, and the demonstration turned violent. More often the violence grew from a confrontation between strikers assembled at a workplace and troops, police, or strikebreakers sent in to thwart or control them.

In France, occasional strikes broke out in the biggest cities as early as the sixteenth century. In the first half of the nineteenth century, several rounds of strikes—notably those of Lyon in 1831 and 1834—bubbled up into bloodily repressed insurrections. But the first sets of strikes approaching a national scale came at the end of the Second Empire, in 1869 and 1870. A major strike movement swept the textile and metal-working plants of Alsace in July 1870, with some 20,000 workers out in the vicinity of Mulhouse. Then:

> Peaceful parades took possession of the streets. First the carpenters: the evening of 4 July, 400 to 500 men "walked through the city, singing, in an orderly fashion." And for three days the processions continued across the city, in groups, men, women, children, marching "in a fairly disciplined way."[32]

Then the demonstrations grew. In a number of towns, the strikers kept the nonstrikers out by force. Eventually the troops came in, and the minor violence ended. Total: a few injuries, a little property damage, perhaps 70 arrests.

Not all strikes were so peaceful, however. During the same period, a number of mining strikes involved pitched battles between troops and demonstrators. In the course of a strike of 15,000 miners around St. Etienne in June 1869, the troops killed 13 and wounded another 9 members of a crowd which attacked them; this encounter went down in history as "the massacre of La Ricamarie." At Aubin (Aveyron), later in the year, the troops shot 30 to 40 strikers trying to break into a metal-working plant, and managed to kill 14 of them on the spot. The point is not that people sometimes died in the course of these conflicts. It is that both the strikes involving trivial damage and those involving loss of life took essentially the same form.

The tremendous Paris Commune of 1871 broke the continuity of modern collective violence to some extent. Its organization greatly resembled that of earlier Parisian rebellions, and its leitmotifs—local control, communal autonomy, equalization of advantages—went against the prevailing nationalization of political conflict and the formation of special interest associations. But the break occurred as the Prussians marched through northern France, as the government fled, as the rest of the nation, in effect, seceded from Paris. The break was short. With Paris tamed and the national government reinstalled, French people returned quickly to the modern forms of violent conflict.

Later on strikes grew in amplitude and frequency. As they spread, they became increasingly common contexts for collective violence, even though a decreasing proportion of all strikes were violent. After 1890, a number of strikes took on an insurrectionary character, with both the doctrine and the practice of the general strike growing in importance. (It was at just this time that Georges Sorel, in his famous *Reflections on Violence*, placed the "myth of the general strike" at the center of revolutionary action.) And the character of strike activity continued to change as the structure of labor unions, the structure of industry, and the relations of labor management and government all evolved. France's peak years for strike activity— 1906, 1919-1920, 1936, 1947, 1968—have all been years of great social conflict in other regards as well. Each of those crises marked a new stage in the scale and sophistication of conflict.

THE TRANSITION TO MODERN COLLECTIVE VIOLENCE

Unlike the food riot or the *occupazioni*, all this is terribly familiar stuff to the twentieth-century reader. In it he sees the collective violence of his own era. The only reason for reviewing it is to notice the deep differences in character among the primitive, reactionary, and modern forms. They lend importance to the fact that so many Western countries shifted from one type to another rapidly and decisively.

The nature, timing and causes of these shifts from one major type of collective violence to another are complicated, controversial, and variable from one country to another. Just as complicated, controversial, and variable, in fact, as the political histories of European nations. The transformations of collective violence depended on transformations of nonviolent political life. Rather different political systems emerged in different corners of Europe: communist, socialist, liberal-democratic, corporatist. Each had a somewhat different experience with collective violence. Yet everywhere two things happened, and profoundly affected the character of violent protest.

The first was the victory of the national state over rival powers in towns, provinces, and estates; politics nationalized. The second was the proliferation and rise to political prominence of complex special-purpose associations like parties, firms, unions, clubs, and criminal syndicates. The two trends generally reinforced each other. In some countries, however, the state gained power faster and earlier than the organizational changes occurred; Russia and France are cases in point. In others, the organizational revolution came much closer to the nationalization of politics; Germany and Italy fit that pattern. In either case, the times of overlap of the two trends produced the most dramatic changes in the character of collective violence.

Some of the contrast appears in tabulations of violent events occurring in France during the three decades from 1830 to 1860 and three later decades from 1930 to 1960.[33] The representative set of conflicts includes 1,265 events, involving 3,015 formations (distinct groups taking part in the collective violence). The distribution over time appears in Table 3.1. The figures show that France did not, by any means, become a peaceable nation as urbanization and industrialization transformed her

Table 3.1: The Frequency of Violent Events in France, 1830-1860 and 1930-1960

Period	Number of Events	Number of Formations	Formations per Event	Estimated Total Participants (thousands)
1830-1839	285	563	2.2	300
1840-1849	293	734	2.5	450
1850-1860	116	263	2.3	100
1930-1939	336	803	2.4	750
1940-1949	93	221	2.4	200
1950-1960	169	431	2.6	350

between 1830 and 1960. The two decades from 1850 to 1860 and 1940 to 1950 produced the fewest violent events; what actually happened is that during two extremely repressive regimes (following Louis Napoleon's 1851 coup and during the German occupation and Vichy government of the 1940s) there was almost no open large-scale violence. If we were to omit the large, if unsuccessful, rebellion which greeted Louis Napoleon's seizure of power, the 1850s would look preternaturally calm. The large numbers for the 1930s include the factory occupations of 1936 and 1937. Even without them the depressed thirties would look like troubled times. So would the prosperous fifties. In boom and bust, the French continue to fight.

We can look at the distribution of formations taking part in the violent events in Table 3.2. The figures show a decided decline in the participation of the ordinary, mixed crowd without any well-defined political or economic identity, and a compensating rise in the participation of crowds labeled as supporters of particular creeds and programs. We find no marked change in the involvement of repressive forces in collective violence, but see an important shift of the task of repression from military forces to police. "Natural" groups like users of the same market (who were typical participants in food riots, invasions of fields, and other small reactionary disturbances) disappeared completely over the 130-year span.

Altogether, our table shows the rise of specialization and organization in collective violence. Just as industry shifted its weight from the small shop to the large factory and population rushed from little town to big city, collective violence moved from the normal congregations of the communal groups within which people used to live most of their lives toward the deliberate confrontations of special-purpose associations. Collective violence, like so many other features of social life, went from a communal basis to an associational one.

As a consequence, the average size of incidents went up. Table 3.3 presents measures of magnitude for the 1,265 violent events in the sample. The figures, of course, describe the average event, not the total amount of violence a decade produced. They show a distinct rise in the average number of people taking part in a violent encounter, despite a strong tendency for events to narrow down to a single day. As the burden of repression shifted from the army to the police, interestingly enough, the use of widespread arrests declined while the number of people hurt stayed about the same. Relative to the number of participants, that meant some

Table 3.2: Formations Participating in French Violent Events, 1830-1860 and 1930-1960

Type of Formation	1830-1839	1840-1849	1850-1860	1930-1939	1940-1949	1950-1960
Simple crowd	16.8%	17.4%	9.1%	1.6%	4.1%	1.8%
Ideological crowd	13.7	9.1	12.5	47.8	19.9	34.2
Guerrillas, bandits and paramilitary forces	3.7	1.0	20.2	2.1	1.8	1.4
Public officials[a]	7.8	11.8	17.5	1.5	4.1	1.8
Military	16.8	13.5	9.9	3.1	9.5	2.1
Police	5.3	8.9	10.3	17.5	20.8	30.7
Military and police	4.8	4.9	6.1	6.8	8.1	3.9
Occupational group	16.7	17.3	3.9	14.9	27.1	17.1
Users of same market, fields, woods, or water	2.5	4.4	1.9	0.8	0.0	0.0
Others	11.9	11.9	7.6	4.0	4.5	6.9
Total	100.0	100.2	99.0	100.1	99.9	99.9

a. *Includes formations consisting of public officials plus police and/or military.

Table 3.3: Magnitudes of Violent Events in France, 1830-1860 and 1930-1960

	1830-1839	1840-1849	1850-1860	1930-1939	1940-1949	1950-1960
Mean number participating	1,093	1,482	923	2,202	2,410	2,197
Mean person-days expended	1,895	2,584	1,518	2,223	2,386	2,184
Person-days per participant	1.7	1.7	1.6	1.0	1.0	1.0
Percentage lasting more than one day	16	18	24	4	4	5
Mean killed and wounded	28.2	17.6	33.0	19.4	185.2	23.0
Mean arrests	30	30	139	23	23	84

decline in the average demonstrator's chance of being killed or wounded. The main message, once again, is that collective violence persisted as France became an advanced industrial nation, although the predominant forms of collective violence changed in fundamental ways.

The twentieth-century figures from France include almost no primitive violence. By the beginning of the century, the primitive forms had been fading slowly through most of Western Europe for three centuries or more. In at least some countries, however, the transition from predominantly reactionary to predominantly modern forms of collective violence occurred with striking rapidity. In England, the reactionary forms were already well on their way to oblivion by the time of the last great agrarian rising, in 1830, although they had prevailed 30 years before. In Germany, demonstrations and strikes seem to have established themselves as the usual settings for collective violence over the two decades after the Revolution of 1848.

The situation was a bit more complicated in Italy, because of the deep division between North and South. The transition to modern forms of collective violence appears to have been close to completion in the North at unification. By the time of Milan's infamous *fatti di Maggio* of 1898, in which at least two policemen and 80 demonstrators died, the newer organizational forms unquestionably dominated the scene. In the South, mixed forms of the food riot and tax rebellion were still appearing at the end of the century. Within ten years after that, however, even in rural areas the agricultural strike and the organized partisan meeting or demonstration had become the most regular producers of violence on the larger scale.

Spain, as usual, is the significant exception: while the country as a whole displays the long-run drift from primitive to reactionary to modern forms of collective violence, it also displays a marvelous array of regressions, mixtures, and hesitations. Surely the country's erratic industrialization, uncertain, fluctuating unification, and exceptional military involvement in politics lie behind its differentiation from the rest of western Europe in this respect. Spain, as Gerald Brenan says,

> is the land of the *patria chica*. Every village, every town is the centre of an intense social and political life. As in classical times, a man's allegiance is first of all to his native place, or to his family or social group in it, and only secondly to his country and government. In what one may call its normal condition Spain is a collection of small, mutually hostile, or indifferent republics held together in a loose federation. . . . Instead of a slow building-up of forces such as one sees in other European nations, there has been an alternation between the petty quarrels of tribal life and great upsurges of energy that come, economically speaking, from nowhere.[34]

Thus Spain becomes the exception that proves the rule. For the rule says the shift from predominantly reactionary to predominantly modern forms of collective violence accompanies the more or less durable victory of the national state and the national economy over the particularisms of the past. In Spain, that victory was not durable, and the forms of violence wavered.

The precise timing and extent of the shift from reactionary to moderen forms of collective violence in these countries remains to be established. For France, it is fairly clear that the shift was barely started by 1840, but close to complete by 1860.

Furthermore, France experienced great, and nearly simultaneous, outbreaks of both forms of collective violence in the years from 1846 through 1851. The well-known events we customarily lump together as the Revolution of 1848 and the less-known but enormous insurrection of 1851 stand out both for their magnitude and for their mixture of reactionary and modern disturbances, but they came in the company of such notable outbreaks as the widespread food riots of 1846-1847, the Forty-Five Centime Revolt of 1848-1849, and the unsuccessful coup of 1849.

If this account of the transition from reactionary to modern collective violence in western Europe is correct, it has some intriguing features. First, the timing of the transition corresponds roughly to the timing of industrialization and urbanization—England early, Italy late, and so on. Furthermore, the most rapid phase of the transition seems to occur together with a great acceleration of industrial and urban growth, early in the process: England at the beginning of the century, France of the 1850s, Germany of the 1850s and 1870s, Italy of the 1890s.

Second, there is some connection between the timing of the transition and the overall level of collective violence in a country. Over the last 150 years, if we think in terms of the frequency and scale of violent events rather than the turnover of regimes, we can probably place Spain ahead of France, France ahead of Italy, Italy ahead of Germany, and Germany ahead of England. France is in the wrong position, and the contrast much less than the differences in reputation for stability or instability, but there is some tendency for the latecomers (or noncomers) to experience greater violence. If we took into account challenges to national integration posed by such peoples as the Catalans, and differences in the apparatus of repression, the connection would very likely appear even closer.

The information we have on hand, then, suggests that the processes of urbanization and industrialization themselves transform the character of collective violence. But how? We have a standard notion concerning the life cycle of protest over the course of industrialization and urbanization: an early stage consisting of chaotic responses to the displacements and disruptions caused by the initial development of urban industry, a middle stage consisting of the growth of a militant and often violent working class, a late stage consisting of the peaceful integration of that working class into economic and political life. This scheme is largely incorrect. Certainly we must correct and expand it to take account both of other groups than industrial workers and of the connections between industrialization and urbanization as such and changes in the political system as such. For the information concerning the character of collective violence we have already reviewed raises grave doubts whether the underlying process producing and transforming protest was one of disintegration followed by reintegration, and whether the earlier forms of protest were so chaotic as the scheme implies.

The experience of France challenges the plausible presumption that rapid urbanization produces disruptions of social life which in turn generate protest. There is, if anything, a negative correlation over time and space between the pace of urban growth and the intensity of collective violence. The extreme example is the contrast between: (a) the 1840s, with slow urban growth plus enormous violence and (b) the decade after 1851, with very fast growth and extensive peace. Cities like St. Etienne or Roubaix, receiving and forming large numbers of new industrial workers, tended to remain quiet while centers of the old traditional crafts, such as Lyon and Rouen, raged with rebellion. When we can identify the participants in political conflicts, they tend to grossly underrepresent newcomers to the city and draw especially from the "little people" most firmly integrated into the local political life of the city's working-class neighborhoods. The geography of the conflicts itself suggests as much. It was not the urban neighborhoods of extreme deprivation, crime, or vice, George Rudé reports, "not the newly settled towns or quarters that proved the most fertile breeding-ground for social and political protest, but the old areas of settlement with established customs, such as Westminster, the City of London, Old Paris, Rouen, or Lyons."[35] The information available points to a slow, collective process of organization and political education—what we may at least loosely call a development of class consciousness—within the city rather than a process of disruption leading directly to personal malaise or protest.

As a consequence of this process, the great new cities eventually became the principal settings of collective violence in France. Futhermore, collective violence moved to the city faster than the population did. Even at the beginning of the nineteenth century, the towns and cities of France produced a disproportionate share of the nation's collective violence. Yet tax rebellions, food riots, and movements against conscription did occur with fair regularity in France's small towns and villages. After these forms of contention disappeared, the countryside remained virtually silent for decades. When rural collective violence renewed, it was in the highly organized form of farmers' strikes and marches on government buildings. This sequence of events was, to some extent, a result of urbanization.

Early in the nineteenth century, the expansion of cities also incited frequent rural protests—obviously in the case of the food riot, more subtly in the case of other forms of collective violence. We have some reason to believe that groups of people who were still solidly established within rural communities, but were losing their livelihoods through the concentration of property and the urbanization of industry, regularly spearheaded such protests. The most important groups were probably the workers in cottage industry. Their numbers declined catastrophically as various industries—especially textiles—moved to the city during the first half of the century. Large numbers of them hung on in the countryside, doing what weaving, spinning, or forging they could, eking out livings as handymen, day-laborers, and farmhands, railing against their fate. Within their communities, they were able to act collectively against power looms, farm machines, tax collectors, and presumed profiteers.

Slowly before midcentury, rapidly thereafter, the increasing desperation of the French countryside and the expanding opportunity for work in the new industrial cities drew such men away from their rural communities into town. That move cut them off from the day-to-day personal contacts which had given them the incentive and the means for collective action against their enemies. It rearranged their immediate interests, placed them in vast, unfamiliar communities, and gave them relatively weak and unreliable relations with those who shared common interests with them.

The initial fragmentation of the workforce into small groups of diverse origins, the slow development of mutual awareness and confidence, the lack of organizational experience among the workers, and the obstacles thrown up by employers and governments all combined to make the development of the means and the will for collective action a faltering, time-consuming process. Collective violence did not begin in earnest until the new industrial workers began forming or joining associations—trade unions, mutual aid societies, political clubs, conspiratorial groups—devoted to the collective pursuit of their interests. In this sense, the short-run effect of the urbanization of the French labor force was actually to damp collective violence. Its long-run effect, however, was to promote new forms of collective action frequently leading to violent conflicts, and thus to change the form of collective violence itself.

This happened in part through the grouping together of large numbers of people sharing a common fate in factories, urban working-class neighborhoods, construction gangs. Something like the class-conscious proletariat of which Marx wrote began to form in the industrial cities. This new scale of congregation combined with new, pressing grievances, improving communication, the diffusion of new organizational models from government and industry, and grudging concessions by the authorities to the right of association. The combination facilitated the formation of special interest associations. At first workers experimented with cramped, antique, exclusive associations resembling (or even continuing) the old gilds; gradually they formed mutual aid societies, labor exchanges, unions, national and international federations.

The new associations further extended the scale and flexibility of communication among workers; they made it possible to inform, mobilize and deploy large numbers of men fast and efficiently in strikes, demonstrations and other common actions. These potentially rebellious populations and their demanding associations proliferated in the big cities, in the shadows of regional and national capitals. They therefore posed a greater (or at least more visible) threat to the authorities than had their small-town predecessors. The authorities responded to the threat by organizing police forces, crowd-control tactics and commissions of inquiry. The associations, in their turn, achieved greater sophistication and control in their show of strength. The process took time—perhaps a generation for any particular group of workers. In that longer run the urbanization of the labor force produced a whole new style of collective violence.

The experience of the industrial workers has one more important teaching for us. In both reactionary and modern forms of collective violence, participants commonly express their feeling that they have been unjustly denied their rights. Reactionary conflicts, however, center on rights once enjoyed but now threatened, while modern conficts center on rights not yet enjoyed but now within reach. The reactionary forms are especially the work of groups of people who are losing their collective positions within the system of power, while the modern forms attract groups of people who are striving to acquire or enhance such positions. The reactionary forms, finally, challenge the basic claims of a national state and national economy, while the modern forms rest on the assumption that the state and the economy have a durable existence—if not necessarily under present management. In modern disturbances, people contend over the control and organization of the state and the economy.

What links these features together historically? The coordinate construction of the nation-state and the national economy simultaneously weakened local systems of power, with the rights and positions which depended on them, and established new, much larger arenas in which to contend for power. In western European countries, as locally based groups definitively lost their struggle against the claims of the central power, reactionary conflicts dwindled and modern conflicts swelled. The rapid transition from one to the other occurred where and when the central power was able to strengthen rapidly or to expand its enforcement of its claims. Accelerating urbanization and industrialization facilitated such an expansion by providing superior means of communication and control to the agents of the central power, by drawing people more fully into national markets, and by spreading awareness of, and involvement in, national politics. In the process, special purpose associations like parties and labor unions grew more and more important as the vehicles in the struggle for power, whether violent or nonviolent. Thus urbanization and industrialization affected the character and the incidence of collective violence profoundly, but indirectly.

THE LOGIC OF COLLECTIVE VIOLENCE

Before rushing to clamp this analysis of European collective violence onto current American experience, we should pause to notice how much of it is an *historical* analysis—helpful in sorting out the past and identifying the context of the present, but not in predicting the future. Categories like primitive, reactionary, and modern have more kinship with timebound terms like Renaissance, Liberalism, or Neolithic than with rather timeless concepts like urban, clan, or wealth. I would not argue for a moment that forward-looking protests are necessarily larger in scale than backward-looking ones, although that has been the usual experience of Western countries for several centuries. For those were centuries of growth and centralization, in which to look backward *meant* to lean toward the smaller scale. As a general statement, the analysis is too one-dimensional.

To take the problem out of time, we must deal with at least two dimensions. One is the organizational basis of routine political life. To simplify the problem, we might distinguish between politics based on small-scale, local, traditional groupings (*communal* politics) and politics based on large-scale organizations formed to serve one well-defined interest (*associational* politics). Then we could say that both the primitive and the reactionary forms of collective violence spring from communal bases, although under differing circumstances, while the modern forms of collective violence develop from an associational base. In the primitive and reactionary cases, the links among those who join together in collective action—whether violent or not—come from traditional, localized, inherited, slow-changing memberships. The rhythm of collective violence therefore follows the rhythm of congregation and dispersion of existing communal groups; market days, holidays, harvest days produce more than their share of violence. In the purely modern case, on the other hand, deliberately created formal organizations provide the crucial links. The organizations help shape the aspirations and grievances of their members, define their enemies, determine the occasions on which they will assemble and the occasions on which they will confront their antagonists, and thus the occasions on which violence can occur. The communal/associational distinction is one of the hoariest in the study of social life, and it turns out to apply to such apparently antisocial behavior as violence.

We have to consider another dimension: the relationship of the groups involved to the existing structure of power. Again simplifying radically, we might imagine a division among groups unrepresented in the existing structure of power, groups in the process of acquiring positions in the structure, groups holding defined positions in that structure, and groups in the process of losing defined positions. Then it would be right to say that on the whole primitive conflicts involve groups holding defined positions in a (certain kind of) structure of power, reactionary conflicts involve groups losing such positions, and modern conflicts involve groups acquiring them.

Strictly speaking, these are not types of violence. The distinctions do not apply to acts of violence, or even to the collective actions characteristically producing violence. They sort out groups of people into differing political situations. Their relevance to violence as such rests on a simple argument: a population's organization and political situation strongly affect its form of collective action, and the form of collective action stringently limits the possibilities of violence. Thus each type of group takes part in a significantly different variety of collective violence.

That clarification gives us the means of putting the two dimensions together. We discover that there are some other possible types not discussed so far:

	RELATION TO STRUCTURE OF POWER		
	Acquiring position	Maintaining position	Losing position
ORGANIZATIONAL BASE	Communal	? *Primitive*	*Reactionary*
	Associational *Modern*	?	?

It is not so hard to fill in two of the blanks. There are really two varieties of modern collective violence, a frenzied variety on the part of people like the suffragettes who are trying to storm the system, and a more controlled but massive show of strength by groups like parties already established in the system. Violent movements of protest like Poujadism, on the other hand, resemble those I have called reactionary except that they have an associational base. That suggests placing them in the lower right-hand corner: the characteristic collective violence of groups losing position in a system built on an associational basis.

As for acquiring position in a communal system, common sense says it can't be done. But we might throw common sense aside and speculate that the millenarian, transcendental, and fanatical movements which rack backward areas from time to time provide men with the means of acquiring totally new identities through religious conversion. That would lead us to expect these other-worldly protests to turn into modern protests as the organizational basis shifts from communal to associational. Some features of millenarian movements in such European areas as Andalusia and Southern Italy lend this speculation a snippet of plausibility, but it is still only a speculation.

We have filled in the boxes. The table now looks like this:

RELATION TO STRUCTURE OF POWER

	Acquiring position	Maintaining position	Losing position
Communal	*Other worldly?*	*Primitive*	*Reactionary*
Associational	*Offensive*	*Interest-group*	*Defensive*

ORGANIZATIONAL
BASIS

The boxes are not air-tight. We can easily locate groups standing halfway between the communal and associational forms of organization, or just barely maintaining their political positions. Organized criminals come to mind as an example of the first; languishing protest parties as an example of the second. The point of the scheme is to suggest that their usual collective actions, and therefore their usual forms of collective violence, will also fall halfway between those of their neighbors in the table.

All this box-filling would be no more than a scholastic exercise if it were not possible to draw some interesting further hypotheses from the discussion. The first is that, regardless of their organizational basis, groups acquiring position are likely to define their problem as the achieving of rights due them on general grounds but so far denied, groups losing position to define their problem as the retention of specific rights of which they are being deprived, and groups maintaining position to pay less attention to rights and justice. Second, the actions of those acquiring or losing position are likely to be more violent than those maintaining position. Third, a larger proportion of collective actions on a communal basis result in violence, because the associational form gives the group a surer control over its own actions, and thus permits shows of force without damage or bloodshed. While historically the shift from communal to associational bases for collective violence did not, by any means, stop the fighting, it did bring into being a number of alternative nonviolent mechanisms for the regulation of conflicts: the strike, the parliament, the political campaign.

So when does this line of reasoning lead us to expect that collective violence will be widespread? It suggests that over the very long run the transformation of a population, a movement or a society from a communal to an associational basis of organization diminishes its overall level of violence, but only over the very long run. If we were to consider external war as well as internal civil disorders, even that timid inference would look dubious. The scheme implies much more definitely that collective violence clusters in those historical moments when the structure of power itself is changing decisively—because there are many new contenders for power, because several old groups of power-holders are losing their grips, or because the locus of power is shifting from community to nation, from nation to international bloc, or in some other drastic way. Violence flows from politics, and more precisely from political change.

The extent of violence depends on politics in the short run as well. Violence is not a solo performance, but an interaction. It is an interaction that political authorities everywhere seek to monopolize, control or at least contain. Nowadays almost all collective violence on a significant scale involves the political authorities and their professional representatives: policemen, soldiers, and others. That happens, first, because the authorities make it their business to intervene and thus maintain their monopoly on the use of force; second, because so much collective violence begins with a direct (but not necessarily violent) challenge to the authorities themselves.

As odd as it may seem, authorities have far greater control over the short-run extent and timing of collective violence, especially attacks on persons rather than property, than their challengers do. That is true for several reasons. The authorities usually have the technological and organizational advantage in the effective use of force, which gives them a fairly great choice among tactics of prevention, containment and retaliation. The limits on that discretion are more likely to be political and moral—Can we afford to show weakness? Could we fire on women and children?—than technical. If the criterion of success is simply the minimization of violence, repression often works. In recent European experience, few countries have been freer of civil disorder than Spain, a normally turbulent nation, when Spain was under the tight dictatorships of Primo de Rivera and Franco. In the heydays of the German and Italian fascists, virtually the only violence to occur was at the hands of government employees.

The authorities also have some choice of whether, and with how much muscle, to answer political challenges and illegal actions which are not intrinsically violent: banned assemblies, threats of vengeance, wildcat strikes. A large proportion of the European events we have been surveying turned violent at exactly the moment when the authorities intervened to stop an illegal but nonviolent action. This is typical of violent strikes and demonstrations. Furthermore, the great bulk of the killing and wounding in those same conflicts was done by troops or police rather than by insurgents or demonstrators. The demonstrators, on the other hand, did the bulk of the damage to property. If we sweep away the confusion brought on by words like "riot," "mob," or "violence" itself, a little reflection will make it clear that this division of labor between maimers and smashers follows logically from the very nature of encounters between police and their antagonists.

All this means that over the short run, the extent, location, and timing of collective violence depend heavily on the way the authorities and their agents handle the challenges offered to them. Over a longer run, however, the kinds of challenges they face and the strength of those challenges depend rather little on their tactics of crowd control and a great deal on the way the entire political system apportions power and responds to grievances.

Discussions of these matters easily drift into praise and blame, justification and condemnation, fixing of responsibility for violence. If, when, where, and by whom violence should be permitted are inescapably difficult questions of moral and political philosophy. My review of European historical experience has not resolved them. Its purpose, after all, was the more modest one of sketching social processes lying behind the actual occurrence of collective violence in Western countries as they have existed over the last century or so. Yet the fact that the analytic and historical questions drag us so close to political philosophy underlines my main conclusions: collective violence is part and parcel of the Western political process, and major changes in its character result from major changes in the political system.

If that is the case, very recent changes in the character and locus of violent protest bear careful watching. Through much of Europe, students have reached a level of activism and anger never before equalled; the French Events of May, 1968, were only the most spectacular episode of a long series. Separatist movements long thought dead, ludicrous or at least under control—Welsh, Scottish, Breton, Basque, Croatian, Slovak, Flemish—have sprung up with energy. Demands for autonomy, *cogestion,* insulation from state control, which virtually disappeared from European political debate a half-century ago, now appear to be growing rapidly. Of course it is possible that the wide-spread emergence of autonomist themes in collective violence is a coincidence, a passing fancy or simply my misreading of the character of the new movements. If none of these is the case, we might consider the possibility that they record a transfer of power away from the national state, perhaps in part because its own weight keeps it from dealing with the most burning aspirations of its own citizens, and in part because power is devolving to international blocs of states. Then we might be witnessing a transformation comparable in scope to the nineteenth-century shift from reactionary to modern forms of collective violence. These are speculations, but they, too, emphasize the political significance of violence.

I leave it to the well-informed reader to apply this analysis of European experience to the civil disorders of contemporary America. Naturally, analogies immediately come to mind. Studies of ghetto riots of the 1960s produced a picture of the average rioter which much resembles what we know of many nineteenth-century urban conflicts: the predominance of young males, the overrepresentation of long-time residents rather than recent migrants, the relative absence of criminals, and so on. But why search for easy analogies? The chief lesson of the European experience is not that riots are all the same. Far from it! What we have seen, instead, is a close connection between the basic political process and the predominant forms of conflict, both violent and nonviolent. That makes it hard to accept a characterization of American ghetto riots as "mainly for fun and profit."[36] It raises doubts about attempts to reduce recent student rebellions to one more expression of adolescent anxiety. It makes one wonder whether the recent revival of violent and nonviolent separatist movements in such different Western countries as Belgium, Canada, Spain, France, and Great Britain indicates some larger change in international politics. For the basic conclusion is simple and powerful. Collective violence belongs to political life, and changes in its form tell us that something important is happening to the political system itself.

AFTERTHOUGHTS, FROM THE SEVENTIES

The near-decade since these reflections went to press have added a great deal of collective violence to the world's record. In the same time, reams of writing about violence have also appeared. It is easy for scholars to confuse the two, the more so because scholarly writing tends to drift with the current of events: guerrilla warfare in the 1950s, riots in the 1960s, terrorism in the 1970s, who knows what in the 1980s. Yet in looking back at essays on violence—or, more generally, on conflict and collective action—written during the crises of the late 1960s, we ought to ask two separate questions: (1) In the light of later scholarship, how well do those essays stand up now? (2) Do they help us understand anything that has happened in the world since then?

The last person you would want to ask for an unbiased answer to these questions is the author of the essay. After all, the author has a lot at stake. If he is mainly a scholar, he is probably skilled at smoothing out the inconsistencies between things he said in the past and things he says now. If he is mainly an activist, he is probably adept at making things he said in the past seem to be reasonable steps on the way to the position he now advocates. If your author, like me, is one of those scholars who turned out (often fearfully and sometimes grudgingly) for the demonstrations and picket lines of the late 1960s and early 1970s, you might reasonably expect him to defend the correctness of whatever he wrote in 1969.

Consider yourself fairly warned: In general, the arguments of this 1969 paper still look valid to me, but you should check them out for yourself. As it happens, since 1969 scholarly sentiment has shifted toward the sort of formulation I was offering them. Interpretations of collective violence as an expression of group derangement and of individual fury have lost much of the popularity they once had. In their place have proliferated treatments of collective violence as a form, or as an outcome, of rational action.[37] On the whole, scholars have come to reject the notion of a sharp separation between routine politics and violent conflict. Instead, they have devoted a great deal of energy to tracing the connections between violent and nonviolent struggles for power.[38] Furthermore, historical and comparative studies of collective violence have flourished in the last decade; social scientists have taken up historical analyses with enthusiasm, as historians have somewhat more guardedly adopted concepts and models of contemporary social-scientific work.[39] As a result of all these changes, essays in the style of 1969's *Violence in America* have become quite common.

None of this means, to be sure, that the discussion of collective violence has lapsed into tidy, boring consensus. Students of conflict, a contentious lot themselves, have moved from wrangling over *whether* collective violence is a normal, rational phenomenon to discussing *how* rational it is, and what sort of rationality it involves.[40] No single, powerful theory of violence has appeared to sweep away disagreement. On the contrary, the weakening of their common opponent—arguments portraying collective violence as an expression of irrational sentiments released, or even caused, by massive social change—sharpened the differences among three different lines of argument: (1) theories in the tradition of Max Weber, stressing the importance of shared beliefs (however "rational") in the orientation of collective action, including violent actions; (2) theories in the tradition of John Stuart Mill and the utilitarians, stressing the role of rational individual calculation; (3) theories in the tradition of Karl Marx, stressing the significance of economically rooted interests and solidarities in a wide variety of conflicts.[41]

In the process, North American scholarly attention has broadened from violence as such to a wide range of conflict and collective action. No doubt one reason for the declining preoccupation with violence itself was the subsiding of the sensational conflicts of the 1960s: ghetto rebellions, campus revolts, protests against American war-making in Southeast Asia. In the relatively calm period which has ensued in North America (although certainly not in the world as a whole), editors have grown bored with essays on violence, foundations have lost interest in financing research on violence, students have ceased flocking to lectures on violence. Researchers, writers, and professors—sensitive to the loss of their audience, alert to new opportunities, and not much more resistant to fashion than anyone else—turned their attention to other, more current issues. The dwindling band who stuck with the study of collective violence found, furthermore, that they could make much more sense out of violent actions by connecting them deliberately to their nonviolent context. With some dissent from psychologists and ethologists who sought to trace collective violence back to individual aggression, and from there to fundamental characteristics of the human organism, most specialists adopted some idea of violent conflict as a special case, or outcome, of a broader process which was not intrinsically violent: collective action in general, conflict in general, and so on. The Weberian, Millian, and Marxian theories on which they leaned encouraged them to expand the range of their analyses. So a combination of waning public interest in violence with partly autonomous intellectual developments broke up the once-prosperous industry of violence analysis, and regrouped its remaining entrepreneurs in other nearby enterprises.

All things considered, these changes were beneficial. They reduced the prevalence of snappy slogans and quick fixes in the study of violent conflict. They tipped the balance toward sustained, careful inquiries, including intensive case studies, controlled comparisons and broad historical analyses. They brought about a recognition that violence is not a phenomenon *sui generis*, but a contingent outcome of social processes which are not intrinsically violent. In particular, the further research and reflection strengthened the idea that collective violence, generally speaking, appears as a by-product of political processes: as a by-product of struggles for power, of contention over the authoritative allocation of collective costs and benefits, of efforts to defend or augment collective rights. Since that idea lay at the center of my 1969 essay, I could only applaud the new direction of work in the field.

Nevertheless, the formulations of that 1969 essay leave many problems unsolved, and some of them obscured. To start with the most important: the classification of violent events into *primitive, reactionary,* and *modern* types has turned out to be a useful preliminary sorting device, but then to cause more and more trouble as analysis proceeds. The scheme gains its plausibility and utility from the rough correlation of several quite different features of violent events: the form of action (e.g., intervillage fights vs. strikes), the sort of social groups involved (e.g., peasant communities vs. political parties), the relationship of the groups involved to the rights and privileges at issue (e.g., defending threatened, long-established rights vs. claiming rights never yet enjoyed) and the tendency of one type to take over from another (e.g., the contemporaneous decline of reactionary events and rise of modern events). In the Western experience of the last few hundred years, those correlations are strong enough to make a simple summary useful: primitive forms of collective violence gave way to reactionary ones, which in turn ceded their place to modern forms of collective violence.

Then the complications begin. Even in the Western historical experience, the correlations are only rough. The strike, for example, does indeed enjoy a historical connection with special-purpose workers' associations, has indeed served particularly to advance new claims, and did indeed begin to supersede a number of older forms of worker action during the nineteenth century. But strikes have often served defensive purposes: holding off wage cuts, resisting the firing of union organizers, stopping speedups, and so forth. Once a form of action is available, people adapt it to their own interests. That is true not only of the strike, but also of the artisans' brawl, the demonstration, and many other forms of action which commonly produced violence.

The second complication is just as weighty. The primitive/reactionary/modern scheme advertises itself as a classification of violent actions. Looked at closely, the advertising is misleading on both counts. First, the basic actions which identify most of the forms involved are *not violent*. Even the action we loosely call "machine-breaking" actually consisted, for the most part, of a sequence in which a group of workers demanded that an employer stop using a labor-saving machine, threatened punishment if he did not comply with their demand, and only broke up the machine when repeated demands, entreaties, and threats failed to produce the desired results. When it comes to such forms of action as demonstrations and mocking ceremonies, the great majority of cases have occurred without violence; in general, violence has only occurred when rival groups, authorities, or repressive forces have tried to stop the action of the demonstrators or mockers.

In addition, the events classified as primitive, reactionary, and modern are not really actions, but *inter*actions. A food riot is nothing at all without a baker, merchant, or city official to attack, a strike nonexistent unless a boss is somewhere on the scene. If that point seems obvious, its implications are not so self-evident. For it means that no explanation based entirely on the experiences of the rioters or strikers can be adequate; at a minimum, an adequate explanation of a strike includes an account of the behavior of the workers, an account of the behavior of the employers, and an account of their interaction. The portrayal of primitive, reactionary, and modern forms of collective violence offered earlier in this chapter emphasizes the experiences of historical underdogs very strongly. It therefore lacks an analysis of the actions of their opponents, and an account of interactions between underdogs and their opponents. As an unintended result, the lopsided argument ends up suggesting that collective violence is an expression of underdog experience alone—exactly the sort of conclusion the chapter set out to attack.

The chapter's basic argument has at least one major defect: it offers only the vaguest identification of the *interests* on which people have historically been prepared to act collectively. Despite some concrete discussion of the rights and interests at issue in such events as invasions of fields and tax rebellions, I eventually sum up the central processes involved as the loss, maintenance, and acquisition of political power. Another of those classifications which serves usefully as a first approximation, but becomes a burden when pushed very far. Let me leave aside the possible misunderstandings generated by using the word "political" so broadly. The real trouble lies elsewhere: although in any given country in a given period there are standard processes by which various groups lose, maintain, or acquire power, and although those processes do indeed account for much of the ebb and flow of collective violence, people rarely fight about power in general. They fight about the particular rights, privileges and opportunities to realize their interest which *constitute* their power, or which their power guarantees. For lack of a systematic discussion of those interests, the earlier discussion gives the impression that power, sheer power, serves as an end in itself.

Over the historical experience discussed in this chapter, two large processes made the greatest difference to the interests of ordinary people. One was the expansion of capitalist property relations, the other the rise of the national state. Increasingly, ordinary people worked for wages, those who controlled capital made the basic production decisions, and the entire range of goods, services and property people needed to survive became available to buyers who could pay the price. That growth of capitalism attacked the interests of small producers, of people who survived by relying on communal rights in forests and fields, and many others. It created new groups of workers and employers with quite different interests and rivalries. We have seen the expansion of capitalism operating concretely in the food riot and the invasion of fields, but also in the strike. The state also grew, and momentously: superseding local governments and squashing local rights, demanding taxes, supplies, and conscripts, building up armies and bureaucracies. That process, too, attacked old interests and established new ones. We have seen state-making at work concretely in the tax rebellion and the anticonscription riot, but also in the demand for female suffrage. The expansion of capitalism and the rise of the national state together created the world we live in. They set the frame for the changing forms of collective action, and therefore of collective violence. They did so by transforming the basic interests people considered worth fighting for, and the means they had of acting on those interests. Collective violence was no more than a contingent by-product of these momentous processes. Yet the connection between the character of the by-product and the character of the processes generating it was—and is—very strong. As a result, the history of collective violence reflects the history of human collective experience as a whole.

NOTES

General. At different times, the Social Science Research Council and the Canada Council have supported the research reported in this paper. In recent years, the National Science Foundation has been its principal source of financial support. A host of people have helped with the research; for the material in this paper I am especially indebted to Priscilla Cheever and Louise Tilly. Summaries of different aspects of our work and bibliographies of detailed reports appear in John Boyd, R.A. Schweitzer, and Charles Tilly, "British Contentious Gatherings of 1828" (Ann Arbor: Center for Research on Social Organization, University of Michigan, 1978; CRSO Working Paper 171); Edward Shorter and Charles Tilly, *Strikes in France, 1830-1968* (Cambridge, England: Cambridge University Press, 1974); Charles Tilly, ed., *The Formation of National States in Western Europe* (Princeton, N.J.: Princeton University Press, 1975); Charles Tilly, Louise Tilly, and Richard Tilly, *The Rebellious Century, 1830-1930* (Cambridge, Mass.: Harvard University Press, 1975); Charles Tilly, *From Mobilization to Revolution* (Reading, Mass.: Addison-Wesley, 1978).

In revising this paper for the new edition of *Violence in America,* I have cleaned up some editorial slips and obscure passages, substituted better data for the preliminary results concerning French collective violence reported in the first version, brought the notes up to date, and written a brief epilogue. Anyone who takes the trouble to compare the old text with the new will discover that, sensitized to my language by recent feminist exhortations, I have changed a number of masculine nouns (e.g., "men") into neutral or collective forms (e.g., "people).

1. Marc Bloch, *Les caratères originaux de l'histoire rurale française* (Paris: Colin, 1952), I, 175.

2. J.L. and Barbara Hammond, *The Village Labourer* (London: Longmans, 1966), 241-242.

3. Elie Halévy (E.I. Watkin and D.A. Barker, trs.), *England in 1815* (New York: Barnes and Noble, 1961), 148.

4. Graham Adams, Jr., *Age of Industrial Violence, 1910-1915* (New York: Columbia University Press, 1966), 132-136.

5. Hammond and Hammond, op. cit., 242-243.

6. Bruce M. Russett and others, *World Handbook of Political and Social Indicators* (New Haven, Conn.: Yale University Press, 1965), 99-100.

7. Antonio Gramsci, *Il Risorgimento* (Torino: Einaudi, 1950), 199-200.

8. The general logic of this distinction (if not the precise formulation or the exact wording) appears in E.J. Hobsbawm, *Primitive Rebels* (Manchester: Manchester University Press, 1959). It also underlies much of the argument of George Rudé, *The Crowd in History* (New York: John Wiley, 1964).

9. Thorstein Veblen, *Imperial Germany and the Industrial Revolution* (Ann Arbor: University of Michigan Press, 1966), 50.

10. *Le Constitutionnel*, November 19, 1835.

11. M. Dorothy George, *London Life in the Eighteenth Century* (New York: Harper and Row, 1964) 280.

12. Rudolf Stadelmann and Wolfram Fischer, *Die Bildungswelt des deutschen Handwerkers um 1800* (Berlin: Duncker and Humblot, 1955), 71.

13. Philippe Ariès, *Centuries of Childhood* (New York: Vintage, 1965) 317-318.

14. Ibid., 318-319.

15. A.J. Peacock, *Bread or Blood* (London: Gollancz, 1965), 79.

16. Ibid., 81.

17. Here and later in the chapter I have relied especially on an unpublished paper by Louise Tilly, "Popular Protest in the Risorgimento: 1850-1860" (University of Toronto, 1967); see also Chapter 3 ("Italy") in Tilly, Tilly, and Tilly, *The Rebellious Century*.

18. Karl Marx, "The Class Struggles in France, 1848-1850," in Marx and Engels, *Selected Works* (Moscow: Foreign Languages Publishing House, 1958), I, 213.

19. Hammond and Hammond, op cit., 261-262.

20. E.J. Hobsbawm, "Le agitazioni rurali in Inghilterra nel primo ottocento," *Studi Storici*, 8 (April-June 1967): 278.

21. E.P. Thompson, *The Making of the English Working Class* (London: Gollancz, 1964), 530.

22. Ibid., 543.

23. Charles Kingsley, preface to *Alton Locke* (London: Macmillan, 1887), xcii.

24. Edward Shorter, "Middle Class Anxiety in the German Revolution of 1848," *Journal of Social History*, 2 (1969): 189-215.

25. Louis Chevalier, *Classes laborieuses et classes dangereuses* (Paris: Plon, 1958), 469.

26. F.C. Mather, *Public Order in the Age of the Chartists* (Manchester: Manchester University Press, 1959), 128.

27. Alan Silver, "The Demand for Order in Civil Society: A Review of Some Themes in the History of Urban Crime, Police, and Riot," in David J. Bordua, ed., *The Police: Six Sociological Essays* (New York: John Wiley, 1967), 12-13.

28. Joseph Hamburger, *James Mill and the Art of Revolution* (New Haven: Yale University Press, 1963), 147.

29. Mather, op. cit., 21.

30. G.D.H. Cole and Raymond Postgate, *The British Common People, 1746-1946* (London: University Paperbacks, 1961), 490.

31. Ibid., 453-454.

32. Fernand L'Huillier, *La lutte ouvrière à la fin du Second Empire* (Paris: Colin, 1957; Cahiers des Annales, No. 12), 65.

33. Our procedure consisted of reading through two national newspapers for each day of the six decades and pulling out each reported event involving some violence (wounding, property damage, or seizure of persons or property over resistance) in which at least one participating formation had 50 members or more. As well as we can determine, a sample thus assembled overweighs events in cities, and especially in Paris, but in a relatively constant fashion. The descriptions of the events coded come not only from the newspaper accounts but also from historical works and French archival material. More details on procedures appear in *The Rebellious Century* and *From Mobilization to Revolution*, both cited above, and in Edward Shorter, *The Historian and the Computer* (Englewood Cliffs, N.J.: Prentice-Hall, 1971); Charles Tilly, "Methods for the Study of Collective Violence," in Ralph W. Conant and Molly Apple Levin, eds., *Problems in the Study of Community Violence* (New York: Frederick A. Praeger, 1969); Charles Tilly, "How Protest Modernized in France, 1845 to1855," in William Aydelotte, Allan Bogue, and Robert Fogel, eds., *The Dimensions of Quantitative Research in History* (Princeton, N.J.: Princeton University Press, 1972); Charles Tilly, "Quantification in History, as Seen from France," in Jacob M. Price and Val Lorwin, eds., *The Dimensions of the Past* (New Haven, Conn.: Yale University Press, 1972).

34. Gerald Brenan, *The Spanish Labyrinth* (Cambridge, England: Cambridge University Press, 1967), 1x.

35. George Rudé, "The Growth of Cities and Popular Revolt, 1750-1850, with Particular Reference to Paris" in J.F. Bosher, ed., *French Government and Society, 1500-1850: Essays in Memory of Alfred Cobban* (London: Athlone Press, 1973), 190.

36. Edward C. Banfield, "Rioting Mainly for Fun and Profit" in James Q. Wilson, ed., *The Metropolitan Enigma* (Cambridge, Mass.: Harvard University Press, 1968), 283-308.

37. Some recent examples are Herbert Hirsch and David Perry, eds., *Violence as Politics* (New York: Harper and Row, 1973); Robert M. Fogelson, *Violence as Protest: A Study of Riots and Ghettos* (Garden City, New York: Doubleday, 1971); David Snyder and William R. Kelly, "Industrial Violence in Italy, 1878-1903," *American Journal of Sociology*, 82 (1976): 131-162; Yoshio Sugimoto, "Quantitative Characteristics of Popular Disturbances in Post-Occupation Japan (1952-1960)," *Journal of Asian Studies*, 37 (1978): 273-291; for bibliographies and reviews of the literature, see Kenneth W. Grundy and Michael Weinstein, *The Ideologies of Violence* (Columbus, Ohio: Charles E. Merrill, 1974); James C. Holmberg, "The Rush to Violence in Social Analysis: A Review Essay," *Historical Methods Newsletter*, 4 (1971): 88-99; Michael J. Kelly and Thomas H. Mitchell, "Violence, Internal War and Revolution; A Select Bibliography" (Ottawa, Canada: Norman Paterson School of International Affairs, Carleton University; Bibliography Series, 3; revised version, 1977); Terry Nardin, "Conflicting Conceptions of Political Violence" in Cornelius P. Cotter, ed., *Political Science Annual*, Vol. 4 (Indianapolis: Bobbs-Merrill, 1972).

38. Examples: Anton Blok, *The Mafia of a Sicilian Village* (New York: Harper and Row, 1974); Daniel Chirot, *Social Change in a Peripheral Society* (New York: Academic Press, 1976); Joe R. Feagin and Harlan Hahn, *Ghetto Revolts* (New York: Macmillan, 1973); William A. Gamson, *The Strategy of Social Protest* (Homewood, Ill.: Dorsey, 1975); Ted Robert Gurr, Peter N. Grabosky, and Richard C. Hula, *The Politics of Crime and Conflict: A Comparative History of Four Cities* (Beverly Hills: Sage Publications, 1977); Henry A. Landsberger, ed., *Rural Protest: Peasant Movements and Social Change* (London: Macmillan, 1974); John Wilson Lewis, ed., *Peasant Rebellion and Communist Revolution in Asia* (Stanford: Stanford University Press, 1974); David Sabean, "The Communal Basis of Pre-1880 Peasant Uprisings in Western Europe," *Comparative Politics*, 8 (1976): 355-364; Michael Schwartz, *Radical Protest and Social Structure* (New York: Academic Press, 1976); Joseph Spielberg and Scott Whiteford, eds., *Forging Nations: A Comparative View of Rural Ferment and Revolt* (East Lansing: Michigan State University Press, 1976).

39. See Ronald Aminzade, "Revolution and Collective Political Violence: The Case of the Working Class of Marseille, France, 1830-1871" (Ann Arbor: Center for Research on Social Organization, University of Michigan, 1973; CRSO Working Paper 86); Yves-Marie Bercé, *Croquants et Nu-Pieds: Les soulèvements paysans en France du XVIe au XIXe siècle* (Paris: Gallimard/Julliard, 1974); J.P.D. Dunbabin, *Rural Discontent in Nineteenth-Century Britain* (New York: Holmes and Meier, 1974); John Foster, *Class Struggle and the Industrial Revolution. Early Industrial Capitalism in Three Towns* (London: Weidenfeld and Nicolson, 1974); Douglas Hay et al., *Albion's Fatal Tree: Crime and Society in Eighteenth-Century England* (New York: Pantheon, 1975); Dirk Hoerder, *Crowd Action in a Revolutionary Society: Massachusetts, 1765-1780* (New York: Academic Press, 1977); Michelle Perrot, *Les ouvriers en grève* (Paris: Mouton, 1974; 2 vols.); Walter J. Shelton, *English Hunger and Industrial Disorders: A Study of Social Conflict during the First Decade of George III's Reign* (London: Macmillan, 1973); Robert D. Storch, "The Policeman as Domestic Missionary: Urban Discipline and Popular Culture in Northern England, 1850-1880," *Journal of Social History*, 9 (1976): 481-509; E.P. Thompson, " 'Rough Music': Le Charivari anglais," *Annales; Economies, Sociétés, Civilisations*, 27 (1972): 285-312; Alfred F. Young, ed., *The American Revolution* (DeKalb: Northern Illinois University Press, 1976).

40. See Richard A. Berk, "A Gaming Approach to Crowd Behavior," *American Sociological Review*, 39 (1974): 355-373; Richard Maxwell Brown and Don E. Fehrenbacher, eds., *Tradition, Conflict and Modernization: Perspectives on the American Revolution* (New York: Academic Press, 1977); James S. Coleman, *The Mathematics of Collective Action* (Chicago: Aldine, 1973); Peter K. Eisinger, "The Conditions of Protest Behavior in American Cities," *American Political Science Review*, 67 (1973): 11-68; Norman Frolich, Joel A. Oppenheimer, and Oran R. Young, *Political Leadership and Collective Goods* (Princeton, N.J.: Princeton University Press, 1971); Sandor Halebsky, *Mass Society and Political Conflict* (Cambridge, England: Cambridge University Press, 1976); Max Heirich, *The Spiral of Conflict: Berkeley, 1964* (New York: Columbia University Press, 1971); Douglas A. Hibbs, Jr., "Industrial Conflict in Advanced Industrial Societies," *American Political Science Review* 70 (1976): 1033-1058; John D. McCarthy and Mayer N. Zald, *The Trend of Social Movements in America: Professionalization and Resource Mobilization* (Morristown, N.J.: General Learning Corporation, 1973); Clark McPhail and David L. Miller, "The Assembling Process: A Theoretical and Empirical Examination," *American Sociological Review*, 38 (1973): 721-735; Anthony Oberschall, *Social Conflict and Social Movements* (Englewood Cliffs, N.J.: Prentice-Hall, 1973); David Snyder, "Institutional Setting and Industrial Conflict: Comparative Analyses of France, Italy and the United States," *American Sociological Review*, 40 (1974): 259-278; William H. Overholt, "An Organizational Conflict Theory of Revolution," *American Behavioral Scientist*, 20 (1977): 493-520; Michael Useem, *Protest Movements in America* (Indianapolis: Bobbs-Merrill, 1975); Louise White, "Rational Theories of Participation," *Journal of Conflict Resolution*, 20 (1976): 255-278; Kenneth I. Wilson and Anthony Orum, "Mobilizing People for Collective Political Action," *Journal of Political and Military Sociology*, 4 (1976): 187-202.

41. For an effort to sort out theories of collective action into these lineages, see Tilly, *From Mobilization to Revolution*, Chapter 2.

Chapter 4
A Comparative Study of
Fragment Cultures

LOUIS HARTZ

The paradox of the fragment[1] cultures in respect to violence and legality is that they heighten consensus by shrinking the European social universe but at the same time discover new sources of conflict which Europe does not have. Some of these sources are inherent in the process of fragmentation itself, as with colonial revolution, but mainly they are to be found in the encounter of the fragment with new groups, Western and non-Western, as its history proceeds. In the end, to deal with these, the fragment is faced with the problem of transcending the new morality which it has established.

It is not hard to see how the migration of a group from Europe heightens social consensus. The group does not have to deal with other groups possessing different values. Thus the French Canadian corporate community does not have to deal with the Enlightenment, and the American middle class does not have to deal with the institutions of the feudal order. Indeed the new intensity of shared values is matched precisely by an escape from Europe's social revolution and all of the violence it contains. The guillotine is missing in the fragment cultures. To be sure, there will be some disorder in the process of forging the new society and the shrunken consensus it contains, as with "frontier lawlessness" or ethnic strife, but these matters can be fairly well contained. It is in the nature of the migration culture that it leads to a new sense of social peace based upon a new sense of community. And when these emotions are fortified by the spirit of a new nationalism, as they almost always are, the moral world of the fragment is secured in an unusually powerful way.

Technically the violence involved in the colonial revolution should have all of the transience of a frontier situation, since it is more or less an instrument for completing fragmentation. And indeed in a liberal culture like that of the United States, or even in a case like India where a native liberal elite revolts, the revolution has the effect of clarifying the situation. But this need not always be so, especially in the feudal cultures where the imperial order may itself represent a vital part of the domestic legitimacy system of the fragment. Latin America is a case in point. The national

---

AUTHOR'S NOTE: *Louis Hartz is professor of government and politics at Harvard. His books include* The Liberal Tradition in America *(New York: Harcourt, Brace and World, 1955); and* The Founding of New Societies *(New York: Harcourt, Brace and World, 1964).*

revolutions there, by abolishing a Spanish monarchy on which the spirit of authority depended, opened up a vacuum into which the military entered.

One would not suppose that the clash of one European settlement with another would have the same temporary character as the clash of migrants with a mother country, since this is a matter not of separation but of permanent connection. Moreover the very fact that each of the fragments is building its new and shrunken sense of community, fortified by nationalism, exacerbates the matter of the relationship. Indeed if we wish to measure what the fragment has avoided in the way of Europe's social revolution we can look at a country like Canada, where bourgeois and feudal cultures confront one another, but as "nations" rather than classes. This means, to be sure, a situation potentially much more explosive than the European, but this very fact drives from the outset toward some federal solution which would be unthinkable within England or France themselves insofar as the relations of classes are concerned. We are, of course, reminded here that in the interfragment confrontation the distance of the social values the fragments enshrine from one another is important. But we must not make too much of this. For the South African case shows us that where the fragments are really quite similar in social and national substance, Holland and England being parts of a North European cultural complex, extraneous factors such as race can enter into the relationship of the fragments and literally explode it.

Actually, for all of the tension between the English and the Dutch which resulted from the racial issue in South Africa, the underlying fact about the attitude of the fragment toward the non-European is that he is outside a consensus of values, European in character, which despite their limited social circumference all of the fragments share. And under these circumstances, a common European violence in relation to the non-European is almost inevitable. The aborigine, at whatever stage of culture, is the first to encounter it. Whether he is simply exterminated, or shoved off into reservations, or incorporated along Latin American lines into the fragment system, force becomes inevitable. Nor is this wholly a transient frontier matter, even in countries like Australia where the simple method of extermination was widely used. Aboriginal groups survive, creating issues of conscience and of policy alike. And of course in the Latin American situation, where the aboriginal elements become vital parts of the culture, their existence helps to define the very categories of social strife.

The same principle of violence holds even when the non-European is imported, as is the case with the African slave in all parts of the fragment world save Africa itself. Indeed the process of importation yields a major and peculiar form of violence in its own right, since there are the horrors involved in the voyage from Africa, a kind of "forced fragmentation," which matches, curiously, the more spontaneous movements on the part of the European populations themselves. We must not forget, however, that the European fragment values themselves seek to absorb slavery into their own definitions of legitimacy, and this profoundly conditions the nature of the force associated with it. Feudal fragments, such as those of Brazil, instinctively seek to legitimize slavery along hierarchical lines, whereas bourgeois fragments like that of the United States oscillate between "property" and "personalty" as categories for the African. This oscillation, needless to say, has revolutionary implications, both for the European and the African in the United States, as the Civil War and its aftermath fully reveal.

The effort to "abolish" or "digest" the Indian and the African obviously has limits as a technique for cultural relatedness. It cannot easily be applied to the world at large which is descending on the fragments in the twentieth century as it is upon all nations. Ironically, this experience brings the fragment into contact with the very revolutionary process it escaped at the time of migration, for the European revolution has been transferred, albeit in changed fashion, to large areas of the globe. That transfer is, to be sure, a phase of the European cultural fragmentation itself, which the new societies share, and there is a common theoretical bond here between the United States, India, and even Japan. But the differences are also immense, since the Enlightenment fragments of Europe in these instances usually work within the context of the most powerful traditionalisms. It is at this point, where 1789 returns, as it were, that the European settlement cultures face most vividly the challenge of transcending their perspectives. Whether they can meet this challenge, without descending into irrational violence at home and abroad, is still an open question. Perhaps a consolation is to be found in their record of federal invention, not merely in two fragment cultures like the Canadian but within single fragment societies like the United States. Certainly, for the nations born of the drive of European groups to live separately, the fragment cultures have shown a remarkable concern with the institutional technique of "living together."

MIGRATION AND CONSENSUS

Let us look more closely at the process by which the fragments create a special sense of community out of their own contracted social substance. The fact that this process can override frontier disorders of a domestic kind is testimony to its force. But it will always be in contrast to the European social revolutions that the fragments escape, in contrast to their barricades and their civil wars, that the new spirit of consensus will be centrally measured. This is not merely a matter of escaping the old regime, or as in the feudal cases of French Canada and Latin America escaping the Enlightenment itself. Flight from the immediate enemy is, to be sure, a critical matter. But when the pilgrims leave, they leave not merely an opposing group; they leave a total historical process, whose interactions generate constantly new results. Thus the integrity of the new fragment consensus is protected, by virtue of the same stroke of movement, from the enemies of the future as well as the past.

The threat of socialism illustrates this process almost everywhere. Since that subversive movement requires a mixture and a confrontation of both feudal and bourgeois elements, neither the feudal nor the bourgeois fragments can produce it; Marx is missing both in French and English Canada, despite the strain of the CCF, although he blossoms in France and England, where the fragments of North America interact on a class basis and keep the social revolution moving. This is a hidden source of unity within Canada as it is between Canada and the United States, for surely it would be a matter of concern throughout North America if any area within it produced something like a Bolshevik Revolution. The problem of Castro in a later and different context may give us a hint of this. To be sure, western Europe does not itself produce many victorious revolutionary socialisms, but the Marxian force is a factor there, continuing the 1789 revolution, which most of the fragment cultures escaped. Historically, if the world of Boston and the world of Quebec are both to exist, even Harold Laski has to be excluded from their borders.

This is not to deny that labor violence can take place in the fragment cultures, as the Molly Maguire movement will show. But it is to deny that this violence will symbolize a major trend of proletarian revolution. Historically, the working class is typified by the AFL in the United States and English Canada and by Catholic syndicates in French Canada. Nor does the Australian case, where a series of major strikes in the 1890s led to the victory of the Labor Party, really disprove our point. For the fragment root of the culture of Australia was proletarian, even to some extent Chartist, so that socialism was an inherent outcome of its history—as, let us say, Jacksonian democracy was an inherent outcome of the bourgeois culture of the United States. In this sense the upheavals at the turn of the century in Australia have something in common with Dorr's Rebellion in Rhode Island, manifestations in line with the fragment ethic, helping it forward, rather than challenging it in a subversive way. The Australian experience shows us that the process of European settlement can embrace more in the way of ideology than conservatism or liberalism, but it does not disprove the proposition that all settlements, in their own ideological terms, escape social revolution and go forward to a new experience of moral consensus.

That consensus is bound to be fortified by nationalism, because it is the only substitute the fragmented European has for the European national identity he has lost. How else can the migrant Puritan regain a sense of national wholeness than by calling the Puritan ethic itself the American way of life? This process varies in intensity from fragment to fragment depending of the clarity of the ideological substance, and the relationship to the European homeland. But it is to be found everywhere, even in English Canada where the ambiguities of the fragment identification are legendary. Of course, where it appears in extreme form, it produces itself a moral vigilantism which borders on the violent. "Americanism" in McCarthyite form or French Canadianism in Duplessis form can be terrifying things. But it is interesting that these are always "law and order" movements, and the label is not wholly meaningless. While there is a sad paradox in men being harried by movements boasting lawfulness, the fact is that such patriotic crusades do express, in pathological form, the normal spirit of legalism in the fragment world. That spirit rests on the new and contracted consensus arising out of migration. If an excess of national emotion sends militants off in the pursuit of subversive phantoms, then the legalism of the fragment has, in some sense, no right to complain. Here is a curious case of "law and order" against itself.

We must not overlook the role of fragment nationalism in containing the tensions implicit in new immigration, for by converting the fragment ethic into a source of national identity it permits the immigrant to "belong" simply by subscribing to it. To be sure, ethnic struggles are historic in the United States despite "Americanization." In other fragment cultures, where the blossoming of fragment nationalism has been inhibited, the "melting pot" has worked even less effectively. Indeed it might even be argued, insofar as strife is concerned, that in societies like English Canada or Latin America, where ethnic separatism tends to persist, violence is itself minimized, since the homogenizing moral force which would hurl groups into contact with one another is limited. Canada is interesting on this count because there is a tendency for the newcomers of recent times, taking their cue from the Federal relationship of French and English, to rationalize explicitly the maintenance of their own identity. But after all of this has been said, and the complexities of the matter noted, it remains a fact that the conversion of the fragment ethic into a national code always contributes something to immigrant belonging. And the reason is that national membership is transmuted thereby from something inscrutable and unattainable into somthing doctrinal and embraceable. You cannot become an Englishman by subscribing to Magna Carta, but you can make at least some progress toward becoming an Australian by subscribing to the open egalitarianism of the national legend.

Politics betrays the new consensus, indeed rests upon it. When one says that the fragment cultures escape social revolution, one automatically says many things about their political sytems. Their political struggles are usually not ideological, save in the sense that the national ideology is occasionally brought into play against subversives. It is illuminating to see how this principle works out in Australia, where even the socialism of the Labor Party relaxes into a pragmatism nourished by the general egalitarian consensus. What this often means, indeed, as once again the Australian experience illustrates, is a positive distrust of the intellectual, the ideologizer. This will be accentuated in fragment cultures of an intrinsically democratic type, for there the death of ideology coincides with an exaltation of the popular mind. In a relatively stratified bourgeois fragment such as the English Canadian there is a bit more place for the intellectual elite, and in the feudal fragments, leaving aside the habit of clerical leadership, there is a larger place as well. Given the torn fabric of Latin America, which was penetrated by French thought in the eighteenth century, we actually begin to get something like an "intelligentsia"—a phenomenon rare indeed in the new society.

All of this is merely to return us to the special spirit of legalism injected into the fragment world by the tighter moral consensus which, as against Europe, it contains. Pragmatism is close to legalism, since it flourishes on the basis of a moral settlement which adjudication also requires. *Inter arma leges silent.* Nor does one need to concentrate on the courts alone here, for the spirit to which I am referring can have its incarnation in religion and in clerical establishments, also, as in the case both of French Canada and Latin America. What is at issue is a sense of the presence of objective norms nourished by the fact that the competition of norms has been narrowed and even eliminated through the process of flight from Europe. Surely it is clear enough that this emotion conquers the initial spirit of chaos in the new society, even in an instance like the American, where the saloon and the badman are parts of the national legend. Of course the frontier outlaw in the United States is himself a kind of heroic individualist, far more in tune with the bourgeois ethos than a Bolshevik revolutionist, which is one of the reasons why the legend can nurture him. But even if we account him a deviant, his meaning lies in his transience. The roads are inevitably paved in the Western town and the chamber of commerce takes over.

Indeed it is in the United States, with all of its Jesse James tradition, that the peculiar legalism of the fragment culture appears most vividly. The lucidity of the Puritan consensus creates the basis for nothing less than the remarkable power of judicial review of the Supreme Court, a power resting on the notion that there is enough moral agreement in the political world to permit the adjudication of even its largest questions. Surely nothing reveals more clearly the escape of the fragment from the revolutionary ideological turmoil of Europe than the presence of that power. The very notion of "sovereignty," that ally of all revolutionary enterprises, has to be missing where the higher law is so liberally applied. But if this is the case, if the Supreme Court is a projection of the fragment consensus, the question will always exist as to how far it can control that consensus when, for reasons of patriotism or cultural anxiety, the consensus gets out of hand. Can "law and order" really be protected against itself?

LEGITIMACY AND COLONIAL REVOLT

There will always be a question as to whether the colonial revolutions in the fragment world are not themselves "social revolutions," enactments of a peculiar 1789. But even though we face up to every social aspect of these upheavals, we have to insist that this is not the case. The colonial revolt is tied in with migration, the very process of social escape. And if the violence it engenders can cut in various directions, either the continuing turmoil of Latin America, for example, or the relative peace of the United States, it remains a fact that neither result can be understood apart from the exigencies of the imperial experience.

I have said that in the Latin American case the removal of the Spanish king through imperial revolt impaired the legitimacy structure of the fragment itself. Since efforts to produce New World monarchies failed, save in the case of Brazil where in fact it was a migrant Portuguese monarchy itself which served the purpose, the gap was soon filled by the legendary caudillo. There is no doubt that the feudal fragment has a peculiar vulnerability here, because of its authority needs. Of course these can be met inside the fragment itself, as they were for the most part in French Canada, which was able, out of its own elite, to manufacture a fairly stable system, despite the reliance on Paris. However, it is worth noting that the French Canadian order was not put to the Latin American test on this count. French rule was abolished not by revolution but by external conquest, and the British supplied by their imperial authority much of the direction that they had destroyed on the French side. Nor, in terms of power itself, was the shift from the French to the British on this count as significant as might seem. The French Catholic ethos was in fact prenational, rationalizing authority per se, and it made an accommodation to the conquerors doctrinally possible. French Canada in this connection has not been forced to "stand on its own feet" as a feudal fragment as Latin America has.

Ideally, of course, even in the feudal case, colonial revolt should enhance the integrity of the fragment ethic by completing the escape from European enemies. It is merely a sign that there has not been a full social migration when imperial institutions serve domestic needs. In the case of the American Revolution we have an illustration of this fulfilling aspect of colonial revolt, and nothing brings out more vividly the contrast with Latin America than the issue of monarchy itself. By the time of the Revolution the British monarchy, for all of the reluctance of the colonists to break with it, had ceased to be a major factor in the legitimacy system of the American colonies. Due in part to imperial neglect, and in part to the growth of self-governing institutions, the American system was practically complete in its own terms. Paine celebrated American reality in *Common Sense*. That pamphlet was later translated in Latin America, but in a context, of course, entirely distinctive. Which reminds us, in addition to the differences in the monarchical question, of the differences in the whole doctrinal setting of revolution. In the United States the liberalism of revolutionary doctrine carried forward the intrinsic liberalism of the culture, whereas in Latin America it contradicted not only the initial feudal ethos but also the drive of the creole revolutionary leaders themselves, who remained elitist. It clarified the fragment spirit here, confused it there.

All of this, of course, is why the transition to republican government was easy in the United States, lacking further violence, Napoleonic coups, palace revolts. In the Latin American case the failure to develop domestic monarchs continued the legitimacy gap, but in the United States, had such an effort been successful, it would have impaired the evolving spirit of legitimacy itself. This, undoubtedly, despite all of the rumors at the time, is why no serious attempt at a "restoration" did take place. Certainly, under these circumstances, there was no need either for a military substitute for the monarchical figure, and once again despite rumors and a plot or two, this was why a caudillo dictatorship did not develop. The "critical period" of American history was, in fact, a period in which the American fragment was moving toward larger cultural stability, a wider articulation of its own original meaning. The Constitutional Convention of 1787 was a climax to this process, even if most of the men attending it seem to have been so worried that they did not understand the fact. The fundamental law these men forged, which could have gone the way of French or Latin American constitutions, has lasted down to the present day.

So here was a case, yearned for but never achieved in the theories of great social revolution, where violence was a "transitional" stage toward a purer legality. Surely in other fragment situations where the break with the mother country was not decisive there have been tensions and ambiguities which in the United States were resolved once and for all in the eighteenth century. Surely, too, as both Canada and Australia well illustrate, the persistence of the imperial connection qualifies and inhibits the full conversion of the fragment essence into a new nationalism, a new "way of life." In these terms one can repeat the proposition that the Latin American outcome is the "pathology" of the fragment revolutionary process, a situation traceable to the intrusion of extraneous imperial connections into the domestic heart of the fragment. And in these terms also one can say again that the process is to be associated not with the Jacobins of Europe but with the Mayflower voyage and the Pizarro trip.

FRAGMENT COMPETITION: FEDERALISM

The more one explores the nature of the fragment ethic and its expanding consensus, the more obvious it is that when fragments confront one another, the possibilities are explosive. We are in fact dealing with emergent "nations," compounded out of the class substances of Europe, armed with nationalisms more sensitive than those of Europe because more ideological, more doctrinal. French Canada, put alongside the Protestantism of the English, is loaded with the latent dynamite of the holy war. When one adds to the situation the possibility of clashes over other issues, such as the racial issue of South Africa, one has a potential for struggle exceeding in significance any involved in the relationship to the mother country. No wonder that, in order to contain it, there has to be the most delicate kind of federal diplomacy.

Nor must we assume that, as European class ethics confront one another, the rivalry of the European nationalisms themselves is entirely forgotten. Certainly the struggles that are possible over language are as intense as any in the interfragment relationship. To be sure, devotion to language can reflect attachment merely to a neutral carrier of culture, rather than to the nationalism of Europe, and it would be a mistake to exaggerate its importance in European terms. All of the fragment languages vary from those of the mother countries, reflecting indeed the very simplifying processes by which the fragment itself becomes a distinctive nation. No one would seriously say that Afrikaans, the most dramatic of the linguistic variations, elicits the ardor of its support in South Africa because of the memory of Holland. But after this has been conceded, and the central importance of the fragment culture itself is stressed, the European sentiment cannot be wholly excluded. The fragment cultures, for all of their distinctive nationalist claims, have a manner of giving themselves away on this score, as, for example, when they always seem to prefer immigrants from the country of their own origin.

There can be little doubt that interfragment competition, in its own way, enhances the process by which the fragment converts its culture into nationalism. Without the English Canadian, would the French Canadian define his personality so vividly in nonbourgeois terms? To be sure, the normal nationalizing processes would be at work, as against France itself, and the articulation of the Canadian soul in terms of the rejection of Voltaire and Robespierre would go forward. But the challenge of British merchants in the eighteenth century exacerbates, clearly, the conservative tendency which begins with the migration from France in the seventeenth. Nor does the peculiar "prenational" character of the feudal ethos to which I have referred in the French Canadian case, which in fact assists the reception of British authority, alter this fact. The submission to British monarchy as a formal authority affair is one thing, the preservation of French Canadian cultural integrity can be another. The two can exist within that ethos. But even here we must not overstate the case. There was resistance to the British, as with Papineau and the Rebellion of 1837. Nor does the fact that this resistance also took place in the English sector itself, as part of the drive for representative government, alter the point. What can be a democratic struggle in English Canada, as Papineau himself tends to reveal, can be a nationalist struggle in French.

Of course substantive alliances can be forged across the lines of the fragment, and these can betray numerous facets of the interfragment situation. In Canada the fact that French "reform" forces were interested in the preservation of Catholic corporate culture made a link with the English radicals difficult, though the elites of seigneurial and clerical power often got together rather handily with the Family Compact forces of English conservatism. Indeed the latter relationship, understand-able in light of the stratified nature of the English bourgeois fragment, was probably more solid than anything worked out between the fragments in South Africa after the conquest, even though there the cultural similarities were greater than in the Canadian case. The problem of the African instantly exploded the situation within the context of a common Protestant, North European background. And yet one cannot help noting that the gradual surrender of the English to the Dutch in the racial area, after the Boer War and into the present period, meant that that area itself could yield a substantive bond. Cultural surrender is always a possibility, though least likely in the case of the "first" fragment, i.e., the Dutch or the French, since the sense of fragment nationhood goes back farther in these cases.

Given the limits to the substantive synthesis of the fragments, federalism emerges automatically as a method for containing their relationship, a concession to the fact that we have left the class world of Europe and entered upon "international relations." This federalism, needless to say, must be distinguished from that in single fragment cultures, such as the United States and Australia, where size, settlement, and diversity of a different kind lead to decentralized structures. Federalism in the latter instances is far more "successful," since it is underwritten by the fragment consensus itself: when the consensus is impaired, as in the case of the South and the Civil War in the United States, it encounters troubles that approximate the interfragment type. But for all such troubles, there is no doubt that the efforts at authentic cultural federalism in the fragment world represent one of its greatest achievements. Where in general that world has narrowed the horizon of men, here is an instance in which it has broadened it also. Where the legalism of that world has tended to rest on the most explicit cultural agreements, here is a case where a legalism has arisen resting on the ethos of cultural diversity itself.

And yet is it really true to say that in the interfragment situation the moral consensus is fully missing? All of the fragments involved in Canada and South Africa are European. That is no minor matter, especially in societies which know also the North American Indian and the African. The truth is, the cultural federalism of the fragment experience, if it is not underwritten by the unity of a single fragment ethos, is underwritten by the common norms of the European experience. That may be why it is possible at all. When we move to the non-European, coming out of alien and simpler societies, violence begins to flourish on a grand scale.

THE IMPACT OF ABORIGINAL CULTURES

Technically it is not true to say that legalism breaks down completely when the non-European is involved, since in and through the treatment of the aborigine there are manifestations of fragment morality, as when the Spanish Catholic ethos protects the native or even the American bourgeois ethos speaks of an "Indian treaty." But given the threat of the stone age aborigine both to the explicit class morality of the fragment and to its implict Europeanism, there are bound to be limits to the application of such norms. The fragment exterminates the aborigine, closes him off into separate areas, or absorbs him into its own social order on a certain level. And in all of these cases it uses force in full measure.

It vividly reveals the European edge of the moral conscience of the fragment that, when it comes to extermination, even fragments drenched in the Enlightenment ethic engage in the practice happily. Indeed, it is interesting to note that the brutal record established by the Australians in this respect coincided with a culture of the socially "radical" type. In Tasmania the aboriginal element was wiped out completely. Of course the Enlightenment morality, and above all its Puritan progenitor, has an exclusivity about it both in terms of the "democracy" and in terms of the "damned" which can lead to quite unexpected brutalities. The record here, in contrast to that of the feudal cultures, may have some of the distinctive quality it has in the realm of African slavery. Of course there is always the final pang of conscience in the Enlightenment cases, stemming from the retrospective inclusion of the aborigine into the Lockean community, which produces legislative results.

The method of isolating the aborigine is closely tied in with the violence of the "Indian war" itself, since as a result of that war he is driven off into separate territories. The social principle, moreover, is practically the same in both cases: protection of the morality of the fragment by a kind of Hebraic nonintercourse with the alien culture. When the idea is implemented by a conscious "reservation" policy, the culture of the European fragment has usually triumphed so fully in the land that the desperate fears which inspired the separatist drive in the first place are usually forgotten. Latin America represents, to be sure, a special problem here, because the presence of isolated Indian tribes, in the context of a culture which has incorporated the Indian, can involve a serious issue for the integrity of the state system itself. The Indian question in Mexico or Peru casts a curious light on fragment "separatism."

But we must not assume, of course, that the Latin American approach to the Indian was lacking in violence. Indeed the same type of extermination crusades which prevailed elsewhere are to be found in both the Spanish and the Portuguese cases where Indian tribes, as in Brazil or Chile, were unwilling to cooperate in terms of cultural incorporation. And incorporation itself was a violent process, involving a social upheaval for the Aztec and the Inca more drastic than anything to be found in the revolutions of Europe. Granted that there were reciprocities in these cultures on which the Iberians could rely, as in the systems of authority, religion, and production, still these were far from the social unities which linked all classes within the more advanced European order. Latin America, though feudal in substance, arises out of a great "social revolution," if we wish to use the term in this connection.

Of course, like all great enterprises of social renovation, this one was not wholly successful, remarkable as many of its achievements were. Nor was this entirely because certain aboriginal groups could not be absorbed into the Iberian system, or even because aboriginal practice, as in religion and elsewhere, persisted in sublimated form despite Europeanization and Christianization. It was also because the Indian groups that were absorbed, and hence made to serve as feudal substitutes, were left with racial scars that distributed the organic life of the Iberian order. If racial issues are more "social" in Latin America than elsewhere, it is probably true to say, without being deliberately paradoxical, that social issues are on the whole more racial. Certainly the tensions that arose historically on this score were very great, and in any assessment of the impairment of the feudal consensus in Latin America, they must be included in the record no less than the institutional ruptures arising from the breakdown of the imperial order. The Spaniards showed an absorptive genius here that the British did not—for whatever reason, feudal values, Iberian history, or the accidents of Indian culture—but they paid the price of a basic continuing problem for it. They have been denied the luxury of resolving the Indian problem by intermittent episodes of retrospective guilt.

One thing, in any case, is clear. Whether the European fragment destroys, isolates, or incorporates the aborigine, the record is vivid with bloodshed. Here is the ironic compensation it experiences for leaving its enemies in Europe behind, that it encounters even stranger antagonists abroad. The encounter brings out all of the hidden values it shared with others in the old country, its basic Europeanism, and doing so, unleashes a violent energy that transcends even that which produced the guillotines of the Old World. But insofar as the aboriginal victims of that violence are concerned, they are met by the fragment in the course of its travels, almost as a matter of happenstance. What of the non-European whom the fragment deliberately imports, the African slave?

SLAVERY AND ITS AFTERMATH

The African, of course, is open to all of the violence reserved for the non-European, but being imported as a slave, he will not in the nature of things, save possibly in South Africa, experience extermination or isolation. He will enter the fragment community on some incorporative basis, and this means that fragment legality will instantly encounter a problem with him. On the basis of the aboriginal experience in Latin America, one can predict the outcome here, an effort as in Brazil to bring the black man like the Indian into the Iberian feudal system. But in the North American case, where the Indian has not been absorbed and where above all the Enlightenment norm prevails, the African produces a novel issue. It is one of the most complex issues in the entire pattern of fragment legality.

It is easy to forget the violence involved in the initial acquisition of the slave. In part, this is because the European is ordinarily not responsible for his capture, that work being done in Africa itself; there are no "Indian wars," save possibly again in South Africa, designed to obtain the slave. To be sure, the European enters the process at the point of migration from Africa, and he presides over what is probably the most brutal episode in the entire early process, the slave passage, but this is not easy to remember for another reason. Voyages in their nature are forgotten, since the children of the men who take them never relive the experience. In this sense, the fragmented African is like the fragmented European, the product of an act neither can recall, which reminds us of a most significant matter: that master and slave encountered each other in the Western hemisphere when both were in the process of movement, both in the process of leaving an "old world" behind. True enough, the Mayflower voyage is celebrated, the passage of the slave repressed, but not all of the energy of all the patriotic societies in the hemisphere have been able to intrude the initial European voyage into its active life. Who really cares about a trip from England to Plymouth, however "important," which not even the tourist agencies advertise?

Memory does begin, however, at the point of landing, for here the pattern of fragment life itself takes shape. And whether one views the matter from the standpoint of the European or the African, violence is at its heart. To be sure, because the experience of slavery was present in Africa itself, albeit in a manner quite different from that which came to prevail in the New World, there was a receptivity to it on the part of the African which did not exist, say, among Indian tribes like the Iroquois. It is a legendary fact that the African was imported in precisely those areas of the New World where the aboriginal population would not serve the labor purpose. But this does not alter the fact of force which pervaded the slave relationship. It was there, implicit or explicit, from the instant of purchase to the instant of death.

Of course, this is precisely where the morality of the fragments themselves appear, for the way in which a culture distributes the legitimate use of force is the clue to its ethical life. Feudal Iberia mitigated force theoretically in the slave relationship by feudalizing and Christianizing it, whatever the actual brutality of the system was. But the liberal spirit of the North Americans, being classless, actually precluded this. Human beings being equal; the slave must be somehow inhuman, a true object of property in the Lockean sense, and this produced a theoretical indifference to the force exerted against him. Of course slave codes existed limiting the power of the master, but they had a doctrinal incongruity in the liberal system which, ironically, they lacked in the feudal. And yet there was the inevitable other side of the coin. Accept the humanity of the slave in the liberal scheme, and you must instantly give him all of the rights accorded his master. He moves, without a theoretical moment of waiting, from bottom to top. That was the curiously revolutionary oscillation contained, insofar as the African was concerned, by the Declaration of Independence.

However complex the cause of the American Civil War, that oscillation was reflected in it. The radicalism of the liberal ethic, hidden beneath Supreme Court legalism in a fragment context, exploded in the bloodiest episode the fragment had seen. The Court could not prevent this, as its ultimate failure in the Dred Scott case showed, for what was at stake was the meaning of the very consensus on which its power rested. And yet the clash here took place, for all of the activity of the black man, mainly within the European population; the violence of the slave relationship, because it could not be digested by the fragment morality, was transferred to a struggle among the masters themselves. That struggle ended with the emancipation of the African, the termination of legalized force against him, but it did not bring him fully into the Lockean community. Despite the fixed and continuing radicalism of the liberal demand, and even despite Reconstruction amendments which were written into the fundamental law itself, an ambiguous situation was the result.

That situation, however, was as unstable as the initial situation out of which the war had come. Given social change and the world impact in the twentieth century, the radicalism of Jefferson would reassert itself, this time with the African himself as the most militant carrier of it. The violence of slavery, exploding within the European fragment in the nineteenth century, is turned by the black man against the fragment in the twentieth. However, the rioting in the streets was preceded by the desegregation decisions of the Supreme Court, which reminds us that the black man is still working with the moral materials of the fragment establishment. To be sure, there is a Black Power, separatist overtone to the black battle, which holds out the thought of a two-fragment federalism of the Canadian type or a kind of reverse bantustanism of the South African sort. But so far this has not crucially challenged the Jeffersonian base of the civil rights movement which binds the black man to the

European fragment itself, gives him allies within it and a weapon vastly more powerful than any he can find in another formula. In a fairly pure liberal fragment culture like the American, when you have the Declaration of Independence on your side you come close to having all that there is.

THE AMERICAN PARADOX

Certainly the most effective method for dealing with black violence in the United States is to bring the black man finally fully into the Lockean world, to make him a complete part of consensus and legality. And yet this brings us to a paradox found everywhere in the fragment world, that while the most immediate resources for healing fragment wounds lie in the fragment ethic itself, the impact of a unifying globe requires also that that ethic be transcended. In the American case it has been proven that a blind Wilsonian pursuit of the Declaration of Independence is not the best method for handling world reality. On the other hand, insofar as the black man is concerned, there is this consolation, which reminds us of the peculiar relationship a liberal fragment has to the forces at work on the international scene today. The American Lockean drive to include the blacks coincides with a world movement also designed to establish their equality, and it is even a fact that African nationalism has itself entered as an influence into the civil rights movement. To be sure, there is a difference between social revolution in Africa or Asia and final purification of an absolute liberal ethos derived from the Mayflower. The difference is at the heart of the matter. But we are still dealing with types of "equality," and there ought to be possible an accommodation between them.

Surely when we look at the feudal fragments, with their traditionalized elitist instincts, we see the meaning of this point. The racial hierarchies of Latin America, granted that they are "feudalized," do not fall under the impact of an American civil rights impatience. Of course feudalism itself elicits a deep current of social change, and in this sense Latin America is closer than other fragment cultures to the "underdeveloped" world, as is French Canada. But it is the historic power of the fragment which resists this change. We must not forget that in the international sphere the feudal cultures of both North and South America have also been able to yield quite a considerable worship of Salazar, Franco, and even Hitler.

It will always be ironic that, as they confront the revolutionary world of the twentieth century, the settlement cultures I have discussed here confront products of the European cultural fragmentation itself, sharing basic aspects of their own experience. Whether in Africa or China, it is the migration of European ideas which has disturbed the globe. But despite all the connections here, even that in the case of the American blacks, the "return to revolution" on the part of the fragments poses the most serious problems of understanding for them. Even the very Enlightenment ethos that most of them have can, in this context, be a special source of bitterness and violence. It is doubtful whether men fight more fiercely over the acceptance of the idea of "equality" than over the method of its application.

But one thing is certain. The world will never be reduced through violence by the settlement cultures to the limits of their own ethical outlook. To be sure, it is remarkable how "successful" violence was in this connection in the past, as with mother countries, Indians, Africans. Indeed, given this record, it is perhaps not surprising that the instinct of blind ferocity keeps asserting itself. But sooner or later all of the fragments will have to discover that if the Chinese cannot be deserted as Europe was deserted, neither can they be eliminated like the Iroquois.

An intensified federal outlook, greater than any generated within or among the fragments in the past, is inevitably needed. But if this takes place, what will the fragment have lost? It will have lost some of the cozy warmth of its own shrunken consensus, some of the high righteousness of its own sense of "law and order." Surely the world offers compensations for this. What the fragment nations have missed is the experience of cultural diversity, and this is precisely what a federal perspective on Africa and Asia can yield. In our century the settlement cultures have been entrapped by the world they tried to escape. But if they have the courage to accept that world, they will discover a reward even greater than any they found in Kansas or Quebec.

NOTE

1. I use the term "fragment" here to describe societies arising from the movement of European population, the principle being that the settlers represent a part of the total culture of Europe. Theoretically, the cultural fragmentation of Europe also includes narrower European imperial settlements and the carrying forward of European ideas by native groups as in India or Japan. I shall refer occasionally here to the latter cases, but mainly I shall be concerned with the fragment experience as it applies to societies based significantly on European population, specifically the United States, Latin America, Canada, South Africa, and Australia. For the general theoretical background I am using, see my discussion in Chs. 1-3 of *The Founding of New Societies* (New York: Harcourt, Brace and World, 1964).

Chapter 5

Violence in American
Literature and Folklore

KENNETH LYNN

Recurring themes of violence in American literature and folklore bear witness to the continuing violence of American life. The cruel practical jokes and bloodthirsty tall tales of frontier humorists tell us a good deal about what it was like to live on the cutting edge of a wilderness. The burning cities of Ignatius Donnelly's *Caesar's Column*, Jack London's *The Iron Heel*, and other social novels of the turn of the century reflect in their flames the revolutionary discontent of farmers and industrial workers in the 1890s. Mark Twain's *Pudd'nhead Wilson*, Melville's "Benito Cereno," and Richard Wright's *Native Son* measure the racial animosities with which black and white Americans have been struggling since the seventeenth century. The war novels of Stephen Crane, and of Hemingway and Dos Passos, register the central experience of life "in our time."

American literature and folklore have great significance, therefore, for all those who are interested in the violent realities of our society. The trouble, however, with the way in which these materials have been used by historians, sociologists, anthropologists, and psychiatrists is that literature has been assumed to be nothing less (or more) than a mirror image of life. The effects of fictional conventions on representations of reality have been ignored, as have the needs of authors and audiences alike for the pleasures of hyperbolic exaggeration. Furthermore, by extrapolating violent incidents out of their literary contexts, social scientists have not taken into account either the mitigating dreams of peace which are threaded through the very bloodiest of our novels and stories, or the comic juxtapositions which take the curse off many of the most unpleasant episodes that the American imagination has ever recorded.

The false impressions created by social scientists have been reinforced by certain literary critics who have used their judgments of American literature as a basis for making larger judgments about American society. The errors of these critics have not

AUTHOR'S NOTE: *Kenneth S. Lynn was a member of the English department at Harvard from 1955 to 1968. Since 1969, he has been professor of history at Johns Hopkins. His books include* Mark Twain and Southwestern Humor *(Little, Brown, 1959),* William Dean Howells: An American Life *(Harcourt Brace Jovanovich, 1971),* Visions of America *(Greenwood Press, 1973), and* A Divided People *(Greenwood Press, 1977).*

proceeded out of any lack of literary subtlety, but rather out of their wish to be recognized as cultural messiahs. The messianic strain in modern literary criticism has been in any case very strong, embracing such diverse commentators as T.S. Eliot, Northrop Frye, F.R. Leavis, and Marshall McLuhan, but it has been particularly strong among commentators on American literature. From D.H. Lawrence in the 1920s to Leslie Fiedler in the 1960s the desire of literary critics to lead a revolution in American values has been continuing and powerful, and this desire has led them to insist that violence is the dominant theme of American literature, that American literature is more violent than other literatures, and that the violence of our literature has become more deadly with the passage of time. For the first stage in a revolution is to prove its necessity, and what better evidence could be offered as proof of the sickness of historic American values than the unqiue and obsessive concern of our literary artists with themes of blood and pain? To the messianic critics, the indictment of American books has opened the way to the conviction of American society.

The question of American literary violence thus needs reexamination. By looking closely at certain representative examples, from the humor of the old Southwest to the tragic novels of our own time, we may be able to measure more accurately than heretofore both the extent and the significance of violence in American literature and folklore.

When we consider the humorists of the region between the Alleghenies and the Mississippi River, which in the 1830s and 1840s was known as the American Southwest, we are immediately struck by the theoretical possibility that the literature of violence in America has been written by losers—by citizens who have found their political, social, or cultural position threatened by the upward surge of another, and very different, group of Americans. For the Southwestern humorists were professional men—doctors, lawyers, and newspapermen, for the most part—who were allied on the local level with the big plantation owners and who supported on the national level the banker-oriented Whig party of Daniel Webster and Henry Clay; and what bound these writers together as a literary movement, what furnished the primary animus behind their violently aggressive humor, was their fear and hatred of Jacksonian democracy. Longstreet, Thompson, Kennedy, Noland, Pike, Cobb, Thorpe, Baldwin, Hooper: all the best-known humorists of the old Southwest were agreed that Andrew Jacksonism stood for a tyrannical nationalism which threatened to obliterate states' rights; for a revolutionary politics which by 1860 would democratize the constitution of every Southern state except South Carolina; and for a new spirit of economic competitiveness which everywhere enabled poor white entrepreneurs to challenge the financial supremacy of the bankers and the planters, even as Faulkner's Snopes clan would crawl out of the woodwork after the Civil War and take over the leadership of the biggest bank in Yoknapatawpha County.

Augustus Baldwin Longstreet's *Georgia Scenes* (1835) established the basic literary strategy of Southwestern humor, which was to define the difference between the emotionally controlled, impeccably mannered, and beautifully educated gentleman who sets the scene and tells the tale and the oafish frontiersmen who are the characters within the tale. By keeping his narrators outside and above the barbaric actions they described, Longstreet (and his successors) drove home the point that Southern gentlemen stood for law and order, whereas Jacksonian louts represented an all encompassing anarchy. However hot-tempered the author might be in private life (and Judge Longstreet was only one of many Southwestern humorists who had a notoriously bad temper); however much the hideously cruel, eyeball-popping fights they described gave vent to their own sadistic sense of fun; whatever the political satisfaction that they secretly derived from the spectacle of Jacksonians clawing and tearing at one another; the literary mask of the Southwestern humorists was that of a cool and collected personality whose thoughts and conduct were infallibly above reproach. Politically and socially, the humorists had a vested interest in maintaining that mask.

They also had a vested interest in enlarging upon the violence of backwoods bully boys, riverboat toughs, and other representatives of the new democracy. Because the more inhuman his Jacksonian characters were made to appear, the severer the gentleman-narrator's judgment of them could become. No matter how much lipservice they paid to realism as a literary ideal, there was a built-in, political temptation to exaggerate the truth which Whig humorists found impossible to resist. One and all, they wrote comic fantasies, which the historian of American violence will cite at his own risk.

Even those social scientists who are aware that the purported reality described by a story must always be understood as a projection of the story teller's mind generally distort the meaning of Southwestern humor by taking its violence out of context. Doubtless, as I have already suggested, the humorists' fascination with scenes of violence tells us a good deal about the frustrations and fear of the Southern Whig mind. Yet if we set out to calculate the total imaginative effect of, say, Longstreet's *Georgia Scenes,* we find that the "frame" devices which encapsulate the stories within a gentleman's viewpoint and the balanced, rational, Addisonian langue of the gentleman-narrator's style remove a good deal of the horror from the stories. As in Henry Fielding's *Tom Jones,* a novel of which Judge Longstreet was very fond, violence becomes funny rather than frightening, sanative rather than maddening, when it is seen from a certain elevation, when it is understood by the audience to be a kind of marionette show that is controlled by, but does not morally implicate, the master of ceremonies.

In the years after 1850, when relationships between the sections steadily deteriorated and the South gave way to a kind of collective paranoia, Southwestern humor finally lost its cool. Instead of speaking through the mask of a self-controlled gentleman, the humorist of the new era told his sadistic tale in the vernacular voice of the sadist himself. Whereas Judge Longstreet had been at pains to keep his distance, imaginatively speaking, from the clowns he wrote about, George Washington Harris gleefully identified himself with the prankster-hero of *Sut Lovingood's Yarns* (1867)—for in a world ringed by enemies, the only hope of survival which a paranoid imagination could summon up was to strike first, an ungentlemanly act of which Longstreet's narrator would have been manifestly incapable. Just as the Whig party disappeared after the mid-1850s, so did the literary persona who had incarnated Whiggery's conservative ideals. In his place there arose a grotesque child-hero who was the literary equivalent of the fire-eating, secessionist spirit which increasingly dominated Southern politics after 1855. The vernacular narration of young Sut Lovingood is not intended to remind us of the virtues of modern behavior—indeed, just the reverse. For Sut's humor blocks intellectual awareness in order to release a tremendous burst of vindictive emotion; he is concerned not to instruct society, but to revenge himself upon it. A rebel without a cause, Sut tells us much about the rebels of the lost cause of 1861-1865.

Yet in the overall picture of Southwestern humor, *Sut Lovingood* is the exception, not the rule, a rare instance of the sadistic humor of the frontier being expressed in a manner unqualified by any kind of stylistic or formal restraint. For the most part, the humorists of the old Southwest had a more ambivalent attitude toward violence. Clearly, they were fascinated by it, no matter what they said to the contrary. The way in which the narrators of their stories linger over the details of physical punishment indicates that there was a lurking hypocrisy in the law-and-order stance of the humorists. However, in dealing with Southwestern humor, the historian of the Whig mind must be as careful about leaping to exaggerated conclusions as the historian of Jacksonian reality. If the humorists were hypocrites to a degree, they were also sincere to a degree. If they secretly delighted in the human cockfights they pretended to deplore, they also were genuinely committed to a social standard of moderation in all things. This commitment was expressed in the literary qualities of their writing. In Southwestern humor, the style was, in a very real sense, the man.

Another striking outburst of violent stories in American literature occurred in the social fiction of the turn of the century. Thus Ignatius Donnelly's widely read novel, *Caesar's Column* (1891) projects a dystopian vision of American society in 1988. At first glance, New York City is a smokeless, noiseless, dream city, with glass-roofed streets, glittering shops, and roof garden restaurants. But beneath the surface, the narrator of the novel (a white visitor from Uganda) discovers that the city, like the nation at large, is engaged in a deadly social struggle between a ruling oligarchy, which maintains itself in power with a dirigible fleet armed with gas bombs, and a brutalized populace, made up for the most part of a sullen-tempered, urban proletariat, but also supported by a degraded peasantry. The story climaxes in a lurid account of the definitive breakdown of the social order, which occurs when the looting and burning of the city by a revolutionary organization called the Brotherhood of Destruction raged beyond the control of the oligarchy's troops. The number of corpses littering the streets finally becomes so great than an immense pyramid of dead bodies is stacked up and covered with cement, partly as a sanitary precaution and partly as a memorial to the violence. In the end, the entire city is put to the torch, and except for a small band of Christian socialists who escape to Africa, the entire population is consumed in the holocaust.

The apocalyptic fury of the novel relates very directly to the political hysteria of the 1880s and to the agricultural and industrial unrest of the 1890s—to the fears of an anarchist takeover, for example, that swept the nation after the Haymarket riot in Chicago in 1886, and to the bitter, bloody strikes at Homestead, Pennsylvania, and Pullman, Illinois, in the mid-1890s. The novel is also a startling prophecy of the events of the summer of 1967 in Newark and Detroit. Yet in the very act of calling attention to these resemblances between literature and life, we are also confronted with the important difference, which is that the novel is much more extreme than the reality. As in the case of the Southwestern humorists, Ignatius Donnelly was not a mere seismograph, passively recording social shocks, or even forecasting them;

rather, he was a man who had been driven to become a writer by the experience of political loss, and the apocalyptic darkness of his novelistic vision tells us more about Donnelly's state of mind than it does about American society, past or present.

A political reformer from Minnesota, Donnelly had been deeply upset in 1889 by the overtly corrupt practices of the legislature in his state. In addition to this commitment to good government, Donnelly was a Populist, who combined a concern for the deteriorating economic position of the Midwestern farmer with a political and moral concern that American life was coming to be dominated by its big cities. If the demographic trends of his time continued, Donnelly realized, they would reduce the importance of the farm vote and would spread the spirit of corruption that had so appalled him in the Minnesota legislature. In equating the spread of urbanism with the spread of corruption, and in envisioning damnation and destruction as the ultimate penalty of city life, Donnelly revealed himself, in the judgment of Richard Hofstadter, as a sadist and a nihilist. *Caesar's Column* is "a childish book," so Hofstadter has written, "but in the middle of the twentieth century it seems anything but laughable: it affords a frightening glimpse into the ugly potential of frustrated popular revolt."[1] Donnelly's novel is thus for Hofstadter a key to the provincial spirit of Midwestern America, a spirit ruled by suspicions of the East, distrust of intellectuals, and hatred of Jews, and given to raging fantasies of Babylonian destruction. The violence depicted in *Caesar's Column* may never have been matched by the social data of American history, but Hofstadter would contend that the sado-nihilism of the American hick is very much a part of the emotional actuality of our civilization, and that Donnelly's novel is expressive of a profoundly dangerous phenomenon.

Yet Donnelly's ambivalent view of the city—a place on the one hand of glittering amusement and technological marvels and on the other hand of social exploitation and spiritual degradation—is a view he shares with a vast number of American writers from all centuries of our history, all sections of the country, and all ranges of literary excellence from the least memorable to the most distinguished, the most intellectual, and the most cosmopolitan. The urban imagery summoned up by Hawthorne and Melville in the 1850s is characterized by starkly symbolic contrasts of blazing light and sinister darkness, as is the imagery of *New York By Gaslight* and other trashy books of the period. E.P. Roe's bestselling novel, *Barriers Burned Away* (1872), which depicts the great Chicago fire as a judgment upon a wicked city, is part of an incendiary tradition which not only includes Donnelly's mediocre novel, but Part IV of T.S. Eliot's *The Waste Land* (1922). Clearly, what Donnelly was expressing in his novel was a frustration which fed into a familiar American concern, at heart, a religious concern, with the question of whether honor, charity, and other traditional values of Western civilization were capable of surviving in the modern city. That Donnelly gave a gloomy answer does not necessarily prove that his political frustration contained an "ugly potential" of violence. It is, indeed, more likely that the ending of his novel was a religious strategy that went back through Hawthorne and Melville to the Puritans. By issuing a jeremiad which warned of the terrible consequences of abandoning the Christian life, he hoped to bring an urban America back to the faith of its fathers.

Jack London's *The Iron Heel* (1905) also ends cataclysmically. Although the plot of the socialists to overthrow capitalism in America has been led by the dynamic Ernest Everhard (whose medium size, bulging muscles, and omnivorous reading habits recall Jack London himself), the awesome power of the ruling oligarchy—the so-called Iron Heel—is too much for the outnumbered revolutionaries. At the climax of the book, the slum classes—for whom Everhard and his fellow socialists feel nothing but contempt—go pillaging through the city. However, this act is the self-indulgent gesture of a degenerate, racially mongrelized mob which does nothing to benefit the military position of the gallant elitists of socialism. According to the novel's twenty-seventh-century editor, 300 years of bloodletting were to pass before the Iron Heel is finally overthrown and the Brotherhood of Man established.

The question at once arises as to why London, after building up his hero as a superman, should have permitted him to be defeated, especially since he was an exponent of the same revolutionary cause as Everhard was. The answer has seemed unavoidable to some readers that London was interested in violence for violence's sake, even if it meant denying himself the pleasure of a socialistically happy ending. However, the confusion which London displayed in his ideological writings suggests another explanation for the ending of *The Iron Heel*. For these ideological writings reveal that London was as committed to a belief in the competitive ethic of American success as he was to socialism, and that he was hagridden by the conviction that the victory of socialist principles would lead to social rot, because it would terminate competition between individuals; consequently he found it imaginatively impossible to write a novel depicting the triumph of the socialist revolution. To portray Everhard and company in charge of a socialist America would have meant that London would have been forced to show his autobiographical hero presiding over a society characterized by declining production, degenerating racial stocks, and decaying institutions.

It is not surprising, therefore, that even though *The Iron Heel* is supposedly edited by a man living under the reign of the Brotherhood of Man in the twenty-seventh century, no description is given of how this socialist Utopia is organized or operated, no hint is offered as to the steps that have been taken to avoid social decay. Unable to portray a paradise that he knew in his heart was really a hell, London found it an easier imaginative task to concentrate on describing the defeat of the socialist revolution. To lament the defeat of socialism was infinitely easier than to pretend to rejoice in its triumph.

A third possible explanation for the ferocious violence of *The Iron Heel's* conclusion is that it reflected London's awareness of all the disappointments that American radicals had suffered in the course of his lifetime. The Greenback movement had gone nowhere, except to oblivion; the Supreme Court had reversed the Granger cases; the Populists had never become anything more than a regional movement; in the climactic election of 1896, Bryan had been badly beaten; and Eugene Debs had polled a disappointing number of votes in the presidential elections of 1900 and 1904. London's socialist hopes were simply overwhelmed by his inability to forget the bitter lessons of recent American history: in the new era of Standard Oil trust and other big-business combinations, American radicals could scarcely by optimistic.

All three explanations of London's novel are equally compelling. Unquestionably, London was neurotically fascinated by tests of mental and physical endurance; long before his suicide, his mind was thronged with images of violent death. To literary critics interested in establishing the sickness of the American psyche, London's personal life simply reinforces their thesis that his novels and stories are obsessed by violence. Because it damages their thesis, these critics ignore the fact that violent endings offered London a means of resolving his contradictory ideological commitments to success and socialism—and that therefore the conclusion of *The Iron Heel* ought to be understood as a literary strategy which enabled a philosophically troubled writer to resolve his ambivalence and complete his books. Equally damaging to the interpretation of *The Iron Heel* as symptomatic of an author's (and a nation's) psychological illness is the fact that a socialist novelist who foresaw the continuing hegemony of capitalist combinations in America was simply being realistic. Can we really be sure that the ending London gave his novel represented anything else than his unwillingness to fool either himself or his readers about the changes of building a socialist Utopia in twentieth-century America? The apocalyptic fury with which *The Iron Heel* concludes may well have been the sign of London's sanity as a social prophet, rather than of his psychological imbalance.

Writing about the experience of modern war begins in American literature with Stephen Crane in 1895. Our first modern conflict had ended 30 years before, but for a generation after the Civil War American writers had either ignored or romanticized that terrible struggle. The one exception was John W. DeForest's novel, *Miss Ravenel's Conversion from Secession to Loyalty* (1867), which had portrayed the fighting in grim and realistic detail. However, *Miss Ravenel* had been a failure, commercially speaking, and in the wake of its failure there arose a genre of writing called the intersectional romance, which typically told of a wounded Union Army officer being nursed back to health by a predictably beautiful Southern belle, whom he finally led to the altar. Even the literary reminiscences of soldiers who had served in the war told a good deal less than the whole truth. Thus the *Century* magazine's notable series of military recollections, "Battles and Leaders of the Civil War," represented only an officer's eye view of what had in fact been a democratic war won by a mass army. The same fault afflicted Ambrose Bierce's otherwise superbly honest *Tales of Soldiers* (1891). Before Crane published *The Red Badge of Courage* (1895), only a very minor writer named Wilbur F. Hinman had recorded, in a comic novel entitled *Corporal Si Klegg and His "Pard"* (1887), how the violence made possible by modern military technology had affected the men in the ranks.

That Crane should have been impelled to measure the impact of the war on ordinary Americans was certainly not the result of his own experience of violence, for he was not even born until 1871, six years after the close of the war, and in the course of his middle-class New Jersey boyhood had never heard a shot fired in anger. What fascinated him about the Civil War was what also fascinated him about the submarginal world of the Bowery, which he had come to know during his salad days as a reporter on the New York *Herald*. Like the seamiest of New York's slums, the most tragic war in our history represented American life *in extremis*, and such representations suited Crane's subversive frame of mind.

Political and social events of the early 1890s had revealed to Crane an enormous disparity between the official version of American life as conveyed by such popular authors of the day as James Whitcomb Riley and Thomas Bailey Aldrich, and the often brutal realities that were attendant upon the nation's transformation into an urban and industrial civilization. The effect of this revelation on a young man who had already been engaged throughout his youth in a Tom Sawyerish rebellion against his middle-class upbringing was to turn him against all the optimistic beliefs in the pursuit of happiness, the inevitability of progress, etc., which most Americans cherished. Revolted by blandness and complacency, Crane went in search of misery and violence—in the lower depths of Manhattan; in sleazy bars down Mexico way, where he was nearly murdered one scary night; on the battlefields of Greece, where he served as a correspondent covering the Greco-Turkish War; and again as a war reporter in Cuba, where he differentiated himself from Richard Harding Davis and other correspondents by the risks he took, by the deliberate way he exposed himself to the fire of Spanish rifles.

In the world of his imagination, Crane craved the same experiences, and he often wrote of them before he had lived them. *Maggie. A Girl of the Streets* (1893), the story of an East Side girl whose descent into prostitution concludes with her descent into the East River, was largely worked out before Crane quit college and went to live in New York, just as *The Red Badge of Courage* was published before he saw Greece or Cuba. For his books were not *reportage*; they were works of art which endeavored to make the American novel relevant to a new generation of socially skeptical readers, as the works of Zola, Crane's literary idol, had done for the French novel. The restlessness, the guilt, and the itch to change things that impelled middle-class, urban Americans into the Progressive movement of 1901-1917 were first manifested in the fiction of Stephen Crane in the mid-1890s. Paradoxically, a body of work dominated by a black humor and an ironic style, and by scenes of violence often culminating in horridly detailed descriptions of dead bodies, had a life-giving effect, a revitalizing effect on American art and politics. For his mordant skepticism about official American culture and all his efforts to flee—both spatially and spiritually—from the world he had been brought up in, Crane was really a middle-class spokesman. Unlike the Whig humorists of the 1830s or the Utopian novelists who were his contemporaries, Crane was not a loser in American life. He was, rather, an outsider, who had assumed his critical role by choice rather than necessity. Whereas Judge Longstreet and his fellow humorists had lamented a way of life, a scheme of values, that was irrevocably passing out of the national scene, and whereas Jack London and Ignatius Donnelly were lamenting an American civilization that would never come to be, Crane offered violent versions of a modern war we had already fought and would fight again, and of a city which has been the archetype of our collective life from his own time to the present. As with most outsiders in American life, including the runaway Tom Sawyer, rebellion was a halfway house for Stephen Crane and violence a means of ultimate accommodation.

The violence of Ernest Hemingway's early novels and stories are expressive, so we have been told, of a far more cruel, pointless, and degrading war experience than the Civil War that Stephen Crane conjured up out of talking with veterans and reading the *Century* magazine. Why this should be so is not entirely clear, inasmuch as the Civil War was infinitely more costly to our soldiers and to our people. Indeed, the violence of Hemingway's fiction has become so famous as to obscure the fact that none of his stories, and none of the stories of Dos Passos or E.E. Cummings or any other American writer who served overseas in the First World War, come anywhere near matching the butchery described in Erich Maria Remarque's *All Quiet on the Western Front*, Henri Barbusse's *Under Fire*, Guy Chapman's *A Passionate Prodigality*, and other European chronicles of the Great War. In only one way are the novels of the Americans more nightmarish than those of the European writers. Hemingway, Dos Passos, and company did not, and indeed could not, outrival the details of endless horror that four years in the trenches had etched in Guy Chapman's or Erich Remarque's memory. Yet Remarque and the other European writers also paid grateful tribute in their books to the psychological comforts of mass comradeship, whereas the heros of Hemingway and Dos Passos are loners who feel lost in the midst of the crowd. They may find one other kindred spirit, generally Italian, or possibly a girl friend, generally British, but they know nothing of the group feeling that Remarque and the European writers were grateful to. A desolate sense of alienation is the special mark of the best American fiction to come out of the First World War. In seeking to assess the meaning of the violence expressed by the "lost generation" writers, we must therefore reckon with the loneliness which accompanies it and which gives it its peculiarly devastating and memorable effect.

Perhaps the alienation may be explained by the very special role which our writers played in the war. For the striking fact is that unlike their literary equivalents in England, France, and Germany, the American writers were not soldiers but ambulance drivers or some other kind of auxiliary. Malcolm Cowley worked for military transport; Hemingway was with the Red Cross in Italy; Dos Passos and Cummings were with the Norton-Harjes ambulance unit, and so were Slater Brown, Harry Crosby, and other young men who would achieve some kind of literary distinction in the 1920s. They were in the war, but not of it; involved and yet not involved. They could not pay tribute to the comradeship of the trenches because they had never really experienced it, they had never really belonged.

But this is only a partial explanation of the loneliness recorded in their fiction. For it does not answer the question of why they became ambulance drivers in the first place. And here we come to the heart of the matter. For their enlistment as ambulance drivers was not so much a cause of their alienation as an expression of it. They were outside the mainstream of American life, already suspicious of what Hemingway would later call the "sacred words," before they ever landed in Europe. The war did not cause them to feel lonely, but rather confirmed and intensified a preexistent feeling of not fitting in. When these future ambulance drivers had been high school and college students in the period 1900-1917, they had been disgusted by the discrepancy between the consistently idealistic theory and often grubby practice of America in the Progressive era. Ironically, the young men whose imaginations had been kindled by the violence of Stephen Crane in the 1890s had become the adult establishment 20 years later, and thus in turn became the target of a new generation of rebels—who also chose to express their dissent from the going values of society by means of violence. That the younger literati of 1917 sought out the war did not mean that they were patriotically responding, as millions of other young men in America were, to the high-flown rhetoric of Woodrow Wilson. Dos Passos, a political radical, went to Europe in order to witness the death throes of capitalism. Hemingway, who already knew that the woods of northern Michigan contained truths undreamed of in the suburban philosophy of his native Oak Park, Illinois, made his way to the front line at Fossalta diPiave because he knew that that line offered a great opportunity to a young writer who was seeking—as Stephen Crane had before him—for materials with which to rebuke his middle-class American heritage. When fragments of an Austrian mortar shell hit him in the legs, and he was hit twice more in the body by machinegun fire, he found his materials with a vengeance. Thereafter a wound was to become the central symbol of nearly all his work and the consequences of a wound his recurrent theme. In many ways a highly personal testament, Hemingway's work also captures, in hauntingly symbolic terms, the permanently scarring effects of the First World War on American society. In so doing, the violent expression of an outsider has become the means by which generations of modern Americans have understood themselves. Originating as a criticism of peace-time America, Hemingway's violence turned into an explanation of what twentieth-century warfare has done to us as a people. Leslie Fiedler would have it that Hemingway's concern with violence signifies a pathological inability to deal with adult sexuality,[2] but this interpretation ignores the fact that violence has an intrinsic importance in our history, especially in this era of global wars—as Hemingway precociously understood from childhood onward.

The literature dealing with race relations is very different from all other expressions of violence in American writing. Even in Hemingway's most tragic stories, his protagonists make a separate peace which for a fleeting time is a genuine peace; the universe of pain inexorably closes down on them again, but the memories of happiness remain as a defense against despair and madness. However, with the notable exception of *The Adventures of Huckleberry Finn* (1884), in which Huck's memory of his life on the raft with Nigger Jim sustains him against all his sordid encounters with the slave-owning society on shore, the important American books on race are unredeemed by such recollections. The sanative qualities of Southwestern humor are also missing from this literature, as are the long-range hopes of social justice that arise out of the ashes of *The Iron Heel* and *Caesar's Column*. "Benito Cereno," Melville's brilliant short story of the early 1850s; Mark Twain's mordant novel, *Pudd'nhead Wilson* (1894); and Richard Wright's smashingly powerful *Native Son* (1940): these three representative works offer us no hope whatsoever for believing that the violence and the hatred, the fear and the guilt that separate black and white Americans from one another will ever end. As I have tried to indicate, the nihilism that has been imputed to works dealing with other aspects of American violence is highly debatable, as is the charge that the violence of American literature is sick, sick, sick, because it really stands for our alleged maladjustment to sex or some other cultural sickness. In the literature of racial violence, however, terms like "nihilism" and "sickness" seem very applicable, indeed.

What hope, for instance, does Melville offer us in telling the story of "Benito Cereno"? The kindness and compassion of Don Benito are not sufficient to keep his black servant from putting a razor to his master's throat, and while Don Benito does manage to escape from violent death, he is unable to shake the shadow of his racial guilt. Haunted by the hatred that the revolt of his slaves has revealed, but powerless to expiate a crime that is far older than himself, Don Benito dies, the very image of the impotent white liberal, on the slopes of the aptly named Mount Agonia.

The tragic hopelessness of Melville's story becomes in *Pudd'nhead Wilson* one of the later Mark Twain's bitterest jokes. With his superior intelligence, *Pudd'nhead Wilson* is able to solve a bewildering racial crime: his exposure of the fact that the "Negro woman" who has murdered one of the leading white men of the town is in reality a man, Tom Driscoll, whose entire life has been a masquerade in white face, is a masterpiece of detective work. Even more impressive is Wilson's discovery that the masquerade was made possible by Tom Driscoll's light-skinned Negro mother, who switched a white baby and her own baby into one another's cradle, a deception made possible by the fact that both babies had the same white father. Yet finally, *Pudd'nhead Wilson* is a helpless man. His superior intelligence is powerless to overcome the accumulated racial crimes of American history. To be sure, his trial testimony sends the black masquerader to jail and thence to the auction block, where he is sold to a slave trader from "down the river." But if Wilson's testimony succeeds in condemning a black man, it does not succeed in freeing a white man. For the real Tom Driscoll, who has been a slave for 20 years, is not restored to freedom by being given back his identity. Thanks to what society has done to him, he can neither read nor write, nor speak anything but the dialect of the slave quarter; his walk, his attitudes, his gestures, his bearing, his laugh—all are the manner of a slave.

Mark Twain's awareness of the interwoven strands of sex and violence in the racial tragedy of American life is amplified in *Native Son* into a terrifying story of sexual temptation, murder, and legal revenge. The crippling fears of the white man that dominate Bigger Thomas's mind have their white counterparts in the hysterically antiblack editorials in the Chicago newspapers and the demonic racism of the police. Nowhere in this implacable novel does the author give us any grounds for belief in the possibility of genuine communication and mutual trust between the races.

It is, of course, possible that "Benito Cereno" has no other reference than to the darkness into which Melville's mind descended after 1851, *Pudd'nhead Wilson* no other reference than to the celebrated misanthropy of the later Mark Twain, *Native Son* no other reference than to Richard Wright's own tortured soul. Yet it is significant that these extraordinarily gifted writers, two white, one black, agree so completely about the insolubility of American race hatred. Conceivably, their fictions reveal not only the tragic thoughts of three authors, but the tragic truth of American society as well.

NOTES

1. Richard Hofstadter, *The Age of Reform* (New York: Vintage, 1955), 70.
2. Cf., *Love and Death in the American Novel* (New York, 1960), 125, 175, 186, 304-309, 341, 350-352.

Part 3
Issues of Violent Conflict in
American History

Part 3 contains essays that focus on six issues that have dominated much of America's domestic collective violence: frontier vigilantism, industrial labor, race relations, Indian policy, antiwar agitation, and revolutionary terrorism. Three of the six center primarily on questions of the extension of civil rights to groups—i.e., union organization and collective bargaining for workers, political and economic rights for blacks, and the balance between normal and special rights for native Americans. The other three concern broad areas of public policy that have led to violence—i.e., the maintenance of public order on the frontier, opposition to unpopular wars, and terrorism by radical minorities. These involve broader questions of often competing rights and obligations, such as the right to security of life and property versus the right to criminal due process, the right of conscience to reject immoral war-making versus the equal obligation to take up arms in defense of the national interest, the right of revolution versus the right of citizens in a democratic state to be protected from terrorism. Although the potential for violence associated with all six of these issues remains unpleasantly salient today (urban vigilantism and police strikes are no strangers to our headlines), they cluster in three overlapping historical epochs. Frontier vigilantism surged primarily in the nineteenth century and labor violence erupted in the latter nineteenth and early twentieth centuries. Racial violence spanned a century from the 1860s to the 1960s, bridging two attempts at reconstructing race relations, while antiwar agitation joined the civil rights issue to endow the 1960s with its uniquely tumultous character. Finally, while relationships with Indians is probably the oldest source of intergroup violence in American history, and radical revolution was the seed of our national birth, protest by native Americans and noisy campaigns of revolutionary terrorism have come of age in the 1970s.

PUBLIC ORDER ON THE FRONTIER

In Chapter 4, Louis Hartz argued that all the European fragment cultures tended to generate a kind of violence-prone moral vigilantism from their collision with frontier conditions. Yet while all of the fragment cultures created by the great international migration encountered frontier conditions which reacted upon the transplanted culture, in none was the admixture of imported values, frontier environment, and time so uniquely structured to maximize the impact of the frontier as in the United States. The essential ingredients were relatively modern liberal-capitalist values and a sufficient expanse of accessible and desirable land which would allow the frontier encounter to be repeated and prolonged.

In Latin America, both the feudal values of Spain and Portugal and the difficult topography combined to blunt the frontier experience. Similarly, in Canada, the settlers of the St. Lawrence River Valley carried prerevolutionary French cultural luggage, and the inhospitable Laurentian Shield deflected pioneers southward into the United States; when railroads opened the Canadian prairie provinces to British settlement in the late nineteenth century, the frontiersmen came directly from the more traditional East and the process of settlement was not nearly as prolonged as was the American experience. Siberia was settled by Czarist peasants. In Australia, pioneers pushed through the gaps in the Great Dividing Range only to discover the vast arid expanse of the outback. But in the United States an interminable stream of relatively propertyless individuals, armed with bourgeois-liberal values and a powerful acquisitive instinct, marched 3,000 miles to the Pacific in an epic migration lasting two and a half centuries.

The unique American character forged in the process, as Frederick Jackson Turner and his disciples have explained, was characterized by an intense individualism and an almost fanatical equalitarianism. The "new man" was democratic, optimistic, mobile, nationalistic, and hospitable to change. But he was also criminally wasteful, and at the core of his individualism was a materialistic philosophy which enshrined property rights and held them to be largely immune from governmental or public control. Hence, his equalitarianism was flawed by an inconsistency which held that such barriers to his acquisition as red Indians and Mexicans were exempt from the democratic embrace, and horse thieves were exempt from due process. Although the American frontier has been officially closed for over two-thirds of a century, its impact on our national character has been deep and abiding.

The deeply rooted tradition of vigilantism that was nurtured for so long by the American frontier experience has never comported well with the official commitment of the revolutionary young republic to a quest for "ordered liberty" through due process of law. Furthermore, this American quest for ordered liberty has itself been an ambivalent one. Our dual commitment to liberty and equality—a commitment symbolized by the Declaration of Independence and the Constitution—has always embodied a fundamental conflict, for liberty and equality are often contradictory goals. Born in rebellion against traditionally constituted authority, the new republic's noble task of constructing "a government of law, not men" has always been complicated by the unalterable reality that men must fashion, interpret, and enforce their laws.

That the origins of the venerable American vigilante tradition can be traced to the Revolutionary era is both symbolic and instructive. An authority on the South Carolina Regulators of 1767-1796, Richard Brown observes in Chapter 6 that the new spirit of populist vigilance, which was muted in our earlier environment of colonial deference, was logically nurtured by the democratic ethos of the Revolution. But because vigilantism constitutes at best an extralegal enforcement of community mores, its proponents have perforce constructed a defensive rationale based upon the "higher law" doctrine of the rights of revolution, self-preservation, and sovereignty.

The American vigilante tradition has been linked in the popular mind with the frontier, and it is true that the frontier's characteristic lack of effective agencies of law enforcement clearly invited and to a degree legitimized vigilante justice. Implicit in this view is the assumption that vigilantism should subside with the disappearance of the frontier. But Brown points out that as a flexible human institution, vigilantism was easily adapted to respond to the demands of an urban and industrial America. Symptomatic of this transition to a modern "neovigilantism" was the greatest of all vigilante movements: the San Francisco Vigilance Committee of 1856. Neovigilantism may be distinguished from the older frontier model not only by its urban environment but also, revealingly, by its victims. Whereas the old vigilantism sought to chastise mainly horse thieves, counterfeiters, outlaws, and badmen, the victims of neovigilantism have characteristically been ethnic, racial, and religious minorities, union organizers, and political radicals. Modern vigilance groups have frequently been supported by prestigious community leaders, often with the tacit support of the police. The tenacity of this American tradition, together with its institutional flexibility, suggests that its resurgence in future times of trouble is a distinct and sobering possibility.

The unmatched ethnic diversity of American immigration and the protracted American encounter with the frontier forged a national character that mirrored that contradiction between the American creed and American practice that Gunnar Myrdal has labeled "the American Dilemma." That contemporary urban industrial America continues to reflect ethnic animosities and a vigilante impulse is testimony to the persistent virulence of our ethnic pluralism and our frontier legacy.

THE RIGHTS OF INDUSTRIAL LABOR

A cursory glance at the histories of Western Europe and the United States during the past two centuries suggests that working-class demands for resolution of economic and related political grievances have been the most common and persistent source of turmoil, if not of revolution or civil war. In the United States workers seldom made political demands as they so often have in Europe, but the chronicles of conflict between them and their employers have been extraordinarily bloody, seemingly more so than those of any industrial nation in the world. Although many historical instances of labor violence in America have been examined in detail, the study by Professors Philip Taft and Philip Ross, below, is the first to examine systematically the cumulative records of American strike violence. The core of their study is an interpretative chronicle of violent strikes from the 1870s to the present. Labor violence was unquestionably pervasive and intense, occurring in every region of the United States, in almost every type of industry, and with great frequency in almost every decade from the 1870s to the 1930s. At one of its peaks, between 1902 and 1904, the loss of life reportedly exceeded that of the ghetto riots and rebellions of 1964-1968 in both absolute and relative terms. The most common immediate causes of violent labor conflict were employers' denial of the right of labor to organize and their attempts to break strikes. Employers and unions were both guilty of violence. In the majority of cases, however, including the most bloody ones, overt violence was initiated by the armed guards hired by employers or by local law enforcement officers and deputized citizens acting in consort with employers. Such action was not always taken without legal justification. Community and legal norms in the nineteenth and early twentieth centuries generally approved the use of force to guarantee employers an absolute right to exercise authority over their means of production—a right with which workers nonviolently interfered by establishing picket lines against nonunion workers and suppliers. The use of violence to enforce this right inspired retaliatory violence by the workers again and again.

The outcome of labor violence in the United States very seldom favored the workers or the unions. Hundreds of workers were killed, thousands injured, tens of thousands jailed or forcibly expelled from their communities. The unions most involved in violent disputes usually lost their organizational effectiveness, and their leaders and organizers were constantly harassed. Despite this dismal record, violence in American labor disputes persisted for several generations. Yet in the contemporary United States, expressions of workers' grievances have been muted. Strikes are no longer likely to be bloody affrays but tests of economic strength played out by labor and management following mutually accepted rules. The circumstances of the passing of violence seem even more dimly perceived than its origins. But it is evident that some patterns of events, some balance among increased economic well-being, coercion, accommodation, and regulation, have led to the abatement of violent economic-based conflict. We know, for example, that employers and government often responded forcefully to worker protest, and that their responses sometimes minimized protest, sometimes exacerbated it. Concessions by either employers or government were slow to come and, when they were made, were seldom in direct response to violence. The more specific questions concern the circumstances in which specific kinds of coercion were effective, the extent to which various kinds of protest were successful for those who made them, either in the short or the long run, and the merits of different kinds of accommodation for minimizing grievances and disruptive protest.

No final answers can be given to these questions, but persuasive evidence about some of them are provided in Chapter 7. The means by which working-class protest and violent labor-management conflict were defused may hold some general and specific lessons for the expression and resolution of contemporary discontents.

This is also the place to caution against optimistic assumptions that all labor-management conflicts in the future will be settled peaceably. We are now in a cycle of conflict between organized public employees and public authorities, who do not always accept workers' right to strike. The use of bargaining measures, such as strikes and "job action" slowdowns and sick-ins by police, firemen, sanitation and postal workers, teachers, and air traffic controllers may invite retaliation, violent confrontations, and ultimately undercut public authority. Moreover, there is no warrant for assuming permanent harmony in labor-management relations in all of private industry. Sporadic violence accompanied the widespread coal strike of winter 1977-1978, a strike which was prolonged and bitter in large part because miners felt that union leadership had sold out to management. This is a common suspicion of workers in industries where management and labor negotiators have worked out collegial bargaining relationships and may lead to internecine strife within unions. More serious is the prospect that a major depression, or persistence of "stagflation," will intensify workers' grievances to the point that they overwhelm existing arrangements for resolving labor-management conflict. The historical record in Europe and America seems to speak against this possibility because it shows that labor conflict usually has increased during prosperity and declined during hard times. Nevertheless, the possibility must be considered that what has worked to minimize labor-management conflict during 40 years of relative progress and prosperity in America may not work in times of economic crisis.

RACE RELATIONS

Racial violence in America has clustered around both ends of the post-Civil War century. The first Reconstruction was largely a failure, as Southern white intransigence and terrorism defeated the short-lived crusading of war-weary Northern whites and out-gunned Southern blacks. In Chapter 8, political scientists G. David Garson and Gail O'Brien consider four alternative explanations of Reconstruction violence—the biological, cultural, sociological, and political—and conclude that the flow and ebb of racial violence was primarily determined by political conditions. Racial peace was clearly purchased at the price of racial equality, and the grisly moral was reinforced that violent means work when public opinion strongly supports or at least acquiesces in its ends.

The failure of the first Reconstruction set the stage for a century of racial violence that witnessed a fundamental transformation: blacks basically began as victims and ended as aggressors. In Chapter 9 sociologist Morris Janowitz traces this evolution of race riots through three stages. First, a half-century ago, the typical race riot in American cities was an interracial clash on the boundaries of expanding black neighborhoods, one in which whites more often than blacks took offensive action. Second, during the Second World War, these communal clashes began to give way to large-scale riots, wholly within the black community. Often triggered by a police incident, the outbursts resulted in a clash between the local population and officers and agents of the larger society, with implied overtones of political protest. Because the outbursts resulted in widespread looting, they can be described as commodity riots. Third, by the late 1960s, this form of racial violence began to decline, being replaced by a new form: a more selective, terroristic use of force against whites by small, organized groups of blacks with crude ideological motives.

Each stage in the transformation or racial violence in the United States—from communal, to commodity, to political—has carried with it elements of the next stage. Each stage is an expression of the social structure of the United States and the position of blacks in this social structure. Janowitz is concerned with why, when, and through what processes such violence ebbs as well as flows. He argues that the agencies of social change and social control are crucial in accounting for the occurrence and form of urban racial outbreaks. The impact of two such agencies is examined: the patterns of intervention and the consequences of law enforcement crucially condition the sequence and extent of the riot; while the mass media have both an immediate impact on the contagion of riot behavior and a long-term effect on the social structure.

OPPOSITION TO WAR

Psychoanalysts no sooner popularized the concept of displacement than some scholars made an analytic leap of faith to propose that wars represented a displacement of aggressions within the community onto foreign enemies. Conflict theorists, relying more on reason than faith, suggested that in the face of external conflict, members of a community were likely to join ranks and minimize their differences. Some factually oriented sociologists and political scientists pointed out that unsuccessful wars had frequently led to revolutionary movements: for example, in Russia in 1917, in Bavaria the next year, and in Italy several years after that. Opponents of the war in Vietnam suggested that the increase in domestic turmoil in the late 1960s was the work of those who took their cues from the international actions of the government.

Some cautions, but no definitive answers, for grand theorizing about connections between external and internal conflicts are suggested by the examination of the historical and contemporary experience of the United States in Chapter 10. Robin Brooks points out that some of the wars the United States has fought have been accompanied by direct internal protest, others not. When specifically antiwar protest has occurred, its immediate sources have been the belief that a particular war was unjust, and resentment against its contingent requirements of conscription and material support. Opposition on both grounds was especially widespread during the Civil War, in both the North and the South; during the Second World War, and during the Vietnam War. In the latter two wars the protesters seldom resorted to violence on their own initiative. They were however frequent targets of retaliatory violence by groups of outraged citizens and by the police and military. Despite the historical continuity of American antiwar protest, and especially in light of the patterns of severe governmental response. Brooks concludes that anti-Vietnam protest was of such an unprecedented magnitude and reflected such a broad constituency that historical guidelines have little to tell us.

AMERICAN INDIANS

The dramatic surge of Red Power militancy by radical American Indians, which in 1972 led to the occupation of the Bureau of Indian Affairs building in Washington by members of the American Indian Movement, and culminated the following year in the violent occupation and seige of Wounded Knee, South Dakota, raised both new and ancient questions concerning the United States' historically most violence-plagued minority. Long devastated by the invading white man's warfare, disease, and vices, America's Indians, as unique wards of the state, have also suffered from periodic pendulum swings in federal policy, which alternated radically between emphasizing the Indians' special rights and protections (in the collective diplomatic metaphor of treaties with Indian nations), and opposite policies that were grounded in assumptions of assimilation and acculturation (in the individual metaphor of the Americanization of immigrants). Despite the noble rhetoric of the Northwest Ordinance of 1787, which pledged that Indian lands and property should never be taken from them without their consent, and Chief Justice John Marshall's pledge of beneficent wardship in *Worcester v. Georgia* (1832), which recognized their undisputed possession of the land "from time immemorial" and their retention of the natural right of self-government even in wardship status, the relentless expansionism of the new nation produced an Indian policy marked by the Indian Removal Act of 1830, the "Trail of Tears," military subjugation, and confinement to Western reservations. Then the Dawes or Allotment Act of 1887, which was premised on assumptions of the undesirability of collective tribal life and the desirability of assimilationist, homesteader norms, led to a half-century of depredation and decline. Indian tribes lost 86 million of their 138 million reservation acres and the Indian population was reduced to perhaps half of its approximate peak of 922,000 (including 73,000 in Alaska but excluding 220,000 in Canada) in aboriginal North America.

The revival of social conscience during the New Deal, however, produced another turnaround in the form of the reformist Indian Reorganization Act of 1934, which scuttled the disastrous severalty of the Dawes allotment program in favor of increased tribal self-government and the revival of ancient customs and religious practices. Then with the more conservative 1950s came another switch, with Eisenhower Republicanism emphasizing termination of dole-like federal services. Yet again, during the 1960s, Presidents Kennedy, Johnson, and Nixon attempted to grasp the nettle. And whatever the fickle federal policy, social and economic forces were luring approximately half of the resurgent Indian population off the reservations to the cities, where aggressive Indian consciousness and radicalism contrasted sharply with the conservativism of the reservations' tribal elders, with their client relationship to the federal bureaucracy. In Chapter 11, sociologist Jeanne Guillemin offers a thoughtful and balanced analysis of the complexities, dilemmas, and paradoxes of the "Indian Problem," with special attention to the surge of Indian militancy on the heels of the liberationist 1960s, and the sociology and politics of the government's response to growing and often conflicting demands in a context of protest and violence.

TERRORISM AND REVOLUTION

The most exotic form of violence to afflict America during the late 1960s and early 1970s was the use of terrorist bombings, murders, and a handful of dramatic kidnappings on behalf of revolution and national liberation. Bombings and assassinations have been common enough in the country's historical experience, but never before had they been so concentrated nor accompanied by such outpourings of radical rhetoric against militarism, capitalism, racism, and oppression. The international sources of inspiration for revolutionary terrorism are analyzed by political scientists J. Bowyer Bell and Ted Robert Gurr in Chapter 12. They argue that militant ideologies of national liberation are almost wholly irrelevant for Americans, excepting Puerto Ricans and, possibly, Hispanos in the Southwest. The ideology and practice of revolutionary terrorism by other groups has proven politically ineffectual, even counterproductive. For most of the people involved, whether in the Weather Underground, the Symbionese Liberation Army, or the George Jackson Brigade, terrorism has been a way of acting out personal and political anguish, a kind of public therapy which has fascinated rational media audiences but has attracted neither sympathy nor support for revolutionary causes.

Chapter 6
The American Vigilante Tradition

RICHARD MAXWELL BROWN

The vigilante tradition, in the classic sense, refers to organized, extralegal movements, the members of which take the law into their own hands. The first vigilante movement in American history was in 1767. From then until about 1900, vigilante activity was an almost constant factor in American life. Far from being a phenomenon only of the Western frontier, there was much vigilantism in the eastern half of the United States. Although the first vigilante movement occurred in Piedmont, South Carolina, in 1767-1769, most of the Atlantic Seaboard States were without significant vigilante activity. But beyond the Appalachians there were few states that did not have vigilante movements. There may have been as many as 500 movements, but, at the present, only 326 are known.[1]

American vigilantism is indigenous. There were "regulators" in early-eighteenth-century London, who formed a short-lived official supplement to London's regular system of law enforcement,[2] but there was no connection between London's legal regulators and the South Carolina's Back Country Regulators of 1767, who constituted America's first vigilante movement. From tie to time in Europe there appeared movements or institutions (such as the *Vehmgericht* of Germany and *Halifax law* of the British Isles)[3] which resembled American vigilantism, but these phenomena did not give rise to a vigilante tradition either on the Continent or in the British Isles. European expansion in other areas of the world has, similarly, failed to produce anything quite like the American vigilante tradition. Perhaps the closest

AUTHOR'S NOTE: *Richard Maxwell Brown is Beekman Professor of Northwest and Pacific history at the University of Oregon. Formerly he taught at Rutgers University and the College of William and Mary. He is author of* The South Carolina Regulators *(Harvard University Press, 1963) and* Strain of Violence: Historical Studies of American Violence and Vigilantism *(Oxford University Press, 1975). He has edited several other volumes, the most recent of which is* Tradition, Conflict, and Modernization: Perspectives on the American Revolution, *coedited with D.E. Fehrenbacher (Academic Press, 1977). He is continuing his research on American vigilantism and is also at work on a book on the Mussel Slough conflict, upon which Frank Norris based his novel,* The Octopus.

This chapter is from Strain of Violence: Historical Studies of American Violence and Vigilantism, *by Richard Maxwell Brown. Copyright © 1975 by Oxford University Press, Inc. Reprinted by permission.*

thing to it was the *commando* system (against marauding *kaffirs*) of the Boer settlers
in South Africa; the *commandos*, however, were more like the Indian-fighting
rangers of the American frontier than the vigilantes.[4]

Vigilantism arose as a response to a typical American problem: the absence of
effective law and order in a frontier region. It was a problem that occurred again and
again beyond the Appalachians, and it stimulated the formation of hundreds of
frontier vigilante movements.[5] On the frontier, the normal foundations of a stable,
orderly society—churches, schools, cohesive community life—were either absent or
present only in rough, makeshift forms. The regular, legal system of law enforcement
often proved to be woefully inadequate for the needs of the settlers.

Fundamentally, the pioneers took the law into their own hands for the purpose of
establishing order and stability in newly settled areas. In the other settled areas, the
prime values of person and property were dominant and secure, but the move to the
frontier meant that it was necessary to start all over again. Upright and ambitious
frontiersmen wished to reestablish the values of a property holder's society. The
hurtful presence of outlaws and marginal types, in an area of weak and ineffectual law
enforcement, created the specter and, often, the fact of social chaos. The solution
was vigilantism. A vigilante roundup of ne'er-do-wells and outlaws followed by their
flogging, expulsion, or killing not only solved the problem of disorder but had an
important symbolic value as well. Vigilante action was a clear warning to disorderly
inhabitants that the newness of the settlement would provide no opportunity for the
erosion of the established values of civilization. Vigilantism was a violent sanctification of the deeply cherished values of life and property.

Because the main thrust of vigilantism was to reestablish, in each newly settled
area, the civilized values of life, property, and law and order, vigilante movements
were usually led by the frontier elite. This was true of the greatest American vigilante
band—the San Francisco vigilance committee of 1856—which was directed by the
leading businessmen of the city. Again and again, it was the most eminent local
community leaders who headed vigilante movements.

"Vigilance Committee," or "Committee of Vigilance," was the common name of
the organization, but, originally—and far into the nineteenth century—vigilantes
were known by the now obsolete term of regulators. Variant names for vigilante
groups were "slickers," "stranglers," "committees of safety," and, in central Texas,
simply, "mobs." (In this study, "vigilante" will be used as a generic term to cover all
phases of the general phenomenon of vigilantism.) The duration of vigilante
movements varied greatly, but movements that lasted as long as a year were long-
lived. More commonly, they finished their business in a period of months or weeks.
Vigilante movements (as distinguished from ephemeral lynch mobs) are thus
identifiable by the two main characteristics of (1) regular (although illegal)
organization and (2) existence for a definite (often short) period of time.

I

The first American vigilante movement—the South Carolina Regulators, 1767-
1769—did not occur until 160 years after the first permanent English settlement at
Jamestown. The reason for the late appearance of the phenomenon was the slow pace

of frontier expansion. It was well into the eighteenth century before the settlement of the Piedmont began on a large scale, and, at the time of the Revolution, the settlement of the Piedmont was just coming to a close. Thus, frontier expansion proceeded at a snail's pace in the colonial period, and it was possible to provide adequate systems of law enforcement for the slowly proliferating pioneer communities. The one exception to this pattern of orderly frontier expansion occurred in the South Carolina Piedmont in the 1760s.

Newly settled and recently devastated by the Cherokee Indian War, the South Carolina Back Country of the 1760s was typical of later American frontier areas. As sketched in the previous chapter, this war so disrupted social organization that, by the mid-1760s, the whole of the Back Country was being terrorized by gangs of outlaws. A two-year campaign by the regulators restored law and order, albeit violently. Regulator violence had become so brutal, however, that a countermovement of "Moderators" was organized. The latter, along with the provincial government's provision for district courts and sheriffs, caused the regulators to disband voluntarily in 1769.[6]

An American tradition had begun, for, as the pioneers moved across the Appalachians, the regulator-vigilante impulse followed the sweep of settlement toward the Pacific. The model for dealing with frontier disorder established by the South Carolina Regulators was utilized over and over again by American settlers.

Geographically, American vigilantism divides into Eastern and Western halves, and they are similarly distinct, chronologically. Eastern vigilantism mainly came to an end in the 1860s, whereas Western vigilantism began in the 1850s. Eastern vigilantism fell between the Appalachian Mountains[7] and the ninety-sixth meridian, whereas Western vigilantism stretched from the ninety-sixth meridian to the Pacific.[8] The humid Mississippi Valley, Great Lakes, and Gulf Coast regions furnished the main scenes of Eastern vigilantism; Western vigilantism took in the arid and semiarid Great Plains and the Rocky Mountains and the Pacific coast. Eastern vigilantism was a response, chiefly, to frontier horse thieves, counterfeiters, and ne'er-do-well whites. West of the ninety-sixth meridian the vigilantes were concerned largely with disorder in mining camps, cattle towns, and open ranges.

In early-nineteenth-century America, horse thieves and counterfeiters seemed to go together, and when they did, a vigilante movement was not far behind. The vulnerability of the settler to horse theft needs no comment, but counterfeiting as a frontier evil is a bit less familiar. The money problem made itself felt at the national level in the age of Jackson in a number of famous issues, such as the Bank War, but it was no less a problem in the backwoods and border country. Not only did the frontier suffer from a money shortage, which counterfeiters as well as wildcat bankers tried to fill, but the frontier felt the lack of money especially in regard to the purchase of federal public land. Added to the lively demand for cash at the land office was the chaotic condition of the paper money system. The lack of an effective system of federal paper money and the plethora of private bank notes meant that never before or since in our history was counterfeiting easier.[9]

Horse thieves commonly organized into gangs, stealing horses in one area and disposing of them hundreds of miles away—preferably across state lines.[10] For obvious reasons, counterfeiting operations were best carried on in the same way, and it was simple to combine the two. The link between counterfeiting and horse theft affected the geographical distribution of regulator and vigilante movements. The latter tended to be found in wilderness areas, close to state lines, or near Indian borders—all were places favored by horse thieves and counterfeiters.

From the 1790s, and well into the nineteenth century, vigilante activity was generally local in Kentucky, Tennessee, Indiana, and Illinois.[11] Thereafter, there were four major peaks or waves of vigilantism. They occurred in the early 1830s, the early 1840s, the late 1850s, and the late 1860s. The first wave, from 1830 to 1835, took place mainly in the lower Southern states of Alabama and Mississippi, where Captain Slick's bands operated against horse thieves and counterfeiters[12] and vigilantes attacked gamblers and the alleged Murrell conspiracy.[13] The second wave, in the early 1840s, included the Bellevue vigilante war in Iowa,[14] the east Texas Regulator-Moderator conflict,[15] the northern and southern Illinois Regulators,[16] and the Slicker War of the Missouri Ozarks.[17] The vigilante wave of the early 1840s may have been a response to a shift in outlaw elements (caused by the 1830-1835 vigilante campaign) from the Lower Mississippi River region of Alabama, Mississippi, Arkansas, and Louisiana to the Upper Mississippi area (northern Illinois, eastern Iowa, and the Missouri Ozarks) and to the trans-Mississippi Southwest (east Texas).

The third peak of vigilantism, from 1857 to 1859, included the Iron Hills and other vigilante movements of Iowa,[18] the northern Indiana Regulators,[19] the San Antonio[20] and New Orleans[21] vigilantes, and the *Comités de Vigilance* of southwest Louisiana.[22] The movements of the late 1850s may have been inspired by the San Francisco Vigilance Committee of 1856,[23] which was well publicized throughout the nation. The fourth and final wave of vigilantism occurred in the immediate post-Civil War period (1866-1871) with major movements erupting in Missouri,[24] Kentucky,[25] Indiana,[26] and Florida[27] in a reaction to postwar lawlessness.

The nature of the natural resources of the West determined the types of frontier disorder that gave rise to vigilantism. Repeated strikes of precious and valuable metals in the Sierras and Rockies set off mining rushes that brought miners and others into raw new camps and towns by the thousands. In such places the law was often absent or ineffectual, with vigilantism the result. The other great natural resource of the West was the grassy rangeland of the Great Plains, the mountain plateaus, and the river valleys. The open-range system afforded an irresistible attraction to cattle and horse thieves, who, in turn, invited vigilante retaliation.

Beginning with the first significant vigilantism in the gold-rush metropolis of San Francisco in 1849, and continuing for 53 years down to 1902, there were at least 210 vigilante movements in the West. No vigilante movements in American history were better organized or more powerful than the San Francisco vigilance committees of 1851 and 1856. The San Francisco movements had an immense impact on American vigilantism in general, and on California vigilantism in particular. During the 1850s the San Francisco committees were copied all over the state in the new mining towns (Sacramento, Jackson, etc.) and in the old Spanish cities (Los Angeles, Monterey, etc.). Of California's 43 vigilante movements, 27 movements occurred in the 1850s.[28]

Montana was a most significant vigilante state. It had two of the most important movements in the history of vigilantism: the influential Bannack and Virginia City movement of 1863-1865 (which popularized the term "vigilante" in American English)[29] and the 1884 movement in northern and eastern Montana, which Granville Stuart led against horse and cattle thieves in a human roundup that claimed 35 victims and was the deadliest of all American vigilante movements.[30] In addition, Montana, from the 1860s to the 1880s, was in the grips of a territorywide vigilante movement with headquarters, apparently, in the territorial capital, Helena.[31]

Texas had 52 vigilante movements—more than any other state. There were two important ante-bellum movements (Shelby County in east Texas, 1840-1844; San Antonio, 1857 and later), but the majority (at least 27 movements) occurred in violence-torn central Texas in the post-Civil War period from 1865 to 1890.[32] There were dozens and dozens of vigilante movements in most of the other Western states; only Oregon and Utah did not have significant vigilante activity. The 16 movements in Colorado were headed by the Denver vigilantes of 1859-1861.[33] New Mexico had three strong vigilante movements in Albuquerque (1871-1882),[34] Las Vegas (1880-1882),[35] and Socorro (1880-1884).[36] The Butler County vigilantes, who enlisted almost 800 members and claimed eight victims, formed the most notable of Kansas's 19 movements.[37] To the north, Nebraska had 16 vigilante movements that were topped by the Sidney vigilantes (1875-1881) and the Niobrara region vigilantes (1883-1884), who accounted for two and six fatalities, respectively.[38] Wyoming vigilantism, swift, brutal, and deadly, began with two movements in the wild railroad boomtowns of Cheyenne and Laramie (1868-1869) and came to a climax with vigilantism's most famous failure, the cattlemen's regulator movements, which precipitated the Johnson County War of 1892.[39]

If the Eastern and Western vigilante movements are compared, it can be seen that there were about twice as many vigilante movements in the West (210) as in the East (116). (Here the figures probably understate the ubiquity of Eastern vigilantism. Regulator activity was general in the early years of settlement in Kentucky, Tennessee, Indiana, and Illinois, but records of only a few of those movements have survived.) The ratio of large, medium, and small movements in the West was about 1:2:2; in the East it was approximately 1:1:1. Of the 729 known victims killed by vigilantes, about five-sevenths were dispatched by Western vigilantes.

There were 81 large movements; they extended, chronologically, from 1767 to 1897. Fifty-nine of the 81 large movements were clustered in the period from 1850 to 1889; 49 movements occurred in the mid-century decades from 1850 to 1879 when the nation was wracked by Civil War violence in the East and the tensions of rapid frontier settlement in the West. About three-fifths (190) of all vigilante movements took place after 1860, and 180 of them were concentrated in the three decades from 1861 to 1890. By the same token, about five-sevenths (511) of all the killed victims of vigilantism perished after 1860.[40]

Behind the statistics lies the impact of vigilantism on the American consciousness. The original South Carolina Regulator movement of 1767-1769, with its success in restoring order in the Back Country, recommended itself to the pioneers who crossed the Appalachians and populated the Mississippi Valley. Hence the regulator method was applauded as a tool for establishing frontier social stability until, in the 1840s, three anarchic movements in southern Illinois, the Missouri Ozarks, and east Texas gave regulators an increasingly bad name. Soon thereafter, in 1851 and 1856, the restrained San Francisco vigilance committees restored to vigilantism an enormous prestige, which it retained through the remainder of the century. Countless vigilante movements from coast to coast modeled themselves upon the San Francisco vigilance committees. One of these was the vigilante movement of the gold camps of Bannack and Virginia City, Montana (1863-1865), which in turn had something of the same effect on American attitudes as the earlier South Carolina and San Francisco movements. Thomas Dimsdale's classic book, *The Vigilantes of Montana* (1866), not only spread the fame of the Montana movement but was a veritable textbook of the vigilante method.

Significant vigilante activity did not always involve a formally organized movement with officers, trials, etc. By the latter half of the nineteenth century the ritual-like action of organizing a vigilante movement had been carried out so many times on so many frontiers that to many settlers it often seemed an unnecessary delay to swift lynch-law justice. A local consensus in favor of immediate vigilante action without any of the traditional formalities produced *instant vigilantism*, which was more prevalent in the West than the East. Many of the "one-shot" vigilante actions in Western states were the result of instant vigilantism, which existed side by side with more formally organized vigilantism. Instant vigilantism meant that the public mind had long since been made receptive to vigilante action when general conditions of a particular crime seemed to warrant it. The ritual process of organization had been gone through so many times, the rationale of vigilantism was so well understood, and the course of action so obvious on the basis of past precedents that the settlers readily proceeded to the lynching.

Instant vigilantism seems to have occurred in all the Western states but Oregon and Utah, and it was particularly effective in California. In the Golden State, regular vigilante action took 101 lives, but the toll of instant vigilantism from 1851 to 1878 was almost as high, amounting to 79 lives.[41] On a lesser scale, instant vigilantism occurred in other Western states, where time and again, precipitate lynchings were justified by vigilante tradition.

II

Settlers ordinarily desire new opportunities but not social innovation. Their main desire is to recreate the life they left behind them, reconstructing the communities from which they came. This is no great problem for entire communities that migrate en masse. The Pilgrim settlers of Plymouth, Massachusetts, and the Mormon migrants to Great Salt Lake, Utah, are notable cases of "colonized" new communities.

More common have been the "cumulative" communities of inhabitants thrown together helter-skelter by the migration process.[42] The migrants to San Franciso, California, in 1849 and after furnish an example of the cumulative new community. San Franciscans came from all over the world and were an immensely diverse lot. The only thing that united them, initially, was their desire to profit from the California Gold Rush.

Basic to the reconstruction of the community is the reestablishment of the old community structure and its values. To the extent that both are achieved, an orderly and stable new community life will be achieved. Although American frontiersmen of the nineteenth century came to their new localities from all points of the compass and were usually unknown and unrelated to each other, most came from essentially similar communities. The typical American community of the eighteenth and nineteenth centuries possessed a social structure of three levels.[43]

(1) The upper level consisted of leaders and their families. Included were well-to-do businssmen, the most eminent professional men, affluent farmers and planters, and prominent men of whatever occupation. This was the local elite, and in it were concentrated the community leading men.

(2) The middle level included the men of average means: farmers, craftsmen, tradesmen, and less eminent lawyers, teachers, and other professionals. The industrious, honest middle level formed the core of the community. In this sector resided the legendary but real American yeoman.

(3) The lower level included the honest poor and also those who were either marginal to or alienated from the remainder of the community. *In* but not really *of* the community (and spurned by it) were the ne'er-do-well, shiftless poor whites. They constituted a true *lower people*; they were viewed with contempt and loathing by the members of the upper and middle levels who could not abide their slatternly way of life, their spiritless lack of ambition, their often immoral conduct, and their disorganized family life.[44]

The lower people were not outlaws but often tended to lawlessness and identified more with the outlaw element than with the law-abiding members of the community. The outlaw element lived on the fringes of the community. In some cases they sprang from the lower people, but they were also men of good background who chose the outlaw life or drifted into it. They were alienated from the values of the community, although some occasionally joined respectable community life as reformed men.

A community has behavioral boundaries just as it has geographic boundaries. When a new community establishes its geographic boundaries, it must also establish its behavioral boundaries. The latter represent the positive, mutual values of the community.[45] The values that supported the three-level community and the basis upon which it rested were the related ideals of life and property. The American community of the eighteenth and nineteenth centuries was primarily a property-holder's community, and property was viewed as the very basis of life itself.

The vigilante leaders were drawn from the upper level of the community. The middle level supplied the rank-and-file. Outlaws and alienated lower people represented the main threat to the reconstruction of the community and were the principal targets of the vigilantes.

In the cumulative new communities of frontier America, the alienated lower people and the outlaws met the representatives of the middle and upper levels in social conflict. The former wished to burst their subordinate bounds and take over the new communities. In sociological terms the outlaws and the hostile lower people (but not the honest poor) constituted a "contraculture."[46] They rejected the respectable values of life and property and wished to upset the social structure in which the upper- and middle-level men were dominant. The relative weakness of social bonds in the new settlements was their opportunity. On the other hand, men of upper-level background or aspirations were determined to establish and strengthen the community structure in which they were dominant. In this they had the support of the middle-level inhabitants, and, with them, they mounted vigilante campaigns to quell the insurgent outlaws and lower people.[47]

The danger of a takeover of newly settled areas by the alienated, outcast elements of society was a real threat. Whether or not the alleged Murrell conspiracy of the lower Mississippi Valley in the 1830s actually represented a concerted plot of white outlaws to raise a gigantic slave rebellion in the interest of an "underworld" dominion of the region, the phenomenon revealed the sensitivity of lawful society to the large numbers, aggressiveness, and alienation of the outlaws of the region. In southern Illinois, in the 1840s, the "Flathead" element of horse thieves, counterfeiters, brigands, slave stealers, and Ohio River-bottom dwellers triggered a violent regulator reaction.[48] In east Texas, in the late 1830s, a similar combine of horse thieves, counterfeiters, slave stealers, and "land pirates" incited a countermovement by the regulators.[49] By 1841, a group of outlaw gangs had virtually taken over the Rock River counties of northern Illinois until challenged by the regulators in that year.[50] Much earlier, in South Carolina in the middle 1760s, a disorderly mixture of demoralized Indian war veterans, "straggling" refugee whites, "crackers," mulattoes, and outlaw horse thieves and counterfeiters well-nigh ruled in Back Country until honest men reacted in the regulator movement.[51] West of the Mississippi and Missouri in the raw, new mining camps, cattle towns, railheads, and open ranges, the same threat emanated from the professional "badmen" and outlaw gangs, the "blackleg" element, and the always troublesome rustlers and horse thieves. These and other challenges were thus met head on by the vigilantes.

The masonic lodge was often found in frontier communities, and the relationship between freemasonry and vigilantism was frequently an intimate one. Typical was the situation in Bannack, Nevada City, and Virginia City, Montana, rough, new mining camps in 1863-1864. There the leading members of the active vigilante movement of the winter of 1863-1864 seem initially to have formed a bond as a result of their common membership in the masonic lodge.[52] The like happened elsewhere. The same impulse—desire to participate in the upper-level dominance of the community—often caused the same person to join the masonic lodge (usually an elite local organization) and enlist in a vigilante movement. In Montana, Texas, and elsewhere, freemasonry was often the shadowy background for the organization of a local vigilante movement.[53]

Sometimes the members of the upper level did not wait for an overt crime outbreak but formed a vigilante organization to prevent an outbreak and cement the three-level community structure. Thus, Thomas G. Wildman of Denver, Colorado, wrote back East on September 8, 1859:

> There is to be a Vigilance Committee organized in the town this evening. All of the leading men of the town has signed the Constitution, and its object is a good one. . . . It is thought that stabbing and drunkenness will be rampant here this winter, and we think that the rowdies and gamblers will be more careful when they find out that we are organized and that all the first men of the town are determined to punish crime.[54]

To the men of Butler County, Kansas, in 1870-1871, vigilante action was the cornerstone of community construction. After killing eight men, they justified their action by declaring, "it has become a question whether honest men of the country shall leave, or this gang." Invoking "self-preservation" as "the first law of nature," they asserted that "however much we deplore the further use of violence in order to secure life and property. . . we shall not hesitate to do justice to the guilty if it is necessary."[55]

James Hall described the challenge which outlaws and lower people presented in the early years of the settlement of the Midwest:

> We had whole settlements of counterfeiters, or horse thieves, with their sympathizers— where rogues could change names, or pass from house to house, so skillfully as to elude detection—and where if detected, the whole population were ready to rise to the rescue. There were other settlements of sturdy honest fellows, the regular backwoodsmen in which rogues were not tolerated. There was therfore a continual struggle between these parties—the honest people trying to expel the others by the terrors of the law, and when the mode failed, forming *regulating* companies, and driving them out by force.[56]

An example of the problem was the bandit and "blackleg" community of the tamarack thickets and swamps of Noble County in northern Indiana. William Latta, William D. Hill, and George T. Ulmer were the pioneer founders and leaders of this illicit community, which thrived for 25 years. The banditti and their blackleg allies were sworn to uphold each other. They robbed, murdered, stole, gambled, burned buildings, and made and sold counterfeit money. They exerted a pernicious influence on the sons and daughters of their respectable neighbors, leading many young men and women into lives of crime, debauchery, and prostitution. Finally, in 1858, 2,000 regulators rose and scattered the blacklegs and outlaws once and for all.[57]

The loathing of upper-level men for the lower element—the contraculture—of the frontier was stated with feeling by Thomas Dimsdale, who cried that "for the low, brutal, cruel, lazy, ignorant, insolent, sensual and blasphemous miscreants that infest the frontier we entertain but one sentiment—aversion—deep, strong and unchangeable."[58] At times the deep aversion expressed itself in grisly ways. Such an incident occurred in Rawlins, Wyoming, in 1881, where Dr. John E. Osborne (a future governor of Wyoming) attended the hanging of the brutal Western outlaw, Big Nose George Parrott (or Parrotti). After the hanging, Dr. Osborne skinned the corpse and tanned the skin. The skin thus preserved was made into various mementos (including a pair of shoes that were put on years-long exhibit in a Rawlins bank), and, in effect, constituted an upper-level trophy in tribute to the community values of life and property held by such men as Dr. Osborne.[59]

Vigilante movements varied in size from the 12 to 15 members in Pierre, South Dakota, to the 6,000 to 8,000, who belonged to the San Francisco vigilance committee of 1856. Of the 326 documented vigilante movements, information has survived on the number of members in 50 movements. There were 13 movements of small size, varying from 12 to 99 members. At the other extreme were nine movements ranging in order of size downward from 6,000-8,000 members to 700 members: San Francisco (1856), South Carolina (1767-1769), Attakapas region of Louisiana (1859), northern Indiana (1858), northern Illinois (1841), Idaho City,

Idaho (1865), Bald Knobbers of Missouri (1885-1887), Butler County, Kansas (1870-1871), and Denver, Colorado (1859-1861). Predominant were the 28 movements, spread from 100 to 599 members—these were the movements of medium size. Thus, the typical vigilante movement was one of from one hundred to several hundred members. When we consider that the majority of American vigilante movements took place in new frontier localities of small population, the typical participation of from one hundred to a few hundred members underscores the extent to which the community as a whole participated in these movements.[60]

The characteristic vigilante movement was organized in command or military fashion and usually had a constitution, articles, or a manifesto to which the members would subscribe. Outlaws or other malefactors taken up by vigilantes were given formal (albeit illegal) trials, in which the accused had counsel or an opportunity to defend himself. An example of a vigilante trial is found in the northern Illinois regulator movement of 1841. Two accused horse thieves and murderers were tried by 120 regulators in the presence of a crowd of 500 or more. A leading regulator served as judge. The defendants were given a chance to challenge objectionable men among the regulators, and, as a result, the number of regulators taking part in the trial was cut by nine men. Two lawyers were provided—one to represent the accused and one to represent the "people." Witnesses were sworn, an arraignment was made, and the trial proceeded. In summation, the prosecuting attorney urged immediate execution of the prisoners. The crowd voted unanimously for the fatal sentence, and, after an hour allotted to the two men for prayer, they were put to death. The accused were almost never acquitted, but the vigilantes' attention to the spirit of law and order caused them to provide, by their lights, a fair but speedy trial.

Sentences of whipping and explusion were common in the early decades of vigilantism, but, as time passed, killing—usually by hanging—became the customary sentence. Through 1849 there are only 88 documented fatalities resulting from vigilante action. In the next decade, 105 persons were killed by vigilantes, and it was at about this time—the 1850s—that the transition in the meaning of the term "lynching" from whipping to killing was occurring. The change, from whipping and expulsion to killing, in vigilantism, made firm in the 1850s, was accentuated during the remainder of the century; from 1860 to 1909 vigilantes took at least 511 lives.

The number of victims of the 326 organized vigilante movements upon which this chapter focuses is only a part of the total number of lynch-law fatalities in American history. Included in the larger context are the victims, also, of the unorganized, ephemeral lynch mobs. Attempts to arrive at a grand total are doomed to only partial success, since in the centuries-long history of American lynch law, much evidence has been suppressed, lost, or scattered. Still, available figures (although understating the total number of those actually killed) do afford a reasonable approximation of the number of those who thus lost their lives: 729 persons executed by organized vigilantes, 1767-1909; 4,730 persons executed by unorganized lynch mobs, 1882-1951; with 5,459 the grand total.

Since the grand total of 5,459 does not include the victims of the first and third Ku Klux Klans, nor the vigilante, lynch mob, White Cap, and Night Rider fatalities not compiled, a round total of 6,000 is probably closer to reality. Legal executions no doubt surpassed extralegal executions in the pre-Civil War period (as they have in the twentieth century), but with the wave of black lynchings in the South after Reconstruction, plus the continued widespread application of vigilantism in the West, the pattern was reversed in the late nineteenth century: during the period from 1883 to 1898, the number of persons lynched annually easily surpassed the yearly total of legal executions.[61]

Of the 326 known vigilante movements, 141 (43 percent) were responsible for the death of 729 victims. Of the movements by category (i.e., large, medium, small), the large movements were, as might be expected, the most deadly, the medium movements less so, and the small movements hardly at all. Thus, the overwhelming number of deaths attributed to organized vigilantism, 704 (or 97 percent of the total of 729), were exacted by 122 large and medium movements, which, however, amounted to only 37 percent of all 326 vigilante movements.

The tendency among the 141 vigilante movements taking lives was to stop after claiming four or fewer victims. The most lethal of all vigilante movements was that in Montana in 1884 led by Granville Stuart; it accounted for 35 lives. The 10 other vigilante movements that killed 16 or more victims were, in descending order of deadliness, those of Lewiston, Idaho (1862-1864, 1871); Bannack and Virginia City, Montana (1863-1865); the entire Montana Territory (1862-1884); San Saba County, Texas (1880-1896); Madison and Hinds counties, Mississippi (1835); southern Illinois (1846-1849); Shackelford County, Texas (1876-1878); San Antonio, Texas (1857-1865); South Carolina (1767-1769); and the combined city of Cheyenne and Laramie County, Wyoming (1868-1869).

Although the trend was for the large movements to kill the most victims, it was not always necessary for a powerful movement to take a large number of lives. Often a vigilante movement could achieve its aims by taking only one or a few lives. The greatest of all vigilante movements (San Francisco, 1856) killed only four men. Two other significant movements—the northern Illinois regulators of 1841 and the northern Indiana regulators of 1858—executed only two men and one man, respectively. The fearful example of one or two hangings (frequently in conjunction with the explusion of lesser culprits) was on many occasions enough to bring about the vigilante goals of community reconstruction and stability.[62]

Vigilante leaders wished to establish and strengthen the three-level community structure (in which they would be dominant) and the values of life and property that supported it. Specifically, they wished to check disorder and crime, but in some situations the threat of the latter was slight. In such cases, their desire to use vigilantism underscored their basic, implicit goals of implanting community structure and values.

All this they wished to achieve as cheaply as possible. They were the typical frontier entrepreneurs. Their enterprise in commerce or land was often speculative, and they frequently skated on economic thin ice. The delicate balance of their own personal finances could be easily upset; hence they had a lively awareness of the cost of public services and a yen to keep them down, lest, as substantial taxpayers, their own circumstances should suffer. No better resolution of the conflicting goals of public order and personal wealth could be found than vigilantism, which provided a maximum of the former at minimum cost to the ambitious and well-to-do.

The typical vigilante leaders were ambitious young men from the old settled areas of the East. They wished to establish themselves in the upper level of the new community, at the status they held or aspired to in the place of their origin. Two notable but representative examples of aggressive young vigilante leaders were William Tell Coleman and Wilbur Fisk Sanders.

Coleman was head of the San Francisco vigilance committee of 1856 and was 32 years old at the time. His father had been a Kentucky lawyer and legislator but died a bankrupt when the son was only nine. The future vigilante, deprived of the opportunity for an education, spent his early years moving restlessly about the Midwest (Illinois, Missouri, and Wisconsin) in a fruitless quest to regain the upper-level status of his father. Arriving overland in California in 1849, at the age of 25, Coleman embarked on a career, which, by 1856, found him to be one of San Francisco's most successful importers. His participation as a vigilante leader was, in effect, an action to cement his position in the upper level of the new city and to consolidate the three-level social system there.

Wilbur Fisk Sanders was the courageous and incisive prosecuting attorney of the vigilantes at Virginia City, Montana, in 1864. Like Coleman, Sanders came from an upper-level background but had not yet made firm his own position. He was 29 when he served as a vigilante and had not long before accompanied his uncle, Sidney Edgerton (who had been appointed territorial chief justice by Lincoln), from Ohio to Montana. Sanders's vigilante service did much to establish the three-level system in chaotic early Montana, and it was the beginning of one of the most spectacular careers in the territory. Sanders went on to become one of the leading lawyers and top Republican politicians in Montana. He founded the Montana Bar Association and, in 1889, was elected one of Montana's first two U.S. senators.[63]

III

In frontier areas, law and order was often a tenuous thing. Outlaws—singly or in gangs—headed for the new areas and took every advantage they could of the social disorganization stemming from the newness of the settlement and the weakness of the traditional institutions of state, society, and church.

Law enforcement was frequently inadequate. Throughout most of the nineteenth century (and not just on the frontier) it was restricted to the immediate vicinity of county seat, town, or township.[64] Localities lacked the economic resources to support constables, policemen, and sheriffs in long pursuits of lawbreakers. A really large expenditure of funds on the pursuit, capture, jailing, trial, and conviction of culprits could easily bankrupt the typical frontier county or town.

There was also the handicap of poor transportation. The mobility of sheriffs and others was only as rapid and flexible as their horses could afford. A fugitive, having gained any sort of lead, was difficult to catch. The development of the railroad was a help but was not without its disadvantages. The officer was bound to the fixed route of the railroad. There were large gaps, also, between the railroad lines—gaps into which the fugitives unerringly headed. In the hinterland stretches not served by the railroads, the authorities were forced to make their way over poor roads and disappearing trails.

Linked with inadequate law enforcement was an uneven judicial system. Through fear, friendliness, or corruption, juries often failed to convict criminals.[65] The lack of jails (in the early days) or their flimsy condition made it nearly impossible to prevent those in custody from escaping.[66] The system presented numerous opportunities for manipulation by outlaws, who could often command some measure of local support. Whenever possible, outlaws would obtain false witnesses in their behalf, pack juries, bribe officials, and, in extreme cases, intimidate the entire system: judges, juries, and law enforcement officials.[67] Such deficiencies in the judicial system were the source of repeated complaints by frontiersmen. They made the familiar point that the American system of administering justice favored the accused rather than society. The guilty, they charged, utilized every loophole for the evasion of punishment. Compounding the problem was the genuinely heavy financial burden involved in maintaining an adequate "police establishment" and judicial system in a sparsely settled and economically underdeveloped frontier area.[68]

For many a frontiersman, vigilantism was the solution to these problems. W.N. Byers, an old Denver, Colorado, vigilante of 1860 reminisced:

> We never hanged on circumstantial evidence. I have known a great many such executions, but I don't believe one of them was ever unjust. But when they were proved guilty, they were always hanged. There was no getting out of it. *No, there were no appeals in those days; no writs of errors; no attorneys' fees; no pardon in six months. Punishment was swift, sure and certain.*[69]

Vigilantism could never have become such a powerful force in nineteenth-century America without having gripped the mind and emotions of Americans. This it did through a system of ideas and beliefs that emerged as the ideology of vigilantism. There were several elements in it.

In the nineteenth century the doctrine of "vigilance" suffused America in a way that had not been the case before or since. To be vigilant in regard to all manner of things was an idea that increasingly commanded Americans as the decades passed. The doctrine of vigilance provided a powerful intellectual foundation for the burgeoning vigilante movements, and, in turn, vigilante movements reinforced the doctrine of vigilance.

Vigilance committees were formed early for a host of things having nothing to do with the problem of frontier disorder. In 1813-1814, the leading men of Richmond, Virginia (headed by Chief Justice John Marshall), organized a committee of vigilance whose purpose was home-guard defense against a possible British attack during the War of 1812.[70] The attack never came, but the idea of vigilance did not die. In 1817, when Pensacola, Florida (at that time still under Spanish rule but soon to become American) was threatened by a ship of Mexican filibusters, the citizens established a committee of vigilance for home defense which, however, like that of Richmond was never put to the test.[71] American settlers in Texas on the eve of the Texan Revolution founded committees of vigilance in Nacogdoches, and other localities, in 1835-1836 by way of preparing for the looming hostilities with the Mexican mother country.[72]

The doctrine of vigilance had thus been utilized in regard to the early-nineteenth-century crises of war and expansion; so, too, was it put to the service of sectional interests as the North and South moved toward confrontation in civil war. Possibly the first "vigilance committee" involved in the sectional issue was that of the Ohio county of Meigs, which lay across the Ohio River from western Virginia. In 1824, Meigs County men organized a vigilance committee to prevent Virginians from pursuing fugitive slaves into their locality.[73] As early as 1838, Philadelphia and New York had vigilance committees to aid fugitive slaves. In the 1850s, Northern vigilance committees of this sort became increasingly common as they proliferated in response to the Fugitive Slave Act in Boston, Syracuse, Springfield, and smaller cities.[74] The South, conversely, fostered the founding of antiabolition vigilance committees as early as 1835 in Fairfax County, Virginia. Such committees spread throughout the South in the 1840s and 1850s.[75] By that time in Dixie abolitionists constituted an illusory threat at best. But the antiabolitionist vigilance committees probably helped increase the sectional solidarity of the South.

The doctrine of vigilance was not restricted to the great issues of war and sectional controversy but impinged upon the prosaic world of commerce. Thus, in a presage of the modern Better Business Bureau, the Merchant's Vigilance Association of New York City was organized in 1845 "to investigate and expose abuses in trade" and "to prevent frauds."[76] In time, the doctrine of vigilance merged with the earlier regulator tradition (that went back to the South Carolina Back Country) and the result, by the 1840s and 1850s, was the vigilance committee dedicated to the eradication of frontier crime and turbulence.

Although the doctrine of vigilance was the context for the organizing of many vigilante movements, the vigilantes, knowing full well that their actions were illegal, felt obliged to legitimize their violence by expounding a philosophy of vigilantism. The philosophy of vigilantism had three major components: self-preservation, the right of revolution, and popular sovereignty. Reinforcing the three-fold philosophy of vigilantism was an economic rationale for vigilante action. All these elements—the doctrine of vigilance, the vigilante philosophy, and the economic rationale—composed the ideology of vigilantism.

By the middle of the nineteenth century, self-righteous vigilantes in as widely separated locales as Washington Territory, Montana, Missouri, and Louisiana were routinely invoking "self-preservation" or "self-protection" as the first principle of vigilantism. Thus the June 1, 1856, Vigilance Committee of Pierce County, Washington Territory, justified its existence by citing "self-preservation [as] the first law of society, & the basis upon which its structure is built."[77] The French Acadians of the Louisiana Comités de Vigilance were no less sure of their ground when, on March 16, 1859, they declared, as a basis for taking the law into their own hands, that "self-protection is supreme."[78] The same note was struck by Thomas J. Dimsdale in his classic contemporary account when he stated that for the honest Montana miners of Bannack and Alder Gulch (1863-1864) the depredations of the "road agents" had narrowed the question down to "kill or be killed." Under the principle that "self-preservation is the first law of nature" the vigilantes "took the right side."[79] The very same language—"self-preservation is the first law of nature"—headed the resolutions of the Johnson County vigilance committee as it organized against post-Civil War horse thieves, murderers, and robbers in Warrensburg, Missouri, on February 28, 1867.[80]

The right of revolution was crucial, since vigilantes were well aware that their illegal action was, in effect, a blow at established authority. In order to deal with horse thieves and counterfeiters in Illinois in 1816-1817, "the people," Governor Thomas Ford later wrote, "formed themselves into *revolutionary tribunals* . . . under the name of regulators."[81] Vigilante penmen cut right to the heart of the matter by unequivocally invoking the right of revolution. A Louisiana *Comité de Vigilance* proclamation of March 16, 1859, explicitly avowed its character as a "revolutionary movement."[82] The authorized historian of the *Comité*, Alexander Barde, cited the American Revolution as a justified popular insurrection and precedent for the movement he described. To condemn the vigilance committee in the context of intolerable conditions of lawlessness (analogous to the lack of justice that brought on the Revolution of 1776), said Barde, would be "to condemn our history" and to say "that if Nero governed us, we should submit to Nero."[83]

Most vital to the philosphy of vigilantism was the democratic ideal of popular sovereignty, whose origins went back to the era of the American Revolution. Aside from factors stated at the beginning of this chapter, an additional reason for the failure of vigilantism to appear before 1767 was the lack, up to that time, of a mature belief in democracy. The emergence of the popular-sovereignty doctrine in the revolutionary period was linked to the transition from deferential to democratic social values in America, a process that took from the time of the Revolution to the age of Jackson. By the latter age (which coincided with the firm establishment of the vigilante tradition), the rule of the people was acknowledged by all but the most skeptical and reactionary.

"Popular sovereignty" was much more than a slogan used by the ambitious Democratic party politician, Stephen A. Douglas, as an answer to the thorny problem of slavery in the territories; it represented a belief shared deeply by Americans of whatever political persuasion. The regulators of the predominantly Republican party counties of La Grange and Noble in northern Indiana saw no inconsistency (as they prepared for a lynch-law drive) in stating as the first of their Resolutions on January 9, 1858:

> Whereas, We are believers in the *doctrine of popular sovereignty*; that the people of the country are the real sovereigns, and that whenever the laws, made by those to whom they have delegated their authority, are found inadequate to their protection, it is the right of the people to take the protection of their property into their own hands, and deal with these villains according to their just desserts.[84]

The same idea was put a bit more pithily in 1902 when the following jingle was found pinned to the body of a man hanged by the vigilantes of Casper, Wyoming:

> Process of law is a little slow.
> So this is the road you'll have to go.
> Murderers and thieves, Beware!
> PEOPLE'S VERDICT.[85]

"The *right of the people* to take care of themselves, if the law does not," said Professor Bigger of the local normal school to the Johnson County, Missouri, vigilantes in 1867, "is an indisputable right."[86] Hence, to nineteenth-century Americans the rule of the people was superior to all else—even the law. Vigilantism was but a case of the people exercising their sovereign power in the interest of self-preservation.

The economic rationale of vigilantism was tied to elite dominance of local vigilante movements. Thus, although vigilantism rested on a bedrock democratic premise, the vigilante operation in practice was often not democratic. Ordinary men formed the rank and file of the vigilante organization, but usually its direction was firmly in the hands of the local elite. The local vigilante leaders often paid the highest taxes, and they had the customary desire to whittle down the tax rate and keep local expenses in check. From this point of view there was a persuasive economic rationale, for vigilante justice was cheaper, as well as quicker and more certain, than regular justice. This was a theme that the vigilantes sounded time and again.

In 1858, northern Indiana regulators paraded under a banner that said, simply, *"No expense* to the County."[87] A Denver *Tribune* reporter probed opinion in Golden, Colorado, in 1879 after a recent vigilante lynching and found that "on every side the popular verdict seemed to be that the hanging was not only well merited, but a positive gain to the county, saving it at least five or six thousand dollars."[88] The redoubtable vigilance committee of Las Vegas, New Mexico, was (like many others) dominated by the leading local merchants. One night in the early 1880s the vigilantes entered the local jail, took out all the inmates, and chased them out of town. The reason for the expulsion was economy in government, as the inmates—"petty thieves, bunko men, and would-be badmen—were eating their heads off at the city's expense."[89] On September 3, 1887, the Meeker (Colorado) *Herald* praised a local vigilance committee and said, "We approve of this method of dealing with 'rustlers' as it is expeditious and saves the county the expense of prosecuting such cases."[90]

IV

Two "models" of vigilante movements developed. One was the "good" or socially constructive model, in which the vigilante movement dealt with a problem of disorder straightforwardly and then disbanded. The result was an increase in the social stability of the locality; the movement was, thus, socially constructive. The other model was the "bad" or socially destructive one, in which a vigilante movement encountered such strong opposition that the result was an anarchic and socially destructive vigilante war. Some movements were run according to the ideal theory of vigilantism whereas others were not. Some were socially constructive; others were not.

The socially constructive movement occurred when the vigilantes represented a genuine community consensus. Here a majority of the people either participated in the movement or approved of it. Vigilantism of this sort simply mobilized the community and overwhelmed the unruly outlaws and lower people. The community was left in a more orderly and stable condition, and the social functions of vigilantism were served: the problem of community order was solved by the consolidation of the three-level social structure and the supporting community values.

Although the methods used were often harsh and arbitrary, most vigilante movements—large and small—conformed to the socially constructive model. One of the best examples was the northern Illinois regulator movement of 1841. The northern Illinois movement confronted a classic threat to community order: an agglomeration of outlaw gangs were nearing control of the area. With the regular government virtually powerless, the respectable leaders of the community upper level took the law into their own hands with the help of the middle-level farmers.

Since 1835, the situation in the Rock Valley of northern Illinois had gone from bad to worse. Several gangs of horse thieves and counterfeiters found the Rock River country a convenient corridor for illicit operations in Wisconsin, Illinois, Iowa, and Missouri. The Driscoll and Brodie gangs had made Ogle and De Kalb counties a virtual fief. The Oliver gang dominated Winnebago County. The Bliss-Dewey-West ring waxed strong in Lee County, while the Birch gang of horse thieves ranged in all quarters. By 1840 the desperadoes were numerous enough to control elections in Ogle County and to similarly threaten other counties. One summer the outlaws even went so far as to burn down the newly constructed courthouse at Oregon, Illinois.

Finally, in April, 1841, 15 "representative men" of Ogle County formed the first regulator company. In no time at all the counties were dotted with regulator squads, but the most vigorous were those of Ogle. The regulators embodied the social, economic, and political prestige of Ogle County: John Phelps was the county's oldest and wealthiest settler and the founder of the county seat, Oregon. Peter Smith combined a bank presidency with the ownership of 1,600 acres of land. The farmers who made up the bulk of the movement were substantial property holders; they had taken up government land claims ranging from 240 to 600 acres. These solid citizens brooked no opposition. They burned the Rockford *Star* to the ground soon after it published an antiregulator editorial. But, on the whole, the local elite kept the movement well under control. Having accomplished their purpose in a campaign of whipping, hanging, and firing squads, the regulator companies disbanded. Socially they left the Rock Valley in a better state than before they organized.[91]

The northern Illinois regulator movement exhibited the major characteristics of the successful frontier vigilante movement. It was organized in a rational way. Mass participation of respectable men was the mode, but the movement was dominated, clearly, by the social and economic elite of the area. The regulators were implacable in their war on the outlaws and unrelenting in the face of opposition. Although the Rockford *Star* opposed the regulators, no antiregulator coalition, as a whole, developed. The outlaw gangs were isolated and broken up. The vigilante leaders desired the assurance of their position at the upper level of their communities but were not power mad. With the outlaw threat put down, peace and order reigned.

In the socially destructive model, the vigilante movement resulted in anarchy. Because there was no community consensus behind the vigilante movement, strong opposition appeared, and civil conflict flared. In the socially constructive model, opposition to the vigilantes was narrowly restricted to outlaws and lower people who could gain no support from the remainder of the community. For the vigilantes to be stymied, a large antivigilante coalition was necessary. The formation of an antivigilante coalition almost inevitably condemned the community to a chaotic internecine struggle between the vigilantes and their opponents.

Respectable men did not join the antivigilante coalition because of any great sympathy for the outlaws and lower people. They were impelled into opposition by things the vigilantes did or stood for. Sometimes two or three powerful local families would join the antivigilante movement. In some cases, a family had been carrying on a feud of sorts with a leading vigilante family.[92] Sometimes a local political party or faction went into the antivigilante movement, because the vigilantes were dominated by the rival party or faction.[93] In the 1830s-1850s, if the leading Democrats of a community, for example, were found among the vigilantes, the antivigilante coalition would probably attract the local Whigs. Political rivalries were often linked to vigilante strife, for, in many instances, vigilante leaders harbored political ambitions and were not above using the movement to further their personal ambitions.[94] Economic rivalries among community leaders also were a factor in antivigilante and vigilante alignments; mercantile competition sometimes caused a leading storekeeper to go into the opposition if his rival were a vigilante.[95] Thus personal, family, political, and economic antagonisms accounted for a ready-made vigilante opposition in some communities.

At other times, vigilante extremism drew into opposition decent men who otherwise probably would not have opposed vigilantism. The best of vigilante movements usually attracted a fringe of sadists and naturally violent types. Often these men had criminal tendencies and were glad to use the vigilante movement as an occasion to give free reign to their unsavory passions. It was always a problem for vigilante leaders to keep these elements under control, and sometimes a movement was taken over or seriously skewed by these social misfits. Sadistic punishment and torture, arbitrary and unnecessary killings, and mob tyranny marked vigilante movements that had truly gone bad.[96] When this happened, many sound and conservative men felt they must oppose the vigilantes with whose original objectives they had probably felt no quarrel.

Examples of the socially destructive model of vigilantism did not occur as often as the constructive model, but when they did extremely violent conflicts tended to appear. Among the leading instances were the east Texas regulators (versus the moderators), 1840-1844; the southwest Missouri Slickers (versus the Anti-Slickers), 1842-1844; and the southern Illinois regulators (versus the Flatheads), 1846-1850.[97] Sometimes an antivigilante coalition arose which, although unable to match vigilante strength, was able to call in outside help, and hence could define the limits of vigilante power. The antivigilante Law and Order faction in San Francisco, in 1856, played this role. The vigilantes there would have liked to have hanged Judge David S. Terry but did not dare do so, for the Law and Order faction would almost certainly have obtained federal action against the vigilantes.[98] Similarly, the moderators in the South Carolina Back Country, 1769, were not strong enough to overturn regulator domination, but they did check the movement and bring its excesses to an end.[99]

If a socially destructive model of vigilantism gained power, the moral standing of the vigilantes and the opposing coalition tended increasingly to be compromised. As the struggle became more violent, the respectable men of the antivigilante coalition put a higher premium on the violent talents of the outlaw element with which they otherwise had nothing in common. So, too, did the original vigilantes themselves recruit and acquire a criminal fringe, which they put to mercenary use. With the community descending into bloody chaos, wise and prudent men left if they could. The opposing movements tended to fall more and more into the control of the worst and most extreme of their adherents. When this occurred, the desperate neutral residents would beseech state authorities for the intervention of the militia, and the "war" would subside fitfully in the presence of state troops.[100]

The regulator-moderator war of east Texas (1840-1844) was representative of this degenerate, socially destructive vigilante situation. The scene was the redland and piney wood country of east Texas in the days of the Lone Star Republic. The center of the conflict was Shelby County. Fronting on the Sabine River, where it formed the boundary between Louisiana and Texas, Shelby County lay in an old border area that had never been known for peace and calm. In 1840, the regulator movement arose as a quite honest and straightforward attack on a ring of corrupt county officials who specialized in fraudulent land transactions. The rise of the regulators was probably inevitable in any case, for the county had long wilted under a plague of counterfeiting, horse thievery, slave stealing, and common murder and mayhem. The regulators, however, overplayed their hand, especially after their original leader, Charles W. Jackson, was killed and replaced by the nefarious adventurer, Watt Moorman. Bad elements infiltrated both the regulators and their opponents, the moderators, but, by comparison, the latter seemed less obnoxious. Some honorable and level-headed citizens like John W. Middleton stayed with the regulators to the end, but an attitude of wild vengefulness came to be more characteristic of the band. The early group of ne'er-do-wells among the moderators dwindled. As more and more citizens were forced to take sides, many joined the moderators, reacting to the sadism and vindictiveness of the swashbuckling Watt Moorman, who affected a military uniform and blew great blasts on a hunting horn to summon his henchmen.

The original reasons for the founding of the regulator movement were all but forgotten. The war became a thing in itself, a complexity of personal and family feuds that was consuming the area in blood lust. Several attempts to restore peace failed. Complete anarchy was the situation in 1844 when an all-out battle between two armies of several hundred men each was forestalled only by the dramatic intervention of Sam Houston and the militia. After four years, 18 men had been killed and many more wounded. A stream in the vicinity was called "Widow's Creek." The killing of so many leaders and the exhaustion of the survivors probably explain why the war was not revived after Sam Houston and the militia withdrew. Ex-regulators and ex-moderators warily fought side by side in separate companies in the Mexican War, but for 50 years east Texans were reluctant to discuss the episode lest old enmities be rekindled.[101]

Vigilantism characteristically appeared in two types of situations: (1) where the regular system of law and order was absent or ineffective, and (2) where the regular system was functioning satisfactorily. The first case found vigilantism filling a void. The second case revealed vigilantism functioning as an extralegal structure of justice that paralleled the regular system.

Why did vigilantes desire to erect a parallel structure when the regular one was adequate? There were a number of reasons. By usurping the functions of regular law enforcement and justice or, at times, duplicating them, vigilante action greatly reduced the cost of local government. As taxpayers, the vigilante leaders and the rank and file benefitted from the reduction in public costs. Second, the process of community reconstruction through the recreation of social structure and values could be carried on more dramatically by a vigilante movement than was possible through the regular functioning of the law. A vigilante hanging was a graphic warning to all potentially disruptive elements that community values and structure were to be upheld.

The sort of impression that vigilantes wanted to make was that received by young Malcolm Campbell, who arrived in Cheyenne, Wyoming, in 1868 at the age of 28. No sooner had he arrived than there were four vigilante hangings. "So in rapid succession," he recalled, "came before my eyes instances which demonstrated the strength of law [as carried out by vigilantes], and the impotence of the criminal. Undoubtedly, these incidents went far in shaping my future life and in guiding my feet properly in those trails of danger where I was later to apprehend some of the most dangerous outlaws of the plains."[102] (Campbell later became a leading Wyoming sheriff.)

Finally, the vigilante movement sometimes existed for reasons that were essentially unrelated to the traditional problems of crime and disorder. The San Francisco vigilance committee of 1856 is one of the best examples of the vigilante movement as a parallel structure. The San Francisco vigilantes spoke of a crime problem, but examination of the evidence does not reveal a significant upsurge of crime in 1855-1856. The regular authorities had San Francisco crime well under control. Fundamentally, the San Francisco vigilantes were concerned with local political and fiscal reform. They wished to wrest control of the government from the dominant faction of Irish-Catholic Democrats. The vigilantes actually left the routine enforcement of law to the regular police and intervened only in a few major cases. The parallel structure of the vigilante movement was utilized to organize a reform political party (the People's party) and to shatter the Irish-Catholic Democracy faction by exiling some of its leading operatives.

Sometimes the regular and parallel structures were intertwined. Law enforcement officials often connived with vigilantes. Here a sheriff or police chief was not taken by surprise when a vigilante force bent on a lynching converged upon his jail, for he had helped plan the whole affair. Appearances were preserved, usually, by a token resistance on the part of the law officer, but it was well known in the community that he had shared in the vigilante plot.

Why would men violate their oaths and subvert their own functions as officers of the law? For some men the reason was that they were little more than hirelings of the local vigilante elite to whom they were beholden for office. Other officers were large landholders or businessmen themselves; they shared the vigilantes' desire to keep down governmental costs. Little interested in legal niceties, vigilante-minded law officers were happy to have a bad man disposed of quickly, cheaply, and permanently by a lynching.

American vigilantism has been paralleled by a number of related movements. Such movements as the three Ku Klux Klans, the White Caps, and the Night Riders were illegal and usually violent. One legal, nonviolent movement existed side by side with vigilantism from the late eighteenth to the early twentieth century. This was the anti-horse thief movement. It is now almost forgotten, but hundreds of thousands of Americans from New England to the Rio Grande belonged to it.

The anti-horse thief movement consisted of local societies, clubs, and associations of men—mainly farmers—who banded together to detect and pursue thieves, especially horse thieves. The anti-horse thief societies were much like vigilante movements in respect to organization, objectives, and types of members. There was one crucial difference: they did not take the law into their own hands. Instead, they restricted themselves to the detection and pursuit of culprits whom, after capture, they dutifully turned over to local law enforcement officers. They eventually came to incorporate themselves under state law, and some states granted them constabulary powers.

The first anti-horse thief societies arose spontaneously just after the revolutionary fighting had ended.[103] The first such society was probably the Northampton Society for the Detection of Thieves and Robbers organized in Massachusetts in 1782. By 1800, similar groups had been founded along the Atlantic coast from Rhode Island to Delaware. The movement thrived in the northeastern United States as a legal supplement to regular law enforcement. It was vital and long lived in New Jersey—a typical state—where over 100 local societies were founded from 1788 to 1915. Official approval of the New Jersey societies was unstated until 1851, at which time the legislature explicitly approved organization of the societies; later it granted them the power of arrest. The societies flourished until the establishment of township police departments in the 1890s lessened the need for them. Inauguration of the state police in 1921 rendered them wholly unnecessary. Here and there they still exist but only as nostalgic social organizations.

The experience of New Jersey and the Northeast with the anti-horse thief movement was duplicated in the Mid- and Southwest. The movement got underway in Indiana in 1852 with the legalization of regulator bands as anti-horse thief societies. After the Civil War, the movement grew rapidly, and an interstate combine, the National Horse Thief Detective Association (with headquarters in Indiana) spread into Ohio and Illinois.[104] A similar development was seen across the Mississippi, where a movement that began in northeast Missouri in the 1860s had, by the 1890s and later, become the farflung Anti-Horse Thief Association with thousands of local chapters and over a hundred thousand members in Kansas, Oklahoma, Missouri, and Arkansas.[105]

Eventually the anti-horse thief movement succumbed to the automobile. The latter supplanted the horse as the means of transportation the members had joined together to protect. And the automobile immensely increased the range, mobility, and effectiveness of local law enforcement, thereby rendering obsolete the anti-horse thief society as a supplemental crime-fighting agency.

V

In the short run, the vigilante movement was a positive facet of the American experience. Many a new frontier community gained order and stability as the result of vigilantism that reconstructed the community pattern and values of the old settled areas, while dealing effectively with crime and disorder. A host of distinguished Americans—statesmen, politicians, capitalists, lawyers, judges, writers, and others—supported vigilantism by word or deed. Some of them were personally involved in vigilante movements; usually this was when they were younger men, but, in later life, they never repudiated their actions.

Men who were actually vigilantes or had expressed strong approval of specific vigilante movements included two presidents of the United States (Andrew Jackson, Theodore Roosevelt), five U.S. senators (Alexander Mouton, Louisiana; Francis M. Cockrell, Missouri; Leland Stanford, California; William J. McConnell, Idaho; Wilbur Fisk Sanders, Montana); eight governors of states or territories (Mouton, Louisiana; Stanford, California; McConnell, Idaho; Augustus C. French, Illinois; Fennimore Chatterton and John E. Osborne, Wyoming; Miguel A. Otero and George Curry, New Mexico); and one minister to a foreign country (Granville Stuart, Montana, minister to Uruguay and Paraguay). Prominent writers who were outspoken in their support of vigilantism included historian Hubert Howe Bancroft, novelist Owen Wister, and university president and diplomat Andrew D. White.

The nineteenth-century American elite walked a tightrope in regard to vigilantism. Most of the elite held conservative social and economic views and were not attracted by the revolutionary and democratic rationales of vigilantism, but, as late as the First World War, members of the American elite looked with favor upon the vigilante tradition. In 1918, a group of distinguished writers formed an organization to promote the war effort. Significantly, they chose to call themselves "the Vigilantes." Invoking the vigilante heritage, their pamphlet announced:

> There has been a disposition to associate the Vigilantes with those beloved rough-necks of the early California days, who established order in frontier towns and camps by methods distasteful to tender souls. We find no fault with this. In fact, we are rather proud of being linked up with the stern and vigorous pioneers who effectually squelched the anarchists and I.W.W. of their day.

The membership list of the Vigilantes was a "Who's Who" of the writers of the day. Among those who belonged were Hamlin Garland, Booth Tarkington, Ray Stannard Baker, Irvin S. Cobb, Edgar Lee Masters, Theodore Roosevelt, and many others.[106]

The classic era of vigilantism had attracted the participation and support of elite Americans as well as rank and file frontiersmen. It came to an end around the turn of the century, but the vigilante tradition lived on into the twentieth century. In fact, it was extended into new areas of American life. Thus arose the later phenomenon of the new vigilantism, or neovigilantism.

Neovigilantism grew mainly after the Civil War and was largely a response to the problems of an emerging urban, industrial, racially and ethnically diverse America. The transition from the old to the new vigilantism was heralded by the San Francisco vigilance committee of 1856, which used the methods of the old vigilantism on the victims of the new. Virtually all the features of neovigilantism were present in the San Francisco movement of 1856. Neovigilantism was to be frequently urban rather than rural, as was the case in San Francisco. The old vigilantism had been directed mainly at horse thieves, counterfeiters, outlaws, badmen, and lower people. Neovigilantism found its chief victims among Catholics, Jews, immigrants, blacks, laboring men and labor leaders, political radicals, and proponents of civil liberties. The actions and overtones of the San Francisco movement were strongly imbued with the passions and prejudices that came to be features of the neovigilantism.

The San Franciscan vigilantes were ethnically biased; their ire focused on one group: the Irish. The vigilantes were anti-Catholic; their hero and martyr was the anti-Romanist editor, James King of William, and most of their victims in 1856 were Catholics. Although their ranks included laborers and mechanics, there was a distinct social class tinge to the 1856 movement: middle- and upper-class merchants were aligned against the lower-class supporters of the San Francisco Democratic machine. Last but not least was a disregard for civil liberties. Angered by the arguments of John Nugent of the San Francisco *Herald*, who came out in favor of regular justice, the merchant vigilantes of '56 quickly organized an advertising boycott that transformed the *Herald* overnight from the strongest to the weakest of the city's major dailies.

Allegedly concerned with a crime problem, the San Francisco vigilantes of 1856 were, in actuality, motivated by a desire to seize control of the municipal government from the Democratic political machine that found the nucleus of its support among the lower-class, Irish-Catholic workers of the city. Basic to the vigilante movement was the desire to establish a business-oriented local government, which would reduce expenditures, deprive the Irish-Catholic Democrats of access to municipal revenues, and lower taxes. To a considerable extent, the San Francisco vigilante episode of 1856 represented a struggle for power between two religious, class, and ethnic blocs. Thus, the vigilante leadership of upper- and middle-class, old American, Protestant merchants was aligned against a political faction supported by Irish-Catholic lower-class laborers. Such were the social and economic tensions that typically enlisted the violence of neovigilantism.

The protean character of neovigilantism precludes an extensive discussion of it. Only significant tendencies are noted here. Blacks have been the targets of three distinct Ku Klux Klan movements over a more than 100-year period, going back to 1867.[107] Catholics and Jews were singled out for verbal attack by the second Ku Klux Klan (of the 1920s), but the bulk of Klan violence in the 1920s seems to have been leveled against ne'er-do-well white Anglo-Saxon Protestants, who did not measure up to the puritanical Klan moral standards, and was similar to the White Cap movement, which violently regulated the immoral and shiftless from 1887 on into the twentieth century. Immigrants were repeatedly the victims of neovigilantism. One of the most spectacular instances was the lynching of eleven Sicilians in New Orleans in 1891.[108] Laboring men and labor union organizers (many of whom were immigrants) were frequently the subjects of vigilante violence when they were striking or attempting to organize.

Political radicals have often undergone vigilante harassment; one of the most striking examples was the arrest of thousands of Communists and radicals in the "Red raids" of January 1, 1920.[109] The raids were carried out under the color of law, but the whole action resembled nothing so much as a giant vigilante roundup. Proponents of civil liberties have at times fallen afoul of a quasi-vigilante spirit manifested in such waves of intolerance as the "McCarthyism" of the early 1950s.

During the turbulent, riot-torn, crime-ridden 1960s and early 1970s, three sectors of the American public have become vigilante-prone: (1) Members of the black enclaves, North and South, who have felt the need for self-protective organizations against white harassment and violence. The Deacons for Defense and Justice of the middle and late 1960s illustrate the neovigilante spirit among black people. (2) White residents of urban and suburban neighborhoods, who have felt threatened by a possible incursion of black rioters and looters. The predominantly Italian-American membership of a North Ward Citizens' Committee (founded in 1967) of Newark, New Jersey, emerged as a leading example of this neovigilante impulse. (3) Residents of urban neighborhoods beset by crime. The Maccabees (1964-1966 and later) of Crown Heights, Brooklyn, arose as the prototype for this species of modern vigilantism. Although the Maccabees were mainly white (their core was composed of Hasidic Jews reacting against black street crime), black organizations similar to the Maccabees have appeared in high-crime black neighborhoods where they have been especially active in recent years against drug dealers.

These vigilante movements of the 1960s and early 1970s have differed from classic vigilantes in the sense that the current movements have not ordinarily taken the law into their own hands. (Since 1970, however, there have been reports that black and Puerto Rican vigilantes have executed drug dealers in New York City.) Instead, the main activity has been patrol action around neighborhoods in radio-equipped automobiles (linked to a central headquarters) for the purpose of spotting, reporting, and discouraging criminal acts against the residents of their communities. Characteristically, these up-to-date vigilantes cooperate with the police, but not always: the black organization of Deacons for Defense and Justice was formed, in part, to deal with white police harassment in black sectors in small cities of the deep South, whereas, as indicated, recent black and Puerto Rican urban vigilantes have supposedly levied summary justice on ghetto drug pushers. Despite frequent cooperation with police, the contemporary movements are in the authentic vigilante tradition, for they are associations in which citizens have joined together for self-protection under conditions of disorder. While usually not usurping the law, these movements have been commonly viewed as vigilantes by the public, the authorities, and themselves.[110]

VI

Despite the existence of some anarchic, socially destructive vigilante movements, the effect of vigilantism—as noted above—was to enhance social stability and order in frontier areas. Moreover, American opinion generally supported vigilantism; extralegal activity by a provoked populace was deemed to be the rightful action of good citizens. Thus, from the short-run perspective of frontier development the paradoxical aim of vigilantism—to uphold the law by breaking the law—was not only achieved but applauded. Yet a long-range view of vigilantism casts doubt on its positive impact. We are and always have been a law-abiding people, but pervasive respect for the law has been counterpointed by a widespread spirt of lawlessness. Americans have long felt that intolerable conditions justify defiance of law and ultimately, if required, revolution.

The vigilante tradition has powerfully fostered American lawlessness. A part of the heritage of hundreds of American communities from the Piedmont to the Pacific, vigilantism—like the American Revolution—has taught the lesson that in certain cases defiance of law pays. The typical vigilante took the law into his own hands sincerely (but paradoxically) in the interest of law and order. He desired social stability and got it. But was it purchased at too high a cost?

Yes, said the principled opponents of vigilantism, who hammered home a philosophy of antivigilantism that went as far back as the opposition to the original South Carolina movement of 1767-1769. From the very beginning, antivigilante theorists cogently argued that due process of law was a precious Anglo-American legacy, that true law and order meant observing the law's letter as well as its spirit, and, finally, that the only way to obtain real and lasting law and order was to pour all one's power and substance into making the regular system work.

One trenchant opponent of the San Francisco Vigilance Committee of 1856 noted that "if the same energy which prompted the formation of the Committee and organized the armed force that assaulted the jail had been directed to strengthen the regular course of justice as public opinion can do it, there would have been no need for the [vigilante] outbreak. . . . The precedent is bad, the law of passion cannot be trusted, and the slow process of reform in the administration of justice is more safe to rely on than the action of any revolutionary committee, no matter how great may be the apparent necessity," he continued. "Better to endure the evil of escape of criminals than to inaugurate a reign of terror which to-day may punish one guilty head, and tomorrow wreak its mistaken vengeance on many innocent lives," he concluded.

Aside from the danger of vigilante action extending to extremism, the critics of vigilantism were upset by its fundamentally subversive character. A southern Illinois opponent of the regulator movement in Pope, Johnson, and Massac counties, Richard S. Nelson, charged in 1847 that by attacking citizens and taking their property, the Regulators had violated "those great principles of civil liberty" upon which the Illinois state constitution was based. Nelson also turned the vigilante justification of popular sovereignty against them by noting that, in forcing elected county officials to leave the county or surrender their offices, the regulators had "made a direct attack upon the sovereignty of the people."[111] There is no doubt, however, that, for all the plausibility of Nelson's invocation of popular sovereignty against vigilantism, the appeal to popular sovereignty was made much more often by vigilantes than by their opponents.

Occasionally, vigilante opponents discussed what they thought were the sociological causes of the crime and turbulence that led to vigilantism. The Reverend William Anderson Scott was a courageous opponent of the powerful San Francisco vigilantes of 1856. In a sermon entitled "Education, and not Punishment, the True Remedy for the Wrong-Doings and Disorders of Society," Scott called for industrial education for the lower classes and for urban eleemosynary institutions as means of eradicating the root sources of crime. "You may depend upon it," he insisted, "the stream of blood will never be staid [sic] while men take the law into their own hands."[112]

Americans have for generations been ambiguous in their attitude to law. In one sense, Americans are a law-abiding people of exemplary character. But the many organized movements in our history that have openly flouted and ignored the law (revolutionary Whigs, Northern abolitionists, Southern filibusters, regulators, vigilantes, Ku Klux Klansmen, White Caps, lynch mobs, etc.) show that lawlessness has been rife. In 1837, the young Abraham Lincoln delivered an address on "The Perpetuation of Our Political Institutions" and found that the chief threat came from "the increasing disregard for law which pervades the country—the growing disposition to substitute the wild and furious passions in lieu of the sober judgment of courts, and the worse than savage mobs for the executive ministers of justice."[113]

The key to the apparent contradiction between our genuine lawfulness and the disregard for law emphasized by Lincoln lies in the selectivity with which Americans have approached the law. Going back to the colonial period and the patriotic resistance to the British mother country, "the Americans," observed James Truslow Adams, "had developed a marked tendency to obey only such laws as they chose to obey. . . . Laws which did not suit the people, or even certain classes, were disobeyed constantly with impunity."[114] Perhaps in the long run the most important result of vigilantism has been the subtle way in which it has persistently undermined our respect for law by its repeated theme that the law may be arbitrarily disregarded— that there are times when we may choose to obey the law or not.

NOTES

1. Many small vigilante movements undoubtedly left no traces; this seems to have been especially true in the old Northwest and old Southwest in the first 20 or 30 years of the nineteenth century. The 326 movements, presently known, are listed in Appendix 3 of my *Strain of Violence* (New York: Oxford University Press, 1975).

2. [Charles Hitchin], *The Regulator . . .* (London, 1718); Christopher Hibbert, *The Road to Tyburn . . .* (Cleveland, 1957).

3. Hubert Howe Bancroft, *Popular Tribunals* (San Francisco, 1887), Vol. I, pp. 2-6.

4. James G. Leyburn, *Frontier Folkways* (New Haven, 1935), p. 219.

5. There have indeed been urban as well as rural vigilante movements. The greatest of all American vigilante movements—the San Francisco vigilance committee of 1856—was urban. Vigilantism has been by no means restricted to the frontier, although most typically it has been a frontier phenomenon.

6. Richard Maxwell Brown, *The South Carolina Regulators* (Cambridge, Mass., 1963). See, also Ch. 3, *Strain of Violence*.

7. Aside from the South Carolina Regulators there was little vigilante activity in the original 13 states of the Atlantic seaboard. The North Carolina Regulators (1768-1771) did not constitute a vigilante movement, but rather embodied a violent agrarian protest against corrupt and galling local officials and indifferent provincial authorities.

8. The 96th meridian coincides, approximately, with both physiographic and state boundaries. Physiographically it roughly separates the humid prairies of the East from the semiarid Great Plains of the West. The states of Minnesota, Iowa, Missouri, Arkansas, and Louisiana fall into the province of Eastern vigilantism. The states of North and South Dakota, Nebraska, Kansas, and Oklahoma mainly fall into the area of Western vigilantism. In Texas the 96th meridian separates east Texas from central and west Texas, but for the sake of convenience all Texas vigilantism (along with that of the Dakotas, Nebraska, Kansas, and Oklahoma) has been included under the heading of Western vigilantism.

9. Lynn Glaser, *Counterfeiting in America* . . . (New York, 1968), Ch. 5. On the relationship between counterfeiting and the frontier money shortage, see Ruth A. Gallaher, "Money in Pioneer Iowa, 1838-1865," *Iowa Journal of History and Politics*, 31 (1934): 42-45. The use of counterfeit money for public land purchases is revealed in *Counties of Warren, Benton, Jasper and Newton, Indiana: Historical and Biographical* (Chicago, 1883), p. 458.

10. See, for example, Randall Parrish, *Historic Illinois* . . . (Chicago, 1906), pp. 405-406; Charles Edward Pancoast, *A Quaker Forty-Niner* . . . , ed. Anna P. Hannum (Philadelphia, 1930), pp. 103-104.

11. William Faux, *Memorable Days in America* . . . |1823| (*Early Western Travels*, ed. Reuben G. Thwaites, Vols. 11-12; Cleveland, 1905), Vol. 11, pp. 293-294; John L. McConnel, *Western Characters* (New York, 1853), pp. 171-175; William N. Blane, *An Excursion through the United States and Canada during the Years 1822-1823* (London, 1824), pp. 233-235; Robert M. Coates, *The Outlaw Years* . . . (New York, 1930).

12. James W. Bragg, "Captain Slick, Arbiter of Early Alabama Morals," *Alabama Review*, 11 (1958): 125-134; Jack K. Williams, "Crime and Punishment in Alabama, 1819-1840," ibid., 6 (1953): 14-30.

13. Williams, "Crime and Punishment in Alabama," p. 27; James E. Cutler, *Lynch-Law: An Investigation into the History of Lynching in the United States* (New York, 1905), p. 99; H.R. Howard, comp., *The History of Virgil A. Stewart* (New York, 1836); Edwin A. Mills, "The Mississippi Slave Insurrection Scare of 1835," *Journal of Negro History*, 42 (1957): 48-60; David Grimsted, "The Mississippi Slave Insurrection Panic, 1835" (unpublished paper, Southern Historical Association, Atlanta, 1973).

14. John E. Briggs, "Pioneer Gangsters," *Palimpsest* 21 (1940): 73-90; John C. Parish, "White Beans for Hanging," ibid., 1 (1920): 9-28; Harvey Reid, *Thomas Cox* (Iowa City, 1909), pp. 126, 154-155, 165-167; Jackson County Historical Society, *Annals of Jackson County, Iowa*, 2 (1906): 51-96.

15. C.L. Sonnichsen, *Ten Texas Feuds* (Albuquerque, 1957), Ch. 1; Lela R. Neill, "Episodes in the Early History of Shelby County" (M.A. thesis, Stephen F. Austin State College, 1950), pp. 77-153 and passim.

16. On the northern Illinois regulators, see Alice L. Brumbaugh, "The Regulator Movement in Illinois" (M.A. thesis, University of Illinois, 1927), pp. 3, 5-27, and William Cullen Bryant, *Letters of a Traveler* . . . (New York, 1850), pp. 55-68. Two of the most important sources on the southern Illinois regulators are Brumbaugh, "Regulator Movement," pp. 29-65, and James A. Rose, comp., Papers Relating to the Regulator and Flathead Trouble in Southern Illinois (bound typescript in Illinois State Historical Society, Springfield).

17. James H. Lay, *A Sketch of the History of Benton County, Missouri* (Hannibal, Mo., 1876), pp. 46-61. Pancoast, *Quaker Forty-Niner*, pp. 101-121. J.W. Vincent, "The 'Slicker War' and Its Consequences," *Missouri Historical Review*, 7 (1912-1913): 138-145.

18. *The Iowan*, 6 (1958): 4-11, 50-51. Jackson County Hist. Soc., *Annals*, 1 (1905): 29-34; *The History of Clinton County, Iowa* (Chicago, 1879), pp. 437ff.; Paul W. Black, "Lynchings in Iowa," *Iowa Journal of History and Politics*, 10 (1912): 151-209; Orville F. Graham, "The Vigilance Committees," *Palimpsest*, 6 (1925): 359-370.

19. M.H. Mott, *History of the Regulators of Northern Indiana* (Indianapolis, 1859); Weston A. Goodspeed and Charles Blanchard, eds., *Counties of Whitley and Noble, Indiana: Historical and Biographical* (Chicago, 1882), pp. 33-37, 63-73.

20. Among many sources, see Dorothy K. Gibson, "Social Life in San Antonio, 1855-1860" (M.A. thesis, University of Texas, 1937), pp. 122-131.

21. George A. Ketcham, "Municipal Police Reform: A Comparative Study of Law Enforcement in Cincinnati, Chicago, New Orleans, New York, and St. Louis, 1844-1877" (Ph.D. dissertation, University of Missouri, 1967), pp. 148-150.

22. Harry L. Griffin, "The Vigilance Committees of the Attakapas Country; or Early Louisiana Justice," Mississippi Valley Historical Association, *Proceedings,* 8 (1914-1915): 146-159; Alexander Barde, *History of the Committees of Vigilance in the Attakapas Country* [1861], trans. and ed., Henrietta G. Rogers (M.A. thesis, Louisiana State University, 1936).

23. An earlier important vigilante movement in San Francisco was that of 1851; see Mary Floyd Williams' *History of the San Francisco Committee of Vigilance of 1851: A Study of Social Control on the California Frontier in the Days of the Gold Rush* (Berkeley, 1921); George R. Stewart, *Committee of Vigilance: Revolution in San Francisco, 1851* (Boston, 1964); Bancroft, *Popular Tribunals,* Vol. 1, pp. 201-428.

24. *The History of Johnson County, Missouri* (Kansas City, 1881), Ch. 15; *History of Vernon County, Missouri* (St. Louis, 1887), pp. 348-349; *History of Greene County, Missouri* (St. Louis, 1883), pp. 497-501.

25. Lewis and Richard H. Collins, *History of Kentucky* (Louisville, 1924), Vol. 1, pp. 198-209; E. Merton Coulter, *The Civil War and Readjustment in Kentucky* (Chapel Hill, 1926), p. 359.

26. Wayne G. Broehl, *The Molly Maguires* (Cambridge, Mass., 1965), pp. 239-240, describes the Seymour, Indiana, vigilance committee of 1867-1868.

27. Ralph L. Peek, "Lawlessness and the Restoration of Order in Florida" (Ph.D. dissertation, University of Florida, 1964), pp. 91, 105-108, 111, 125-126, 149-150, 216-220.

28. See, especially, Bancroft, *Popular Tribunals,* Vol 1, pp. 441ff., and the California listing in Appendix 3 of *Strain of Violence.*

29. Thomas J. Dimsdale, *The Vigilantes of Montana* . . . (Virginia City, Mont., 1866); Nathaniel Pitt Langford, *Vigilante Days and Ways* (Boston, 1890); Hoffman Birney, *Vigilantes* (Philadelphia, 1929).

30. Granville Stuart, *Forty Years on the Frontier,* ed. Paul C. Phillips (Cleveland, 1925), Vol. 2, pp. 195-210; Michael A. Leeson, *History of Montana: 1739-1885* (Chicago, 1885), pp. 315-316.

31. Montana Territory Vigilance Committee, *Notice!* (broadside, Helena, Mont., Sept. 19, 1865). Leeson, *History of Montana,* pp. 303-316.

32. See Ch. 8, *Strain of Violence.*

33. Among many sources, see Jerome C. Smiley, *History of Denver* . . . (Denver, 1901), pp. 338-350.

34. Albuquerque *Republican Review,* Feb. 18, 1871. Santa Fe *Weekly New Mexican,* Nov. 13, 22, 1879; Victor Westphal, "History of Albuquerque: 1870-1880" (M.A. thesis, University of New Mexico, 1947), pp. 64-65; Bernice A. Rebord, "A Social History of Albuquerque: 1880-1885" (M.A. thesis, University of New Mexico, 1947), p. 34.

35. Miguel A. Otero, *My Life on the Frontier* (New York and Albuquerque, 1935-1939), Vol. 1, pp. 181-206; Vol. 2, pp. 2-3; Santa Fe *Daily New Mexican,* Mar. 12, 25-26, Apr. 13, 1881.

36. Erna B. Fergusson, *Murder & Mystery in New Mexico* (Albuquerque, 1948), pp. 15-32; Chester D. Potter, "Reminiscences of the Socorro Vigilantes," ed. Paige W. Christiansen, *New Mexico Historical Review,* 40 (1965): 23-54.

37. On the Butler County vigilantes, see A.T. Andreas, *History of the State of Kansas* . . . (Chicago, 1883), pp. 1431-1432, and Correspondence of Governor J.M. Harvey, File on County Affairs, 1869-1872 (MSS in Archives Department of Kansas State Historical Society, Topeka). Materials on Kansas vigilantism are also to be found in Nyle H. Miller and Joseph W. Snell, *Why the West Was Wild* . . . (Topeka, 1963), and Genevieve Yost, "History of Lynching in Kansas," *Kansas Historical Quarterly,* 2 (1933): 182-219. See, also, Robert R. Dykstra, *The Cattle Towns* (New York, 1968).

38. On the Sidney vigilantes, see Grant L. Shumway, ed., *History of Western Nebraska* . . . (Lincoln, 1921), Vol 2, pp. 152-157, and Bryan T. Parker, "Extra-Legal Law

Enforcement on the Nebraska Frontier" (M.A. thesis, University of Nebraska, 1931), pp. 53-54, 62-63. On the Niobrara region vigilantes, see Parker, "Extra-Legal Law Enforcement," pp. 63-65.

39. J.H. Triggs, *History of Cheyenne and Northern Wyoming* . . . (Omaha, 1876), pp. 14, 17-18, 21, 23-27; J.H. Triggs, *History and Directory of Laramie City* . . . (Laramie, 1875), pp. 3-15. The classic (but far from flawless) contemporary account of the Johnson County War by the antiregulator Asa Shinn Mercer was *The Banditti of the Plains* . . . (Cheyenne, 1894). Outstanding is Helena H. Smith's *The War on Powder River* (New York, 1966). General treatments of Western vigilantism are found in Bancroft's *Popular Tribunals*, Vol. 1, pp. 593-743; Wayne Gard's *Frontier Justice* (Norman, 1949), Ch. 14; Carl Coke Rister's "Outlaws and Vigilantes of the Southern Plains," *Mississippi Valley Historical Review*, 19 (1933): 537ff.

40. The state-by-state detail in regard to Eastern and Western vigilantism is summarized in Table 5-2 in Richard Maxwell Brown, "The American Vigilante Tradition," p. 164, in Hugh Davis Graham and Ted Robert Gurr, eds., *The History of Violence in America* (New York, 1969). The decade-by-decade chronological statistics of vigilante movements and the number of their victims appear in Tables 5-3a, 5-3b, and 5-6d in ibid., pp. 165 and 175.

41. The instant vigilantism toll of 79 men was gained from an analysis of Bancroft's narrative in *Popular Tribunals*, Vol. 1, pp. 515-576.

42. The distinction between "colonized" and "cumulative" new communities was formulated by Page Smith in *As a City upon the Hill: The Town in American History* (New York, 1966), pp. 17-36.

43. The following sketch of the three-level American community structure is based upon my own research and recent studies of American society. Among the latter are Jackson Turner Main's *The Social Structure of Revolutionary America* (Princeton, 1965) and, for the nineteenth century, Stephan Thernstrom's *Poverty and Progress: Social Mobility in a Nineteenth Century City* (Cambridge, Mass., 1964); Ray A. Billington's *America's Frontier Heritage* (New York, 1966), Ch. 5; Merle Curti's *The Making of an American Community* (Stanford, 1959), pp. 56-63, 78, 107-111ff., 126, 417ff., 448.

44. On the marginal "lower people" of the South (where they have been labeled "poor whites," "crackers," and so on), see Brown, *South Carolina Regulators*, pp. 27-29, and Shields McIlwaine, *The Southern Poor White from Lubberland to Tobacco Road* (Norman, 1939), a literary study, For lower people in the North, see Bernard De Voto, *Mark Twain's America* (Boston, 1932), pp. 54-58, and George F. Parker, *Iowa Pioneer Foundations* (Iowa City, 1940), Vol. 2, pp. 37-48.

45. Kai Erikson, *Wayward Puritans: A Study in the Sociology of Deviance* (New York, 1966), Ch. 1.

46. J. Milton Yinger, "Contraculture and Subculture," *American Sociological Review*, 25 (1960): 629, holds that a contraculture occurs "wherever the normative system of a group contains as a primary element, a theme of conflict with the values of the total society." See also David M. Downes, *The Delinquent Solution: A Study in Subcultural Theory* (New York, 1966), pp. 10-11.

47. See, for example, De Voto, *Mark Twain's America*, pp. 58-62; Parker, *Iowa Pioneer Foundations*, Vol. 2, pp. 37-48, 247-265.

48. See Howard, *History of Virgil A. Stewart*; Mills, "Mississippi Slave Insurrection Scare"; Grimsted, "Mississippi Slave Insurrection Panic," on the alleged Murrell plot. On the Flatheads, see Brumbaugh, "Regulator Movement," pp. 28-65; Rose, Papers Relating to Regulator and Flathead Trouble; Charles Neely, *Tales and Songs of Southern Illinois* (Menasha, Wis., 1938), pp. 7, 35, 41; Norman W. Caldwell, "Shawneetown: A Chapter in the Indian History of Illinois," *Journal of the Illinois State Historical Society*, 32 (1939): 199-200.

49. See note 101, below, for sources.

50. See note 91, below, for sources.

51. Brown, *South Carolina Regulators*, pp. 27-37.

52. Langford, *Vigilante Days*, Vol. 1, pp. 320-324. Howard A. Johnson, "Pioneer Law and Justice in Montana," Chicago Corral of the Westerners, *Brand Book*, 5 (1948-1949): 10.

53. About frontier Masons in Texas, the late Walter Prescot Webb wrote that "they believed in the law and aided in preserving order, often in ways best known to themselves." James D. Carter, *Masonry in Texas ... to 1846* (Waco, 1955), p. xviii.

54. Thomas and Augustus Wildman, Letters, 1858-1865 (MSS in Western Collection, Beinecke Rare Book and Manuscript Library, Yale University, New Haven).

55. *Cowley County Censor* (Winfield, Kan.), Jan. 7, 1871.

56. David Donald, ed., "The Autobiography of James Hall, Western Literary Pioneer," *Ohio State Archaeological and Historical Quarterly*, 56 (1947): 297-298.

57. Mott, *Regulators of Northern Indiana*, pp. 6-7 and passim.

58. Dimsdale, *Vigilantes of Montana*, p. 116.

59. Fred M. Mazulla, "Undue Process of Law—Here and There," *Brand Book of the Denver Westerners*, 20 (1964): 273-279. Dr. Osborne became governor of Wyoming in 1893.

60. Membership figures are cumulated in Tables 5-4 and 5-5 in Brown, "American Vigilante Tradition," p. 172.

61. The source for the lynch-mob total of 4,730 is Jessie P. Guzman et al., eds., *1952 Negro Year Book: A Review of Events Affecting Negro Life* (New York, 1952), p. 277. The grand total of 5,459 represents some double counting of victims, but this is more than offset, undoubtedly, by unknown (and thus uncounted) victims. Like the grand total, the total of documented vigilante victims (729) understates the actual undocumented total, which may be as high as 1,000. For the excess of annual lynchings over annual legal executions, 1883-1898, see Cutler, *Lynch-Law*, Chart 1, opposite p. 162.

62. The statistics on vigilante killings in this and preceding paragraphs are cumulated in Tables 5-6a through 5-6d in Brown, "American Vigilante Tradition," pp. 174-175.

63. Allen Johnson, Dumas Malone et al., eds., *Dictionary of American Biography* (New York, 1928-1958), Vol. 4, pp. 295-296; A.B. Scherer, *"The Lion of the Vigilantes": William T. Coleman and the Life of Old San Francisco* (Indianapolis, 1939). On Sanders: *Dictionary of American Biography*, Vol. 16, pp. 336-337.

64. See, for example, Anthony S. Nicolosi, "The Rise and Fall of the New Jersey Vigilant Societies," *New Jersey History*, 86 (1968): 29-32.

65. "Uses and Abuses of Lynch Law." *American Whig Review*, May 1850, p. 461. Pancoast, *Quaker Forty-Niner*, pp. 103-104. Brumbaugh, "Regulator Movement," pp. 9-11.

66. Dwyn M. Mounger, "Lynching in Mississippi, 1830-1930" (M.A. thesis, Mississippi State University, 1961), p. 9.

67. Brumbaugh, "Regulator Movement," pp. 10-11.

68. James Stuart, *Three Years in North America* (Edinburgh, 1833), Vol. 2, pp. 212-213; Williams, "Crime and Punishment in Alabama," p. 26.

69. Smiley, *History of Denver*, p. 349. (Emphasis mine.)

70. "The Vigilance Committee: Richmond during the War of 1812," *Virginia Magazine of History and Biography*, 7 (1899-1900): 225-241.

71. Harris G. Warren, "Pensacola and the Filibusters 1816-1817." *Louisiana Historical Quarterly*, 21 (1938): 816.

72. See, for example, Documents relating to the Committee of Vigilance and Safety of Nacogdoches, Texas, Jan. 3, 1835 to Dec. 5, 1937 (transcripts in University of Texas Archives, File Box B 15/40).

73. *Hardesty's Historical and Geographical Encyclopedia ... of Meigs County, Ohio* (Chicago, 1883), pp. 273-275.

74. Wilbur H. Siebert, *The Underground Railroad from Slavery to Freedom* (New York, 1898), pp. 71ff., 326ff., 436-439. See, also, Larry Gara, *The Liberty Line: The Legend of the Underground Railroad* (Lexington, 1961), pp. 99, 104-109.

75. John Hope Franklin, *The Militant South* (Cambridge, Mass., 1956), pp. 87-90; Gara, *Liberty Line*, pp. 157-158.

76. *National Police Gazette*, Sept. 17, 1845, p. 5.

77. Pierce County, Washington Territory, Vigilance Committee, Draft of Compact, June 1, 1856 (MS in Western Collection, Beinecke Rare Book and Manuscript Library, Yale University, New Haven).

78. Griffin, "Vigilance Committees of Attakapas," pp. 153-155.

79. Dimsdale, *Vigilantes of Montana*, p. 107.

80. *History of Johnson County*, pp. 372-373.

81. Thomas Ford, *A History of Illinois from Its Commencement as a State in 1818 to 1847* [1854], ed. Milo M. Quaife (Chicago, 1945-1946), Vol. 1, pp. 10-11.

82. Griffin, "Vigilance Committees of Attakapas," pp. 153-155.

83. Barde, *History of the Committees*, pp. 26-27.

84. Mott, *Regulators of Northern Indiana*, pp. 15-18.

85. Alfred J. Mokler, *History of Natrona County, Wyoming 1888-1922* . . . (Chicago, 1923).

86. *History of Johnson County*, pp. 372-373.

87. Mott, *Regulators of Northern Indiana*, p. 17.

88. *Denver Tribune*, Dec. 30, 1879, cited in John W. Cook, *Hands Up* . . . (Denver, 1897), p. 103.

89. Otero, *My Life*, Vol. 2, p. 2-3.

90. Pamphlet No. 342, Document No. 37 (typescript, State Historical Society of Colorado, Denver), pp. 118-119.

91. Brumbaugh, "Regulator Movement," pp. 3, 5-27. Bryant, *Letters of a Traveller*, pp. 55-68.

92. For example, the Turk family (Slickers) vs. the Jones family (anti-Slickers) in southwest Missouri. Lay, *History of Benton County*, pp. 46-61.

93. For example, in the southwest Missouri Slicker conflict the Slickers were mostly Whigs, and the anti-Slickers were mostly Democrats. Pancoast, *Quaker Forty-Niner*, p. 104. In the southern Illinois Regulator-Flathead struggle, the factor of local political rivalry was important. Parker B. Pillow, Elijah Smith, and Charles A. Shelby, Regulators and political "outs," were in conflict with a Flathead "in" faction led by Sheriff John W. Read. Report of Governor Augustus C. French, Jan. 11, 1847, and *Sangamo Journal*, Jan. 28, 1847—both in Rose, Papers Relating to Regulator and Flathead Trouble. See, also, Brumbaugh, "Regulator Movement," pp. 66, 69. Political factionalism also contributed to the Regulator-Moderator strife in Shelby County of east Texas where a political "in" faction of old pre-Texas Revolution settlers (Moderators) was opposed by a political "out" faction of post-revolutionary newcomers (Regulators). Neill, "Shelby County," pp. 75-77.

94. For example, in later years San Francisco's 1856 vigilance committee leader, William T. Coleman, criticized Charles Doane (the grand marshal of the vigilantes) for running for sheriff on the People's party ticket. Coleman felt that vigilante leaders, such as Doane, should not run for office. William T. Coleman, Vigilance Committee, 1856 (MS, ca. 1880, in Bancroft Library, University of California, Berkeley), p. 139.

95. In New Mexico's Lincoln County War of 1878-1879, the McSween-Tunstall-Brewer mercantile faction organized (unsuccessfully) as Regulators against the dominant Murphy-Dolan mercantile faction. William A. Keleher, *Violence in Lincoln County: 1869-1881* (Albuquerque, 1957), pp. 152-154. Maurice G. Fulton, *History of the Lincoln County War*, ed. Robert N. Mullin (Tucson, 1968), pp. 137-142ff.

96. In addition to the east Texas regulators (see below), other movements that fell into sadism and extremism were, most notably, the southern Illinois regulators and the southwest Missouri Slickers. There were other movements of this stripe; even in well-controlled movements, the element of sadism and extremism often crept in in a minor way. The problem was inherent in vigilantism.

97. The east Texas regulators are discussed later. For the southern Illinois regulators see *passim* and note 16, this chapter, and for the southwest Missouri slickers see *passim* and note 17, this chapter.

98. See San Francisco *Daily Town Talk*, Aug. 8-9, 1856. Political factionalism was a factor in the 1856 San Francisco vigilante troubles. By and large, the vigilante leaders were composed of old Whigs and Know-Nothings who were in the process of becoming Republicans. The political "ins" who controlled San Francisco and whom the vigilantes attacked were the Irish-Catholic Democrats led by David C. Broderick. The "Law and Order" antivigilante faction tended to draw its strength from the southern-oriented wing of the California Democratic party. Unlike most San Francisco vigilante leaders, William T. Coleman was a Democrat, but as a Kentuckian he maintained a life-long devotion to the principles of Henry Clay and, hence, had much in common with the many vigilante leaders who were also oriented to Henry Clay nationalism as Whigs, Know-Nothings, or Republicans.

99. Brown, *South Carolina Regulators*, Ch. 6. Down to about the 1850s opponents of regulators and vigilantes were often called "moderators."

100. For a nineteenth-century paradigm of vigilante movements gone bad, see "Uses and Abuses of Lynch Law," pp. 462-463.

101. Sonnichsen, *Ten Texas Feuds*, Ch. 1; Neill, "Shelby County," pp. 77-153 and *passim.*

102. Robert B. David, *Malcolm Campbell, Sheriff* (Casper, Wyo., 1932), pp. 18-21.

103. On the anti-horse thief movement in the Northeast and in New Jersey, see Nicolosi, "New Jersey Vigilant Societies," pp. 29-53.

104. On the National Horse Thief Detective Association of Indiana and neighboring states, see J.D. Thomas, "History and Origin of the National Horse Thief Detective Association" in *Journal of the National Horse Thief Detective Association*, 50th annual session (Union City, Ind., 1910), pp. 19-20, and Ted Gronert, *Sugar Creek Saga . . .* (Crawfordsville, Ind., 1958), pp. 140, 256-257.

105. On the Anti-Horse Thief Association of the trans-Mississippi Midwest and Southwest, see Hugh C. Gresham, *The Story of Major David McKee, Founder of the Anti-Horse Thief Association* (Cheney, Kan., 1937), and, especially, the Association's newspaper, the *A.H.T.A. Weekly News* (with variant titles) for 1902-1943, on file in the Kansas State Historical Society, Topeka. A recent study is that of Patrick B. Nolan, "Vigilantes on the Middle Border: A Study of Self-Appointed Law Enforcement in the States of the Upper Mississippi from 1840 to 1880" (Ph.D. dissertation, University of Minnesota, 1971). The A.H.T.A.'s membership was largest in Kansas with the Indian Territory (now eastern Oklahoma) also heavily represented. There were also substantial memberships in Oklahoma Territory, Missouri, and Arkansas. A number of other states had smaller enrollments. Late in the history of the organization, long after it had passed its peak, Illinois had a large membership.

106. *The Vigilantes* (New York, 1918), pp. 5, 8-14. This pamphlet was probably written and compiled by the Vigilantes' managing editor, Charles J. Rosebault. The Vigilantes were aided by leading American capitalists who served as "underwriters" or associate members; among them were George F. Baker, Jr., Cleveland H. Dodge, Coleman Dupont, Jacob H. Schiff, Vincent Astor, Elbert H. Gary, Simon Guggenheim, Dwight Morrow, and George W. Perkins.

107. On the first Ku Klux Klan: Allen W. Trelease, *White Terror: The Ku Klux Klan Conspiracy and Southern Reconstruction* (New York, 1971). On the second Klan: David M. Chalmers, *Hooded Americanism* (Garden City, N.Y., 1965); Charles C. Alexander, *The Ku Klux Klan in the Southwest* (Lexington, 1965); and *Crusade for Conformity: The Ku Klux Klan in Texas, 1920-1930* (Houston, 1962); Kenneth T. Jackson, *The Ku Klux Klan in the City: 1915-1930* (New York, 1967).

108. In one sense the mass lynching was a classic vigilante response to a crime problem (the Italians had apparently been members of the Mafia and involved in the killing of the New Orleans chief of police), but the element of strong anti-Italian ethnic prejudice was crucial to the episode and typical of neovigilantism. See Joseph L. Albini, *The American Mafia: Genesis of a Legend* (New York, 1971).

109. See William Preston, *Aliens and Dissenters* (Cambridge, Mass., 1963), which contains examples of neovigilante attacks on workers, immigrants, and radicals. See, also, John W. Caughey, ed., *Their Majesties the Mob* (Chicago, 1960), pp. 1-25, 100-205.

110. Brown, "American Vigilante Tradition," pp. 201-208; Harold A. Nelson, "The Defenders: A Case Study of an Informal Police Organization," *Social Problems*, 15 (1967-1968): 127-147; Gary T. Marx and Dane Archer, "Citizen Involvement in the Law Enforcement Process: The Case of Community Police Patrols," *American Behavioral Scientist*, 15 (1971-1972): 52-72. Contemporary vigilantism worldwide is treated by H. Jon Rosenbaum and Peter C. Sederberg in "Vigilantism: An Analysis of Establishment Violence," *Comparative Politics*, 6 (1973-1974): 541-570, and in a forthcoming interdisciplinary collection edited by H. Jon Rosenbaum and Peter C. Sederberg, *Vigilante Politics: Pro-Establishment Violence in the Contemporary World*, to which I have contributed "The History of Vigilantism in America." I have also plumbed, much more briefly, contemporary American violence and vigilantism in historical context in "The History of Extralegal Violence in Support of Community Values" (a publication of my testimony before the National Commission on the Causes and Prevention of Violence in 1968), pp. 86-95, in Thomas Rose, ed., *Violence in America: A Historical and Contemporary Reader* (New York, 1970), and "An Escape from Paranoia." *American West*, Jan. 1970, p. 48.

111. Editorial in the New York *National Democrat* quoted in Bancroft, *Popular Tribunals*, Vol. 2, pp. 554-555; *Illinois State Register* (Springfield), Jan. 1, 1847 (transcript in Rose, Papers Relating to Regulator and Flathead Trouble).

112. William Anderson Scott, *A Discourse for the Times Delivered in Calvary Church, July 27, 1856* (San Francisco, 1856). On Scott: Clifford M. Drury, *William Anderson Scott: "No Ordinary Man"* (Glendale, Calif., 1967).

113. John G. Nicolay and John Hay, eds., *Complete Works of Abraham Lincoln* (New York, 1905), Vol. 1, pp. 35-50. In his address Lincoln dwelled on the ubiquity of "mob law" in the 1930s and specifically cited the Mississippi vigilante actions in 1835 in Madison and Hinds counties and Vicksburg as well as a case of lynch law in St. Louis.

114. James Truslow Adams, "Our Lawless Heritage," *Atlantic Monthly*, 42 (1928): 736. In recent years a prime example of arbitrary disregard of the law has been the idealistic tactic of civil disobedience. See Abe Fortas, *Concerning Dissent and Civil Disobedience* (New York, 1968), Chs. 4-5. See, also, *Strain of Violence*, Ch. 6, dealing with "lawless lawfulness."

Chapter 7
American Labor Violence
Its Causes, Character, and Outcome

PHILIP TAFT and PHILIP ROSS

The United States has had the bloodiest and most violent labor history of any industrial nation in the world. Labor violence was not confined to certain industries, geographic areas, or specific groups in the labor force, although it has been more frequent in some industries than in others. There have been few sections and scarcely any industries in which violence has not erupted at some time, and even more serious confrontations have on occasion followed. Native and foreign workers, whites and blacks have at times sought to prevent strike replacements from taking their jobs, and at other times have themselves been the object of attack. With few exceptions, labor violence in the United States arose in specific situations, usually during a labor dispute. The precipitating causes have been attempts by pickets and sympathizers to prevent a plant on strike from being reopened with strikebreakers,[1] or attempts of company guards, police, or even by National Guardsmen to prevent such interference. At different times employers and workers have played the roles of aggressors and victims. Union violence was directed at limited objectives; the prevention of the

AUTHORS' NOTE: *The late Philip Taft was a member of the economics department at Brown University from 1937 to 1968. After his retirement he held visiting positions at a number of universities, including the University of Chicago and the University of Texas. During his long career he served on wage boards and state government commissions and was a prolific author. Among his many books were* History of Labor in the United States, 1896-1932, *with Selig Perlman (Macmillan, 1935);* Organized Labor in American History *(Harper and Row, 1964);* Labor Politics American Style *(Harvard University Press, 1968); two volumes on the American Federation of Labor; and* Rights of Union Members and the Government *(Greenwood Press, 1975). He died in 1976. A posthumous study,* Labor in Alabama, *is forthcoming from Greenwood Press.*

Philip Ross has been on leave since 1976 from the New York State School of Industrial and Labor Relations at Cornell University, serving as Industrial Commissioner for the State of New York. He also has served as a consultant to a number of federal agencies, including the National Labor Relations Board and the Departments of Commerce and Transportation. His publications include The Government as a Source of Union Power *(Brown University Press, 1965) and* The Labor Law in Action: An Analysis of the Administrative Process *(National Labor Relations Board, 1966).*

The research reported in this chapter was supported by a grant from the Ford Foundation. This is an abridged version, prepared by the editors, of a longer chapter, which appeared in the first edition of Violence in America.

entrance of strikebreakers or raw materials to a struck plant, or interference with finished products leaving the premises. While the number of seriously injured and killed was high in some of the more serious encounters, labor violence rarely spilled over to other segments of the community.

Strikers, no matter how violent they might be, would virtually always seek to win the sympathy of the community to their side, and therefore attacks or even incitements against those not connected or aiding the employer would be carefully avoided. Such conduct was especially common in the organized strikes, those which were called and directed by a labor organization. Strike violence can therefore be differentiated from violence that is stimulated by general discontent and a feeling of injustice. Moreover, the unions were normally anxious to avoid violence and limit its impact because, simultaneously with the strike, the organization might also be operating under a contract and negotiating with other employers in an attempt to solve differences and promote common interests. Unions seek and must have at least the grudging cooperation of employers. No major labor organization in American history ever advocated violence as a policy, even though the labor organizations recognized that it might be a fact of industrial life.

Trade unions from the beginning of their existence stressed their desire for peaceful relations with employers. However, minority groups within the labor movement or without direct attachment to it advocated the use of violence against established institutions and also against leaders in government, industry, and society. The union leader might hope to avoid violence, but recognized that in the stress of a labor dispute it might be beyond the ability of the union to prevent clashes of varying seriousness. They might erupt spontaneously without plan or purpose in response to an incident on the picket line or provocation. Those who saw in violence a creative force regarded the problem differently; they had no objectives of immediate gain; they were not concerned with public opinion. They were revolutionaries for whom the radical transformation of the economic and social system was the only and all-consuming passion.

The most virulent form of industrial violence occurred in situations in which efforts were made to destroy a functioning union or to deny to a union recognition.

THE INFLUENCE OF IDEOLOGY

There is only a solitary example in American labor history of the advocacy of violence as a method of political and economic change. In the 1880s a branch of anarchism emerged that claimed a connection with organized and unorganized labor and advocated individual terror and revolution by force. The principle of "propaganda by the deed," first promulgated at the anarchist congress in Berne, Switzerland, in 1876, was based upon the assumption that peaceful appeals were inadequate to rouse the masses. This view could be interpreted as a call upon workers to create their own independent institutions, such as trade unions, mutual aid societies, and producer and consumer cooperatives. However, almost from the beginning this doctrine was interpreted to mean engaging in insurrectionary and putschist activities, and in terror directed against the individual.[2]

Social revolutionary views were not widely accepted in the United States during the 1880s, but the difference between the moderates and the militants, which divided the European movement, was also in evidence here. As early as 1875, education and defense organizations (*Lehr und Wehr Vereine*) were organized in Chicago, and they soon spread to other cities. Members met regularly and drilled with arms. It was the issue of using arms which was largely responsible for the split in the Socialist Labor Party in 1880, and the more militant social revolutionaries gradually approached the anarchist position on politics and violence.

An attempt to unite the scattered groups of social revolutionaries was made by the Chicago conference of 1881 and was unsuccessful. The meeting adopted a resolution recognizing "the armed organizations of workingmen who stand ready with the gun to resist encroachment upon their rights, and recommend the formation of like organizations in all States."[3] This was only a prelude to the convention held in Pittsburgh in 1883, dominated by Johann Most, a German-born revolutionary who had served prison terms in a number of countries. Most had come to the United States in December 1882, and transferred his journal, *Freiheit*, to New York. Through the spoken and written word he became the leader of the anarchists in the United States and the leading figure of the predominantly immigrant revolutionaries.

In typically socialist fashion, the congress explained the causes of the evils afflicting modern society. Since all institutions are aligned against him, the worker has a right to arm himself for self-defense and offense. The congress noted that no ruling class ever surrendered its privileges and urged organization for planning and carrying out rebellion. Capitalists will not leave the field except by force. These ideas had some influence among a limited number of workers, largely immigrants. Most himself did not favor trade unions, regarding them as compromising organizations, and even refused to support the eight-hour movement in the 1880s. Anarchists, however, were active in union organizations and some regarded them as the ideal type of workmen's societies. Albert Parsons, August Spies, and Samuel Fielden, all of them defendants in the Haymarket Trial, had close connections with a part of the Chicago labor movement.

The anarchists were not all of the same view, but many of them including Most not only advocated the formation of armed societies, but published materials on the making of explosives. *Revolutionary War Science (Revolutionäre Kriegswissenschaft)* is a treatise on the use of arms and the making of what we would call "Molotov cocktails." There is little evidence that these suggestions were ever taken seriously by many workers, and the anarchist movement's greatest influence in the United States was in the 1880s. Even at the height of their influence the anarchists had few supporters. Whatever violence took place in the United States cannot be traced to the thinking of Most of any of his workers. In fact, even then it was widely believed that the armed societies were engaging in playing a game, and that they represented little danger to the community. It is quite certain that violence in labor disputes was seldom inspired by the doctrine of "propaganda by the deed," whose self-defeating nature convinced many of its exponents of its fallacy. In this regard, experience was a more potent force than moral considerations and governments reacted to these terrorist methods with savage repression. One of the few incidents of anarchist violence in the United States was an attack by Alexander Berkman on Henry Frick during the Homestead strike. The boomerang effect of this action was to transform the hated Frick into a folk hero when, though wounded, he fought off his attacker. The assassination of William McKinley by the anarchist Czolgosz is another example. Most did not repudiate the tactic, but laid down conditions for its use that were critical of Berkman's conduct.

THE PRACTICE OF VIOLENCE IN THE 1870s AND 1880s

Repudiation of theories did not eliminate the practice of violence from the American labor scene. The pervasiveness of violence in American labor disputes appears paradoxical because the great majority of American workers have never supported views or ideologies that justified the use of force as a means of reform or basic social change, nor have American workers normally engaged in the kind of political activity that calls for demonstrations or for physical confrontation with opponents. Through most of its history, organized labor in the United States has depended largely upon economic organizations—unions—for advancement through collective bargaining, and upon pressure politics and cooperation with the old parties for achieving its political aims. Yet we are continually confronted with examples of violent confrontations between labor and management. Does industrial violence reveal a common characteristic with basic causes and persistent patterns of behavior, or is it a series of incidents linked only by violence? Labor violence has appeared under many conditions, and only an examination of the events themselves can reveal their nature and meaning.

The Strikes and Riots of 1877

The unexpected strikes and riots which swept over the United States in 1877 with almost cyclonic force began in Martinsburg, W. Va., after the Baltimore Ohio Railroad had announced its second wage cut in a relatively short period. The men left their trains and drove back those who sought to replace them. Governor Henry W. Mathews called upon President Rutherford B. Hayes for federal assistance, and the latter, despite his reluctance, directed troops to be sent.[4] Federal troops had a calming influence on the rioters in Martinsburg, but two days later, on July 20, Governor John Lee Carroll of Maryland informed the President that an assemblage of rioters "has taken possession of the Baltimore Ohio Railroad depot" in Baltimore, had set fire to it, and "driven off the firemen who attempted to extinguish the same, and it is impossible to disperse the rioters." Governor Carroll also asked for federal aid.[5]

Order was restored immediately by federal tropps, but Governor Carroll then appealed for help in putting down a disturbance at Cumberland. Requests also were made for troops to be sent to Philadelphia, where the authorities feared outbreak of rioting. The most serious trouble spot, however, was Pittsburgh, where the attempt to introduce "double headers" was the cause of one of the more serious disturbances of the year. The changes might have been accepted if they had not followed cuts in pay and loss of jobs—both caused by declining business. Open resistance began, and when a company of militia sought to quell the disturbance it was forced to retreat before the mob and take refuge in a railroad roundhouse where it was under constant attack. A citizens posse and federal troops restored order.

Railroads in Pennsylvania, New York, and New Jersey suffered almost complete disruption. The Erie, New York Central, and Delaware Lackawanna Western, and the Canada Southern operating in Ohio, Pennsylvania, and New York States were struck on July 24, idling about 100,000 workers. Federal and state troops were used to suppress rioting, and sometimes the state police were themselves the cause of violence. After 13 persons were killed and 43 wounded in a clash between militia and citizens in Reading, Pa., for example, a coroner's jury blamed the troops for an unjustified assault upon peaceful citizens.

In Ohio the railroads were blocked, but the governor's plea for federal aid was not met. In the end the state authorities, assisted by the National Guard and the citizens' committees succeeded in quelling the disturbances at Zanesville, Columbus, Toledo, and Cleveland, but it was nearly the middle of August before order had been completely restored. The strikes and rioting moved westward and Indiana and Illinois were affected. In the face of a threatened strike, the governor of Indiana refused to appeal for federal troops and the latters' duties were limited to protecting federal property and enforcing orders of the federal courts. Work on the railroads entering Chicago was suspended, and rioting broke out in the city. On the 26th of July a bloody skirmish between the police, National Guardsmen, and a mob resulted in the killing of 19 and the wounding of more than 100 persons. It started with resistance of a mob to the attempts of the police to clear the streets, and it ended when the police and militia charged the crowd.

The riots of 1887 mirrored deeply felt grievances generated by several years of unemployment and wage cuts. All the rioting cannot be attributed to striking workmen and their sympathizers. Railroads, urban transportation systems, and trucking are among the industries that are almost completely exposed to attack during a labor dispute. They operate in the open, and it is difficult to prevent attacks by strikers and sympathizers upon working personnel and property. The strikes and riots of 1877 were, however, a violent protest against deteriorating conditions and the suffering and misery endured during a great depression. The widespread and ferocious reaction has no parallel in our history, but there are others of lesser magnitude that were important in shaping labor-management relations.[6]

There is no evidence that the riots of 1877 brought reforms in the handling of railroad disputes, which was the initial cause of the disturbances. They did demonstrate that the United States would not escape the trials and tribulations affecting other industrial nations, and that more attention must be given to the problems that industrial societies tend to generate. It was, however, more than a decade later that the first hesitant step was taken by the federal government to provide a method of adjusting labor disputes, a method that was never tried. Not until the Erdman Act of 1898 did the federal government provide a usable procedure for settling labor-management disputes on the railroads. An added provision guaranteeing railroad workers protection of the right to organize was declared unconstitutional by the U.S. Supreme Court when challenged by a carrier, *Adair v. United States*, 1908.

1885-1886: The Southwestern Railroad Strike and Others

The railroads were the scene of another extensive strike in 1885-1886, although it was comparatively a mild contest. The southwestern strike was a two-stage affair. It began in March 1885 in the shops of the Missouri Pacific Railroad, when a demand by an assembly of the Knights of Labor for the restoration of a wage cut of the previous year was not met. Intervention of the governors of Kansas and Missouri ended the walkout. The strike had the support of citizens along the right of way, and no violence took place during the walkout. In the next year the Knights of Labor had another encounter with Jay Gould, who controlled the southwestern roads, and another settlement was reached. However, the parties were not happy with the settlement, and in January of 1886 another strike was called by assemblies of the Knights of Labor. This time the company rejected compromises, and the sheriff of the area around Parsons, Kan., reported, on March 27, 1886, that efforts to move trains "were forcibly resisted. . . Many agents had been 'killed' and disabled, and a serious wreck had occurred."[7] Four hundred troops were ordered to Parsons by the governor. In Fort Worth, Tex., a train proceeding under guard encountered a switch open and men hiding beside the track. An exchange of fire resulted in the wounding of three policemen and a striker.[8] Troops were ordered to the scene of the trouble. On April 9, 1886, the sheriff of St. Clair County, Ill., where East St. Louis is located, reported: "There is shooting going on . . . between a force of deputies and the mob." Six men and a woman were killed, and it was later established that the deputies had fired rifle shots into a crowd and then escaped to St. Louis. This incident started as a result of the determination of the Louisville and Nashville Railroad to operate its trains out of East St. Louis, Ill. It fortified its determination by the employment of a large force of guards following the forcible efforts of strikers and sympathizers to close down railroad operations at this point. On April 9 an attempt to move a coal train encountered opposition from armed men. A posse directed the mob to disperse, and attempted to arrest a man.

> The squad of deputies was then furiously assailed with stones, as is alleged by the deputies, several of them being struck. One of the deputies raised his rifle, fired, and a man was seen to fall. The showers of stones and pistol-shots from all directions began to rain upon the officers, who returned the fire with their guns and pistols, with deadly effect, into the crowd. The firing was kept up until the crossing was clear, the people fleeing panic-stricken and rushing into houses in every direction for protection and safety. . . .
>
> Bloodshed was succeeded by incendiarism.[9]

About 40 railroad cars were burned. At the request of the sheriff, a large force of state troops was sent to East St. Louis, and they succeeded in restoring order.

Despite railroad violence, strikes in 1886 were generally peaceful. The U.S. Commissioner of Labor reported that in the year 1,572 strikes took place involving 610,000 workers. Some employers, including powerful ones, were likely to refuse to deal with a labor organization representing their employees. Workers were not then any more than now inclined to give up their unions without a struggle, and employers who refused to deal with the organizations of their workmen began to rely on local and state governments for assistance during labor disputes. Although the great majority of strikes were peaceful, whether they succeeded or failed to obtain their objectives, the possibility of violence tended to be smaller in contests in which union recognition was not an issue. Under such circumstances the employer was likely to regard the strike as a temporary rupture of relations between himself and his labor force. When recognition was in question, the employer might seek to demonstrate that the strikers could be replaced and that their cause was lost. For the workers, the issue was not only the demands for which they struck, but the possibility that they would be replaced by newly hired workmen. Employers were therefore anxious to have the support of additional police and state troops if possible. An obliging sheriff might, as in the Chicago stockyards strike of 1886, plead for the sending of troops, who upon their arrival would find the community peaceful and threats of disorder nonexistent.

This use of troops was not always unquestioned. General C.H. Grosvenor on March 19, 1875, submitted a resolution requesting the governor to inform the House, "what, if any, public reason or necessity existed for the calling out, arming and sending to Nelsonville, the Ohio Independent Militia, on the 11 and 12 of June 1874." It was called out during a strike of coal miners. "The statute of Ohio provides for the organization of the independent militia, and the Governor is ex-officio commander-in-chief; but he has no power to call out the militia until an exigency has arisen which requires the presence of troops." Grosvenor denied the existence of riot or disorder:

> Was there insurrection or not? The Governor says there was not. Was there invasion? Nobody pretends it. Was there any resistance to the enforcement of law? There was not. If there was no riot or insurrection, if there was no invasion, if there was no resistance to civil authority, then the Governor of this State has no jurisdiction to call upon these companies, and his order was in violation of law, and without the authority of law.[10]

LABOR VIOLENCE IN THE 1890s

Not all violence was inspired by employers. While employer obduracy might lead to rejection of recognition, such conduct was in itself legally permissible. Had workers passively accepted such decisions, the level of violence in American labor disputes would have been reduced. Workers were, however, unwilling to watch their jobs forfeited to a local or imported strikebreakers. Employers could shut down their plants and attempt "to starve" their employees out of the union. Such a policy might have worked, but employers cognizant of their rights and costs frequently refused to follow such a self-denying tactic. As a consequence violence initiated from the labor side was also prevalent. In the 1890s violent outbreaks occurred in the North, South, and West, in small communities and metropolitan cities, testifying to the common attitudes of Americans in every part of the United States. While workers might react against the denial of what they regarded as their rights, the outcome of their violent behavior seldom changed the course of events. Serious violence erupted in several major strikes of the 1890s, the question of union recognition being a factor in all of them. As will be noted below, the Homestead strike, which was a defensive action in behalf of an existing and recognized union, and the Pullman strike, which was called in behalf of other workers denied recognition, also failed. Violence in the Coeur d'Alene copper area eventually led to the destruction of the Western Federation of Miners in that district. Violence was effective in the Illinois coalfields only because the community and the governor were hostile to the efforts of two coal producers to evade the terms of a contract acceptable to the great majority of producers in Illinois.

Although steel workers in Pennsylvania and copper miners in Idaho had different ethnic origins and worked under dissimilar conditions, each reacted with equal ferocity to the attempts of their employers to undermine their unions.

Homestead

In Homestead, Pa., the domineering head of the Carnegie Steel Co., Henry C. Frick, used a difference over wages and a contract expiration date as an excuse for breaking with the union. When the union called a strike against the demands of Frick, the latter was ready to bring in a bargeload of Pinkerton operatives to guard his plant from the harassment of union pickets. Frick's plan became known, and the guards were met by several hundred steelworkers. In the battle to land the guards from the barges, two Pinkertons and two strikers were killed. Another attempt to land also ended in failure. Eventually the Pinkertons were forced to surrender and some were severely mauled by strikers and sympathizers. At the plea of the sheriff, the governor ordered 7,000 troops to Homestead. Leaders were arrested, but juries refused to convict.

While the violence was temporarily successful in holding off the landing attempted on July 4, it was unable to change the outcome of the contest between the union and Frick. Under the cover of the protection given to him by the National Guard, he was able to open his mills. Furnaces were lit on July 15, and the company announced that applications for work would be received until July 21. The following day a large force of nonunion men entered the plant. Ultimately the union was defeated, and according to a leading student of the steel industry of another generation, John A. Fitch, the union never recovered from its defeat in Homestead. The steel workers were fearful of Frick's attempt to break the union. The hiring of several hundred Pinkertons and their stealthy efforts to land convinced the strikers that a serious movement to destroy their organization was on the way, and the use of the hated Pinkertons sharpened their anger. An investigation by the U.S. Senate noted: "Every man who testified, including the proprietors of the detective agencies, admitted that the workmen are strongly prejudiced against the so-called Pinkertons and their presence at a strike serves to unduly inflame the passions of the strikers."[11]

Coeur d'Alene

Organization of the metal miners in the Coeur d'Alene region in Idaho was followed by the mine operators' establishment of an association after the miner's union had won a wage increase. A lockout was called several months after the miner's success, and every mine in the area was closed down. An offer of lower wages was rejected. The strikers were not passive. Strikebreakers were urged to leave or were forcibly expelled; court injunctions against violence were ignored. In July 1892 the situation deteriorated. A union miner was killed by guards, and it brought an attack by armed miners upon the barracks housing guards employed by the Frisco mill. It was dynamited, and one employee was killed and 20 wounded. An attack on the Gem mill followed and although five strikers were killed and more wounded, the mill surrendered. The guards gave up their weapons and were ordered out of the county. Armed with Winchesters, the armed strikers marched on Wardner, where they forced the Bunker Hill mine to discharge its nonunion contingent.

At the request of the governor, who sent the entire National Guard, federal troops were sent to restore order. The commanding general ordered all union men arrested and lodged in a hastily built stockade or bullpen. The commander of the state militia removed local officials sympathetic to the strikers and replaced them with others favorable to his orders. Trains were searched and suspects removed. Active union men were ordered dismissed from their jobs. The district was treated like a military zone, and companies were prohibited from employing union men. About 30 men were charged with conspiracy, and four were convicted, but subsequently released by the U.S. Supreme Court. Nevertheless, the miners were able to win recognition from all but he largest of the mining companies, which set the stage for a more spectacular encounter seven years later.[12]

The Pullman Strike

Railroad strikes have been among the more violent types of labor dispute. Normally, railroad workers are not more aggressive than other workers. However, railroads cover large open areas and their operations are always open to the rock thrower or the militant picket who may take it upon himself to discourage strikebreaking. A sympathy strike by the newly organized American Railway Union with the workers in the Pullman shops led to a widespread suspension of railroad service in 1894. What stands out in this bitter clash is the sympathy that the losing struggle generated among thousands of railroad workers. The refusal of the Pullman Co. to discuss the restoration of a wage cut with its employees was interpreted as an example of corporate arrogance. Like 1877, 1894 was a depression year, and many workers were without a job or income.

The strike started in May, and the American Railway Union, meeting in convention the following month, sought to bring about a settlement of the differences. When the American Railway Union imposed its boycott upon Pullman equipment, its action was challenged by the General Manager's Association, made up of the executives of the 24 railroads entering Chicago. Special guards were engaged, federal marshals were appointed to keep the trains moving, and if an employee refused to handle Pullman equipment he was discharged. Attempts to operate with strikebeakers led to fearful resistance. Rioting was widespread, and at the request of the railroads and advice of Attorney General Richard Olney, federal troops were sent to Chicago, over the protests of Governor John B. Altgeld. Every road west of Chicago felt the impact of the strike. Clashes between strikers and strikebreakers brought out federal or state troops in Nebraska, Iowa, Colorado, Oklahoma, and California. Although the loss of life and property was not as serious as during the disturbances of 1877, the Pullman strike affected a wider area. An estimated 34 people were killed and undetermined millions of dollars were lost in the rioting connected with this conflict.

The immediate cause of the violence was the determination of the General Manager's Association to defeat the sympathy strike. The responsibility for violence rests largely on the behavior of George Pullman, whose attitude was similar to those held by many industrialists. He was unwilling to allow his workers the slightest influence upon the decisions of the company which greatly affected their welfare. Like other firms, the Pullman Co. was suffering losses of business as a result of the depression, and it may not have been able to meet the demands of its employees. It could, however, have conferred in good faith and explained its position instead of following a policy of peremptory rejection and dismissal of those who had asked for a reconsideration of a wage cut. Pullman's attitude, shared by many industrialists, tells us something about the cause of violence in labor disputes. Arrogant, intransigent, unwilling to meet with their employees, owners depended upon their own or the government's power to suppress protest. Behind the powerful shield they could ignore the periodic outbreaks by their labor force; they knew that these seldom were strong enough to gain victory.

Coal Miners' Strikes

Three separate incidents involving coal-mining violence illustrate the fragility of peaceful methods in this industry. In two of the three cases, the use of force did not end in failure, but there were exceptional circumstances in each. Much depended upon the attitude of the authorities and the sympathies of the public. Free miners in Tennessee were able to control changes in the system of working convict labor in the coal mines. Leasing of convicts for work in the mines was begun in 1865, and the competition of these men, who had no influence on their working conditions or pay, was a threat to the free miners. Other grievances also played a role. Payment of wages by scrip, absence of checkweighmen at the mines, and the use of yellow dog contracts were sources of protest. When the free miners went on strike in 1891, the companies introduced convict labor as replacements. On July 21, 1891, hundreds of armed miners demanded that convict workers leave the mining camps at Briceville and Coal Creek. State troops were ordered into the area, but the governor agreed to the discontinuance of convict labor in the mines.[13]

Violence was also a factor in the settling of the coal miners strikes in Alabama in 1894. A month after the strike started, miners in Johns, Adger, and Sumpter were ordered to leave the company houses. The company "strategy in breaking the strike was to import Negro labor to work in the mines. During the strike's first week, 100 Negroes were brought from Kansas."[14] On May 7, 1894, a band of armed men invaded the Price mine at Horse Creek "blowing up boilers, burning supplies and destroying property." On July 16, in a gunfight at Slope, five miles from Birmingham, three black strikebreakers and a deputy were killed. Troops were ordered into the area by the governor and remained there until August 14, when the strike was settled.[15]

In 1897, the United Mine Workers of America tried again to establish itself as the bargaining agent for the bituminous coal miners. Despite the UMW low fortunes and virtual lack of resources, a national strike was called on July 4. Although unsuccessful in West Virginia, the union was able to establish bargaining rights in Indiana, Illinois, Ohio, and western Pennsylvania. The central competitive field agreement was developed, which aimed at a wage scale which would allow operators from all of the above regions to operate on the basis of rough equality. Not all operators were willing to go along with the arrangement.

Most serious was the outcome of the attempt of the Chicago-Virden Coal Co., Virden, Ill., to carry on operations with strikebreakers. On October 12, 1898, the company attempted to land a carload of strikebreakers. A report of the company's intention had reached the strikers, and many of them lined the sides of the tracks carrying loaded rifles. However, the train did not attempt to discharge its cargo at the railroad station, but moved ahead to a stockade. Shots had been exchanged between the miners and the occupants of the car, and when the car reached the stockade, guards firing rifles rushed out. In the exchange of fire 14 men, eight of them strikers, were killed and a number of others wounded. Governor John B. Tanner denounced the company and sent National Guardsmen to Virden. They restored order, and prevented a group of strikebreakers from landing in the city the day after the riot.[16] A similar but nonviolent sequence involving the Pana Coal Co. had occurred the previous year. The two recalcitrant companies eventually signed the central competitive agreement, but without the support of the governor the outcome might have been different.

These coal strikes were exceptional in that the use of force did not fatally injure the union. As the full chronicle of labor disputes demonstrates, violence was rarely a successful union weapon, despite the fact that it was ordinarily a defensive measure employed against guards or strikebreakers who were attempting to destroy the effectiveness of a strike.

The importance of public opinion in supporting labor's side of a dispute has seldom won for unions the help or neutrality of public authorities in a context of labor violence. In the strike against convict labor, the governor had and exercised his power to eliminate the cause of the strike. In the Illinois coal strike, the coal companies had broken ranks with other employers by refusing the terms of a negotiated agreement. Moreover, the violence was directed against armed outsiders who were brought into the community to replace local miners. But as the next section shows, in general, violence in labor disputes was likely to lead to repression by public force.

A completely different outcome followed the second act of the Coeur d'Alene story. In 1892, the union signed all of the companies except the Bunker Hill and Sullivan, which over the years remained a holdout. In the spring of 1899, Edward Boyce, president of the Western Federation of Miners, visited the area and began a campaign to bring that company into line.

In April 1899, a Northern Pacific train was seized at Burke, Idaho. At Gem, where the engineer was compelled to stop, dynamite was loaded on the train. Others joined the train at Wallace, and the engineer was then ordered to switch his train onto the tracks of the Oregon Northern Railroad and proceed to Wardner. Masked men got off the train, proceeded to the Bunker Hill and Sullivan mill and, after dispersing the guards, destroyed the mill, inflicting damages of about a quarter of a million dollars. Governor Frank Steunenberg, on learning of these events, requested federal aid, the Idaho National Guard being on duty in the Philippines.

Federal troops were dispatched and the state auditor, Bartlet Sinclair, was directed by the governor to take command. He jailed every member and sympathizer of the union that could be found. All were, in his opinion, morally guilty of the dynamiting. Makeshift jails were used until the prisoners had constructed a stockade where they were lodged. Local officials sympathetic to the miners were removed, and others friendly to the company replaced them. Sinclair was determined to root out the Western Federation of Miners. A permit system was instituted under which applicants for work were required to repudiate the union by agreeing that it was a criminal conspiracy. The secretary of the Burke local union was tried for conspiracy to murder and was convicted and sentenced to prison. Ten others were convicted of interfering with the U.S. mail. Most of the miners were kept in the bullpen until November 1899, but the military occupation of the district continued until April 1901, when a new state administration ended it. The miners' leaders imprisoned by the state were also pardoned, but the union never regained its vigor in the Coeur d'Alene area. The violence against the company boomeranged; it did not serve the union's interest. The lesson that can be derived from the episodes in the Coeur d'Alene area is that violence is a risky tactic for those who need public tolerance if not public support in behalf of their demands, no matter how just or righteous their cause.[17]

THE DECADE BETWEEN 1900 AND 1910

The first decade of the twentieth century witnessed expansion of union membership, which increased opportunities for conflicts with employers. As in previous periods, strikes were on occasion marked by violence. The prospect of violence was heightened by rising employer resistance to union objectives. The signs of this new employer response consisted of the founding of many employer associations, the beginning of the open-shop campaign, and the use of citizen alliances as assault troops on union picket lines.

Pennsylvania Anthracite Coalfields

Violence in Illinois and in the Coeur d'Alene was carried out primarily by native or Americanized workers. Through the 1870s the Pennsylvania anthracite area was dominated by English-speaking workers: Americans, English, Scotch, Irish, and Welsh were the principal sources of labor.[18] By 1900, large numbers of eastern and southern Europeans had come into the area, and the English-speaking ratio in the population had dropped from 94 percent in 1880 to 52 percent in 1900.[19] With the destruction of the Knights of Labor and the Amalgamated Association of Anthracite Miners, no counterweight to the companies' power existed. Absence of checkweighmen, the existence of the company store, and the complete domination of the area by the coal companies were unrestrained evils. Nothing better demonstrates the abuse of power than an attack in 1897 upon miners who had struck against the high prices at the company store and were peacefully marching from Hazleton to Latimer. The sheriff and a force of deputies met the marchers on the road and ordered them to disperse. When they failed to obey instantly, the sheriff ordered his deputies to fire on the unresisting paraders. Eighteen were killed and 40 seriously wounded, and many of the killed and wounded were shot in the back. The sheriff and several deputies were tried for murder, but were acquitted.[20]

In 1900, the United Mine Workers of America was able to challenge successfully the anthracite coal operators. Although the union had only about 7 percent of the miners in the area in the organization, it called a strike in September of 1900. There was only one serious clash between strikers and guards, which led to the death of a strikebreaker. Immediately 2,400 troops were sent into the area by the governor. The strike was settled on terms not unfavorable to the union, and the single violent encounter played no role in the outcome.[21] Peace in the anthracite mines was brought about by political pressure but also by the skillful leadership of John Mitchell, the president of the United Mine Workers. Mitchell had always deplored the use of violent methods and constantly pleaded for negotiations as a peaceful means of settling labor disputes. He further recognized the importance of retaining public sentiment on the strikers' side, and he was determined to prevent the use of widespread prejudice against the southern European immigrant worker to defeat them. This strike was, however, only a skirmish; the anthracite workers were to face a more serious trial two years later.

When negotiations between the operators and the union broke down in April 1902, it appeared that the strike would be more violent than the preceding one. A more aggressive spirit was evident among the men, and the companies appeared to be equally determined to scotch further progress of the union. Hundreds of commissions for iron and coal police to guard mining property were issued, and the companies decided to recruit strikebreakers and operate during the strike. In a summary of violence at the end of September, the New York *Tribune* claimed that in the disturbances arising out of the strike, 14 had been killed, 16 shot from ambush, 42 others severely injured, and 67 aggravated assaults had occurred; 1 house and 4 bridges were dynamited, 16 houses, 10 buildings, 3 washrooms around mines, and 3 stockades were burned; 6 trains were wrecked and there were 9 attempted wrecks, 7 trains attacked, and students in 14 schools went on strike against teachers whose fathers or brothers were working during the strike.[22]

Despite the extent of violence, it is doubtful whether it had any decisive effect on the outcome of the strike. In insisting that the strikers were prevented from working because of union intimidation, the operators claimed that the mines would be opened and fully manned if adequate protection were granted. The governor of Pennsylvania sent the entire National Guard of the state into the anthracite area, but their presence did not increase the output of coal. This demonstration that the tieup was not the result of coercion but of the determination of the miners to bargain through a union ended the impasse.

What made the union victory possible was the conciliatory attitude of Mitchell. Firm on essentials, he was ready to compromise on details. Careful not to antagonize public opinion, he emphasized the justice of the miners' cause, the right of men to bargain collectively over the terms of employment. Mitchell and his subordinates always pleaded for peaceful behavior, and while the advice was often honored in the breach, neither he nor any other leaders could be attacked for advocating destruction of property or assaults upon persons which, had they done so, would have given employers a powerful argument with which to sway public sentiment.

The Colorado Labor War

The use of force to settle differences was more common in the Western mining camps at the turn of the century than in Eastern manufacturing or even mining communities. In the West there was a tendency for violence to erupt on a larger scale. The tendency for each side to resort to force to settle differences led to a gradual escalation of the level of violence, which reached a point where the Western Federation of Miners faced the combined power of the Mine Operator's Association, aided by the state government and a private employer's group, the militant Citizen's Alliance. It was an unequal struggle in which men were killed and maimed; union miners imprisoned in the bullpen; union halls, newspapers, and cooperatives sacked; and many strikers deported. There is no episode in American labor history in which violence was as systematically used by employers as in the Colorado labor war of 1903 and 1904. The miners fought back with a ferocity born of desperation, but their use of rifles and dynamite did not prevent their utter defeat.

The war opened in 1903. It started with a peaceful withdrawal from work in the Colorado City mill of the United States Reduction Refining Co., after demands for a wage increase and union recognition had been rejected. The strike quickly spread to the other mines and mills in the area. Although no reports of lawlessness had been made, the governor sent in several companies of militia at the request of the sheriff. Although settlement was made, with the assistance of the governor, the manager of the United States Reduction Refining Co. refused to accept its terms. District No. 1 of the Western Federation of Miners on August 3, 1903, called strikes in mines shipping ore to the refineries of the United States Reduction Refining Co. This was denounced by the Colorado Mine Owners Association as an "arbitrary and unjustifiable action" which "mars the annals of organized labor, and we denounce it as an outrage against both the employer and the employee."[23]

The association announced that it was determined to operate without the cooperation of the federation and, in response to a plea from the operators, state troops were sent to Teller County, where Cripple Creek was located, on September 3, 1904. At the same time a strike for shorter hours was going on in Telluride, and troops were sent into that area, although no reports of trouble were published. Active union men were arrested through September, lodged in a bullpen for several days, and then released. The militia officers took umbrage at an editorial in the *Victor Record*, and arrested its staff, who were held for 24 hours in the bullpen before they were released.[24]

The first significant violence attributed to the strikers was the blowing up of the Vindicator mine in Teller County, in which two were killed. Martial law was declared in Teller County and the military informed the editor of the *Victor Herald* that editorial comments would be censored. When the union secured a writ of habeas corpus directing the military to bring an arrested miner before a state court, the governor suspended the writ "on the ground of military necessity."[25] Deportations of strikers were begun, and temporarily halted by an order from a state court. The military obeyed this court order. When 16 men were killed by the fall of a cage at the

Independence mine at Victor, bitter feeling increased. Violation of safety rules was blamed by the union for the accident.

By February 2, 1904, conditions in Teller County were sufficiently close to normal for the governor to withdraw troops. The mining companies then put into effect a "rustling-card" system that required applicants for employment in mines and smelters to obtain a card authorizing them to seek work. Each time a person changed jobs he had to procure a new card, which gave the mining companies an opportunity to blacklist all who did not meet their standards. The strike dragged on, and on June 6, 1904, while nonunion miners were returning from work, a charge of dynamite exploded under the Independence railraod station, killing 13 and seriously wounding 16. After the explosion, the Citizen's Alliance went into action. County and city officials sympathetic to the union were forced to resign, and a roundup of union members and sympathizers started. They were placed in a bullpen, and many of them were later deported to Kansas and New Mexico. The commander of the militia, General Sherman Bell, set up a commission to decide the fate of the prisoners held in the bullpen. A person's attitude towards the Western Federation of Miners determined whether he would be released or deported. On July 26, 1904, the governor ended military rule and left the field to the Citizen's Alliance. During its tenure, since June 8, the commission examined 1,569 men, recommending 238 for deportation and 42 for trial in the criminal courts; the rest were released from the bullpen.[26] Gradually, normal conditions were restored, but the union continued its nominal strike until December 1907, when it was called off.[27]

Simultaneously with the Cripple Creek strike, the union was directing another in the San Juan area of Telluride County, Colo. The same scenario was played here. Troops were sent into the area soon after the calling of the strike in September 1903. Censorship, deportations, and arrests accompanied the troops. The union fought a losing battle, and the Telluride Miner's Association announced it would never employ members of the Western Federation of Miners. When the resistance of the strikers was broken, the governor withdrew the state troops, but by that time the Citizen's Alliance could itself handle deportations and assaults.[28]

The effect of this organized violence upon the miner's organization is summarized by Sheriff Edward Bell of Teller County, and a leader in the campaign against that union. After the assaults and deportations had broken the back of the resistance, the sheriff announced:

> The danger is all past. There are less than 100 of the radical miners left in the Cripple Creek district. The rest have been deported, or have left the district because they were unable to gain employment. They can never get work again. The mine owners have adopted a card system by which no miner can gain admittance to a mine unless he has a card showing that he does not belong to a union.[29]

The miners were no easy victims. They resisted as well as they could, but they faced the overwhelming power of the mine operators aided by the business community, the governor, and the courts.[30]

A Collection of Urban Strikes

The Chicago teamsters' strike of 1905 was one of the more violent of the decade. Although it lacked the dramatic confrontations typical of the Western mining camps, the strikers' constant clashes with strikebreakers, guards, and police resulted in a number of deaths, hundreds of injuries, and the arrest of 1,108 persons. The teamsters' strike started on April 6, 1905, as a sympathetic walkout in defense of a small union of clothing cutters. It lasted 106 days and involved 4,500 out of the more than 38,000 union teamsters in Chicago. During the strike, 1,763 special policemen were added to the Chicago police department. The sheriff of Cook County employed 913 extra deputies, and an additional 4,157 unpaid deputies were recruited for strike duty, largely from the business community. The police department reported that 14 deaths and 31 injuries were caused by firearms; there were 202 other casualties. The police brought 930 cases against strikers, and 178 against nonunion men who had been arrested. Constant demands were made upon the governor for state troops, and the President of the United States was asked to send federal aid. Both requests were rejected. Strikebreakers were brought from other cities, and professional strike guards and police rode the wagons delivering goods to boycotted firms. The entire business community was united against the union, and hundreds of thousands of dollars were raised to fight the walkout. In the end, the union was forced to surrender without attaining any of its demands. It was a serious loss which had repercussions within the teamster's union as well as the Chicago labor movement.[31]

Many disputes in this period took place which failed to attract national attention because of the fewer numbers of employees involved and the smaller economic importance of the firms. The significance of these minor strikes lies not only in their demonstration of the ease with which violence arose in the industrial arena, but in the dispersion of violence in virtually every part of the country. No region or industry can claim a monopoly on violent confrontation, although labor disputes in some industries were more susceptible to the exercise of force.

Strikes in municipal transportation services were often accompanied by riots and general disorder.[32] Attempts to replace strikers by operating with new employees could easily lead to rioting, because surface cars often passed through neighborhoods which strongly supported the strikers. Disturbances on open streets could also be joined by sympathizers and even uninvolved seekers of excitement. Two of the more violent transit strikes in this period occurred in Philadelphia and Columbus, Ohio.

The issue in dispute on the Philadelphia transit lines was the continued existence of the local of the Amalgamated Association of Street Railway Employees, with which the Philadelphia Rapid Transit Co. had an agreement. The union had been recognized in 1909 as a result of pressure by local politicians who wished to avoid a controversy in the midst of a municipal campaign for public offices. However, the company encouraged the establishing of the Keystone Carmen, a company-dominated union, and at the same time discharged 173 members of the regular labor organization. When no bargaining agreement was reached, the union called a strike, and the company countered by importing strikebreakers and guards under the direction of James Farley, a notorious street fighter and supplier of armed guards during strikes. In the first days of the strike, the police and private guards were helpless against mobs who roamed the streets wrecking cars and smashing windows;

the company claimed 298 cars had been destroyed, and more than 2,000 windows broken. Much of the violence during the Philadelphia dispute was caused by traveling pickets and their sympathizers. The guards were, however, inured to violence and engaged in it themselves. In Philadelphia on March 8 "a band of 'strikebreakers,' men furnished by private detective agencies . . . for temporary use, took a car down the crowded thoroughfare at high speed shooting into the crowds on the sidewalk and wounding several persons."[33] Eventually the strike was settled with the abandonment of the legitimate union and the estalishment of a company-dominated organization.[34]

A strike in Columbus, Ohio, in 1910 was also caused by the unwillingness of a rapid transit company to deal with a union established in that year. Intervention by the state board of arbitration resulted in a temporary agreement, but it was ended by a union charge of bad faith after the company discharged a number of union men. Many members of the police force refused to ride on the streetcars and protect strikebreakers. The "first few days of the strike was attended with riots from the downtown streets in which men were pulled from cars and beaten, cars stoned, trolley ropes and wires cut."[35] The company imported 450 trained guards and strikebreakers from Cleveland, and the strike "settled down to guerrilla warfare. Cars have been stoned and dynamited in all parts of the city; attempts have been made to blow up car houses where non-union members are quartered and the public intimidated from riding by systematic picketing and boycotting."[36] At the request of the local authorities, troops were sent into the city on July 28, 1910. "While enroute to Columbus, a sympathizer of the lawless conditions in Columbus deliberately wrecked the first section of the Fourth Infantry train."[37] A number of men were injured, but the violence subsided after the arrival of troops, and service was resumed.

Two clothing industry strikes in this period surrounded by considerable violence ended with the recognition of the unions involved. In New York City the International Ladies' Garment Workers' Union was able to win collective bargaining rights in the New York market after two strikes, each in a different branch of the industry. On November 22, 1909, almost 20,000 workers in the dress and waist industry, the large majority of whom were young women, went out on strike. The walkout lasted until February 15, 1910. The settlement of the strike was followed by the cloak-maker's walkout, involving more than 50,000 workers. In this strike both sides engaged in considerable violence. The employers engaged dozens of private guards, and the union countered by hiring its own strong-arm men. This strike was successful and marked the beginning of permanent collective bargaining in the ladies' garment industry in New York. Pressures to reach an agreement came from sources outside the industry, including the Jewish community, which found the internecine struggle between Jewish employers and employees highly distasteful.

A much more violent encounter was the strike of the men's clothing workers in Chicago during the same year. Beginning on September 22, 1910, as a protest against a cut in rates paid for the stitching of seams, the strike spread and eventually involved virtually all of the 40,000 workers employed in the Chicago market. The United Garment Workers of America, the union with jurisdiction in the trade, took over direction of the walkout, but the industry was unwilling to deal with a labor organization. Police were active in breaking picket lines, and considerable violence ensued. On December 4, the first picket was killed, and another eleven days later. A private detective escorting strikebreakers was killed in the first days of January, and before the strike ended four others were killed. The strike lasted 133 days, during which 874 arrests were made, mostly of union pickets or their sympathizers. It succeeded in gaining union recognition from Hart, Schaffner & Marx, one of the leading firms in the Chicago market, recognition which was later expanded to the entire industry. The Hart, Schaffner & Marx decision to accept collective bargaining in large part arose from one partner's strong personal distaste of the violence generated in this dispute.[38]

Private and State Troops

In Pennsylvania, every railroad in 1865 and every colliery, iron furnace, or rolling mill in 1866 was granted by statute liberty to employ as many policemen as it saw fit, from such persons as would obey its behests, and they were clothed with all authority of Pennsylvania, were paid such wages and armed with such weapons as the corporation determined—usually revolvers, sometimes Winchester rifles or both—and they were commissioned by the governor.[39]

Appointments under Pennsylvania's Coal and Iron Police Act were made without difficulty. Corporations would file requests, and as a rule no investigation of the need for such appointments or restrictions on the behavior of those selected were made. In 1871 a fee of $1 was charged for each commission issued. From then until 1931, when the coal and iron police were abolished, the mining companies of Pennsylvania were able to utilize police under their own control in labor disputes. "There was no investigation, no regulation, no supervision, no responsiblity undertaken by the State, which had literally created 'islands' of police power which was free to float as the employers saw fit."[40] The Pennsylvania system was not duplicated elsewhere. In its stead, in other states sheriffs and other local officials were authorized to appoint persons paid by the employer for strike and other private police duty.

On numerous occasions mercenaries were guilty of serious assaults upon the person and rights of strikers, and their provocative behavior was frequently an incitement to violence and disorder. Their presence, when added to the special deputies and company policemen and guards, increased substantially the possibility of sanguinary confrontations in strike areas.[41] Furthermore, the availability of private police figured in many events which have been ignored in American labor history. These would include the expulsion of organizers from a county, the forceful denial to union organizers of the opportunity to speak in company towns, and the physical coercion of individual employees because of their union affiliation or sympathies.

As we have seen, outbreaks of labor violence frequently required the intervention of state troops, whose activities in restoring order usually resulted in defeating the strike. This lesson was not lost to some employers, who, with the connivance of local public officials, secured military aid in situations where violence was absent or insignificant. During the general strike of silk workers in Paterson, N.J., in 1902, it was claimed that the mills faced an attack by a mob. At the request of the sheriff, troops were sent to the city on June 19. They found no disorder, and left after nine days.[42]

A more flagrant instance of misrepresentation took place in the Goldfield, Nev., dispute between the Industrial Workers of the World (IWW) and the craft unions. Trouble started when the IWW announced that members of the carpenter's union would have to join the IWW by March 7 "or be thrown off the job and run out of town. The carpenters did not submit their applications, but did carry guns to work on the morning of March 7. The IWW in the face of this armed opposition was to call off all the helpers from the jobs where A.F. of L. men were employed."[43] Tension increased, and at the request of the governor, President Theodore Roosevelt sent federal troops to Goldfield. The President also appointed a commission to investigate the disturbance. It said:

> The action of the mine operators warrants the belief that they had determined upon a reduction in wages and the refusal of employment to members of the Western Federation of Miners, but that they feared to take this course of action unless they had the protection of Federal troops and that they accordingly laid a plan to secure such troops and then put their program into effect.[44] The commission found no basis for the statement that "there was a complete collapse of civil authority here."[45]

The same course of events took place in two other widely separate cases. In a strike at the National Fireproofing plant at Raritan, N.J., troops were sent during a strike in November 1908. Although no violent incident or threats had been made, the sheriff asked the governor to send troops. His request was met, but they stayed only a few days. It may be that the sheriff feared that violence would follow, since the strikers were mostly Poles, Hungarians, and other southern Europeans.[46] At almost the same time, state troops were summoned to a tunnel job in McCloud, Calif. The sheriff had informed the governor that strikers had taken over the "powder house, undoubtedly for use as bombs or like service." The sheriff claimed the strikers threatened to kill anyone who went to work. Troops were sent and they helped the sheriff arrest the leaders of the strike. When this was accomplished, the troops left.[47]

Campaigns of Violence by Unions

Despite explicit repudiation of force as an accepted tactic, a number of unions pursued systematic campaigns against opponents. These campaigns were directed against workers who refused to join a given labor organization, against employers, or both. One such campaign was carried on by the Western Federation of Miners against mine managers, company agents, and public officials. Harry Orchard, a member of the federation, confessed to the commission of many crimes, including the murder of Governor Frank Steunenberg of Idaho on December 30, 1905, at the alleged orders of the chief union officers.

The outstanding example of a campaign of force is the one conducted by the International Association of Bridge Structural Iron Workers in the first decade of the century against some employers. When the National Erectors' Association decided in 1906 that it would no longer continue its agreement with the union, the latter turned to terror and dynamite. In the first few years of the open-shop fight, about 100 nonunion ironworkers and company guards were assaulted, three guards being killed. Between 1906 and 1911, about 100 structures were damaged or destroyed by charges of explosives.[48] Luke Grant, who studied this episode for the Commission of Industrial Relations, concluded "that the dynamite campaign was ineffective as far as it was directed against the National Erectors' Association and that it weakened the influence of the organization with some independent employers." Others believed that the campaign kept the small contractors in line.[49] Moreover, Grant was convinced that the dynamiting campaign did the union a great deal of harm. "It stirred the public mind as few labor wars have done."[50] The "main reason for the resort to dynamite is found in the uncompromising attitude of the open-shop employers. The American Bridge Co. offered to compromise in the early stages of the fight and the union representatives rejected the terms of the compromise." After that the attitude of the employers was unyielding. Every effort on the union side to bring about a conference, after it realized the mistake that had been made, proved unavailing.

> Without a conference, no settlement of the strike was possible. For the union it meant either unconditional surrender or a fight to the finish. There was no middle course open while the employers refused to confer. . . . When the hopelessness of the situation became apparent to the union officials, resort was made to the destruction of property. Diplomacy was out of the question, so dynamite was tried. It proved to be a colossal blunder, as was the rejection of the peace terms offered in the beginning of the fight.[51]

INDUSTRIAL VIOLENCE 1911-1916

These six years rank among the most violent in American history, except for the Civil War. Although the origins of violent encounters were not different from those in the past, they frequently attained a virulence seldom equaled in industrial warfare in any nation. This was as true of many small disputes as it was of the major confrontations in Michigan copper and the West Virginia and Colorado coalfields.

The Illinois Central Shopmen's Strike

This strike differed from others in which serious violence took place in that union recognition was not the cause of the conflict. Single crafts had been recognized by this carrier for a number of years, but the carrier refused to negotiate a common contract with the system federation, a central body of several crafts. Following the establishment of the Railway Employees Department, the Illinois Central Railroad was requested, in June 1911, to deal jointly instead of singly with the Machinists', Steam Fitters', Railway Clerks', Blacksmiths', Boilermakers', and Sheet Metal Workers' Unions. The carrier refused, and a strike was called on the entire line of the Illinois Central. The railroad decided to replace the strikers. Violence was reported all along the right of way of the carrier. In Mississippi, one of the more important areas served by the Illinois Central, violence erupted at a number of points. When a train carrying strikebreakers arrived at McComb on October 3, 1911, it was met by about 250 armed men who opened fire on the new arrivals. Ten men were killed, cars were burned, and strikebreakers were afterward removed from the strike zone by militia called in by the governor. Demonstrations against those working were also carried on. On January 17, 1912, five black laborers employed as helpers at McComb were fired upon while returning from work; three were killed, the others wounded. Strikebreakers were temporarily escorted out of the strike zone.[52] The shops at Water Valley, Miss., were attacked and the governor ordered troops to that community on October 6, 1911. Serious violence was reported in New Orleans and a company guard was killed at Athens, Tex., and a guard and strikebreaker at the Illinois Central roundhouse at Houston, Tex. In Clinton, Ill., Carl Person, a leader of the strike, killed a strikebreaker who had brutally assaulted him. Person was tried for murder and acquitted on the ground of self-defense.[53] Despite the strike's formal continuance until June 28, 1915, it was in effect lost within several months after its start.

IWW Strikes and Violence

Despite its temporary advocacy of direct action, and sabotage, the strikes of the IWW were not particularly violent. In 1912-1913, the IWW led two textile strikes in the East, and an affiliate, the Brotherhood of Timber Workers, operating in Louisiana, struck for improved wages and in working conditions in the Louisiana timber area. An exchange of gunfire between pickets and guards before the Gallaway Lumber Co. at Grabow, La., resulted in the killing of three union men and a company guard. A score of others were wounded. Several companies of troops were sent into the area and remained three days. A clash between strikers and strikebreakers at Merryville, on November 14, brought state troops into the area. The trouble ceased with their arrival, and the business community was anxious that the troops remain. More than 1,000 men were on strike, and "the people in the area were mostly in sympathy with the strike." It was, however, insufficient to help the strikers win. Several of the leaders were indicted for murder, but they were later acquitted.

The textile strike in Lawrence, Mass., including more than 25,000 workers, was the most important IWW-led strike and made a deep impression on contemporary observers.[54] Refusal of employers to offset the loss of wages that followed the reduction of hours required for women workers by a recently enacted law was the cause of the walkout on January 11, 1912. As the workers belonged to no union, they invited the general organizer of the IWW, Joseph Ettor, to aid them. He succeeded in having specific demands formulated and presented to each employer of the strikers. Troops were sent into the city, and their number was increased as the strike continued. At the same time, the governor of Massachusetts sought to have the state board of arbitration settle the dispute. The strikers were willing, but the American Woolen Co., the largest employer, refused to participate. A number of clashes between pickets and the militia took place, and in one a woman was killed. The strike continued until March 12, and was ended by the offer of a wage increase. Although the strike was a victory for the textile workers, the IWW was unable to gain a permanent foothold in Lawrernce or in the textile industry. While arrests are not necessarily a measure of strike violence, it is interesting that in Lawrence during the strike, more than 350 arrests were made. Several were sentenced to two years in prison; 24 to one year; and 22 were fined.

While the IWW strikes in the East represented forays into geographical areas where the union had few members, the strike in the Wheatland, Calif., hop fields took place in the union's natural habitat. The workers in the strike were typical of the IWW membership. The strike began on August 13, 1913, as a spontaneous protest against the miserable conditions at the Durst brother's ranch, where several thousand pickers had assembled awaiting the beginning of the season. Through extensive advertising, several thousand pickers had been attracted to the ranch in search of employment. Even by the standards prevailing in migrant-worker camps, living conditions were very bad there. Inadequate toilet facilities, charges for drinking water, absence of housing for many hundreds, and the low sanitary state of the campsite caused sufficient dissatisfaction that the migrants elected a negotiating committee. Richard Ford and Herman Suhr, members of the IWW, were on the committee. Demands for improvements in sanitation and an increase in the price of picking were made, and the committee, headed by Ford and Suhr, met with one of the Durst brothers. Durst flicked his glove across Ford's face and rejected the demands. The resident constable then tried to arrest Ford. When a warrant was insisted upon, the constable left and returned with the district attorney of the county and several deputy sheriffs. An attempt to arrest Ford led to an argument which ended in general shooting. The district attorney, a deputy sheriff, and two hop pickers were killed. The next day the militia arrived, but quiet had already been restored.[55] Ford and Suhr and two others were tried for murder, and the first two were convicted and sentenced to prison. The affair ended without improvements, although it stimulated a legislative investigation.

Although IWW strikers were not unusually violent, the reputation of the IWW made its members an easy target for repressive action by the authorities. The two bloodiest episodes in the life of the IWW were in Everett and Centralia, Wash., each connected with the attempt to organize lumber workers. The Everett confrontation started when the Lumber Workers Industrial Union No. 500 opened a hall in Everett in the spring of 1916, in an effort to recruit members. Street meetings were prevented and the sheriff deported the speakers and other members of the IWW to Seattle on a bus. It is of some interest to note that a speaker who advocated violence at a meeting at the IWW hall in Everett was later exposed as a private detective. For a time the deportations were stopped, but they were resumed in October 1916. An estimated 300 to 400 members were deported by the sheriff and vigilantes from Everett. On October 30, 1916, 41 IWW men left Seattle by boat. They were met by the sheriff and a posse, seized, and made to run the gauntlet between two rows of vigilantes who beat their prisoners with clubs.

On November 5, 1916, the IWW in Seattle chartered a boat, the *Verona*, and placed an additional 39 men on another vessel. The chartered boat set out for Everett. Having been informed of the attempt of the IWW to land peacefully, the sheriff and about 200 armed men met the chartered vessel at the dock. The sheriff sought to speak to the leaders. When none came forward and the passengers sought to land, a signal to fire into the disembarking men was given by the sheriff. Five members of the IWW and two vigilantes were killed, and 31 members of the IWW and 19 vigilantes were wounded by gunfire. The *Verona* and the other vessel carrying members of the IWW returned to Seattle without unloading at Everett. Almost 300 were arrested, and 74 were charged with first-degree murder. The acquittal of the first defendant led to the dismissal of the case against the others.[56]

Another tragedy occurred in Centralia, Wash., a lumber town of almost 20,000 inhabitants. Several times the IWW sought to open a hall in that community, but in 1916 the members were expelled by a citizen's committee, and two years later the IWW hall was wrecked during a Red Cross parade. With dogged persistence the IWW opened another hall. When threats were made to wreck it, the IWW issued a leaflet pleading for avoidance of raids upon it. During the Armistice Day parade in 1919, members of the IWW were barricaded in their hall and when the hall was attacked, opened fire. Three members of the American Legion were killed, and a fourth died from gunshot wounds inflicted by Wesley Everest, himself a war veteran. Everest was lynched that night by a citizen mob. Eleven members of the IWW were tried for murder. One was released, two were acquitted and seven were convicted of second degree murder. A labor jury from Seattle that had been attending the trial claimed that the men fired in self-defense and should have been acquitted.[57] It is not necessary to attempt to redetermine the verdict to recognize that the IWW in Everett and Centralia was the victim, and the violence was a response to attacks made upon its members for exercising their constitutional rights.

Two Major Labor Wars

West Virginia. The West Virginia and Colorado coal strikes of 1912-1914 were fought with an unrelenting fury that shocked the conscience of the country. Since 1897 the United Mine Workers of America had held contracts for the majority of bituminous coal miners, but union efforts to organize the expanding West Virginia mines failed a number of times after the beginning of the central competitive field agreement in 1898. Conscious that the failure to organize West Virginia constituted a serious threat to the union-held fields, the union sought greater recognition in the Paint Creek district, and a wage increase. Rejection by the operators led to a strike on April 20, 1912. Later the miners in the Cabin Creek district joined the walkout.

Guards provided by the Baldwin-Felts detective agency entered the area in large numbers and began evicting strikers from company-owned houses. On June 5, the first miner was killed, and nine guards were indicted for murder. Miners and Baldwin-Felts guards fought a pitched battle at Mucklow, on July 26, in which twelve men, mostly guards, were killed. The governor sent several companies of militia into the strike area, and arrests of strikers began. The military force was withdrawn at the end of 30 days, but with an increase in violence, it was reimposed on October 12. A military court was established which tried and sentenced strikers. Complaints by miners against the behavior of company guards led to the appointment of a citizens' commission by the governor. It reported that company guards had been guilty of "denials of the right of peaceable assembly, free speech, many and grievous assaults on unarmed miners, and that their main purpose was to overawe the miners and their adherents, and if necessary beat and cudgel them into submission."[58] The commission also charged that the miners were not entirely innocent and it held that their efforts to bring the West Virginia area under union control was an important cause of the troubles.

The mines were reopened in September with the assistance of imported workmen. Sporadic violence continued, with the tent colonies housing the dispossessed miners as a target. On February 7, 1913, an armored Chesapeake Ohio train, the "Bull Moose Special," attacked the tent colony in Holly Grove and poured more than 200 shots into the village. Quinn Morton, the general manager of the Imperial Co. who was in charge of the train, was accused of saying: "We will go back and give them another round." When testifying before a committee of the U.S. Senate, Morton was asked if he, "a cultured gentleman, approves the use of a machine gun on a populous village." In retaliation, an armed contingent of miners moved towards Mucklow, and fought a battle with guards in which twelve miners and four guards were killed. Martial law was then declared for the third time. The U.S. Senate committee criticized the denial of the rights of the miners, but it held the union was not blameless for the tragedy in the coalfields. A new governor was elected 1912, and in April 1913 he proposed a compromise, which the union hesitantly accepted. A few concessions were made, but the union was not recognized and soon dispersed.

War in Colorado. The Colorado coal industry was virtually nonunion. A number of efforts to establish collective-bargaining relations had been made, but all failed. In 1913 the United Mine Workers of America tried again, and Frank J. Hayes, vice president of the union, came to Colorado and enlisted the aid of Governor Elias Ammons towards obtaining a conference with the mine operators. The governor tried and failed. Further efforts to gain a conference were made by the union, and when they did not succeed, a strike was called on September 25, 1913. An estimated 8,000 to 10,000 miners left their jobs, and they and their families left their company-owned houses for the tent colonies which the union rented. In the meantime the companies had been preparing for the strike. "Spies, camp marshals and armed guards infested the mining camps and the city of Trinidad. In Huerfano County alone, 326 men, many imported from other states, had been commissioned as deputy sheriffs."[59]

Before the strike, a union organizer had been shot by a detective employed by the Colorado Fuel Iron Co. A marshal employed by the same company was killed on September 24. On October 7, 1913, after an exchange of shots between strikers and guards, the latter attacked the tent colony at Ludlow and killed a miner. On October 17, a party of mine guards attacked the tent colony at Forbes, killing a miner and wounding a young boy. Three strikers were shot and killed and one was wounded at Walsenberg several days later when a group of guards fired into a striker's meeting. On the following day, a battle was fought between armed miners and a contingent of guards at Berwind Canyon, which ended with the killing of a guard. Another battle between strikers and guards was fought there without reported casualties. An armored train, the "death special," was outfitted and while on the way to Ludlow, it was shot up by armed miners who killed the engineer. The train was forced back. On October 27 strikers attacked a building sheltering guards at Forbes Junction.

While the fighting was going on, Governor Ammons was trying to bring about a settlement. Failing in the attempt, he sent the entire National Guard to the strike zone. Their arrival was not opposed by the strikers, who felt that troops would behave better than company guards. The governor, while directing that protection be accorded to property and those who wished to work, advised against the use of troops in assisting in the importation of strikebreakers. More than 2,000 guns of strikers were turned in at the request of the commanding general. Others were, however, kept in reserve. Great pressures were exercised on the governor for stronger measures against the strikers and he capitulated by allowing Gen. John C. Chase, the head of the militia, to carry out a policy of repression.

Chase had been the commander in the metalliferous miner's strike in 1903-1904, and his union animosity was well known. Militiamen began harassing strikers, many of whom were arrested and detained for long periods of time. At the request of the state federation of labor, the governor appointed an investigating committee, which found that militia men had abused strikers and their wives and daughters. It reported that many of the guards had been allowed to join the National Guard, replacing regular members who were anxious to return to their homes and occupations. These men hated the strikers, and were not averse to assaulting and even killing them. The committee requested the removal of Chase as partial to the mine owners, and charged that many militiamen were guards on the payroll of the mine owners, and that the entire contingent had shown consistent bias in favor of the employers.

During February and March of 1914 there were few clashes, but it was believed that the presence of a congressional investigating committee in the state had a moderating influence on behavior. Most of the guard was accordingly withdrawn, but a troop of 35 men was left at Ludlow and Berwind Canyon. This was a tough group, made up mostly of company guards and professional adventurers, whose commander was a Lt. K.E. Linderfelt, whose animosity to the strikers was well known. On April 20 the Ludlow tent colony was attacked by the soldiers under Linderfelt and five men and a boy were killed by rifle and machinegun fire. The militiamen then fired the tents, and 11 children and two women were smothered. The tents were stripped of all portable things of value. Hundreds of women were driven from this colony of 1,200 people to seek shelter in the ranches and homes of the area. Three prisoners, including Louis Tikas, the Greek leader of the strike, were shot by the troops, ostensibly while trying to escape. The militiamen had one fatality.

Two days later, the Colorado labor movement notified President Woodrow Wilson that it had called on the workers of the state to arm themselves and to "organize the men in your communities in companies of volunteers to protect the workers of Colorado." The call was signed by the heads of the state federation of labor and the miners' union. A "military camp of strikers was established. . . . Inflamed by what they considered the wanton slaughter of their women, children and comrades, the miners attacked mine after mine, driving off or killing the guards and setting fire to the buildings."[60] In one action, 200 armed strikers left their base near Trinidad and attacked the mining camp at Forbes. Burning buildings, they poured deadly fire into the camp, killing nine guards and one strikebreaker; the strikers lost one man. Twenty-four hours later, federal troops arrived, and the fighting ended. "During the ten days of fighting, at least fifty persons had lost their lives, including twenty-one killed at Ludlow."[61] The Ludlow war ended with a total of 74 dead.

Despite the bloodshed, no recognition of the union was granted. Efforts of President Wilson to achieve permanent peace were in vain. A large number of miners, including John R. Lawson, the head of the miner's union in Colorado, were indicted. The latter was convicted of murder, but the verdict was overturned by the Colorado Supreme Court. The Ludlow war, one of the more tragic episodes in labor's history, failed to dissolve the adamantine opposition to unionism, which had become a fixed and immovable article of faith among many of the great industries of the United States.[62]

VIOLENCE IN LABOR DISPUTES DURING AND AFTER THE FIRST WORLD WAR (1917-1922)

Strike statistics, which were published by the Commissioner of Labor beginning with the year 1881, ceased to appear in 1905, and were resumed by the U.S. Bureau of Labor Statistics in 1915. The number of strikes between 1917 and 1922 was high compared with the following decade. The influence of wartime demand for labor, the dislocations which accompany wartime economic activity, the sharp rise in union membership, and reduced unemployment all exercised an influence on the potential for labor violence. Strikes tended to be shorter during wartime, but with the ending of hostilities the country experienced severe tension in the labor market. Several factors accounted for heightened labor discontent. Union membership rose sharply between 1916 and 1920, from 2,772,000 to 4,881,000. Considerable dissatisfaction existed as a result of rises in the cost of living during wartime and the general malaise that war normally generates. Many employers who had accepted union organization as a wartime necessity or as a result of government fiat were now anxious to rid themselves of labor organizations. This is evident from the power of the campaign by antiunion employers who espoused the American Plan of Employment, a program designed to support employers opposing the presence of unions in industry. The large accretion of union members also brought demands for changes in union policy and for the use of more aggressive tactics in labor disputes.

The Lynching of Frank Little

Despite the growth of strikes, the levels of violence during World War I were low, and the violence was mainly directed against strikers. In Butte, Mont., during the 1917 copper strike, the room of Frank Little, a member of the general executive board of the IWW, was invaded by a group of masked men. He was seized and hanged on a trestle. The strike itself had been called for improvement in the terms of employment and for the abolition of the "rustling card," a notice allowing the holder to seek employment in the mines which aided in the enforcement of a blacklist against union members. The governor requested troops, and federal soldiers arrived in Butte on September 10, 1917. The troops remained until December 18, 1917, and were returned to Butte on February 7, 1919, during a strike against a wage reduction led by the IWW. They departed 10 days later. The third appearance of federal troops was during the miner's strike of April 1920. They remained in the city until January 1921.[63]

The Arizona Deportations

During the First World War, strikes in most of the Arizona copper mines were called by the Industrial Workers of the World, or the International Union of Mine, Mill & Smelter Workers, an affiliate of the American Federation of Labor. A common response of employers was to deport the strike leaders and their followers.

Virtually the entire business and mining employer community participated in the deportations of 1,284 men from Bisbee, Ariz., on July 12, 1917. Great discontent with wages and working conditions existed in the Arizona copper county during 1917 and 1918. In addition, the IWW and Mine & Smelter Workers were competing for members among the miners. The latter had originally organized a large number of workers in the Warren district, of which Bisbee was the most important community. It had, however, lost its place to Metal Mine Workers Industrial Union No. 800, an IWW affiliate. A set of demands was drawn up and presented to the companies in the area. They refused to confer with the IWW committee and a strike was called for June 26.[64]

A large proportion of the miners in the Bisbee area responded to the strike call. Testimony showed that there was no violence. In fact, some witnesses claimed that petty crime had diminished because the IWW had told the bootleggers not to carry on their activities during the strike. Nevertheless, a Loyalty League was organized, and several mine managers suggested that the strikers and their sympathizers be deported from the city. The cooperation of Sheriff Harry Wheeler was obtained. On the morning of July 12 the streets of Bisbee were filled with nearly 2,000 men wearing white handkerchiefs on their sleeves. They had been deputized by Sheriff Wheeler. Men on the street were stopped and their business ascertained. Those unable to give satisfactory explanations were seized and taken to the local ball park which served as the assembly point for "undesirables." Homes of known strikers and sympathizers, including some lawyers, tradesmen, businessmen, and property owners, were visited and many were taken into custody. A deputy seeking to arrest a member of the IWW was killed, and his assailant slain by a fellow deputy. This was the only violent incident in the rounding up of 1,284 men.

After two hours in the ball park under a hot Arizona sun, the prisoners were compelled to march between two lines of armed men and to board a cattle train which the railroad provided. According to Fred W. Brown, a voluntary organizer of the American Federation of Labor, the tracks along the first stop of the train were "lined with gunmen" who had left Bisbee and had overtaken the train. Mounted guns stood on both sides of the track and no one was allowed to leave. The train arrived in Columbus, stayed for an hour, and left for Hermanes, where the men were dumped. On the morning of July 14, a company of U.S. soldiers arrived and brought the deportees back to Columbus, where they were provided with food and shelter by the U.S. Government. After eight days, they were allowed to leave. A majority stayed until September; food was cut off on September 12.

During the deportation, no messages were allowed to leave Bisbee. The sheriff then established a screening committee, a "kangaroo court," before which the deportees and others seeking to enter Bisbee had to appear. Many of those who came to seek work or reclaim their clothes and other personal possessions were forced to leave the community, even when they owned property. The President's Mediation Commission, during its inquiry in Arizona, was told by Sheriff Wheeler that he had heard from the chambermaid and others that there was "a plan on foot when they [the strikers] go down in the mines to get their clothing . . . that they were to block those tunnels and keep the men down at work in the mines. I am told these things; I cannot swear to them."[65]

Sheriff Wheeler and 21 leading businessmen were indicted for violating the rights of the deportees by a federal grand jury. The indictment was invalidated by the U.S. circuit court, and the decision was upheld in *United States v. Wheeler*. An indictment by the state for illegal kidnaping was obtained against 244 leading businessmen, Sheriff Wheeler, and many deputies and police officers. One case was tried, and the verdict of acquittal after several weeks of trial led to the dismissal of the charges against the other defendants. President Wilson and the President's Mediation Commission sharply criticized the conduct of the mob guilty of the deportation.[66]

Steel and Coal Strikes

Changes in attitudes were noticeable with the coming of peace. During the war the federal government sought to prevent protracted labor disputes, because they inevitably lowered output. Once the war was over, the restraints of the government in the name of patriotism were no longer effective. Moreover, a large amount of discontent among workers led to an increase in wildcat as well as in authorized strikes. Workers in some industries were trying to fortify bargaining rights that they had gained as a result of government pressure. Unions had carried on more vigorous organizing drives than before the war, and American Federation of Labor affiliates had sponsored a joint campaign for organizing the open-shop steel industry. The organization campaign was successful in enlisting the support of most steelworkers, but a barrier was posed by the refusal of the U.S. Steel Corp. and the smaller companies in the industry to deal with unions. Elbert Gray, on behalf of his own company and the industry, refused to meet with a committee of union officers claiming to represent employees of his company. Neither the pleas of the president of the United States nor clergymen nor any other force would induce him to recede from his position. Reluctantly a strike was called by the cooperating unions, and it turned out to be one of the more bloody of the period. Meetings were suppressed in many steel communities, union organizers and officers harassed, and behind the protection of police and hired guards the companies reopened their plants and were able to compel the unions to surrender without gaining any concessions. Violence was widespread in steel communities, such as Gary, Ind., and state and federal troops were brought in to restore order. In other towns, troops were not required. Twenty people were killed during the strike, and many more injured.

Coal was the center of some of the bloodiest labor disputes after the First World War. Most of the disputes centered around the efforts of the United Mine Workers of America to organize the nonunion counties of McDowell, Mingo, and Logan Counties in West Virginia. In September 1919, armed union miners were set to invade Logan County, but turned back at the request of the governor and district officers of the union in order to preserve peace. A strike for union recognition was called in Mattewan, Mingo County, in May 1920, and in an argument over evictions of miners from company houses, shooting between Baldwin-Felts guards and Sheriff Sid Hatfield left 10 dead, seven of them guards. The strike spread to McDowell County, which was soon caught up in the developing violence. Troops were sent in by the state, and after the killing of six in a battle between miners and deputies, federal troops arrived, but they were soon withdrawn, to be replaced by large numbers of deputies.

In the first months of 1921 it appeared that peace had been restored, but by May each side was arming for renewed warfare. Hundreds of armed miners were determined to march again into Logan County and the sheriff was prepared to prevent their entry. Union officers at first convinced the miners to withdraw and go home, but a report that miners had been ambushed and killed led the miners to re-form their ranks. Several thousand armed miners began a march on Logan County, and the governor called for federal aid. President Warren Harding ordered the miners to disperse and sent 2,100 federal troops to enforce his order. Six hundred miners surrendered to the U.S. Army, and after being disarmed, were released. The arrival of federal troops ended the miner's war. Several hundred were indicted in state courts for sedition and conspiracy, but juries refused to convict. In all, at least 21 people lost their lives. A Senate committee found that both sides were guilty of acts of violence, but the conduct of the union was found "absolutely indefensible. Men have been killed, property had been destroyed, telephone wires cut, trains commandeered and misused, and a march of some thousands of men organized and policies carried out which bordered close on insurrection."[67] But the committee also criticized the system of "paying sheriffs out of funds operators," and the prevention of union members from coming into the area. "There is complete industrial autocracy in this country."[68]

After the breakdown of an interstate conference with the United Mine Workers in summer of 1922, the coal operators informed the president of the United States that, given adequate protection, they could operate their mines despite a prospective strike. Thereupon the president appealed to the governors of 28 states to provide adequate policing so that the mines would start producing.

> The Governor of Pennsylvania sent more than 1,000 state troops to the strike fields of Western Pennsylvania for guard duty. The Governor of Colorado sent troops to the coal fields of that state. The Governor of Kentucky did likewise. Troops patrolled the highways. They broke up union meetings. They refused to permit miners to stop in the streets and roads to talk to each other. The Governor of Indiana sent 800 troops into Clay and other counties to afford protection while coal was being produced.[69]

The National Guard was also on duty in New Mexico and Utah and at a number of points in other states. The War Department dispatched federal troops at the request of the governors to the following states: West Virginia, Pennsylvania, Tennessee, Wyoming, Utah, New Mexico, Oklahoma, Kansas, and Washington.[70]

The bloodiest encounter during the coal strike occurred near Herrin, Ill. One of the operators, the Southern Illinois Coal Co., was allowed to uncover dirt from the overlay on condition that no coal would be shipped. The company had dealt with the union, as did all the operators in the Illinois District No. 12, United Mine Workers of America. The miners employed left their jobs, as did all others in the district, when the union issued a strike call. Later during the strike the company broke relations with the union and began mining coal. The workers whom it had imported were supposed to be members of the Shovelmen's Union. When John L. Lewis was asked about the organization, he replied that it was an "outlaw" organization, meaning it was unaffiliated. William J. Lester, head of the company, in addition to carrying on mining, had imported a number of guards. Three miners who approached the mining operation, presumably for a conference, were killed. Miners in the neighboring town armed themselves, and in the latter part of June sprayed the mining area with gunfire and stormed the stockade. Those who surrendered were beaten and shot to death, including Lester. Twenty-one, three of them strikers, died in this attempt to create a nonunion enclave in District No. 12, which had been completely unionized since 1898.[71]

Apart from Herrin, in which troops were not used, there was little violence associated with the coal strike. This lack of violence was due essentially to the success of miners in shutting down operations completely and the fact that reopening of the mines took place under the protection of state and federal troops. The inability of the coal operators to resume production despite military protection compelled them to resume bargaining with the United Mine Workers, which led to an agreement.

Railroad Disputes

The Shopmen's Union had greatly expanded as a result of favorable treatment they received from the government during the war. The return of the railroads to private management after the war led to the establishment of the Railway Labor Board, which authorized several general wage cuts. Rank-and-file pressures forced the unions, against the wishes of some of their leaders, to call a national strike on July 1, 1922, in which 400,000 men participated. The National Guard was sent to a number of points, although there were no reports of violence or intimidation. In Missouri the entire Guard was mobilized, and units were sent "to Franklin, Moberly, Macon, Poplar Bluff, and Chaffee, these being prominent railroad centers."[72] Since no violence was reported, it can only be assumed that the troops were used as either a precautionary device or as an attempt to overawe the strikers. The Kentucky Guard was sent to two localities and soldiers of the Illinois militia were called out at three points in connection with the railroad strike. Three other states—Kansas, Texas, and Idaho—sent troops to two railroad centers within each state. In addition, the entire National Guard of California was mobilized for service in the railroad strike of 1922 "in readiness for possible trouble . . . but were not placed on active duty."[73]

The shopmen's strike did not force the carriers to suspend operations. The operating crafts were not asked to respect the picket line and worked throughout the strike. As a result, the spectacular assaults of the strikes in 1877 and 1894 were absent. Nevertheless, there was a large amount of serious violence during this walkout. In the application for a restraining order, the United States charged that 20 persons had been killed in a number of incidents stretching across the entire country. The government also claimed that assaults with deadly weapons upon strikebreakers had taken place in 27 states and that sabotage had been practiced against railroad structures or the right-of-way in 20 states. Specifically, these included the dynamiting of bridges, the wrecking of trains, the derailment of others, the throwing of bombs. These episodes resulted principally in damage to property; a derailment in Worcester, Mass. was an exception, leading to the death of two persons and injury to 30 others.[74] Reported acts of intimidation ranged from the use of profanity to threats of death and violence not only against the workman but against his wife and children . . . bombing, painting with yellow paint, and the writing of inflammatory words upon the workman's house. The secondary boycott, which forced merchants not to sell to workmen; kidnapping and abductions, followed by tar and feathers or whipping and beatings, which resulted in bleeding backs and broken bones; robberies; forcible withdrawal from work and even from the cities; bombing of roundhouses and trains and throwing of bombs near workmen; firing bridges and the homes of workmen; sending of letters and circulars containing threats, abusive and insulting language; picketing, which included clubbings and beatings whenever there was no officer present . . . terrorism by mobs; persuasion under threat of violence; the nightly shootings by large crowds of men with high-powered rifles into railroad shops in which men were working; forcible entrance into the railroad shops, whereupon they destroyed and damaged engines and railroad property, and dragging the women out, beat them and sent away with instructions never to return.[75]

The widespread violence did not change the outcome. The leaders were dubious about the success of the strike, and they went along because of pressure from the rank and file. Violence began almost at once because the carriers decided, at the beginning, upon replacing the strikers. The strikers reacted with savage violence in many places, but their acts were unable to reverse the defeat which they faced. The strike failed everywhere. Among the major contributing causes were the unremitting hostility of the federal government, which secured sweeping injunctions based upon the Sherman Anti-Trust Act, and the decision of the operating brotherhoods to cross picket lines and run the trains.

THE PERIOD BETWEEN 1923 AND 1932

Union membership sharply declined between 1920 and 1923, from the high point of 4,881,000 in 1920 to 3,622,000 in 1923. Union activity similarly declined. Even more consequential than the decline in membership was the loss of elan and confidence that overcame the labor organizations as a result of repeated lost strikes. In effect, the removal of government protection made many of the wartime's gains temporary, and numerous employers reverted to a nonunion status. Although membership did not fluctuate sharply through the rest of the decade, the failure to make substantial gains in a generally prosperous period reflected a low level of organizing capacity, which was in turn a sign of loss of confidence.

The number of strikes dropped sharply, and while they varied from year to year, the number in 1928 was below those of any year of record since 1884. The years from 1920 through 1932 reveal the same experience, a moderate number of strikes. One result was a lowering of the level of industrial violence, although it erupted in the Chicago building trades as a result of the efforts of the business community to compel the building trades to accept an arbitration award of Judge Kenesaw M. Landis. The award followed an agreement between the Chicago building trades unions and the building trades contractor associations to allow Judge Landis to settle their differences over wages. Judge Landis' award was rejected by the unions on the ground that he had exceeded the powers under which he acted as an arbitrator. Employers denied the charge, and, with the support of the entire business community, decided to ignore the union's protests. When the contractors began to operate with new recruits, they found many of them assaulted and equipment and jobs damaged or dynamited. Two watchmen at one of the jobs were killed, and many others, workmen and pickets, were injured. The fight over the Landis award lasted from 1923 to 1926, when the industry returned to its former relationships. It is difficult to determine the role of force in this sequence of changes. Many contractors found the award unworkable because it made bidding more difficult, and they welcomed participation in wage-setting and work rules enforcement.

The low strike level elsewhere in the country reduced the possibilities for violent confrontations, although the governors of Indiana, North Carolina, and Rhode Island each sent state troops to the scenes of strikes.[76] In none of the three cases was violence reported. As usual, continuous strife took place in the bituminous coal industry. In Colorado, the Industrial Workers of the World notified the state industrial commission that a strike would be called in 30 days unless the operators made concessions. Thereupon the city council of Walsenberg ordered all members of the IWW out of town, and a mob led by the mayor wrecked the IWW headquarters. The companies refused concessions and a strike was called on October 18, 1927. During the strike a new constabulary was established, and on November 21 the constables, against the wishes of the Rocky Mountain Fuel Co., appeared before the Columbine, owned by the latter company, and ordered the cessation of picketing. When the pickets refused, and some rocks were thrown at the constables, they empited their guns at the pickets, killing six and wounding a number of others.[77] During a parade of strikers to a meeting with the Industrial Commission, on January 12, 1928, the lines were ordered to disperse. Shooting began, and a boy and a striker were killed.

This strike attracted nationwide attention but it was much less significant than the efforts of the bituminous coal miners to maintain their union in the coal fields of Pennsylvania, West Virginia, and Ohio. Investigating the reported abuses, a U.S. Senate committee noted:

> Everywhere your committee made an investigation in the Pittsburgh district we found coal and iron police and deputy sheriffs visible in great numbers. In the Pittsburgh district your committee understands there are employed at the present time between 500 and 600 coal and iron police and deputy sheriffs. They are all very large men; most of them weighing from 200 to 250 pounds. They are all heavily armed and carry clubs usually designated as a "black jack."

> Everywhere your committee visited they found victims of the coal and iron police who had been beaten up and were still carrying the scars on their faces and heads from the rough treatment they had received.[78]

There were also a number of textile strikes in the South, which attracted more than ordinary attention because of the resistance to the unions shown by the industry. In 1927, troops were sent to Hendersonville, N.C., during a textile strike because of the reported threats of violence.[79] Strike leaders were kidnaped and run out of town during a strike at Elizabethtown, Tenn., in April 1929. An attempt to organize the employees of the Marion Manufacturing Co., Marion, N.C., led to a strike of 1,000 hosiery workers on July 11, 1929. Workers employed at the Clinchfield mills joined the strikers after one month. As a result of sporadic clashes, Governor Max Gardner sent the militia to the area on August 11. The troops arrested 148 strikers, charging them with rioting. On September 11 the strike was called off, and the men returned to work, but as a result of a dispute over work payment, the night shift went on strike on October 2. The strikers remained before the mill gates seeking to notify the day shift that a strike had been called. Without warning deputies fired into the line of pickets, killing 6 and wounding 24. The militia, which had been withdrawn, was sent back to Marion. The sheriff, 12 deputies, and 2 mill officials were arrested and charged with homicide. Eight were tried and acquitted, although all the dead and wounded had been shot in the back.[80] In addition to the above, constant violence accompanied mine labor disputes in Kentucky's Harlan and Bell Counties in 1931 and 1932.

Many strikes during this period involved agricultural workers. Imperial Valley was the scene of an extensive strike in 1930 under the auspices of the Agricultural Workers Industrial Union, a Communist-dominated organization. Sixteen participants were indicted for criminal syndicalism, of whom six Mexicans were convicted; the others were paroled. Organization drives in California by the Cannery & Agricultural Workers Industrial Union in 1933 met with some success. A union demand for 35 cents an hour was the major strike issue. Violence occurred during disorders in El Centro on January 9, 1933, but was suppressed. In the onion fields of Hardin County, Ohio, in June 1934, 800 workers went on strike. Okey O'Dell led in forming the Agricultural Workers Union, AFL. Shortly thereafter he was abducted and beaten, and ordered not to return to the area. The strike was lost. On September 7, 1934, 67 persons were arrested, but the grand jury would not indict.[81]

THE NEW DEAL

Between 1933 and 1937 the labor movement underwent profound changes internally as well as in its relations to employers. For the first time in peace-time history, union organizations had the attention and approval of the federal government. Influenced by the labor legislation of the first years of the Roosevelt administration, unions began to expand, and by 1937 more members were enrolled in unions than at any time in history. The increases in union membership were reflected in a doubling of strikes between 1932 and 1933, and another doubling from 2,172 in 1936 to 4,740 in 1937. Almost half of the strikes in 1937 were for union recognition.

Coal Again

The increase in strikes increased the number of occasions for clashes between workers, strikebreakers, and the police. Violence occurred in the coal areas in a number of states where organization was progressing rapidly, with the most serious episodes occurring in the captive mine districts of Pennsylvania and in Kentucky, where resistance to new unionizing drives was carried on by deputies on the payroll of the mine companies.[82]

The bloody character of coal labor disputes brought out the National Guard in Indiana, New Mexico, and Utah, as well as in Ohio, where the death of a miner at Sullivan was responsible for the presence of state troops. The prime reason for calling up the Guard appeared to have been actual or threatened clashes between strikers and their replacements.[83]

The most sanguinary episodes took place in Kentucky, where coal operators in Harlan and Bell counties continued aggressive resistance to unionization that they had used in the past. Neither changes in public or worker sentiment, nor government suasion could soften their determination to keep their operations on a nonunion basis. Soon after the enactment of the National Industrial Recovery Act, the United Mine Workers sought to organize the miners employed by the U.S. Coal & Coke Co., a subsidiary of the U.S. Steel Corp. at Lynch, a mining community in the eastern part of Harlan County. The union succeeded in establishing a local in June 1933. After a time an open meeting was held in Cumberland, and two members of the Lynch police force stood in front of the hall and noted who was present at the meeting from their town. Subsequently, men were discharged, and in July and August 1933, the police department of Lynch purchased tear gas, 41 rifles, 21 revolvers, and 500 cartridges. A company union was also formed. Under this pressure, organizing was suspended.[84]

When the contract between the Harlan County Coal Operators Association and the United Mine Workers of America expired, in April 1934, armed deputies and company guards were in full command. Peaceful meetings of the miners were suppressed, union miners were severely beaten, and organizers driven out of town. After the enactment of the National Labor Relations Act in 1935, renewed efforts to organize were undertaken by the United Mine Workers, which had contracts with three coal companies in Harlan County. In September 1935, miners in 13 camps went on strike. A union member was kidnapped and compelled to leave the county. The union was not at this time successful in organizing, and abandoned its efforts temporarily.[85] When a new organizing drive was launched in 1937, the sheriff increased the number of his deputy sheriffs to 163, only three of whom were paid from public funds. At first no violence was used against union organizers.[86] They were not, however, able to obtain lodgings at some hotels, and in one instance tear-gas bombs were thrown into the place where organizers were staying. On February 8, 1937, as a group of organizers were driving through the countryside, they were fired upon from a car and one of the occupants was wounded. The driver of the organizer's car accelerated his speed and managed to escape into a garage. The incident had been witnessed by three small boys who related what they had seen to Lloyd Clouse. After being warned to keep quiet, Clouse was shot and killed on April 24, 1937, by a deputy. Marshall Musick, a union organizer who had lived in Evarts for 14 years, was forced to leave town because he feared he would be killed after he had been warned and shot at several times. After Musick had left, his son was killed by a volley fired through the window of his house.[87]

On November 27, 1937, the National Labor Relations Board found the Clover Fork Co. guilty of discriminating against members of the United Mine Workers of America, and found the Harlan County Coal Operators Association guilty of coercion and restraint of workers. The decision was upheld by the Circuit Court of Appeals for the Sixth Circuit.

> As a result of this decision, the other coal companies of Harlan County, which had not abandoned the unyielding attitude toward the union, settled their disputes with the union. On August 19, 1938, the Harlan County Coal Operator's Association signed an agreement with the United Mine Workers extending the terms of the Southern Appalachian contract to the Harlan County Coal Operators Association.[88]

Peace was finally established in the Kentucky coal mines.

Violence in 1934

The increase in demands for recognition brought about by a rapidly growing union membership led to violence on many picket lines. In 1934, state troops were called out in connection with the national textile strike during September. The major reason for the violence and the use of troops appears to have been the determination of employers not to deal with the union. This was the basic impediment to a peaceful settlement in the national textile strike, the San Francisco longshoremen's strike, and the Minneapolis teamsters and the Kohler strikes of that year, which were the centers of the most serious violence. The first two are described below.

The 1934 strike that involved the largest number of workers took place in the cotton textile industry after the convention of the United Textile Workers of America had demanded a general wage increase and other improvements in working conditions. When all proposals for meetings were rejected by the industry, a strike was called on August 31, 1934. The workers in Alabama commenced their walkout earlier, on July 15, and an estimated 20,000 in 28 mills were reported on strike. In Alabama, the president of the Decateur local was shot and two of his aides were beaten. The National Guard was sent to Chambers and Lee counties. In Georgia, complaints of roving pickets were made at the beginning of the strike. Clashes between pickets and strike guards led the governor to proclaim martial law, and to set up an internment camp. In a fight between strikers and guards at Trion, 2 were killed and 24 wounded. In North Carolina, a number of pickets and strikebreakers were wounded, and the governor sent troops to the strike zone. The troops were directed to "afford protection to those citizens who wanted to work and were being denied that privilege. . . . This policy extended to the protection of strikers and other citizens whose action and conduct was within their legal rights; this thought with reference to picketing."[89] Throughout the strike, 5,000 state troops were active in New England, and an estimated 2,000 strikers were interned in Georgia. The strike cost 15 lives, and an unestimated number of wounded by gunfire and other means.[90] The textile strike was completely lost.

Unions in the Pacific coast seafaring and longshore industry, which had been largely eliminated in the 1920s, were reestablished in 1933, but negotiations between unions and their employers did not move on an even keel. At best, the shipowners and stevedore companies accorded the labor groups grudging recognition and waited for an opportunity to eliminate the unions. In the spring of 1934 no agreement could be reached with the Pacific coast longshoremen, who were then affiliated with the International Longshoremen's Association. At the same time, the seagoing unions made demands for recognition. The demands of both groups were rejected by the employers, and the longshoremen and seamen struck, respectively, on May 9 and May 16, 1934. After several plans for ending the walkout had failed, a movement for reopening the San Francisco port was undertaken by the Industrial Association. On July 3 trucking operations were begun, and several trucks loaded with cargo were taken through the picket lines. On the following day the Belt Line Railway, a state-owned line, was attacked by strikers and sympathizers. Governor Frank Merriam then sent the National Guard into the city to restore order. On July 6 the worst riot of the strike, and the encounter that was to bring on a local general walkout, took place. Two pickets were killed and many injured. The San Francisco Labor Council then sponsored the general strike, which lasted from July 15 to July 19 and was called off after employer concessions resulted in full recognition of the Longshoremen & Sailor's Union, and union control of hiring halls.

3. Strikes and Violence in 1935 and 1936

The year that witnessed the enactment of the Wagner Act showed little abatement of employer resistance to union organization. In all parts of the country, in small and large disputes alike, governors were increasingly inclined to dispatch their troops to cope with strikers. Four disturbances that brought state troops to the strike scene were in coal and metalliferous mining, in addition to two in the lumber industry, and four in textiles. Troops also were sent to a strike in a meat-packing plant in South Dakota, and to another in an engine plant in Freeport, Ill. A streetcar strike in Omaha, Neb., and the general strike in Terre Haute, Ind., accounted for the other incidents.[91]

Mining and textiles contributed most of the serious violence in 1935. An attempt to launch a dual union in the anthracite-coal fields caused serious conflict in that area between followers of the new and the old union. Clashes between the adherents of the United Anthracite Miners of Pennsylvania and the United Mine Workers of America resulted in a riot in which two were killed on February 14, and a large number injured. Even more serious was the fight at the Glen Alden collieries at Nottingham, Pa., on May 31, 1936. Five were killed and 21 hurt in this encounter. The United Anthracite Miners finally disbanded in October 1936.[92] One or more strikers were killed in each of at least 16 other local strikes throughout the country and in a variety of industries.

The violence that was common in the textile industry in 1934 continued into the following year. At La Grange, Ga., the National Guard was sent to maintain order after a disturbance during a strike which started in March. At the Monmouth textile mill in Union, S.C., a foreman and constable were killed during a riot on June 19. At Pelzer, S.C., a woman was killed and 22 persons were wounded when the sheriff and his deputies fired into a crowd of pickets. The sheriff was denounced for his unnecessary use of force. Troops were sent into the area, and a number of deputies were arrested. Later the parties worked out an agreement for ending the walkout.[93]

According to the Chief of the National Guard Bureau of the U.S. War Department, state troops were called out 11 times in 1936 in connection with labor disputes.[94] These troops were used in three textile strikes, in a coal strike, and an Idaho lumber workers strike, in a match factory in Cloquet, Minn., and in a clothing factory in New York State.[95] Troops were mobilized in Pekin, Ill., during a walkout at the plant of the American Distilling Co., but the threat of a general strike prevented their use. The most violent walkouts in 1936 were in the coal, steel, and textile industries, at least from the point of view of persons killed, one or two deaths occurring in each of seven strikes in these and other industries.

Violence in Labor Disputes in 1937

By 1937, unions had been for four years the beneficiaries of government legislation to protect their rights to organize and to bargain. Despite this, using the index of people killed in labor disputes, this year was one of the more bloody in the history of American labor violence. One dispute, the Little Steel strike, accounted for 16 deaths and many others seriously injured. In addition, an estimated eight other people died in industrial disturbances.[96]

The worst episode of the steel strike took place "in a stretch of flat, waste, sparsely inhabited prairie land east of and adjacent to the South Chicago plant of the [Republic] steel corporation."[97] From the beginning of the strike, the police interfered with peaceful picketing; however, after Mayor Edward Kelly announced picketing would be permitted, 16 pickets were allowed before the gates. According to his testimony, an anonymous source had informed Capt. James L. Mooney, who was in charge of police in the factory area, that the strikers planned to march into the steel plant on Memorial Day. Because its pickets had been arrested by the police, the union had called a protest meeting on May 30. The meeting was held, and a motion to establish a mass picket line before the plant was adopted. As the marchers reached the police lines, a discussion followed "for a period of from four to ten minutes."[98] Within less than a minute thereafter "the strikers were in full retreat, in haste and confusion, before the advancing police lines. . . . Within that brief space of time, ten of the strikers received fatal gunshot wounds, thirty others were wounded by bullets and some sixty others received lacerations and contusions of varying intensity. Thirty-five police received minor injuries."[99] The Senate committee found

> That the provocation for the police assault did not go beyond abusive language and the throwing of isolated missiles from the rear ranks of the marchers. We believe that it might have been possible to disperse the crowd without the use of weapons. . . . From all the evidence we think it plain that the force employed by the police was far in excess of that which the occasion required. Its use must be ascribed either to gross inefficiency in the performance of the police duty, or a deliberate effort to intimidate the strikers.[100]

The extent of the violence throughout the strike is summarized in La Follette committee reports. It found that the riots which occurred at Republic Steel Corp. plants during the Little Steel strike of 1937 resulted in the following: total gunshot wounds, 37; injuries other than gunshot, 202; buckshot wounds, 1; birdshot wounds, 17; established and possibly permanent injuries, 19; dead, 16, for a total dead and injured of 283. In addition, one policeman received a bullet wound, two birdshot wounds; injuries, 37; for a total of 40.[101] It was the opinion of Robert Wohlforth, the secretary of the La Follette committee, that during the Little Steel strike

> a mobilization of men, money and munitions occurred which has not been approached in the history of labor disputes in recent times. Although known to be incomplete, the committee has assembled data showing that a total of 7,000 men were directly employed as guards, patrolmen, deputy sheriffs, National Guardsmen, city police and company police on strike duty. Over $4,000,000 was expended directly attributable to the strike. A total of $141,000 worth of industrial munitions was assembled for use.[102]

The violence in the Little Steel strike came largely from the aggressive behavior of the police and company guards. The strike was lost on the picket line and, in this respect, resembled the pattern of past events in the steel and many other industries. However, the union gained recognition and with it collective bargaining was established in Little Steel, as a result of the application and enforcement of the Wagner Act by the NLRB and the courts.

VIOLENCE IN 1938-1939

The year 1937 saw the last of the great strike spectaculars in which the clash of armed forces or large-scale assaults led to heavy casualties. Violence continued to accompany some labor disputes, and each year produced new victims, but the level of violence was substantially and permanently lowered. In all, there were six deaths in the course of labor disputes in 1938. In 1939 there was a striking decline in the use of militia in labor disputes. The Kentucky National Guard was sent to protect the Malan-Ellison Mine in Harlan, where a dispute had arisen. Three miners were killed in Harlan and one more elsewhere before the trouble subsided. Another dispute over the signing of a contract led to the wounding of seven men, two of them officers of the Hart Coal Co.[103] Five deadly disputes elsewhere resulted in the deaths of an equal number of men.

VIOLENCE IN 1940-1946

By 1940, union organizations entered into a new phase of growth and security. Strikes took on more and more their contemporary character of an economic conflict attended with minor violent episodes. This period was one of serious turbulence in the labor market, and the shift to war production was accompanied by widespread dislocations. The subsequent reconversion to a peacetime economy was a challenge to the new industrial relations. The continual increase in union membership and union strength resulted in record-high numbers of strikes over important issues at the end of this period.

In 1940, there were seven deaths in labor disputes. While people were killed in most of the subsequent years, the incidents which generated violence were sporadic clashes and usually involved few workers. Private guards were involved in only two fatal disputes in this seven-year period. The first occurred during 1940 in a building trades strike, when a picket was shot in the back by two guards, both of whom were indicted.[104] The other incident, the wounding of a picket who later died, occurred at the Phelps-Dodge plant on July 30, 1946.

The coal industry continued to produce a disproportionate share of violence. In 1940, one man was killed and two were wounded while peacefully picketing a coal mine in Ohio. "The tragedy roused the miners to a high pitch and the killer decided to remain in jail for the time being under the protection of the sheriff. He said he fired because one of his brothers was assaulted."[105] In 1942, nine killings took place in three separate incidents in the Kentucky coal mines. In April the president and vice president of the coal company at Middleboro were shot to death along with a miner and a deputy sheriff.[106]

A rising share of violent clashes was caused by jurisdictional disputes. In June 1940, a nonstriking bus driver, who was a member of the Amalgamated Association of Street Railway & Motor Coach Employees, was killed in a jurisdictional dispute with the Brotherhood of Railroad Trainmen. The Amalgamated eventually defeated the trainmen in an NLRB representation election.[107] One of the more grave disputes of 1941 took place in a suburb outside of St. Louis, Mo., and involved a fight between unionized and unorganized building tradesmen. One man was shot to death, four were wounded, and a number of others were beaten in a battle between the two groups.

The National Guard was seldom employed during this period. Alabama sent the militia to restore order in 1941 at the Utica Mills at Aniston, to Gadsden for eight days at a strike at the Republic Steel plant there, and on two occasions to police strike activities at the Tennessee Coal & Iron Railroad.[108] The sporadic and at times accidental nature of the remaining violent disputes is readily apparent in enumerating several of them. An organizer for the International Ladies' Garment Workers' Union in New York City was killed in 1940 after a scuffle with the owner of a nonunion shop.[109] Soon after this, the IBEW conducted a strike at the Triangle Conduit & Cable Co. in Brooklyn, N.Y., where, seven weeks after the start of the strike, 2,000 pickets tried to prevent the entrance into the plant of strikebreakers. One of the pickets died "of a heart attack brought on by the excitement." Later, several local officers were indicted for rioting.[110]

There was only one reported death in a labor dispute in 1942, another in 1943, and one more in 1945. An unusually bloody affair took place at a strike on the Toledo, Peoria & Western Railroad in the same year. The cause of the strike was the attempt of the railroad's president, George McNair, to compel changes in work rules. All service trades and shop employees went out on strike and two of the strikers as well as McNair were killed. The latter was shot by an assailant who was never caught.[111]

THE POST-TAFT-HARTLEY ACT PERIOD (1947-1962)

The passage of the Taft-Hartley Act in 1947 had numerous causes, including a continuing resentment by some employers' groups of the Wagner Act, the postwar strike wave, and patent abuses by some unions. Whatever the consequences of the newly imposed legal restraints upon union activities may have been, the Taft-Hartley Act did not in any significant way dimish the protection accorded to unions by the Wagner Act. Public policy in support of the principles and procedures of collective bargaining remained unchanged. Changes in union membership responded more to the level of employment and unemployment than to the changes in the laws governing labor-management relations.

Violence, however, was not completely erased from the labor-management scene and several strikes appeared to resemble outwardly the industrial disputes of another day. However, even those in which violence took place lacked the ferocity of the battles of the pre-Wagner Act days. These incidents seem to demonstrate that the potential for violence is always present in industrial disputes in the United States, but they do not, in most instances, show the relentless bitterness of Homestead, Pullman, Ludlow, and many other affrays which desecrated the industrial landscape of earlier periods. Using fatalities as an index of violence, the comparative numbers are very small considering the high number of labor disputes, and even more the millions of workers who are covered by collective-bargaining agreements peacefully renewed at periodic intervals (see Table 7.1).

Table 7.1: Number Killed and Wounded and Number of Times Milita Was Called in Labor Disputes (1947-62)

Year	Location	Killed	Wounded[a]	Militia
1947		0	0	0
1948	Maryland	1	0	0
	Illinois, Iowa	3		1
1949	Kentucky	1		
1950	Tennessee	1	4	1
	Alabama	1		
1951	Georgia	1	0	1
	Arkansas	1		
	Tennessee	1		
1952		0	0	0
1953	West Virginia	1	4	
	Pennsylvania	1		
	Southern RR. States	1	b	
1954				
1955	Louisiana	1		
1956				
1957	Tennessee	2	7	
1958	New York	1	2	
	Florida	2	2	
1959	Kentucky	4		1
	Louisiana	1	1	
1960	Wisconsin	1		
1961	New York	1		
1962	Tennessee	3		

a. Statisics available usually in connection with strikes involving fatalities.
b. Several.

As in the past, violent strikes in this period exhibit little if any regularity. But some differences emerge that largely confirm certain trends in 1940-1946. There is decreasing resort to the National Guard, and assaults on strikers by company guards have been all but eliminated. Industries such as coal that have been a fertile source of past violence have become pacified and no longer provide exceptional bloody episodes. Geographically, violence continues to be widely dispersed, although the data suggest that violence tends to occur more frequently in the South and Midwest and less often in the Northeast and the Far West. Most of the deaths in these strikes were accidental, in the sense that violence was not part of a systematic campaign by either the union or the employer. Some deaths were a result of a brawl between pickets and strike replacements, which has been the single most important source of all strike violence. Indeed, many strikes that had been peaceful were converted to battles on the first day that a back-to-work movement started. Occasionally, violence took place away from the struck facility, sometimes under circumstances in which it is difficult to disentangle personal elements from the labor controversy.

To be sure, there were strikes which had all the hallmarks of past struggles. The national strike of the CIO Packinghouse Workers against several packing companies in 1948 was accompanied by killings, disorder, and the National Guard. In this strike, the police in Kansas City, Kans., raided the union hall, destroyed furniture, and attacked those present. In 1955, during a strike on the Louisville & National Railroad, injuries and a death resulted from clashes between pickets and strike-breakers. Bridges were dynamited and rolling stock damaged, and the railroad was the victim of continual vandalism.

By and large, however, the most publicized strikes in this period, while bitter and prolonged and full of disorder and assaults, did not result in killings. These strike spectaculars—Kohler, Square-D, Perfect Circle, Southern Bell—were all wide-spread and usually accompanied by minor acts of violence, which in a few cases were quite grave and resulted in more or less extensive amounts of property damage. The worst of these strikes was that involving the Perfect Circle Co. and the UAW, in which both sides were plainly guilty of violence. The Perfect Circle Co. was the only employer of this group that did not settle the strike by beginning or resuming collective bargaining relationships with its union. However, it should be noted that in due time this company eventually recognized the union that had been decertified in three out of its four plants after the strike.

CONTEMPORARY VIOLENCE

The most informative source of the extent of contemporary violence is found in the records of the National Labor Relations Board. In Section 8(b)(1)(A) of the Taft-Hartley Act, Congress gave the Board power "to proceed against union tactics involving violence, intimidation and reprisal or threats thereof."[112] In interpreting this section, the Board commented that "Congress sought to fix the rules of the game, to insure that strikes and other organizational activities of employees were conducted peaceably by persuasion and propaganda and not by physical force, or threats of force or of economic reprisal."[113] In fiscal 1968, the Board closed twelve cases after the entry of a Board order or court decree in which unions had been found to have engaged in some act or acts of violence. Moreover, 14 Board regional offices for the same period closed informally 38 other such cases.[114] These regions handle roughly half of the agency's total case load and include New England, parts of metropolitan New York and Chicago, the industrial areas of Pittsburgh and Detroit, the southeastern states, the Midwest, and part of Texas, and the Far West. On the assumption that the unreported half of the United States would have exhibited about the same number of violent labor cases, we may conclude that there were 80 to 100 cases of unlawful acts with some degree of violence committed by labor unions and involving the NLRB in this 12-month period.

An example of present-day violence occurred during a labor conflict between District 50, United Mine Workers, and a manufacturer of iron castings in a small Michigan city. Despite a long history of collective bargaining, a strike of the 85 employees for a new contract that took place on March 13, 1967, lost its peaceful character on March 30 when some pickets were armed with baseball bats. It was alleged that an employer representative and two strike replacements were assaulted by several pickets and formal complaints were made to the police. The employer had been operating the plant at a reduced scale using supervisors and hiring strike replacements from any source. The alleged assailants were not union officers, but the Board imputed agency responsibility to the union on the grounds that this conduct took place under a controlled picket line. The regional office settled the case informally with the union and the employer, on the grounds that the picketing was otherwise peaceful, that no further violence was reported, and that a local court had issued a temporary restraining order directed against the violence. The settlement agreement provided for the usual remedy within the scope of normal Board procedures, that is, the agreement of the union to cease its unlawful activities and post a notice to its members to this effect. The strike continued after the closing of the case and the company's operations remained unaffected by the peaceful picketing.

The pattern of illegal activities which constitutes violence and coercion subject to the jurisdiction of the Labor Board rarely varies. Frequently there is some blocking of plant ingress and egress, occasionally the laying of nails "by persons unknown" on the plant driveway, sometimes allegations that sugar or other foreign material is put in the gas tanks of company and nonstriking employees' vehicles, accusations of object throwing which may include rocks, eggs, or paint, some physical scuffling or pushing, and always the making of threats. Damage to company plant is rarely observable in these cases, although vehicles standing in the street appear to be fair game. In very few cases does more violence take place, such as physical assaults or the following and harassing of drivers of company trucks on the highways and at stops. In several cases, union pickets were found in front of the homes of working employees with signs imputing the worst sins of humanity to those who cross picket lines. In all cases but one the union's coercive conduct was limited in time and ceased after the filing of a charge with the Board or the obtaining of a state court injunction. Indeed, in 11 cases of the 38 formally adjusted cases, court orders were obtained by the employer.

The existence of Board machinery for determining a union's representation status has eliminated this issue from its previously predominant role as a cause for strikes. The number of such cases involving coercive union behavior is very low. Two situations involved the International Ladies' Garment Workers' Union, which established a number of pickets in front of a small plant during an organizational campaign. In both cases, the sole unlawful activity, which was corrected by the filing of the charge, was interference with free movement to and from the plant.

The reduction of union-caused violence cannot be exclusively attributed to the impact of section (8)(b)(1)(a), although this section has a direct bearing upon such unlawful acts. With rare exceptions, as is noted in our description of Board cases, local law enforcement agencies supported by state courts are able to control union violence. The power of the state, now as in the past, is usually competent to protect employers' property interests, including the safeguarding of free ingress to and egress from a struck plant. However, in the event of a breakdown of local law enforcement, the board is empowered under section (10)(j) of the Taft-Hartley Act to secure an injunction from a federal district court. Since 1947 there have been eleven occasions where such an injunction has been obtained. In all of these cases, uncontrolled mass picketing and large-scale incidents of violence and threats of violence were responsible for the Board's intervention. It also should be noted that the enforcement of a federal court order is invariably swift and effective. Of course, the significance of section (10)(j) cannot be measured alone by the number of times it was used. The prospect of its use, as observed in one of the board cases discussed above, is ordinarily sufficient to stop violent behavior.

Attempts were made to secure additional data on violence from such obvious sources as local police departments and the U.S. Department of Justice. Police manuals from a number of cities throughout the country revealed that police departments were highly sensitive to the disorders inherent in labor disputes and a number of cities specified in considerable detail appropriate police procedures. All of these were directed at insuring open picket lines and freedom of movement of people and goods across them. At the same time, police officers were cautioned to maintain neutrality and impartiality in maintaining order. The records of the Labor Board indicate that these instructions were ordinarily executed with considerable fidelity, although the enthusiasm with which police carried out their orders varied with local conditions. There were times when police allegedly turned their backs at minor outbursts of picket line violence; on the other hand, unions charged that the contrary often took place. In one Board case a union representative claimed: "Any time a driver either refused or hesitated to make a delivery, the police showed up." We were given access to the full records of a major northern industrial city's police department which revealed an almost complete absence of labor violence over a four-year period. During this time only one arrest was made, and that involved a fist fight between a picket and a customer of a struck store.

We were also given summaries of major complaints of labor violence made to the Federal Bureau of Investigation from 1961 to 1967. The Department of Justice informed us that most of the other complaints were about small-scale damage to property whose isolated nature and remoteness in affecting commerce precluded federal action. Property damage was also the most significant characteristic of the major complaints of labor violence made to the Federal Bureau of Investigation from 1961 to 1967. The use of dynamite was reported in 1961 and 1963 during a jurisdictional dispute on the Great Lakes. Explosions were reported on the Wabash Railroad in 1963, and on the New York Central Railroad in the same year. The most serious incidents of property damage occurred during disputes with employers with extensive and exposed property holdings. A strike of the IBEW against the Alabama Power Co. in 1966 was accompanied by 50 acts of sabotage, including the draining of oil from transformers, placing of chains across powerlines, severing of guy wires on transmission line poles, the destruction of power equipment by gunfire, and the like. Also in 1966 a labor dispute between the Oil, Chemical & Atomic Workers' Union and the United Fuel Gas Co. was followed by dynamiting 24 company pipelines in West Virginia and Kentucky as well as other property damage.

In none of the above disputes did personal injuries or deaths occur. Assaults against individuals took place, however, in four strikes. For example, a strike among employees of a Florida telephone company in 1967 witnessed several dynamiting incidents and the shooting of several employees. The assailants and the circum-stances surrounding these incidents are unknown to the writers. A serious recent violent strike involved steel hauler owner-operators in 1967, whose dissatisfaction with the Teamsters Union to which they belonged generated more than 50 serious incidents of violence. In their attempt to secure better representation, the dissident teamsters attempted to intimidate other drivers by acts of violence, including the throwing of fire bombs and rocks. One death and another serious injury were reported.

From time to time the newspapers report outbreaks of strike violence such as in the 1962 Florida East Coast Railroad strike and in the 1968 dispute between the Steelworkers Union and the Lone Star Steel Co. in Texas. The latter strike was marked by beatings, shootings, and threats and required the intervention of the Texas Rangers. It is noteworthy that in describing this strike in its story heading, the *Wall Street Journal* said: "Shades of the 1930s: Violent Steel Strike Rocks a Steel Producer in Texas."[115]

The diminution of the level of violence is attested to by its relatively scant treatment in congressional hearings since 1947. The essential concern of proponents of labor reform during the Taft-Hartley hearings was to deprive employees guilty of violence, threats, sitdown mass picketing, and other forms of intimidation of their reinstatement rights. It should be noted that past court decisions, in some instances overruling the Board, had eliminated the act's protection for employees engaging in the above practices. The McClellan committee's 1956-1959 investigation of improper union and employer activities found no evidence of large-scale violence except in few cases such as the Kohler and Perfect Circle cases. However, the Landrum-Griffin Act of 1959 contains prohibitions against threats and acts of violence and intimidation arising out of the management of internal union affairs. This is one of the least violated sections of the Landrum-Griffin Act. Other federal statues which touch upon labor violence, such as the Hobbs Act,[116] have given rise to a handful of cases.

A fundamental purpose of the national labor policy, first enunciated by the Wagner Act and confirmed by its subsequent amendments in the Taft-Hartley and Landrum-Griffin Acts, was the substitution of orderly procedures for trials of combat. But in balancing the public interest in the peaceful settlement of industrial disputes with the freedom of labor and management to work out their problems in light of their needs and experience, the law did not outlaw the exercise of economic force. Indeed, by endorsing collective bargaining, the NLRA explicitly acknowledged that tests of strength, i.e., the infliction of economic harm, with all its costs and hardships, is superior to such alternatives as compulsory arbitration.

However, this approval of the strike, the picket line, and the maintenance of hard bargaining lines by employers and unions was limited by the establishment of specified rules of conduct imposed on all parties. Some subjects were removed as bargaining issues and are not subject to economic pressures. Foremost among these was the question of union recognition and with it the concomitant mutual obligation to bargain in good faith. The wishes of a majority of employees within an appropriate bargaining unit determined whether or not collective bargaining was to begin, and this determination could not be lawfully qualified or limited.

The workings of the majority-rule principle can best be appreciated by applying it to the major disputes of the past. Members of the bargaining committee that approached the Pullman company were fired and Pullman refused to deal with any committee of his employees. Charles Schwab, head of the Bethlehem Steel Co., announced during the 1910 strike, "I will not deal with union committees or organized labor," an attitude reiterated for the entire industry in 1919. This position was taken by employers in Michigan Copper, in the coal industry of Colorado and the major coalfields in West Virginia, and by others in the more violent strikes. Some employer associations were hostile to the principle of dealing with unions, and these groups included the leading firms in many industries. Because employer refusal to meet and deal with unions was the major cause of past violent labor strikes, the effective enforcement of the Wagner Act reduced sharply the number of such encounters.

This diminution of labor violence was not a temporary phenomenon but endured the strains of major and minor wars, a number of business cycles, and substantial changes in national and local political administrations. Moreover, the social and economic environment in post-New Deal America was scarcely conducive to the pacific resolution of disputes of any kind. The reconversion of American industry after the Second World War brought on the greatest strike wave in our history. Yet, these mammoth strikes were accompanied by virtually no violence, completely at variance with the experience after 1918.

The contribution of the NLRA in sustaining the reduction in the number and severity of sanguinary labor clashes went beyond prescribing enforceable bargaining behavior. The law supported the right of labor unions to organize, but only on condition of avoidance of violence. Violence on a picket line is always latent but tends to surface when the employer recruits replacements and attempts to operate. Today, as always, employers have the legal right to move goods and people freely across a picket line and the duty and practice of police has tended to safeguard this right. Moreover, employees who engage in violence forfeit the protection of the act, which is a restraining influence upon them. The diminution of violence on labor's side has correspondingly lowered the propensity of employers to resort to force as either a defensive or aggressive tactic.

SUMMARY AND CONCLUSIONS

The United States has experienced more frequent and bloody labor violence than any other industrial nation. Its incidence and severity have, however, been sharply reduced in the last quarter of a century. The reduction is even more noteworthy when the larger number of union members, strikes, and labor-management agreements are considered. The magnitude of past violence is but partially revealed by available statistics. One writer estimated that in the bloody period between January 1, 1902, and September 30, 1904, 198 persons were killed and 1,966 injured in strikes and lockouts.[117] Our own independent count, which grossly understates the casualties, records over 700 deaths and several thousands of serious injuries in labor disputes. In addition, we have been able to identify over 160 occasions on which state and federal troops have intervened in labor disputes.

The most common cause of past violent labor disputes was the denial of the right to organize through refusal to recognize the union, frequently associated with the discharge of union leaders. Knowledge of workers' resentment at their inability to join unions encouraged employers to take defensive measures during strikes and lockouts. These measures often included the hiring of guards who, by their provocative behavior, often created the very conditions they had been engaged to minimize.

The melancholy record shows that no section of the United States was free from industrial violence, that its origin and nature were not due to the influence of the immigrant or the frontier, nor did it reflect a darker side of the American character. Labor violence was caused by the attitudes taken by labor and management in response to unresolved disputes. The virtual absence at present of violence in the coal and copper mines, breeding grounds for the more dramatic and tragic episodes, are eloquent testimony that labor violence from the 1870s to the 1930s was essentially shaped by prevailing attitudes on the relations between employer and employee. Once these were changed, a change accomplished partly by legal compulsion, violence was sharply reduced.

Employer Violence

Employers and unions were both guilty of violence. Employer violence frequently had the cover of law. No employer was legally bound to recognize the union of his employees. He has and always had the right to defend his property and maintain free access to the labor and commodity markets. In anticipation of trouble, the employer could call on the community police force, and depending upon size and financial ability, supplement them with protective auxiliaries of his own. Such actions usually had public support, for the employer was exercising a recognized right to self-defense, despite widespread recognition by many public leaders in and out of government of the desirability, need, and justice of collective bargaining. In the absence of the authority and effective sanctions of protective labor legislation, many employers fought unionism with every weapon at their command, in the certainty that their hostility was both lawful and proper.

Union Violence

Facing inflexible opposition, union leaders and their members frequently found that nothing, neither peaceful persuasion nor the intervention of heads of government, could move the employer towards recognition. Frustration and desperation impelled pickets to react to strikebreakers with anger. Many violent outbreaks followed efforts of strikers to restrain the entry of strikebreakers and raw materials into the struck plant. Such conduct, obviously illegal, opened the opportunity for forceful police measures. In the long run, the employer's side was better equipped for success. The use of force by pickets was illegal on its face, but the action of the police and company guards were in vindication of the employers' rights.

The effect of labor violence was almost always harmful to the union. There is little evidence that violence succeeded in gaining advantages for strikers. Not only does the rollcall of lost strikes confirm such a view, but the use of employer agents, disguised as union members or union officials for advocating violence within the union, testifies to the advantage such practices gave the employer. There were a few situations, in areas made vulnerable by their openness such as a strike in municipal transportation or involving teamsters, where violence was effective in gaining a favorable settlement. Even here, however, such as in the teamsters strike in Chicago in 1905, the violence often failed. The most sensational campaigns of the Western Federation of Miners to bring their opponents to heel by the use of force were unsuccessful, and the union was virtually driven out of its stronghold. The campaign of dynamiting of the Iron Workers' Union ended in the conviction of the McNamaras. Subsequent convictions of a number of union leaders, including its president, who were convicted of transporting dynamite and of conspiracy in the federal courts, almost wrecked the union. The campaign of violence carried on by the molders against the members of the antiunion National Founders Association failed to change the latter's policy.[118]

The right to organize was not retained in Homestead, or won in Pullman, the Colorado metal mines, Coeur d'Alene, or in the steel mills in 1919, although the sacrifice by union members, especially the rank and file members, was great. In fact, the victories gained by violent strikes are rather few, for the use of violence tends to bring about a hardening of attitudes and a weakening of the forces of peace and conciliation. A community might be sympathetic to the demands of strikers, but as soon as violent confrontations took place, the possibility was high that interest would shift from concern for the acceptance of union demands to the stopping of violence.

It is the violent encounters that have provided organized labor with its lists of martyrs, men and women who gave their lives in defense of the union and collective bargaining. The role of martyrdom is not for us to assay, and may be useful in welding the solidarity of the group. The blood of the martyr may be the seed of the church, but in labor disputes it is doubtful if the sacrifices have been worth the results obtained. The evidence against the effectiveness of the violence as a means of gaining concessions by labor in the United States is too overwhelming to be a matter of dispute.

Except for contemporary examples, we have not dealt with the numerous minor disturbances, some of them fairly serious, that were settled by the use of the normal police force. We have also generally avoided the many instances in which organizers and active unionists were denied their right to remain in communities or were the victims of local vigilante groups. We know that union organizers could not enter the closed coal towns, and that labor speakers could neither hire a hall nor speak in a public square in many communities. A number of coal counties in Kentucky and West Virginia built what amounted to an iron wall against the invasion of union organizers. The situation became worse during strikes. In the 1919 steel strike, the mayor of Duquesne, Pa., announced that "Jesus Christ could not hold a meeting in Duquesne," let alone the secretary-treasurer of the American Federation of Labor.

Sitdown Strikes

Some recent apostles of violence as a method of social reform point to the sitdown strikes in the 1930s as proof of the value of such tactics. The sitdown strike was the usual suspension of work, but instead of the employees leaving the premises of their employer, they remained within the plant. The tactic itself is not a violent one, although it is obviously an unlawful trespass upon another's property. However, these tactics were used against employers who had refused to grant recognition to the union, which during the great sitdown strikes in the plants of General Motors and the Chrysler Corp. were in violation of the National Labor Relations Act. As a matter of fact, the sitdown strikes were exceptionally peaceful, given the circumstances, and there was only one serious confrontation between strikers and company guards during the strike at General Motors and, by the standards of the time, it can be described as a minor altercation. The beneficiaries of violence accompanying a sitdown strike are abundantly clear from the events surrounding a conventional recognition strike by the UAW against the Ford Motor Co.'s Rouge plant on April 1, 1941. According to the union, the company—

> tried to take an illegal sitdown strike at the plant to discredit the genuine strike and to obscure the legal demands of the Ford workers. A federal conciliator and a Ford advertising director, however, revealed that the sitdowners were a thousand strike-breakers hired by Ford to stage a demonstration of riot and disorder.[119]

The company's attempt to use the sitdown as a basis for state and federal armed intervention was unsuccessful.

As a matter of fact, violence was used against the automobile workers who used the sitdown tactic. Not only were many discharged for joining the union, but the attack upon Walter Reuther and Richard Frankensteen and others by a group of thugs under the direction of Harry Bennet, in charge of security at the Ford Motors Plant, was one of the more serious incidents in the organization of the industry. In ruling that sitdown strikers lost the protection against discharge for union activity guaranteed by the National Labor Relations Act, the U.S. Supreme Court said: "The seizure and holding of the buildings was a thing apart from any acts of sabotage. But in its legal aspect the ousting of the owner from lawful possession is not essentially different from assault upon the officers of an employer."[120] For our purposes, however, the distinction between a trespass and a physical assault is meaningful and important regardless of their legal equivalence. Once it became known that by participation in a sitdown strike a discharged worker forfeits his reinstatement rights under the law, the use of this tactic virtually ceased, and it has not been widely used since the above decision.

The Persistence of Violence

We are, however, confronted with a paradox in that violence in labor disputes persisted even though it seldom achieved fruitful results. With few exceptions, labor violence was the result of isolated and usually unplanned acts on a picket line, or occurred during a prohibited parade or demonstration protesting employer obduracy or police brutality. It might also start by attempts of pickets to prevent the transportation of strikebreakers or goods, and a clash would follow police interven-tion. Where the employer refused to deal with the union, the possibility of eventual violence was always high. The desire of the American worker for union representa-tion took place in the teeth of employer opposition that was able to impose heavy sanctions for union activity. The reproduction of conditions in which violence is spawned inevitably was followed by outbreaks of violence. Violence could be successfully repressed by superior forces but it could not be eliminated until its causes were removed.

The Reduction in Violence

The elimination in 1933 of the most important single cause of violence, refusal to recognize the union for purposes of collective bargaining, came about at the time when union membership was lower than it had been for 15 years. The first step taken was the adoption of section (7)(a) in the National Industrial Recovery Act, which guaranteed workers in industries operating under codes of fair competition the right to organize and bargain collectively through their own representatives. This provision was only partially effective in protecting the right to organize, but it was a significant beginning. Its successor, the National Labor Relations Act, with its amendments, has been on the books and upheld by the Supreme Court for almost a half a century. The sharp decline in the level of industrial violence is one of the great achievements of the National Labor Relations Board.

It may have been a fortunate coincidence that the labor laws guaranteeing the right to organize were enacted at the time the character of business management was changing. The professional business executive, who has increasingly come to dominate management, is not inclined to regard his business in the same sense as the head of a family-developed firm. He is more flexible in his thinking and more responsive to social and political changes. It may not be an accident that some of the bitterest contemporary labor disputes—Kohler and Perfect Circle, for example— took place in family-held businesses. The professional business leader is more detached, more pragmatic in his reactions, and knows that American business has sufficient resilience to adapt itself to free collective bargaining. The performance of American industry since the end of the Second World War demonstrates that union organization and collective bargaining are not incompatible with satisfactory profits and a high rate of technological change.

Violence has greatly diminished, but it has not entirely ceased. Between 80 to 100 proven charges of violence or coercion are closed annually by the National Labor Relations Board. In addition, reports of violence of varying seriousness appear periodically in the press. The charges that come before the Board that we have examined are largely based upon threats and generally minor picket-line incidents. Yet in none of them did deaths or serious injuries occur, and nearly all of them, if they had taken place prior to the 1930s, would have been ignored in our study. Had we taken note of all the threats and picket line incidents prior to the 1930s, our study would have reached unmanageable proportions. Present-day violence is by and large the result of accidental and random events which occasionally erupt in a picket line confrontation.

Prospect of Reversion to Past Patterns of Violence

Has widescale violence been permanently erased from American industry? The reduction in violence in labor disputes has been accompanied by sharp increases in violent behavior in other areas of American life. This is no accident. The conditions that gave rise to past labor violence have been eliminated and a restoration of these conditions would lead to a reversion in conduct. 'Any tampering with the complex mechanism that governs our contemporary labor policy is an invitation towards unharnessing of the forces of violence and hate that we have successfully mastered.

Labor and Other Forms of Violence

Can one draw more general conclusions from the labor experience, or are they peculiar to the problems of workers seeking to establish unions in industry? On many occasions the union operated in a hostile community, while minorities carry on their protests in their own friendly neighborhoods. Nevertheless, in both situations the reaction of the majority is likely to be decisive. There have been times where public sentiment was so strongly on the labor side that no matter what violence it committed, it ran no risk of estranging local public sentiment. Such was the case in Virden and in the far more questionable situation in Herrin. Usually, however, violence led to the alienation of public opinion and sometimes to a shift in public sentiment to approval of severe actions against the strike. The evidence is clear that the absence of violence committed by unions would not have retrieved many lost strikes. However, it appears highly probable that the advocacy or the practice of organized and systematic violence on the union side would have prevented the enactment of the New Deal Labor legislation.

There is no evidence that majorities will supinely accept violence by minorities. The fact that rioters are fighting for a just cause or reacting to oppression has not, in the case of labor, led to the condoning of violence by the public. The desirability of collective bargaining had, prior to the 1930s, been endorsed by a number of public bodies, and all twentieth-century presidents of the United States. Such views are also sponsored by leading students in the field, legislators, clergymen, and others. Such approval did not save labor from severe repression.

It appears to us that it is a gross confusion of the problem to emphasize the creative character of violence as a guide to the behavior of minorities suffering from serious inequities and injustice. Creative violence obviously refers to the successful revolutions in England, the United States, France, and Russia. It appears to us that such a view is completely irrelevant if it is not vicious and highly misleading. We are concerned not with revolutionary uprisings, which such a view implies, but how a minority can achieve belated justice. Although we believe that minorities can obtain little through violence, we are also convinced, on the basis of labor experience, that violence will continue unless attention is paid to the removal of basic grievances.

In some respects the violence in the ghettos resembles the kind that surrounded labor disputes; it arises without prior planning and out of isolated instances that may not repeat themselves. It is also highly probable that violence of this kind will be unproductive or even counterproductive, in that it will antagonize many who would normally support the claims of minorities for equal justice and opportunity. Yet the labor analogy with racial minorities can be pushed too far. Labor's grievances were specific and could be met by single or groups of employers with concessions. The adverse effects of granting these concessions were small, injured few people, and employers could generally pass on any added costs to consumers. On the other hand, to the extent that the grievances of minorities are of a general nature and the meeting of their demands impinges upon the privileges of wide sections of the community, the resolution of their disputes is apt to be met with greater opposition.

NOTES

1. For a long period of time strikebreakers were not regarded as replacements.

2. Jean Maitron, *Histoire du Mouvement Anarchiste en France* (Paris: Societe Universitaire D'Editions et de Libraire, 1961), 67-69.

3. Quotation is from Henry David, *History of the Haymarket Affair* (New York: Russell and Russell, 1958), 73; see also John R. Commons and associates, *History of Labour in the United States* (New York: Macmillan, 1918), 291-293.

4. The exchange of letters between Governor Mathews and the President are in *Federal Aid in Domestic Disturbances, 1877-1903*. S. Doc. 209, 57th Cong., 2d session, 315.

5. Letters in *ibid.,* 317.

6. See Robert V. Bruce, *1877: Year of Violence* (Indianapolis: Bobbs Merrill, 1959); J.A. Dacus, *Annals of the Great Strikes* (St. Louis: Schammell, 1877); Edward Winslow Martin, *The History of the Great Riots* (Philadelphia: National Publishing Co., 1877).

7. *Fifth Biennial Report of the Adjutant General of the State of Kansas, 1885-86*, 53-54.

8. *Investigation of Labor Troubles in Missouri, Kansas and Texas and Illinois*, H. Rept. 4174, 49 Cong. 2d sess., 1887, pp. IV-V.

9. *Biennial Report of the Adjutant General of Illinois to the Governor and Commander-in-Chief, 1885-86*, 21, 22, 27, 30, 32.

10. Speech of Gen. C. H. Grosvenor of Athens County to Ohio House of Representatives, Mar. 10, 1875, 3, 9, 15.

11. Quotation is from *Investigation of Labor Troubles.* U.S.S. Rept. 1280, 52d Cong., 2d sess., pp. XII, XIV. See also *Employment of Pinkertons*, H. Rept. 2447, 52d Cong., 2d sess.

12. *Report of the United States Industrial Commission*, Washington, 1901, vol. 12, p. 490; George Edgar French, "The Coeur d'Alene Riots," *Overland Monthly*, July 1895, 33-34; Selig Perlman and Philip Taft, *History of Labor in the United States* (New York: Macmillan, 1935), vol. 4, 17-173.

13. A.C. Hutson, Jr., "The Coal Miners' Insurrection of 1891 in Anderson County, Tennessee," *The East Tennessee Historical Society's Publications*, No. 7, 1935, 103-121.

14. Robert David Ward and William Warren Rodgers, *Labor Revolt in Alabama: The Great Strike of 1894* (Southern Historical Publications No. 9, University of Alabama, 1965), 68.

15. *Biennial Report of the Adjutant General of Alabama*, 1894, 52, 62; Ward and Rodgers, op. cit., 111.

16. *Biennial Report of the Adjutant General of Illinois to the Governor and Commander-in-Chief, 1899-1900*, 6-7; *Eighteenth Annual Report of the Illinois Bureau of Labor Statistics, 1899*, II-III.

17. See Vernon H. Jenson, *Heritage of Conflict* (Ithaca, N.Y.: Cornell University Press, 1950), pp. 13-14; Selig Perlman and Philip Taft, *History of Labor in the United States, 1896-1932* (New York: Macmillan, 1935), vol. 4, 184-186; Report of the United States Industrial Commission, vol. 12, 469-470; *Coeur d'Alene Labor Troubles*, S. Doc. 140, 56th Cong., 1st sess., 65; *Coeur d'Alene Labor Troubles*, H. Rept. 1999, 56th Cong., 1st sess., 69-125.

18. The Molly McGuires, a terrorist organization that operates in the anthracite area at this time, was not a bargaining organization. Made up of Irish miners, it exercised vengeance against arrogant mine bosses of British origin and others who came into its disfavor. It did not direct demands for improvements in working conditions, although it issued warnings against oppressors. Whatever its connection with the labor movement may have been, we know that this group was destroyed and many of its leaders hanged.

19. Frank Julian Warne, *The Coal Mine Workers* (New York: Longmans, 1905).

20. New York *World*, Sept. 11-12, 1897; Also see Edward Pinkowski, *The Latimer Massacre* (Philadelphia: Sunshine Press, 1950).

21. New York *Tribune*, Sept. 23, Sept. 27, 1900.

22. New York *Tribune*, Sept. 30, 1902; Perlman and Taft, op. cit., 44; Robert J. Cornell, *The Anthracite Coal Strike* (Washington: Catholic University Press, 1957); Frank J. Warne, *The Slav Invasion and the Mine Workers* (Philadelphia: Lippincott, 1904); *Report to the President on the Anthracite Coal Strike of May-October, 1902,* Anthracite Strike Commission (Washington: U.S. Government Printing Office, 1903).

23. *A Report on Labor Disturbances in the State of Colorado from 1880 to 1904.* S. Doc. 122, 58th Cong., 3d sess., 112.

24. Ibid., 182-187.

25. Ibid., 192-193.

26. Ibid., 295.

27. Ibid., 325.

28. Ibid., 168-169, 200-201, 205.

29. Ibid., 325.

30. See Vernon Jensen, *Heritage of Conflict* (Ithaca: Cornell University Press, 1950); Benjamin McKie Rastall, *The Labor History of Cripple Creek District,* University of Wisconsin Bulletin No. 198 (Madison, 1908).

31. The information on violence is from the police reports sent to the Bureau of Labor by Frank L. Palmer and Ethelbert Stewart, both of whom were present at different times during the strike in Chicago, and reported regularly to the Commissioner of Labor. The papers were examined in the National Archives, Washington, D.C. They are in the Papers of Ethelbert Stewart.

32. *Report of the Adjutant General of the State of New York,* 1902, pp. 61-62.

33. *The Public,* March 18, 1910, 253.

34. Harold J. Howland, "The War in Philadelphia," *The Outlook,* March 5, 1910.

35. *Electric Traction Weekly,* Sept. 10, 1910, 993.

36. Ibid, 994.

37. *Annual Report of the Adjutant General to the Governor of the State of Ohio,* 1910, 5.

38. *The Clothing Workers of Chicago, 1910-1922* (Chicago: Amalgamated Clothing Workers of America, 1922); Perlman and Taft, op. cit, pp. 304-308. A year later, the Cleveland garment workers sought recognition, and their efforts were accompanied by rioting and shooting, including the killing of a picket. C. E. Ruthenberg, "The Cleveland Garment Workers," *International Socialist Review,* Sept. 1911, 136.

39. *Labor Conditions in the Anthracite Regions of Pennsylvania, 1887-1888,* H. Rept. 4147, 50th Cong., 2d sess., 136-167.

40. J.P. Shalloo, *Private Police* (Philadephia: The American Academy of Political and Social Sciences, 1933), 61.

41. See report of the *Committee on Education and Labor Pursuant S. Res. 266* (74th Cong.), S. Rept. 6, Part 2, 76th Cong., 1st sess., 1939; *Report of United States Commission on Relations,* S. Doc. 415, 64th Cong., 1st sess., 1916, 92-98.

42. *Report of the Adjutant General of the State of New Jersey for the Year Ending October 31, 1902,* 25.

43. *U.S. H. Doc. 607,* 60th Cong., 1st sess., 17.

44. Ibid, 22.

45. Ibid, 23.

46. *Report of the Adjutant General of the State of New Jersey for the Year Ending October 31, 1909,* 15-16.

47. *Biennial Report of the Adjutant General of California,* 1910, 50-51.

48. Luke Grant, *The National Erectors' Association and the International Association of Bridge and Structural Iron Workers* (Washington: U.S. Commission on Industrial Relations, 1915), especially 107-148.

49. Ibid., 125.

50. Ibid., 130.

51. Ibid., 136-137.

52. *Report of the United States Commission on Industrial Relations* (testimony of Charles F. Markham, president of Illinois Central), vol. 10.

53. The violence is described in sections dealing with the Harriman and Illinois Central strikes in ibid.

54. *Annual Report of the State Board of Conciliation and Arbitration in Massachusetts, 1912,* 31; *Report of Massachusetts Adjutant General for 1912,* 7; *Report on Textile Strike in Lawrence, Massachusetts,* S. Doc. 870, 62d Cong., 2d session; *Hearings on the Strike at Lawrence, Massachusetts,* H. Doc. 671, 62d Cong., 2d sess.

55. *Report of the Adjutant General of the State of California, 1914,* 45-46; *Proceedings of the 15th Annual Convention of the Convention of the California State Federation of Labor,* 1914, 72-73.

56. Walker C. Smith, *The Everett Massacre* (Chicago: I.W.W. Publishing Co., 1917), deals with the issue from the IWW point of view. Also, Perlman and Taft, op.cit., 390-392.

57. Ralph Chaplin, *The Centralia Conspiracy* (Chicago: I.W.W. Publishing Co., 1924); *The Centralia Case,* Joint Report on the Armistice Day Tragedy at Centralia, Wash., Nov. 11, 1919, issued by the Department of Research and Education of Federal Council of Churches, the Social Action Department of the National Catholic Welfare Council, and the Social Justice Committee of the Central Conference of American Rabbis, 1930; Ben Hur Lampman, *Centralia Tragedy and Trial* (Tacoma, Wash., 1920).

58. *Investigation of Conditions in Paint Creek Coal Fields of West Virginia in Pursuance of S. Res. 37,* S. Rept. 321, 63d Cong., 2d sess., contains the commission's report. Quotation is on 238.

59. George P. West, *Report on the Colorado Strike* (Washington: U.S. Commission on Industrial Relations, 1915), 31.

60. Ibid., 133.

61. West, op. cit., 135. West was an investigator for the U.S. Commission on Industrial Relations and was acquainted with the facts. The figure on the dead women from Luke Grant, "The National Erectors Association," 131.

62. Perlman and Taft, op. cit., 336-342; Philip Taft, *Organized Labor in American History* (New York: Harper & Row, 1964), 259-262; *Final Report and Testimony Submitted to Congress by the Commission on Industrial Relations,* Vols. 6, 8, 9. Also Barron B. Beshoar, *Out of the Depths* (Denver: Golden Press, n.d.), 180-194.

63. *Monthly Labor Review,* Sept., 1941, 569.

64. *Transcription of the Hearing of the President's Mediation Board.* Held at Bisbee, Ariz., Nov. 1-5, 1917, 239-240.

65. Ibid., 160.

66. *Report on the Bisbee Deportations Made by the President's Mediation Commission to the President of the United States,* Nov. 6, 1917.

67. *West Virginia Coal Fields.* Hearings before U.S. Senate Committee on Education and Labor, 67th Cong., 1st sess., 7, 52, 873.

68. Ibid., 6. See also Winthrop D. Lane, *Civil War In West Virginia* (New York: Huebsch, 1921).

69. *United Mine Workers Journal,* Aug. 15, 1922, 7-8, 9-10.

70. *Monthly Labor Review,* Sept., 1924, 570.

71. Paul M. Angle, *Bloody Williamson* (New York: Knopf, 1952) deals with this episode.

72. *Report of the Adjutant General of Missouri*, Jan. 10, 1921.

73. *Annual Report of the Chief of the Militia Bureau*, 1923, 58-65.

74. The information is from the Bill of Complaint Exhibit No. 3, *U.S. Railway Employees Department, American Federation of Labor, etc.*, in U.S. District Court for the Northern District of Illinois Eastern Division, 124-128, 139-143.

75. *Appendix to Annual Report of Attorney General of the United States for the Fiscal year 1922* (Washington: U.S. Government Printing Office, 1924) 20.

76. *United Mine Workers Journal*, Mar. 15, 1926, p. 11; Harriet L. Herring, "12 Cents, the Troops and the Union," *The Survey*, Nov. 15, 1923, 199-200; *Annual Report of the Chief of the Militia Bureau*, 1927, 68.

77. Daniel J. McClurg, "The Colorado Coal Strike of 1927—Tactical Leadership of the IWW," *Labor History*, 82-85; *Biennial Report of the Adjutant General of the State of Colorado to His Excellency the Governor*, 1928, 26-28.

78. *Conditions in the Coal Fields of Pennsylvania, West Virginia, and Ohio*. Hearings before the Committee on Interstate Commerce, U.S. Sen., 70th Cong., 1st sess., pursuant to S. Res. 105.

79. *Report of the Adjutant General of the State of North Carolina*, July 1, 1926, to Dec. 31, 1927.

80. New York *Times*, Oct. 3-5, 12, 1929; *The Marion Murder* (New York: National Executive Committee of the Conference for Progressive Labor Action, 1929).

81. *The Struggle for Civil Liberty on the Land* (New York: American Civil Liberties Union, no date), 24-25, 27-28.

82. Captive mines produced coal only for the use of owners, such as steel and public utility companies.

83. New York *Times*, Oct. 5, 10, 11, 1933.

84. *Violation of Free Speech and Rights of Labor: Private Police Systems, Harlan County, Kentucky*, report of the Committee on Education and Labor pursuant to S. Res. 266 (74th Cong.). A resolution to investigate violations of the right of free speech and assembly and interference with the right of labor to organize and bargain collectively, Feb. 13, 1939, 47-48.

85. Ibid., 79.

86. Ibid., 83.

87. Ibid., 98-104.

88. Ibid., 112.

89. *Report of the Adjutant General of the State of North Carolina, January 1, 1933-December 31, 1935*, 12.

90. Ibid., 447-449. See also New York *Times* through August and September 1934 for detailed coverage of the textile strike situation.

91. Walter Wilson, *Call Out the Militia* (New York: American Civil Liberties Union, 1938), 28.

92. New York *Times*, Feb. 1, 15, Mar. 31, May 14, Oct. 27, 1935.

93. New York *Times*, Sept. 3-8, 1935.

94. *Report of the Chief of the National Guard*, 1936, 16.

95. Wilson, op. cit., 29.

96. President Thomas Girdler, of the Republic Steel Co., testified before the La Follette Committee in August 1938, and stated that his industrial relations policy had succeeded. Senator Robert M. La Follette commented: "Mr. Girdler, in connection with the success of his industrial-relation policy, the record of this investigation shows that the steel strike of 1937 cost the country sixteen lives and 307 persons were injured." *Hearings before a Subcommittee on Education and Labor*, U.S. Senate, 75th Cong., 3d sess., pt. 34, 13889.

97. *The Chicago Memorial Day Incident.* S. Rept. 46, pt. 2, 76th Cong., 1st sess., 1937, 3.

98. Ibid., 18.

99. Ibid., 18.

100. Ibid., 39.

101. *Hearings Before a Subcommittee of the Committee on Education and Labor,* U.S. Senate, 75th Cong., 3d sess., pt. 34, 13968.

102. Ibid., pt. 28, 11497.

103. New York *Times*, July 17, 28, Aug. 29, Nov. 9, 11, 1939.

104. Denver *Post*, May 23, 1940.

105. St. Louis *Dispatch,* July 25, 1940.

106. New York *Times,* Apr. 16, 1941.

107. Los Angeles *Times,* June 9, 1940.

108. *Quadrennial Report of the Adjutant General of Alabama,* 1942, 87-88.

109. New York *Times,* May 10, 1940.

110. Brooklyn *Eagle,* Sept. 24, 1940.

111. Oklahoma City *Oklahoman,* Apr. 21, 1946.

112. *NLRB* v. *Drivers, etc.,* 362 U.S. 274 at 290.

113. *Perry Norvell Co.,* 80 NLRB 225 at 239.

114. We have examined all of the Board's case files in which a finding has been made of union-caused violence or coercion.

115. *Wall Street Journal,* Oct. 30, 1968.

116. The Hobbs Act inhibits the use of or threat of force to transport money in interstate commerce.

117. Slason Thompson, "Violence in Labor Disputes," *World's Work,* Dec. 1904.

118. *Final Report and Testimony of the Commission on Industrial Relations,* S. Doc. 415, 64th Cong., 1st sess. (Washington: U.S. Government Printing Office, 1916), vol. 1, 242-244.

119. "We Work at Ford's—A Picture History," UAW-CIO Ford Dept., Detroit, Mich., 1955, 45.

120. *National Labor Relations Board* v. *Fansteel Metallurgical Corp.,* 306 U.S. 240.

Chapter 8
Collective Violence in the Reconstruction South

G. DAVID GARSON and GAIL O'BRIEN

In 1871 a group of black citizens of Kentucky petitioned the United States Senate for relief from the "organized bands of desperate and lawless men mainly composed of soldiers of the late Rebel Armies," who, "under armed discipline and disguised and bound by Oath and secret obligations, have by terror and force subverted all civil society among the Colored people."[1] The Secret societies, the guerrilla bands, the fears of black uprisings, the clashes with the army of occupation, all combined to create an era of violence in the American South so extensive in scope that it can scarcely be detailed.[2]

Why do such periods of violence occur? Is it primarily because of the frustration and bitterness at war's end? Or economic disorganization and personal ruin? The absence of civilized repression over traditionally violent men? A conscious struggle for power? The answer to this question undoubtedly involves many layers of explanation—economic, sociological, political, and cultural. Moreover, focus on one layer need not preclude the causal importance of any other. The task of social scientists, however, is not to identify any one cause of periods of violence, nor is it simply to accumulate a lengthy list of all the factors involved, but rather to determine which are the more proximate causes of violence and which the more remote.

ALTERNATIVE EXPLANATIONS OF RECONSTRUCTION VIOLENCE

At the most general level, there are four explanations of Reconstruction violence—the biological, the cultural, the sociological, and the political. The biological perspective suggests that freeing the black man constituted the liberation

AUTHORS' NOTE: *G. David Garson is professor and head of the department of political science at North Carolina State University at Raleigh. His books include* Group Theories of Politics *(Sage Publications, 1978), and* Power and Politics in the United States *(Heath, 1977).*

Gail W. O'Brien is assistant professor of history at North Carolina State University at Raleigh; her publications have appeared in the North Carolina Historical Review *and V. Burton and R. McMath (eds.),* Nineteenth Century Southern Communities *(Greenwood Press, 1978).*

of a more primitive and violent race, leading to anarchy and terror countered by vigilance groups who restored order by force. A variant contends that the war lowered the levels of civilized repression necessary to confine the aggressive instincts of all men, that this led to violence from many levels of society, and was ended by the gradual reemergence of the planned repression of peaceful civilization.[3]

A cultural explanation looks to the two hundred plus slave revolts and perhaps beyond that to African warfare to see violence as a traditional means of political articulation by black men, not rooted in race but in custom. An entirely compatible explanation would emphasize dueling, lynch law, and other customary forms of violent behavior in white culture for sources of Reconstruction violence. On the other hand, a social conditions argument looks not to the distant past, but instead finds the roots of violence in the devastation of war which brought in its wake widespread foreclosures and confiscations, hunger and the transiency of large segments of the population.[4]

A final perspective, the political, leads to an emphasis on conflict of interest in an unregulated situation. This argument can be formulated in several ways. Reconstruction violence may be interpreted as a movement by Northern whites and by blacks to intimidate the defeated Southerners, who, after recovering, formed their own secret societies to regain lost power. At the same time, it may be viewed as resulting from the unwillingness of Southern whites generally to share power with blacks or, more specifically, as the unwillingness of prewar Southern white leaders to share power with blacks or lower-class Southern whites in the postwar era. Within these frameworks, then, more or less emphasis may be given to the black-Northern, Southern white, or Southern white elite share of the violence.[5] It is the general thesis of this essay that political considerations are the most proximate causes of violence during Reconstruction.

AN HISTORICAL ANALYSIS OF COLLECTIVE VIOLENCE DURING RECONSTRUCTION

In distinguishing the more proximate from the more remote causes of violence, it is necessary to determine first the type(s) of violence one wishes to investigate and then the frequency of such instances over time. It is assumed that the pattern of frequency will illuminate the more proximate causes.

This study focuses upon instances of *collective violence* and attempts to determine the frequency of such events through a thorough search of the *New York Times* and the relevant academic literature. Collective violence is defined as an event that involves at least fifteen people, not including lawful officials, and results in damage to property or injury to persons. It does not include assaults on single individuals or families, terrorism, arson, or bombings committed by individuals or small groups. Nor does it include nonviolent forms of coercion or lynchings not also involving riots.

The data probably represent a fraction even of the cases of collective violence in this period. For example, four disturbances in 1867 and three in 1868 were detailed for Tennessee. Yet Brigadier General John R. Lewis, Assistant Commissioner of the Freedman's Bureau for Tennessee, reported in October 1866 to Commissioner Oliver O. Howard that thirty-three freedmen had been murdered in that state since

April 1865. Additional reports for the same time span indicated twenty-nine murders in Arkansas, twenty-four in South Carolina, at least seventy in Louisiana, and nineteen in Kentucky.[6] While the vast majority of these crimes probably fall below our criteria of rioting, it should be noted that these reports, as well as reports of other forms of violence, such as whipping, beating, and stabbing, seem generally to correspond to the trends in collective violence which are quantitatively documented in Table 8.1.

As seen in Table 8.1 crowd violence did not occur randomly by year in the postwar South; instead, it rose in the years 1865-1867, peaked in 1868, declined in the years 1869-1871, and rose again in the midseventies, though never again reaching the 1868 level.

Table 8.1: Frequency of Race-Related Riots During Reconstruction, 1865-1877[a]

Year	Riots[b]
1863	1
1864	-
1865	4
1866	6
1867	9
1868	19
1869	4
1870	1
1871	3
1872	7
1873	5
1874	7
1875	3
1876	10
1877	0
1878	0
1879	1
1880	1
1881	0
1882	1
1883	0
TOTAL	82

a. Years 1863-64 and 1878-83 are presented for comparison.
b. Includes cases (14) drawn from sources other than the New York *Times*.

On preliminary inspection of Table 8.1 it is clear that some of the explanations mentioned earlier fit the frequencies better than others. A biological explanation generates, for example, an expectation of maximum violence at the close of the war, with a gradual decline thereafter. Similar predictions derive from the cultural conditions explanation. Removal of the lawful system of repression of a violent culture would presumably imply a maximum of violence at the time when that system was in greatest disarray, immediately after the war. Violence, however, was not greatest immediately after the war, nor was the annual frequency a matter of simple gradual decline.

A social conditions explanation, emphasizing deprivation and frustration, fares a little better. It might explain the peak of violence in 1867-1868 by the severe recession of that year, although it fails to explain the absence of a peak of violence amid the devastation prevailing at the close of the war. Also, a deprivation argument would predict significantly more violence in the two years following the panic of 1873 compared with the two preceding, but this is not the case. And a primary emphasis on social conditions would certainly fail to explain the sudden decline of race-related disturbances in the several years following 1876.

Of all the explanations, political considerations appear to be the strongest correlates of collective violence during Reconstruction. Almost 44 percent of the riots in Table 8.1, for example, occurred in the three election years 1868, 1872, 1876, while many of the remainder could have stemmed from political tensions. One must, of course, analyze carefully the disturbances in the election years to see if a political explanation conforms to the available data. Additionally, one must explain the large number of disturbances in non-election years, as well as the relative absence of rioting in the years after 1876.

Close scrutiny of the disturbances suggests that collective violence in the Reconstruction South progressed through three distinguishable phases: from (1) anomic violence of the immediate postwar era, similar to that described by DuBois, into (2) violence sanctioned and legitimized by figures of authority, and, after a period of "politically used" crowd violence, into (3) a phase in which leaders lost control of the situation and violence got out of hand. In the latter stage, authorities frequently became involved in usually successful efforts to restrain violence. The phase of anomic violence was confined largely to 1865, while the second phase of sanctioned violence was in evidence in most states by 1866 and reached its peak in 1868. Sanctioned violence recurred in some localities on into the 1870s, but in most states the third phase can be dated from 1869.

In terms of frequency of collective violence, relatively few instances occurred in the anomic stage as competitive groups formed to fill the political arena; the number increased as clashes between political groups occurred, and it subsequently declined when one side was defeated or a regrouping of forces was necessary. The frequency pattern of riots observed in Table 8.1 occurred, then, because political struggles climaxed in several Southern states simultaneously. Not surprisingly, these struggles often occurred in election years. For example, of the nineteen riots occurring in the presidential election year 1868, three-fourths took place in four states: Louisiana, Arkansas, Georgia, and Tennessee. Similarly, a conjunction of political factors in Louisiana in 1873-1874, Mississippi in 1874-1875, and South Carolina in 1876 largely explains the rise in riots in the midseventies. This is not to suggest that politically used crowd violence did not occur in other Southern states. Certainly, the evidence suggests that it did, but it was the occurrence of riots in the states just listed that accounted for most of the variation observed in Table 8.1. It should be noted that these dates do not necessarily mark the end of Republican rule in these states but the times when Democratic politics became the most extreme, to the point of armed militancy.

Anomic Violence

Although engendered by racial hatreds, the four riotous disturbances found in 1865 reflected the anomie of the war's close. The first riot reported in 1865, for example, followed rumors of an attack by black troops on Irishmen. A party of black soldiers "aided by some debauched country blacks" reportedly entered into a violent fight with whites over "a widow lady, near the city [Augusta, Georgia], who at the time had several young ladies staying with her." The disturbance was stopped by other federal troops after six blacks had been killed or fatally wounded.[7] In September 1865, ex-Confederate guerrillas near Springfield, Tennessee, killed one black and tortured or injured others in "indiscriminate robbery and murder" in that city. In December 1865, a small riot was precipitated at Clarksville, Tennessee, when a policeman attempted to arrest a black soldier. Several were wounded in the fray, allegedly led on the white side by "a notorious guerrilla." On Christmas Day a riot occurred in Alexandria, Virginia, in which 14 blacks were killed and 2 whites injured, in unclear circumstances.

While this level and type of violence is in accord with the anomic variety, it should be emphasized that a rather general movement against blacks had already begun in the South in 1865, even if it was not reflected in rioting. For example, John Hope Franklin noted black conventions held to protest the treatment of blacks at New Bern, Norfolk, Petersburg, Vicksburg, Alexandria, Nashville, Richmond, Raleigh, and Jackson between May and October 1865.[8] These were both in anticipation of and in response to the passage by Southern legislatures in the summer and fall of 1865 of reactionary Black Codes, as well as to physical threats.[9]

Politically Sanctioned Crowd Violence

Following the anomic violence of the war's end, many authority figures, primarily white conservatives but also radicals, found it to their political advantage to legitimate the grievances and often violent methods of some of their followers. In emphasizing the sometimes neglected political relation between authority and violence, however, it would be entirely wrong to give the impression that motivation to violence comes from above. "Permission to hate," a term used by C. Vann Woodward in characterizing this period, presumes prior hostility. It suggests neither a tight conspiracy to commit violence nor, on the other hand, merely violence by individuals. While it is in fact impossible to know now what the underlying causes were that motivated violent individuals in this period, one can discern from the existing literature what Neil Smelser describes as "a structurally conducive setting," a setting permissive of hostility and prohibitive of other responses.[10]

Of the five riots discovered in 1866 for example, only one, that in Brenham, Texas, was not encouraged by local authorities. In Natchez, Tennessee local police proved so unneutral that the local (federal) army post commander desired to disarm them, but he was overruled by General Wood.[11] In May there was an important riot in Memphis, lasting two days and resulting in the death of 46 blacks and the wounding of one white.[12] In this one-sided riot the police, the representatives of local public authority, showed such criminal unneutrality that the state legislature placed them under state commissioners. After the riot the local newspaper, the Memphis

Avalanche, implicitly praised the rioters, saying, "Thank heaven the white race are once more rulers of Memphis."[13].

A riot at New Orleans on July 30 was not dissimilar. As with an earlier riot at Norfolk, Virginia, it grew out of an attack by whites on a black-radical political parade. Tension was high in New Orleans because of a convention held there to consider depriving certain Confederate veterans of their vote and extending the franchise to freedmen. The meeting had been convened by anti-Confederate forces attempting to outflank planters in the legislature who were trying to organize their own reactionary constitutional convention. Local leaders publicly stated their opposition to the convention of July 30. Du Bois noted "A prominent judge harangued the grand jury against the meeting. The mayor told the general in command of the U. S. Army that he proposed to prevent the assembly."[14] Mayor Monroe, who was also head of a secret society called "The Southern Cross," organized a mob, armed them, and proceeded with them to the State House and there "shot down people who were in the hall." Blacks and supporters beat back the police three times but were overwhelmed. Thirty-four to fifty blacks were killed and up to two-hundred were wounded. General Sheridan called it "an absolute massacre by the police . . . a murder which the mayor and police perpetrated without the shadow of necessity."[15] Afterward the local grand jury condemned the convention, charged it with exhorting blacks to kill whites, blamed the military for wrongly protecting the convention from the local police, and implicitly upheld the rioters.

In the final riot uncovered in 1866, that of August 30 in Shipley, Maryland, the New York *Times* reported that organized "desperadoes" screamed "What about New Orleans!" as they attacked a black Methodist camp meeting. This attack on the Methodists (who were associated with antislavery and prosuffrage positions) resulted in the murder of a white minister, and came during a campaign by the Unconditional Union Party, publicly supported by Governor Swain in the Baltimore newspapers, to oppose black suffrage. A lieutenant testified before a congressional committee that the "respectable people" of Maryland often "countenanced" the violence of others against the black.[16].

Given the psychological conditioning of the prewar era when Southern whites learned patterns of domination, while Southern blacks, free as well as slave, supposedly learned submission, it is not surprising that Southern conservative whites frequently constituted the aggressors in postwar confrontations. Additionally, when one considers that conservatives also possessed most of the material means for aggression and that they easily believed that a "black revolution" was "imminent," it is certainly not unexpected that they instigated much of the crowd-related violence.[17]

This was the case despite the fact that conservatives convinced many of their followers (and no small number of subsequent historians, see note 5) that violent activities on their part were a *response* to aggressive radicals. Yet those who would link rioting with friction between conservatives and alledgedly problack federal troops would have to explain why, at the time when the number of troops was declining, the number of riots rose from four in 1865 to six in 1866 to nine in 1867 to nineteen in 1868. Furthermore, it has proved impossible to document any cases of rioting growing out of the activities of the Union Leagues, organizations formed from 1862 in the South to promote Republicanism among blacks.

Still, black resistance to local conservative authorities, particularly in Southern cities, was not unknown and neither were inflammatory remarks by radical leaders. For example, in July, 1867, a Southern newspaper claimed that radicals instigated a riot at a Conservative meeting in Rogersville, Tennessee, at which the Conservative candidate for governor was speaking. Also in the same month, Brigadier General Cooper reported that state guards had been fired on by armed mobs and "outlaws" in several places, "in an attempt to keep the country in a reign of terror."[18]

Similarly, in May 1867 in Richmond, Virginia, the release of a white man but not a black, both of whom had been arrested for fighting, led to blacks rescuing their comrade and stoning the police. The New York *Times* reported a black's belief that such ad hoc attempts to secure justice were sanctioned by the new politics of the city: "We gwine [sic] to do as we please; isn't Judge John C. Underwood here to protect us?" Revealingly, this riot came just after a convention in April in which the radical leader James W. Hunnicut, in making a move for dominance in the Republican party had made "incendiary speeches" attacking the reactionary legislature for passing vagrancy laws and asserting that blacks were being treated unjustly in the courts. Even more significant, just prior to the riot, radical leader Lewis Lindsay had made statements to the effect that "before any of his children should suffer for food, the streets of Richmond should run knee-deep in blood; and he thanked God that Negroes had learned to use guns, pistols, and ramrods," On the white side, the Richmond *Enquirer* stated three weeks before the riot that "The Negroes openly avow sentiments which deserve death upon the gallows."[19]

Not infrequently clashes encouraged by authorities led to the development of *organizations* that sought to use violence. Such organizations, often sanctioned by authorities, further escalated the possibility of riots. The Freedmen's Bureau reported that groups like the Jayhawkers, Regulators, and Black Horse Cavalry, formed as early as 1866 in Georgia, had the approval of some authorities and intimidated the remainder.[20] In May 1867, the first convention of Ku Klux Klan was held at Nashville. At this "national" meeting the prestige of Confederate hero General Nathan B. Forrest was conferred on the Klan by his acceptance of the office of Grand Wizard of the Invisible Empire.[21] Forrest instituted a series of Fourth of July parades to demonstrate Klan strength.

Not surprisingly, the encouragement of violent actions by authority figures and the concomitant mobilization of individuals into groups intensified as elections approached. With an upcoming state election and a concomitant acceleration of Klan activity in Tennessee, for example, violent conflicts soon occurred. In May, 1867 a riot occurred at a radical convention in Brownsville in which three blacks and two whites were shot. All observers reported a noticeable increase in racial animosity. Two days after the Fourth of July a parade and rally of black radicals, members of the Union League, were attacked by white and black Conservatives in Franklin, Tennessee, south of Nashville. It was reported that the mayor knew of the attack in advance but did nothing to prevent it.[22] As the presidential election of 1868 approached, similar clashes occurred in other Southern states,[23] illustrating the high point of the phase of sanctioned violence.

RACIAL VIOLENCE, 1868:
LOUISIANA, ARKANSAS, AND GEORGIA

Louisiana. Du Bois noted, "The whole South was in a blaze of excitement about the 1868 election. Tremendous and frequent meetings were held in every city and parish in Louisiana . . . Secret semi-military organizations were set . . . It was believed that if Seymour and Blair were elected, Reconstruction would be overthrown."[24]

At the end of September a riot occurred at Opelousas, in St. Landy Parish after the Seymour Knights (a Democratic organization) severely whipped Republican editor Emerson Bentley, a "carpetbagger," for articles published in the St. Landry *Progress.* Bentley fled to New Orleans, but a rumor spread that he had been killed. Blacks flocked to Opelousas and clashed with local whites in a disturbance in which four blacks and perhaps one white person were killed. Local authorities disarmed the blacks and jailed eight, who were later taken from the jail and murdered. The shooting of blacks continued for two days. Democrats asserted that twenty-five to thirty blacks were killed; Republicans claimed over two hundred.[25]

Rioting also occurred at Caddo, Louisiana, while in nearby Bossier Parish armed bands of whites pursued and attacked blacks, killing 40 (Democratic version) to 120 (Republican version), after a complex series of incidents culminated in the murder of two local whites by blacks. In New Orleans the rioting of whites against black suffrage led local authorities to exclude blacks from the election in return for ending white rioting. This action led to the resignation of blacks from the police force. Ten blacks and seven whites were reported killed in the rioting.[26]

Although the rioting sometimes, as in the clash of blacks and Italians in St. Bernard Parish (neighboring New Orleans), grew out of specific, nonpolitical, racial enmities, the general connection with elections in 1868 is suggested by the abrupt end to crowd violence found in 1869 (one riot was found in which a mob led by a Democratic editor destroyed the offices of a Republican editor), 1870, and 1871 (no riots found). One important reason noted by Du Bois was that Republican Governor Warmuth secured power by an 1869 law to "at his discretion throw out any votes anywhere in the state on any pretext."[27] By making elections a foregone conclusion, the incentives to voter intimidation and election violence were temporarily removed. The conflict was not resolved by this means, of course, and crowd violence appeared with dramatic force in the elections of 1872, and especially in 1873 and 1874.

Arkansas. A peak of crowd violence was also reached in Arkansas in 1868. There, pro-Union men had been quick to institute Isaac Murphy governor at a convention held on January 4, 1864. The Conservatives adopted the strategy of tolerating Murphy while seeking Democratic control of the legislature, which they secured in 1866. The legislative commission to Washington seeking to secure readmission emphasized the "importance, the absolute necessity, of remaining quiet, of preserving good order, and a quiet submission to and a rigid enforcement of the law everywhere within the limits of the state." A local newspaper editorialized: "There is no provocation which should induce [the people of Arkansas] to lose their self-possession and make imprudent or passionate remarks. They should allow the Butlers, Stevenses and the Sumners do all the bullying."[28] The Republicans began a massive effort to organize their party and register votes, beginning in 1866 and nominating a slate of candidates in April, 1867.

At about this time General Forrest came to Arkansas to promote the Ku Klux Klan, securing General Albert Pike as the Klan's influential promoter in the state. Although Klan activity began at least in April, it appears to have been organized too late to have had great influence on the radical victory in June, based in part on intensive party organizing and depending on the federal disfranchising of many ex-Confederates who had voted Democratic in 1866. Although Clayton became the Republican governor of the state, violence became widespread by the end of the year. Federal troops and law officers were attacked near Rocky Comfort, and four militia were killed by a mob of citizens in Augusta, Arkansas. Also in October, Reconstruction Congressman James Hind was killed in Monroe County. Clayton noted that prosecutions were impossible because of the Klan's influence with local authorities, even to the point of being assured of control of jury selection.[29]

For his part, Clayton used the militia vigorously. As early as April, 1868, the *Daily Republican* printed that the militia was to be armed and given the duty of enforcing Republican policies in the state.[30] The federal military was twice asked by local merchants to intervene in Arkansas to stop the "depradations" of the state militia, but these complaints were only turned back over to Clayton.[31] Clayton even used men like Col. William Monks of Missouri with his some 60 men to control the Klan, in spite of complaints of brigandage.[32] Following Tennessee's lead, stringent Ku Klux laws were passed in 1870, but in Arkansas they were better enforced by the state militia. Similarly, a Ku Klux dissolution order issued by Forrest in 1869 and the federal Anti-Ku Klux laws of 1870 and 1871 applied in Arkansas as well, with similar mixed effects.[33] Not insignificant was a rather effective spy system developed by Clayton against the Klan.[34]

Georgia. In Georgia blacks and radicals had begun organizing in 1866 before passage of the Reconstruction acts with large meetings in Macon, Savannah, and Augusta. The constitutional convention which met at Atlanta in December was dominated by whites, but the constitution it promulgated provided for the enfranchisement of blacks and was adopted in April by a small majority of 18,000 votes. Although a Republican, Rufus B. Bullock, was elected by the narrow margin of 7,171 votes in the gubernatorial election; he was an ex-Confederate officer who had lived in the South before the war. The closeness of the parties was reflected in Republican control of the governorship but not of the legislature, which proceeded in July to reject Bullock's nominees for U.S. Senate and Congress, replacing them with Conservatives and moderates. Georgia was restored to the Union by the Omnibus Bill of June 25, but the legislature, asserting its independence further in September, 1868, expelled its black members and set in motion a train of events leading to Georgia's again coming under military rule.

It was at this time, Du Bois noted, that "The outrages of the Ku Klux Klan on Negroes became widespread."[35] General John B. Gordon, reputed to have been the state Grand Dragon of the Ku Klux, testified that "in 1868 I was approached and asked to attach myself to a secret organization in Georgia; I was approached by some of the best citizens of the state."[36] On the other side, some violent threats by pro-Union forces were also noted in Savannah and Macon.

The most notable riot occurred at Camilla, Georgia, on September 19, 1868. From 150 to "several hundred" blacks, depending on the account, marched on the town. Led by two white Republican candidates for office, they were demonstrating for the right to vote. The local sheriff, attempting to stop the demonstration, returned to town for reinforcements, and in the second confrontation a shot was fired, setting off a disturbance in which eight or nine blacks were killed and about thirty wounded; in comparison, two whites were wounded and none killed.[37] In November there was an election disturbance at Savannah after black Republicans reportedly tried to prevent black and white Democrats from voting. After the elections, blacks near Savannah attempted to assert control over two plantations. In August, 1869, General A. H. Terry reported, "In many parts of the state there is practically no government. The worst of crimes are committed and no attempt is made to punish those who commit them. Murders have been and are frequent; the abuse in various ways of the blacks is too common to excite notice. There can be no doubt as to the existence of numerous insurrectionary organizations known as Ku Klux Klans."[38]

Terry was given military command over Georgia on Christmas Eve, 1869. The legislature was reorganized with a Radical majority, and troops were used to keep order in numerous localities. Violence declined in the state after the campaign of 1868 and the reestablishment of military rule at the end of 1869. The political result, however, was a moderate-conservative coalition which gained two-thirds of the seats in the elections of 1871. As in other states white authorities then turned away from the forms of violence which had served their earlier purposes. Bullock, fearing impeachment, resigned in Octber, 1871.

SANCTIONED RACIAL VIOLENCE, 1872-1876

As in 1868, relatively high crowd violence levels during the mid-1870's resulted largely from clashes between competing groups in specific states: Louisiana, 1873-74; Mississippi, 1874-75; and South Carolina, 1876.

Louisiana, 1873-1874. As noted in the previous section, Governor Warmuth had taken control of elections in Louisiana and, through this control, removed the incentive to influence them by force. This obviously shaky solution quickly broke down. As early as the campaign of 1872 the anti-Warmuth Republicans were being urged to armed revolt, and Grant was forced to send troops to establish in office the regular Republican candidate Kellogg over the claims of his rival, John McEnery, an "anti-Negro" Democratic candidate backed by the planters and, as it happened, by Warmuth himself.[39].

Indeed, in the early months of 1873, Louisiana did not have an effective state government. The McEnery forces, though not in possession of the state house or armory, claimed to be the legal government of the state. As it became clearer and clearer that the Kellogg government was to prevail, violence increased. On March 5, McEnery forces, reportedly including militia units, attacked and took over New Orleans police stations until thrown back by reinforcements after one man was killed and a dozen wounded. The following day the McEnery legislature was taken over and its members arrested by armed police. Similar disorders occurred in other parishes. In Colfax the Kellogg sheriff mobilized a previously disbanded black militia to oust his fusion ticket (Democratic) rival; the fusion sheriff marched on the town on Easter Sunday with a force of some 150 men and surrounded the courthouse where the blacks had taken refuge, set fire to the building, and shot those who fled or tried to surrender. Some 60 to 100 blacks were reported killed. In St. Martinsville "rebels" skirmished for control of the local government for several days until their leader was arrested and their forces broken by a metropolitan force sent from New Orleans.[40]

By the summer of 1874, the Democratic resistance to the "illegal" Kellogg government had taken the form of the organization of the White Leagues, which varied by place from traditional parties to organized, drilled bodies. A major disturbance occurred in August at Coushatta when six white Republicans surrendered to local forces after a bloody fray; the next day they were shot while being transported, at their own will, but bound, out of the county. This outrage caused the parish to be placed under military rule, although U.S. troops were not sent in until over a month later.

The major instance of crowd violence was an attempted revolution in New Orleans in September. Here White League forces led by D. B. Penn, an ex-Confederate claiming the lieutenant-governorship under the McEnery ticket, placed Frederick N. Ogden in charge of the militia and succeeded in taking the city on September 14, with only 14 deaths on their side and 44 on the government side. The attempted revolution was sparked by Kellogg's policy of seizing privately held arms and by Penn's campaigning for Kellogg's overthrow. On September 15, Grant issued a proclamation upholding the Kellogg government, a proclamation enforced by federal troops on September 17, without resistance. After this defeat Conservative leaders "frowned on intemperate expression and provocative action, in an earnest and partially successful effort to have a campaign and election of such a sort that the results could not be overturned on charges of intimidation and violence."[41] The election results, after being much contested and having become involved in federal mediation, led to a Conservative house and a Radical senate (the governorship was not up for election until 1876). The continuing repudiation of violence by Louisiana Democratic leaders assured a relatively low level of violence throughout the remainder of Reconstruction, even in the bitter election of 1876, which brought Francis T. Nicholls, a conservative, to the governorship.

Mississippi, 1874-1875. In Mississippi the Constitution of 1868 was defeated by a narrow margin, partly, Du Bois suggested, because Republicans failed to appeal sufficiently to blacks by ignoring them in nominations. Consequently, Mississippi was not admitted to the Union, there was no competition of presidential electors in 1868, and hence much less violence than in other states. General Adelbert Ames became provisional governor under a military appointment, and under his direction another election was held in November, 1869. After rioting in three or four counties, the Constitution was passed, minus the provisions which had restricted white suffrage. Under this legislature and the one elected in 1871 Republicans were in the majority, although blacks were not.

The new legislature soon angered many whited by proposals for mixed schools. In 1870-1871 the Ku Klux Klan reappeared, burning a number of schoolhouses and intimidating teachers. In 1872 and 1873 Senators Ames and Alcorn carried on a bitter feud in which the former emphasized the latter's intent to allow blacks to be killed "by the hundreds" if elected governor. Between this election and November 1875, when Conservatives gained control of the state, opponents of Ames carried on "the Mississippi plan, as it came to be called, [which] was based not on the use of force but on the ever-present possibility that it might, and would be used if necessary. Its leaders planned, with the greatest care, to avoid violence of the sort which might cause federal intervention."[42]

This policy of "brinksmanship" with regard to violence often led over the brink in the 1874-1876 period in Mississippi. In Vicksburg, violence erupted when 500 "taxpayers" forced the town's Republican sheriff and black chancery clerk out of office and installed their own; black militia, acting on Ames's order, marched to confront the armed citizens, but both sides agreed to withdraw. The blacks were fired upon and a number killed as they withdrew.[43] Violence of the Vicksburg type occurred elsewhere in the state in 1874, but these incidents were minor compared to those in 1875, when "Nearly all the Democratic clubs in the state were converted into armed military companies," according to black Congressman John R. Lynch.

In that year the most notable crowd violence occurred at Clinton, where 500 armed whites fired upon a mass meeting of blacks; in the following week over a score of blacks were killed in race clashes in the country. The governor sought federal aid and was refused; the legislature then authorized the purchase of additional weapons, and the governor called for the mobilization of the militia. The Democratic *Clarion* responded, "The time has come when the companies that have been organized for protective and defensive purposes should come to the front. . . . Let every citizen hold himself in readiness to join one of these companies."[44] The governor was forced to sign a "peace agreement" with the Democrats in the face of the threat of open revolution in the state; the black militia was disbanded and Democratic intimidation was given a free hand. The Democrats, particularly Chairman James George, tried to restrain violence, as "we are nearly through now and are sure to win. Don't let us have any trouble of that sort on our hands."[45]

Although there were only a few scattered election riots, intimidation was widespread, and in several counties the Republican vote literally disappeared. The result was a Democratic sweep which President Grant termed "chosen through fraud and violence as would scarcely be accredited to savages."[46] In spite of a disturbance like that at Artesia in 1876, where U.S. troops were sent in to calm a fight resulting from a political meeting, violence seems to have fallen off sharply after the counterrevolution of 1875 — after, that is, state Conservative leaders had ended their endorsement of armed militance and ended their exaggerated grievances justifying action under arms.

South Carolina, 1876. Finally, in South Carolina violence reached a peak in 1876. In that state there seems to have been a conscious imitation of the "Mississippi plan"; in fact, General Wade Hampton, the Democratic nominee for governor, had resided in Mississippi since the end of the war and had only returned to South Carolina in 1876. As in Mississippi, however, violence soon erupted. In Hamburg, South Carolina, for example, seven black militiamen were killed in a riot that broke out during the trial of the militia's captain for blocking a public highway. Republican candidate Daniel Chamberlain wrote a letter to Grant anticipating "a campaign of blood and violence" and calling for vigorous federal action. Local newspapers condemned this move and the reaction became more aggressive in tone. As in Mississippi, Democratic leaders discouraged "actual violence . . . because of its probable effect in bringing federal intervention," while at the same time "The Democrats of the state were organized into Rifle Clubs."[47] Radical candidates were forced by these clubs to share their platforms with Democrats. Armed parades of marching Democrats were held in many of the county towns. By September there were "well-organized attacks by large groups of armed Democrats against groups of Negro Republicans" in Ellentown. Local Democratic leader General Gary stated: "The shot-gun policy is to plainly tell the Negroes that the whites are again in control of the state. . . . I, for one, would first shoot Chamberlain, Elliot, Pattersib and such carpetbaggers, and second the miserable white native scalawags, and lastly the black leaders generally." The U.S. District Attorney complained that "These [rifle] clubs have created and are causing a perfect reign of terror; the only safety for Negroes is in their signing a statement pledging themselves to vote Democratic."[48] Some 17 to 30 or more blacks were killed at Ellentown in the riot and aftermath.

Blacks occasionally responded violently. A sheriff was reported bushwacked and some plantation buildings burned by blacks prior to a radical clash in September near Robbins, South Carolina. At Beach Island, however, Democratic "red shirts" reportedly "rode the night before the election all through the settlement firing pistols and shotguns . . . [on election day] colored men were shot at and the Republican Supervisor of Election was driven away from the polls."[49] In Hamburg, scene of the initial riot, 75 Democratic redshirts led by A. P. Butler broke up a Republican meeting and drove the speaker from town; on election day they surrounded the polls and "colored men were struck and everything that could be done by yells and threats was done to prevent the Republicans from voting."[50] A postelection riot occurred in Charleston, focusing on an attack on a Republican ex-congressman. Alfred Williams, close to the Hampton Redshirts, summarized the election: "the Democrats cheated and intimidated and bribed and bulldozed and repeated where they could and the Republicans did likewise."[51]

The Democrats claimed a very narrow victory for Tilden and Hampton, while the Republican Board of Canvassers threw out the returns from Edgefield and Laurens counties for fraudulence, assuring a Hayes-Chamberlain victory. The result was a dual state government, eventually resolved in favor of the Democrats in the "corrupt bargain" of that year, whereby Hayes was supported by Southern Democratic electors in return for the end to Republican regimes in South Carolina and Louisiana. In conferring with Grant, Hampton promised an end to violence. With regard to race-related violence, the promise was kept: crowd violence ground dramatically to a virtual halt after 1876.

Uncontrolled Crowd Violence and the Withdrawal of Sanction by Authorities

Although sanctioned racial violence continued long after 1868, a reaction against the excesses of crowd violence against blacks soon set in.

In contrast to the politically oriented violence in Louisiana, Arkansas, and Georgia in 1868, the three disturbances found in Tennessee in that year illustrate the tendency of such violence to exceed the political bounds originally expected. In Franklin, Tennessee, a mob of armed whites shot a storekeeper suspected of being a black leader and his white assistant. In western Tennessee the Ku Klux Klan's raiding of homes of people with Union sympathies led to the sending of troops. In Lewisburg a band of white men terrorized blacks until they were dispersed by black militia which led to further violence a week later.[52] Additional examples of excesses are shown in Kentucky, where as late as 1873 and in spite of Democratic control of the government, secret bands were reported imperiling white-owned agriculture by driving the cheap black labor force from certain sections of the country-side, and in Baltimore where a riot occurred at a black picnic.[53]

Once political rioting became terroristic mob action, it usually tapered off as authorities who had hitherto initiated, sanctioned, defended, or tolerated it began to disavow it. Thus, crowd violence declined in the period around 1870 not only because these were not presidential election years, but also because hitherto friendly authorities and leaders began to "clamp down" on agents of violence. Forrest's order of 1869 ordering the disbanding of the Klan in Tennessee was explicit in its repudiation of the violent excesses that had grown up in the name of that organization. Also in 1869, former Tennessee Governor Neill Brown, a Conservative, published in the Nashville *Banner* an appeal to the Klan, holding "whatever may have been their motive in the beginning, admitting the insecurity of life and property, those times had passed away."[54] By 1871, such comments by Conservative Southerners seem not to have been uncommon.

No instances of crowd violence were found in Tennessee in the years 1870 and 1871 after the Conservative victory and the resignation of Republican Governor Brownlow to become a U.S. Senator. The one riot found in 1872 dealt with a white attack on a black picnic, with no indication of political factors. No riots were found in 1873; in the remaining four years through 1877, only two more riots were found, both in 1874. The first involved the storming of a jail in Trenton, Tennessee, and the subsequent massacre of six of sixteen blacks arrested for the kidnapping of a white man. The Memphis *Appeal,* described as "a strong Democratic newspaper," condemned the affair, likening it to the "insane" parties of armed blacks in some parts of the state.[55] The second event occurred when a black man's quarrel with the mayor led the mayor's friend to shoot the black outright. The resistance to arrest led to a shoot-out in the streets of Somerville, Tennessee. Although possibly related, especially in the latter case, to tension involved in the 1874 elections, the three riots found in Tennessee in the period after 1868 represent a distinctly different and declining phase of violence in Tennessee and, indeed, in the South.[56] This phase has already been discussed, of course, in connection with rioting in Arkansas, Georgia, Louisiana, Mississippi, and South Carolina in the midseventies as well as in 1868.

CONCLUSION

While it cannot be proven that crowd violence either started or declined because of the actions of authorities, it may be shown that such an hypothesis is plausible, even when examined in some detail, for collective violence did not occur randomly by year in the postwar South. Instead, it was intimately linked to the politics of various states where authorities, contesting for power (primarily Democratic but also Republican), elicited and legitimized it, then sought to restrain its excesses.

In this paper we have tried to show, without undue simplification, the hypothesized pattern. According to this pattern, anomic crowd violence, characteristic of the immediate postwar period, changed to politically used crowd violence, legitimized by political leaders, notables, or editors, i.e., figures of authority on one or both sides. This type of violence then frequently got out of hand and resulted in leaders on both sides, including even Ku Klux Klan leaders, becoming involved in usually successful efforts to restrain it. Riots subsequently ended, almost abruptly, when one of the political contenders was defeated, as eventually happened with Republicans in all of the Southern states. This was the case even though hated symbols—blacks and Republicans—remained on the scene.

The ups and downs of the annual frequencies of crowd disturbances may be explained by the conjunction of political conditions underlying violence in several states. These conditions were most likely to occur in presidential election years, and, to a lesser extent, in all even-numbered election years. A peak was reached in 1868 largely because of political machinations in Louisiana, Arkansas, Georgia, and Tennessee. Collective violence declined then around 1870 because this was not a crucial election year, because both Republican federal and state officials and Ku Klux Klan and Conservative leaders were trying to restrain the violent excesses that had grown up, and, more importantly, because events in most Southern states had by this time resulted in defeat of one side or made necessary a regrouping of forces. Crowd violence then rose again in the midseventies because of political conditions in Louisiana, 1873-1874, Mississippi, 1874-1875, and South Carolina, 1876.

In short, collective violence played an important role in the political developments of the Southern states as they underwent the reconstruction process. Without the war, without economic problems, without race hatreds, without many other factors, crowd violence would not have occurred in the South. But the *variation* of race-related instances of crowd violence during Reconstruction cannot be explained by these biological, social, and cultural factors. Instead, it is best explained by the strange political relationship among authorities, followers, and violent means. And it is this last point which students of American politics might well ponder, for rarely, indeed almost never, in the annals of American history has violence been used to such an extent to subvert the political process.

NOTES

1. Joanne Grant, *Black Protest: History, Documents and Analysis* (Greenwich, Conn.: Fawcett, 1968), 155.

2. For recent discussions of violence in the postwar South, see Allen W. Trelease, *White Terror* (New York: Harper and Row, 1971); and John A. Carpenter, *Sword and Olive Branch: Oliver Otis Howard* (Pittsburgh: University of Pittsburgh, 1965), particularly 127-135.

3. The work of Annie Cooper Burton, daughter of a Ku Klux Klan member, who linked Reconstruction violence to a crusade by public-minded men to control the disorderly elements leased upon the South by the war, typifies the biological perspective. Annie Cooper Burton, *The Ku Klux Klan* (Los Angeles: Warren T. Potter, 1916).

4. Journalist Edward A. Pollard incorporated both a cultural and a sociological explanation in his work in 1873 by attributing Reconstruction violence to the extension of prewar "lynch law" enhanced by the Southerners' need for scapegoating born of defeat and ruin during the war. Edward A. Pollard, *The Key to the Ku Klux* (publisher unknown, 1873; Widener Library, Harvard University US 6340.27). In a more sophisticated sociological explanation, black historian W. E. B. Du Bois divided Southern violence into several phases: simple postwar disorder, a labor war to force black laborers to work on owners' terms, a labor war between black and white workers competing for the same jobs, and finally explicitly racist violence by an alliance of white workers and capitalists against the black race through secret organizations. W. E. B. Du Bois, *Black Reconstruction in America 1860-1880* (New York: World, 1964; orig. pub. 1935).

5. William A. Dunning and his students at Columbia University, writing around the turn of the century, emphasized the black-Northern share of the violence, while more recent works viewed Southern Conservative whites as the primary aggressors. William A. Dunning, *Reconstruction, Political and Economic, 1865-1877* (New York: Harper and Row, 1907). Some of Dunning's students include James W. Garner, *Reconstruction in Mississippi* (Gloucester, Mass.: Peter Smith, 1901); J. G. De Roulhac Hamilton, *Reconstruction in North Carolina* (New York: Columbia University, 1914); and Mildred Thompson, *Reconstruction in Georgia* (New York: Columbia University Press, 1915). Those writing in the Dunning tradition compose a far more lenghty list. For a helpful introduction, see Vernon L. Wharton, "Reconstruction," *Writing Southern History,* Arthur S. Link and Rembert W. Patrick, eds. (Louisiana State University Press, 1965), 298-304 and particularly footnote 25, p. 304.

More recent works include op. cit., Du Bois; Francis B. Simpkins, "New Viewpoints of Southern Reconstruction," *Journal of Southern History,* 5 (February 1939): 49-61; John Hope Franklin, *Reconstruction: After the Civil War* (Chicago: University of Chicago Press, 1961); Trelease, op. cit., Carpenter, op. cit.

Howard K. Beale in a 1940 article injected a class element into the debate by suggesting that the unnaturalness of Reconstruction stemmed from the fact that poor whites got an opportunity to rule for the first time in Southern history, and a number of works, including that of Cooper, cited the role of the "better sort" in forming secret, violent societies. Howard K. Beale, "On Rewriting Reconstruction History," *American Historical review,* 45 (July 1940): 807-827.

6. John A. Carpenter, "Atrocities in the Reconstruction Period," *Journal of Negro History,* 47 (April 1962): 242-244.

7. "Georgia Correspondence," *National Intelligencer,* 5, Jan. 1866, quoted in Walter L. Fleming, ed., *Documentary History of Reconstruction* Vol. I (New York: McGraw-Hill, 1966; orig. pub. 1906), 91.

8. Franklin, op. cit., 228. See also New York *Times*, Sept. 28, 1865, 4:1; 30 Dec., 1865, 4:1.

9. For challenges to the older view that "relative order" prevailed during Presidential Reconstruction, see Jesse Parker Bogue Jr., "Violence and Oppression in North Carolina During Reconstruction, 1865-1873" (unpublished Ph.D. dissertation. University of Maryland, 1973) and W. McKee Evans, *Ballots and Fence Rails: Reconstruction on the lower Cape Fear* (New York: W. W. Norton, 1966).

10. Neil Smelser, *Theory of Collective Behavior* (New York: Free Press, 1962), 226-227.

11. James F. Sefton, *The United States Army and Reconstruction, 1865-1877* (Baton Rouge: Louisiana State University Press, 1967), 89.

12. Franklin, op. cit., 62.

13. Franklin, op. cit., 63.

14. Du Bois, op. cit., 464. See also New York *Times*, Sept. 31, 1866, "Great Riot."

15. Franklin, op. cit., 64.

16. Report of the Joint Select Committee, op. cit., 270. See also New York *Times*, Sept., 1, 1866, 1:4.

17. Rumors of black rebellions and subsequent reprisals by whites were a common feature of the antebellum South. Such fears continued to sweep the white South in the post-war period. For an investigation of one such instance, see Dan T. Carter, "The Anatomy of Fear: The Christmas Day Insurrection Scare of 1865," *Journal of Southern History*, 42 (Aug. 1976): 345-364.

18. New York *Times*, Aug. 5, 1867, 1:7 Rogersville; see also New York *Times*, July 8, 1867; July 13, 1867; August. 23, 1867; May 18, 1867.

19. Du Bois, op. cit., 539-541. See also Claude G. Bowers, *The Tragic Era: The Revolution after Lincoln* (Boston: Houghton Mifflin, 1929), 207; New York *Times*, May 10, 1867.

20. Fleming, op. cit., Vol. 2, 360.

21. Davis, op. cit., Ch. 4. For an additional example of the legitimization of Klan activities by authority figures, see William Harris, "The Security of the New Order," Ch. 12 in *Day of the Carpetbagger: Republican Reconstruction in Mississippi* (Baton Rouge: Louisiana State University Press, 1979).

22. New York *Times*, May 15, 1867, Brownsville.

23. Tennessee also experienced several riots in 1868 which are discussed in the following section.

24. Du Bois, op. cit., 474.

25. Robert Selph Henry, *The Story of Reconstruction (New York: Bobbs-Merrill, 1933), 341. New York Times*, Oct. 6, 1868 7:2; Oct. 7, 1868 8:1; Oct. 8, 1868 8:1; Oct. 13, 1868 2:2.

26. New York *Times*, Oct. 25, 1868, 1:2; Oct. 27, 1868, 1:1; Oct. 28, 1868, 3:1; Oct. 29, 1868, 1:1; Nov. 2, 1868, 5:3; Nov. 7, 1868, 1:7.

27. Du Bois, op. cit., 478, New York *Times*, Jan. 1, 1868, 1:1.

28. Stanley F. Horn, *Invisible Empire: Story of the Ku Klux Klan, 1866-1871* (Boston: Houghton Mifflin, 1939), 244.

29. Ibid., 247-248, New York *Times*, Oct. 31, 1868, 1:2; Nov. 18, 1868, 1:4; 18 Dec., 1868, 1:2.

30. Bowers, op. cit., 369.

31. Sefton, op. cit., 217.

32. Fleming, op. cit., 2, 73-76.

33. David M. Chalmers, *Hooded Americanism: The History of the Ku Klux Klan* (Chicago: Quadrangle Books, 1965), 19. Chalmers argues that the liquidation order was largely effective in Arkansas, Tennessee, Georgia, Alabama and Mississippi.

34. Horn, op. cit., 261-262.

35. Du Bois, op. cit., 503.

36. Horn, op. cit., 170.

37. Horn, op. cit., 174. New York *Times*, Aug. 22, 1868, 1:7; Aug. 23, 1868, 1:3; Aug. 28, 1868, 5:3; Oct. 6, 1868, 1:5; Oct. 10, 1868, 1:2.

38. Horn, op. cit., 176. New York *Times*, Nov. 4, 1868, 8:3; Jan. 4, 1869, 1:6; Jan. 6, 1869, 2:5, 7:2; Jan. 7, 1869, 1:2.

39. This complex turn of events is recounted in Du Bois, op. cit., 478-483, and in Henry, op. cit., 276-492.

40. New York *Times,* March 6, 1873, 1:4; May 7, 1873; May 8, 1873; May 9, 1873; May 17, 1873; May 30, 1873; April 16, 1873, 1:1.

41. henry, op. cit., 527.

42. Henry, op. cit., 544; Du Bois, op. cit., 685.

43. Allen, op. cit., 199-200.

44. Allen, op. cit., 200.

45. Henry, op. cit., 548.

46. Du Bois, op. cit., 685.

47. Henry, op. cit., 567.

48. New York *Times,* Oct. 10, 1876, 1:7; Oct. 16, 1876, 1:1, 1:3.

49. New York *Times*, Nov 29, 1876, 5:2.

50. New York *Times,* Nov. 20, 1876, 5:2.

51. Henry, op. cit., 574. New York *Times*, Nov. 29, 1876, 5:2; Nov. 21, 1876, 1:3; Sept. 22, 1876, 1:4; Nov. 29, 1876, 5:2; Nov. 9, 1876, 1:4.

52. Davis, op. cit., 107. New York *Times*, Aug. 19, 1868 Franklin; Dec. 8, 1868, western Tenn.; Dec. 16, 1868 5:4 Lewisburg.

53. New York *Times*, Nov. 8, 1872, 1:4; July 10, 1873, 1:6.

54. Horn, op. cit., 375.

55. New York *Times*, Aug. 30, 1874, 5:4.

56. New York *Times*, July 15, 1872, 2:5; Aug. 30, 1874, 5:4; Sept. 12, 1874, 1:3; Aug. 9, 1974 1:3.

Chapter 9
Collective Racial Violence
A Contemporary History

MORRIS JANOWITZ

INTRODUCTION

Understanding the causes and consequences of racial violence and of race riots in particular is a most difficult task. One's moral outrage thwarts reasoned exploration of the complex reality involved and produces oversimplified accounts and explanations. In 1968, the *Report of the National Advisory Commission on Civil Disorders* (The Kerner Commission) was published.[1] It was based on an extensive series of public hearings and a massive collection of documentation, and on the results of a wide range of studies completed by social scientists. Yet only one year later, in 1969, Allen D. Grimshaw, one of the most careful students of race riots, in *Racial Violence in the United States* already reflected the assessment of many scholars in his statement that the commission erred when it sought to isolate the single most important cause for the racial disorder in the 1960s.[2] He pointed out that the Kerner Commission concluded that the most fundamental factor in causation is "the racial attitude of white Americans, and the impact of that attitude on their behavior toward black Americans." Grimshaw, on the other hand, held that "they [the members of the Kerner Commission] have not confronted the meaning of the structural sources of violence, although they have identified them—they have not attempted to cross the bridge linking psychological and sociological perspective."[3] This essay, based on materials which I collected for the subsequent presidential inquiry on violence, the National Commission on the Causes and Prevention of Violence, is an effort to develop historically based analysis of the structural and institutional roots of collective racial violence involving the interplay of the sociological and psychological dimensions.[4].

My point of departure was that race riots are the dramatic hallmark of the injustices of race relations in the United States. They have an explosive, destructive, and amorphous character which makes generalization very difficult. As a form of "collective behavior," their natural history is not easily recorded or analyzed. Students of race relations believe that one of the most adequate and comprehensive

AUTHOR'S NOTE: *Morris Janowitz is Lawrence A. Kimpton Distinquished Service Professor at the University of Chicago. He is well known for his broad-ranging sociological research on the dynamics of prejudice and social change, public opinion and the mass media, the military, urban violence, and race relations. His most recent book on social organization is* Social Control of the Welfare State *(University of Chicago Press, 1977).*

studies of a particular race riot still remains that prepared by the Chicago Commission on Race Relations on the Chicago rioting of 1919—the result of the careful work of the late Charles S. Johnson, done under the supervision of Robert E. Park of the University of Chicago.[5] Nevertheless, it is possible to present a sociological interpretation of changed patterns of collective racial violence in the United States over the half century from the First World War to the Vietnam era. The history of race riots reflects not only the expanded aspirations of blacks but also the techniques that have been used to maintain their inferior social position. The history of race relations in the United States has been grounded in a system of law enforcement which has denied to blacks due process and equal protection, and which therefore has weakened the legitimacy of law-enforcement agents, especially in the lowest-income black areas.

The transformation in the patterns of collective racial violence in urban areas during the 50-year period falls into three different phases. First, the typical race riot of the period of the First World War and immediately thereafter, the *communal* riot, was an interracial clash, an ecologically based struggle at the boundaries of expanding black neighborhoods. Second, during the Second World War communal riots began to give way to large-scale outbursts within the black community. These riots represented a form of collective behavior against the agents and symbols of the larger society. They can be described as *commodity* riots because of the extensive looting that gives symbolic meaning to these outbursts. The commodity-type riots reached a high point during the period 1964-1967. Much of the writings by social scientists during those years about these conflicts appear superficial in retrospect because the authors were unable to develop a sense of historical perspective. In particular, the prediction of chronic and extensive collective racial riots proved to be in error. Instead, the summer of 1968 emerged as a turning point, as the incidence of racial outburst declined markedly. A third period came into being; it was characterized by a new form of essentially *political* racial violence: a more selective, terroristic use of force with political overtones, again directed mainly against whites, by small, organized groups of blacks. But by 1972 with the end of the Vietnam era, even such violence was more symbolic than actual.

The form and extent of collective racial violence, it is assumed, are expressions of the social structure and the agencies of social change and social control. Therefore, in particular, the role of the police and law-enforcement agencies and of the mass media in fashioning patterns of collective urban violence will be explored.

A central "sociological assumption" supplies a point of departure. While there is considerable evidence to support it, still it is best to consider it as an assumption: Social tensions generated by discrimination, prejudice, and poverty offer essential but only partial explanations of black mass rioting in the urban centers of the United States. Social conditions conducive to collective violence have been much more widespread than the actual selective outbursts. Allen Grimshaw concluded in 1962 that "there is no direct relation between the level of social tension and the eruption of social violence."[6]

It is not necessary to accept all that this proposition implies because the evidence is not that solid, and, more important, because significant "indirect relations" may well have operated. It is enough to reemphasize the obvious fact that in the United

States, social tensions exist where riots break out, and to accept Grimshaw's alternative formulation that "in every case where major rioting has occurred, the social structure of the community has been characterized by weak patterns of external control."[7] Because of widespread potentials for racial violence, in the language of sociology the agencies of social change and social control are crucial in accounting for actual urban racial outbreaks.[8] Moreover, the manner in which outbursts are handled and controlled deeply influences race relations and subsequent patterns of violence.

On the whole, statistical studies designed to account for which cities have been struck by riots have not been highly rewarding. But one carefully matched comparison of riot and nonriot cities by Stanley Lieberson and Arnold R. Silverman, covering 76 race riots between 1913 and 1963, confirms and amplifies Grimshaw's formulation.[9] For the period before the new wave of riots of the mid-1960s, they found (a) no support for the contention that rapid population change accompanies riots; (b) no confirmation for the hypothesis that unemployment level is a direct factor, but rather that encroachment of blacks on the white occupational world evidently tends to increase chances of riots; and (c) no support for the notion that race riots are a consequence either of low black income or relatively large black-white discrepancies in income. Nor, for that matter, does poor black housing serve to distinguish riot cities from nonriot cities.

Their evidence does, however, support "the proposition that the functioning of local government is important in determining whether a riot will follow a precipitating incident." Thus, (a) cities with more racially integrated police forces had fewer riots; (b) cities with more representative forms of local government (for example, citywide election of councilmen versus district elections) had fewer riots; and (c) cities with a large percentage of blacks who were self-employed in retail trade, such as store, restaurant, or tavern owners—that is, cities with stronger independent middle-class business groups—had fewer riots. In short, these measures were indicators of the articulation of blacks into the social and political fabric of the metropolitan community, reflecting stronger and more viable patterns of social control.

If one is interested in the institutional aspects of race riots, it is also necessary to focus attention on (a) the professional and organizational limitations of law-enforcement agencies, and (b) the impact of the mass media. The record of law-enforcement agencies over the last half-century has been one of inadequate equal protection for minorities and limited capacity for dealing with urban disorders, with noteworthy exceptions and with slowly and definitely increasing levels of profes-sionalization. Likewise, the growth of the mass media, especially television, has not been accompanied by increased standards of performance. To the contrary, the impact of the mass media, in their lack of a constructive role in describing problems of social change, plus their imagery of violence and their treatment of riots and law-enforcement agencies, has made a positive contribution to violence.

FROM "COMMUNAL" TO "COMMODITY" RIOTS

Racial violence has a history as old as the nation itself. The institution of slavery was rooted in a ready resort to violence.[10] After the Civil War the political control of the freed black was enmeshed in a variety of illegal forms of resort to violence. For purposes of this analysis, the particularly devastating and explosive outbreak of mass racial riots can be thought of as a distinct phenomenon, although any effort at categorization is a tricky and elusive intellectual effort. The draft riots of the Civil War had clear racial overtones. But "modern" riots can be traced to racial outbreaks generated during the First World War and again during the Second World War. There were, of course, riots during the interwar period, but the heaviest concentration was during wartime years. The riots of this historical era need to be distinguished from the outbursts that took place during the 1960s.

During the First World War and its aftermath, the "modern" form of the race riot developed in Northern and border cities where the black was attempting to alter his position of subordination. These outbreaks had two predisposing elements. First, relatively large numbers of new migrants—both black and white—were living in segregated enclaves in urban centers under conditions in which older patterns of accommodation were no longer effective. The sheer expansion in the black population was an essential factor. The riots were linked to a phase in the growth and transformation of American cities. Second, the police and law-enforcement agencies had a limited capacity for dealing with the outbreak of mass violence and often conspired with white rioters against the black population.

The riots of this period could be called "communal" riots or "contested area" riots. They involved a form of ecological warfare because they were a direct struggle between the residents of white and black areas. The precipitating incidents would come after a period of increasing tension and minor but persistent outbursts of violence. For example, the Chicago riot of 1919 was preceded by two years of residential violence in which more than 27 dwellings were bombed. Typically, the precipitating incident would be a small-scale struggle between white and black civilians—often in a public place, such as a beach or in an area of unclear racial domain. In the major riots of the large cities, tension and violence spread quickly throughout various parts of the larger community. Deaths and injuries were the result of direct confrontation and fighting between whites and blacks.

Within a few hours the riot was in full swing, and continued intermittently with decreasing intensity for several days. Whites invaded black areas, and very often the riot spread to the central business district where the white population outnumbered the blacks. Much of the violence took place on main thoroughfares and transfer points as blacks tried to return to their homes or sought some sort of refuge. Symbolically, the riot was an expression of the impulse of some elements of the white community to "kick the Negro back into his place."

Despite the wide areas that were engulfed and the number of casualties inflicted, the whites involved were limited to very small groups or nuclei of activists, often encouraged by vocal bystanders to take the initiative. White youth gangs and their leaders were in the forefront in a number of cities. Blacks fought back in time, but they seldom invaded white areas. According to available documentation, the whites were armed mainly with bricks and blunt sticks, and they fought with their fists. There were a limited number of hand guns (pistols) and rifles. On occasion, blacks were better armed because they had more of these weapons, and knives as well. These riots had many incidents of direct, personal, and brutal stuggle between the contestants.

The personalized aspect of the violence can be inferred from reports such as that of the Chicago Commission, which stated that "Without the spectators, mob violence would have probably stopped short of murder in many cases."[11]

Gunshots were directed at specific and visible targets, often where one side had overwhelming superiority. Nevertheless, deaths by beating and mauling greatly outnumbered those from gunshots. Newspaper reports of snipers were exaggerated. In the East Chicago riots of 1917 there was only one case of repeated gunfire, and in Chicago in 1919 the commission found one such serious incident and a number of more scattered occurrences, as blacks sought to retaliate against white marauders passing by in automobiles. In fact, instead of the term "sniper" fire, the reports of the First World War period speak of occasional "volley firing."

During these riots, rumors about specific incidents of racial strife were spread by word of mouth. Newspapers contributed to racial tension by frequently and repeatedly publishing inflammatory reports, such as one Chicago report that blacks slaughtered a defenseless white child. As the riots often lasted for several days, news reports served to recruit white activists from other parts of the city and even from out of town. Editorial efforts to calm public opinion and to demand effective law enforcement developed slowly and hardly balanced the inflammatory contents of news columns.

Restoration of civil order required the police to separate the two groups and to protect the enclaves of blacks from whites. Frequently the police were deficient in their duties and occasionally assisted white rioters. In any case, they were not prepared for such outbreaks. State militias or federal troops were used repeatedly and generally displayed higher professional standards. Without overlooking the casualties caused by the police themselves, the fundamental anatomy of these riots was a communal clash between blacks and whites.

During the Second World War the pattern of rioting underwent a transformation which took full form with outbreaks in Harlem and Detroit in 1943, in Brooklyn in 1964, in Watts in 1965, and in Newark and Detroit in 1967. For lack of a better term, the change has been from "communal" riots to "commodity" riots.[12] The Detroit riot of 1943 conformed to the communal or contested area pattern. It involved concentrations of recently arrived black migrants, and the precipitating incident occurred in a contested area, Belle Isle. Violence spread rapidly and produced clashes between blacks and whites. The Harlem riots of 1943, on the other hand, contained features of the new type of rioting.[13] The black population had a higher concentration of long-term residents. Most important, it was a riot that started within the black community, not at the periphery. It did not involve a confrontation between white and black civilians. It was an outburst against property and retail establishments, plus looting—thus the notion of the commodity riot. The retail establishments were owned mainly by outside white proprietors. Deaths and casualties resulted primarily from the use of force against the black population by police and National Guard units. Some direct and active participation by white civilians may take place in such a riot, as was the case in Detroit in 1967, but this is a minor element.

THE NATURAL HISTORY OF COMMODITY RIOTS

There have been repeated efforts to describe the various stages in the natural history of race riots, especially the commodity-type riots.[14] In assessing these research efforts, two considerations must be kept in mind. First, the type of intervention by law-enforcement officers has deeply influenced the anatomy of race riots in the United States. During the period of the intial communal riots, the effectiveness of local police forces varied greatly, reflecting their high degree of decentralization. The increased ability of local police to seal off contested areas reduced the prospect of communal riots. Since the riots of the First World War there has been a gradual growth in the capacity of local police to prevent riots at the periphery of the black community, but not without conspicuous exceptions. The use of radio communications and motorized local police have been the essential ingredients of control. Most Northern cities have witnessed a steady and gradual expansion of black residential areas, accompanied by bitter resentment and continous minor outbreaks of violence, including bombings. But the police almost daily contain these tensions, which might otherwise explode into communal riots.

The capacity of local enforcement agencies to repress "border" incidents has not been matched with a capacity for controlling the outbreak of violence within the black community. The outbreak of commodity riots produced very different police responses in various communities, ranging from highly effective and professional behavior to weak and irresponsible action that exacerbated rioting and prolonged tension. Thus the stages of a riot are not predetermined but partly reflect the pattern of intervention of law-enforcement agencies.

Second, it is, of course, difficult to document accurately the natural history of a riot and especially the behavior of rioters in a commodity riot. The President's Advisory Commission on Civil Disorders (Kerner Commission) sponsored a variety of social research studies on the riots of the 1960s, which focused mainly on the attitudes of the public and the rioters. The methodology of the sample survey was emphasized, which does not make possible a full analysis of the dynamics of the "collective behavior" of a racial riot.[15] While teams of investigators are required to collect basic documentation, the natural history and anatomy of a riot are probably best assessed by a single person who is concerned with cross-checking sources. S.L.A. Marshall has demonstrated how a single investigator can reconstruct a complex and fluid military battle by afteraction group interviews,[16] but this procedure has not generally been applied to race riots. The most comprehensive analytic account of a commodity riot has been presented by Anthony Oberschall in his study of the Watts, California riot.[17]

From all sources, one conclusion emerges, namely the absence of organized conspiracy in commodity riots. But the absence of organized conspiracy does not mean the absence of a pattern of events. Thus Jules J. Wanderer's analysis of 75 riots during the period 1965-1967 demonstrates the recurring pattern of events in these outbursts. By means of the Guttman scale technique, Wanderer demonstrated a consistent cumulation of a configuration of "stages" as a riot progresses from low to high intensity.[18] The difference from one outburst to another involved the extent to which each one proceeded through the various stages of increased and intensified collective behavior.

The motivation in commodity riots was clearly not desperation generated by starvation, such as in food riots in India during famines. One is struck by the repeated reports of the carnival spirit that pervades the early stages of a commodity riot. The new type of rioting is most likely to be set off by an incident involving the police in the ghetto, where some actual or believed violation of accepted police practice has taken place. The very first phase is generally nasty and brutish; the police are stoned, crowds collect, and tension mounts. The second stage is reached with the breaking of windows. Local social control breaks down, and the population recognizes that a temporary opportunity for looting is available. The atmosphere changes quickly, and positive enthusiasm is released. But all too briefly. If the crowds are not dispersed and order restored, the third stage of the riot is the transformation wrought by arson, firebombs, and sniper fire, and countermeasures taken by police and uniformed soldiers.

There can be no doubt that the countermeasure deeply influenced the course of the rioting—even in some cases prolonging the period of reestablishing order. One is struck by the great variation in local response to escalated rioting and in the skill and professionalism of the police forces in their counterefforts. Differences in policy strategy have been partly accidental and partly the result of conscious policy, since law enforcement officials have a past record to draw on, and since during the 1960s they became continuously alerted to the possibility of riots. Thus, for example, there were wide differences in response patterns to early manifestations of disorder by local police in the 1960's. In Detroit, Ray Girardin, a former police reporter who became police commissioner, explicitly acknowledged that he followed a loose policy in the early phase of the Detroit rioting, assuming that local civilian black leadership would contain the disorder. He cited his previous experience in which this approach had worked effectively.

By contrast, the operational code of the police in New York City under Commissioner Howard Leary during that period was to intervene with that amount of manpower judged appropriate for early stages of the confrontation. The objective was to prevent the spread of contagion. The procedure was as follows: special steps were taken to prevent routine police performance from developing into incidents that might provoke tension. But if an incident became the focal point for tension and a crowd gathered, the police responded early and in depth in order to prevent the second stage from expanding. Numerous police were sent to the scene or kept in reserve nearby. The police sought to operate by their sheer presence, not to provoke further counteraction. They sought to prevent the breaking of windows and the starting of looting that would set the stage for an escalated riot. If actual rioting threatened, one response was the early mobilization of local national guard units and their ready-reserve deployment in inner-city garrisons. In part, this was designed to reduce the time required for their deployment on city streets; in part it was a policy that enabled local police to commit their reserves with the surety of having a supporting force available.

Whereas the communal riot involved a confrontation between the white and black communities, the commodity riot, especially as it entered the final destructive phase, represented a confrontation between the black community and law-enforcement officials of the larger society. The extent of the exchange of gunfire emerged as one of the most problematic dimensions. Reports in the mass media of the use of weapons during and immediately after the riots by the rioters were exaggerated, according to the investigations of the Kerner Commission.[19] In fact, the deaths inflicted by sniper fire were few. For example, it is reported that five of 43 deaths during the Detroit disorder were linked to sniper fire, and in Newark, two of 26 deaths.[20] These observations did not involve comparisons with earlier riots or an assessment that the gunfire contributed to conditions in which extensive arson developed. In fact, direct comparisons with the communal-type riots underline the greater dispersal of firearms and the much more intense use of firepower. They were escalated riots because of the more extensive but still scattered use of weaponry.

There are no adequate statistics on the distribution of weapons in the hands of participants before a particular riot. But there is clear evidence that over the years the sale and home storage of firearms has continually increased, made possible by affluence and the absence of adequate gun-control legislation, and stimulated by fears of racial violence. These trends have occurred both in white and black communities. As Zimring has demonstrated in the case of personal violence, the sheer availability of weapons tended to escalate racial conflict.[21] In addition to the already available arms, a significant stock of weapons appears to have been accumulated during actual rioting in particular areas. Important sources of supply have been looted, including sporting goods stores, general merchandise establishments, and pawn shops.

During this third phase of the commodity riots, when sniper fire developed, it usually involved single individuals, and occasionally groups of two or three persons. There was little evidence of forethought by rioters in the deployment of weapons for effectiveness or mutual fire support. Supporting fire by such snipers could have rendered them much more destructive. In isolated cases there was evidence of limited coordination and planning of firepower, but these cases are of minor importance in accounting for the firepower encountered by law-enforcement officers. The crucial impact of the sniper fire derived from its interplay with arson activities. Sniper fire immobilized fire-fighting equipment, and this permitted widespread destruction by fire which in turn contributed to more rioting and more sniper fire. This dimension was absent in the older communal riots. In this sense, the commodity riots were escalated in intensity and sheer destruction as compared with the communal outbreaks. They were escalated also in the sense that the mass media rapidly disseminated the image and reality of mass fires and widespread looting on a scale not found in the earlier riots. The spread of fire was frequently facilitated by various incendiary bombs of a home-made nature. These fire bombs have also been used as antivehicle bombs, but generally with little effectiveness.

The phase of scattered sniper fire presented, in some respects, a type of quasi-military situation. But the notion of an insurrection had little meaning, for snipers had no intention and were not capable of holding territory, nor were they part of a scheme to do so even temporarily. In riots during the 1960s, sniper fire frequently exposed inexperienced police officers and National Guard units to unaccustomed dangers. Personal risk was clearly present, as the scattered source of fire often enveloped the law-enforcement units. This envelopment fire, especially from behind, led to the use of the term "guerrilla tactics," but the guerrilla concept is really not relevant because guerrillas are part of an organization; proceed with a plan, prepare paths of withdrawal, and develop sanctuaries.

The police personnel were at times surrounded and, in the absence of effective command and control, were exposed to an environment that most of them had not previously experienced. Their behavior was conditioned by the feeling of unreality and the physical disruption of the rioting situation, and they often responded with indiscriminate and uncontrolled fire. Overresponse and excessive firepower by police and National Guard units in turn contributed to the escalation of the rioting.[22] The immediate result was that police officers exposed numerous civilians to danger. Such fire did not suppress snipers, who can only be eliminated by carefully directed countersniper procedures, including direct verbal appeals to surrender with the guarantee of personal safety. In fact, the initial counterfire actually mobilized new rioters.

The summers of 1964 through 1967 demonstrated wide variations in the capacity of National Guard units to respond to and assist local police. On the whole, National Guard units had received little specific training in riot control, and the content of such training did not appear to have been particularly germane to actual problems. The level of National Guard effectiveness derived from their general military preparedness. The performance of National Guard units in Newark and in Detroit was judged by expert observers to have been deficient. By contrast, the behavior of units in Baltimore and in Milwaukee was reported to be much more in accordance with the requirements of the constabulary function, namely, the minimum use of force to restore civil law and due process. The basic problem was fire control and an effective communications network. On the other hand, federal troops used in Detroit were highly professional units with extensive training which clearly displayed a higher degree of unit control and were less prone to use unnecessary fire. The superiority of the federal troops reflected past experience and indicated that more effective military training per se (even without additional civil disorder training), and more effective officers, produced more appropriate responses.

There was some evidence that one index to National Guard effectiveness is the extent of integration of the units. Because of their fraternal spirit, most National Guard units have been able to resist federal directives, and in 1967 blacks accounted for less than 2 percent of their personnel. In those cases where integration took place, it meant that the units were seen as more legitimate by the local population. Moreover, units that were forced to integrate were more likely to be concerned with these issues. For example, units in Detroit and Newark were not integrated, while Chicago-based units employed during the summer disturbances of 1965 were integrated and had black officers.

PARTICIPATION IN COMMODITY RIOTS

The extent of participation and the social characteristics of the rioters were revealing indices of underlying factors in the social structure that condition these collective outbursts. There is every reason to believe that in the commodity riots of the 1960s a larger number of blacks and a greater percentage of the population of riot-torn communities actively participated in the outbursts than was the case during the older, communal-type confrontations. The commodity-type riots took place within the confines of the black ghettos, which have grown greatly in size and population since the First World War. Within these massive ghettos during the hours of the most intensive outbursts, it appeared as if social controls were momentarily suspended. The sheer size of the ghettos and the greater remoteness of the outside community contributed to this breakdown and to the "mobilization" of numbers. It is understandable that in the second phase of milling and looting, many residents were swept up by the sheer contagion of events, especially where law officers stood by passively while stores and shops were being looted.

The societal context also had radically changed during the period of transition to commodity riots. Through the mass media, the demands of the black population had received widespread and favorable publicity, and there was considerable sympathy in the nation for their plight. The civil rights movements had achieved strong legitimacy, and within the black community there was increased sensitivity about minority status. All these factors contributed to the intensity of and participation in the actual rioting.

The size of the groups rioting and their percentage of the available population, as well as their social characteristics, became matters of public debate. The Kerner Commission devoted efforts to probing these questions and refuting the claim that only a very tiny percentage—for example, less that 1 percent—of the black population was involved in riot-torn communities.[23] The commission argued that the riots included a much larger active group who were generally representative of lower-class slum dwellers and therefore could not be characterized as a tiny criminal element. The size of the rioting group could be estimated from direct observation, a most hazardous approach; from extrapolations of arrest data—a technique that probably underestimated the number of activists; or from self-reports gathered by sample surveys after the riots—an approach that grossly overstated the case. On the basis of different available sources, it was estimated that between 10 and 20 percent of the potential population was involved in the riots of 1967. The lower figure of 10 percent appears to be more accurate, although even this estimate is open to serious question. Aside from the reliability of the data, the question hinges on the differing definitions of participation. To speak of even 10 percent participation is to include those persons who were caught up momentarily in the collective processes of the riot as the contagion spread.

Although there are numerous statistical and methodological weaknesses in the various analyses of the arrest data and sample surveys, the findings are relevant for describing the social characteristics of the rioters. All sources agree that women were a significant minority of the activists in the commodity riots, reflecting a broadening of the base of involvement as compared with the communal riots, which were mainly a men's affair. Interestingly enough, the police tended to arrest few women, either because their infractions of the law were minor or because they believed that women were not at the core of the riot.

As expected, the bulk of the rioters were young males between the ages of 15 and 34 whose skill levels were low. In a social profile of the 496 black males arrested in Detroit, the typical participant has been characterized as "a blue-collar worker in a manufacturing plant where he earned about $120.00 a week. Although currently employed, he had experienced more than five weeks of unemployment in the past year. He had not participated in a government training or poverty program."[24] In some groups of arrested black youths, the unemployment level reached almost 40 percent. In addition, among samples of those caught up in the riots and arrested in 1967, previous arrest records were found comparable to the equivalent age groups in the black population at large. The explanation for this finding was that it is very common for young black males to have an arrest record—in some categories, a majority.

Clearly, these data indicate that the activists were not a tiny minority of chronic law offenders nor highly unrepresentative in terms of selected social background characteristics. The full personal and social dynamics of these riots will probably never be adequately described, for involvement relates not only to demographic and social characteristics but to patterns of primary and informal group structures of the ghetto community, as well as social personality and attitude. Some clues can be drawn from the observation of various surveys that the participants overrepresented single men who lived outside the family units. These were persons who were less subject to the informal group stuctures of family life and more a part of informal street and community life. Anthony Oberschall is one of the few analysts who sought to identify the role of youth gangs in riots, in his case, Watts.

> Another informant who has been close to some of the gangs in South Los Angeles reported, however, that gang members, in an effort to prove their claims upon leadership in a certain territory and in competition with each other, were vying for leadership over the crowds during the riots, and this meant among other things actively participating in the skirmishes against the police, breaking into the stores and setting them on fire.[25]

Yet in other cities, especially in Chicago in 1968, gang leaders were active in seeking to dampen tensions and violent outbursts. It has been reported that those arrested early in a riot as disorderly persons tended to be younger, unemployed, and native-born in the locality, and thus differed from the looters, who tended to be older, less unemployed, and Southern-born.[26] In other words, the looters, who joined the riots after they were underway, were more integrated into the adult occupational world.

In contrast to the "criminal interpretation," the alternative formulation of the commodity riots as a form of political insurrection is equally inadequate, if by insurrection is meant an armed social movement with an explicit set of goals. The very absence of evidence of prior planning—either rightist or leftist—would weaken such an interpretation. In 23 disorders studied by the Kerner Commission, none were "caused by, nor were they the consequence of any plan or conspiracy."[27] But more important, it is striking that during the riots of 1964-1967 there was a remarkable absence of visible leadership—either existing or emergent—that sought to press for collective demands. The leadership and supporters of the civil rights movement were not centrally involved in the riots. The emphasis of the civil rights organizations on issues such as school integration, access to public accommodation, and voting rights was less directly relevant to the immediate lives of slum dwellers, who were mainly concerned with the welfare system and with immediate employment opportunities. The impact of the riots of 1967 on the civil rights movement was drastic in that it made the movement's demands more militant and more oriented to lower-class needs. But clearly the leaders of the civil rights movement were not activists in these outbursts. If anything, the riots occurred because of the inability of the civil rights movement to accomplish sufficient social change in the slums, although the movement made a decisive contribution in intensifying aspirations and group consciousness.

Many participants, after the riots, could consciously verbalize their social and economic dilemmas and link their life situation to their behavior. In interviews they had a tendency to highlight "police brutality" as an underlying cause. Of course, most who participated merely took the event as a given fact of life and offered little explanation for their involvement. In contrast to the communal riots, where the black response was a direct and primitive struggle for survival, the commodity riots had overtones which might be called parapolitical, in the sense that group consciousness pervaded this particular form of collective behavior. On balance it can be said that by 1967 the commodity riot was a form of collective action, which on occasion was large-scale and included a broadly representative segment of the lower socio-economic class of the urban community. Regardless of the amount of sympathetic interest they mobilized among middle-class blacks, the commodity riots were a "violent lower-classs outburst."[28]

An additional aspect of participation was the active involvement of those in the black community who sought to dampen or inhibit the spread of the riots. In official reports they have come to be described by the awkward and unfortunate term "counterrioters." In the communal riot, such a role was not possible; paradoxically, such behavior by blacks during a commodity riot was the result of an increase in the integration of blacks into the larger social structure as compared with the period of communal rioting. Already in the Harlem riot of 1943, more than 300 blacks were given Civilian Defense insignias and armbands, and used as deputies. For the summer of 1967, the Kerner Commission reported that in all but six of 24 disorders they investigated, blacks were actively on the streets attempting to control rioters.[29]

In some cities, political and community leaders sought to address gathering crowds. In others, religious leaders and community workers walked the streets urging persons to disperse, while still other local residents assisted police and firemen in their tasks. Some of these activities were officially recognized and even sanctioned by the local authorities, but most of the efforts seem to have been without official sponsorship. It is difficult to evaluate the effectiveness of these efforts, especially in communities where extensive rioting broke out. But they had the greatest effect in the communities that were on the verge of rioting and in which rioting was avoided.

DECLINE IN RIOTS, 1968-1969

The summer of 1968 was a turning point in the era of communal riots. The trend in racial conflict from 1964 to 1967 was one of continued, and even expanded, outbreaks that appeared to reach a climax with the massive destruction of Newark and Detroit.

In the winter and spring months of 1968, the outlook for the summer of that year was bleak. Racial tensions remained high. Extremist and even moderate leaders anticipated even higher levels of violence, and a variety of analysts agreed. One of the writers for the Kerner Commission, assessing the findings of public opinion polls, stated that "on the eve of the summer of 1968, these responses are anything but reassuring."[30] The tensions generated by the Vietnam War had continued. There was no new massive national response to the social and economic needs of the black community, except in the important employment sector, where industrial corporations began to abandon rigid recruitment and training procedures and to engage an increasing number of inner-city personnel with the expectation of developing their qualifications on the job. Community relations were made more difficult by extremist statements by some isolated police officers who spoke of the necessity of a "tough" policy and of their plans to use heavier hardware for control purposes. The tragic assassination of Dr. Martin Luther King, Jr., was a final element in the prelude to the summer of 1968.

But race relations during the summer of 1968 had a different character than these anticipations. In October 1968 the Department of Justice released a report by Attorney General Ramsey Clark which revealed a decline in the scope and intensity of racial riots. Quantitative measures of riots are difficult to construct, but these appear to be of relatively high validity. The definitions were carefully worked out and the same data collection procedures were used to compare the months of June, July, and August 1967 with the same months of 1968. The results showed a decline in "major" disturbances from eleven to seven, and of "serious" ones from 35 to 18, while minor outbursts increased slightly from 92 to 95. The most dramatic indicator of the decline was the drop of deaths from 87 to 19. To some degree, these data understate the full decline from 1967 to 1968, since the category "major" riots included all riots that lasted longer than twelve hours and included more than 300 persons. Very large-scale riots, such as Newark and Detroit, were absent in 1968. Likewise, there was a marked decline in estimated property damage, from $56 million in 1967 for three riots in Cincinnati, Newark, and Detroit, to $4 million for all damage during June, July, and August 1968.

The summer of 1969 passed with even fewer outbursts than 1968. There were seven riots, but none of these was major by 1967 standards, while serious incidents dropped to 16 and minor disorders totaled 74. One hypothesis to account for the short-term and immediate pattern was that the development of new tactics and new organizations permitted more effective expression of black interests and black solidarity. Another hypothesis is that improved police-community relations and higher levels of police professionalism also contributed to the decline. The available data seem to indicate that, while minor outbreaks continued, interaction between the police and the black community was able to reduce and contain larger and more widespread riots.

Under pressure of political and community leadership, many police officials took initial steps to improve communications with the black communities through devices, such as special conferences, the assigning of officers of community relations, and improved police training. Criticism of the police in some communities and their relative success in others led to more professional behavior. The advocates of deescalation had more and more influence; the slogan of the Kerner Commission, "manpower and not firepower," spread widely as new police doctrine. Older doctrines of riot control, which emphasized weaponry and technical characteristics, gave way to newer and more reasoned approaches. Police departments sought to improve their internal communications and their ability to mobilize manpower. They sought to strengthen supervision and control in the field and emphasized the need for restraint. There was a much more professional response to the problem of sniper fire, in that police were instructed not to respond with indiscriminate firepower. There was progress toward deescalation of police response to more appropriate levels. Despite the publicity given to those few police officers who spoke about the need for tanks and Mace, the major trend in local police work was in the opposite direction.

The limitation on professional competence of the local police to deal with problems of urban racial violence in part reflects the particular system of law enforcement that has developed in the United States. Deeply influenced by British institutions, the nation did not develop a strong national police force with responsibility for the control of civil disorder—as had France, for example. Yet the United States has experienced extensive civil disorders throughout its history, and the country found its equivalent to a *gendarmerie* in the state militia and later in the National Guard. The National Guard is a part-time force, which was essentially organized and trained for national defense purposes, so it seldom developed professional standards for local police support. The result has been that in both labor disputes and in race riots, federal troops have performed with higher levels of effectiveness than the Guard, not because of specialized training for the task but because of generally better organization.

The division of responsibility between local, state, and federal agencies has greatly limited the conditions under which federal troops would intervene in a riot. In the Detroit riots of July 1967, federal troops were not deployed upon the request of state and local authorities, but only after a presidential representative, former Assistant Secretary of Defense Cyrus Vance, had personally inspected the city and certified the need for federal troops. There was local criticism that this procedure unduly delayed the dispatch of troops. The office of the President has had to struggle to avoid premature commitment of federal troops whenever local authorities feel under pressure, at the same time maintaining the credibility of swift federal intervention if required. As a result, the Department of the Army established a Directorate for Civil Disturbance Policy and Operations to oversee such involvements. Greater use was made of federal troops in 1968 than in 1967. These troops underwent specialized training, but it was their general organizational effectiveness and command structure that enabled them to operate with the greatest restraint. They very seldom made use of their weapons; their sheer presence was mainly responsible for limiting riot behavior. (For example, in the Washington, D.C., riot, at most 15 bullets were fired.) In fact, there were numerous occasions on which the local population welcomed the arrival of federal troops, with the clear implication that they preferred not to be policed by local personnel.

With the degree of reliance placed upon the National Guard, it became abundantly clear during the summer of 1967 that racial integration in these units had to be pressed with much greater vigor. It had been federal policy to encourage such integration, and, in fact, all black units were disbanded; but the recruitment of blacks into the National Guard lagged. Where integration of blacks into Guard units had taken place, it was the result of state and local political leadership. Therefore, on August 10, 1967, the President's Commission on Civil Disorders unanimously issued a set of recommendations to produce short-term improvements in riot control.

These recommendations called for increased recruitment of black personnel into the National Guard, the establishment of standards for eliminating inferior officers, and greater reliance on specialized training. As the need for federal intervention declined drastically after 1968, federal policies began to have an impact on the National Guard, especially in the area of improved training, while the extent of integration in the Guard improved only slowly.

POLITICAL VIOLENCE

Each stage in the transformation of racial violence already carries with it the elements of the next stage. In the midst of the rioting of 1967, while the mass media forecast persistent and increasing rioting, individual social science analysts anticipated a marked decline in such outbursts and an emergence of a more selective, more delimited form of violence.[31]

In the decade after 1968, riots at the level of Newark and Detroit did not take place in the United States. As black enclaves developed in suburban areas, limited forms of communal riots between blacks and whites, especially centering in high schools, became a reality in these areas. But the essential trend was that escalated rioting and the rioting of commodity looting after 1967 gave way to more specific, more premeditated, and more regularized uses of force. It was as if the rioters learned the lesson emphasized in the mass media, that mass destruction achieves too few tangible benefits. New outbursts appeared to be more goal-directed—a diffuse goal at times; at other times a very specific one. It is almost appropriate to describe these outbursts as political violence or political terror, or even conspiratorial violence. It is not inaccurate to describe them as a shift from expressive outbursts to a more instrumental use of violence. Those involved were persons who came to believe that white society could not be changed except by persistent violence.

The participants were likely to be persons who had taken part in previous collective outbursts. There was an element of organization, at least to the extent that activists were concerned with personal survival and avoidance of the police, and to the extent that the targets seemed to be selected, and the patterns repeated for a specific purpose. The local school was a particular target. Violence took the form of harassment of white schoolteachers active in union work, assaults on teacher picket lines during strikes, or small-scale outbursts at the neighborhood schoolyard. Housing projects, especially integrated housing projects, were subject to rifle fire and fire-bombing. On occasion sniper fire was directed against police officers. These incidents were created for the purpose of developing solidarity in local gangs and in paramilitary groups. The United Auto Workers union reported the use of terror tactics, including knifings and physical assault, against both white and black workers in the Detroit area. The union identified one responsible group, the League of Revolutionary Black Workers, in its documentation.[32]

The object of these new tactics seemed to be to establish a vague political presence. Conspiratorial overtones were involved, and the assaults spilled over against social agencies and local political leaders. The line between random outbursts and these forms of political violence or political terror is difficult to draw, but these outbursts often took place with the explicit appeal of "Black Power."

Traditional youth gang activities tended to resist political orientations, but signs of conscious political orientation became more visible.

Dramatic manifestations of the phase of political violence, or conspiratorial violence, were the shoot-outs which occurred with police personnel during the summer of 1968 in New York City, Cleveland, Pittsburgh, Oakland, Los Angeles, and elsewhere. The degree of prior planning in these incidents is difficult to ascertain, but selection of police personnel as specific targets is obvious. In some cases the action appears to have been a response to presumed harassment by the police. In other cases the police were responding to a call for help. In still other cases police cars were attacked without warning. For example, on September 29, 1968, a man wearing a "black cape lined with orange walked up to a police car in Harlem . . . and without provocation, opened fire on two patrolmen, wounding them both."[33] Other incidents developed around a police action, such as the removal of a disabled vehicle. Generally these incidents seemed to involve loosely and informally organized groups. The Black Panther organization found itself in repeated gun battles with the Oakland police during these years. A shoot-out in Cleveland on July 26, 1968, created such community tension that Mayor Carl B. Stokes responded with the unprecedented withdrawal of white police officers and the deployment of black officers and 500 black community leaders to maintain peace. This procedure was rapidly terminated.[34] The incident which subsequently generated extensive national attention was the planned assassination of the black Superintendent of Schools in Oakland by an organized terrorist fragment.

These tactics of violence were, in effect, a new form of "defiance" politics. In the past, organized criminals, including groups which penetrated political party organizations, used violence to extract a financial toll from slum communities. These traditional groups confined violent outbursts to the maintenance of their economic privilege. The new practitioners of political violence and political terror were more open in advocating violence and opposing the larger society. They represented an effort to achieve goals much broader and vaguer than those of the racketeer, with crude ideological overtones and especially a desire to carry violence into the white community.[35]

It is very difficult to contain terroristic eruptions of political violence. The tactics and plans are more secret, and official surveillance and covert penetration are the only techniques of management. The forms of organization are those of a combination of a conspiratorial and predatory gang and a paramilitary unit with overtones of a "liberation" outlook. The more secret and cohesive the group, the greater the problems of surveillance. Even though these types of paramilitary groups break into factions, the task of control is extremely difficult.[36] The task becomes even more complex and troublesome when these surveillance agencies develop the conception, as they often do, that to collect information is not enough. They sometimes assume that they must act as active agents of control, particularly in spreading distrust within these terrorist organizations. The task becomes endless and dangerous if the officials become interested simply in playing a game, or develop an interest in maintaining the groups which they are supposed to be monitoring.[37]

With the decline of commodity riots, the United States experienced a series of dramatic and persistently violent actions involving black paramilitary groups, such as the Black Panthers, the Black Liberation Army, and Black Muslims, including violent confrontations between such groups and police and criminal justice officials. The mass media served to increase the visibility of these armed confrontations. In retrospect, the tactics of law enforcement officials, as they struggled to deal with such violent tactics can be judged as having increased racial tensions and prevented effective conflict resolution. Among the most conspicuous episodes were the armed assaults on the Black Panthers by police officers in December 1969 in Chicago, and in 1972, the shootings in Baton Rouge when the police sought to disperse an impromptu rally by black militants. In the thrust to repress political violence, police officers at times were also involved in harassment as well as lapses in judgment and professional standards.

The symbolism of these confrontations was that of national liberation movements, especially since a few publicity-drenched leaders visited and resided for specific periods in "radical" African states—for example, Eldridge Cleaver went to Algeria and Stokely Carmichael to Guinea. While there are no adequate statistics, it does appear that after the withdrawal of U.S. troops from Vietnam in 1972, the extent of acts of political violence and related police confrontations declined to a considerable degree. Certainly the amount of mass media attention decreased as their news value diminished. But the amount of mass media coverage is hardly a satisfactory index to the frequency of this type of political violence.

While the failure of the larger society to meet the needs of the black community contributes to an environment in which conspiratorial violence will continue to erupt, such violence, once begun, has a life of its own. Small groups of terrorists have on historical occasion been able to achieve important goals and political objectives, but it is hazardous to speculate about the conditions under which they are able to succeed.[38] In the past they appear to have succeeded when they were struggling against a political elite that ruled by terror and without a broad base of support. In the contemporary period, terrorist movements have assumed great importance in nations where political institutions have become ineffective. Neither of these conditions is applicable in the United States. Instead, it may well be the case that political violence by black groups will have counterproductive features. In the United States, only limited amounts of political violence can be employed before a point of diminishing return is reached for both the user and the social order in which it is applied.[39] But in any case, the more precise observation needs to be offered that in the United States the extensive riots of the 1960s left only a tiny residue of violent political activism in the black community.

THE EFFECT OF THE MASS MEDIA

Another important institution of social control with special relevance for collective racial violence is the mass media.[40] A debate on this issue has raged among social scientists since the early 1930s when the Payne Foundation underwrote a group of University of Chicago social scientists in the first large-scale study of the impact of the mass media, in this case the consequences of movies on young people and especially on deviant, asocial, and violent behavior of young people.[41]

The mass media both reflect the values of the larger society and are agents of change and devices for molding tastes and values. It is a complex task to discern their impact, for they are at the same time both cause and effect. Controversies about the mass media focus particularly on the issue of their contribution to crime and delinquency and to an atmosphere of lawlessness. Among social scientists it is generally agreed that the effects of the mass media are secondary as compared with the influence of family, technology, and the organization of modern society. But differences in the meaning and importance attributed to this "secondary factor" among social scientists are great. "Secondary" can mean still important enough to require constructive social policy, or "secondary" can mean that a factor is trivial and unimportant.

Two separate but closely linked issues require attention. First, what are the effects of the mass media, with their high component of violence, on popular attitudes toward authority and on conditioning and acceptance of violence in social relations? Second, what have been the specific consequences of the manner in which the mass media have handled escalated racial rioting since Watts? The managers of the mass media run their enterprises on a profit basis, and one result has been that the content of channels of communication, especially television, in the United States has had a distinctly violent flavor as contrasted with other nations. Self-regulation of the mass media in respect to violence has not been effective except to some extent in the comic book industry.[42]

In my judgment, the cumulative evidence collected by social scientists over the last 30 years has pointed to a discernible, but limited, negative impact of the media on social values and on personal controls required to inhibit individual disposition toward aggressive actions.[43] Other students of the same data have concluded that their impact is so small as not to constitute a social problem. Many studies of media impact are based on limited amounts of exposure, as contrasted with the continuous exposure of real life. Other studies make use of ex post facto sample surveys which are too superficial to probe the psychological depths of these issues. More recent research using rigorous experimental methods and more sophisticated methods of analyzing survey data have strengthened the conclusion that high exposure to violence content in the mass media weakens personal and social controls.[44] These new findings include the results of probing fantasy and psychological responses of young people after exposure to violence content.

The issue runs deeper than the concentration on violence in the mass media. It involves an assessment of the mass media's performance in disseminating a portrayal of the black and social change in depth. It also involves the access that the mass media extends to the creative talent of the black community. The Kerner Commission emphasized the lack of effective coverage of the problems of minority groups by the mass media and the absence of minority-group members, especially blacks, in operating and supervisory positions in these enterprises. The events of the riots and the recommendations of the Kerner Commission on this aspect of the mass media produced "crash" programs to recruit and train minority personnel. The contents of the media, including advertising, have become more integrated in the subsequent decade, and a long-run impact on public opinion has been likely, especially among younger persons.

It is also necessary to assess the television coverage of the riots themselves and the impact of this coverage on social control. For example, the National Advisory Commission on Civil Disorders sought to probe the immediate impact of the mass media coverage of the riots of the summer of 1967 both on the black community and on the nation as a whole. It commissioned a systematic content analysis study which, despite its quantitative approach, did not effectively penetrate the issue or even satisfy the commission. The content study sought to determine if "the media had sensationalized the disturbances, consistently overplaying violence and giving disproportionate amounts of time to emotional events and militant leaders."[45] The conclusion was negative because of findings that, of 837 television sequences of riot and racial news examined, 494 were classified as calm, 262 as emotional, and 81 as normal. "Only a small proportion of all scenes analyzed showed actual mob action, people looting, sniping, setting fires, or being killed or injured." Moderate black leaders were shown on television more frequently than were militant leaders. Equivalent findings were reported for the printed media.

But such a statistical balance is no indicator of the impact of the presentation. Even calm and moral presentations of the riots could have had an effect on both black and white communities; more certainly, persistent presentation of "hot" messages, even though they constitute only a part of the coverage, would have an impact. The commission therefore modified and in effect rejected its own statistical findings and more appropriately concluded that (1) "there were instances of gross flaws in presenting news of the 1967 riots"; and (2) the cumulative effect was important in that it "heightened reaction." "What the public saw and read last summer thus produced emotional reactions and left vivid impressions not wholly attributable to the material itself." The commission concluded that "the main failure of the media last summer was that the totality of its coverage was not as representative as it should have been to be accurate."

The extensive escalated "commodity-type" riots warranted massive coverage according to existing standards of mass media performance. The coverage was so extensive that there was an imbalance in presenting the total scene in the United States, and, in particular, a failure to cover successful accomplishments by community leaders and law-enforcement agencies. In fact, there were overtones in the coverage of racial violence which conformed to the "crime wave" pattern of news. The result was to give spot coverage to violent events that would not have been reported under "normal" circumstances.

Thus television served as the main instrument for impressing the grim realities of the riots onto the mass consciousness of the nation. On-the-spot reportage of the details of even minor riots and their aftermath was extensive and was buttressed by elaborate commentaries. If the fullest coverage of these events was considered necessary as a basis for developing constructive social policy, the costs of such media coverage should not be overlooked. It is impossible to rule out the strong contention that detailed coverage of riots had an effect on potential rioters. Such a contention does not rest on the occasional instance in which the television camera has focused on the riot scene and led either rioters or police to play to the television audience. Of greater importance was the impact of pictures of the rioting on the wider audience. Again we are dealing with a process of social learning, especially for potential participants. Rioting is based on an element of contagion which involves the process by which the mood and attitudes of those who are actually caught up in the riot are disseminated to a larger audience. Television images served to spread the contagion pattern throughout urban areas and the nation. Large audiences saw the details of riots, the manner in which people participated in them, and especially the ferment associated with looting and obtaining commodities, which was so much at the heart of riot behavior. Television presented detailed information about the tactics of participation and short-term gratifications.

A direct and realistic account of the tactical role of the mass media, particularly television, can be obtained from specific case studies, such as reported in depth by Anthony Oberschall on the Watts riot:

> The success of the store breakers, arsonists, and looters in eluding the police can in part be put down to the role of the mass media during the riot week. The Los Angeles riot was the first one in which rioters were able to watch their actions on television. The concentration and movements of the police in the area were well reported on the air, better than that of the rioters themselves. By listening to the continuous radio and TV coverage, it was possible to deduce that the police were moving toward or away from a particular neighborhood. Those who were active in raiding stores could choose when and where to strike, and still have ample time for retreat. The entire curfew area is a very extended one.[46]

The mass media disseminated the rationalizations and symbols of identification used by the rioter; they also reinforced and spread a feeling of consciousness among those who participated or sympathized with extremist actions, regardless of the actions' origins. In particular, television offered them a mass audience far beyond their most optimistic aspirations. Knowledge of the riot would spread in any case, but immediate, extensive, and detailed coverage both speeded up the process and gave it a special reality. On balance, I would argue that these images reinforced predispositions to participate and even to legitimate participation. To be able to generate mass media coverage, especially television coverage, became an element in the motivation of the rioters. The sheer ability of the rioters to command mass media attention was an ingredient in developing legitimacy. In selected intellectual circles in the United States, a language of rationalization of violence developed. The mass media served to disseminate a popular version of such justification. Commentaries on television were filled with pseudo-sociological interpretations and the rioters themselves were given ample opportunity to offer suitable rationalizations.

When rioting was of the contested-area variety, prior to 1943, the newspapers were the major news medium. In many areas they developed an operational code, informally and formally, to deal with news about rioting. The practice was to apply an embargo on news about a riot during the actual period of the riot; a story would appear after the event. The goal was to prevent the newspapers from serving as a means for mobilizing rioters, as was the case in the riots of Chicago in 1919. With the growth of television and the intensification of competition between the press and television, this practice broke down.

The riots projected a new element in the mass media imagery of the black, if only for a limited period of time. Until the Second World War the mass media served to reinforce the system of segregation by casting the black exclusively in a minority position as well as by describing and characterizing him as weak. This portrait served to mobilize and reinforce aggressive sentiments and emotions against him. The extremely prejudiced person is more disposed to release his aggression if he believes that the object of his aggression is too weak to respond to his hostile feelings and emotions.[47]

Since 1945 and especially since 1960 the mass media have been helping to modify the imagery of the black and thereby to weaken prejudiced symbolism. The advances of the black in economic, social, and political life have supplied a basis by which the mass media could project a more realistic and more favorable picture of blacks. The reasoned and moral arguments in defense of racial equality by black and white leaders provided the subject for extensive editorial commentary in the mass media. Mass media images of blacks were enhanced by the role of black troops in the Korean War and by the increasing presence of the black as policeman. Regardless of black leadership opinion on the war in Vietnam, the black soldier's role has served to modify in a positive direction the image of the black man in both white and black communities. The early phase of the civil rights movement, with its emphasis on orderly and controlled demonstrations, served also to alter the symbolism of the black from that of a weak, powerless figure. The climax of this phase of change, as presented by the media, was the dramatic March on Washington in 1963 led by the late Dr. Martin Luther King, Jr. As an event in the mass media, it was unique. The national media were focused on a predominantly black assemblage moving in an orderly and powerful fashion. In a real sense, it was a symbolic incorporation of blacks into American society because of the heavy emphasis on religion and its setting in the nation's capital.

In the elimination of prejudiced imagery, blacks in the United States obviously have had to face much greater psychological barriers than any other minority group. Hostility and prejudice formed on the axis of color run deep. Nevertheless, the secular trend in negative stereotypes toward blacks from 1945 to 1975 has shown a dramatic decline, and the mass media have had an effect on this trend.[48]

The mass media view of blacks as a group growing in strength and direction was for the moment shattered by the period of extensive rioting. Instead, a partial image of explosive irrationality was dramatized. The use of sheer strength for destructive purposes rather than to achieve a goal that the white population could define as reasonable and worthwhile served only to mobilize counterhostility and counter-aggression. With the passage of time, these images faded as the mass media focused on reporting in depth the realities of the black community and the processes of social change at work, and the long term but incomplete increase in racial tolerance continued again.

ON THE EXPLANATION OF COMMODITY RIOTS

In the aftermath of the commodity riots, social scientists have vigorously pursued quantitative studies seeking to account for these patterns of collective violence.[49] In the main, these empirical efforts have been based on a version of the concept of relative deprivation and some have been formulated as manifestations of "revolutionary" violence.[50] It is commonplace to ground "theories" of relative deprivation in the classic writings of Marx and de Tocqueville. For Marx revolutions would occur when the socioeconomic environment was deteriorating, while for de Tocqueville revolutionary outbreaks would occur when a repressive government loosened its political control and generated expectations which it was unable to satisfy. James C. Davies has emphasized that both formulations can be fused into a J-curve theory.[51] In his view, violent political outbursts take place "when a prolonged period of objective economic and social development is followed by a short period of sharp reversal."[52]

The energetic efforts to apply the concept of relative deprivation to race riots has not produced impressive, consistent, or adequately compelling results.[53] First, one must keep in mind that these outbursts of race riots are not "revolutions" or efforts to create revolutions. They are forms of collective violence. They are rooted in economic and social conditions, but they must be understood in terms of the structure of society and its institutions.

Second, the relative deprivation concept is too general to handle the full range of multivariate elements operative in conditioning psychological attitudes and in fashioning the institutional structure of race relations. Third, there is a considerable body of social indicators, including attitude data, which has encouraged social scientists to apply systematic and refined methods of quantitative analysis. But unfortunately the data are not adequate for the task, so these efforts are often inconclusive.[54]

In the end, various thoughtful social scientists have come to adhere to a narrower and more diffuse conclusion. The "precision" of the relative deprivation approach gives way to the idea that revolution, violent revolt and, correspondingly, race riots are manifestations of "ambiguity, fluctuation and uncertainty of condition."[55] These conditions "contribute to one's susceptibility to be mobilized for revolt." Such a conclusion seems reasonable and compatible with common sense, but it is hardly trenchant or profoundly clarifying. Rather than the synthesis offered by James C. Davies, I find the original and competing formulations of Marx and de Tocqueville more suggestive and more useful in assessing the available research on collective racial violence, especially concerning both the rise and decline of the commodity-type riots. For the period of the spread of the commodity-type riot, the modification of the proposition of de Tocqueville is the more appropriate. The growth of militant attitudes and violent behavior is linked to a modest increase in economic and social circumstances which generated "rising expectations" and which was strengthened by more political appeals and "promises" that were not fulfilled. In the interplay between psychological and sociological elements, the existing institutional structure thwarted required societal change and resulted in ineffective social control.

The decline of the commodity-type riots also reflects the perspective inherent in de Tocqueville's analysis. Clearly, the larger society and its institutions which penetrated the local community immediately sought to improve the relative socioeconomic position of blacks in American society. Although the efforts to secure increased employment for low-income blacks and related education-training programs had some direct effects, there was no "instant" alteration in the position of the black citizenry.

The persistence of extensive collective violence, as anticipated by some analysts, failed to occur. The decline in rioting as the most limited basis for political violence in the black community was not the direct result of a drastic restructuring of the life chances of blacks or other minority groups. However, there was sufficient institution-building and accommodation to maintain effective levels of political legitimacy. Black leaders were more directly incorporated in public decision-making and administrative posts—from the local community to the national level. The number and visibility of elected black officials increased dramatically as blacks expanded their electoral participation.[56] The reality and symbolism of the accommodative politics which emerged during and in the aftermath of the commodity riots had their direct and immediate consequences. There can be no doubt, as carefully documented by William J. Wilson, that the consequence of these efforts was, in the decade of the 1970s, to assist middle-class, college educated blacks to a greater extent than those in the bottom strata of American society.[57] As of the writing of this essay in 1978, the fate of the black under class still remains problematic despite the vast growth of social welfare expenditures.

Thus one can speak of a "natural history" of a movement in the 1960s toward increased discontent, leading to violent outbursts and followed by a process of institutional negotiation and adjustment. But this process was hardly predetermined in its outcome—which seems implied in the J-curve conception. It was the result of the voluntaristic actions of elites and institutional groups—both black and white.

The history of the race riot is thus more than an account of the change from communal to commodity-type conflict to politically based violence. It is more than the history of the gross inadequacies of the system of law enforcement and the limitations in the performance of the mass media. It is, in part, an answer to the question posed by Ralph Ellison, the black novelist: "But can a people live and develop for over three hundred years simply by reacting?"[58] The black outbursts have been more than a reaction to police brutality and a double standard of legal justice. In a symbolic sense, they are expressions of energies to participate in and transform the larger society. In all phases of life, the blacks are no longer merely reacting but acting.

NOTES

1. *Report of the National Advisory Commission on Civil Disorders* (Washington, D.C.: U.S. Government Printing Office, 1968). See also James S. Campbell, "The Usefulness of Commission Studies of Collective Violence," *Annals of the American Academy of Political and Social Science,* 391 (September 1970): 168-76; Jeffrey K. Hadden, "Reflections on the Social Scientist's Role in Studying Civil Violence: Introduction to a Symposium," *Social Science Quarterly,* 51 (September 1970): 329-38.

2. Allen D. Grimshaw, *Racial Violence in the United States* (Chicago: Aldine, 1969), 4. In this volume Grimshaw presents an overview of the state of social science research on collective racial violence as of 1969.

3. Ibid. 5

4. Morris Janowitz, "Patterns of Collective Racial Violence," in Hugh Davis Graham and Ted Robert Gurr, U.S. eds., *Violence in America: Historical and Comparative Perspectives* (Washington, D.C.: U.S. Government Printing Office, 1969), 317-37.

5. Chicago Commission on Race Relations, *The Negro in Chicago: A Study of Race Relations and a Race Riot* (Chicago: University of Chicago Press, 1922). For another riot of that period that has been documented in depth, see Elliott M. Rudwick, *Race Riot at East St. Louis, July 2, 1917* (Carbondale, Ill.: Southern Illinois University Press, 1964).

6. Allen D. Grimshaw, "Factors Contributing to Colour Violence in the United States and Great Britain," *Race,* 3 (May 1962): 3-19. See also Robin M. Williams, " Social Change and Social Conflict: Race Relations in the United States, 1944-1964," *Sociological Inquiry,* 35 (winter 1965): 3-25.

7. Allen D. Grimshaw, "Actions of Police and Military in American Race Riots," *Phylon,* 24 (fall 1963): 271-89.

8. Morris Janowitz, "Sociological Theory and Social Control," *American Journal of Sociology,* 81 (July 1975): 82-108.

9. Stanley Lieberson and Arnold R. Silverman, "Precipitants and Conditions of Race Riots," *American Sociological Review,* 30 (December 1965): 887-98.

10. John Hope Franklin, *The Militant South, 1800-1861* (Cambridge: Harvard University Press, 1956).

11. The Chicago Commission on Race Relations, *The Negro in Chicago,* 23.

12. See also Allen D. Grimshaw, "Lawlessness and Violence in America and Their Special Manifestations in Changing Negro-White Relationships," *Journal of Negro History,* 44 (January 1959): 52-72.

13. Alex L. Swan, "The Harlem and Detroit Riots of 1943: A Comparative Analysis," *Berkeley Journal of Sociology,* 16 (1971-72): 75-93.

14. See, for example, Hans Mattick, "The Form and Content of Recent Riots," *Midway* (summer 1968): 3-32.

15. See Allen A. Silver, "Official Interpretations of Racial Riots," *Urban Riots: Violence and Social Change, Proceedings of the Academy of Political Science,* 29 (July 1968): 146-58.

16. S.L.A. Marshall, *Men Against Fire* (Washington, D.C.: Infantry Journal, 1947).

17. Anthony Oberschall, "The Los Angeles Riot of August 1965" *Social Problems,* 15 (winter 1968): 322-34.

18. Jules J. Wanderer, "1967 Riots: A Test of the Congruity of Events," *Social Problems, 16* (fall 1968): 193-98.

19. *Report of the National Advisory Commission on Civil Disorders* (New York: Dutton, 1968), Ch. 15.

20. Arnold Katz, "Firearms, Violence and Civil Disorders," mimeographed paper, Stanford Research Institute (July 1968), 10.

21. Frank Zimring, "Is Gun Control Likely to Reduce Violent Killings?" *University of Chicago Law Review,* 35 (summer 1968): 721-37.

22. Louis G. Goldberg, "Ghetto Riots and Others: The Faces of Civil Disorder in 1967," *Journal of Peace Research,* 5 (1968): 120.

23. Robert M. Fogelson and Robert B. Hill, "Who Riots? A Study of Participation in the 1967 Riots," *Supplemental Studies for the National Advisory Commission on Civil Disorders* (Washington, D.C.: U.S. Government Printing Office, July 1968), 221-48.

24. *The Detroit Riot: A Profile of 500 Prisoners* (Washington, D.C.: Department of Labor, March 1968).

25. Oberschall, "Los Angeles Riot of August 1965," 335.

26. Sheryl M. Moinat, Walter J. Raine, Stephen L. Burbeck, and Keith K. Davison, "Black Ghetto Residents as Rioters," *Journal of Social Issues,* 28 (1972); National Advisory Commission on Civil Disorders, *Supplemental Studies,* 239; Jeffrey M. Paige, "Political Orientation and Riot Participation," *American Sociological Review,* 36 (October 1971): 810-20.

27. National Advisory Commission on Civil Disorders, *Supplemental Studies*, 239.

28. Oberschall, "Los Angeles Riot of August 1965," 329.

29. *Report of the National Advisory Commission on Civil Disorders*, 7.

30. Ibid., 243.

31. See Morris Janowitz, *The Social Control of Escalated Riots* (Chicago, University of Chicago Center for Political Study 1968). In this study the formula of use of "manpower" rather than "firepower" was also developed.

32. New York *Times*, March 13, 1969, 22.

33. New York *Times*, September 29, 1968.

34. For a list and analysis of 25 reported sniping incidents in July and August 1968, see *Riot Data Review* (Lemberg Center for the Study of Violence), No. 3 (February 1969): 1-38.

35. See Harold Cruse, *The Crisis of the Negro Intellectual* (New York: Morrow, 1967), 347-401, for an analysis of the ideologies of violence in the black community. The activities of two groups of racial terrorists, the Black Liberation Army and the Symbionese Liberation Army, are described in Ch. 12 of this book.

36. Paul Blackstock, *The Strategy of Subversion* (Chicago: Quadrangle, 1964).

37. Gary Marx, "Thoughts on a Neglected Category of Social Movement Participants: The Agent Provocateur and the Informant," *American Journal of Sociology*, 80 (September 1974); 402-42.

38. See Barrington Moore, Jr., "Revolution in America?," *New York Review of Books* (January 30, 1969) for an analysis of the conditions limiting violent revolution in the United States.

39. Paul Blackstock, "Anarchism, Manipulated Violence and Civil Disorder," unpublished manuscript, 1968.

40. Paula B. Johnson, David O. Sears, and John B. McConahay, "Black Invisibility, the Press, and the Los Angeles Riot," *American Journal of Sociology*, 76 (January 1971): 698-721; Terry Ann Knopf, "Race Riots, and Reporting," *Journal of Black Studies*, 4 (March 1974): 303-27.

41. See W. W. Charter, *Motion Pictures and Youth* (New York, 1933).

42. See *Christian Science Monitor*, October 4, 1968, for details of a survey conducted by that newspaper's staff.

43. Morris Janowitz, "Societal Socialization: Mass Persuasion," in *The Last Half Century: Societal Change and Politics in America* (Chicago: University of Chicago Press, 1978), 320-63.

44. *Television and Growing Up: The Impact of Televised Violence*, Report to the Surgeon General, U.S. Public Health Service, from the Surgeon General's Scientific Advisory Committee on Television and Social Behavior (Washington, D.C.: U.S. Government Printing Office, 1972).

45. *Report of the National Advisory Commission on Civil Disorders*, 202.

46. Oberschall, "Los Angeles Riot of August 1965," 335-36.

47. For a discussion of this psychological mechanism, see Bruno Bettelheim and Morris Janowitz, *Social Change and Prejudice* (New York: Free Press 1964).

48. Angus Campbell, *White Attitudes Toward Black People* (Ann Arbor, Mich.: Institute for Social Research, 1971) 130.

49. William R. Berkowitz, "Socioeconomic Indicator Changes in Ghetto Riot Tracts," *Urban Affairs Quarterly*, 10 (September 1974): 69-94; Milton Bloombaum, "The Conditions Underlying Race Riots as Portrayed by Multidimensional Scalogram Analysis: A Reanalysis of Lieberson and Silverman's Data," *American Sociological Review*, 33 (February 1968): 76-91; Bryan T. Downes, "A Critical Reexamination of the Social and Political Characteristics of Riot Cities," *Social Science Quarterly*, 51 (September 1970): 349-60; and "Social Characteristics of Riot Cities: A Comparative Study, *Social Science Quarterly*, 49 (Decem-

ber 1968): 504-20; William Breithaler Ford and John H. Moore, "Additional Evidence on the Social Characteristics of Riot Cities," Social *Science Quarterly,* 51 (September 1970): 339-48; Stanley Lieberson and Arnold Silverman, "The Precipitants Underlying Conditions of Race Riots," *American Sociological Review,* 30 (December 1965): 887-98; Jerome L. McElroy and Larry D. Singell, "Riot and Nonriot Cities: An Examination of Structural Contours," *Urban Affairs Quarterly,* 8 (March 1973): 281-302; Seymour Spilerman, "The Causes of Racial Disturbances: A Comparison of Alternative Explanations," *American Sociological Review,* 35 (August 1970): 627-49; Jules Wanderer, "An Index of Riot Severity and Some Correlates," *American Journal of Sociology,* 74 (March 1969): 500-05; Donald I. Warren, "Neighborhood Status Modality and Riot Behavior: An Analysis of the Detroit Disorders of 1967," *Sociological Quarterly,* 12 (summer 1971): 350-66.

50. Abraham H. Miller et al., "The J-Curve Theory and the Black Urban Riots," *American Political Science Review,* 71 (September 1977): 964-82.

51. James C. Davies, "Toward a Theory of Revolution," in Barry McLaughlin, ed., *Studies in Social Movements* (New York: Free Press, 1969), 85-109.

52. Ibid., 86, Also see Ch. 16.

53. Clark McPhail, "Civil Disorder Participation: A Historical Examination of Recent Research," *American Sociological Reviews,* 36 (December 1971): 1058-73.

54. Abraham H. Miller et al., "The J-Curve Theory. . ." passim.

55. Ibid., 980.

56. Philip Converse, "Changes in the American Electorate," in *The Human Meaning of Social Change,* Angus Campbell and Philip E. Converse, eds. (New York: Russell Sage Foundation, 1972), 326-31.

57. William J. Wilson, *The Declining Significance of Race: Blacks and the Changing American Institutions* (Chicago: University of Chicago Press, 1978).

58. Ralph Ellison, *Shadow and Act* (New York: Random House, 1964), 315.

Chapter 10
American Indian Resistance and Protest

JEANNE GUILLEMIN

The popular and not entirely inaccurate view of the impact of Western civilization on American Indians is that a larger, expanding society wrought havoc on aboriginal groups. From the seventeenth-century defeat and dispersal of New England Indians to the nineteenth-century atrocities of Sand Creek and Wounded Knee, historical emphasis has been on the ultimate subjugation of native tribes, and has given little attention either to the underlying causes or to the contemporary survival of many groups. Yet any perspective which limits itself to only the overt hostilities which punctuate the long history of Indian-white relations obscures the cumulative effect of nearly 400 years of colonization and native rule. Focus on the victimization of American Indians also renders paradoxical the recent dramatic increase in their numbers and the present social viability of many reservations and urban communities.

This is not to deny the brutalities and violence which are an integral part of colonial history, for every phase of frontier expansion was marked by Indian resistance and bloodshed. Nor is it to say that inequities no longer characterize contemporary Indian-white relations. Racial discrimination, augmented by cultural and linguistic dissimilarities, has deeply affected Indian education, employment and, on an individual level, personal self-esteem. But public fascination with the military defeat of Indian groups can prevent a constructive understanding of the why and wherefore of frontier violence and contemporary incidents of Indian protest.

Far from being short-lived and spontaneous phenomena, each overt conflict between Indians and whites has been the product of complex social forces and, in the aftermath of conflict, neither side has been able to escape its common history or the fact that both continue to live in the same society. The contact of aboriginal groups with the dominant society did not end with the military defeat of Western tribes; instead, Indian-white relations were reformulated. Put most briefly, the old relationship of colonial settlers to native tribes was salvaged from the debris of continental expansion and translated into a standardized reservation system. As

AUTHOR'S NOTE: *Jeanne Guillemin is an associate professor of sociology at Boston College. She has written extensively on the life-ways and political circumstances of Indians in North America, including* Urban Renegades: The Cultural Strategy of American Indians *(1975). In 1978-1979 she was a Congressional Fellow of the American Anthropological Association.*

America evolved from a string of colonial outposts to a federal government, the format for Indian-white contact changed and, with it, the kind of overt conflict which was most likely to erupt.

Underneath the complex history of North American settlement by Europeans we can discern three phases of Indian resistance and protest. Basically these phases were determined by the growth of a centralized government capable of ordering social relations between native tribes and white society. Although many years separate the first European contacts with Indians and later white intrusions into the continental interior, the relative influence of domestic national authority had at least as much effect on the shape of conflict as the date of contact. Whenever and wherever national authority operated, it was a third party to conflict between Indians and private white citizens, and in some circumstances it could have positive and peaceable influence.

As nationalism developed among the white populations of the United States and Canada, the idea that native Americans should be administered emerged and grew stronger, and finally displaced the earlier and more limited goal of aboriginal conquest. Therefore, regardless of when any group of Indians first laid eyes on white intruders, the categories by which it would be governed were well-defined by the second half of the nineteenth century. Keeping these facts in mind, we can discern the following phases of Indian-white relations: (1) the sixteenth-through mideighteenth-century colonization of the Northeast; (2) the growth of urban industrialization and nationalism which characterized westward expansion in the nineteenth century; and (3) the rise of large-scale bureaucracies on federal and state levels, a predominant characteristic of modern economics and politics.

Within each of these phases, the dynamics of specific hostilities between Indians and whites are understandable in terms of the answers to four interconnected questions about their comparative strengths. What kind of political and military organization characterized conflicting native and white groups? Which of the two had the best access to the technology of warfare? At a very fundamental level, did the sheer numbers of Indians or whites give either an advantage over the opposing side? And, finally, what were the economic motivations which justified lighting the fires of armed violence? The interplay of these four factors—leadership, technology, demography, and economic motivation—becomes clearer when we look systematically at each era of Indian-white relations.

COLONIAL SETTLEMENT vs. INDIAN ALLIANCES

The fragmentary evidence available on the earliest Indian-white contacts in the Northeast indicates that the worst effects of European intrusion were felt many years in advance of any open warfare. Contagious diseases, such as smallpox and venereal disease, decimated coastal Indian communities during the sixteenth century and those not destroyed by disease were forced to adapt to the traders and fishermen who were the source of their troubles. Involvement in the fur trade often spelled another round of catastrophes, as Indians came to rely on European food and clothing, which was inferior to native versions and occasionally contaminated. The result was an increase in malnutrition and pulmonary diseases, such as tuberculosis and pneumonia.[1]

Despite epidemics and disease, or perhaps as a result of them, there was considerable mobility and defensive reorganization among aboriginal groups. From the perspective of the American colonial historian, the sixteenth century was a time when, from Jamestown to Port Royal, a secure European foothold was being established in North America. An Indian historian might just as well point out the development of significant native alliances in the Eastern hinterlands, north and south. The Iroquois were the best-known and most long-standing example, but other military alliances developed to counteract colonial expansion. At various points, in fact, the balance between Indian war parties and colonial militia favored the former who, like other guerrilla forces, knew the terrain and had (through trade) access to the same weaponry as their enemies.

Why, then, were coastal Indians not able to contain the settlers at Jamestown or deter the colonization of Penn's Woods or defeat the Massachusetts Bay Colony in King Philip's War (1675-1676)? The answer is less related to comparative political and technological assets than, on the one hand, to population growth in the new colonies, and, on the other, to the moral fervor which added incentive to white economic expansion. While plans to entice immigrants to the New World met with varying success, the rising birth rate in European colonies validated each endeavor and lent a naturalistic justification to strategies for growth. The moral determination of colonial leaders is well illustrated in the orations of the Reverend John Cotton, John Mason, and others, which leave no room for doubting that the extermination of the "savages" was necessary. Unfortunately, we do not have extensive documentation of Indian exhortations to war; what is available suggests that their goals were to stem a rising tide rather than to annihilate their offensive neighbors.

The form of violence which characterized colonial conflict could scarcely be categorized as warfare on the scale of contemporary European wars or even the War of Independence. Skirmishes, raids, and minor retaliations are all that historical records reveal and all that could be possible under the circumstances of colonial life. Even King Philip's War, with its prepossessing title, is revealed in detail as little more than a series of surprise attacks on rural enclaves, both native Indian and English ones. It was only after the American Revolution that the military intervention of the state changed the scale of retribution. In 1779 President Washington ordered army troops to lay waste the villages of the New York Iroquois, partly in reprisal for their lack of support for colonial forces and partly to prevent random, violent conflicts with white settlers. Before Sullivan's Raid, which became the popular name of the campaign, violence and destruction were the outcome of local-level competition— settlers vying with Indians for land, tribes competing with other tribes for trade routes, Europeans competing with each other for both land and commerce.

STATE INTERVENTION AND THE INTERNAL FRONTIER

Although the new federal government had the legal right to intervene in Indian-white relations, military intervention after punishment of the Iroquois occurred outside the Northeast at the expanding frontiers of the nation. In the Southeast, Indians fought on both sides of the United States-Spanish struggle for dominance. Then, in a series of "Indian Wars" in the early part of the nineteenth century, former allies and foes were effectively dispersed by army troops. With a growing European market for cotton and agricultural products, the South's plantation system began expanding not only toward Florida but westward toward the Mississippi and the port of New Orleans. One imperative of this expansion was the removal of land-holding Indians in the Carolinas and Georgia. Between 1820 and 1840, the U.S. Army was in charge of the displacement of more than 30,000 Southeastern Indians, forcing many of them to march to territory beyond the Mississippi on the infamous "Trail of Tears," whose hardships cost dearly in terms of native lives.[2] This use of federal troops constitutes the first in a long series of events in which the War Department, acting in the name of national progress, intervened in Indian-white affairs.

Concerning the social organization of the internal frontiers—the plantation South and the U.S. and Canadian West—one myth needs to be dispelled. The impression is often given that white population growth, similar to that felt by Northeastern Indians, precipitated the displacement and segregation of other tribes. In actuality, the antebellum South was a closed system in which relationships between the dominant white caste of owners and the subservient caste of black slaves would have been severely troubled if population density had approached that of the North. Even with the westward expansion of the plantation system, Southern families tended to maintain dynastic control of property inheritance and paternalistic control of their workers. The immigration of surplus populations from Europe was discouraged, both by law and by custom, as a threat to social equilibrium.

Following the Civil War, the division between the growing urban Northeast as the producer and consumer of manufactured goods and the rest of the continent, including Canada, as the supplier of raw materials for industry emerged with great clarity. In the West in particular, there developed a kind of imperial policy whereby government support was given for the extension of commerce and investment. True to the form of nineteenth-century European imperialism, the establishment of dominion over the West required a certain amount of manpower, but not settlement by large numbers of conventional citizens. To the contrary, the work of mining, trade, ranching, lumbering, and railroad-building required and attracted men who were adventuresome and also superfluous to the societies from which they had emigrated. Hannah Arendt's comment on those who implemented British imperial rule in South Africa applies as well to those who populated the American West in approximately the same epoch: "The world of native savages was a perfect setting for men who had escaped the reality of civilization."[3]

Nor was this kind of frontiersman, whatever his work, likely to have made a permanent escape; much of the chaos associated with the "Wild West" was due to the shifts in population which took place as mines opened and closed, railroad work began or stagnated, and land sales boomed or collapsed.

Following the Louisiana purchase, Mississippi trade brought rifles and other artifacts of civilization to the mounted Indian warriors of the West and made them, for a time at least, formidable foes. At each border of the Western frontier, the conflicts between Indians and whites were initially on a scale which suited a thinly distributed but mobile population. Each side had its horsemen and raided the other's more defenseless sectors, the unprotected native encampment and the undefended farming family.

Rather than protecting a large influx of settlers, army troops dispatched to the West were commissioned to put an end to the activity of white rowdies, many of whom were little more than teenagers, and to confine troublesome, nomadic Indians to a circumscribed area, separate from their non-Indian adversaries. Although this was the stated goal of the U.S. Cavalry, its installations and specific duties were never far from the purpose of protecting commercial interests. The building of army forts in the West followed the path of trade routes, and orders from Washington were invariably related to one or another difficulty regarding outlaw or Indian interferences in railroad construction, cattle-ranching, mining, etc.[4]

The West of Billy the Kid and other outlaws was eventually tamed by the presence of the army, the institution of the federal marshal, and the establishment of local courts and police. The latter institutions became a successful means of imposing civil order during the last part of the century, when a respectable bourgeoisie replaced the fluctuating, predominately male population of the early frontier. As for Indian tribes, there was no law which accounted for them; their resistance to being confined to reservations was interpreted as a declaration of war. The journals and reports of army officials give the impression that Indians were, in fact, subject to a moral judgment which paralleled the civil process of arrest, review, and incarceration. In contrast to white outlaws, who were individually guilty of criminal behavior, Indians were perceived as groups, whose customs were irremediably savage, requiring government restrictions on their mobility. When Indians resisted confinement, as the Nez Perce did in 1877 under the leadership of Chief Joseph or as the remnants of Sioux groups loosely organized around Sitting Bull did in 1890, army reaction was as intrepid as if convicted criminals had escaped jail and were running free in a crowded city.

That punishment was being meted out to whole communities of natives, only some or none of whom had had a hand in hostilities, was not lost on all army officers; some saw a protective function for Indians in the institution of reservations. But such reflections can hardly be taken as more than humanistic asides which have little bearing on the army's actual duties. Otherwise, we would have found the U.S. Cavalry as a protectionist force in California, where from the 1840s through the 1870s miners and roustabouts carried out a wholesale slaughter of that region's native population. The civil disorder of California mining camps and boomtowns posed no threat to continental expansion. In its very repressiveness, it secured a vital economic ingredient: immigrant Chinese labor to work on the railroads and in frontier towns.

The need to confine native tribes to reservations or to exterminate them became ever more pressing in the last quarter of the nineteenth century, a time of marked fluctuations in the national economy. As Fred Shannon and other historians have seen it, the federal government's role in the West was heavily influenced by businessmen and private corporate interests with surplus capital to invest in land and industrial enterprises.[5] For example, Congress was persuaded to sell public lands, including territory granted by treaty to Indians, as part of a plan to relieve urban crowding in the Northeast. The visions of many thousands of settlers finding a new life for themselves in homesteading never became reality; most public land was acquired by land speculators and eventually by investors in large-scale agriculture or industry. Even as public and Indian lands were being put on the auction block, competition with corporate enterprise was forcing small farmers off the plains and back to urban centers.

In addition to private economic imperatives, the conquest of Indian tribes became a matter of national pride. News of Custer's "last stand" reached the East just at the time of the nation's centennial celebration and touched off newspaper diatribes against "savage warriors" and public demonstrations in support of the federal militia. Added to this, the image of the frontier family beset by savage Indians bolstered public support for army "wars" against Indian tribes. Reports of Indian attacks on settlers, even if retaliatory, fired public sentiment, though the opening of the West was directed largely by the pragmatic concern of investors. The financial instability of the national economy, which was just beginning to gauge itself to large-scale corporate organization, lent a frenetic imperative to the army's mission; the presence of disruptive elements which might jeopardize economic development was even more intolerable under uncertain market conditions. By legitimate and illegitimate avenues, the demands of private industry had their impact on federal policy and the pace and viciousness of Western Indian conquest was stepped up accordingly.

FEDERAL GOVERNMENT-TRIBAL RELATIONS

Although the Bureau of Indian Affairs (BIA) was established in 1834, the modern federally administered reservation system developed in the decades following the Civil War. Its characteristics are those of any large, rationally organized corporate bureaucracy, the same form which now orders American political, economic, and educational institutions, with the important difference that the clients of this bureaucracy are exclusively Indian. The bureaucratization of Indian-white relations has lent enormous complexity to an already complicated past, mainly by involving conflicting interest groups in attempts to undo the Gordian knot of what has been commonly phrased as the "Indian problem."

Even before the final defeat of the plains Indians, the War Department's control of Indian matters was being supplanted by progressive educators and missionaries concerned with the fate of native tribes.[6] Once the difficult business of restricting native groups to reservations had been accomplished, and town, county, and state governments were capable of imposing civil order in surrounding areas, the military presence was unnecessary. The task of the federal government, as formulated by liberal educators, became to incorporate surviving Indians into the national polity. Along lines similar to those proposed for integrating immigrants, programs were devised for teaching English, sewing, and small-scale farming in tribal communities, with the added touch of conversion to Christianity. None of these efforts to bring civilization to Indians could be described as unique; the history of missionary activities in North America extends over many years and virtually all regions. The notable transition, which was complete by 1900, was political administration according to religious and moral principles. The salvation of Indians, long a concern of humanists and missionaries, became the goal of modern federal policy.

Military leaders, especially during the Grant administration (1869-1877), struggled to maintain control of the Bureau of Indian Affairs, but they offered only a static, protectionist maintenance of native reservations. The government's difficulty was to iron out the many irrational aspects of its relationship to diverse Indian groups, and a military guard was not only insufficient to the task, but a reminder of a major dilemma: that in the land of equal opportunity, some people were not free. The promise of liberal educators was to set in motion an evolutionary scheme whereby even defeated "savages" might eventually progress to a condition of individualistic autonomy, thereby validating the egalitarian ethos of the state and also demonstrating the beneficience of the central government. In addition, progressive programs resolved the side issue of healing the wounds of bitter warfare conducted within national boundaries; for, in addition to troubling national economic expansion, renegade Indians were a symbolic threat to national integrity, literally the "enemy within" in an era already dominated by civil war.

The institution of a bureaucratic administration and the fostering of progressive programs were and still are only a partly rational overlay on an unresolved paradox. To begin with, the federal government's relationship is with tribes, not individuals, and constitutes an extraordinary admission of obligations. By definition, the corporate nature of tribal recognition is in opposition to the ordinary civil status of the man on the street. Also, as the trustee of tribal welfare, Washington claimed jurisdiction over Indian life and land in a way it did not do over any other local community. The justification for this is an historical one, and to terminate the obligations would require a denial of national historical facts, beginning with early congressional assumption of responsibility for treaties contracted by the British prior to the American Revolution.

Furthermore, issues of race and racism hang heavily over past and present relations between tribes and the federal government. The goal of a standardized relationship to Indian groups, one which dismisses the importance of cultural differences, geographic locale, and population size, is inherently racist, being based on no other fact than racial category. Yet movement towards this goal has been characteristic of federal decision-marking since the inauguration of progressive reforms in the late nineteenth century.

At the same time, the business of Indian administration fell to civil servants, a sector of government which has increased dramatically over the course of this century. The civil servant has been involved in Indian affairs on at least two levels, as the office workers in Washington and as the local or regional Indian agent. Until very recently, the Bureau of Indian Affairs official was likely to be a white man charged with the peculiar duty of native rule, a political anomaly in a nation based on democratic representation. Although altruistically motivated, Bureau employees and the Bureau itself have long been the objects of criticisms echoing Mannoni's argument that all colonial bureaucrats have a vested interest in oppression.[7]

Present Indian policy is not far afield from its nineteenth-century mission, although the interpretation of needed improvement on reservations has taken a decidedly pragmatic turn. The present Indian problem is defined in economic terms, as a lack of education, of employment qualifications, of administrative skills, of technological expertise, of captial—in short, as poverty.[8] Statistics on tribal education, health, and unemployment are so consistently below the national average that few people, in or out of government, express surprise that the conditions of this particular minority should read like the Book of Job. It is almost assumed, with a fatalism uncharacteristic of government officials or the American public, that Indians must be the victims of circumstance. There is no particular logic behind any such assumption, only the vague notion that, once defeated *by* this nation, Indians must remain defeated as long as they are *in* this nation.

Conversely, politically active and articulate Native Americans are constantly faced with the obstacle of American preoccupation with war and violence. The dominant society's reactions to any kind of public protest veers either toward sympathy for the dead victims of militarism or toward a fear that the resurrected enemy might, justifiably or unjustifiably, still seek to retaliate. Were these only the occasional attitudes of a public which has been manipulated by media images, then Indian spokesmen could profitably direct their statements to some more rational and informed audience. But where the audience might be expected, in academia or in Congress, few have been able to overcome their own cultural biases in order to make level-headed appraisals of current Indian-government issues.

CONTEMPORARY INDIAN POLITICS AND ECONOMICS

A realistic assessment of the contemporary Indian situation must take into account several basic facts. The first is that there is no one group of Native Americans. There are literally hundreds of separately recognized tribes and bands in the United States and Canada, all of them sufficiently dispersed that they cannot constitute a single political collectivity. The diversification of Indian interest groups is not strictly along linguistic or cultural lines; that one belongs to a group with a particular name may be more important in determining relationships with outsiders, Indian and non-Indian, than adherence to traditional ways. The distinction between a Cherokee and a Navajo, or between an Iroquois and a Hopi is likely to be drawn by them on the basis of identification with a particular history of community and kinship.

There are, in addition, other social divisions which defy any analyst's power to generalize about Native Americans. The migration of Indians to industrial centers, which began in large numbers during the Second World War, presents a distinction between those adults who are directly involved in wage labor and those who remain engaged in the reservation economy, which is underwritten by government monies. The frequent mobility of urban Indians between city jobs and reservation communities, sometimes over long distances, has been well documented.[9] Nevertheless, there exists an obvious dichotomy between those for whom the reservation holds no hope of adequate employment and those who as tribal council members, BIA administrators, or employees of local industry are able to remain in or near reservations. While the dichotomy resists definition in terms of social class, there is a tendency for the economically secure reservation adults to be older and politically more conservative than their relatives in the city. Of late, as Eastern Indian groups have endeavored to organize themselves as tribes and land-holders, there has also been evidence of still another dividing line, between treaty-recognized Western tribes and the newly established organizations of the East.

On the positive side of dependency status, the Indian Health Service has had remarkable success in reducing infant mortality rates and generally extending the lifespan of individual Indians. Federal housing has also improved and widespread participation of many Native Americans in the national labor market has put Indian standards of living at an all-time high, though still below that of other Americans. The increase in the Indian population is at about 3 percent a year, a faster rate of growth than for any other population segment. This continuing trend towards a younger population sets Indians at odds with the "greying of America" which is being felt in the dominant society. Given the paucity of economic opportunities on reservations, it seems almost a certainty that today's Indian children will be tomorrow's urban workers. And because federal administration of human services and welfare is itself deeply invested in supporting tribal communities, much in the same way that welfare departments rely on their clients, it is predictable that at least some of them will live on reservations as tribal administrators or welfare recipients.

Despite their geographic dispersal and cultural diversity, Indians have been administered as if they constituted a single, homogeneous body. If we follow René Maunier's definition of colonization as "education by legislation,"[10] the federal government has been set on the same course of colonial policy for the past 100 years, attempting in successive programs to impose standardized legal codes over local custom. At first, the progressive educators who directed the Bureau of Indian Affairs attempted to abolish traditions. In the next most significant phase of Indian administration, New Deal legislators supported an adaptation of constitutional representation to existing tribal leadership organizations, with the result that many of today's tribal governments have an identical political structure and articulate in precisely the same way with the central government. In Canada, the stipulations of tribal treaties, rather than legislatively approved programs, have produced approximately the same effects.

The relationship of American Indians to the federal government is more complex than that of any colonized population to the metropolitan power or even than that of other nationalized aboriginal populations, such as Mexican Indians, for whom a structural model of internal colonialism has been proposed.[11] The complexity lies in the bureaucratic division of labor between the Department of the Interior, which manages Indian land and trust funds, and its subordinate, the Bureau of Indian Affairs, which was the administrative prize won by liberal educators from the army. Unlike the tenancy of large numbers of Mexican mestizos and their counterparts in other Latin American nations, the trustee-ward relationship of Washington to native tribes provides for a system of direct federal jurisdiction, to the exclusion of private individuals, corporations, and other levels of government.

Legally, most Indian tribes own a land base; but this does not mean that they have more than usufructuary rights over it. Many tribes have funds held in trust for them by the federal government; but this does not mean that, corporately or individually, the capital value of such funds is freely available to them. The trustee responsibilities of the Department of the Interior are, in part, involved in keeping tribal assets protectively out of the control of tribes. In the normal routine of its management of public lands, however, Interior has leased Indian land and subsurface rights at less-than-cost prices to large national industries and local corporations.[12]

Meanwhile, Indian business ventures which were approved by the government have succumbed to what appears to be inevitable failure. The most recent failure in a long line of investments, most of which were in reservation agriculture and factories, has been the promotion of tourist centers. According to a recent article on the front page of the *Wall Street Journal*, a combination of the energy crisis, inexperience, and bad luck have resulted in millions of dollars in deficits.[13] With every failure, the guardianship role of Interior is augmented, for neither the government nor Indian tribal organizations are prone to risk taking. At the heart of such failures is the vulnerability to which every small business is prone in an age of mega-corporations. Even with capital assured, the affordable margins of error remain narrow, updating and maintaining a competitive technology is costly, and weathering market lows produces an often fatal strain. There are special difficulties which affect exclusively Indian enterprise. Few Indians have the technical training and administrative skills and experience necessary to make a going concern of agribusiness, industry, or resorts. Reliance on government specialists needs to be examined for possible conflicts of interest; indeed, tribes tend to employ private consulting firms to aid them in economic development projects. The touchy problem of tribal factionalism adversely affecting business organizations has yet to be fully considered, although in-group conflict reportedly contributed to problems in tourist resort management. Tied to this issue of competition is a number of unanswered questions concerning the "spin-off" phenomenon: of the handful of Indians who go on to graduate and professional education, how many return to the reservation community? How many prefer the rewards offered by private corporations? How many prefer to work in the higher echelons of government?

Among tribes such as the Navajo, the Crow, the Cheyenne, and others, whose lands are known to be rich in industrial fuels and minerals, concerted efforts have been made to claim more complete control of land use than the federal government has ever permitted. The Crow and Blackfeet have had direct dealings with private corporations concerning access to their natural resources. Led by the Navajo, they and other Western tribes have had independent talks with the Organization of Petroleum Exporting Countries (OPEC) and conducted themselves more as sovereigns than dependents.

Where, if anywhere, such activity will lead is uncertain. That it can severely disrupt the present nature of the majority of reservation economies is unlikely, for these have become firmly entrenched as "sustained enclaves," part and parcel of programs of federal human services.

INDIAN POLITICAL ACTIVISM

Given the control which the federal government exercises over tribal government and economics, Indians might be expected to be politically passive. Yet beginning with the implementation of the 1934 Indian Reorganization Act (IRA) the geographic dispersal of tribal leaders has been countered by a growing consciousness of how similar the problems of their communities are and how much of that similarity is based on restrictive federal policies which affect them in identical ways. The standardization of the tribal council form, coupled with efficient modern communication and transportation, was bound to produce such a recognition of shared political fate.

Added to this has been the urban experience of many Indians who joined the wartime labor market and the armed forces after having been exposed to the self-governing emphasis of the New Deal Indian policy. Living off-reservation put them in contact with other minorities and whites, and as standards of living rose, so did a sense of being a part of American society. The establishment in 1944 of the National Congress of American Indians as the first lobby run by and for native people was a direct outcome of both the politicizing effects of the IRA and the general new awareness of a larger national context for Indian issues.

Since then, the trend towards pan-Indian organization has continued, usually in areas of special need—education, health care, family counseling—which in many ways parallel the humanistic orientation of the BIA. Many pan-Indian organizations, while they may escape the "blaming the victim" syndrome, have not based their activities on any radical critique of American society in general or of the federal government in particular. Nor have many been known to address the American public at large as a potential pressure group. Instead, their attention has been directed toward key offices in government and in Indian communities.

The significant exception to this is the Indian Red Power movement which took hold during the late 1960s.[14] Essentially an urban movement, its most active membership was drawn from among young, relatively well-educated Indians, who criticized the American power structure and demanded national attention to the Native American cause. Although the form of public demonstration which they used was identical to the demonstrations of early proponents of civil rights for blacks, the list of grievances was markedly different from that of other minorities. Violation of treaties, misuse of land, neglect of human services, restrictions on tribal leadership—these and other accusations of oppression were directed at the federal government before nationwide media audiences. The seizure in 1969 of Alcatraz Island by the "Indians of All Tribes" was the first Red Power demonstration to receive prolonged media coverage. This was followed by protests in different areas around the country which were either sites of historical moment, such as Mount Rushmore and Plymouth Rock, or the focus of Indian rights disputes, as in upper New York State, northern California, Washington State, Wisconsin, and Colorado.

While the Indians of All Tribes in San Francisco and the American Indian Movement were seeking to gain public support, it is doubtful that these early demonstrations did more than bring out latent sympathies which were not translated into active political support. The Indians who occupied Alcatraz Island received hundreds of cartons of old clothes from well-wishers; but a plan to create an urban center for the Bay Area's thousands of Native Americans never received a serious hearing. Other important decisions concerning land claims, fishing rights, and treaty obligations were handled, as usual, behind closed doors in Washington and in state courts.

Red Power activism did have the effect of alerting Congress to a vocal new interest group, a different kind of Indian than the tribal council leadership and Washington lobbyists. However, with the election of a Republican administration in 1968 and the winding down of the War on Poverty, legislation to remedy the particular inequities which existed for Indians was apparently not forthcoming. Despite the fact that tribes had benefitted only intermittently from antipoverty programs, it seemed that Indian activists had arrived at a congressional well already run dry.

Still, the preceding decade had generated high expectations of reform within a climate of increasing political activity against the federal government by antiwar demonstrators. Looking at both the victories of black civil rights leaders and the growing momentum of protest against the Vietnam War, a young, articulate, and media-conscious Indian leadership had scarcely anything to lose. The efforts they put into national organization and the dramatic staging of protests appeared to pay off when support for legislative reform was declared not by any congressional leader but by the President-elect, Richard Nixon.

Relying on a brief requested from author Alvin Josephy, Jr., on July 8, 1970, Nixon delivered to Congress what is now recognized as a landmark address on Indian affairs. He spoke directly to the issue of a complementary relationship between the national government and tribal organizations, advocating a reversal of former injustices and a redistribution of authority within the BIA. Noting the inherent conflict of interest between the Department of the Interior's protection of national interests and its duty to protect the interests of Indians, Nixon proposed to solve this structural problem by increasing the power of the White House at the expense of both the Interior and Justice Departments, beginning his proposal with what can now, in post-Watergate times, be recognized as a classic comment on the workings of the federal administration:

> Every trustee has a legal obligation to advance the interests of the beneficiaries of the trust without reservation and with the highest degree of diligence and skill. Under present conditions, it is often difficult for the Department of the Interior and the Department of Justice to fulfill this obligation. No self-respecting law firm would ever allow itself to represent two opposing clients in one dispute; yet the federal government has frequently found itself in precisely that position. There is considerable evidence that the Indians are the losers when such situations arise. More than that, the credibility of the federal government is damaged whenever it appears that such a conflict of interest exists.[15]

The power of the "imperial presidency" was amply proven in the months that followed Nixon's statement. In line with his advocacy of native autonomy, Nixon appointed as Commissioner of Indian Affairs, Louis Bruce, an Indian who also happened to be a wealthy New York State businessman. Bruce took his position and the President's proposals perhaps more seriously than was expected. He increased the proportion of younger Indians within the ranks of the Bureau and at the same time initiated measures to reduce by half the number of people working in the Washington office to disperse administrative power to regional offices and tribes.

Although the BIA under Bruce could be perceived as a more beneficent institution, the combination of Nixon's programs and Bruce's diligence only seemed to underscore the fact that real decision-making went on at higher levels of the Interior Department. In mid-January 1971, for example, Interior approved the construction of the trans-Alaskan pipeline before working out any compensation to the Alaskan natives whose land and mineral rights were in question. In the Southwest, the crucial allocation of water and irrigation rights to reservation communities was prevented by Interior's commitment to state interests in monopolizing that resource. During the same year, Interior granted numerous exploration permits and strip-mining leases to private industries so that the energy potentials of reservations lands might be explored. For one reservation, that of the Northern Cheyenne in Montana, more than half of its 433,000 acres was threatened by strip mining. The Bureau of Indian Affairs had essentially no influence in regulating any of these matters. Instead, in both the Interior and Justice Departments, a complicated array of administrators, planners, engineers, and lawyers became the governmental managers of Indian lands, although the legitimate system of appeal open to native tribes stopped at the level of Commissioner of Indian Affairs.

THE TRAIL OF BROKEN TREATIES

The "increasing scent of victory in the air" which Indian spokesman Vine Deloria had noted in 1969 had, by 1972, been actualized in the difficult task of Bureau reorganization, in the new pursuit of grievance compensation, and the persistence of pan-Indian organizations. But as Nixon's first term drew to a close, frustration with the limits of legitimate appeal, concern with the executive interpretation of Indian policy, and the desire for still more action, prompted the combined efforts of eight activist Native American organizations to stage a public demonstration, "The Trail of Broken Treaties," in Washington.[16]

The original plan was to have four automobile caravans travel cross-country and meet in the capital during the week of November 2-9, preceding the presidential elections. American Indians could not have had two candidates more sympathetic to their cause. The Democratic candidate, Senator George McGovern, had long been a congressional spokesman for native rights. President Nixon had effectively mobilized a weak Congress to legislate BIA reforms and was campaigning for a second term on a strong "return the government to the people" platform. The function of the demonstration was not to educate either McGovern or Nixon, but to elicit an even greater commitment while the candidates were in the public eye. The event of a national election guaranteed maximum media coverage, which the protest organizers reasoned would give them the support of a national audience. They intended to make those who could affect legislation, including congressmen, declare themselves in favor of Indian affairs reform with the American polity as a witness: "We seek a new American majority—a majority that is not content merely to confirm itself by superiority in numbers, but which by conscience is committed toward prevailing upon the public will in ceasing wrongs and in doing right."[17]

There is no evidence to suggest that the Washington demonstration was meant as a criticism of executive action. To the contrary, in the first of the 20-point proposal the Indians brought to the capital, a return to a treaty-making relationship between the federal government and Indian "nations," was advocated so that "the President may resume the exercise of his full constitutional authority for acting in the matter of Indian Affairs."

However, by its very form, the assembly implied a critique of the Chief Executive who, on the eve of a predicted landslide victory, dispatched White House personnel and the Secretary of Interior to handle the situation. Once in Washington, the several hundred Indians who had joined the demonstration were shunted about between presidential aides, who feared a bad media image, and Interior officials, who refused to accept the Caravan leadership as legitimate representatives of American Indian interests.

When prearranged facilities for housing and food proved insufficient, the Trail leaders appealed to the BIA, but the Interior persisted in its disavowal of protest. On November 2, participants in the caravan spent the day milling about the Bureau building while the principal organizers met with Commissioner Bruce and C. Harrison Loesch, an Assistant Secretary of the Interior. At four p.m., guards on regular duty attempted to clear Indians from one area; but they refused to leave until negotiations were successfully completed and instead evicted the guards. A general panic spread throughout the building and the siege began.

During the week-long occupation of the Bureau building, attempts to discredit the Trail leadership continued to come from the Interior and, as a complementary face-saving strategy, attempts to placate the Indians were directed by the White House. A federal court order was served on the demonstrators on November 3, but no attempt was made to evict them. The hour of forced eviction was progressively delayed while meetings went on between Indian leaders and Interior and Justice officials; in the interim, the rhetoric of AIM leaders in particular, grew more militant and reports of vandalism within the building spread. Ultimately, it was Leonard Garment, as assistant to John Erlichman, presidential advisor on minority affairs, and Frank Carlucci, a middle-level appointee to the Office of Management and Budget, who concluded negotiations on November 6 and directed that funds be given to individual Indians to aid their exit from Washington. They recommended no prosecution against the demonstrators and diplomatically promised attention to the proposals of the Trail leaders.

The repercussions of the BIA occupation were immediate. While public sympathy was once again enlisted for American Indian activists, the reactions of American Indians ranged from virulent opposition to a sequence of peaceful demonstrations across the nation in support of the Trail proposals. The most conservative reaction came from heads of tribal councils, who resented any attempt to circumvent their authority. In a press release issued the very day that negotiations were completed, Interior Secretary Rogers Morton stated:

> For the honor and dignity of 480,000 reservation Indians, all Americans should understand that the protestors are a small splinter group of militants. They do not represent the reservation Indians of America. The National Tribal Chairmen's Association, composed of duly-elected officers of each tribe, has advised me through its Executive Director, Mr. William Youpee, that this illegal intrusion has no meaningful support in the Indian community. In addition, numerous Tribal Chairmen have sent telegrams or issued statements condemning the seizure.

The vandalism which occurred during the seizure of the Bureau building was universally deplored, although the exact amount of damage was never objectively gauged. From the government's point of view it was the destruction of some Bureau files and the absconding with others which marked the Trail demonstrators as lawbreakers. Through the arbitration of Hank Adams, one of the more moderate organizers of the caravan, the stolen file documents were returned, but the occupation itself and the destruction of government information intensified government surveillance of Indian activists. Militant AIM leaders, such as Russell Means and Dennis Banks, found themselves with the enemy on two flanks, conservative Indian leaders on one side and the FBI on the other.

Three months after the BIA occupation, in a direct sequel to that confrontation, AIM members and supporters began their occupation of the site of the Wounded Knee massacre of 1890 to protest corruption in local tribal governments and Indian oppression by the federal government.[18] The decision to occupy the Sioux village of Wounded Knee was not influenced by the historical event alone. Returning with other Oglala Sioux to the Pine Ridge reservation, Russell Means had received a hostile reception from tribal president Richard Wilson. Wilson succeeded in having Means arrested by a special BIA officer and used his special powers to harass the Indian activists. In towns and cities adjacent to the reservation area, riots and brawls involving Indians, whites fearful of AIM, and the police broke out.

In the midst of this disruption, the "Second Battle of Wounded Knee" began with a statement that the 200 Indians within a hastily constructed garrison would, if necessary, fight to the death. Government overreaction to the event was nothing short of spectacular. An array of FBI agents, federal marshals, BIA and state police descended on Pine Ridge with tanks, machine guns, and airplanes and spent the next two-and-a-half months in a parody of warfare. The leaders of the occupation suffered not the martyrdom they had declared themselves willing to undergo, but a demoralized surrender—and worse, a round of court indictments which rendered the leadership of the Red Power movement incapable of action.

SELF-DETERMINATION ON POLICY IN INDIAN AFFAIRS

If the Trail of Broken Treaties signaled the beginning of the end of Red Power militancy, it also accelerated federal reoganization of the Bureau of Indian Affairs, and ushered in the present era of self-determination policy. In the aftermath of the occupation, Assistant Secretary Loesch and Commissioner Bruce were both suspended, and other Bureau personnel were dispersed among several different floors of the main Interior building. In 1975 an interim committee of Indians and government officials, the American Indian Policy Review Committee, was set up to compile evidence on which to base administrative reform. As a "cooling off" mechanism, the committee operated very effectively by providing an open forum for Indian grievances in cities and on reservations across the country. After two years it produced what is fundamentally a reiteration of old problems, undistinguished by innovative suggestions for solutions.

As the commission was doing its work, Congress passed the 1975 Indian Self-Determination and Educational Assistance Act, which provides for increased tribal autonomy in local reorganization of government, schooling, and "physical plant" management of the reservation community. The presumption is that most Indian tribal councils, given the option between creating and running their own programs and having the BIA remain in charge of reservation services, will choose the former.

Since approval of Indian contracts rests with the secretary of Interior or with the secretary of Health, Education, and Welfare, the Bureau has obviously been relegated to a back seat in the future of Indian affairs.

Reflected in the Self-Determination Act is another trend related to the diminishing influence of the BIA. Many government departments, special offices, and congressional committees are involved in some fashion or another with Indian policy, whether in social assistance, engineering, urban organizations, veterans administration, or a host of other programs. This is an inevitable outcome of the proliferation of the federal civil service, which accelerated under the Kennedy administration and continues to the present. Though the results of the 1975 act have not yet been reckoned, it is also presumed that funding for Indian contracts will be multichanneled and involve offices and personnel beyond the Bureau.

Finding critics of the self-determination policy is difficult. Indian advocates are pleased at the potential for tribal self-government. Government employees favor it as a less cumbersome method of minority funding. Even staunch supporters of terminating federal trustee responsibilities are able to discern in it incentives for free enterprise and the American way which could eventually disburden Washington of its Indian tribes.

The more cynical, including me, Russel Barsh, Ronald Trosper, and others,[19] have noted that the Self-Determination Act presents an illusion of progress and some real pitfalls. One of its major provisions is against any program which would affect reservation land use or tribal funds, the special province of Interior. The 1975 act, then, maintains the dichotomy between community and land management by shutting doors on programs to create viable reservation economies, as opposed to those which run exclusively on government funds.

The self-determination policy in general fails to address the conflict of interest issue inherent in Interior's supervision of reservation land and trust funds. With "autonomy" being distributed through regional BIA offices to tribal governments, the Washington Bureau lacks the power to challenge decisions made in the national interest but against Indians. At a time when the search for and development of domestic sources of energy borders on the manic, Interior is itself caught between environmental preservation and national industrial needs. A deflection of Indian tribes to tasks, such as rewriting their constitutions and planning new schoolhouses, is perhaps the easier way. But there are too many tribal groups on Western reservations feeling competitive pressures for their resources from business and state governments for federal officials to ignore.

Although they live on federal land, reservation Indians also rely to some degree on local towns—where they shop, go for entertainment, or work—and must deal with county and state politics. Over the last five years, concurrent with the influx of a large population to the West and Southwest, a backlash has emerged, one in which the special status of Indians is condemned everywhere from the cafes in new boomtowns created by petroleum and mining companies to the floor of the U.S. Congress. Yet the federal government, ostensibly a protector of Indian rights and virtually the only respector of historical treaties, has yet to address worsening relations on the state and local level and to institute forums for arbitration. Instead, in the absence of a strong executive and mobilized Congress, courts have become the arbiters of conflict, deciding each case in terms of justice instead of the necessary coexistence of conflicting parties.

More than previous legislation, the Self-Determination Act involves Indian tribes in the techniques of contracting and the politics of grantsmanship without curtailing the inefficiencies in funding distribution which have long plagued them. In 1973, Senator Edward Kennedy opened hearings on Indian education with a statement which might just as well be made about other program areas: "Indian educators and tribal leaders, as well as parents and teachers, have been unable to discover what portion of the funds appropriated for the Indian education programs really reaches and benefits Indian children." [20] The participation of many federal offices in Indian affairs programs plus the disbursal of funds through regional offices represent an organizational diffusion that is uncharacteristic of other federal agencies. The latter, over the last decade, have reversed earlier trends towards decentralization on the grounds that consolidation improves efficiency. In spite of congressional hearings on accountability in Indian affairs, the present complexity of reservation administration is so great that, as in hearings on corporate monopolies, finding one individual to testify that he or she actually understood the entire system would be next to impossible.

If and when tribal councils shall be asked to account for contract and grant funds is a touchy subject. AIM accusations of tribal council corruption have been pushed aside; the federal government is even less interested in local-level reservation politics than in the internal order of the Third World countries to which it gives aid. To date, the Departments of Interior and HEW have not been restrictive in approving projects; yet it is impossible that tribes can avoid paying the hidden prices of a dependence on contracting. The greatest of these is not in writing the first proposal, but in the requirements of future funding. First, since the majority of problems which contracts can address are in the area of human services, some deprived group or groups—alcoholics, drug users, the old, the ill, undereducated children—must continue to be publicized to insure the renewal of funds. Second, renewed funding depends to some degree on measures of success or at least a positivistic estimate of the original project. Perhaps it is more accurate to say that tribal leaders must present themselves as "successful," i.e., as infallibly stable, capable of administrative organization, and in control of their communities. Such strategies may sound familiar to those who know the work of Rosalie and Murray Wax, George Castile and Ernest Shusky, which touches on the negative effects of previous legislation.[21] What the future bodes is even more rigidity and positivism in tribal government. Unfortunately, one of the first signs of the contract syndrome is a firm resistance to critical evaluation, so that even sympathetic outsiders are intolerable unless they are willing to participate in the unreality of propaganda. The greatest potential loss to tribal organizations is the right to learn by ordinary processes of trial and error.

What happens to tribal governments is only one-half the picture of contemporary Indian reality. The other half lies in the as yet unfelt reactions of young Native Americans who, better educated and more sophisticated than any previous generation, have been confronted with a frustrating and sometimes frightening assortment of experience and information: the dismal history of Indian-white relations, the political martyrdom of Banks, Means, and other Red Power leaders, tribal factionalism and malfeasance, small-town racism and big-city discrimination and, everywhere, the loss of dignity through poverty—if not one's own, then the poverty of one's relatives and one's people. If their sanity prevails, their anger is restrained but not diminished, and their temptations to martyrdom are overcome, this generation of Native Americans could very well prove to be its own salvation.

NOTES

1. A.G. Bailey, *The Conflict of European and Eastern Algonkian Cultures 1505-1700* (St. John, N.B.: Publications of the New Brunswick Museum, 1937), 75-83. See also C. Ford, "Colonial Precedents of Our National Land System as It Existed in 1800," *Bulletin of the University of Wisconsin*, 352, History Series, 2 (1910): 321-478.

2. Mary E. Young, *Redskins, Ruffleshirts and Rednecks: Indian Allotments in Alabama and Mississippi 1830-1860*, (Norman: University of Oklahoma Press, 1961).

3. *Origins of Totalitarianism* (New York: Harcourt Brace, 1951), 190.

4. F.P. Prucha, *Broadax and Bayonet: The Role of the United States Army in the Development of the Northwest, 1815-1860* (Madison: State Historical Society of Wisconsin, 1951); and, by the same author, *The Sword of the Republic: The United States Army on the Frontier* (New York: Macmillan, 1969).

5. Fred A. Shannon, "The Homestead Act and Labor Surplus," *American Historical Review*, 41 (1936): 637-651. For further details on Indian land take-over by speculators and corporate businesses, see Pauls W. Gates, "The Homestead Law in an Incongruous Land System," *American Historical Review*, 41 (1936): 652-81.

6. C.B. Cowing, *Populist, Plungers, and Progressives* (Princeton, N.J.: Princeton University Press, 1961); Robert W. Mardock, *Reformers and the American Indian* (St. Louis: University of Missouri Press, 1971).

7. O. Mannoni, *Prospero and Caliban: The Psychology of Colonization* (New York: Praeger, 1964).

8. See Sar A. Levitan and William B. Johnston, *Indian Giving: Federal Programs for Native Americans* (Baltimore: Johns Hopkins University Press, 1975).

9. Joan Ablon, "Relocated American Indians in the San Francisco Bay Area: Social Interaction and Indian Identity," *Human Organization*, 23 (1964): 296-304; Jeanne Guillemin, *Urban Renegades: The Cultural Strategy of American Indians* (New York: Columbia University Press, 1975); Peter Z. Snyder, "The Social Environment of the Urban Indian," in *The American Indian in Urban Society*, Jack O. Waddell and O. Michael Watson, eds. (Boston: Little, Brown, 1971), 207-243.

10. René Maunier, "The Diffusion of French Law in Algeria," in *Independence Convergence and Borrowing in Institutions, Thought and Art*, Harvard Tercentary Publications (Cambridge: Harvard University Press, 1937), 80-88.

11. P.G. Casanova, "Internal Colonialism and National Development," *Studies in International Comparative Development*, 1, 4 (1965): 27-37; Rodolfo Stavenhagen, "Classes, Colonialism and Acculturation," *Studies in International Comparative Development*, 1, 7 (1965): 53-77.

12. See the updated analysis of Indian land-leasing by Robert Bee and Ronald Gingerich, "Colonialism, Classes and Ethnic Identity," *Studies in International Comparative Development*, 12, 2 (1977): 7-93.

13. Bruce Koon, "Indian Tribes Find Great White Father is Big Loss Leader," *Wall Street Journal*, April 21, 1978.

14. Alvin Josephy, Jr., *Red Power: The American Indian's Fight for Freedom* (New York: McGraw-Hill, 1971).

15. Ibid., 226.

16. For information on the organization for the demonstration, see *BIA I'm Not Your Indian Anymore* (Rooseveltown, N.Y.: Akwesasne Notes, n.d.).

17. Ibid., 9.

18. Robert Burnett and John Koster, *The Road to Wounded Knee* (New York and Toronto: Bantam, 1974).

19. Jeanne Guillemin, "The Politics of National Integration: A Comparison of United States and Canadian Indian Administrations," *Social Problems*, 25, 3 (1978): 319-32; Russell L. Barsh and Ronald L. Trosper, "Title I of the Indian Self-Determination and Education Assistance Act of 1975," *American Indian Law Review*, 3, 2 (1976): 361-95.

20. Quoted in Burnett and Koster, op. cit., 275.

21. M.L. Wax and R.H. Wax, "The Enemies of the People," in *Institutions and the Person: Essays Presented to Everett Cherrington Hughes*, H.L. Becker, et al., (eds.) (Chicago: Aldine, 1968); G.P. Castile, "Federal Indian Policy and the Sustained Enclave: An Anthropological Perspective," *Human Organization*, 33, 3 (1974); 219-27; Ernest Shusky, "Development by Grantsmanship: Economic Planning of the Brule Sioux Reservation," *Human Organization*, 34 (1975): 227-36.

Chapter 11
Domestic Violence and America's Wars
An Historical Interpretation

ROBIN BROOKS

INTRODUCTION

This essay analyzes the domestic protest and violence that erupted in response to American involvement in the nine major wars carried on by the United States since 1775: the Revolution, the War of 1812, the Mexican War, the Civil War, the Spanish-American War, the First and Second World Wars, the Korean War, and the War in Vietnam. The focus is further limited to include only those conflicts with a clearly antiwar component—e.g., the New York City Draft Riots of 1863—while excluding the racial violence of the First and Second World Wars and the ghetto rebellions. Violence initiated by opponents of the war or by those who support it— whether civilians, police, or military—is examined, but not technically nonviolent events like the legal repression of draft resisters or the relocation of Japanese-Americans in 1942. Further, a distinction is made between violence that in effect represents support for the other side in internecine conflicts like the Civil War or the American Revolution, and violence arising from opposition to war beyond America's borders or to the means by which it is carried on. The inquiry seeks to understand why there have been so few antiwar riots in the American past, despite much opposition to American wars, and to draw some conclusions about similarities and differences between antiwar violence during the Vietnam conflict, and that in our past.

HISTORICAL RETROSPECT

The Revolution

The American Revolutionary era is replete with violence involving mobs and unofficial bodies of men. Before the actual outbreak of the Revolution, numerous violent outbreaks occurred: the Boston Massacre, the Gaspé incident, the regulator movement, tenant riots in Westchester County, N.Y., and the mobbing of Stamp Act

AUTHOR'S NOTE: *Robin Brooks got away with being a slightly violent radical in the late 1960s and is now professor of history and American studies at San Jose State University. He served as Fullbright Professor to India in 1975-1976. His interest is in social and cultural history, especially in environmental history, and he is currently at work on a cultural history of the 1960s.*

collectors, to cite just a few. During the war itself, bloody conflicts between Tories and Whigs occurred frequently in New York, the Carolinas, and along the frontier. But these seemed to have involved less opposition to the war itself than a taking of sides in a civil war. None of them, I believe, fits the criteria of an antiwar riot.

The so-called "Fort Wilson" riot, in Philadelphia, October 4-6, 1779, is somewhat more difficult to categorize. The origins of the Fort Wilson riot might be described as a popular movement to punish some opponents of war, but it quickly moved beyond that limitation. After the British evacuated Philadelphia, early in 1779, popular resentment against suspected Tories mounted. The suspects included some Quakers, at once conscientious opponents of war, but also British sympathizers and wealthy merchants. When the Pennsylvania government's appointed committee did not seem to be acting effectively, the popular militia moved to take the law into its own hands. Its committee, composed of one man from each company, moved swiftly against Tories—and also against "engrossers, monopolizers, and those who sympathized with them, as well as certain lawyers who had appeared as counsel for the accused at the Tory trials."[1] Placards appeared, denouncing several prominent leaders of the Revolution, among them Declaration of Independence signers Robert Morris (speculating in flour) and James Wilson (lawyer for the Tories).

The militia committee and its sympathizers, after attempting in vain to find leaders among prominent radicals like painter Charles Wilson Peale, set out to punish the evildoers. After arresting several suspects, including a number of Quakers, they headed toward the home of James Wilson. Wilson's friends, among them some of the most prominent Philadelphia Whigs, had armed and barricaded themselves in his house. The mob approached, and one of its leaders, a ship's joiner, disclaimed any intention of attacking Wilson; he explained that they supported the constitution of Philadelphia, but that "the laboring part of the city had become desperate from the high price of the necessaries of life."[2] The procession marched on and had mostly passed Wilson's house when a member of the garrison, a Captain Campbell, opened a window and waved a pistol at the crowd. Who fired first is not known, but in the exchange of shots Campbell was mortally wounded. A battle ensued with casualties on both sides, quelled only when the Philadelphia Light-Horse Cavalry, led by General Joseph Reed, the state's chief executive, charged upon and dispersed the mob.

Twenty-seven of its number were jailed, while Wilson and his fellow defenders left town. Many returned—Wilson prudently accepted his friends' counsel to stay away—to organize plans for dealing with the militia, whose officers had proposed violent measures to free their friends. This action was forestalled when the militiamen were set free on bail, and General Reed managed to conciliate both sides. Ultimately no one was prosecuted, as the Assembly declared an act of amnesty for all implicated persons. In summation, the riot was only peripherally connected with opposition to war, and more clearly a case of class or economic conflict.[3]

In Dutchess County, N.Y., during July 1776, and again in Columbia County in August 1777, farmers took up arms against Revolutionary authorities, and were suppressed after some fighting. But is it not possible to discern from the fragmentary surviving records whether they acted out of opposition to the war per se, which fell harshly upon them in requisitioning goods and supplies and in sometimes requiring military service as proof of loyalty, or whether their actions were simply an expression of economic grievances or of loyalty to His Majesty George III.[4] Nor can we find clear-cut evidence of civilian riots against the British authorities occupying New York and other cities. On balance, it appears there was very little antiwar violence of any kind that might usefully be compared to that of our own time.

The War of 1812 and the Mexican War

The War of 1812, in contrast, is neatly organized for the purposes of our study. It furnished one major and one minor riot, plus a fine scholarly explanation of the sources of social cleavage of the day.

The Baltimore Federalist newspaper, the *Federal Republican*, published a harsh critique of President Madison and the Republican Party for the declaration of war against Britain, just a few days after the event. A loyal mob promptly destroyed the editor's house and his press, forcing him to flee to the District of Columbia. But other Baltimore Federalists, taking a principled stand for freedom of the press and their right to express their antiwar opinions, arranged to have another issue of the paper (published in Washington) circulated in Baltimore and carrying a Baltimore address on the masthead. They shut themselves up in the house they named, armed, and prepared to defend their rights. On July 27, 1812, the mob attacked the 20 defenders. After a sharp battle, in which some of the attackers were killed or wounded, the mob brought up cannon. The mayor's intervention, with cavalry, halted the action. He then persuaded the Federalists to go to jail to await trial. Inexplicably, the troops protecting the jail were called off—other members of the city militia had refused to serve—thereby exposing the prisoners to renewed attack. The mob—led by two butchers—broke into the jail, took out the prisoners, and beat them savagely. Eight were beaten into insensibility and tossed into a heap in front of the jail, from where the mob refused to allow them to be removed until noon the next day. General Lingan, a hero of the Revolution, was beaten to death. General Henry Lee, former Governor of Virginia, colleague of Washington, and father of Robert E. Lee, nearly suffered the same fate; almost two months later he could neither talk nor eat solid food. Other Federalists were manhandled and tortured for hours before finally escaping or being released. No punishment was visited upon the mob.[5]

In direct response to this event, New Englanders opposed to the war took revenge on one of their own. On August 3, 1812, Massachusetts Congressman Charles Turner, who had voted for war, returned to his home in Plymouth. In addition to being a Republican congressman, he was also Chief Justice of Sessions for Plymouth County. This made no difference to his antiwar Federalist neighbors, who seized him on the main street and kicked him through the town.[6]

Neither Henry Adams, in his great history of the period, nor the histories of any of the major towns record any other mob action during the War of 1812. But Roger N. Brown, in *The Republican in Peril: 1812* offers an explanation of the bitter cleavage in politics. He contends that Federalists and Republicans were deeply divided, each certain that the other side had the worst motives—for going to war or for opposing it—in mind, and that each side was prepared to go to almost any lengths to frustrate its enemies: "Republican and Federalist views of party opposites are largely false . . . wild parodies of the truth." Such views stem from "personal inexperience with political parties that encouraged men to identify opponents with their fears." What experience they had, "derived as it was from history and the factional contests of the colonial period, instinctively presumed prolonged opposition to rest on selfish, even traitorous motives. . . . Eighteenth-century political thought extolled the blessings of the harmonious commonwealth and condemned sustained organized party activity" for ignoring the common good in pursuit of power.[7]

Given such sharp polarization as Brown describes, why do we find such little violence during the War of 1812? One explanation might lie in the comparatively high degree of consensus within each section; e.g., Baltimore was overwhelmingly Federalist, so that no opposition dared raise its head after the riots. But such an explanation does not explain why violence did not flare up in the marginal areas. Perhaps a more useful explanation might run counter to Brown's, to suggest that many people did not care much about the war one way or the other, while the open, legitimate, and effective channels of expression—the press and the political system—afforded adequate outlets for the concerned minorities.

At least this is the explanation offered by Charles G. Sellers for the lack of antiwar riots during the Mexican War.[8] (There may have been some such incidents, but a sampling of the press and periodicals, diaries, town histories, and other secondary accounts does not reveal any of which I am aware.) The Mexican War also elicited sectional cleavage, very similar to that of 1812, with New England largely opposed and the South and West largely in favor. But because political opinion could easily be translated into effective protest and political movements, Sellers suggests, there would be little cause for riots on the part of those opposed to the war. Since the actual fighting from the outbreak of the war until the capture of Mexico City lasted less than 18 months and produced an uninterrupted string of U.S. victories, we might speculate that antiwar protests would be less than desperate while prowar groups could afford to be tolerant of misguided scrupulousness.

The Civil War

The Civil War, of course, is quite another matter. Replete with all sort of violence arising from opposition to the war, both North and South, it confronts the historian with the need to make fine distinctions about the purposes of the participants. Only a few days after the firing on Fort Sumter had initiated the conflict, some 10,000 Confederate sympathizers in Baltimore, carrying the Stars and Bars at their head, attacked approximately 2,000 Union troops from Massachusetts and Pennsylvania who were passing through "mobtown" en route to Washington, D.C. The soldiers opened fire to protect themselves, but it took the resolute action of the Baltimore police to enable them to escape the fury of the mob. At least twelve citizens and four soldiers died in the affray. Yet this conflict belongs properly to the history of the Civil War itself, rather than to the category of antiwar violence.[9] Subsequently French S. Evans, who had been a well-known newspaper editor before the war, fled Baltimore to escpe an irate mob prepared to punish him for the expression of pro-Union sentiments.[10]

Similarly, many actions of Unionists in the South might properly fall within the category of pro-Northern demonstration rather than that of antiwar protest. Georgia

Lee Tatum's *Disloyalty in the Confederacy* tell us that in almost every state of the Confederacy, conscription roused bitter opposition among the poor whites. The German areas of Texas, the mountains of Appalachia and the Ozarks, and the swamps of Florida all became centers for deserters and the disaffected from which guerrilla warfare emanated and into which Confederate recruiting officers and provost marshals could venture only with the escort of the army. Let us consider three events which might be considered as reflecting in some measure antiwar violence.

Western North Carolina was originally a source of loyalty to the Confederacy. But when the conscription law omitted owners of 20 or more slaves from its purview, disaffection flared up. W.W. Holden, editor of the Raleigh *Standard*, became the leader of the antiwar movement in the state, writing editorials that came perilously close to treason in the eyes of many. On September 9, 1863, a detachment of Georgia troops en route through Raleigh attacked the office of the *Standard*. The next day a Unionist mob attacked and destroyed the Raleigh *State Journal,* the pro-Confederate paper in town. Although Governor Vance maintained a neutral attitude during this period of strife, Holden ran against him as a peace candidate for Governor in 1864. Those voting for Holden in some areas where pro-Confederate sentiment still ran strong found themselves subjected to what one of the state's historians euphemistically called "violent unpopularity."[11]

German settlers around Austin, Texas, generally opposed the Confederate cause. Draftees at Industry, Texas (in Austin County), in December 1862, attacked a Confederate officer and drove him away, after they organized armed bodies to defend themselves, threatening to destroy those of their fellow Germans who were loyal to the Confederacy.[12] At the same time, citizens of Randolph County, in northern Alabama, defied the Conscription Act. Led by their very active Peace Society, an armed mob raided the county jail forcibly to free arrested deserters.[13]

Opposition to conscription proved to be the major source of mob violence in the North, too. German immigrants in Port Washington, Wisconsin, attacked a draft commissioner, destroyed draft machinery, and sacked the homes of prominent Republicans until dispersed by troops. This story could be repeated in almost every Midwestern state. One enrolling officer was killed in Indiana, another in Wisconsin. An Irish mob in Chicago manhandled a U.S. marshal.[14]

But the most notorious case of all was the great New York City Draft Riot, of July 13-17, 1863, one which dwarfs by comparison all contemporary racial or antiwar violence. Estimates of the size of the mobs, which fought police, militia, and federal troops, run as high as 50,000. Its most recent chronicler suggests total deaths were as many as 1,300 and damage above $5 million, while acknowledging that these must remain imprecise estimates. Official records list 18 persons killed by the rioters, 11 of them blacks; but more than 70 persons, most of them black, were reported missing, and many of them were never accounted for. Nor is there agreement about the general causes of the riot. The Conscription Act, of course, provided the occasion, as it went into operation only two days before the eruption of the riots. But the vicious persecution of blacks by the mobs, largely made up of poor Irish immigrants, indicates that the identification of the Civil War with the cause of emancipation was a major factor, compounded by competition for jobs and status at the bottom of the urban pecking order. Class animosity entered into the equation, too, because the $300-exemption clause made the war into "a rich man's war but a poor man's fight."[15]

New York City was not the only center of antidraft rioting in the East. Irish miners in the anthracite coalfields of Pennsylvania rioted; so did Connecticut draftees.[16] But the draft was not the only source of antiwar violence during the Civil War; the organized peace movement in the North also led to violence.

Clement Vallandigham, Ohio Peace Democratic congressman, proved the main focus of antiwar agitation in the North. On May 1, 1863, Union troops arrested Vallandigham in his hometown of Dayton for a speech denouncing the war. A mob of his sympathizers burned down the proadministration paper, the Dayton *Journal* (and when the fire got out of hand, a good bit more of the town). Federal troops were called in to quell the rioting, and did so after killing one member of the mob. In Indianapolis that same month, a pro-Vallandigham rally was broken up by armed soldiers with considerable violence erupting, none of it fatal.[17]

Many antiwar demonstrations and rallies suffered a similar fate. As early as August 16, 1861, veterans (of three months' service) broke up a peace meeting in Saybrook, Connecticut. At Stepney, in the same state, loyalists from Bridgeport led by P.T. Barnum and sewing-machine heir Elias Howe, Jr., attacked a meeting and tore down its peace flag. Returning to Bridgeport, despite the pleas of Barnum and Howe, the mob, now swelled to over 8,000, destroyed the Copperhead Bridgeport *Farmer*.[18] Other Copperhead papers like the Columbus [Ohio] *Crisis*, the Dubuque [Iowa] *Herald*, and the Chicago *Times* suffered from attacks by soldiers and civilians. But in both Connecticut and in the Midwest, federal crackdowns on the peace movement—involving violation of due process for those arrested by suspension of habeas corpus and arbitrary incarceration without trial—succeeded in destroying organized peace activity in the North.[19] David Donald has ascribed the greater ability of the North than the South to suppress opposition to an excess of democracy in the Confederacy; I suspect that the victories of Grant and Sherman in 1863 and 1864 also played a large part, insofar as "nothing succeeds like success."[20]

The Spanish-American War

The Spanish-American War—John Hay's "splendid little war"—was effectively over in three months. It had been enormously popular to begin with, and cost only 379 battle casualties (although more than 5,000 Americans died from disease and food poisoning), so it should be no surprise to discover that there was no antiwar violence. Curiously, there was considerable opposition in high places to the war's imperial fruits—the annexation of Puerto Rico, the Philippines, etc. Mark Twain, Andrew Carnegie, William James, House Speaker Thomas Reed, and E.L. Godkin, editor of the *Nation*, were all active in the Antiimperialist movement. But none of these men could have—and none showed the slightest interest in—organized popular antiwar violence, and none was forthcoming from any other source.[21]

The First World War

Opponents of War, 1917-1918, by H.C. Peterson and Gilbert C. Fite, provides an outstanding treatment of antiwar violence during the First World War. The persistence and scale of violence, as well as the social base of opposition to this war, make it the nearest thing to a parallel with the anti-Vietnam war struggle. But it differs sharply with the latter in that almost every case of violence occurred when patriotic mobs attacked opponents of war. From the long and appalling list of incidents compiled by Peterson and Fite, I could find only the following two in which the initiative for violence appeared to originate with the antiwar movement.

An anticonscription meeting of 2,000 persons in New York City on June 15, 1917, almost led to a riot. Word that soldiers and sailors had surrounded the hall and intended to question members of the audience as they came out caused a near panic. According to the New York *Times* report, the servicemen who tried to block the doors were hit by flying wedges of the audience, and cursed by more than 10,000 more onlookers outside the hall.[22]

More serious was the "Green Corn Rebellion" of eastern Oklahoma. Before the outbreak of war, poor tenants and sharecroppers had formed the Working Class Union, a syndicalist organization associated with the Industrial Workers of the World. In August 1917, several hundred of these farmers assembled, intending to march on Washington, take over the government, and stop the war. They expected to be joined by many thousands more who objected to the war and the draft across the country. While waiting for other WCU members to rally to them, they subsisted on unripe green corn. They had cut some telegraph wires and attempted without success to destroy railroad bridges, when they were attacked and dispersed by patriotic posses. Some 450 antiwar farmers were arrested; many were released but minor offenders were sentenced to incarceration from 60 days to two years, and the leaders drew three- to ten-year sentences.[23]

In all the other cases Peterson and Fite record, violence was initiated by patriots. In Boston, in July 1917, 8,000 Socialists and other radicals staged an antiwar parade. Sailors and soldiers, attacking in regular formations upon command by an officer, broke up the parade; the paraders were beaten and the Socialist party headquarters raided. None of the approximately 10,000 persons involved in the attack was arrested; ten of those attacked were.[24] In Collinsville, Illinois, a young man of German birth, registered as an enemy alien and professing Socialist leanings—but with no record of having opposed the war overtly—was lynched by a drunken mob. When its leaders were indicted, their attorneys called their act a "patriotic murder," and the local jury acquitted them after 25 minutes' deliberation.[25]

At Rutgers University, in the only case of a campus riot I have found prior to the Vietnam conflict, fellow students demanded that Samuel Chovenson, an antiwar Socialist, speak at their Liberty Loan rally. When he refused, they stripped him, covered him with molasses and feathers, and paraded him through New Brunswick.[26] Berkeley, California, also had its riot, although it was not primarily a campus affair: a mob attacked religious pacifists, burned down their tabernacle (a tent), and dunked them in their baptismal tank—whereupon the authorities arrested the pacifists and jailed them.[27]

A major source of opposition to the first World War was the People's Council of America for Peace and Democracy. Its meetings were broken up in Philadelphia, Wilmington and Chicago. When pacifist minister Herbert Bigelow, a Socialist, attempted to speak under the council's auspices in Newport, Kentucky, a mob seized, bound and gagged him, drove him 20 miles into a forest and lashed him repeatedly with a blacksnake whip on his bare back. The Assistant Attorney General of the United States commented that no statement against the attackers would be considered unless it was by a "responsible citizen," while the dean of the University of Minnesota Law School, denouncing the People's Council, said that "wartime was no time to quibble about constitutional rights and guarantees."[28] When Irish opponents of the war paraded carrying a red flag in Butte, Montana, on June 6, 1917—the day after the draft law went into effect—patriotic citizens, reinforced by the police and by the state militia with fixed bayonets, dispersed the demonstration. Twenty arrests were made, all of demonstrators.[29] Elsewhere, sailors and soldiers broke up a Philadelphia anticonscription meeting.[30]

The Industrial Workers of the World, advocates of direct action and sabotage in the interest of revolutionary syndicalism, pose a special problem of interpretation. They had been the most militant and violent opponents of the American capitalist system, especially in the West, before the war. As revolutionaries, they were hardly pacifists, but they sharply opposed the war as a war for big business. In this circumstance patriotism became the cover under which the enemies of the IWW could destroy it. Mass jailings, beatings, and deportations of "Wobblies" took place in Arizona, Montana, and other states. In Butte, patriotic vigilantes seized IWW organizer Frank Little, dragged him through the streets tied behind their automobile until his kneecaps were scraped off, then hanged him to a railroad trestle. The New York *Times* commented, on August 4, 1917, that the lynching was "deplorable and detestable," but noted that "IWW agitators are in effect and perhaps in fact, agents of Germany. The Federal government should make short work of these treasonable conspirators against the United States."[31]

For the *Times*, then and subsequently, the only alternative to lynching was federal suppression of dissent against the war. The *Christian Science Monitor* agreed. It editorialized on May 4, 1918: "The most regrettable thing about the whole matter is that, owing to the failure of the state and federal courts to deal adequately with the problem, private citizens are left, in self-protection, to take the law into their own hands." Governor Lowden of Illinois, U.S. Attorney General Gregory, and other members of the cabinet, and many senators and congressmen agreed. The upshot was the Sedition Act, a sweeping amendment to the Espionage Act, aimed to muzzle all except "friendly" criticism of the government, the armed forces, the constitution, the flag and the war. Its signature into law by President Wilson on May 16, 1918, led to some 1,500 arrests, effectively superseding mob action against opponents of war as it effectively wiped out all expression of dissent.[32]

Peterson and Fite provide an appropriate conclusion: they note that "a strong minority bitterly resented the war and conscription," but (as Attorney General Gregory said) "their propaganda was almost immediately suppressed and destroyed."[33]

The Second World War

The Second World War was totally unlike the First World War. Norman Thomas, veteran Socialist and pacifist leader, reported in 1943:

Now it is true that there has been almost no interference by legal authorities or by mobs with public meetings. There has been . . . no parallel to the wholesale arrests under the Espionage Act. . . . In every previous war in which we have engaged there has been organized opposition of various strength. Last time, despite rigorous suppression, opposition was persistent and by no means confined to enemy sympathizers. Opposition to active participation in this war, strong before Pearl Harbor, completely dissolved after the surprise attack by Japan and the Japanese and German declarations of war against the United States.

Roger Baldwin, director of the American Civil Liberties Union (itself formed to protect pacifists in their expression of antiwar opinions during the First World War), agreed fully with Thomas. He noted that firm, effective government action has "tended to allay fear and to create the conviction that any movements obstructive of the war are well in hand."[34] As a result, he found, "we experience no hysteria, no war-inspired mob violence, no pressure for suppressing dissent, no activity of a secret political police, no organization of virtuous patriots seeking out seditious opinion, and no hostility to persons of German or Italian origin." He did note the hostility to persons of Japanese origin, but commented that "while painfully in evidence, [it] is largely confined to the Pacific Coast and smaller communities in the West."[35]

Attorney General Earl Warren of California, testifying before a congressional hearing concerned with the forcible removal of these same Japanese-Americans, warned that "my own belief concerning vigilantism is that the people do not engage in vigilante activities so long as they believe that their Government through its agencies is taking care of their most serious problem." Only if they believe that that is not happening do they "start taking the law into their own hands." Mr. Warren, in asking for this racist action—Japanese removal—was also making an important point about our treatment of serious dissent in wartime: either the government suppresses it legally, or the people will suppress it violently. Despite the long, uncertain course of the Second World War, its origins guaranteed that there would be such little dissent that the people could tolerate what the government did not suppress.[36]

The Korean War

The Korean War appears as an excellent example of consensus through crackdown. Like the War of 1812, the Korean War generated one brief flash of opposition. On August 2, 1950, New York City opponents of the war, mostly leftist, held a rally despite refusal by the police to grant them a permit. The rally drew a few thousand people, but they were quickly dispersed by a heavy police force. The New York *Times* reporter noted that "some of the demonstrators who refused orders to disperse were badly beaten by the police. Some were charged by mounted police who rode onto crowded sidewalks. On the whole, however, the police used restraint."[37] There were two other newsworthy incidents, both comparatively minor: Four workers in the Linden, New Jersey, plant of General Motors attempted to hand out antiwar leaflets at the plant. Their fellow employees beat them and threw them out of the plant, GM refused to rehire them, and the United Auto Workers expelled them from the union.[38] In San Francisco, a meeting of Harry Bridges's Longshoremen's Union erupted into a riot when Bridges tried to substitute a peace resolution for one supporting the actions of the United States in Korea. (A Senate committee reported that it was seeking ways to jail Bridges, and his deportation hearing followed almost immediately.)[39] Unlike other conflicts, the Korean War began during a period of greater peacetime repression than the country had ever known; as a result the government itself, with committees of the House and Senate playing a role equal to or greater than that of the administrative branch, played an enormous role in quashing dissent, leaving very little room for the efforts of would-be vigilantes.[40]

The War in Vietnam

And so we come down to the present. Violence in the early stages of the War in Vietnam resembled the model of the Korean War and most American wars, in that peaceful demonstrators were attacked by citizens or by the police. In October 1965, demonstrators in Berkeley, California, declared their intention to close down the Oakland Army Terminal by massive, nonviolent action. They were easily turned aside, without violence, by the massed Oakland police on the borders of that city. Violence erupted when members of the Hell's Angels motorcycle gang attacked seated demonstrators, but this was quickly quelled by the same Oakland police. Subsequently, nonviolent pickets were attacked repeatedly while picketing the Port Chicago, California, naval facility, and draft-card burners in Boston were beaten by a Boston mob. As late as April 1967, antiwar demonstrations took the form of peaceful protest marches (with no violence in San Francisco and very little in New York), but there was a reversion to type during the summer of 1967, when pickets protesting the appearance of President Johnson at the Century-Plaza Hotel in Los Angeles were badly beaten by police. The demonstrators were overwhelmingly a nonviolent group, although they did include a few activists who provoked the police onslaught by jeers and intemperate language.[41]

But the events of "Stop-the-Draft Week"—October 16-22, 1967—appear to be something of a watershed. In California, radical student leaders announced that they would close the Oakland Selective Service Induction Center "by any means necessary." But tactical divisions reflecting opposing principles within the anti-Vietnam movement led to a division of labor. On Monday, October 6, members and sympathizers of "the Resistance" sat in nonviolently and were arrested nonviolently. On Tuesday, several thousand students and other radicals attempted physically to seal off the induction center, and were violently dispersed by the Oakland police. Few were arrested, but many were beaten or gassed in response to their token resistance (those who resisted nonviolently, and newsmen, seemed to bear the brunt of the police onslaught). Wednesday saw a return to nonviolence, and when Thursday passed almost without any demonstration, it appeared that the protesters faced an inglorious defeat. But inexplicably, Friday became a day of new, escalated tactics by the militants. Instead of trying to stand up to the police, some 15,000 activists dispersed all over the neighborhood in the vicinity of the induction center. They dragged parked cars into intersections and overturned them there or deflated their tires; they blocked traffic with potted plants and trash cans; and by fleeing and regrouping they easily avoided the superior power of the police. These mobile tactics succeeded in sharply reducing physical violence against the demonstrators.

If "the capture of intersections" delayed the work of the induction center scarcely an hour or two, the demonstrators regarded their actions as a moral victory. Beyond their ingenious tactical innovations, the militants had also embarked on a new stage in opposition to the war: no longer was the leadership of the movement in the hands of the nonviolent opponents of war, but rather the initiative lay with the activists who, in words at least, claimed the right to self-defense and even to take the offensive against the enemy—although in fact they were singularly unsuccessful in effectively opposing police violence with violence of their own.

The crowning event of Stop-the-Draft Week was "The Siege of the Pentagon," on Saturday and Sunday, October 21-22. Here again, a classically nonviolent demonstration, numbering 50,000-100,000, had to share the stage with demonstrators who proclaimed their intention to use force, though the advocates of violence were in much smaller proportion to the rest than at Oakland. Most of the action during the day was nonviolent, but in the small hours of the night, soldiers and federal marshals beat many of the young demonstrators severely.[42]

Taken together, the Oakland and Pentagon riots indicated a change in focus on the part of radical opponents of the war. Until then most opponents of the war had tacitly accepted the legitimacy of American institutions by submitting voluntarily to the penalties for civil disobedience; now, however, many of the dedicated radical opponents of the war had denied legitimacy to the institutions as well as to the war, thus expressing their rejection of the notion that justice is to be found at the heart of the American system.[43]

This new tendency dominated the events of the next months, as the scene of violence shifted to the campus. Beginning with a riot which developed when police broke up a demonstration against Dow Chemical Co. at San Jose State College, in November 1967, violent confrontations between students and police occurred repeatedly, with recruitment by Dow Chemical, the CIA, and the Armed Forces triggering the action. Among the sharper struggles were those at the Universities of Wisconsin and Iowa, Cornell, Long Beach State College, and San Francisco State College, culminating in the Columbia riots of May 1968. Two points may be noted:

(1) The student protesters verbally expressed their determination to stop Dow et al. by any means necessary, thereby inviting the violence.

(2) In almost all cases the students committed violence against property, whereas the police beat up the (ineffectually) resisting students.[44] Certainly this new pattern obtained in the two major riots of 1968: the Columbia riots of May, where radical students, acting in cooperation with blacks, seized buildings and were violently dispossessed, and in the Chicago convention riots of August 1968. The last are particularly instructive as examples of the new pattern.

A handful of militant activists uttering vocal threats to "destroy the system" succeeded in provoking massive police attacks against an irresolute mass of young people who shared the militants' description of the illegitimacy of "the system," but were not seriously prepared to move beyond rhetorical dedication to revolutionary goals. Whether this state of affairs will long obtain is open to question, but at present there appears to be an enormous gap between the perception by tens of thousands of radical students that both the war and "the system" are illegitimate, and their readiness—however stridently proclaimed—to act in accordance with that perception. Their inability to act is not so much a matter of attitude as it is a matter of their lack of effective power. But this in turn rests on the present unwillingness of other millions of American college students (who agree with the radicals about the wrongness of the war, as shown by their support of Eugene McCarthy and other peace candidates) to act outside "the system" (and their support of McCarthy, who insisted he was trying to give them an alternative within it, shows this point, too).[45]

The present equilibrium is quite unstable. It is highly unlikely that large numbers of students can be persuaded to accept the legitimacy of the present war. Therefore, continuation of the status quo in Vietnam is likely to have the effect of persuading them to accept the radicals' proclaimed identity between the war and "the system." In such a case, violent repression like that which took place at Chicago will only increase their acceptance of the legitimacy of violent resistance—though the facts of power in America may limit such actions to one or another form of guerrilla tactics like those of Oakland's Friday, October 20, 1967, riots. On the other hand, rapid termination of the war in Vietnam—by negotiated peace and withdrawal—would serve effectively to isolate the radicals by apparently undermining the major premise of their argument that war and imperialism are necessary concomitants of "the system."

CONCLUSION

Violent conflict arising from opposition to the Vietnam War has followed a course quite different from that in earlier wars, the only possible exception being antiwar violence in the Confederacy. For the crucial fact seems to be that antiwar rioting shows no signs of diminishing. In attempting to explain this fact, the study of the past is of some help, if only to point up contrasts. Other wars have been unpopular, at least in some sections—the War of 1812, the Mexican War, and the Spanish-American War—without evoking significant violence. But each of these was relatively short. Furthermore, in each there were effective channels for opposition short of violent protest; today opponents can demonstrate peacefully, but such demonstrations seem to make little inroads upon an unresponsive political structure (the failure of the peace candidacies of McCarthy and Kennedy, which had promised to open such channels, will undoubtedly heighten the sense of frustration which is one component of violent protest). Unresolved minority tensions, like those of the Civil War, undoubtedly heighten the intensity of domestic conflict. Apart from the War of 1812 and the Korean War (and of course the Confederacy), American arms have won decisive victories, and both of these conflicts came to a halt much more rapidly than the present conflict. Other wars have had prestigious people in opposition, or have been opposed by dedicated and well-organized radicals, or by a large part of a social group (workers in the First World War), or by significant ethnic or sectional minorities—the Vietnam conflict has all of these in tandem.

But there is much that is without historical parallel. In no previous American war have youth and students been significantly in opposition; previously they were a major source of patriotic sentiments. And with the single exception of the losing effort of the Confederate South, in no previous war have its opponents been able to see their case gaining increasing popular support. Nor is there any example of such widespread opposition to an American war coming from the academic and literary community.

For a conclusion we might look to St. Thomas Aquinas. He defined a just war as one meeting three qualifications: the ruler must be legitimate; the cause must be just; and the means employed must be proportionate to the ends in view. Apart from civil wars, there has seldom been any question about the legitimacy of American government. Every American war has produced a few opponents who thought the cause unjust, but (perhaps duration is of significance in this equation) these have been relegated to one section or ethnic group without greatly changing the attitudes of large patriotic majorities—again the civil wars are an important exception. Proportionality of means to ends first became a question at the beginning of the century, when Mark Twain and other intellectuals denounced the torture of prisoners in the Philippines. But atrocity stories only heightened American patriotism during the First and Second World Wars and the Korean War because Americans or neutrals were the victims of enemy barbarities. Violent opposition to the Vietnam War seems to have begun with the question of proportionality—the questions of napalm, defoliation, saturation bombing, etc.—and to have escalated to the point where a large minority of the American people question the justice of this war, and some begin to question the very legitimacy of "the system" that, in the minds of radical opponents of the war, has produced these effects.

History teaches, when it does, by analogy. That is, we look for similarities in the causal sequence of events which produce like effects. So Americans facing mounting civil disorder and riots during a period of war, arising out of opposition to that war, seek to understand this phenomenon by searching through our past wartime experiences. Unfortunately, the past does not have much to tell us; we will have to make our own history along uncharted and frightening ways.

EPILOGUE: REFLECTIONS FROM ANOTHER TIME

Looking back to the end of the 1960s a decade later, I am struck by how ephemeral the threat of revolution was. At the time it seemed real enough, and scholars were certainly affected by the rhetoric of radical hopes and conservative fears. But how swiftly has real disaffection, expressed as violent action justified by the delegitimization of dominant institutions and values, been transposed into public truce and private selfishness. Our popular mood today is animated by a sullen self-gratification which lacks even the excuse that it is the model for a New Jerusalem. Where have all the flower-children gone? The acid heads, peace marchers and bank burners? And can this altered perspective shed new light on the theme of domestic violence in wartime America?

Events of the sixties, particularly the civil rights movement and the Vietnam protest, opened up a vein of radical scholarship that contrasted sharply with the end-of-ideology consensus of the fifties. Had it coincided with the Civil War centennial we might have been deluged with studies of popular agitation and violence during the Civil War; as it is coinciding with the bicentennial of 1776, we have learned a great deal more about popular behavior during the American Revolution. We cannot say as much for any other conflict. (I can say this confidently. Ten years ago looking for sources was a hit-or-miss proposition; I could not be sure that I had not missed some significant demonstration. But the recent publication—in Germany—of Dirk Hoerder's massive and excellent bibliography, *Protest; Direct Action; Repression: Dissent in American Society from Colonial Times to the Present*, is a boon to researchers that permits me to restrict my comments to selected events.[46]

Looking at the War of 1812, the Mexican War, and the Spanish-American War, three of Harvard's—and the nation's—most eminent historians found no violence at home, or at least none worth mentioning.[47] (The journal literature shows a few incidents of domestic violence in 1812 but none in the other wars.) Nor has anything surprising turned up about the First and Second World Wars or the Korean conflict, although Melvyn Dubofsky's major work on the IWW's history and ideology does clarify how the Wobblies were radical and how radical they were, helping us to understand better why they were suppressed in 1917-1918.[48]

A number of local history journals published articles about dissent and violence during the Civil War, but only James Richardson's *The New York Police* breaks new ground. He carefully explores the class and ethnic sources of antiblack feeling among the Irish draft rioters of 1863. He points out their refusal to accept the legitimacy of the newly professionalized police force, and further suggests that a "police riot" against demonstrators may have triggered the terrible rioting that followed, violence targeted against blacks *and* policemen.[49]

Well before the Bicentennial rituals, radical historians drew upon studies of preindustrial crowds in England and France by George Rudé, Eric Hobsbawm and E.P. Thompson, to write history "from the bottom up." Alfred Young, Staughton Lynd, and Jesse Lemisch presented empirical evidence for class conflict in the Revolutionary era, though Lynd's claim that class struggle was a major theme of the revolution itself was hard to sustain. And Eugene Genovese demonstrated that the "neo-Marxist" ideas of Antonio Gramsci could brilliantly illuminate the plantation South, thereby liberating radical historians from the reductionism inherent in economic determinism, by postulating the mediate term of "ideology" (simply understood as "world view") between social class and behavior.

But the most influential studies of crowd behavior in the Revolutionary era came from Pauline Maier. Maier's work came from Bernard Bailyn's Harvard seminar, and Bailyn equated "ideology" with "false consciousness" or "myth" and inferred popular consciousness from the writings of the Whig élites. Maier's book, *From Resistance to Revolution*, ends with 1776, but in three earlier journal articles she dealt with the Revolution itself. She also used Rudé and Hobsbawm, but went beyond them to show that popular riots had functioned as a sort of safety valve, justifiable under the Lockean argument that "the people were for the most part docile and would only rise up after protracted abuse." But she argues that Revolutionary leaders between 1765 and 1784 worked to redirect popular protest into "orderly 'constitutional' channels," thus becoming "less a precedent for modern mass violence than a stage in the development of the popular, organized politics of the nineteenth century."[50]

Radical scholars preferred to stress the linkage of popular protest movements then and now. They faulted Maier for failing to look at the attitudes of the protesters themselves. To restore that dimension is the purpose of several essays in Alfred Young's anthology, *The American Revolution: Explorations in the History of American Radicalism*, along with several other books and articles, many of them by contributors to his collection. Ronald Hoffman (Maryland and the South), Stephen Patterson and Dirk Hoerder (Massachusetts), Edward Countryman (New York State) and John Alexander and Eric Foner (Philadelphia) have greatly increased our understanding of popular violence during the Revolution. Other essays in Young's collection illuminate pre- and post-Revolutionary mass behavior. All of them follow Maier's lead in describing tensions between Revolutionary leaders and popular mobs, but they treat the question with greater empathy for the lower classes and discover nuances she had neglected.

Hoffman's essay in the Young collection extends to the entire South the theme of his monograph on Maryland politics and economics: he demonstrates widespread and violent disaffection on the eastern shore of Chesapeake Bay (the "Delmarva" peninsula) and in the Carolina Piedmont. He shows how new strivings for equality clashed with traditional patterns of deference among the lower classes as a result of Revolutionary upheaval. And he shows how these upheavals led to parallel strategies of moderation developed by Whig leaders like General Nathaniel Greene and Maryland politician Charles Carroll of Carrollton.[51]

Patterson, Hoerder, and Foner all describe the developing split between popular leaders like Sam Adams and Tom Paine, who strove for "social cohesion, not social conflict" as vital to victory in the Revolution, and their followers, who took to the streets for bread and equality. Patterson notes that the tension between *republican* leaders and *democratic* crowds existed in western Massachusetts as well as in Boston, thereby providing a class underpinning to sectional interpretations of politics.[52] Hoerder's recent monograph considers violence more extensively than does Patterson, and his encyclopedic knowledge of sources undergirds his treatment of crowd behavior and of revolutionary historiography, though his conclusions are in line with Patterson's.[53] And Foner draws upon Alexander's fine description of the "Fort Wilson" riots in Philadelphia, in 1779, but takes us beyond Alexander's conclusion, which relies on the overworked polarity between conflict and consensus.[54]

Anticipating his outstanding study of Tom Paine, Foner explores the ideology of the "artisan-intelligensia" who fanned the Revolutionary fervor of the masses, but drew back from what Paine called the "misguided patriotism" of the "Fort Wilson" rioters, causing an irretrievable split. Paine, like his friends Peale, Matlack, and Rittenhouse, was among the new men whose very rise from obscure origins opened them up to modern notions like freedom of trade and sanctity of property. To the contrary, the rioters justified their actions as congruent with their notion of a "moral economy":

> The urban poor, and many artisans, believed that the operations of the free market worked against their own economic interests. They rejected the emerging doctrine of free trade, so far as it applied to grain, bread, and meat, denying the right of the farmer, merchant, or shopkeeper to an absolute property right in the necessities of life. Indeed, they affirmed the traditional idea of a "just price" for bread, which viewed millers and bakers as servants of the entire community.[55]

Countryman parts company with the others by combining Marxism with the conceptual vocabularly of political scientists like Ted R. Gurr (delegitimization) and Samuel Huntington (political order and breakdown) to analyze New York riots during the Revolution.[56]

Taking their work as a whole, along with other studies in the Young volume about pre-Revolutionary crowds, we see that much of the internal violence during the Revolution was rooted in *class*, meaning that people from the lower orders in town and country came together in struggle, often violent, around common grievances. But there are a number of problems in this work. For instance, Foner suggests that lower-class consciousness may have been a residue from medieval notions rather than an emergent working-class consciousness. Furthermore, although the radicals demonstrate that there were class struggles during the Revolution, they do not show that class struggle was a central causal factor in the Revolution.[57]

Radical historians are faced with a methodological problem that does not concern their fellows. That is, it is not enough for them to depict the past; they must also uncover those forces in the past that are progressive—for how else can their work be a guide to social change in the present? (Aileen Kraditor says it cannot be, but few other radical historians would be willing to surrender their identification with the radical struggles of the past.) But there's the rub. If the rioters at Fort Wilson in 1779 were "misguided patriots," how were they different from the working-class "Hard Hats" who received Nixon's blessings for their attack on antiwar marchers in New York City? Unless further research can show that Southern draft rioters had overcome their traditional antiblack bias, how can we distinguish between their actions and those of the Irish mobs in New York, for both were fighting against class-biased conscription laws? Were Paine and his fellow "radical intelligensia" correct in seeing the struggle for independence from Britain as the long-range goal for the common man that should override the immediate grievances of the popular mob? This last question seems to cry out for comparative analysis: were the Fort Wilson rioters different in kind from the Parisian *sans-culottes* guillotined by Robespierre, the Kronstadt sailors gunned down by Trotsky, the Spanish anarchists smashed by the Popular Front government, or even from the CIA-funded strikers who helped bring down Allende's socialist regime in Chile? Finally, the episodic nature of lower-class violence during the Revolution brings E.P. Thompson's warning to mind: we are justified in talking about *class* when we have consistency over time, but, at any given moment in history we can only speak about the behavior of individuals.

Finally, what about the Vietnam War in light of past wartime disaffection? I am first of all surprised by how little has been done to synthesize the massive amount of data about opposition to the war in Vietnam. Good work has cast light here and there on students, radicals, ideology, politics, media, and culture, but even the most intelligent synthesis, Godfrey Hodgson's *America In Our Time,* lacks a feel for the intense passion and extraordinary hope that animated the era.[58] I do not think the lack of synthesis is due to the superabundance of data—computers could handle that problem. Nor are we too close for perspective any more. Rather, I would follow Hannah Arendt's diagnosis: the responses of most Americans, and certainly their leaders, was for "amnesia" not "amnesty." Historians will note, too, how much

President Nixon did to stimulate that amnesia. By substituting intensified aerial bombing of the entire Indochina peninsula for ground combat, he solved with one slogan—"Vietnamization"—the problems of disaffection escalating toward rebellion at home and an unmanageable army in Vietnam!

I am surprised as well as pleased at how well some of my judgments about violence during the War in Vietnam have held up. My claim that after 1967 something new was happening seems to have been accepted: in the jargon of a political scientist, Michael Stohl, "subordinate segments, after enduring attacks for most of the century, eventually began initiating violence themselves." Stohl also agrees with me that "antiwar violence was directed primarily toward property, while prosystem violence was aimed at individuals."[59]

However, though I had noted the escalation of repressive violence at Chicago (which set the pattern for Kent State), along with most contemporary observers I had expected that such patently unjust acts would strengthen the radical claim that the "system" itself was illegitimate, thereby helping them to build a movement for radical change in America. A few were wiser. William Appleman Williams correctly labeled some of the attempts to provoke confrontation "by any means necessary" as "mindless activism." Barrington Moore observed that the state in America had not lost much of its virtual monopoly of violence, and still held on to the support of the majority of Americans from every class and especially the police.[60] (That the army was becoming quite unreliable as a fighting force in Vietnam may have elicited Nixon's decision to "wind down" the ground war in Vietnam, before the soldiers could bring their disaffection home.) Richard Hofstadter pointed out that the fruits of revolutionary violence were seldom plucked by the lower classes who fought and died, but rather went to the middle classes, the new bureaucrats and the military elites.[61] And Hofstadter's point applies even to the not-so-revolutionary 1960s: the black militants were literally blown away and the student rebels suffered figurative obliteration, taking the dynamic component of the counterculture down with them. Rock entrepreneurs and new-wave psychotherapists, the Dodge Rebellion and the Black Bourgeoisie—not to mention the scholars who won grants and promotions out of the study of violence—did well for themselves; the youthful rebels are now over 30 with only romantic memories for souvenirs.

My observation, in a footnote, that the antiwar movement in its violent phase had a nihilistic quality, seems to me to undercut my claim that it was something new under the American sun. In retrospect, it seems to me that student rebels shared something of the inchoate, spontaneous anger at patent injustice that animated the rioters at Fort Wilson in 1779 and in New York City in 1863. Also like those groups, the New Left, even if it had been successful beyond its dreams, could not have set up any kind of sustained political order to replace the one it wished to overthrow. In this sense the violence of the late sixties was counterproductive and deserves the label of "mindless activism."

But not wholly so. As one who took part in nonviolent demonstrations from Rev. King's March on Washington in 1963 to the first days of Stop-the-Draft week in Oakland in 1967, I shared in the mounting frustration that led many to embrace the new confrontation tactics, including "trashing" against property, which were justified by simple-minded clichés masquerading as revolutionary theory. During a subsequent police riot on my own campus, I even took a swing at a policeman, though I never deluded myself that I was thereby "part of the solution" rather than "part of the problem." Subsequent events, both at home and abroad, leave me convinced (as I was not convinced a decade ago) that violence, even as a last resort in self-defense, is both pragmatically and theoretically inferior to nonviolent resistance as a lever for revolutionary change.

That said, I also believe that the demonstrators of the 1960s, violent as well as nonviolent (with a little help from the people of Vietnam), helped the United States to save its collective soul. Surely they cannot be blamed too much for what we have done with that soul in the self-centered 1970s.

NOTES

1. J. Thomas Scharf and Thomas Westcott, *History of Philadelphia 1609-1884* (*Philadephia: L. H. Everts, 1884*), I, 401.

2. Ibid.

3. Ibid., 401-403. A few weeks later a mob of sailors, complaining of low pay, rioted in Philadelphia, Ibid., 403. Jesse Lemisch, "Jack Tar in the Streets: Merchant Seaman in Revolutionary America," *William & Mary Quarterly,* 3d ser. Vol. XXV (July 1968); 371-407, lists many sailors' riots, but the only one which was an antiwar riot during wartime was a three day antiimpressment riot in Boston, Nov. 17, 1747, during King George's War (391).

4. *Journal of the Provincial Congress* . . . (Albany: T. Weed. 1842), Vol. II, 309-311; *Minutes of the Committee . . . for Detecting Conspiracies* . . . (New York: New York Historical Society, 1924-25.), II 442-443. The Revolutionary authorities in 1778 described the rioters as Tories. See also Richard M. Brown, "Historical Patterns of Violence in America," elsewhere in this volume.

5. J. Thomas Scharf, *History of Maryland From the Earliest Times to the Present Day* (Hatboro, Pa.: Tradition Press, 1967; reprint of 1879 ed.), Vol. III, 3-25. See also Henry Adams, *History of the United States during the First Administration of James Madison* (New York: Scribner's, 1890), Vol. II, 405-408 (Vol. VI of Adams' great *History* of the period 1800-17), says the "well-organized" mob consisted mainly of "low Irish and Germans."

6. Adams, *History,* Vol II, 400.

7. Brown, *The Republic in Peril: 1812* (New York: Columbia University Press, 1964), 181-183.

8. Sellers, personal conversation, Sept. 30, 1968.

9. Scharf, *History of Maryland,* Vol. II, 403-413.

10. Charles L. Wagandt, *The Mighty Revolution: Negro Emancipation in Maryland, 1862-1864* (Baltimore: Johns Hopkins Press, 1964), 28.

11. Georgia Lee Tatum, *Disloyalty in the Confederacy* (Chapel Hill: University of North Carolina Press, 1934), 115, 122, 132-133, citing J. G. De Roulhac Hamilton.

12. Ibid., 46.

13. Ibid., 58.

14. Frank L. Klement, *The Copperheads in the Middle West* (Chicago: University of Chicago Press, 1960), 26-27, 78-80, See also Ella Lonn, *Desertion During the Civil War* (Gloucester, Mass.: Peter Smith, 1966, reprint of the 1928 ed.), 204; and George Fort Milton, *Abraham Lincoln and the Fifth Column* (New York: Collier, 1962; paperback reprint of 1942 edition), 72-73, 116.

15. James McCague, *The Second Rebellion: the Story of the New York City Draft Riots of 1863* (New York: Dial, 1968), 177-179 and passim.

16. Milton, *Lincoln and the Fifth Column,* 109-111; John Niven, *Connecticut for the Union: the Role of the State in the Civil War* (New Haven, Conn.: Yale University Press, 1965), 90.

17. Klement, *Copperheads,* 92, 98. Klement argues that the peace movement was in no way related to any organized pro-Southern scheme; Northern Republican soldier-politicians foisted that canard on the public and on history.

18. Niven, *Connecticut,* 300-302.

19. Klement, *Copperheads,* 88, 320; Niven, *Connecticut,* 302.

20. David Donald, "Died for Democracy," in Donald, ed., *Why the North Won the Civil War* (New York: Collier Books, paperback, 1965; reprint of 1960 ed.), 87-90.

21. Robert L. Beisner, *Twelve Against Empire: the Anti-Imperialists, 1898-1900* (New York: McGraw-Hill, 1968), 10-12 and passim. I have not discovered any antiwar riots arising from opposition to the longer and more severe war of "pacification" of the Philippines, 1899-1902.

22. Peterson and Fite, *Opponents of War, 1917-1918* (Madison: University of Wisconsin Press, 1957), 30-31.

23. Ibid., 40-41.

24. Ibid., 45-46. James Weinstein, *The Decline of Socialism in America, 1912-1925* (New York: Monthly Review Press, 1967), 139-141, lists other cases of mob violence against socialists.

25. Peterson and Fite, *Opponents of War,* 202-204. The Washington *Post* commented: "In spite of excesses such as lynching, it is a healthful and wholesome awakening. . . ."

26. Ibid., 199.

27. Ibid., 197-198.

28. Ibid., 74-79; Weinstein, *Decline of Socialism,* 145, identifies Bigelow as socialist.

29. Peterson and Fite, *Opponents of War,* 28.

30. Ibid., 32.

31. Ibid., 48-60.

32. Ibid., 211-230.

33. Ibid., 41-42.

34. Richard Polenberg, ed., *Americans At War: the Home Front, 1941-1945* (Englewood Cliffs, N.J.: Prentice-Hall, 1968), 94-95, citing Thomas's article in *Common Sense,* Vol. XII (May 1943), 156-159.

35. Polenberg, *Americans At War,* 92-94, citing Baldwin, "Freedom in Wartime," *Report of the American Civil Liberties Union* (June 1943), 3-6.

36. Polenberg, *Americans At War,* 102, citing Warren's testimony before the House of Representatives, *National Defense Migration Hearings* (Washington, 1942), Vol. XXIX, 11010-11019.

37. New York *Times,* Aug. 3, 1950, 1. There is no secondary account of this period that treats this issue.

38. Ibid., Aug. 1, 1950, 13; Sept. 15, 1950, 18.

39. Ibid., July 12, 1950, 16; July 13, 1950, 22.

40. Two incidents will help to illustrate the temper of the times. Four men and one woman drew six-month and one-year jail sentences for having painted the words "Peace" and "No H-Bomb" on a Brooklyn park entrance—before the outbreak of the Korean War. The judge accused them of stabbing our men fighting in Korea in the back. (New York *Times,* Aug. 2, 1950, 6). The Social Science Research Council accepted a $100,000 grant from the Markle Foundation to devise a test for detecting traitors (New York *Times,* Nov. 19, 1951, 25).

41. The riots growing out of our involvement in Vietnam are so much a part of our time (and more fully cataloged in other studies) that I have not documented them separately. The New York *Times Index* is the best guide. I have also used clippings from the San Francisco *Chronicle.* Radical and underground papers like the *Guardian* (formerly the *National Guardian*), the Berkeley *Barb,* the *Mid-Peninsula Observer,* and the Los Angeles *Free-Press,* as well as journals like *Ramparts* and *Liberation,* give the deomonstrators' view of events— some of which I observed at firsthand.

42. Norman Mailer, *The Armies of the Night* (New York: New American Library, 1968); Irving L. Horowitz, "The Struggle Is the Message: An Analysis of Tactics, Trends, and Tensions in the Antiwar Movement" (unpublished MS, 1968), 42, notes that "the level of violence is greatest on the West Coast and in the Berkeley-Oakland-San Francisco area."

43. Ibid., 10, Horowitz says: "The anti-war movement can be considered as an ideology in search of a tactic." I think Horowitz exaggerates the role of ideology in the antiwar movement, while underestimating its nihilism, personified by some of the culture heroes of the New Left: Bob Dylan, the Doors, Arthur Brown, and the Rolling Stones—note the Stones' hit, "Street-Fighting Man."

44. Compare Horowitz, 43.

45. Ibid., 35-36. By "the system," antiwar radicals denote the interrelated complex of political, economic, social and cultural institutions of the United States and the ideology which supports them. [Daniel Walker] *Rights in Conflict* (New York: Bantam Books, 1968).

46. (München: Verlag Dokumentation, 1977), in English.

47. Samuel Eliot Morison, Frederick Merk, and Frank Friedel, *Dissent in Three American Wars* (Cambridge: Harvard University Press, 1970).

48. Melvyn Dubofsky, *We Shall Be All: A History of the IWW* (Chicago: Quadrangle, 1969).

49. James F. Richardson, *The New York Police: Colonial Times to 1900* (New York: Oxford University Press, 1970), 129-146.

50. Pauline Maier, "The Charleston Mob and the Evolution of Popular Politics in Revolutionary South Carolina, 1765-1784," *Perspectives in American History,* 4 (1970): 173-198, esp. 173-74, 186-87. Compare Maier, "Popular Uprisings and Civil Authority in Eighteenth Century America," *William & Mary Quarterly,* 3, 27 (1970): 3-35 "Revolutionary Violence and the Relevance of History," *Journal of Interdisciplinary History,* 2, (1971-72): 119-134; *From Resistance to Revolution: Colonial Radicals and the Development of American Opposition to Britain, 1765-1784* (New York: Alfred A. Knopf, 1972).

51. Ronald Hoffman, "The 'Disaffected' in the Revolutionary South," in Alfred F. Young, ed., *The American Revolution* (De Kalb: Northern Illinois University Press, 1976), 273-316; Hoffman, *A Spirit of Dissension: Economics, Politics and the Revolution in Maryland* (Baltimore: Johns Hopkins University Press, 1973).

52. Stephen E. Patterson, *Political Parties in Revolutionary* Massachusetts (Madison: University of Wisconsin Press, 1973).

53. Hoerder, *Crowd Action in Revolutionary Massachusetts, 1765-1780* (New York: Academic Press, 1977), esp. 335-367.

54. John K. Alexander, "The Fort Wilson Incident of 1779: A Case Study of the Revolutionary Crowd," *William and Mary Quarterly,* 3, 31 (1974): 589-612.

55. Foner, "Tom Paine's Republic: Radical Ideology and Social Change," in Young, ed., *American Revolution,* 187-232 (the passage quoted is at 217). Compare Foner's powerful study of Paine, *Tom Paine and the American Revolution* (New York: Oxford University Press, 1976).

56. Edward Countryman, "Consolidating Power in Revolutionary America: the Case of New York, 1775-1783," *Journal of Interdisciplinary History,* 6 (1976): 645-677.

57. James Hutson makes this point in a review of Young, *William and Mary Quarterly*, 3, 35 (1978): 168-171. I had made the same argument in reviewing Staughton Lynd's monograph on Dutchess County, N.Y. in the American Revolution, "Class Struggle, Then and Now," *Studies on the Left*, 4 (1964): 64-68.

58. Michael Miles, *The Radical Probe* (New York: Atheneum, 1971); Kirkpatrick Sale, *SDS* (New York: Random House, 1973): Garry Wills, *Nixon Agonistes* (New York: New American Library, 1971). See also Peter Clecak, *Radical Paradoxes: Dilemmas of the American Left, 1945-1970* (New York: Harper and Row, 1973); Nigel Young, *An Infantile Disorder? The Crisis and Decline of the New Left* (London: Routledge and Kegan Paul, 1977); Eric Barnouw, *Tube of Plenty: the Evolution of American Television* (New York: Oxford University Press, 1975); Morris Dickstein, *The Gates of Eden: American Culture in the Sixties* (New York: Basic Books, 1977); Godfrey Hodgson, *America In Our Time* (New York: Doubleday, 1976).

59. Michael Stohl, *War and Domestic Political Violence: the American Capacity for Repression and Reaction* (Beverly Hills: Sage Publications, 1976), 94, 120. Daniel Calhoun calls Stohl's book the best of a bad lot of behavioral studies with flawed methodologies: "so many rounds of pseudo-controversy, based on a polite analysis of each other's canned data bases [serving] as elegant ways to avoid measuring the conflict behavior of real social groups," review in *Journal of Interdisciplinary History*, 9 (1978): 189-193.

60. Barrington Moore, Jr., *Reflections on the causes of human misery and upon certain proposals to eliminate them* (Boston: Beacon Press, 1972).

61. Hofstadter, Introduction to Hofstadter and Michael Wallace, eds., *American Violence: a Documentary History* (New York: Alfred A. Knopf, 1970), 10. Compare Douglas T. Miller, quoted in Hugh D. Graham, "The Paradox of American Violence: a Historical Commentary," *Annals of the American Academy of Political and Social Science*, 391 (1970): 81, "much of our historical violence has 'served the dominant establishment'—has generally been 'generated from the top of society, not the bottom, and has aimed at repression, not innovation'."

Chapter 12
Terrorism and Revolution in America

J. BOWYER BELL and TED ROBERT GURR

In the 1970s terrorism became trendy, both in word and deed. But the deeds were nothing new. By other names terrorism has played many parts in American history. On May 4, 1886, a small group of labor militants called a demonstration in Chicago's Haymarket Square to advocate an eight-hour working day. When police attempted to disperse the crowd of 1,500 or so, a bomb exploded. Seven police and four other people died in the explosion and the riot which followed. In the parlance of the day, the organizers were called anarchists, eight of whom were convicted for inciting violence, despite the lack of evidence tying them to the bombing. Had the incident occurred in 1976 journalists would have called the organizers revolutionaries and the bombing terrorism. As it was, the episode entered American history as the Haymarket Riot.[1]

Acts of racial terrorism were an ugly feature of the American landscape throughout the 1960s. In the South white segregationists used bullets, bombs, and torches to intimidate civil rights workers. In Northern cities, late in the decade, young black militants acted out the virulent "off the pigs" hatred of the times by murdering police officers. The police retaliated against their most visible and vocal opponents, the Black Panthers, in a series of armed confrontations and attacks. Segregationists, black militants, and the police all employed the tactics of terrorism:

AUTHORS' NOTE: *J. Bowyer Bell is a senior research associate of the Institute of War and Peace Studies, Columbia University. He has written a number of books based on his first-hand knowledge of contemporary revolutionary movements, including* The Secret Army: The IRA 1916-1970 *(Anthony Blond, 1970);* The Myth of the Guerrilla: Revolutionary Theory and Malpractice *(Knopf, 1971);* On Revolt; Strategies of National Liberation *(Harvard University Press, 1976); and* A Time of Terror: How Democratric Societies Respond to Revolutionary Violence *(Basic Books, 1978).*

Ted Robert Gurr is Payson S. Wild Professor of political science at Northwestern University. His many books and monographs include Why Men Rebel *(Princeton University Press), which won the Woodrow Wilson Prize as the best book in political science of 1970, and* Rogues, Rebels, and Reformers: A Political History of Urban Crime and Conflict *(Sage Publications, 1976).*

The case studies of contemporary American terrorism were prepared by the first author; the second author is responsible for the comparative evidence and interpretation.

they tried to frighten and demoralize their opponents by using sudden, dramatic acts of deadly violence against them.

The tactics called terrorism are ideologically neutral. They can and have been used by any group on behalf of any cause. In American history the Ku Klux Klan used tactics of terror in the Reconstruction South to establish social control over former slaves and their Northern supporters. Vigilantes used similar tactics to establish their version of order on the lawless frontiers. The Molly Maguires, a secret organization of Irish miners, used terror in the hard-coal region of eastern Pennsylvania to oppose the abuses of mineowners and their police.[2] From the Civil War to the Great Depression, owners and managers in dozens of industries used terrorist tactics to intimidate labor organizers and to break strikes.

The only unity in this diversity of historical examples is that the tactics of terrorism virtually never were used in America with revolution in mind.[3] The new element in the 1970s was a distinctive international mythology of revolutionary terrorism. This mythology did not originate in the United States and its impact here has been late, limited, and sometimes ludicrous, But it has contributed some dramatic and unpleasant sideshows to the American political scene.

THE MYTHOLOGY OF REVOLUTIONARY TERRORISM

Paul Wilkinson defines political terrorism as "coercive intimidation." It is "the systematic use of murder and destruction, and the threat of murder and destruction, in order to terrorise individuals, groups, communities or governments into conceding to the terrorists' political demands."[4] Revolutionary terrorism is the variant of terrorism which aims at fundamental political change. These are academic distinctions that emphasize techniques and targets. Those who practice revolutionary terrorism justify their actions in terms of specific, imperative objectives: they seek the liberation of their people, the overthrow of an unjust ruling class. Their cause is an absolute goal, one to which all other ends and means are subordinate. They hold a Manichean vision of the world in which their opponents are irredeemably evil. Revolutionaries thus are justified in killing and instilling terror without moral compunction. Sometimes the revolutionaries speak for a nationality group, fighting against alien rulers. Elsewhere they represent themselves as the vanguard of an oppressed class, struggling against the injustices of their own landowner or capitalist or bureaucratic class.

Nationalist and revolutionary objectives can be pursued by many strategies, including mass political mobilization, nonviolent resistance, and guerrilla warfare. The puzzle is why some revolutionaries take up the ideology and practice of terrorism while others do not. One strategic factor stands out above all others: terrorism is the strategy of the weak. The fewer the revolutionaries are in number, the less their resources in contrast to their opponents, the more likely they are to resort to the politics of atrocity.[5]

It is plausible that terrorism should appeal to small bands of visionaries whose political ambitions far outrun their means. If the alternative is sterile intellectual debate leading into historical oblivion, terrorism is relatively attractive: it is positive, dramatic action that just might strike a weak link in the enemy's political armor. In such circumstances the young intellectuals of Narodnaya Volya—The People's Will—developed the first modern ideology of terrorism in Russia, beginning in 1879. They coupled the philosophy of anarchism to the tactic of assassination and though they failed utterly in their ambition to overthrow the Czarist regime, contributed to a political tradition of resistance that succeeded in 1917.[6] They also provided a model for anarchist terrorism that sputtered fitfully through Europe, the Americas, and parts of Asia for a generation.

Little remains of the nineteeth-century tradition of anarchist terrorism but a faded, almost comical, image of a ragged, bearded bomb-thrower. The contemporary myth of revolutionary terrorism is rooted in the nationalist movements which swept Asia and Africa after the Second World War. Between 1945 and 1970 some 60 new nations came into existence. Seven of them were born directly through armed struggle against colonial powers: Israel (1948), Indonesia (1949), North and South Vietnam (1954), Cyprus (1960), Algeria (1962), and Southern Yemen (1967). Terrorism played a part in all of these wars of national independence, though it was the primary strategy of militants only in Israel, Cyprus, and Southern Yemen. In each of these three cases Britain was the colonial authority, and murder in the streets was only one blood-red thread in a complex plot woven of muddle, pressure, blunder, and compromise.[7] In Vietnam (both in 1945 and 1965) and in Algeria, terrorism was the first stage of revolutionary warfare. Later it was relegated to a supporting role to guerrilla war and conventional ground battles. But terrorism was the first step, and an easy step, and that was the compelling message received by aspiring revolutionaries throughout the Third World.

It is not a myth that sustained campaigns of terrorism contributed to each of these nationalist victories. The myth is the accretion of attitudes and beliefs which cluster around this kernel of historical fact. Acts of terrorism have been given a role out of proportion to their place in the political process that culminated in independence. Nowhere is this more evident than in the 1966 film "The Battle of Algiers," which gives a false aura of victory to the short, bloody, and harshly suppressed terrorist campaign of urban nationalists which preceded the decision to organize rural guerrilla war. Another part of the myth of revolutionary terrorism is the belief that campaigns of violence ultimately will cow threatened people into passive acquiescence. Since unsuccessful terrorist campaigns far outnumber successful ones, it seems evident that terrorist tactics are more likely to stimulate effective resistance than terrified acquiescence.[8] But political myths are mutable. The more sophisticated revolutionary position has translated this present liability into a future asset. They expect by acts of terrorism to provoke their enemy into overreaction, which ultimately will drive alienated supporters of the regime into the revolutionary camp.

The terrorist mythology is exportable as well as mutable. It can be and has been put to the service of any and every nationalism: Breton, Corsican, Croatian, Moluccan, Puerto Rican, Welsh, and most dramatically of all, Palestinian. By a slight twist it also serves the needs of disaffected religious and ethnic minorities. The role of the colonial oppressor has been attributed to the Protestants in Northern Ireland, to Anglo-Canadians in Canada, to white Americans in the United States. By another kind of twist, the myth has been adapted to the situation of Marxist revolutionaries in Western Europe and Latin America. The revolutionary left in these societies is not distinguished by nationality, race, or religion from the nonrevolutionary majority, but Marxism-Leninism identifies the capitalists and their bourgeois supporters as the class enemy of workers and their intellectual vanguard. Thus the capitalist class enemy becomes a natural target for revolutionary terrorists: the techniques of the new mythology have been fitted to an old ideology of class struggle.

The Latin American dispensation of revolutionary terrorism was established in the 1960s. It was one of several modes of revolutionary action, often uses as an alternative or supplement to rural guerrilla warfare. Numbered among the targets were both the domestic elite and North American industrialists and diplomatic officials, who were and are seen as the agents of international captialism. Major campaigns of revolutionary terrorism occurred in Guatemala, from the early 1960s to the mid-1970s; Venezuela, 1962-1963; Brazil, 1968-c. 1972; Uruguay, 1963-c. 1974; and Argentina, from 1969 to the present. In none of these instances did the revolutionaries achieve their intended effects. Their impact was most devastating in Guatemala and Argentina, where revolutionary action provoked the establishment of right-wing terrorist squads with tacit support from the police and military. The result in each country was a civil war of contending terrorisms in which the revolutionary left was virtually annihilated. In Uruguay the Tupamaros suffered much the same fate, but not before that country's long-lived democratic government was swept aside by a military regime which was willing to use unrestrained violence against the Tupamaros and their supporters. If revolutionary mythology is correct, many more Uruguayans should now be sympathetic to the revolutionary cause. The catch is that no Tupamaros remain to lead them.[9]

Revolutionary terrorists in the advanced industrial societies are politically and ideologically more diverse than their Latin contemporaries. Some are the most extreme factions of dissident national, ethnic, and religious minorities. Far and away their largest and most effective campaign to date has been carried out by the Irish Republican Army, beginning in 1969. The political landscape of Northern Ireland has been fundamentally altered as a consequence, though the shape of the ultimate settlement cannot yet be discerned. The purely political terrorists, those operating in the Marxist-Leninist tradition, have been active in half-a-dozen countries at most. Italy's Red Brigades, responsible for the 1978 kidnapping and murder of former Premier Aldo Moro, are now the largest of them and the only ones with any serious prospect of inducing political change. Germany's Red Army Faction (the Baader-Meinhof Group) has had considerable sympathy on the far left but few activists have escaped the tight network of surveillance. Newly democratic Spain has suffered a spate of bombings and assassinations, most of them by Basque nationalists, some claimed by groups on the far left. The Weather People in the United States have gone so far underground that it is no longer possible to distinguish their bombings, if indeed they continue, from the background noise of thousands of bombs annually set off by patriotic American cranks, Mafiosi, labor racketeers, eco-raiders, and high school chemistry students. Britain's terrorists in the mid-1970s were IRA exports, not homegrown products. Moluccan terrorists in the Netherlands were second-generation nationalists, not Marxist revolutionaries. The Japanese Red Army, which staged the Lod Airport massacre in Israel in 1972, was tiny, ephemeral, and operated internationally rather than in Japan. Indigenous revolutionary terrorists have yet to surface elsewhere in the industrial West.[10]

A global sketch of revolutionary terrorism would not be complete without mention of international terrorism, which has some claim to be the most dramatic innovation in violent politics of this generation. Terrorism has long had an international dimension, typified by the assassination of American diplomatic personnel in Latin America and American hijacking of air-liners to Cuba. Irish nationalists have periodically sent terror squads to Britain since late in the nineteenth century, and the Algerian nationalists did the same in France during the Algerian War. The novelty of the new transnational terrorism is that its attacks are carried out on the territory of third parties, or in international air space. The Popular Front for the Liberation of Palestine pioneered the latter tactic in July 1968 when it hijacked an E1 A1 707 flight out of Rome and diverted it to Algiers, then held the crew and some passengers hostage to pressure Isreal to release Palestinian guerrillas. It was a logical tactic for militant Palestinians to choose since their target was a homeland from which they were barred. Eritrean and Croatian nationalists have emulated the Palestinians, and so have other groups attracted less by tactical necessity than by the enormous publicity attendant on international exploits.

International terrorism increased sharply after 1968. A CIA study which counts all incidents with international targets or ramifications identifies 111 incidents in 1968, 282 in 1970, and a peak of 413 in 1976, followed by a decline to 279 in 1977. The tactics chosen varied considerably over time: political highjacking reached a peak with 21 incidents in 1970; by 1977 they had declined to eight. Bombings and kidnappings, on the other hand, reached their peak in the mid-1970s before beginning a decline. This study and others also confirm the common perception that Western democracies are more victimized by international terrorism than any other group of countries. This is the regional location of 2690 international terrorist incidents recorded between 1968 and 1977: the Atlantic Community, 46 percent; Latin America, 28 percent; the Middle East, 16 percent; the rest of the world, 10 percent. Though few of the attacks occured in the United States itself, American property and citizens were victimized in 43 percent of all incidents.[11]

REVOLUTIONARY TERRORISM IN CONTEMPORARY AMERICA

The tactics of terrorism have the sanction of historical usage in the United States. *Revolutionary* terrorism in contemporary America is imitative. Almost without exception the nationalists, radicals, and psychopaths who have perpetrated terrorist acts in the name of revolution in the United States have taken their cues from the international environment. It is revolutionary rhetoric that is alien to America, not the use of violence for political purposes. As a consequence revolutionary terrorism has had little appeal except to marginal groups, so far outside the political mainstream that their actions seem more like staged media events than serious gestures of protest and resistance.

The Ideologues of the Left: From Marx to the Jackson Brigade

In June 1969, the most prominent of New Left organizations in the United States, the Students for a Democratic Society (SDS), held a national convention in Chicago. Most of its members shared a middle-class, white, university background. The glue in the beginning for the SDS and much of radical university politics of the era had been opposition to the war in Vietnam, often expressed in moral as well as political terms. The New Left, and much of liberal opinion in general, was also much concerned about greater social justice, an end to racism, and institutional reform. By 1969 some of the factions beneath the broad umbrella of SDS had become increasingly ideological and militant. Some were deeply immersed in the minutia of Marxist-Maoist ideology. Others were impatient for dramatic action, frustrated that the real revolutionaries of the Third World could wage an armed struggle while they were trapped in "Amerika"—so they spelled it to symbolize its alleged fascist tendencies. The most radical of them were convinced that change was possible only with the end of the existing American system.

The divisions of opinion on how to end the American system and what should replace it were dramatically in evidence at the SDS convention. There was a spate of revolutionary oratory, the citation of appropriate texts, the display of red books, and the insistence on right thinking. The Black Panthers were attacked as more nationalist than revolutionary and charges of racism were exchanged. Ultimately one faction walked out and soon split into the Revolutionary Youth Movement, whose members stressed political agitation, and the Weathermen (later known as the Weather People and Weather Underground), who sought immediate revolutionary action. At the June convention one of the future Weather People, Bernadine Dohrn, had insisted that "We can't just talk about revolution, we have to act." Now reduced to the faithful few, they were absolutely secure in their conviction that, as in Bob Dylan's "Subterranean Homesick Blues," "You don't need a weatherman to know which way the wind blows." And for the Weather People, a gale was blowing them toward action not analysis.

The Weather People's ideological analysis was, especially for their New Left rivals, rather cursory. "Amerika" was a racist-imperialist-capitalist-repressive (later sexist) society that was overextended and under attack from Third World revolutionaries. The Weather People, borrowing from another Dylan song—"The pump don't work 'cause the vandals took the handles"—wanted to be the vandals in the heart of the mother country of imperialism, a country that had bought off the white workingman with color television, imprisoned its youth in school-jails, ground down black people, and institutionalized exploitation. They, like many rebels before them, felt that somehow, someplace, someone must strike the first blow. After that the future could take care of itself.

The first real violence came in Chicago in October, when the Weather People staged a dramatic episode of street theatre. During "Four Days of Rage" they rampaged through the street of the Gold Coast and Loop smashing windshields, breaking store windows, and fighting with the provoked and outraged police. It was a violent, structured display involving risks and the exhilaration of danger intended to show "Amerika" that the revolution was real. Despite the horror of the conservatives and the avid coverage of the networks, the four days indicated something of the nature of the threat: Less than 300 young people (no other group answered their call to Chicago) stage-managing a riot was hardly a terminal threat to the United States.[12]

But the Weather People had more than a mere riot in mind. There were to be attacks on "imperialist" targets: Boston English High School, the Cambridge, Massachusetts police station (after which 23 suspects were arrested), the Harvard Center for International Affairs (and more arrests), and finally bombings against symbolic targets. Bombs have been widely used in America for at least a century, sometimes out of private or public malice, sometimes for the sheer hell of it. The hundreds of explosions and incendiaries in the average year are natural occurrences in an open society that sells dynamite over the counter and automatic rifles by mail order. The most thorough canvass of information on bombings was conducted in 1969-1970 by the Alcohol, Tobacco, and Firearms Division of the Treasury Department which gathered reports from state and local law enforcement agencies. In 15½ months, beginning January 1969, those agencies recorded 975 bomb explosions and 3,355 incendiaries, 1,175 bombs that failed to go off, and more than 35,000 bomb threats. In the 4,330 instances where the bombs went off, the study tried to identify source or issue, with these results:

    64% arose from unknown causes;
    20% occurred during campus disturbances;
     7% were attributed to black extremists;
     5% were attributed to white extremists;
     3% were in aid of criminal activities; e.g. extortion; and
     1% occurred during labor disputes.

If we suppose that most bombings of unknown cause had private motives, the evidence suggests that at most a quarter of American bombings during this period had political objectives—most of the campus bombings and some of the racial ones.[13]

The Weather People could claim responsibility for some of the most dramatic events of the time. March 1970 marked a turning point. On March 6, three large explosions wrecked a four-story townhouse in New York's Greenwich Village. In the burnt-out ruins of 18 West 11th Street, the police found the body of Theodore Gold, 23, a member of the SDS and a leader of the 1968 revolt at Columbia University; Diana Oughton, a wealthy young woman out of Madiera School and Bryn Mawr; and another young man, Terry Robbins. Kathy Boudin, 26, whose parents owned the townhouse, and Cathlyn Platt Wilkerson, 25, escaped and went underground. The townhouse had been a bomb factory.[14] On March 12, bombs caused severe damage to three New York corporate headquarters, and workers had to evacuate twelve others because of bomb threats—there would be more than 400 threats over the next 24 hours. There was a bomb in Albuquerque, New Mexico, under a Reserve Officers' Training Corps building; and in Bel Air, Maryland, a leading black militant, Ralph E. Featherstone, was killed when an explosion wrecked the car he was driving. The Greenwich Village explosion was simply the most spectacular in a month of explosions. By year's end there had been 36 bombings or bomb attempts on property of the federal government alone, with damage estimated at $650,000. The Weather People were responsible for some, and no doubt also contributed to the less dramatic but more disruptive tactic of bomb threats. In the same year 592 such threats forced

226 evacuations of federal buildings at a cost of nearly $4 million in lost working time.[15] The most serious cost of this activity was psychic not material: it was the rising sense of anxiety and revulsion that gripped most Americans.

In the early months of revolutionary bombings, the young terrorists avoided killing anyone but themselves. But on August 24, 1970, the inevitable occurred. In Sterling Hall, the University Mathematics Research Center of the United States Army, at the Madison campus of the University of Wisconsin, Karleton Lewis Armstrong, 24, detonated a fertilizer-and-oil mixture with a stick of dynamite. There was a huge explosion. In the ruins of Sterling Hall, firemen discovered the body of Dr. Robert Fassnacht, who had been working late in his laboratory. Those who had sought to demonstrate their affirmation of life and the evil of war, had murdered the innocent. No matter that Armstrong had allegedly taken every precaution to detonate his device when Sterling Hall was empty, Fassnacht was still dead. The three people on West 11th Street in New York had only killed themselves, but Armstrong had taken an innocent life to dramatize a point, very much a matter of overkill.

The Weather People had gone underground shortly after a war council held at Flint in December 1969. On May 21, 1970, Bernadine Dohrn read a taperecorded declaration of war, later published in the *New York Times,* (May 25) and the *Great Speckled Bird* (June 8). By then, the house on West 11th Street had been demolished, and within a few months the explosion at Sterling Hall would make all but the most militant reconsider the tactics of violence. Still, some did not draw back. The Weather Underground remained more or less intact, spread out across the country in small, circulating cells. Some blended into the much larger half-world of communes, colonies, and flawed utopias established by the counterculture. Others reportedly emulated their enemies in the establishment by establishing false identities and conventional lifestyles as a cover for revolutionary activities.[16] Still others simply dropped out of the revolution, turned off by Fassnacht's death and unpalatable statements from the leaders. At Flint Bernadine Dohrn had praised the senseless and brutal murders by the Charles Manson family: "Dig it, first they killed those pigs, then they ate dinner in the same room with them, then they even shoved a fork into a victim's stomach! Wild!" John Jacobs insisted that "We are against everything that's good and decent." Those who remained in the underground appeared to be acting out fantasies, gripped by self-loathing, turning politics into personal therapy. Some stayed out of necessity, fearing arrest and prosecution if they emerged. Late in the 1970s even some of the fugitives surfaced, apparently finding the prospect of plea-bargained sentences less painful than the paranoia of underground existence.

The Weather Underground seems a rational, almost comfortingly familiar revolutionary organization by comparison with some others who emulated it. On George Washington's birthday in 1974, Samuel H. Lovejoy, an organic farmer, sabotaged a 500-foot-high tower that was part of a planned nuclear power plant. He took full responsibility and announced his reasons in a four-page typewritten statement. In December 1974, Michael H. Brown put a bomb under a bench in the meditation room of the United Nations General Assembly building. In February 1975, the New World Liberation Front claimed responsibility for four bombings, including an explosion in an NBC affilitate television station, in the name of various radical causes. Bombs were placed by the Emiliano Zapata Unit, by the Quarter

Moon Tribe, The Perfect Park Home Grown Garden Society, and yet again by the Weather Underground. A recent campaign in the tradition of the Weather Underground was mounted by the George Jackson Brigade between 1976 and 1978. Named for a militant black inmate who was killed in prison, the Brigade's handful of members carried out a series of robberies and bombings in Oregon and Washington with the avowed purpose of fighting the evils of capitalism in the United States. No one but the police, the victims, and the militants paid much attention. The FBI reported the deadly statistics from all political and private acts of terrorism: 28 killed in the first six months of 1976 with 763 incidents, three more dead than in the first half of 1975 but 255 fewer incidents. The worst incident came in December 1975, when a bomb explosion at La Guardia Airport in New York killed 11 people and injured 75—for this one no one wanted to claim credit. Yet even at its most unattractive and despite the revolutionary rhetoric, the radical underground was content with symbolic bombs; only some Puerto Rican nationalists and the psychopaths seemed seriously interested in killing people.

In fact it was *talking* about revolution coupled with visible, symbolic "deeds" that engendered not only anguish and concern on the part of the authorities but also official violence. The Puerto Rican Young Lords or the Black Panthers were mainly interested in pride and prejudice not guerrilla war. Unfortunately for many of the militants, the police not only took them at their word but also found the provocation of armed and uniformed black men too real for toleration. The subsequent transformation of the Black Panthers from symbolic guerrillas talking revolution to a social service organization concerned with local political power was remarkably swift. Those who wanted war ended up in jail or early graves. In fact, during a turbulent decade of great social and racial change, during an unpopular war, with often unresponsive administrations in Washington, the remarkable result of the rhetoric of revolution, the declarations of war, the berets and shotguns and bombs and prison breaks is that there was so little deadly violence, that so few people were killed coldly and rationally for real political purpose. Again, except for the Puerto Ricans and psychopaths, "revolutionary terrorism" of the American left was a matter of style as much as of substance, of symbol and rhetoric and personal anguish.

The Nationalists: The Latin Connections

If the ideologues of the radical left reveal a great deal about American society and something of the politics of therapy, Latin American nationalists are almost alien to the United States but most assuredly serious revolutionaries. Contending factions among Cubans have made southern Florida an arena for arson, extortion, and bombings—as well as a base for forays against the home island. *El Poder Cubano* (Cuban Power) was the principal U.S.-based Cuban terrorist organization in the 1960s; since then its place has been taken by the Cuban National Liberation Front, and most recently the Command of United Revolutionary Organizations. All have directed their attacks at symbols and supporters of the Castro regime, in the United States and internationally. Some Cubans have become deeply involved in both Central American and South American operations of the right. Accused of the September 21, 1976 murder of the former Chilean Foreign Minister Orlando Letelier in Washington, of providing gunmen for Central American regimes, of involvement in dozens of conspiracies of the right, the Cubans have become a serious American problem but with no direct relation to American politics except for the historic CIA connection. The same is not true, however, in the case of the Puerto Ricans.

The movement for a free Puerto Rico is older than this century and has been a problem for the United States since July 1898. *Independentista* sentiment has had a cyclical history with the cycle lately on the down side. In the 1967 plebiscite on the island's status, the *independentistas* boycotted the vote, which was distributed 60.4 percent for commonwealth, 39 percent for statehood, and 0.6 percent for independence. In the 1972 general elections, the Puerto Rican Independence Party received 4.37 percent of the vote. Revolutionaries have, however, never felt it necessary to poll their constituency. They march to a different drummer, act under a higher law, look into their own hearts to find the dreams of the people. Their people, the *independentistas* feel, have been bought with promises and crumbs from the American table, misguided by ambitious locals who have under the standard of Commonwealth or Statehood betrayed their own. Someone must act to awaken the deluded. Nations are born out of the cauldron, not by plebiscites or petitions, and freedom is won with a sword, not ceded from afar. All the attitudes and platitudes of two centuries of national liberation movements can be found in the militant rhetoric of the ultra-*independentistas*. And unlike the postures and pretensions of the radicals of the American left, the Puerto Rican nationalists have really waged a sustained campaign of liberation with bombs and bullets, no less deadly for its limited support and limited scale.[17]

In 1950, Puerto Rican nationalists attempted to assassinate President Harry S. Truman at Blair House. In 1954 four nationalists took part in a shooting attack from the gallery of the U.S. House of Representatives in which five members of Congress were wounded. In part the shift to armed militancy was the result of frustration with Puerto Rican electoral politics. In 1944 Luis Muñoz Marin and the Popular Democratic Party had won a substantial electoral success with independence as part of the platform. But there was no independence. Muñoz Marin went his own way and the *independentistas* found themselves a tiny, increasingly islolated minority as Muñoz Marin became the first elected governor in 1948 and as the impact of economic development from Operation Bootstrap began to transform the island. The shootings changed nothing. The Puerto Rican Independence Party continued to sustain electoral losses until the late sixties: in 1968, 25,000 votes; in 1972, 52,000; in 1976, 73,000. Yet in 1976 the vote for independence was still only 6.5 percent, and whatever the disappointments of the Commonwealth, few saw any future choice except that between statehood, which President Gerald Ford had advocated as one of his last official acts, and an adjusted Commonwealth status. Very few are required, however, to begin a revolution; and in August 1974, the *Fuerzas Armadas de Liberación* National (FALN) opened their armed campaign against the colonial giant with bombs in Damrosch Park in Lincoln Center, New York.

Operations also continued on the island (although not all the bombing and burning could be attributed directly to the FALN), but the key targets were in the United States, where media coverage guaranteed the maximum impact. The most extensive blitz in 1974 came on October 26 in New York City when, between 2:56 and 3:40 a.m., bombs detonated under a car on Nassau Street, at Eastern Air Lines offices and Banco de Ponce at 10 Rockefeller Plaza, at Lever House, the Union Carbide Building, and Manufactures Hanover Bank. Damage was extensive. But the most deadly explosion occured at 1:35 p.m., January 24, 1975, at Fraunces Tavern, 101 Broad Street in New York, where four people were killed and 55 were injured. The intent was to kill—the explosion occured at the crowded lunch hour—as it had been the previous year when a rookie police officer named Angelo Poggi was maimed by a decoy trap-bomb. The bombing campaign continued through 1975 with explosions spreading to Chicago in June and on October 27 to Washington, where at 2:00 a.m. an explosion caused damage at the State Department Building. Law enforcement authorities attributed 49 blasts to the FALN between the first bomb at Damrosch Park on August 31, 1974, and February 18, 1977, when two explosions, again in New York, damaged the Gulf & Western Building and the Texaco Guide Center in the Chrysler Building. Most of the targets were symbolic exploiters of the island—banks, airlines, transnational companies—and the timing indicated that the FALN was not interested in killing people. Fraunces Tavern was a notable and bloody exception. Largely unnoticed by the media, the campaign continued in Puerto Rico—that is, until a non-FALN operation had national impact. At the Federal Bar Association meeting in Puerto Rico in September 1977, a special Advanced Seminar and Conference on Terrorism and Countermeasures was organized with a variety of academic and police experts invited to participate. A local lawyer was assassinated. The seminar was cancelled. And the academic experts, many for the first time, were exposed to raw terrorism rather than a world of paradigms, aggregate data, and typologies.

There is every indication that the FALN will continue its campaign for an independent Puerto Rico. The organization is so small and buried in the Latin ghettos of a few major American cities that police penetration and intelligence have proven difficult if not impossible. Most Puerto Ricans, of course, abhor the violence, have no interest in independence, and care little for the radical ideology of the FALN. Within the independence movement there is opposition to terrorist violence but some recognition that symbolic bombing is valid because aimed at colonial interests. The case for a free Puerto Rico has been cogently argued by Rubén Berríos Martinez, President of the Puerto Rican Independence Party and no advocate of violence, in the April 1977 issue of *Foreign Affairs*, most assuredly not a normal platform for revolutionaries. There is a more general residue of sympathy and understanding as well. In October 1977, for example, four former governors of Puerto Rico appealed to President Jimmy Carter to release the five jailed Puerto Rican nationalists who were involved in the attack on the House of Representatives in 1954 and on President Truman in 1950. Only the current governor opposed their release. Given the climate of toleration, a heritage of resistence to alien rule stretching back to 1868, and a not-unreasonable goal, the FALN presents the United States with a real and unresolved nationality problem. Worse, because of the prevailing anti-*independentista* sentiment on the island, there may be no resolution in sight. The United States can hardly force independence on a reluctant island in order to end the FALN campaign, and without independence there seems every likelihood that the FALN will continue to inject revolutionary terrorism into the American body politic. That it is low-intensity terrorism, that few have been killed, and that few are likely to be does not make the prospect more pleasing. At least, however, the FALN is explicable in rational, political terms, unlike those who have killed in the grip of millenarian fantasies.

Hispanos are the youngest and fastest-growing minority in the United States and soon will outnumber blacks. Puerto Ricans make up the lesser portion of this Spanish-speaking population. One can speculate whether a potential for revolutionary nationalism exists among the much larger Hispanic population of the Southwest. Spanish dissidents of nothern New Mexico rose in brief rebellion in 1967, in Tierra Amarilla, and the region has been afflicted by rashes of rural arson, but the burning issue is old land claims, not revolution.[18] Militant Chicanos in Southwestern cities have followed a similar trajectory to the Puerto Rican Young Lords and the Black Panthers, from radical posturing to social action. But with these exceptions the Mexican-Americans and the increasing numbers of Mexicans in America have been politically quiescent. It is by no means impossible that some will someday become bitterly disenchanted in their search for the pot of gold at the end of the Yankee rainbow, giving rise to exotic and violent new nationalisms.

Aberrant Conspiracies, Misfits, and Lone Gunmen

America has more than its share of driven, confused, and self-destructive people leading miserable lives who strike out in murderous violence to ease their own anguish. They may embellish their acts with the fashionable phrases of the day—Southern nationalism, revolutionary anarchism, environmental purity—but often this is merely a gloss for personal therapy by recourse to violence. The psychopathic assassin would rather be wanted for murder than not wanted at all. Arthur H. Bremer, who shot and maimed Governor George Wallace in 1972, felt that at least he was mentioned on the Walter Cronkite program, at least and at last he was someone to be noticed. He did not even bother to devise a plausible political rationalization. While Americans in general prefer rational explanation—there must have been an Oswald conspiracy, James Earle Ray could not have acted alone—the United States has long been afflicted with a particular kind of disturbed and deadly individual. The psychological profile fits both men and women as was demonstrated when Squeeky Frome of the Manson Family tried to shoot President Gerald Ford in September 1975. With remarkable frequency these violent loners come from broken homes, are incapable of establishing personal relationships, have serious sexual problems, and rarely have been able to hold jobs for any length of time.[19]

On several occasions in the last decade small groups of such people have coalesced to form the nucleus of deadly conspiracies, rationalizing their actions in radical and revolutionary slogans borrowed from groups with more coherent causes. The Symbionese Liberation Army and the Black Liberation Army are the most dramatic examples. We would expect to find similar personality traits at the center of extremist groups like the American Nazi Party and the New World Liberation Front.

The archetype of such groups in the United States was the Symbionese Liberation Army, which was constituted from the last froth of the lunatic fringe of the 1960s radicalism. Most were guilt-ridden, middle-class university militants playing deadly war games, involved in a fantasy revolution that offered both the exhiliration of real danger and with it the prospect of self-destruction. They were joined under the leadership of the ultimate existential man, Donald DeFreeze—a black, escaped convict who found meaning for his brutalized and bitter life by declaring total war on society. "We are savage killers and madmen," he said in a taped message, "willing to give our lives to free the people at any cost."

The Symbionese Liberation Army was part cult, part radical conspiracy, but most of all a means of group therapy for a dozen misfits who found that together they could reinforce one another's fantasies and lead lives of public desperation. Their revolutionary "deeds" consisted first of the murder in 1973 of Oakland's black Superintendent of schools Marcus Foster, for reasons never made clear even among themselves. It was followed by the February 1974 kidnapping of Patricia Hearst, the premier media event of the decade. Then came another brief kidnapping, two bank robberies, a flawed attempt at shoplifting, and the final blazing shoot-out at 1466 East 54th Street in Los Angeles, brought to television viewers, live, in color, personal, close-up. Their proclamations from General Field Marshal Cinque (Donald DeFreeze) were meandering, ill-assorted radical verbiage. Their demands for immediate free food for the poor showed no grasp of the technical problems of distribution. What they did manage to grasp was the attention of the media, first with the Hearst kidnapping, then the conversion of Patty into Tania, and always the great chase. The gun fight at 54th Street had the inevitability of the final showdown in a classic Western film. The six who died in the flaming ruins—the Los Angeles police SWAT team fired a total of 5,371 rounds—could no longer live together or alone as savage killers and madmen. In the last days they seem almost consciously to have sought release in a final confrontation. The few "soldiers" who escaped, including Tania, were arrested after months of drifting through the underground, still playing at revolution.[20]

Less spectacular but more brutal than the SLA was the Black Liberation Army, which preceded the SLA by two years. Its members were not guilty, driven children of the middle-class but the dregs of the urban ghettos, ex-convicts who had learned haltingly the language of black nationalism and radical politics in cell yards. Emerging into a world without promise, they drifted on the edge of the Black Panther movement, coalescing briefly in small shifting groups, always moving, hiding, isolated even within the ghetto. Almost spontaneously they struck out at the most obvious symbol of the system that had crushed and imprisoned them. For the BLA any police officer, whether black or white, was a blue target.

On May 19, 1971, New York patrolmen Thomas Curry and Nicholas Binetti were in patrol car parked on Riverside Drive watching District Attorney Frank Hogan's apartment building. A car swept past them going the wrong way down the one-way street. The patrol car chased them for six blocks, caught up at 106th Street and pulled alongside. A man on the passenger's side of the car reached across the driver, thrust a .45-caliber sub-machine gun out the window, and opened fire. From three feet the slugs tore through the patrol car. Binetti and Curry were critically wounded; both lived but both were maimed. And on May 19, the police had no idea why they had been shot—no motive, no clues, no witnesses, nothing. Two nights later in Harlem, Patrolmen Waverly Jones and Joseph Piagentini answered a call and then walked back toward their patrol car. They strolled past two young men leaning on car fenders. Once they were past the parked car, the two pulled out guns and fired into the backs of the two patrolmen. Waverly Jones, a black officer, was hit three times in the spine and once in the back of the head. He was dead when he crumbled to the ground. Piagentini went down. The two black men yanked out the policemen's service revolvers and standing over them continued to fire down. Piagentini was hit repeatedly—thirteen times—and died on the back seat of a radio car rushing him to Harlem Hospital. At 8:30 the same night, a package was delivered to the *New York Times* containing the license plate of the suspected getaway car in the Curry-Binetti shooting on Riverside Drive, a live .45-caliber cartridge, and a proclamation headed "All Power to the People" from the then unknown Black Liberation Army. The day after the Jones-Piagentini murders another BLA letter took credit. War, of a sort, had been declared on the police.

On January 27, 1972, patrolmen Gregory Foster and Rocco Laurie were shot to death by three black men in the East Village. Both bodies sprawled on the pavement were shot again and again. In January a radio patrol car in Brooklyn was riddled with automatic fire and two cops wounded. Less than two weeks later three black men riddled another patrol car in Queens. The two patrolmen were wounded. In San Francisco blacks entered a police station and murdered a sergeant with a close-range shotgun blast. Police were ambushed in Atlanta and North Carolina. By then the FBI and the various police forces involved knew a great deal more about the BLA. They were mostly from the ultrafringe of the Black Panthers, almost all with police records—except for one unusual exception, a young woman named Joanne Chesimard, who had been a City College student and was the BLA's one intellectual. Most of the BLA men moved about under shifting aliases, drifting from one city to another, living on the proceeds of bank robberies and holdups, hiding out in abandoned houses, splitting up and meeting again in the ghetto. One by one they were arrested or killed in shoot-outs. Once in prison—and almost all those wanted for murder were eventually caught and imprisoned—their sympathizers repeatedly tried to rescue them. There were four attempts to free the three men sentenced to life for the murder of partolmen Piagentini and Jones, the last in May 1975. By then the BLA had disappeared, although the previous year a tape recording from a group called the Black Liberation Army took credit for the murder of two young white men in Florida. Though the BLA has disappeared into prison, it is not likely to be forgotten, not by the police and not by the black convicts who make up a disproportionate part of the American prison population. Donald DeFreeze had proudly called his army "savage killers and madmen." The Black Liberation Army was just that—savage killers and madmen. The fig leaf of revolutionary proclamations could not hide the fact. Nor can other Americans hide from the fact that the same objective conditions which gave rise to the BLA still exist. It remains to be seen whether the practice of violence in the service of revolutionary rhetoric is only temporarily out of fashion among the black under class.[21]

To a degree the BLA murders were explicable, coming after a decade of militant rhetoric and the souring of the national commitment to greater social justice. In March 1977, an even more bizarre black movement staged one of America's most spectacular "terrorist" incidents, but hardly for revoluationary purposes. On March 9, 1977, at 11:00 a.m., six members of the black Hanafi Muslim sect seized a wing of the B'nai B'rith headquarters in downtown Washington, D.C. Three others took over offices in the Municipal Building and three more took control of the Islamic Center.

At the Municipal Building a black radio reporter was shot and killed, a City Councilman was shot in the chest, and another man was hit with a shotgun blast that paralyzed him from the waist down. At B'nai B'rith, employees were slashed or shot. Even after they had control, several of the Hanafis brutalized their hostages. They were members of a sect led by Hamaas Abdul Khaalis—born Ernest Timothy McGhee in Gary, Indiana—who had a long history of mental instability, not improved when rival Black Muslims murdered his family a year earlier. He had returned home to find the bodies of two adults and five children. At the killers' trial Khaalis was fined $750 for contempt of court, for he found the guilty verdict and life sentences insufficient. Justice had not been done. He wanted restitution, so like others he copied the tactics and techniques of the more spectacular transnational terrorists. The Hanafi struck, seized 134 hostages, and issued their demands: his $750 was to be returned, the film *Mohammed, Messenger of God* closed, and his family's killers handed over to him—the last clearly a nonnegotiable demand. What Khaalis was actually doing was structuring a psycho-drama at the expense of 134 innocent people, so that in a highly compressed period of catharsis, his anger could abate. Fortunately for everyone, there was in Washington a team of excellent hostage bargainers who realized that negotiation not a shoot-out would be possible. Aided by three Islamic ambassadors, the negotiators finally made a deal with Khaalis and after 39 hours the seige was over. The government agreed to let Khaalis remain free without bail pending trial, but he was soon arrested for making threats over a tapped telephone. He still had the $750, but *Mohammad* reopened and the processes of justice ground forward.

With the Hanafi seige we have come a long way from revolutionary terrorism. The only element that remains from the myth of revolutionary terrorism is the technique, which persists like the grin of the Cheshire cat after the body which gave life to it has disappeared. The techniques devised by revolutionary terrorists can be used by anyone with a private or political grudge, as was demonstrated again in suburban Cleveland in 1977. Cory C. Moore seized police captain Leo M. Keglovic and demanded to speak to the President of the United States; he also asked that all white persons vacate the planet. After 46 hours of negotiations the hostage was released and President Carter phoned. Cory Moore and the Hanafis and presidential assassins may commit ruthless acts and disrupt private and public life. It may or may not be appropriate to call them all terrorists, as law enforcement officials are wont to do. But they most certainly are not revolutionary terrorists, nor do they indicate anything about American society except that one of the concomitants of freedom is a vulnerability to violence used as personal therapy.

CONCLUSION

The tactics of terrorism have their political uses. The strong often have found them an effective means of intimidating the weak. American vigilantes, the Klan, and company police historically have used terror to the end in conflicts that are analyzed elsewhere in this book. More quixotic are attempts by the weak to intimidate the strong by violence, hoping even to topple them from power. Many contemporary uses of bombings, hostage-taking, assassination, and hijacking are so motivated. The rationale is provided by a mythology of revolutionary terrorism whose claim to credibility derives originally from the effective use of terror by radical nationalists in struggles to establish a handful of new nations, among them Israel, Vietnam, Algeria, and South Yemen. In all these instances the nationalists had wide support and won because the tactics of terror proved to be a catalyst in the process by which the foreign minority lost its political nerve. With the notable exception of the Palestinians and blacks of white-ruled southern Africa, though, the revolutionary terrorists of the 1970s are minorities of minorities: extremist factions of the nonrevolutionary left in Western democracies, tiny bands of militants among ethnic and religious minorities throughout the world. Their propaganda of the deed can be briefly but dramatically disruptive, and therefore will command far more public attention than a full-page ad in the *New York Times*. But politically such acts are not likely to win them public support or anything more than a mixed and unpredictabled response of repression and concessions, with the emphasis decidedly on the former.

Revolutionary terrorism in the United States has been derived entirely from foreign models. Puerto Rican nationalists have used its rhetoric and tactics in direct emulation of nationalists elsewhere in the Third World. Anti-Communist Cuban nationalists have mounted fitful campaigns of transnational terrorism from the United States in imitation of the Palestinians but with far less impact. Revolutionary terrorism on the political left in the United States has been a pale and feeble distortion of European and Latin practice. Revolutionary aspirations in America in the 1960s and 1970s were confined to a few intellectuals and campus activists. For the most part their interests were rhetorical not practical and their ideological analysis shallow by comparison with more broadly supported groups like the Tupamaros of Uruguay or the Red Brigades of Italy. Moreover the American revolutionaries could not, indeed would not, set aside the tactical liability of their humanitarianism. Revolutionary terrorists who have worked serious political damage elsewhere have had no compunctions about killing; the Weather Underground targeted buildings not people and its capacity to instill terror was sharply limited as a consequence. It is a favorable reflection on American political culture that even its most committed revolutionaries are not prepared to sacrifice all means to their ends.

The most exotic manifestations of revolutionary terrorism in the United States have cropped up in tiny bands of social misfits and outcasts like the Black Liberation Army, the Symbionese Liberation Army, and the Manson gang. Whereas the Weather Underground numbered hundreds of activists and thousands of sympathizers, these groups numbered a few dozens at most and operated without any visible basis of social support. Often as not their members were not only social misfits but psychologically deviant to the point of clinical insanity. The revolutionary rhetoric of these groups was simply a justification for personal therapy through violence, not a serious demand for political change.

If this interpretation is correct, the United States has been spared the worst excesses of revolutionary terrorism first because it has no smoldering internal nationalisms, and second because it has few if any violent-militant revolutionaries. The scattered episodes of revolutionary terrorism of the late 1960s and 1970s seem to have discredited the cause of political revolution even among its past and potential supporters. But the country does have a long, amply documented tradition of the use of violence for more limited social and political objectives, and for purely personal motives. The techniques of terrorism, stripped of their revolutionary rationale, can readily be adapted to these purposes. The helps explain the contemporary spate of hostage-taking, for example by the Hanafi Muslims and by various private individuals. The technique gained visibility from the dramatic exploits of transnational terrorists, which made it attractive to some Americans looking for a dramatic way to vent personal and social grievances.

In the foreseeable future the United States is likely to see more acts of nonrevolutionary terrorism. Whenever a new and dramatic form of violent political action emerges elsewhere in the world a rash of attempts can be expected to follow in the United States, provided they are within the means of the marginal people who are responsible for imitative terrorism. One basic reason why the long-feared advent of nuclear terrorism has not arrived may be that realistic terrorists fear its political repercussions while imitative would-be terrorists lack access to materials and technical skills. Since the United States is regarded as the archenemy in most of the revolutionary eschatologies of the rest of the world, it is possible that some European and Third World revolutionaries may attempt to bring their wars home to America. But indigenous revolutionary terrorism is unlikely on any substantial scale in America, with the single exception of the Puerto Ricans. Savage killers and madmen American society certainly has, but violent revolutionaries, no.

NOTES

1. See Henry David, *History of the Haymarket Affair* (New York: Russell and Russell, 1936, 1958); and Bernard R. Kogan, ed., *The Chicago Haymarket Riot: Anarchy on Trial* (Boston: D. C. Health, 1959).

2. Wayne G. Broehl, Jr., *The Molly Maguires* (Cambridge, Mass.: Harvard University Press, 1964); J. Walter Coleman, *The Molly Maguire Riots: Industrial Conflict in the Pennsylvania Coal Region* (Richmond, Va.: Garrett and Massie, 1936).

3. A brief historical survey of terrorism in the United States is Bernard K. Johnpoll, "Perspectives on Political Terrorism in the United States," in Yonah Alexander, ed., *International Terrorism: National, Regional, and Global Perspectives* (New York: Praeger, 1976), 30-45. On the nonrevolutionary nature of most terrorism in the United States, see National Advisory Committee on Criminal Justice Standards and Goals,*Disorders and Terrorism: Report of the Task Force on Disorders and Terrorism* (Washington, D.C., 1976), Ch. 1.

4. Paul Wilkinson, *Terrorism and the Liberal State* (New York: John Wiley, 1977), 49. A useful general discussion of concepts of terrorism is offered in *Disorders and Terrorism,* 3-7. A more fundamental distinction made by most analysts of political terrorism is between enforcement terror used by political authorities and agitational terror used by their opponents. See Thomas Thornton, "Terror as a Weapon of Political Agitation," in Harry Eckstein, ed., *Internal War: Problems and Approaches* (New York: Free Press, 1964), 71-99.

5. There is an enormous literature on the concepts and practice of contemporary terrorism. Edward F. Mickolus, *Annotated Bibliography on Transnational and International Terrorism* (Washington, D.C.: Central Intelligence Agency, 1976) is an unclassified document that includes 1,277 items. For a bibliographic essay, see J. Bowyer Bell, *A Time of Terror: How*

Democratic Societies Respond to Revolutionary Violence (New York: Basic Books, 1978), 280-285.

6. Narodnaya Volya (People's Will) was a terrorist faction of the Russian populist movement and is described in detail by Franco Venturi, *Roots of Revolution: A History of the Populist and Socialist Movements in the Nineteenth Century Russia* (New York: Grosset and Dunlap Universal Library, 1952, 1966), Ch. 21. Terrorism has more remote historical antecedents and parallels, for example, in the murderous acts of the thirteenth-century Islamic religious sect known as the Assassins, and the Reign of Terror imposed by the Jacobins in revolutionary France. See, for example, Albert Parry, *Terrorism from Robespierre to Arafat* (New York: Vanguard, 1976).

7. A comparative study of national liberation movements which puts the use of terrorist tactics into its larger political context is J. Bowyer Bell, *On Revolt: Strategies of National Liberation* (Cambridge, Mass.: Harvard University Press, 1976).

8. Research by the RAND Corporation shows that contemporary terrorists are likely to have immediate successes. The perpetrators of kidnapping and barricade operations have been able to get some or all their demands met in more than one-third of cases while major publicity is almost assured. See Brian Jenkins, Janera Johnson, and David Ronfeldt, *Numbered Lives: Some Statistical Observations from 77 International Hostage Episodes* (Santa Monica: Rand Corporation, P-5905, July 1977). But a more general study of terrorist campaigns throughout the world shows that they rarely achieve their ultimate political objectives; see Ted Robert Gurr, "Some Characteristics of Political Terrorism in the 1960s," in Michael Stohl, ed., *The Politics of Terror: A Reader in Theory and Practice* (New York: Marcel Dekker, 1979).

9. Three useful comparative studies of revolutionary terrorism and urban guerrilla warfare in Latin America are Ernest Duff and John McCamant, *Violence and Repression in Latin America* (New York: Free Press, 1976); James Kohl and John Litt, *Urban Guerrilla Warfare in Latin America* (Cambridge, Mass.: MIT Press, 1974); and John W. Sloan, "Political Terrorism in Latin America: A Critical Analysis," paper read to the Southwest Social Science Association Annual Meetings, Dallas, March 1977.

10. There are many studies of terrorism in specific Western countries, including some of the contributions in Alexander, op. cit., and Stohl, op. cit. A narrative survey of terrorism as reported in the world press from 1969 through 1974, organized by country, is Lester A. Sobel, ed., *Political Terrorism* (New York: Facts on File, 1975). Bell, op. cit., and Wilkinson, op. cit., are mainly concerned with terrorism in Western democracies.

11. Central Intelligence Agency, National Foreign Assessment Center, *International Terrorism in 1977* (Washington, D.C., RP 78-10255U, August 1978). Other trend studies include David L. Milbank, *Research Study: International and Transnational Terrorism: Diagnosis and Prognosis* (Washington, D.C.: Central Intelligence Agency, RP 76 10030, April 1976); Edward F. Mickolus, "Trends in Transnational Terrorism," in Stohl, op. cit.; Brian M. Jenkins and Janera A. Johnson, *International Terrorism: A Chronology, 1968-1974* (Santa Monica: RAND Corporation, R-1597-DOS/ARPA, March 1975); and *1974 Supplement* (Santa Monica: RAND Corporation, R-1909-1-ARPA, February 1976). Statistics in these studies are not in agreement because they use different definitions, categories, and information sources. The data in the 1978 CIA study appear to be comprehensive and internally consistent, but as in the other studies cited above the CIA data come from newspaper reports, which are not always accurate or complete.

12. A study of the foundations of the New Left is George R. Vickers, *The Formation of the New Left: The Early Years* (Lexington, Mass.: Lexington Books, 1975). A more impressionistic and less reliable account is Alan Adelson, *SDS: A Profile* (New York: Scribner's, 1972).

13. Data from U.S. Senate, *Riots, Civil and Criminal Disorders*, Hearings before the Permanent Subcommittee on Investigations of the Committee on Government Operations, 91st Congress, 2nd Session, Part 24, 1970, 5342.

14. On the transition to terrorism see Thomas Powers, *Diana, The Making of a Terrorist* (Boston: Houghton Mifflin, 1971).

15. Data from "Drive to Halt Terror Bombings," *U.S. News and World Report*, March 15, 1971: 17.

16. The pronouncements and exploits of the Weather Underground can be followed in the underground press, most recently in the Weatherwomen's newsletter *Osawotomie Notes*. A sympathetic retrospective interpretation of the New Left is Nigel Young, *An Infantile Disorder: The Crisis and Decline of the New Left* (Boulder, Colorado: Westview, 1977). A poignant account of life on the run in the underground is provided in two articles by Ron Rosenbaum in *New Times*, "On Board the Underground Railroad," May 30 (1975): 14-29; and "What Makes Abbie Run?" June 13 (1975): 32-41.

17. The case for Puerto Rican nationalism is put by Gordon Lewis, *Puerto Rico: Freedom and Power in the Caribbean* (New York: Monthly Review Press, 1963); and Juan Angel Silén, *We, the Puerto Rican People: A Story of Oppression and Resistance* (New York: Monthly Review Press, 1971); and Rubén Berríos Martínez, "Independence for Puerto Rico: The Only Solution," *Foreign Affairs*, 55 (April 1977): 561-583.

18. See Peter Nabokov, *Tijerina and the Courthouse Raid* (Berkeley: Rampart Press, 1970).

19. On the psychological characteristics of contemporary American killers, see Hans Toch, *Violent Men: An Inquiry into the Psychology of Violence* (Chicago: Aldine, 1969); and Lawrence Zelic Freeman, "Violent Activists," in Ted Robert Gurr, ed., *Handbook of Conflict Theory and Research* (New York: Free Press, forthcoming). An account of the Manson Family and their murders is Vincent Bugliosi and Curt Gentry, *Helter Skelter* (New York: Bantam, 1975). A sociological profile of 350 terrorists in countries outside the United States has been compiled from news sources by Charles A. Russell and Bowman H. Miller, "Profile of a Terrorist," *Terrorism: An International Journal*, 1, (1977): 17-34.

20. Of the many popular accounts of the Symbionese Liberation Army, see especially Vin McLelland and Paul Avery, *The Voices of Guns* (New York: Putnam, 1974); and David Boulton, *The Making of Tania: The Patty Hearst Story* (London: New English Library, 1975).

21. On the Black Liberation Army, see Robert Daley, *Target Blue* (New York: Delacorte Press, 1973).

Part 4
Perspectives on Crime in the United States

INTRODUCTION

Protest, riot, and rebellion contribute little to mortality rates in the United States. Their effects, like their origins, are mainly social and political. Individual acts of violence are far more pervasive and much more likely to disrupt the lives of ordinary Americans. In 1974, when crime rates were at a peak, police recorded one murder, three rapes, 23 major assaults, and 22 robberies for every 10,000 Americans, which represented an increase of greater than 300 percent in little more than a decade. "Crime" is a matter of social and legal definition, of course, but the people of every society recognize violent, unprovoked attacks and theft of personal possessions as *mala in res*, acts which are intrinsically bad. There are no crime-free utopias; some such offenses occur in every reach of every society. But there is much evidence that the incidence of crimes against persons and property varies enormously from one place to another and from one historical era to another. The three chapters in this part describe and interpret some of these variations.

Much recent writing about the crime problems of the United States has centered on the inadequacy of official crime statistics. Since many offenses go unrecorded, especially minor ones, and since police treatment of citizens' reports and offenders varies, it is understandable that many skeptics and critics concluded in the 1960s that the image of rising crime was exaggerated. Some went so far as to argue that the crime problem was a fiction foisted on the public by law-enforcement officials and the mass media.[1] A decade later we have better information on the extent of crime in contemporary America, thanks in part to national survey studies of victims, and we also have better evidence on historical trends in crime in this and other Western countries. The gist of this evidence, some of it surveyed in Chapters 13 and 14, is that the skeptics of the 1960s were all too skeptical. By concentrating on the immediate evidence of imprecision in official statistics, many of them overlooked a real and serious increase in nasty social behavior. We now know that, even though it was not precisely measured by the FBI Uniform Crime Reports, the increase was all too real. Once recognized as a social reality, and studied in context, it becomes clear that it was neither unprecedented, nor inexplicable, nor without remedy.

Two general propositions are advanced by Ted Robert Gurr in discussing the history of violent crime in Chapter 13. First, violent crime seems to have been declining in Western societies for a very long while—in England apparently for seven centuries—but the long-term trend has been temporarily reversed on numerous occasions. The American crime wave of the 1960s was not unique but had historical precedents in the United States and contemporary parallels in almost all other Western democracies. In Britain and Scandinavia, rates of increase in common crime far outpaced the United States during this decade. This raises the second problem, which is how to explain these short-term tidal waves of crime that rise above the declining trend. Two immediately relevant factors are war and temporary increases in numbers of young males, though explanation by no means stops here. The causal conditions seem to be so potent in their criminogenic effects that police, courts, and prisons can do relatively little about them except ride the tide.

But the tides of rising crime *do* subside. Wesley Skogan provides a detailed study of the texture of contemporary American crime in Chapter 14, in which he shows that serious offenses leveled off in 1974 and began an apparent decline. Victimization surveys and official statistics both document the accuracy of many common beliefs about serious crime in America. It is concentrated disproportionately in larger cities, the offenders (and victims) are even more disproportionately black, and the arrestees are mostly young males. The proportion of young women arrested for property crime (but not violent crime) has sharply increased too. The beginnings of a downward trend are closely linked to two conditions. First, large American cities are rapidly losing population. As they do so, their crime rates are falling ever more rapidly, perhaps because the relative conditions of life for remaining residents are improving. Second, the proportion of youths in the 15-26 year bracket, which shot up sharply in the 1960s, has turned downward. Declining birth rates for both whites and blacks point toward a continuing shrinkage in the size of the group which provides such a large share of both offenders and victims of serious crime.

In Chapter 15 Sheldon Hackney addresses a rather different question: why have homicides long been proportionally more common in the Southeastern states than in the North, Midwest, or Far West? This classic study was written in the 1960s and relies mainly on older data, but there is no reason to think that the traditional pattern has changed fundamentally. Southerners, both black and white, are more disposed to homicide (and less to suicide) than black and white residents of other regions. Hackney tests alternative explanations of the pattern but finds that neither racial composition nor poverty, level of urbanization, nor anomie explains away the difference. Instead, he interprets the pattern as evidence of a persisting regional subculture and speculates about the ways in which it came into existence and why it persists. The Southern heritage, he concludes, is one of "grace and violence," and while other scholars have not always agreed with his conclusions, this assessment will continue to stimulate and inform research on the distinctive character of the American South.[2]

NOTES

1. A study which surveys and to some extent shares these skeptical views is Fred P. Graham, "A Contemporary History of American Crime," Ch. 13 in the 1969 edition of *Violence in America*.

2. Other recent studies of violence in Southern culture are John Shelton Reed, "To Live—and Die—in Dixie: A Contribution to the Study of Violence," *Political Science Quarterly*, 86 (September 1971): 429-43; and Raymond D. Gastil, "Homicide and a Regional Culture of Violence," *American Sociological Review*, 36 (June 1971): 412-27. A critical assessment of all these studies is Colin Loftin and Robert H. Hill, "Regional Subculture and Homicide: An Examination of the Gastil-Hackney Thesis," *American Sociological Review*, 39 (October 1974): 714-24.

Chapter 13

On the History of Violent Crime in Europe and America

TED ROBERT GURR

Great social and demographic changes seem to work profound changes on patterns of crime. This is especially true of the most personally threatening kinds of offenses: murder and assault, robbery and rape. Looking back at the historical traces of crime and crime control in Western societies, we can dimly see the shapes of tidal waves of violent crime, many decades apart, which far overshadow the short-run ebbs and flows described as "crime waves" by contemporary journalists and officials. In the United States one of these tidal waves may have crested in the 1970s, as Wesley Skogan argues in the next chapter, but its passing—if indeed it does pass—will leave in its wake a persisting debate about its origins and profound anxiety about the future among crime-scared Americans. What I shall try to do in this chapter is interpret America's experience of violent crime by comparison with what has happened in other Western societies in the recent and more distant past. The historical and comparative record should help dispel the notion that America's contemporary social problems, along with her tattered virtues, are somehow unique. And while this record does not point to unambiguous explanations for rising crime, it does suggest that some common-sense explanations are more plausible than others.

England is the chief source of American legal codes and institutions of criminal justice, so we shall begin there.

THE ENGLISH EXPERIENCE

Crimes against persons and property leave victims, not statistical records. The court records on which most historical analysis relies are a gauge of the success of victims, witnesses, and constables in bringing offenders to justice, not a direct measure of the extent of crime. Some variations in the records may be due to quirks of official procedures or to changing law and judicial practice. Still, most historians are reasonably confident that court records of the most serious offenses correlate with

AUTHOR'S NOTE: *The author is Payson S. Wild Professor of political science at Northwestern University. His many books and monographs include* Why Men Rebel, *which won the* Woodrow Wilson *Prize as the best book in political science of 1970, and* Rogues, Rebels, and Reformers: A Political History of Urban Crime and Conflict *(Sage Publications, 1976).*

the true incidence of crime. They also conclude that when courts record large changes over time in the volume of serious offenses brought to trial, they usually are responding to real changes in the extent of crime.[1]

A recent study of some remarkably complete thirteenth-century records shows convincingly that murderous brawls and violent deaths at the hands of robbers were everyday occurrences in medieval England. The annual murder rates ranged from 10 to 25 per 100,000 population in rural counties—with the average nearer the higher figure than the lower one. The comparable rate for England and Wales now is 1.97 per 100,000 (in 1974) while in the United States it is 9.77 (1974). One remarkable feature of medieval homicide, from our perspective, is that it was most common in villages and isolated farmsteads. The homicide rates in the small cities of Bristol and London were lower by half, just the opposite of our contemporary pattern of crime-ridden cities and orderly towns and countryside.[2]

By almost all accounts the medieval period in all Europe was a violent and brutal age whose chronicles and letters, as Given remarks, are "filled with stories of murder and rapine."[3] In fact his data for England suggest that homicide rates were increasing during the thirteenth century. But then the view is clouded over and nearly 400 years pass before we find another longitudinal study. Beattie has traced the incidence of crime from 1660 to 1800 through the court records of two English counties, rural Sussex and suburban Surrey, which includes London south of the Thames. In this era crimes against persons and property were considerably more numerous in urban parishes than rural ones, judging by numbers of indictments per 100,000 population. Trends were also somewhat different between town and country, suggesting that different socioeconomic forces were at work. But one general pattern stands out. From 1660 to c. 1720 the trend in indictments for serious crimes held steady or declined in both counties. Then, between the 1720s and the 1760s, came a series of sharp but temporary increases, some of them as great as 400 percent: the peaks in urban assault occurred in the 1720s, 1730s, and again in the 1760s; in rural assault in the 1730s; in property crime in the 1740s and 1750s. After these peaks the rates declined for a generation or more, only to begin a sharp across-the-board rise just before 1800.[4] Beattie's study ends here at the threshold of the modern era. Concern about crime in nineteenth-century England was now centered in the cities, above all in London. The disorderly metropolis was the crucible in which present-day English and American policies and institutions of criminal justice were forged.

By the 1820s London was Europe's largest city, the commercial and political hub of the world's most prosperous society and greatest empire. It was also a dangerous, crime-ridden place. Professional robbers and receivers flourished in neighborhoods where it was worth a prosperous man's life and possessions to venture at night. Thousands of street urchins lived by petty theft during the day and slept in the noisome alleyways and courtyards. A contemporary writer summed up London's squalor and disorder when he denounced the city as "the infernal wen."[5]

The criminal laws designed to control the rampant crime of Georgian England had a harsh bite. The death penalty was specified for more than 200 offenses, on the widely accepted principle that severe punishment was an effective deterrent. But no centralized, professional police force existed to catch offenders. Constables, professional "thief-takers," and private citizens hailed petty offenders before magistrates who were seldom trained in law and were often venal. The judges who heard serious cases had neither the legal discretion nor the inclination to be lenient. The defendant's hopes rested with the reluctance of many a jury to convict in capital cases, or the mercy of the crown in commuting his death sentence to transportation to the Australian penal colonies. Such prisons as existed aimed neither to punish nor rehabilitate. Gaols (the Americans spelled it "jails") held debtors and those waiting to be tried or executed; the bridewells put vagrants and other petty offenders to forced labor for the profit of their officials.

Between the 1820s and the 1870s this hodgepodge was transformed into a modern system of criminal justice. A series of parliamentary acts overhauled the criminal law, penalties were prescribed in proportion to the seriousness of the offense, the death penalty was abolished for all crimes except murder and treason. London's patchwork police services of river police and Bow Street runners, constables and parish watchmen, were replaced in 1829 by the centralized Metropolitan Police. The courts were improved. Beginning in the 1850s, child thieves were committed to new reformatories and kept there long enough to receive basic education and work training. Adult offenders were sentenced to long terms in the new convict prisons, where discipline was harsh and rehabilitation piously sought through hard, monotonous labor.

The zeal of London's new "bobbies" showed up at first in increased arrests and convictions. But by the 1850s common crime seemed on the decline and by the end of Queen Victoria's reign in 1901, the city was thought by the English and visiting continentals alike to be one of the most orderly in all Europe. The official statistics suggest to social historians that the trend continued till the late 1920s, when the conviction rate for all indictable (serious) offenses was one-ninth of the eighteen-forties level. Police statistics on known offenses and arrests, first published in 1869, are especially convincing. Known serious offenses fell by an average of 10 percent per decade for 60 years thereafter. The arrest rate for all offenses, serious and petty ones, was down by a ratio of three to one despite a steady increase in the absolute and proportional size of the Metropolitan Police force. Data on convictions show assault down by a ratio of five to one, total theft by four to one, robbery by more than ten to one. Burglary was the only serious offense to go against the trends, thanks to the activities of a small cadre of professional housebreakers who became increasingly successful at eluding the police.[6]

London was the bellwether for all England and Wales. Professional police forces on the London model were established throughout the country by mid-century. Court reform and the new prison system operated nationwide. The incidence of crime may have reached its peak as early as the 1820s, but the peak in official action, as registered by numbers of trials and convictions, occurred in the 1840s. Thereafter all the national indicators of crime and punishment declined steadily, parallel to those of the Metropolitan Police district.

Serious crime reached it lowest recorded ebb in London late in the 1920s. During the Great Depression which followed, burglary thrived while the war years from 1940 to 1945 saw sharp increases in murder, assault, and robbery. In 1945-1946 the ranks of the Metropolitan Police were expanded from their wartime low, and returning veterans, who were responsible for at least part of the crime problem, soon found their ways into jobs or prisons. So serious crime subsided after 1946, but only for a few years. Early in the 1950s an inexorable increase began. In the 25 years after 1950 indictable offenses known to police in London grew by 450 percent, with the nastiest kinds of crimes increasing most sharply. From 1950 to 1974 murders were up 300 percent, rape by 600 percent, assault by 900 percent, and robbery by 1,200 percent. In this period as in the nineteenth century, London led the way for all England and Wales. Countrywide crime rates were lower but the rates of increase were very much the same.

The evidence sketched above points to three great surges of violent crime in England, roughly a century apart. They crested in the mid-1700s, in the 1830s and 1840s, and perhaps in the 1970s. Figure 13.1 shows London's incidence of higher-court convictions for murder and assault from the 1830s, when they averaged 12 per year per 100,000 people, to the 1920s, when they were less than 2 per 100,000. It also shows the sharp increase in murder and manslaughter known to police which began c. 1955 and reached 18 per 100,000 by 1974. Assaults known to police are literally off the graph. In 1950 they were reported at the rate of 13 per 100,000, by 1974 they exceeded 120 per 100,000. This does not mean that the 1970s were more violent in London than the 1830s, since far more offenses come to police attention than ever culminate in convictions. The national trends since 1945 in crimes against persons and serious theft are shown in Figure 13.3. The lowest recorded rate in the 30-year period is set at 1.00 so that each increase of one unit on the vertical axis represents an increase of 100 percent in the rate of crime.

The recent peaks in English crime are so dramatic that they obscure a much longer-term trend which is of equal or greater importance. It is the decline in violent crime, which is evident from the homicide rates summarized in Table 13.1. Homicide rates were three times higher in the thirteenth century than the seventeenth, three times higher in the seventeenth century than the nineteenth, and in London they were twice as high in the early nineteenth century as they are now. The decline in homicide has been particularly great in the towns and rural areas. And though Londoners today are more murderous than in the recent past, the metropolis remains a far safer place than it was in earlier centuries.

This brief survey of the English historical evidence suggests two patterns in need of explanation: the long-run decline in interpersonal violence, and the short-run peaks in serious crimes against persons and property. A plausible one-word explanation for the decline in homicide is "civilization" and all that it implies about the restraint of aggressive impulses and the acceptance of humanistic values. By their own accounts medieval people were easily angered to the point of violence and enmeshed in a culture which accepted, even glorified many forms of brutality and violence. The progress of Western civilization has been marked by increasing internal and external controls on the show of violence. People are socialized to control and displace anger. Norms of conduct in almost all organized activity stress nonviolent means of accomplishing goals. Interpersonal violence within the community and nation is prohibited and punished in almost all circumstances. None of this was true of medieval society, in England or on the Continent, and the changes occurred gradually and selectively. The process contributed not only to the decline in homicide but the decline and ultimate abandonment of executions in most Western

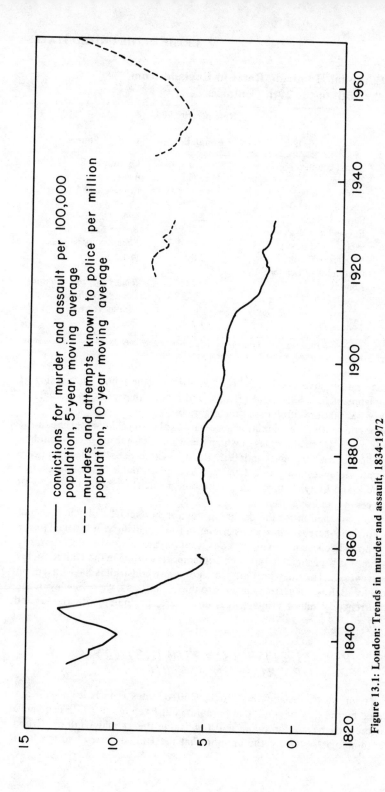

Figure 13.1: London: Trends in murder and assault, 1834-1972

Legend (within figure):
— convictions for murder and assault per 100,000 population, 5-year moving average
--- murders and attempts known to police per million population, 10-year moving average

Source: work cited in note 6, pp. 371-372.

Table 13.1: Annual Homicide Rates in England from
             the 13th to the 20th Centuries

Date	Locale	Rate per 100,000 Population[a]	Source
c. 1250	5 rural counties	c. 20	Given, note 2
c. 1200	London	c. 12	ibid.
1663-65	Surrey County (incl. S. London)	6.1	Beattie, note 4
1722-24	Surrey County	2.3	ibid.
1821-30	England and Wales excluding Middlesex	1.48	British Sessional Papers, various years
1821-30	Middlesex County (incl. most of London)	2.09	ibid.
1921-30	London	0.73[a]	Report of the Commissioner of Police. . . . various years
1966-72	London	1.29[a]	ibid.

a. Rates before 1900 are calculated from committals to trial for murder and manslaughter; rates after 1900 are calculated from cases known to police. Known offenses and committals are only approximately comparable.

societies, the end of slavery and the brutalization of wage labor, the passing of corporal punishment in schools and prisons, and many other positive features of contemporary life that are often taken for granted.[7]

How far does this cultural explanation go toward explaining changing crime rates? It is plausible to apply it to all crimes in which force and violence are used, including assault, rape, armed robbery, and vandalism. But it is scarcely applicable to property crimes without violence, and in fact there is reason to think that offenses like burglary, fraud, and petty theft march to different music: they seem to vary with economic necessity and opportunity.[8]

The cultural explanation for the declining trend in homicidal violence does not explain the episodic increases in serious crimes in English history. It is trivial to say that they occurred because the civilizing constraints on aggression were temporarily relaxed, just as it is superficial to attribute contemporary crime in the United States to "permissiveness." The questions are which of many constraints have eased, on whom, and why. Before suggesting answers to these questions, we review evidence for the occurrence of major crime waves elsewhere, beginning with the United States.

PERSPECTIVES ON THE HISTORY OF CRIME IN AMERICA

Studies of crime's patterns and trends in the United States as a whole have always been hindered by the lack of good, comparable data. Even in the 1960s, some 30 years after the FBI began compiling and publishing the annual Uniform Crime Reports, criminologists were of the opinion that the United States had the least reliable crime data of all Western societies.[9] The key reason is not political malfeasance or bureaucratic ineptitude—though those factors have played a part—but rather the localized character of policing and criminal justice administration in the United States. There are sharp differences among cities and regions in police efficiency, procedures, and statistical recording practices. Only gradually and grudgingly has the reporting of data on offenses known to police and arrests become more uniform across the country. And even now there is no regular, comprehensive reporting on criminal indictments and convictions in the United States, though the English have compiled such data since 1805.

The history of crime in the United States has been most thoroughly studied in cities where urban police and court records exist in greatest depth and detail. We know most about crime trends in Massachusetts, especially Boston and Salem, beginning in the 1820s. The general trend traced by data on arrests is summarized by Roger Lane: "serious crime in metropolitan Boston has declined sharply between the middle of the 19th century and the middle of the 20th." The decline is most pronounced with respect to murder and assault. Boston's murder arrest rate peaked above 7.0 per 100,000 c. 1860 and was less than 2.0 in 1950, as shown in Figure 13.2. The arrest rate for assault declined by a 4 to 1 ratio over the same period. Other offenses show different trends. Rape steadily increased over the century, perhaps because victims became more willing to report offenses. Burglaries and robberies decreased raggedly during the latter part of the nineteenth century but jumped sharply during the First World War and the Great Depression. Moreover the rate of arrests for petty offenses moved pronouncedly upwards from the 1840s onward, almost entirely because of increasing drunk and disorderly arrests. Drunkenness was a dire problem in nineteenth-century American cities, as it was in much of Europe. Tolerated at first, it gained increasing attention from the temperance movement and the police. The rise of professional policing and the decline of serious crime both helped city police in Boston and elsewhere give greater attention to controlling public drunkenness.[10]

Boston's trend of declining serious crime from the 1860s to the 1950s parallels the century of improving public order in London and all England and Wales. Moreover it was accompanied by similar reforms in the criminal justice system, especially the professionalization and expansion of the Boston police. But what the decline actually represents, as we have seen in England, is the ebb from a great wave of crime. The peak in England occurred in the 1830s and 1840s; in Boston and other American cities the upsurge began in the 1850s and crested in the 1870s. In both societies the onset of the waves precedes the introduction of comprehensive systems of recording crime data, so the precise timing, magnitude, and composition of the increase is difficult to ascertain. But the converging evidence of different American studies is convincing about the fact of the wave. Ferdinand's study of Boston begins in 1849, and virtually every arrest indicator he uses shows two sharp increases after 1849, the first peaking in 1855-1859 and the second around 1870, with a lull during or immediately after the Civil War years (see Figure 13.2). The overall rate of increase in arrests for major crime in the 20 years after 1849 was roughly 300 percent.[11] Another study of Boston which uses arrests for property offenses pushes our knowledge back to the 1820s: low crime rates in 1849 were not a fluke but seemingly the result of a gradual decline in property crime that had been underway for a generation.[12] In a parallel study of Salem, Massachusetts, Ferdinand found that assault rates and serious offenses generally went sharply upward in the 1860s and 1870s before begining the now familiar irregular, long-term decline. Powell reports a similar rise in crimes against the person in Buffalo, New York, beginning in the 1850s and peaking out c. 1870.[13] Two other cities whose early arrest data show a rise beginning in the 1850s are New York and New Orleans.[14] In fact I have found no historical study of American crime for this period whose evidence traces any other pattern, though of all the scholars cited only Powell regards the wave as in any way exceptional or worth explaining.[15]

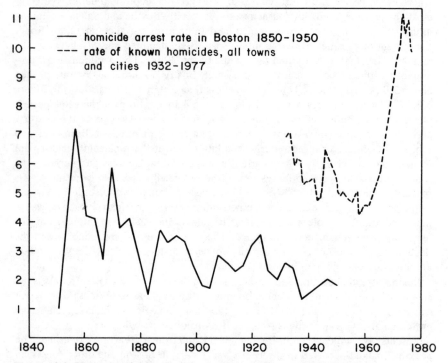

Figure 13.2: Urban homicide trends in the United States per 100,000 population

Sources: Boston: Theodore N. Ferdinand, article cited in note 8, p. 372; all cities: FBI Uniform Crime Reports.

The gradual ebb in urban American crime from 1870 to 1940 is more evident in studies which begin in 1850 than those which begin at the turn of the twentieth century. In the 1920s many Americans were convinced that a crime wave was in progress because, just before the First World War, serious offenses against persons and property began to increase and continued upward until the onset of the Great Depression. The reversal is evident in a number of the city studies cited above and is most clearly documented in a study by Sutherland and Gehlke which spans the period from 1900 to 1930. In five major cities they find that homicide, robbery, and burglary arrests all increased from 1910 to the late 1920s by as much as 500 percent. But they are skeptical about the persistence of the trend and critical of journalistically inspired emotionalism about crime rates.[16] In retrospect, their contention that the crest had passed before 1930 was correct. A later study of Chicago from 1919 to 1939 by Willbach shows that arrest rates for crimes against persons peaked in 1927 followed by a 3:1 decline in the next twelve years. The same author's careful study of New York during this period gives similar results.[17] And the FBI's Uniform Crime Report show that for the country as a whole the period from 1933 to 1940 was one of declining crime.

After 1940 serious crime in the United States followed trends similar to those in England. Personal and property crime both edged up during the Second World War, reaching a plateau in the late 1940s. (In England they declined after the war; in the United States they merely leveled off.) The renewed upward trend which has inspired so much contemporary controversy, fear, and "law and order" crime policies began early in the 1950s. Property crime rates moved up first; the combined rate of known burglaries and armed robberies quadrupled between 1950 and 1974. Crimes against persons did not turn sharply upward until after 1960. The trend in urban murder rates from 1932 to 1977 is compared with Boston's historical record in Figure 13.2. Not much can be made of the difference between Boston and other cities because known offenses and arrests are not precisely comparable. More important is the evidence that the urban murder rate increased by 250 percent between the late 1950s and 1973, the year which marks the apparent peak in violent crime.

The American historical evidence is too shallow to allow us to determine whether there is a long-term secular trend of declining interpersonal violence analogous to England's 700-year trend of falling murder rates. But the evidence of periodic waves of serious crime in both countries is unmistakable. Their most recent crime waves coincided with one another, but historically they did not, which suggests that if the waves have common causes or dynamics, they can operate in ways unique to one society *and* simultaneously among them. Before explanations are considered, we will look for evidence of similar crime trends and waves in crime in other Western societies.

CRIME IN OTHER WESTERN SOCIETIES

England's experience of successful crime control in the nineteenth and early twentieth centuries has parallels in other Western countries. In New South Wales, at literally the opposite end of the earth, colonial officials followed England's lead in reforming criminal justice and the police during the second and third quarters of the nineteenth century, and indicators of serious crime fell by ratios of ten to one and more. Since Australia's crime problems were imported from England in the form of transported convicts, it is scarcely surprising that crime rates fell when the convict population declined simultaneously with the introduction of more rational and humane treatment of offenders.[18] It is more surprising to find in Stockholm—a far smaller city in a very different society—a long-run pattern precisely like that of England and New South Wales. High rates of serious crime and the reforming impulse coincided in Sweden in the second quarter of the nineteenth century and the results were much the same. In the century between the 1840s and the 1930s the rate of convictions for crimes against persons in Stockholm declined by a ratio of about four to one and thefts by five to one. Moreover the most serious offenses declined more sharply than the less serious ones.[19]

Elsewhere in Europe crime trends were rather different. In France, the national rate of convictions for serious property crimes declined irregularly from the 1820s to the early 1960s, with temporary increases during and after the Franco-Prussian War of 1870-1871 and the First and Second World Wars. The rate of serious offenses against the person did not decline, however. Conviction rates for murder and grave assaults were as high in the 1920s as the 1820s, and as low in the 1860s as the 1950s. On the other hand, trials for petty assaults increased throughout the nineteenth century, probably because of increased official attention, not real changes in interpersonal violence.[20] In Germany, which did not become a unitary state until 1871, the property and personal crime rates moved gradually upward from 1882 until just before the onset of the First World War.[21] One consequence of military defeat and demobilization in postwar Germany and the remnants of the Austro-Hungarian Empire was a massive wave of personal and property crime, which subsided later in the 1920s.[22] We remarked above the postwar increase in crime in France, but it was of far lesser magnitude than in Germanic Europe.

The countries most affected by the Second World War also had short-lived "crime waves" during the war and its immediate aftermath, but everywhere the effects were temporary. The most remarkable postwar phenomenon is the near-universality of rising crime in Western societies during the 1960s and early 1970s. The British and North American experience is in no way unique. The late 1940s and early 1950s marked the low ebb of common crime in virtually every English-speaking country. Thereafter the trends were consistently upward. Some data on known offenses in five countries are given in Table 13.2. The rates of offense are quite different in any given year but not too much should be made of the differences since national crime-counting systems differ. Trends within each country are more realiably assessed than absolute differences among them. The trends can be reliably compared and in these countries all of them are strongly positive. In the United States homicides and assaults together increased at an average of 12 percent per year for a generation. Elsewhere the 1950s rates for these offenses were initially lower but the increases have been swifter. The rising trends in theft have been sustained just as long, and averaged between 8 and 14 percent per annum from 1950 to the 1970s. Moreover the most serious forms of property crime—robbery and burglary—rose about twice as rapidly as total theft in all these societies. Ireland seems the most favored country in this comparison. Its relatively low volume of crime may be credited to its Gaelic culture, religious traditionalism, or simply its small urban population. But these conditions did not inhibit the Irish from emulating the growing Anglo-American fondness for mayhem and theft during the 1960s.

Scandinavia provides another set of evidence, with Stockholm serving as a historical laboratory. Unlike London, the Great Depression of the 1930s had little effect on the Swedish capital's crime rates. During wartime, crime in neutral Stockholm rose and then subsided—until about 1950. Since then virtually every category of offense against persons and property has skyrocketed. These are some

Table 13.2: Crime Trends in English-Speaking Countries since 1950

Known Murder and Assaults per 100,000 population

	1950	c.1960	1970s[a]	Average Annual Increase
England and Wales	13.0	32.4	144.3	40%
London	13.0	26.2	123.5	35%
United States	58.0	91.2	237.4	12%
New South Wales	no data	15.5	21.7	4%
Canada	no data	158.2	436.0	13%
Republic of Ireland	5.9	13.7	38.3	24%

Known Theft per 100,000 Population

	1950	c.1960	1970s[a]	Average Annual Increase
England and Wales	847	1,317	3,659	13%
London	1,056	1,942	3,624	10%
United States	1,108	1,786	5,002	14%
New South Wales	no data	604	1,467	14%
Canada	no data	1,408	3,883	13%
Republic of Ireland	346	472	1,065	9%

a. Data for 1974 except England and Wales (1975), United States (1976), New South Wales (1970), and Ireland (1973).

20-year increases in crimes known to police: murder and murder attempts, 600 percent; assault and battery, more than 300 percent; rape and attempted rape, 300 percent; "crimes inflicting damage" (i.e., vandalism), 500 percent; all theft, 350 percent; robberies alone, 1,000 percent; fraud and embezzlement, 700 percent. In 1971, there was one theft reported to police for every eleven inhabitants of the city, which can be compared with 1974 figures of one per 20 Londoners, and one per 18 New Yorkers. In fairness to Stockholmers, they are more likely to report thefts to their trusted police than are cynical New Yorkers. The point remains that the Swedish welfare and criminal justice policies, which reformers credited for the historical improvement in public order, have not inhibited the contemporary rise of urban crime.

Stockholm represents in most severe form a criminal malaise that affected all of Scandinavia. Some comparative data are shown on Table 13.3. At the national level, crimes against persons started up later and more slowly than in Stockholm or the English-speaking countries, but there is no mistaking the presence of an escalating trend. The same is true of property crime. Moreover, we find in Scandinavia a phenomenon familiar from the English-speaking countries: the most serious property offenses have increased far more steeply than common theft. In Sweden, from 1950 to 1974, known theft increased by a multiple of three while the rarer offense of robbery grew tenfold. In Finland, from 1961 to 1973, the proportional increases were: all theft, 275 percent; robbery, 720 percent.

In the heartland of Western Europe that portrait of crime is significantly different in one major respect. There are no long-term increases in murder and assault in the

Table 13.3: Crime Trends in Scandinavian Countries since 1950

Known Assault and Murders per 100,000 Population

	1950	c.1960	1970s[a]	Average Annual Increase
Denmark	41.2	39.2	66.7	2%
Finland	no data	127.9	282.0	9%
Norway	no data	52.4	91.8	5%
Sweden	115.7	126.4	260.7	5%
Stockholm	90.7	266.5	403.2	16%

Known Theft per 100,000 Population

	1950	c.1960	1970s[a]	Average Annual Increase
Denmark	1,922	2,332	4,868	6%
Finland	no data	886	2,850	15%
Norway	no data	748	1,740	9%
Sweden	1,568	2,726	4,958	9%
Stockholm	1,933	4,250	8,215	15%

a. Data 1974-75 except Stockholm (1971).

continental democracies. Congratulations are premature, though, since Germany and France both began to move up in the late 1960s, too recently to certify the existence of an enduring trend. Property crime on the Continent is more of a piece with the English and Scandinavian experience. Theft rates began to rise later, sometime between 1955 and 1965, depending on the country. Since then the official statistics document steadily rising trends into the mid-1970s—with the sole exception of Switzerland, where theft rates have held essentially steady since 1945. These generalization about the continental countries neatly encompass Israel's experience as well.[23]

From the Marxist-Leninist point of view, this evidence of the rising tide of disorder in Western societies is the harbinger of capitalism's long-awaited collapse. The Eastern European commentators who offer this interpretation no doubt are uncomfortably aware that their own societies are suffering a similar affliction. How serious it is neither we nor they can say, since the European Communist states have not published sufficient statistical information to determine the trends.[24]

There is finally the case of Japan, an industrialized democratic society which has had unparalleled success in reducing crime rates—serious crime most of all—during the last two decades. Since 1955, Japan's murder and assault rates have both been halved. Simple theft has been reduced by about a quarter, known white-collar crime has been reduced to one-fifth its former levels, while the robbery rate is scarcely one-tenth of what it was in 1949-1950.

This pattern of change duplicates what happened in England, Sweden, and Australia between the 1840s and the 1920s: as public order improved, serious offenses declined more rapidly than petty ones. And it is the reverse of what has happened in contemporary Western societies, in which serious property crime has increased far faster than petty offenses.

These contrasts and images imply that a fairly high level of petty theft is endemic to prosperous societies, but that serious crime is not. Japan is a case in point. It is a capitalistic society which has had extraordinary success in reducing the incidence of murder, assault, and robbery. The improvement has been a sustained one—some 25 years in duration—and it has taken place in a society undergoing the rapid social and economic changes that elsewhere are assumed to be criminogenic.[25]

EXPLANATIONS OF CRIME

There are many hotly debated explanations of criminal behavior. Some blame the individual: the "criminal" is genetically or morally flawed. At the other end of the spectrum, officials are blamed: they selectively label certain acts deviant and those who engage in them criminal, for whom the stigma becomes a self-fulfilling prophecy.[26]

We want to explain, not individual behavior, but rather the periodic waves of serious crime which punctuate the history of many Western societies. Most explanations are specific to particular societies and periods. Many of them echo prevailing conservative, liberal, or radical views of society. The liberal explanations of rising crime in contemporary English-speaking societies are especially numerous. Substantial social and economic inequalities exist in all these societies, despite their general prosperity. Everywhere the penal system is harshly criticized because prisons are "schools for crime" which brutalize offenders rather than rehabilitating them. The police are often accused of corruption and a heavy-handed disregard for civil liberties. Add to this the special explanations preferred by social analysts confronted with rising crime in particular countries. Britain? Class tensions in a static economy. The United States? An angry black under class, its hopes stirred by promises of a Great Society which never arrived. Ireland? Modernization is eroding traditional acceptance of poverty and authority. Australia? Merely beery, exuberant youths challenging unpopular police.

If there is any universal truth to these kinds of conventional liberal wisdom about the social origins of crime, the Scandinavian countries surely should be more favored than some of the English-speaking nations. They are ethnically homogenous and their social ethos is strongly egalitarian. Their cities are free of slums and their social services are among the best in the world. Economically they have prospered since the end of the Second World War and have had low unemployment. Their police are widely respected, justice is ordinarily even-handed and efficient. Rehabilitation is the central aim of their penal system. But we have already seen that crime in Scandinavia has risen at rates comparable to those of English-speaking societies. Egalitarianism and social well-being may account for their lesser rates of increase in violent crime. They have not inhibited the growth of serious or petty theft in the least.

In pop and radical sociology it has been fashionable to blame rising crime rates on intensified policing and more thorough crime-reporting systems. Contemporary examples of both can be found: there are wide fluctuations in police attention to "victimless" crimes like prostitution and drug abuse, while changes in reporting systems produce abrupt discontinuities in crime statistics.[27] But neither explanation accounts for persistent trends up or down in the rate of common crime. If this explanation for the rising tide of theft and assault were to be taken seriously, we would have to suppose that the police forces of almost every Western society began a sustained expansion in manpower, detection, and crime reporting in the 1950s and 1960s. In none of our city or country studies is there evidence of such changes. These reforms occurred in European societies in the nineteenth century, not in the midtwentieth century, and they coincided with falling rates of common crime, not increasing ones. Also, common crimes come to police attention through reports of private citizens. If rising crime rates in Western societies were due mainly to more conscientious reporting by citizens, the increases would consist disproportionately of petty offenses. But the opposite is the case: serious offenses have increased much more than petty ones.[28]

The "better policing" explanation of rising rates of serious crime since 1950 is largely a myth. It is naive to think that crime statistics depict precisely the real incidence of crime because many victims, especially in high-crime areas, think it is useless to report their losses. But there is little doubt that the long-term trends common to most Western societies reflect real changes in social behavior of large magnitude. This is the social issue most in need of explanation, not the vagaries of police behavior.

The historical circumstances of great crime waves should help us distinguish between plausible and implausible, general and idiosyncratic explanations. Three kinds of social forces seem to be at work. One is modernization, the process by which Western societies were transformed from predominantly rural, agricultural societies into their present industrial, urban shape. Such transitions can be criminogenic if they disrupt traditional patterns of life and thought without replacing them with effective alternatives. And this is evidently what happened to some but not all the rural migrants to European cities in their early stages of growth. The more modern and urban a society becomes, however, the greater its capacity to absorb rural people without criminogenic effect. Modern cities which offer immigrants real economic opportunities, within the framework of a formal network of social control exercised by schools, associations, police, and courts, are not likely to have high rates of crime among immigrants. In fact the immigrants may have less opportunity for crime than in impoverished rural areas. The point is that industrialization and urbanization have complex effects on crime rates. If there is a general pattern—the empirical evidence is sparse and ambiguous—it is a rise in urban crime in the earliest stages of modernization followed by a decline once the process is in full swing.[29]

Modernization is a gradual process, not one that is likely of itself to create a single tidal wave of disorder. The connection between warfare and crime waves is much more precise. In fact, war is the single most obvious correlate of all the great historical waves of crime in England and the United States. A mideighteenth-century wave of crime coincided with Britain's involvement in a succession of wars from 1739 (war with Spain) to 1763 (the end of the Seven Year's War). The upsurge of crime in the early nineteenth century began while Britain was enmeshed in the Napoleonic wars, from 1793 to 1815, and continued through the long and severe economic depression which followed the war's end. Sweden also was involved in the

Napoleonic wars, which may help account for Stockholm's high crime rates in the early nineteenth century. In the United States the peak of urban crime in the 1860s and 1870s coincides with the social and political upheavals of the Civil War. We noted above the great increase in crime which followed Germany and Austria's defeat in the First World War. Lesser crime waves coincided with and followed both world wars in Britain, the United States, and most of the continental democracies.

There are various explanations for the widely observed correlation between war and crime. It has been attributed to wartime social disorganization, postwar economic dislocation, the maladjustment of returned veterans, and also to the legitimation of violence: "some members of a warring society are influenced by the 'model' of officially approved wartime killing and destruction." Archer and Gartner have compared the homicide rates of a large number of nations which participated in one or both world wars and find that the "legitimation of violence" explanation is most consistent with the evidence.[30] Powell offers a somewhat different interpretation of high crime during the American Civil War period, saying that it was due most fundamentally to the collapse of the institutional order. He argues that "The war marked the triumph of industrial capitalism over agrarian and commercial forms of organization," the consequence of which was "extreme disorganization, or anomie . . . . The abnormally high crime rate is but one symptom of the pervasive chaos of the period. However, as the social system began to stabilize in the mid-70s, the crime rate dropped."[31]

A third basic factor that directly influences the extent of both personal and property crime is the size of the youthful population. All records of crime in Western societies, now and in the past, show that young males are disproportionately represented among offenders. If their relative numbers are high in a society or a city, its crime rates are likely to be higher than in societies or cities with older populations. And if the relative number of young males increases substantially in a short time, so will crime. Such changes have occurred periodically in Western societies, often as a consequence of socioeconomic change or war. A population boom was underway in England during the first half of the 19th century thanks to better nutrition and higher birth rates. Concurrently it became the practice of many English rural families to send their adolescent children to the cities to fend for themselves.[32] As a result there was a remarkably high proportion of young males in London's population. In 1841 males aged 15 to 29 made up 13.5 percent of the city's population, a proportion never surpassed from 1821 to the present. The comparable percentages during the low crime years of the early 1920s and early 1950s were 11.5 percent and 9.1 percent, respectively.[33]

The explosion in youth crime in the 1960s and 1970s is closely linked to the profound changes in the age structure in the United States, Britain, and most other Western societies. Birth rates declined to their lowest recorded point in most Western societies during the Great Depression of the 1930s. Then, in the immediate aftermath of the Second World War, they soared upward. In the United States the "silent generation" of 1950s college students might better be called the "small generation" because its members were little more than half as numerous as the college-age population of the late 1960s. The shape and timing of the "age bulge" differ among Western societies and so do their postwar crime trends. The countries which had early and large baby booms, like England and the United States, had early and rapid increases in crime rates, as shown in Figures 13.3 and 13.4. In England and Wales the correspondence between the changing size of the youth population and changing crime rates is particularly striking for property crime. In the United States the correspondence since 1955 is equally close. Germany and Austria (not shown on graphs) provide a marked contrast. They had baby "boomlets" which began later, after economic recovery set in during the 1950s, and were smaller. Their crime rates turned up later and much less sharply. In Japan, however, no correlation is apparent between declining crime rates and changes in the size of the youth population. The latter remained virtually constant from 1946 through 1971.[34]

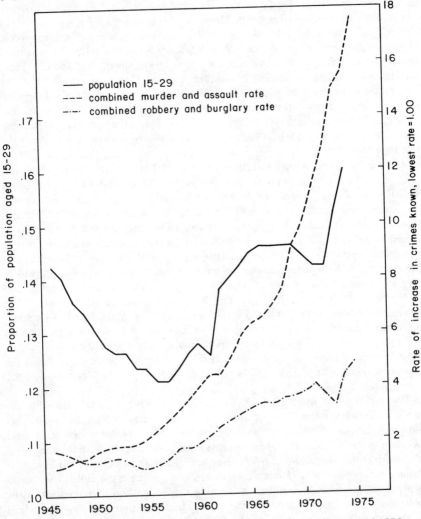

Figure 13.3: Youth population and crime in England and Wales, 1946-1975

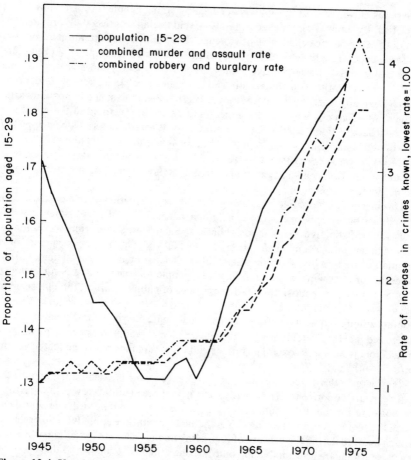

Figure 13.4: Youth population and crime in the United States, 1945-1976

It is not entirely convincing to attribute crime increases of 300 or 500 percent to 50 percent increases in the size of the youthful population. Presumably there are other social forces at work which encouraged a growing proportion of contemporary youths to resort to mayhem and theft. We have seen that international and civil war seem to legitimate interpersonal violence. The 1960s was the decade of revolutionary wars and counterinsurgency, which were glorified, villified, and above all amplified by the media. It was also an era in which politicians and officials publicized their deadly fantasies of nuclear incineration. The mass media saturated a whole generation with violent entertainment. It is plausible to argue that the 1960s saw a significant reversal in the long secular tendency toward restraining and condemning violence. And the people most susceptible to this new tolerance for violence were young people.

Value change in the 1960s went beyond a greater tolerance for interpersonal aggression. Distinctive new "postindustrial" values were articulated on university campuses during the 1960s and soon echoed by young people throughout Western societies. By emphasizing peace, toleration, and social progress they provided an antidote to the public celebration of violence. They also turned attention away from material concerns and celebrated personal liberation and development.[35] But there were distortions of these positive values which were socially more corrosive. The most corrosive form of this alternative ethic might be called aggressive hedonism, which is equally a perversion of traditional Western humanism and of postindustrial values. At its core is a belief that almost any means are justified in the pursuit of personal satisfactions. It resembles a mutation of Western materialism, stripped of its work ethic and generalized from material satisfactions to social and sexual ones. Moreover it often coexists with a sense of resentment against large, impersonal organizations, or indeed any external source of authority that might restrain people from "doing their own thing."

This discussion has come a long way from the consideration of crime waves. The strands can be brought together by concluding that each great wave of violent crime is caused by a distinctive combination of basic social forces. Some crime waves follow from fundamental social dislocation, as a result of which large segments of a population are torn lose from the social fabric. They may be migrants, demobilized veterans, or a growing population of young people for whom there is no social or economic niche. The most devastating episodes of public disorder, though, seem to occur when these kinds of social crises coincide with changes in values. Violent conflict among and within nations seems to legitimate interpersonal violence. I have suggested that the contemporary crime wave which pervades Western societies may be a fallout from a shift toward postindustrial values among college-educated youths of the 1960s and 1970s.

Nowhere in this discussion have major changes in crime been attributed to the police, courts, or prisons. Historically, reform in these institutions was thought to be responsible for the nineteenth-century improvement of public order in European societies like England and Sweden. Yet the same institutions, policies, and practices which evolved during the century of improving public order are essentially the same as those which are now unable to control rising crime. The answer to this apparent paradox is that the criminal law, police, courts, and prisons together can only restrain common crime if they reinforce underlying social forces that are moving in the same direction. These institutions and their policies were effective in turn-of-the-century societies dominated by a self-confident middle class convinced that prosperity in this life and salvation in the next could be achieved through piety, honesty, and hard work. All authorities spoke with the same voice. The institutions of public order were effective because they reinforced the dominant view. They did not merely punish those who transgressed. They were missionaries to the under class, informing them of the moral order through arrest, trial, and imprisonment.

Today, no self-confident consensus on standards of behavior is to be found in most of Western society. There are many self-proclaimed authorities offering may alternatives. Where a solid foundation of social support is lacking, the police, courts, and prisons drift. At worst, the police adopt a siege mentality, hostile to society and offenders alike. The courts devise expedients, such as plea bargaining, which serve administrative efficiency at the expense of both justice and public safety. And the prisons become warehouses which, like the gaols and workhouses of early nineteenth-century England, keep the offender out of circulation for a little while, but only inadvertently punish or rehabilitate him.

There are correctives to crime waves. Uprooted people may be incorporated in the matrix of new institutions or renovated old ones. Traditional values which condemn theft and interpersonal violence may reassert themselves. New values adopted by alienated people, caught between new life ways and old ones, may constrain harmful social behavior in ways even more effective than old values. Methodism is credited with just such effects among the new urban working class of nineteenth-century England, for example. If the Western crime wave of the 1960s does continue to ebb, it will be partly because the invisible hand of hedonism has dictated that an unprecedented proportion of young adults in North America and Europe forego having the children who would become the potential criminals and victims of the 1980s. And the recession in crime may be due in part to a reaffirmation of older moral values and a retreat from the individual freedom and diversity of behavior which flowered in the 1960s. Whatever the reasons, all historical evidence suggests that crime, like economic growth and population size, has finite limits. Call it a law of social gravitation: what goes up beyond supportable limits will eventually come down.

NOTES

General: This chapter is based on research supported by the Center for Studies of Crime and Delinquency of the U.S. Public Health Service and by the German Marshall Fund of the United States. Thanks are due to Tina Peterson for surveying historical studies of crime trends and to Eric Monkkonen for his comments on an earlier draft. The chapter incorporates portions of the author's article, "The Criminal Ethos," which appeared in *The Center Magazine*, 11 (January-February 1978): 74-79.

1. For an evaluation of the reliability of nineteenth-century English crime statistics, see V.A.C. Gatrell and T.B. Hadden, "Criminal Statistics and their Interpretation," in E.A. Wrigley, ed., *Nineteenth-Century Society* (Cambridge: The University Press, 1972): 336-396. A general discussion of the interpretations of different kinds of crime data is Ted Robert Gurr, *Rogues, Rebels, and Reformers: A Political History of Urban Crime and Conflict* (Beverly Hills: Sage Publications, 1976), Ch. 2.

2. James Buchanan Given, *Society and Homicide in Thirteenth-Century England* (Stanford: Stanford University Press, 1977). The records of homicides in thirteenth-century England are probably as accurate as those of any other period before the twentieth century because of strong incentives for local people to report them to the king's justices and equally compelling penalties for failing to do so. The rates' imprecision is due to the lack of accurate population data.

3. Ibid., 35.

4. J.M. Beattie, "The Pattern of Crime in England 1660-1800," *Past and Present*, 62 (February 1974): 47-95.

5. The epithet was applied by the journalist and radical reformer William Cobbett. For a detailed protrayal of the city in this era, see Francis Sheppard, *London, 1808-1870: The Infernal Wen* (London: Secker and Warburg, 1971).

6. This sketch is drawn from David Peirce, Peter N. Grabosky, and Ted Robert Gurr, "London: The Politics of Crime and Conflict, 1800 to the 1970s," in Ted Robert Gurr, Peter

N. Grabosky, and Richard C. Hula, *The Politics of Crime and Conflict: A Comparative History of Four Cities* (Beverly Hills: Sage Publications, 1977), Part II.

7. Given, op. cit., Ch. 1, surveys evidence on the medieval attitudes toward violence. Some evidence for the moderating effect of Enlightenment thought on criminal justice policies is reviewed in Gurr, *Rogues, Rebels, and Reformers*, Ch. II.5. See especially, Norbert Elias, *The Civilizing Process: The History of Manners* (New York: Urizen, 1978—original ed. 1939), 191-205.

8. Many trend and correlation studies show that in the eighteenth, nineteenth, and early twentieth centuries property crime tended to increase during hard times. But from c. 1925 onward in both England and the United States, the pattern is reversed: the greater economic prosperity, the more property crime. Among the studies which report such findings are Gatrell and Hadden, op. cit., 363-376; Theodore N. Ferdinand, "The Criminal Patterns of Boston Since 1849," *American Journal of Sociology* 73 (July 1967): 688-698; Leroy C. Gould, "The Changing Structure of Property Crime in an Affluent Society," *Social Forces*, 48 (September 1969): 50-60; and M. Harvey Brenner, "Effects of the Economy on Criminal Behavior and the Administration of Criminal Justice: A Multinational Study," paper presented to the Conference on Economic Crisis and Crime, United Nations Social Defence Research Institute, Rome, 1975. The last study uses national data for the United States, Canada, England and Wales, and Scotland. Also see Dorothy Swaine Thomas, *Social Aspects of the Business Cycle* (London: Routledge, 1925).

9. Many scholars, officials, and journalists have criticized American crime statistics; see the following chapter by Wesley Skogan. A comprehensive appraisal is Ch. 2, "American Criminal Statistics: An Explanation and Appraisal," in Donald Mulvihill and Melvin Tumin, *Crimes of Violence, Report to the National Commission on the Causes and Prevention of Violence*, Vol. 11 (Washington, D.C.: U.S. Government Printing Office, 1969). For evidence of the politically inspired manipulation of crime statistics in American cities c. 1970, see David Seidman and Michael Couzens, "Getting the Crime Rate Down: Political Pressure and Crime Reporting," *Law and Society* (spring 1974): 457-493.

10. The principal studies of crime in Boston are Sam Bass Warner, *Crime and Criminal Statistics in Boston* (Cambridge: Harvard University Press, 1934); Ferdinand, op. cit.; and Roger Lane, *Policing the City: Boston, 1822-1885* (Cambridge, Mass.: Harvard University Press, 1967). The quotation is from Roger Lane, "Urbanization and Criminal Violence in the 19th Century: Massachusetts as a Test Case," in Hugh Davis Graham and Ted Robert Gurr, eds., *Violence in America: Historical and Comparative Perspectives* (various eds., 1969), Ch. 12, 470 in the Praeger edition

11. Ferdinand, op. cit.

12. Charles Tilly et al., "How Policing Affected the Visibility of Crime in Nineteenth-Century Europe and America," (Ann Arbor: Center for Research on Social Organization, University of Michigan, n.d. [1975]), unpublished ms.

13. Theodore N. Ferdinand, "Politics, the Police, and Arresting Policies in Salem, Massachusetts Since the Civil War," *Social Problems*, 19 (spring 1972): 572-588; Elwin H. Powell, "Crime as a Function of Anomie," *Journal of Criminal Law, Criminology, and Police Science*, 57 (June 1966): 161-171.

14. Tilly et al., op. cit.

15. Powell, op. cit. His interpretation of crime as a consequence of social dislocations is most fully developed in Powell, *The Design of Discord: Studies of Anomie: Suicide, Urban Society, War* (New York: Oxford University Press, 1970), Part 2.

16. Edwin H. Sutherland and C.E. Gehlke, "Crime and Punishment," in *Recent Social Trends in the United States*, Report of the President's Research Committee on Social Trends (New York: McGraw-Hill, 1933).

17. Harry Willbach, "The Trend of Crime in New York City," *Journal of Criminal Law and Criminology*, 29 (1938): 62-75; and "The Trend of Crime in Chicago," *Journal of Criminal Law and Criminology*, 31 (1941): 720-727.

18. Peter N. Grabosky, *Sydney in Ferment: Crime, Dissent, and Official Reaction, 1788-1973* (Canberra: Australian National University Press, 1978).

19. See Peter N. Grabosky, Leif Persson, and Sven Sperlings, "Stockholm: The Politics of Crime and Conflict, 1750 to the 1970s," in Gurr, Grabosky, and Hula, op. cit., Part III.

20. Arthur MacDonald, "Criminal Statistics in Germany, France, and England," *Journal of Criminal Law and Criminology*, 1 (1910): 59-70; Abdul Qaiyum Lodhi and Charles Tilly, "Urbanization, Crime, and Collective Violence in 19th-Century France," *American Journal of Sociology*, 79 (September 1973): 296-318.

21. MacDonald, op. cit.; Vincent E. McHale and Eric A. Johnson, "Urbanization, Industrialization, and Crime in Imperial Germany, Parts I and II," *Social Science History*, 1 (fall 1976): 45-78; 1 (winter 1977): 210-247.

22. Among the most detailed studies ever made of war's impact on crime are F. Exner, *Krieg und Kriminalitaet in Oesterreich* (New Haven, Conn.: Yale University Press, 1927); and M. Liepmann, *Krieg und Kriminalitaet in Deutschland* (Stuttgart: Deutsche Verlags Anstalt, 1930).

23. The foregoing data on postwar crime rates are from Ted Robert Gurr, "Crime Trends in Modern Democracies since 1945," *International Annals of Criminology*, 16 (1977): 41-85.

24. For evaluations of contemporary problems of crime in European Communist states, see Valery Chalidze, *Criminal Russia: Essays on Crime in the Soviet Union* (New York: Random House, 1977); and Ivan Volgyes, ed., *Social Deviance in Eastern Europe* (Boulder, Colorado: Westview, 1978).

25. A recent study which helps account for the Japanese success in dealing with crime is David Bayley, *Forces of Order: Police Behavior in Japan and the United States* (Berkeley: University of California Press, 1976).

26. A recent survey of theories of criminal behavior is Gwynn Nettler, *Explaining Crime* (New York: McGraw-Hill, 1974).

27. For interpretations of crime data as indicators of official behavior see, for example, Clayton A. Hartjen, *Crime and Criminalization* (New York: Praeger, 1974); and Austin Turk, *Criminality and Legal Order* (Skokie, Ill.: Rand-McNally, 1969). A historical study of San Francisco which tests this approach is Eric Monkkonen, "Toward a Dynamic Theory of Crime and the Police: A Criminal Justice System Perspective," *Historical Methods Newsletter*, 10 (fall 1977): 157-165.

28. A more detailed discussion of the relative importance of changing social behavior and changing policies in accounting from crime trends is Ted Robert Gurr, "Contemporary Crime in Historical Perspective: A Comparative Study of London, Stockholm and Sydney," *Annals of the American Academy of Political and Social Science*, 434 (November 1977): 126-134.

29. For historical evidence on the complex relationship between urban growth and crime, see, for example, Lodhi and Tilly, op. cit.; McHale and Johnson, op. cit.; and Powell, *Design of Discord*, Part 2.

30. Dane Archer and Rosemary Gartner, "Violent Acts and Violent Times: A Comparative Approach to Postwar Homicide Rates," *American Sociological Review*, 41 (December 1976): 937-963, quotation 943.

31. Powell, "Crime as a Function of Anomie," 169.

32. John R. Gillis, *Youth and History: Tradition and Change in European Age Relations 1770-Present* (New York and London: Academic Press, 1974), Ch. 2.

33. Decennial data on the youthful proportion of the London population from 1801 to 1971 are given in David Peirce, Peter N. Grabosky, and Ted Robert Gurr, "London: The Politics of Crime and Conflict, 1800 to the 1970's," in Gurr, Grabosky, and Hula, op. cit., 43.

34. These comparisons and Figures 13.3 and 13.4 are based on crime and demographic data gathered and analyzed by the author.

35. The most detailed empirical study of postindustrial values in Western societies is Ronald Inglehart, *The Silent Revolution: Changing Values and Political Styles Among Western Publics* (Princeton: Princeton University Press, 1977). Gillis, op. cit., Ch. 5, discusses the changes in youth subculture during the 1950s and 1960s in historical perspective. A contemporary analysis is Herbert Moller, "Youth as a Force in the Modern World," *Comparative Studies in Society and History*, 10 (April 1968): 237-260.

Chapter 14
Crime in Contemporary America

WESLEY G. SKOGAN

The surge in reported crime in the United States from 1964 to 1974 will be recorded as one of the most portentous political and social facts of that era. That tidal wave of crime signaled an end to the relatively pacific period following the Second World War. Before 1963 the nation's violent crime rate changed little. There was an increase of scarcely two robberies and assaults for each 10,000 persons during the preceding decade-and-a-half. The murder rate actually dropped between 1946 and 1957, and in 1963 stood at only one-third that of the immediate postwar period. The number of property crimes rose very slowly during the same span, and in 1963 they stood at only one-fourth their eventual highwater mark. Then came the turbulent 'sixties, during which an ever-heightening spiral of reported crime and counter-reaction was immeshed in a complex set of political and social events. Crime took off at the same time that the sit-ins of the South moved North, followed by that remora of social change, George Wallace. In 1967 the violent crime rate was twice that of 1963, a figure backlighted by the glare of burning cities. The rate had not quite again doubled by the end of 1973, encouraging Attorney General John Mitchell's proud claim that his government had "decreased it's rate of increase."

To document exactly what happened to crime in the United States following 1963 is a complex problem. As we shall see, there are limits to our measures of crime which make it difficult to know how well they actually reflect the "true" crime rate. This chapter reviews some of the evidence on postwar crime trends, with an eye toward explaining this apparent epidemic. It describes several of the large

AUTHOR'S NOTE: *The author is associate professor of political science at Northwestern University and faculty associate of its Center for Urban Affairs. His articles on police, crime, and public policy have appeared in* Urban Affairs Quarterly, Social Science Quarterly, Criminology, Public Administration Review, *and* Policy Studies, *among others. He has worked extensively on victimization surveys and edited a recent book on the subject,* Sample Surveys of the Victims of Crime *(1976). From 1974 to 1976 he was a visiting fellow at the Law Enforcement Assistance Administration of the U.S. Department of Justice. This chapter was prepared under Grant Number 78-NI-AX-0057 from the National Institute of Law Enforcement and Criminal Justice, Law Enforcement Assistance Administration, U.S. Department of Justice. Points of view or opinions in this document are those of the author and do not represent the official position or policies of the U.S. Department of Justice.*

demographic and economic forces which surged around the crime rate during its precipitous rise during the late 1960s and early 1970s.

The role of demographic change in shaping the volume and nature of crime is clearest in the case of the shifting age distribution of the American population. Crime is a young man's game, and its frequency is greatly influenced by the number of such dangerous specimens about. But in addition, fundamental changes have been taking place in the economic role of women in American society, and those are mirrored in their changing role in crime. Serious crime also is disproportionately a big-city problem. Crime is "overconcentrated" there relative to the size of the urban population, so much so that conditions in our great cities have a significant impact on the overall national crime rate. In the last decade-and-a-half the urban terrain has been changing with increasing rapidity. Some of those changes—principally the depopulation of Northern and Eastern cities and the movement of the population to smaller places in the South and West—may have considerable long-term impact on the nature of the crime problem. Finally, black Americans are substantially overrepresented among those who are apprehended for violent crimes. This leads disproportionate national significance to social and economic trends in the black community. A portion of the increasing crime rate during the later 1960s can be attributed to increasing offense rates by blacks as compared to whites. But in the main, current arrest patterns indicate a reversal of the trend, presaging a decline in crime rates.

As this hints, linking changes in the crime rate to these social and demographic features may provide an explanation for the apparent leveling off of the rate for many serious offenses recently, and perhaps a basis for projecting their modest decline. The seemingly endless succession of increases in reported crime which has characterized the past 15 years now seems to be at an end. This conclusion must remain equivocal, however, for there are severe limitations on our ability to gauge accurately smaller and short-run crime trends. Official crime statistics are affected by citizen actions and bureaucratic routines as well as by offenders. Counts of crime are determined both by "the root causes of crime" and by those who report them, record them, and turn them into grist for the statistical mill.

CRIME TRENDS

Postwar trends in violent and serious property crimes sketch a clear pattern: low rates relative to the size of the population from 1946 to 1964, then a dramatic upturn between 1964 and 1975. During the first period the officially recorded rate of violent crime (incidents per thousand persons in the population) rose from 1.1 to 1.3; during the second it jumped to a high of 4.8, a 336 percent increase. The smallest component of that increase was contributed by the murder rate. Murders are relatively infrequent, and from a low in 1957 of only .04 murders per thousand to a high in 1974 of .10, the homicide rate rose "only" 150 percent. The most common violent crimes are robbery and serious assault (the former involve the use or threat of force to take something, while the latter are attacks with intent to kill or inflict severe injury). Major assaults climbed 375 percent during the postwar period to a high of 2.3 per thousand, while robbery jumped 543 percent to 2.2 per thousand. Reported rape also rose sharply during this period, although like murder this crime makes up a relatively small proportion of all violent crimes. The most serious property crime, burglary (involving unlawful entry of someone's home or place of business), increased 500 percent during the 1946-1975 period, from a low of 2.5 per thousand to a high of over 15 per thousand persons.[1]

While official statistics on crime paint a grim picture of uniformly increasing predation during the 1960s and into the 1970s, they also hold a hint of hope for the future. Most of the rates which have been climbing sharply during the past decade now apparently have slowed their ascent, and several of the most serious of them have evidenced a slight decline. Murder peaked in 1974/1975; in 1976 and again in 1977 rates declined. Rape rates did not increase significantly between 1974 and 1976. Robbery, auto theft and burglary rates fell from 1975 to 1977. Of the serious crimes, only assault continued to rise during this period. These short-term differences were not large, but they followed a decade of sharp year-by-year increases in rates of crime, and there are several reasons to believe that they indicate at least stability in the true crime rate. Advance reports for individual communities for 1977 indicate that patterns of decreasing crime in many large cities are continuing. From 1976 to 1977, the total number of recorded "index crimes" was down in Chicago (by 10,000), New York (by 48,000), Detroit (by 30,000), Philadelphia (by 5,000) and Los Angeles (by 3,000). They were up in Houston, the nation's fifth largest city, but down in San Francisco, Boston, Minneapolis, and San Antonio.[2]

The question is whether those figures can be trusted. Until very recently almost all we knew about the frequency and distribution of crime came from reports that local police agencies filed with the FBI. They forward to Washington the number of incidents which citizens have reported to them, and which they in turn have verified as constituting valid crimes. The FBI publishes these counts, which form the basis for the discussion of changing crime rates above.

It is clear, however, that both decisions by victims to report their experiences to the police and decisions by the authorities to record those complaints are subject to a number of influences which make them problematic indicators of the "true" level of crime. For example, an important determinant of the decision by victims to report property crimes to the police is whether or not they are insured. The number of household insurance policies written each year has been increasing steadily, leading us to suspect the year-to-year comparability of official figures on crimes such as burglary. On the police side, it appears that the more professional departments and those with more resources tend to record most accurately all of the complaints brought to them by citizens. Since the Second World War police departments certainly have become more professional, and their resources have expanded considerably.[3] These factors do not mean that official statistics are useless, though. They give us reasons for skepticism about short-run trends and minute differences in officially recorded rates for specific types of crime. But when we find longer-run trends of change in many categories of crime, of several orders of magnitude, we can be more confident that the aggregate crime indicators reflect real increases in the incidence of offenses and victimization. The 1960s registered just this kind of epidemic change in crime rates.

To trust official statistics to reflect adequately small and short-run changes in crime is a bit riskier. In the previous chapter Gurr argued that trends in the true crime rate should be reflected in shifts in official indicators of its volume, even if the magnitude of the true rate and the official rate differ considerably. The validity of the recent down-trend in the official crime rate reported above need not rest on such a fragile reed, however. Since 1973 the U.S. Bureau of the Census has been conducting national surveys to gauge the frequency of serious crime; while the series is considerably shorter than that which can be constructed from official reports by police agencies, it nicely brackets the time period of concern here, the post-1974 period during which crime rates appear to have leveled off. These surveys have the advantage of being independent of the political and bureaucratic pressures which affect official reports, and they gather extensive data on crimes which citizens did not report to the police in the first place. Thus it is significant that they, like official statistics, also point to a leveling-off in rates for many serious crimes.

The Census Bureau's victimization survey and official crime statistics from the FBI indicate vastly different amounts of crime in America. In 1976, for example, the FBI reported a total of 3,090,000 burglaries, while the victimization surveys uncovered 8,272,000.[4] Thus in order to compare changes in trends since 1973, it is necessary to present figures from the two sources in a common framework. Table 14.1 reports rate trends for six major types of crime, with FBI and Census Bureau figures both indexed at 1975 = 100. Thus figures above or below 100 indicate proportional changes in yearly rates, irrespective of their differences in magnitude.

As Table 14.1 indicates, official reports and surveys agree that all offenses except serious assault dropped between 1975 and 1977. The murder rate (which is not

Table 14.1: Short-Term Trends in Crime Rates (Index 1975=100)

		Index of Rate per Thousand					
Crime	Measure	1973	1974	1975	1976	1977	1978
Murder	Police	90	100	100	92	93	89
Robbery	Survey	98	98	100	96	91	—
	Police	84	96	100	90	87	82
Assault	Survey	104	99	100	103	104	—
	Police	88	95	100	101	108	106
Burglary	Survey	101	100	100	96	96	—
	Police	80	94	100	95	94	90
Auto theft	Survey	97	96	100	85	87	—
	Police	94	98	100	96	97	93

Source: U.S. Department of Justice, *Criminal Victimization in the United States* (Washington, D.C.: U.S. Government Printing Office, yearly); Federal Bureau of Investigation, *Uniform Crime Report* (Washington, D.C.: U.S. Government Printing Office, yearly). Releases for 1978 from the FBI are preliminary. Official rates are per 1000 persons; survey rates are per 1000 persons 12 years of age and older, combining personal or household and commercial victimizations where appropriate. Survey reports for 1978 are not yet available. For 1978, official figures are for the first three months of the year, and are compared here to the first three months of 1977.

measured in the surveys) declined, as did figures for robbery and burglary. Drops in auto theft since 1975 have been substantial. Table 14.1 suggests that only serious assault rates are drifting upward; survey indicators show them to be level between 1973 and 1977, while in official reports they have been climbing yearly.

The significance of Table 14.1 is that at least a leveling-off, and perhaps a decline, in rates for several important crimes is suggested by two quite different sources of data. They both indicate that past trends of skyrocketing rates of serious crime have stabilized and may well be on the decline.

This halt in rising rates of victimization appears to be "across the board," not limited to a few favored groups. One of the most important uses of victimization surveys is to pinpoint key crime problems facing groups in the population. Because they are based on polling sampling techniques, such surveys can give a much more accurate picture than police statistics of the characteristics of both victims and nonvictims, and can compare and contrast the specific risks faced by categories of people. Although year-to-year differences in crime rates for major population groups generally have been small, the latest returns from these surveys generally point to declining rates of victimization for all of them. Table 14.2 presents Justice

Table 14.2: Short-Term Trends in Pattern of Victimization

Victim Attributes	All Violent Crime	Rate of Victimization per Thousand Personal Robbery	All Thefts	Personal Theft	Household Burglary
Whites					
1975	31.6	5.8	97.1	2.6	87.1
1976	31.1	5.5	97.4	2.5	84.0
Blacks					
1975	42.9	14.1	90.3	7.1	129.4
1976	44.4	13.6	86.8	6.3	130.8
Lower income					
1975	38.1	8.7	77.5	4.2	101.7
1976	36.6	8.4	76.0	3.5	101.3
Moderate income					
1975	29.5	5.7	98.5	2.4	83.8
1976	29.7	4.9	94.2	2.0	80.7
Over 65					
1975	7.8	4.3	24.5	3.3	53.8
1976	7.6	3.4	26.0	3.3	50.2
Males					
1975	43.6	9.8	108.1	2.9	na
1976	42.9	9.1	106.2	2.5	na
Females					
1975	23.0	4.0	84.9	3.3	na
1976	23.1	4.0	86.8	3.2	na

Source: U.S. Department of Justice, *Criminal Victimization in the United States: A Comparison of 1975 and 1976 Findings* (Washington D.C., U.S. Government Printing Office, 1977), Tables 3, 4, 6, 9, 10, and 11.

Department findings from their surveys for 1975 and 1976, examining patterns of personal crime and household burglary for several important groups.

With some exceptions—noticeably for blacks—victimization rates in most of the crime categories presented in Table 14.2 declined between 1975 and 1976. Most of the increases, which are slight, are found in the "all violent crime" category, which includes the rising assault counts documented earlier. Robbery declined in all the age/race/sex/income categories analyzed in Table 14.2, as did personal theft (purse snatchings and pocket picking). Petty thefts were up for women, whites and the elderly, but burglary was on the increase only against black households. It was down sharply (as these things go) for the elderly, households with moderate incomes ($7,500 to $15,000 per year), and whites in general. As we saw in Table 14.1, except for assault all of these crimes showed an overall decrease between 1975 and 1976.

The general pattern of victimization presented by Table 14.2 is a familiar one: blacks, the poor, males, and younger persons generally suffer higher rates of victimization than their counterparts. The same pattern describes the plight of big-city dwellers, those with less education, renters, and people living in the North and East. Inequality in the distribution of the burdens of crime remains, and generally falls more heavily upon those who already bear many others as well. On the other hand, the trend line for serious predation seems at least to be leveling off, and it appears that this happy circumstance is enjoyed by many segments of the population.

The question remains, Why? What caused the tremendous upsurge in crime reports during the 1964-1975 period, and to what can we attribute their more recent decline?

While interviews with its victims can tell us much about the frequency of crime and who it strikes, explanations for the crime rate inevitably call for details about offenses and their perpetrators. Until recently those data were available only from police reports on file with the FBI. They record only the race, age, and sex of persons arrested and the jurisdictions in which crime takes place.[5] While this is a relatively limited base for analyzing short-term variations in crime, it does tap many important and shifting features of the demographic terrain which are also related at the individual level to rates of crime.

CRIME AND CITIES

Crime rates are higher in urban areas than in the countryside, and they are higher within central cities than in the suburban towns surrounding them. Relative to the distribution of the population, officially reported crime is overconcentrated in big cities, and this is especially true of violence. Because urban crime rates are so high, big-city crime statistics have a disproportionate impact on nationwide trends. Thus, we should expect changes in urban structure to be reflected in those crime counts. Since 1970, big-city populations have dropped at a faster rate than ever before. In many cities both the total number of crimes and even official crime rates relative to population size have begun to decline.

The relationship between urbanism and crime is well known. Louis Wirth attributed disproportionately high urban crime rates to the heterogeneity, density, and sheer size of big cities.[6] In cities are found people of every economic class and lifestyle, and in their day-to-day commerce there inevitably arise envy, hostility, and conflict. In cities people are thrown together with strangers who they cannot identify but upon whom they must rely. People are anonymous in great cities, and the bonds of family, kinship, history, interdependence, and common fate which serve to control the appetites of individuals in less complex surroundings do not restrain their behavior. Finally, opportunities to commit crime are found more often in cities. There are concentrated warehouses, wholesale trade, truck-docks, banks, shops, liquor stores, late-night facilities, entertainment spas, and provision for vice. All of these attract the attention of potential criminals, and provide them lucrative opportunities to ply their trade.

Table 14.3 indicates the extent to which two types of serious crime, burglary and robbery, are overconcentrated in great cities.

Table 14.3: Concentration of Reported Crime in the Largest U.S. Cities

Year	Percentage of U.S. Population	Percentage of Reported Robbery	Percentage of Reported Burglary
1950	20.8	55.4	33.1
1955	19.6	58.8	32.9
1960	18.5	57.3	30.8
1965	17.7	56.5	28.6
1970	16.9	65.3	31.6
1975	15.4	54.8	23.7
1976	15.3	55.8	23.8

Source: Federal Bureau of Investigation, *Uniform Crime Report* (Washington, D.C.: U.S. Government Printing Office, yearly); U.S. Bureau of the Census, *Statistical Abstract of the United States* (Washington, D.C.: U.S. Government Printing Office, yearly).

The table tracks the 32 largest cities in the United States (in 1970) back to 1950, and forward to 1975. It reports for every five years the proportion of the nation's population which has lived in these cities, and the proportion of the nation's burglary and robbery which was recorded there. From 1950 until 1970 the population of these cities declined slowly, slightly less than 1 percent every five years. Their robbery and burglary counts remained a roughly steady proportion of the nation's total before 1970, although the overconcentration of robbery in the largest cities in 1970 is apparent. Through 1965 there was about three times as much robbery in these cities as one would expect on the basis of their population, and in 1970 three and a half times as much. Overall, through 1970 burglary was about one and a half times as frequent as expected.

These figures mirror the distribution of other violent and property crimes. In 1976, 38 percent of murders, 33 percent of rapes, and 28 percent of serious assaults were reported in these cities, which housed 15 percent of the population. Thirty-eight percent of all auto thefts and 20 percent of larcenies were also concentrated there. Conditions and events in large cities clearly wield a disproportionate influence on national crime totals.

It is significant, then, that one of the most important demographic features of the 1970s has been the increasingly rapid depopulation of great cities. Examination of the recent history of all 157 cities with populations above 100,000 in 1970 reveals the pattern of decline: in 1950 those cities housed 31 percent of the American population, in 1970 that proportion had dropped to 28 percent, and in 1975 to 20 percent.[7] The decline after 1970 in the population of many big cities has been precipitous.

Where these people went, crime rates are lower. They moved to the suburbs and to semirural areas of the fringes of those big cities, and —increasingly—they moved out of major metropolitan areas entirely. Many went South and West, following cheap energy and the good life. With their numbers go more crime, but it is not yet clear that crime rates in these prosperous, low-density, and more hospitable environs will increase beyond those created by simple population growth. And as people leave, crime counts in their old communities have been dropping, often at a *faster* rate than expected. Both official statistics and the Census Bureau's victimization surveys indicate that big-city crime rates are enjoying somewhat of a decline in the mid-1970s. Table 14.3 indicates the official figures for burglary in the 32 largest cities— their share of the national total—dropped about 8 percentage points in the five years between 1970 and 1975, while their population dropped 1.5 percent. Plots of crime trends in major cities indicate that they peaked in 1974, and have traced a mild-to-sharp decline since that time. The victimization surveys set the personal robbery rate in central cities over one million at 19.3 per thousand persons in 1974, and at 18.5 in 1976, a drop of 85,000 robberies. There are fewer people in big cities than ever before, and even crime rates relative to those totals are dropping.

CRIME AND THE AGE STRUCTURE

The bulk of crimes are committed by young people. The traditional "high-risk" years for offenders are 15-25, although there is some evidence that offense rates are growing sharply among younger age groups. Youthful offense rates are highest for property crimes. In 1976, for example, 46 percent of all those arrested for burglary and theft were under the age of eighteen. Only 22 percent of all arrestees for violent crimes were that youthful, however; offense rates for violent crimes were higher among the 18-26 group, and in general violent crimes are committed by wider segments of the population.

These observations lend great significance to the changing demographic structure of the American population. One important aspect of the turbulent 1960s was the growth of the youthful segment of the population. The origins of that growth lay in the "baby boom" which followed the Second World War. Many consequences of the sharp jump in fertility during the 1947-1949 period were felt decades later. Public schools and universities, the job market, and the political system were obliged to cope with mounting claims by the young. Some attribute the cultural transformations of the 1960s to this vast, perhaps "critical," mass of only partially socialized youths.

One of the most direct consequences of the growth of the youthful population was an increase in crime. Table 14.4 details arrest rates for the under-30 population in 1976.[8] The highest-risk age category then was only *16* for property crime; 20-year-olds enjoyed offense rates less than one-half of those only four years younger, and persons over 25 were practically never apprehended for serious property offenses. In the violent crime column the most active group was 18-year-olds, with those 17 and 19 not far behind. Table 14.4 indicates that there are some differences in the age distribution of arrestees for crimes within the violent category. Murder (and serious assault) is common well into the upper reaches of young adulthood, while robbery is most frequently pulled off by those between 16 and 18.

Table 14.4: Age and Arrest Rates for Violent and Property Crimes in 1976

| Age | Arrest Rate per Thousand in Age Category | | | |
	Property Crime[a]	Violent Crime[b]	Murder	Robbery
Under 11	0.97	0.05	0.04	0.02
11-12	10.07	0.66	0.45	0.31
13-14	24.37	2.13	2.12	1.08
15	36.26	4.03	5.45	2.08
16	40.66	5.44	11.78	2.73
17	35.38	5.66	14.04	2.72
18	30.68	5.92	19.36	2.71
19	24.28	5.75	21.08	2.37
20	19.58	5.19	18.96	2.02
21	17.10	5.16	20.53	1.93
22	15.34	4.93	19.93	1.80
23	14.05	4.72	20.16	1.60
24	12.05	4.22	19.97	1.34
25-29	8.72	3.51	17.74	0.96

a. Burglary, larceny, theft, and auto theft
b. Murder, rape, robbery, and aggravated assault

Source: Calculated from data given in: Table 32 of Federal Bureau of Investigation *Uniform Crime Report* (Washington, D.C.: U.S. Government Printing Office, 1977); U.S. Bureau of the Census, *Statistical Abstract of the United States* (Washington, D.C.: U.S. Government Printing Office, 1978, Table 2). Boxes denote maximum arrest rates.

This suggests that, if things remain the same (and we have no reason to suspect that they have not), the crime rate in a jurisdiction should be quite sensitive to the number of youths found there. For the nation as a whole, as the youthful population grows, so should crime.

The effect of the baby boom upon the demographic profile of the nation clearly was reflected in official data on arrestees. Each year following 1952 the proportion of arrestees under 18 rose, and that increase picked up sharply after 1959, when the postwar group began to enter their teens. In 1952 only 8 percent of all arrestees for the FBIs Index Crimes were under 18; in 1962 this figure doubled to 16 percent, and hit 25 percent in 1968. Then the bulk of this cohort passed into the 18-26 age category, and arrests of those under 18 years of age leveled off immediately. In 1976 they were proportionately fewer than the under-18 percentage of 1968.

In the age of "zero population growth," all of this augurs well for projections of the crime rate. This rapid decline in the size of the youthful population—which will be in effect until the 1990s, when *their* teenagers begin to roam—should produce a decline in property, and to a lesser extent violent, crime rates. The impact of our increasing median age (up a year-and-a-half since 1968 alone) will be muted a bit by its uneven distribution, however. In particular, the urban black population is younger than most. The very disproportionate offense rates of young black males, especially for violent crimes (see below) means that their demographic profile has significant impact on the overall crime rate. Thus the violent crime rate should decline more slowly than it appears at first glance. Moreover, as blacks make up a larger proportion of the younger age cohorts, offense rates for youths should continue to rise—but overall there will be many fewer of them, which should reduce the total crime rate.

RACE AND CRIME

Race is one of the most important elements in the dynamics of crime. Blacks frequently are arrested for many property and (especially) violent crimes. Victimization surveys and victim's descriptions to the police of those who "got away" paint a similar picture.[9] At the neighborhood level the volume of crime is strongly correlated with the size of the black population. Thus, trends and conditions in the black community exercise a disproportionate impact on the overall crime rate. There are number of reasons why this should be the case, but as a consequence the fear of crime and concerns about race have become virtually indistinguishable in the minds of many whites. Therefore, it is even more significant that current crime trends include a modest down-turn in rates of arrest for violent crime by blacks, and that demographic trends leading to reduced rates of crime are having significant (although more limited) impacts in the black community.

Table 14.5 indicates the dimensions of the problem. It documents the black proportion of arrestees in several crime categories in 1976. In that year approximately 11.5 percent of the American population was black, yet about 55 percent of all those arrested for murder and 60 percent of all those arrested for homicide were black. Perusal of all 22 crime categories for which the FBI keeps arrest statistics indicates that only in a few categories of juvenile offenses—including runaways (10 percent), vandalism (16 percent), and liquor law violations (10 percent)—were blacks arrested at rates roughly proportional to their share of the population. Arrest rates for blacks were extremely high for more serious violent crimes, and in addition were high (40 percent of the total) for weapons offenses.

At least for those serious crimes, it does not appear that high arrest rates for blacks can be attributed in any substantial way to the propensity of the police to "overarrest" them for actual or imagined offenses. It has been argued that arrest rates for blacks are inflated relative to those for whites, in part because the police typically patrol ghetto areas more intensively and in part because they are more likely to make formal arrests for juvenile and minor adult infractions when black rather than white suspects are involved. However, in the victimization surveys the victims of personal crimes were asked to describe those who preyed upon them. In 1973 they identified 64 percent of all offenders in robberies as black, while official statistics on arrestees set it at 63 percent. For rape the survey figure was 41 percent and the official number was 47 percent. In the case of serious assault the official proportion was 10 percentage points higher than the picture painted by victims, the largest observed discrepancy between the two data sources. Because a number of large steps in the criminal justice system—including citizen reporting of crime, the official recording of complaints, and the ability of the police to catch someone—lie between these observations, they seem to provide powerful evidence that data on arrestees are a useful if indirect *indicator* of the general distribution of offenders in the population.

Table 14.5: Percentage of Arrestees in 1976 Who Were Black

Crime	U.S.	All Cities
Murder	54	62
Rape	47	54
Robbery	59	63
Assault	41	46
Burglary	29	34
Theft	32	34
Auto theft	26	30

Source: Federal Bureau of Investigation, *Uniform Crime Report* (Washinton, D.C.: U.S. Government Printing Office, 1977).

We have already examined two important reasons why blacks are so heavily represented among arrestees: they are city dwellers, and the black population is significantly younger than other groups. America's blacks (and especially those in younger age categories) are disproportionately concentrated in central cities of urban areas, while few are found in their suburban rings. A "critical mass" of persons may have been assembled in the inner cities, which are so isolated from the mainstream economy that they are not much affected by its rewards, or even by its fluctuations. To this must be added the relative youthfulness of urban blacks. In 1976 the median age for whites was nearly 30 years, while for black it was only 24.[10] In addition, there is a litany of income, education, and family status differences between the two populations which are related to criminality in any group. The black urban population shares in overlapping profusion many of the social pathologies which contribute to the breakdown of traditional mechanisms of social control and bring their victims into frequent contact with the police. The consequences of them all can be seen in Figure 14.1, which traces the proportion of arrestees who were black each year since the FBI began reporting modern figures in 1952.

Figure 14.1 suggests that the current overrepresentation of blacks among arrestees for property and violent crimes is a continuation of past trends, but that these trends are changing. The picture for property crimes (here burglary and theft) has remained relatively constant since 1952, with arrest proportion for blacks hovering around 30 percent of the total. For robberies and murders, however, the long-term trend has been for relatively more blacks to be arrested each year, when compared to whites. For robbery, that proportion increased from 53 percent in 1963 to 67 percent in 1972.

These proportions changed at the same time that the overall crime rate was increasing very rapidly and indicate the extent to which violence by blacks contributed to that rise. During the 1963-1972 period, white arrest rates for robbery (arrests per thousand in the U.S. population) increased 74 percent, while arrest rates for blacks went up 194 percent. Increasing black participation in robbery and homicide played an important role in the tremendous increase in violent crime during the 1960s.

What we also see in Figure 14.1 is a pattern of declining arrest totals for blacks as compared to whites during the recent period in which rates for those violent crimes are now dropping. The result has been a rather sharp decrease in the number of arrests of blacks for these crimes relative to their position in the population. At their

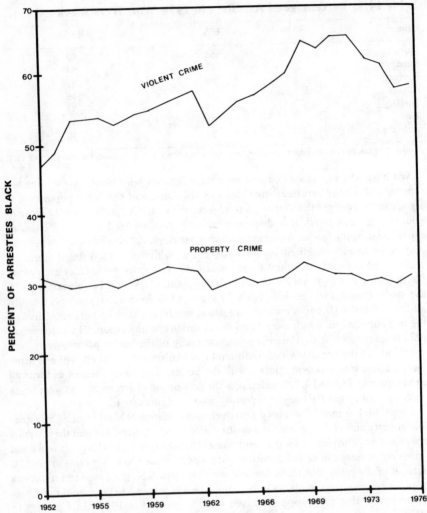

Figure 14.1: Percentages of arrestees for violent and property crime who were black, 1952-1976

Source: FBI Uniform Crime Reports

1972 high, blacks were being arrested for robbery at a rate of 2.5 per thousand, while in 1976 that figure had dropped to 1.5. Virtually the same trend can be observed for murder. As a consequence, in recent years larger proportions of murder *victims* have been white rather than black. Most homicides are intraracial as opposed to interracial affairs, and mortality patterns reflect this fact. Between 1969 and 1976 the proportion of murder victims who were black declined from 55 to 47 percent.

Why this should be the case is less certain. Unfortunately, no data are published from the victimization surveys on changes over time in the attributes of offenders;

however, the data on both offenders and victims of homicides are relatively reliable, and both point to the rise and then fall of black homicide rates during the 1960s and 1970s. One reason for increasing black offense rates during the 1960s, of course, was the relative youth of the black population. The black baby boom peaked later than did that of whites, and during the late 1960s proportionally more blacks than whites were in high-risk offender age categories. Now the median age of the black population is increasing. However, because the fertility level for black females (although reduced) is substantially above that for whites, blacks will continue to contribute disproportionately to the crime count at least into the next century.

WOMEN IN CRIME

As we have seen, one of the determinants of the crime rate is the number of potential criminals in the population. Some high-risk groups, including youths, blacks, and city dwellers, exercise a disproportionate impact upon the overall crime rate despite their minority status. Thus it should be with some trepidation that we turn to the role of women in crime, for numerically they constitute a majority of the population and a vast pool of potential offenders.

Until the mid-1950s the role of women in crime was relatively limited. In the earliest days of systematic reporting only about 10 percent of all arrestees were female. This figure was fairly constant for all types of serious crime, although it was higher for violent than property offenses. Then in the late 1950s the proportion of women arrested for violent crime began to dip. This reflected not a decline in the *number* of female arrestees for crime, but the fact that they were not participating fully in the rising tide of violent crime in the 1960s. In the late 1960s and early 1970s the proportion of arrestees for murder and serious assault who were female averaged about 13 percent, a figure several points below their mark in the early 1950s. These proportions are illustrated in Figure 14.2, which charts the sex distribution of arrestees for violent crime and for simple property offenses (theft, fraud, and embezzlement).

Figure 14.2 shows that increasing female criminality during the 1960s and 1970s was concentrated in property offenses. After 1955 the rate of increase in female property offense rates (arrests per thousand in the population) exceeded that of males, and women now account for nearly one-third of all those arrested for these crimes. As among males, young women are overrepresented in arrest rates for property crimes; this overrepresentation of the young is less extreme, however, and a larger proportion of female than male arrestees for property offenses are adults (60 percent as contrasted to 50 percent, in 1976). These differences in the sexes are not apparent in the case of violent crime; there, virtually equal proportions of male and female arrestees (about 20 percent) fall below voting age.

A number of causes for the growth of female arrest rates have been suggested, ranging from the unwholesome consequences of women's liberation to a decline in chivalry among the policemen. The former presumes that expanded opportunities for women in the criminal sector have resulted from decreases in role differentiation among the sexes, while the latter presumes that the response of policemen to those

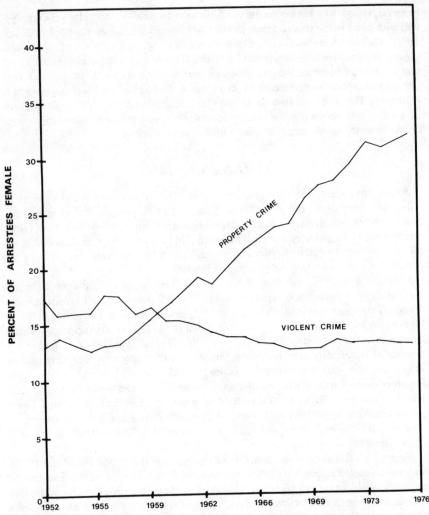

Figure 14.2: Percentages of arrestees for violent and property crime who were women, 1952-1976
Source: FBI Uniform Crime Reports

economic and cultural changes has been, "If they want to be men, we'll treat 'em like men."[11]

The rather early change in arrest patterns for females documented in Figure 14.2 supports the opportunities/role differentiation hypothesis, for it precedes the rhetoric of the women's movement by more than a decade. For a variety of reasons the role of women in the labor force has greatly expanded, and more women than before carry the burden of supporting themselves, and often families as well. This trend is much more apparent among blacks than whites. This means, first, that women are more likely to find themselves in the business world (which will expand opportunities for crimes like embezzlement), and that they are more likely to be tempted by opportunities for "employee theft." At the same time, it renders women more subject to powerful economic pressures, which traditionally have driven some males into crime, including underemployment and unemployment. Because more women entering the labor force take unskilled, low-paying, nonunion, and service jobs, their increased participation in the labor force disproportionately pegs them into occupational categories more vulnerable to those pressures than those of most males. As those who argue that "relative deprivation" breeds crime might point out, this also has led to *increasing* rather than decreasing income differences between working men and women.

Changes in women's economic status thus appear to be a useful explanation for shifts in female arrest patterns in the United States since 1952. While changes in urban patterns, the age distribution, and the status of blacks can be drawn upon to explain generally increasing (and now decreasing) rates of criminality, explanations of significant changes in what women do *relative* to what men do call for the identification of sex-specific social and economic forces of this magnitude.

The trends observed here do not mean that women can be blamed for all of the increase in property crime we have observed during the postwar period. During the period 1956-1976, for example, women rose from 12.6 to 31.2 percent of all those arrested for theft. If instead they had continued to be arrested in their original proportion during the entire span, the total arrest rate for theft still would have increased considerably. If women had continued to assume their modest 1956 role, the arrest rate for theft in the United States in 1976 would have been 378 per 100,000 rather than 423 per 100,000. Changes in women's participation in theft drove arrest rates up 623 percent rather than the 590 percent they "would have" risen if earlier conditions had obtained.

PROGNOSIS

This chapter has painted a rather grim picture of crime in America, but extends a bit of hope for the immediate future. Many of the demographic forces which drove the crime rate to ever higher levels between the early 1960s and the mid-1970s now are following trends which lead us to predict at least stable rates of crime during the next two decades.

First, the age distribution of the nation is shifting. For every 100 arrests for burglary in 1976, 80 were of youths under 25 years of age. Thus, it is extremely important that by 1990 the proportion of the population in the high-risk 15-25 age category will be 16 percentage points lower than it was in 1976, which already was past the peak created by the postwar baby boom. By 2050 the median age of the U.S. population will be a full decade higher than it is now, which augurs well for crime rates in the far future. Not only a simple drop in the size of the high-risk populations is involved in predicting a declining crime rate. For example, the decline in the youthful segment of the population should decrease unemployment rates. Census Bureau figures show that by the end of 1978 there will be a 30 percent drop in the number of persons entering the work force each year, as compared to the late 1960s.[12] As schools become less crowded and as early entry into the job market becomes less competitive, we should find that these mechanisms of social control work more effectively as well.

The continued shift of the American population out of large central cities and away from metropolitan areas, and toward the South and the West, should further discourage the growth of crime. The population is growing in more prosperous (and lower-crime) areas, and declining in many of the very worst places. Depopulation is proceeding at a very fast rate in many of the most famous ghettos in the nation, including Hough, Watts, Woodlawn, and the South Bronx. As whites flee central cities, the housing stock available to blacks increases both in quantity and quality, and has such important side effects as increasing the proportion of black families who are home owners. While these shifts have negative implications for the availability of higher-paying jobs in Northeastern and Midwestern central cities, recent evidence suggests that (outside of the five largest cities, which are in worse shape) the ratio of all jobs to workers in central cities has not been declining in recent years.[13]

All of these positive gains attributable to demographic change accrue more slowly to blacks than to whites, however. The black population is both younger and is continuing to grow, which assures us a relatively large number of high-risk males into the next century. There is increasing unemployment among black youths, and it is increasingly common to find female-headed families in the black community. Both of these ensure low incomes and high welfare enrollment rates, and may point to a continued decline in the effectiveness of informal social controls.

The future of women in crime is most closely tied to variations in the Consumer Price Index. If women continue to lead economically independent lives, and if trends toward female-headed families continue, we should expect upward pressure on the property crime rate. On the other hand, when the violent crime rate began to climb in the mid-1960s the role of women in those crimes relative to men began to decline, for they did not participate in increasing numbers. If the violent crime rate continues to fall, women may take their original place. This would indicate not a change in what they do, but rather the pacification of the male population.

This diagnosis has implications for the treatment of crime. For example, investment in prisons is extremely costly, and we need to think carefully about the wisdom of embarking on massive expansion of our institutional capacity at a time when we can expect continuing stabilization of the crime rate. Changes both in the frequency of crime and the profile of offenders and the types of crime they commit need to be monitored carefully. The difficulties involved in measuring the true level of crime and obtaining an unbiased picture of offenders point up the continued importance of victimization surveys and other independent sources of information on crime. Together with official reports, they enable us to "triangulate" upon the problem, yielding a more reliable picture of its nature. In the 1960s crime was an epidemic; in the 1980s it will be more like a lingering disease. This will call for more subtle readings of society's vital signs before appropriate remedies can be prescribed.

NOTES

1. All data on offically reported crime are drawn from the *Uniform Crime Report*, which is published yearly by the Federal Bureau of Investigation. It reports, among other things, counts of the number of verified crimes of several kinds reported to the police each year, the number of persons arrested for each of about 20 types of crime, and the age, sex, and race of the arrestees. These data are based on reports filed with the FBI by police agencies throughout the country. As discussed in the text, there are many problems with these data. In the main, however, they reveal the same trends and patterns as do other comparable measures of the incidence of crime. They are also the only source of national data on crime prior to 1973.

All data on population have been drawn from the *Statistical Abstract of the United States*, a yearly publication of the U.S. Census Bureau.

2. These data for 1977 and 1978 are unofficial, preliminary releases from the Uniform Crime Reporting Section of the FBI.

3. Wesley G. Skogan, "Citizen Reporting of Crime: Some National Panel Data," *Criminology* 13 (February 1976): 535-549; Wesley G. Skogan, "Crime and Crime Rates," 105-119 in W. Skogan, ed., *Sample Surveys of the Victims of Crime* (Cambridge, Mass.: Ballinger, 1976).

4. U.S. Department of Justice, *Criminal Victimization in the United States: A Comparison of 1975 and 1976 Findings* (Washington, D.C.: U.S. Government Printing Office, 1977); Federal Bureau of Investigation, *Uniform Crime Report* (Washington, D.C.: U.S. Government Printing Office, 1977).

5. Data on the personal characteristics of arrestees have been published by the FBI for many years. Prior to 1952, however, they were drawn from fingerprint cards submitted to the Bureau by local agencies. In 1952, data on arrestees were solicited from all police departments serving cities greater than 25,000; in 1953 this cut-off was reduced to 2,500, and in early 1960s the data was requested from all agencies. Coverage is far from complete. In 1960, agencies covering 60 percent of the U.S. population supplied data, while in 1976 about 84 percent of the population was covered. Coverage is currently lowest in rural areas.

6. Louis Wirth, "Urbanism as a Way of Life," *American Journal of Sociology*, 44 (July 1938): 1-24.

7. U.S. Bureau of the Census, *Statistical Abstract of the United States* (Washington, D.C.: U.S. Government Printing Office, 1978).

8. This mode of analysis was suggested in an unpublished paper by Franklin Zimring, "Dealing with Crime: National Needs and Federal Priorities," a report to the office of Juvenile Justice and Delinquency Prevention, Law Enforcement Assistance Administration, 1975.

9. Lynn Curtis, *Violence, Race and Culture* (Lexington, Mass.: Lexington Books, 1975): Michael J. Hindelang, "Race and Involvement in Crimes," *American Sociological Review* 43 (February 1978): 93-109.

10. U.S. Bureau of the Census, op. cit.

11. Laurel L. Rans, "Women's Crime: Much Ado About. . . .?" *Federal Probation* (March 1978): 45-50; Rita James Simon, *The Contemporary Woman and Crime* (Washington, D.C.: Center for Studies of Crime and Delinquency, National Institute of Mental Health, 1978); Freda Adler, *Sisters in Crime* (New York: McGraw-Hill, 1975).

12. "Fewer Births May Mean Declining Jobless Rate," Chicago *Tribune*, December 16, 1977.

13. Bennett Harrison, *Urban Economic Development* (Washington, D.C.: Urban Institute, 1974).

Chapter 15
Southern Violence

SHELDON HACKNEY

Violence has always been a facet of human experience and a problem for human society. For those interested in determining the cause of violence, and perhaps constructing cures, nothing could be more important than the fact that different societies and different eras produce widely varying rates of violence. Unfortunately for the investigator, even moderately reliable data are available only for the recent past and only for relatively modernized countries. This limits the possibility of cross-national comparisons. For this reason, regional variations within modernized nations become an extremely important source for the comparative analysis of the ecology of violence. The most fruitful area within the United States for such a study is the South, a region with a pattern of violence that stands in striking contrast to that of the nation at large and about which there is a well-developed scholarly literature.

A tendency toward violence has been one of the character traits most frequently attributed to Southerners.[1] In various guises, the image of the violent South confronts the historian at every turn: dueling gentlemen and masters whipping slaves, flatboatmen indulging in a rough-and-tumble fight, lynching mobs, country folk at a bear baiting or a gander pulling, romantic adventures on Caribbean filibusters, brutal police, panic-stricken communities harshly suppressing real and imagined slave revolts, robed night riders engaged in systematic terrorism, unknown assassins, church burners, and other less physical expressions of a South whose mode of action is frequently extreme.[2] The image is so pervasive that it compels the attention of anyone interested in understanding the South.

H.C. Brearley was among the first to assemble the quantitative data to support the description of the South as "that part of the United States lying below the Smith and Wesson line."[3] He pointed out, for example, that during the five years from 1920 to 1924 the rate of homicide per 100,000 population for the Southern states was a little more than two-and-one-half times greater than for the remainder of the United

AUTHOR'S NOTE: *Sheldon Hackney is president of Tulane University. His book* Populism to Progressivism in Alabama *(Princeton University Press, 1969) won both the Beveridge Prize from the American Historical Association and the Sydnor Prize from the Southern Historical Association. "Southern Violence" was originally published in the* American Historical Review, *Vol. 74 (February 1969), 906-925, as well as in the first edition of* Violence in America *(1969, Ch. 14), and is reprinted here by permission of the author.*

States. Using data from the *Uniform Crime Reports* concerning the 1930s, Stuart Lottier confirmed and elaborated Brearley's findings in 1938. He found for this period also that homicide was concentrated in the Southeastern states. Of the eleven ex-Confederate states, Louisiana showed the lowest homicide rate, but it was 74 percent greater than the national average, and no non-Southern state had a higher rate. Interestingly, while murder and assault were oriented to the Southeastern states, robbery rates were highest in the Central and Western states.[4] These findings were replicated in 1954 using data on crime for the years 1946 through 1952.[5] The pattern of high rates of serious crimes against persons and relatively lower rates of crimes against property for the South is consequently quite stable.

At the time that Brearley was setting forth the evidence for Southern leadership in physical aggression against people, another statistical study primarily of American suicide rates revealed that the South was the area whose people had the least propensity to destroy themselves.[6] Austin Porterfield in 1949, using mortality tables from *Vital Statistics,* brought the murder and the suicide indices together and showed that there was a general inverse relationship between the two rates among the states, and the Southern states ranked highest in homicide and lowest in suicide.[7] In 1940, the national average rate of suicide per 100,000 population was 14.4 and of homicide was 6.2, but the old and cosmopolitan city of New Orleans had a suicide rate of 11.1 and a homicide rate of 15.5. Even though some Southern cities exceed some non-Southern cities in suicide rates, the New Orleans pattern of more homicides than suicides is typical of the South. Porterfield comments that "suicide in every non-Southern city exceeds homicide by ratios ranging from 1.19 to 18.60, while suicide rates exceed homicide rates in only 8 of the 43 Southern and Southwestern cities, 5 of those being in the Southwest."[8]

Violence in the South has three dimensions. Relative to the North, there are high rates of homicide and assault, moderate rates of crime against property, and low rates of suicide. The relationship between homicide and suicide rates in a given group is best expressed by a suicide-homicide ratio (SHR = 100 (suicides/suicides + homicides)). The closer the SHR approaches 100, the greater is the proportion of the total number of homicides and suicides accounted for by suicide. The European pattern, shared by white Northerners but not by black or white Southerners, is for suicides to far outnumber homicides so that the SHR is in excess of 80. The ratios in Table 15.1, displayed graphically in Figure 15.1, measure the difference between Southerners and other Americans with regard to violence.

Because the statistics for "the United States" include the statistics for the Southern states, the differences between Southern and non-Southern suicide-murder ratios are understated. Even so, the differences are significant. In the North and the South, but more so in the South, blacks commit murder much more often than they commit suicide. Among white Americans, Southerners show a relatively greater preference than do non-Southerners for murder rather than suicide. The latter pattern is evident in Figure 15.2, which plots white SHR's by state. The Southern and Southwestern states tend to cluster in the upper left part of the graph, signifying high homicide but relatively low suicide rates.

High murder and low suicide rates constitute a distinctly Southern pattern of violence, one that must rank with the caste system and ahead of mint juleps in

Table 15.1: Suicide-Homicide Ratios for
Four Categories of Americans, 1915-64[a]

Year	U.S. White SHR	Southern White SHR	U.S. Black SHR	Southern Black SHR
1915	77.4	62.9[b]	23.7	11.3[b]
1920	69.3	43.4[b]	11.2	05.6[b]
1925	70.9	53.5[b]	09.2	05.0[b]
1930	75.0	61.1[b]	11.9	06.0[b]
1935	76.2	59.9	11.4	06.3
1940	83.3	68.5	09.6	06.5
1945	80.3	66.4	11.1	06.8
1950	82.4	69.8	12.4	09.3
1955	88.3	73.1	15.6	09.7
1960	82.0	74.4	17.0	12.2
1964	81.1	73.2	16.7	11.1

a. Suicide-homicide ratio = 100 (suicides/suicides + homicides). As the ratio approaches 100, it registers the increasing preference for suicide rather than murder among the members of a given group. The ratios were computed from figures taken from: Forrest E. Linder and Robert D. Grove, *Vital Statistics Rates in the United States, 1900-1949* (Washington, 1943), and U.S. Department of Health, Education, and Welfare, *Vital Statistics of the United States,* for the appropriate year.

b. In 1915, only Virginia was represented in the SHR for Southern whites and blacks. In 1920, all of the ex-Confederate states were included in the figures except Alabama, Arkansas, Georgia, and Texas. Arkansas, Georgia, and Texas were still not reporting in 1925, but by 1930 only Texas was excluded. From 1935 on, all Southern states are included.

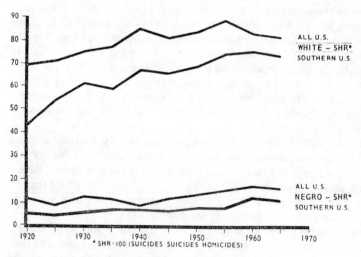

Figure 15.1: Suicide-homicide ratios.

importance as a key to the meaning of being Southern. Why this should be so is a question that has puzzled investigators for a long time, and their answers have been various. When one loyal Southerner was asked by a probing Yankee why the murder rate in the South was so high, he replied that he reckoned there were just more folks in the South that needed killing.

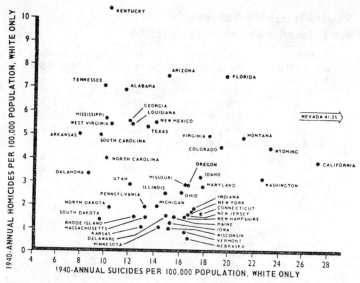

Figure 15.2: Regional homogeneity in homicide-suicide ratios

Few apologies surpass this one in purity, but there is a more popular one that tries to explain the high homicide rates in the Southern states by the extremely high rates of violence among blacks, who constitute a large part of the population. As Table 15.1 indicates, however, Southern whites considered by themselves vary from the national norm in the same direction as blacks, though to a much lesser extent. In addition, Porterfield points out that for the twelve Southern states with the heaviest black population, the coefficient of correlation between serious crimes and the percentage of blacks in the population is − 0.44. There is actually a tendency for states to rank lower in serious crimes as the percentage of blacks in the population increases.[9]

A more sophisticated theory is that Southern white society contains a larger proportion of lower-status occupations so that the same factors that cause lower status groups in the North to become more violent than the rest of society have a proportionately greater effect on the South. The difference in rates would then be accounted for by the numerical bulge in the high-risk group, and only the stratification of society would be peculiarly Southern. Unfortunately for this theory, Southern cities, in which whites show the distinctive pattern of Southern violence, actually have greater percentages of the white population in higher-status jobs than do Northern cities.[10] It is not the class structure that causes the Southern skew in the statistics.

In the same way, the agricultural nature of Southern life might account for the pattern of Southern violence. The fact that the peculiar configuration exists in Southern cities as well as in the countryside could possibly be accounted for by the large migration into the city of people who learned their ways of living and dying in the country. Table 15.2 shows that both homicide and suicide rates are lower for rural districts than for urban areas in the United States. This results in an SHR for the

Table 15.2: Homicide and Suicide Rates by Race and by Size of Population Group, United States, 1940

	U.S.	Cities 100,000 and Up	Cities 10 to 100,000	Cities 2,500-10,000	Rural
Suicide					
(all ages, both sexes): All races	14.4	16.8	15.6	15.1	12.0
White	15.5	17.8	16.4	16.0	13.3
Nonwhite	4.6	7.2	5.8	4.5	3.0
Homicide					
(all ages, both sexes): All races	6.2	7.1	5.7	7.3	5.7
White	3.1	3.2	2.5	3.7	3.3
Nonwhite	33.3	43.3	43.0	51.9	23.1

Source: Forrest E. Linder and Robert D. Grove, *Vital Statistics Rates in the United States, 1900-1940* (Washington D.C.: U.S. Government Printing Office, 1943). Table 24, pp. 534-553.

white population of rural districts considered by themselves of 80.1, as compared with an SHR of 83.7 for the white population of the nation as a whole. The SHR of 68.8 in 1940 for Southern whites, both urban and rural, is significantly lower than the national ratios and indicates that Southern whites were much more given to acting out their aggressions than the white population of either the cities or the countryside in the rest of the nation.

Another way of testing the notion that the rurality of the South may be the root of its strange configuration of violence is summarized in Table 15.3, a comparison of the SHR's of the eleven ex-Confederate states with those of the eleven most rural non-Southern states. The non-Southern states, mostly Western, are closer in time to frontier days and are currently much more subject to instability caused by immigration than are the Southern states, but otherwise the two sets of states are similar enough for purposes of comparison. The percentage of population living in the urban areas of the Southern states ranged from 13.4 percent to 36.7 percent with the mean falling at 26.1 percent, while in the eleven non-Southern states the degree of urbanization ranged from 13.6 percent to 36.7 percent, with the mean at 31.2 percent. In order not to distort the comparison more than necessary, Nevada, with an extraordinary suicide rate of 41.3 per 100,000 population, is omitted from the comparison. At the same time, Virginia and Florida, with very non-Southern SHR's, are retained in the Southern sample. The results still show a significant difference between the suicide-murder ratio of the Southern states and that of the most rural non-Southern states. The strange bent of Southern violence cannot be accounted for by the rural nature of Southern society.

Poverty is also a logical factor to suspect as the underlying cause of the South's pattern of violence. Howard Odum computed that the Southeast in 1930 had 20.9 percent of the nation's population but only 11.9 percent of the nation's wealth.[11] Whether or not the region was poor before it was violent is an undetermined matter. Even more to the point, poverty alone cannot explain high homicide rates. The decline of homicides during business depressions in the United States underlines this argument, as does the fact that crime rates among second-generation immigrants are much higher than among first-generation immigrants despite the fact of increased material welfare.[12] One study has found no significant correlation between crime rates and the proportion of the population on relief by county in Minnesota, whereas there was a strong correlation between crime rates and the degree of urbanization. Like the rural poor in Minnesota, the Japanese of Seattle were poor but honest and nonviolent.[13]

Table 15.3: Suicide and Homicide Rates and Suicide-Homicide Ratios for Southern States and 11 Most Rural Non-Southern States, 1940

Population Group	Suicide-Homicide Ratio
Southern nonwhite	6.7
National nonwhite	12.2
Southern white	68.8
Non-Southern, white rural (11 states)	79.0
National white rural	80.1
National white	83.7

Southern States	White		Rural non-Southern States	White	
	Suicide Rate	Homicide Rate		Suicide Rate	Homicide Rate
Alabama	11.7	6.9	Arizona	15.2	7.5
Arkansas	8.0	5.1	Idaho	17.7	3.3
Florida	19.8	7.5	Iowa	15.2	1.3
Georgia	12.1	5.6	Kansas	13.0	1.1
Louisiana	12.4	5.5	Montana	21.1	4.8
Mississippi	10.1	5.7	Nebraska	16.8	.7
North Carolina	10.4	4.0	New Mexico	14.2	5.7
South Carolina	9.7	5.0	North Dakota	9.7	1.4
Tennessee	10.0	7.1	South Dakota	10.5	1.8
Texas	13.6	5.3	Vermont	16.7	.8
Virginia	18.4	5.0	Wyoming	23.5	4.5
Average	12.4	5.6	Average	15.8	4.2

Source: Forrest E. Linder and Robert D. Grove, *Vital Statistics Rates in the United States, 1900-1940* (Washington, D.C.: U.S. Government Printing Office, 1943), Table 20. All rates per 100,000 population.

Nevertheless, though the data are extremely questionable, there is a significant positive correlation between the SHR for the 56 world polities for which information is readily available and almost every measure of modernization that can be quantified.[14] It is difficult to determine whether it is underdevelopment or the process of change that accounts for this, for scholars have noted that the process of modernization generates conflict and violence of various sorts.[15] For developing as well as for industrialized nations, education is the most powerful predictor of a country's SHR, but indices of industrial and urban activity, along with reflections of the society's general welfare are also significantly correlated with the SHR. This is true for the 56 world polities considered together as well as for the European nations considered as a group and for the non-European countries taken together. That Southerners over the past half century have been growing more similar to non-Southern Americans in their taste in violence as the gap between the nation and the South in economic development has slowly narrowed also argues that there may be no increment of violence in the South that is not "explained" by the relative slowness of the region's development.

Multiple regression analysis offers a technique for testing the possibility that variations in the key indices of modernization operating in an additive fashion might account for the South's particularity in rates of violence. Six independent variables measuring the four factors of wealth, education, urbanization, and age are included in this analysis. Except where indicated below, their values are taken from the *United States Census* of 1940. Urbanization is stated as the percentage of the population living within towns of 2,500 or more; education is measured by the median number of school years completed by persons 25 years old and older; "income" is the state's per capita personal income in dollars for 1940; unemployment is expressed as the percentage of the working force out of work; "wealth" is the state's per capita income in dollars in 1950; and age is the median age of the population. The values of each variable except "income" are recorded by race. "South" is a dummy variable included in the analysis in order to see if any of the unexplained residue of the dependent variable is associated with the fact of its occurring either inside of or outside of the South. All of the ex-Confederate states were assigned the value of one, while all non-Southern states were recorded as zero. The dependent variables that require "explaining" are the suicide rate, the homicide rate, the sum of the suicide rate and homicide rate, and the suicide-homicide ratio. Even though these rates are taken from the most reliable source, *Vital Statistics for the United States,* there may well be large errors between the published rates and the true rates. Some violent deaths are never recorded, and many are improperly classified, but there is no reason to suspect that there has been a long-term, systematic bias in the collection and recording of the statistics for the Southern states. For the purposes of the crude comparison between South and non-South, the *Vital Statistics* are acceptable.

The results of the analysis are summarized in table 15.4. The coefficient of correlation between each of the independent variables and the dependent variable is found in the column labeled "simple." The percentage of the variation in the dependent variable that is associated with, and thus "explained" by, the variation in the independent variable is found by squaring the coefficient of correlation. For example, education is the best single predictor of the white suicide rate. The simple coefficient of correlation of 0.62 between education and suicide in table 15.4 indicates that approximately 30 percent of the variation in the white suicide rate among the 48 states in 1940 is associated with variations in the educational level of the populations. The fact that the correlation is positive means that the suicide rate tends to rise from one state to the next as the educational level rises. Conversely, the negative coefficients of correlation between each of the independent variables, except region, and the white homicide rate indicate that the homicide rate tends to decline as the indices of development rise.

The effect on the dependent variable of all of the independent variables considered together is measured by the coefficient of multiple correlation, R. Thus 72 percent of the white suicide rate and 52 percent of the white homicide rate are explained by seven independent variables operating in an additive fashion. The coefficient of partial correlation expresses the relationship of each independent variable with the unexplained portion of the dependent variable after the independent variables acting collectively have done all the explaining possible. The coefficient of partial correlation for the dummy variable, South, is the most important yield of the multiple regression analysis.

Even though the seven independent variables acting together explain 72 percent of the variation of the white SHR among the 48 states in 1940, 28 percent ($r = -0.53$) of the remaining portion of the variation of the white SHR is associated with the South. This means that the white SHR is lower in the South than can be accounted for by the lower indices of urbanization, education, wealth, and age. Similarly, there is a significant portion of the variation from state to state in the white homicide rate, and in the white suicide rate, that is unexplained by variations in measures of development but that is explained by Southernness.

If the deviation of the South from the national norms for violence cannot be attributed to backwardness, or at least not to the static measures of underdevelopment, there are other possible explanations that should be considered. The concept of anomy, developed by Emil Durkheim in his study, *Suicide*, in 1898, is frequently mentioned as an explanation of both homicide and suicide. Anomy has meant slightly different but not contradictory things to different investigators. It is most generally understood to be a social condition in which there is a deterioration of belief in the existing set of rules of behavior, or in which accepted rules are mutually contradictory, or where prescribed goals are not accessible through legitimate means, or where cognition and socialization have been obstructed by personality traits that cluster about low ego strength.[16] In its manifestation in the individual, in the form of anomy, it is a feeling of normlessness and estrangement from other people. An anomic person feels lost, drifting without clearly defined rules and expectations, isolated, powerless, and frustrated. In this state, there is a strong strain toward deviant behavior in various forms. The problem is that both homicide and suicide are thought to be related to it, and the theory does not predict what sorts of people or what groups will favor one form of behavior rather than another.

To look at Southern violence as the product of anomy in any case would involve a great paradox. The most popular explanation of the high rates of American violence as compared to Europe places the blame on the rapid urbanization, secularization, and industrialization of the United States and on the social characteristics associated with this remarkable growth: geographic and status mobility, an emphasis upon contractual relationships and upon social norms rather than upon personal relationships, competitive striving, and a cultural pluralism that involves a high level of dissonance among the values that everyone tries to put into practice.[17] The South has traditionally served as the counterpoint to the American way of life for the reason that it seemed to differ from the North in these very aspects.[18] Southerners have a

Table 15.4: Multiple Regression Analysis—Violence, Development, and Sectionalism in the United States, 1940

Dependent Variable by State	R Variation Explained	Urbanization		Education		Income		Unemployment		Wealth		Age		South	
		Simple	Partial	Simple	Partial	Simple	Partial	Simple	Partial	Simple	Partial	Simple	Partial	Simple	Partial
White suicide rate	0.72*	.25	-0.64*	.62*	.52	.56*	.14	.22	.33	.53*	.35	.55*	.59*	-0.31	0.42*
White homicide rate	.52*	-.45*	-.24	-.17	.09	-.42	.23	-.13	.26	-.42	-.12	-.58*	.24	.54*	.49*
White homicide-suicide rate	.57*	.07	-.59*	.52	.44*	.36	.20	.15	.35	-.34	.22	-.30	.41*	-.09	.50*
White homicide-suicide rate	.72*	.53*	-.02	.40*	.11	.63*	-.24	.25	-.18	.62*	.29	.76*	.49*	-.68*	-.53*
Nonwhite suicide rate	.30	.08	-.13	.30	.25	.47*	.26	.15	-.09	.34	-.00	.13	-.04	-.34	.08
Nonwhite homicide rate	.25	-.07	-.28	-.19	-.25	-.11	.18	-.17	.21	-.09	-.04	.04	.40*	.28	.37*
Nonwhite homicide-suicide rate	.22	-.02	-.30	-.03	-.12	.13	.27	-.08	.15	.09	-.04	.10	.35	.09	.37*
Nonwhite suicide-homicide rate	.35	.27	.36	.36	.31	.43*	.18	.30	-.11	.36	-.10	.12	-.40	-.36	-.09

* The chances that a random ordering of the data would produce a relationship this strong are less than 1 in 100.

greater sense of history than Northerners, a greater attachment to place, and more deferential social customs. By all reports, Southerners place more emphasis on personal relations and on ascribed statuses than do Northerners. Not only do Southerners prize political and social cohesion, but by most measures the South is much more homogeneous than the non-South.[19] Yet, though the South differs from the North on so many of the factors that supposedly contribute to anomy and thus to violence, the South is the nation's most violent region.

There is one body of theory that would seem to predict higher rates of violence precisely because of the South's homogeneity. Reformulating the observations of George Simmel and Bronislaw Malinowski, Lewis Coser writes that "we may say that a conflict is more passionate and more radical when it arises out of close relationships." "The closer the relationship," so the reasoning goes, "the greater the affective investment, the greater also the tendency to suppress rather than express hostile feelings. . . . In such cases feelings of hostility tend to accumulate and hence intensify." Such a theory fits the empirical observation that individuals who express hostility retain fewer and less violent feelings of antagonism toward the source of their irritation.[20] But Coser himself states that, though conflicts within close relationships are likely to be intense when they occur, "this does not necessarily point to the likelihood of more *frequent* conflict in closer relationships than in less close ones." There are situations in which accumulated hostilities do not eventuate in conflict behavior and may even serve to solidify the relationship.[21]

The frustration-aggression hypothesis involves similar perplexities.[22] For example, one of the alternative ways of adapting to frustration is to turn the frustration inward upon the self. In extreme cases this can result in suicide.[23] A psychoanalyst has concluded after an extensive study that a major portion of Sweden's very high suicide rate is caused by the frustrations arising from a highly competitive, success-oriented society.[24] The general rise in suicide rates in the United States during economic downturns argues that the same mechanism is at work among some segments of the population. Consequently, nothing in the frustration-aggression hypothesis predicts the direction the aggression will take.

There are currently two theories that attempt to explain the generally inverse relationship between homicide and suicide as reactions to frustration. The first, developed by Andrew F. Henry and James F. Short, Jr.,[25] is based on the assumption that both homicide and suicide are the result of frustration-aggression and builds upon Porterfield's initial suggestion that the strength of the relational system might have something to do with an individual's choice of either homicide or suicide.[26] Henry and Short adduce data on the relationship of homicide and suicide rates to the business cycle and to certain statistically distinct groups. They reason that overt aggression against others "varies directly with the strength of external restraint over the behavior of the adult—external restraint which is a function of strength of the relational system and position in the status hierarchy.[27]

Martin Gold has pointed out, however, that contrary to the assumption of Henry and Short, upper-status people are likely to be more restrained by the expectations of others than are lower-status people. Even more damaging is Gold's demonstration that the Henry and Short hypothesis does not correctly predict the greater preference of women for suicide rather than homicide,[28] nor does it correctly predict the fact that suicide rates are lower among the middle classes than at either extreme of the social scale.

The second theory, fashioned by Martin Gold, attempts to relate differences in child-rearing practices to preferences for hostility or guilt as an accommodation to frustration. Specifically, Gold shows that there is a positive correlation between the incidence of physical punishment commonly used in the child-rearing practices of certain groups and the rate of homicide for that group. His conclusion is that physical disciplining of children leads to aggression against others rather than against the self.[29] To confound the theory, restrictive child-rearing practices in Europe evidently do not lead to the physical violence that such practices among the lower classes in America are supposed to produce. There is also considerable doubt that there is a significant class differential in the degree of physical punishment used to discipline children.[30] William and Joan McCord found in their study of juveniles that there was no strong relationship between disciplining methods and criminality except when a child is rejected by his parents or when his parents provide him with a deviant role model. Harsh discipline does less damage than neglect.[31] That there is some causal relationship between the socialization of aggression and a group's SHR is reason enough to suppose that it will provide a fruitful line of research, but before it can be a useful ingredient of an explanation of Southern violence, anthropologists and historians need to know much more about regional differences in child-rearing techniques.

Whether or not the cause can be located in child-rearing practices, several bodies of evidence point to the conclusion that Southern violence is a cultural pattern that exists separate from current influences. For instance, several commentators have suggested that the habit of carrying guns in the South made murder a much more frequent outcome of altercations among Southerners than among Northerners. This argument is buttressed by a 1968 survey, reported in Table 15.5, which showed that 52 percent of Southern white families owned guns, as opposed to only 27 percent of the white families of the non-South. It may be, however, that this differential in gun ownership is the result of a violent turn of mind rather than the cause of violence. This is the implication of the fact that when the House of Representatives in 1968 passed a weak gun-control bill to restrict the mail-order sale of rifles, shotguns, and ammunition by the overwhelming vote of 304-118, representatives of the 11 ex-Confederate states nonetheless voted 73-19 against the bill.[32] It should be noted too

Table 15.5: Percentage of Families Owning Firearms

	Yes	No	Not Sure
Total white	34	65	1
South	52	45	3
Non-South	27	72	1
Total nonwhite	24	70	6
South	34	61	5
Non-South	15	78	7

Source: Survey of national statistical sample by Opinion Research, Inc., for a Columbia Broadcasting System program Sept. 2, 1968.

that some Southern states have relatively strict firearms laws without dramatically affecting their homicide rates.[33] Furthermore, the assault rate is extremely high in the South, indicating that Southerners react with physical hostility even without guns.

A glance at Table 15.4 reveals that for Negroes either the data are grossly skewed or there is little relationship between violence and the selected indices of social welfare. There is the barest hint that, controlling for the selected factors, there is some explanatory value in sectionalism, a conclusion that has independent verification. Thomas F. Pettigrew and an associate found that the major correlate of the rate of black homicide in the North was the proportion of blacks in a given area who had been born and raised in the South and that this was in addition to the effect of migration itself. It had long been known that homicide was much less frequent among Northern than among Southern blacks, but this finding suggests that violence in the South is a style of life that is handed down from father to son along with the old hunting rifle and family Bible.[34]

The great contribution to the discussion of Southern violence made by Wilbur J. Cash in his book, *The Mind of the South,* was precisely this, that Southern violence is part of a style of life that can be explained only historically.[35] According to Cash's own poetic and impressionistic rendering, violence grew up on the Southern frontier as naturally as it grows up on any frontier. Violence was an integral part of the romantic, hedonistic, hell-of-a-fellow personality created by the absence of external restraint that is characteristic of a frontier. The cult of honor, with its insistence on the private settlement of disputes, was one form taken by the radical individualism of the South, but there were other influences at work. The plantation, the most highly organized institution on the Southern frontier, reinforced the tendency toward violence that had been initiated by the absence of organization. This was so, Cash argues, for two reasons. In the first place, whites on the plantation exercised unrestrained dominance over blacks. In the second place, whites were generally raised by blacks and consequently were deeply influenced by the romantic and hedonistic black personality. Cash does not explicitly say what forces produced this black personality, but the implication is that black personality is fixed by the laws of genetics. But if the more likely position is taken that black and white personalities are shaped by environment and experience, then the reader is left with yet another Cashian paradox: violence in the white personality stems at the same time from the effect of being unrestrained and from imitating the black personality which was formed out of a situation of dependency and subordination.

It may be that the mediating variable that brings together the various inconsistencies in Cash's explanation of how violence came to be established in the late ante-bellum period as part of the Southern personality is the absence of law. Not disorganization nor individualism, not dominance nor submission, not lack of restraint—none of these forces played as important a role as the absence of institutions of law enforcement in forcing Southerners to resort to the private settlement of disputes. Cash makes this explicit in his treatment of Reconstruction, the second frontier.

During Reconstruction, according to Cash, Southern whites resorted to individual and collective violence because the courts were dominated by carpetbaggers and scalawags. Though this is logical, it is not consistent with Cash's earlier argument that the growth of law had been inhibited on the ante-bellum frontier by the desire of

Southerners to provide their own justice. Apparently the direction of causation in the relationship between law and violence changes in accordance with the needs of Cash's interpretation.

Just as the first and second Southern frontiers simultaneously promoted social solidarity and individualism, the third Southern frontier, Progress, changed the South in the direction of the American norm of Babbittry while at the same time accommodating continuity in the basic traits of the Southern mind. A further paradox is involved in the impact of progress on the pattern of violence. Because violence originally arose from individualism, Cash says, the growth of towns should have brought a decrease in rates of violence. This decrease did not materialize because progress also brought poverty and poverty destroys individualism. Cash, in effect, argues that individualism produced violence in the ante-bellum period and the loss of individualism produced violence in the twentieth century.

Though Cash failed to produce a coherent theory of Southern violence, he did focus on two factors that are obvious possibilities as the chief motive forces of Southern violence: the frontier experience and the presence of blacks. The American frontier did spawn violence, but it seems improbable that the frontier could have much to do with the fact that in the twentieth century Southern states on the Eastern seaboard have much higher rates of violence than the nation at large. There is also considerable difficulty with the notion that the presence of large numbers of blacks accounts for the great propensity of whites for violence. There is, in fact, very little interracial homicide,[36] and there is no reason to question John Dollard's hypothesis that blacks murder and assualt each other with such appalling frequency because of their daily frustrations in dealing with white men. Because aggressions against whites would call forth extreme negative sanctions, frustrated blacks display their aggressive feelings to other blacks.[37] If this is the case, it is difficult to see how high rates of violence among the dominant white group would also be attributed to the white-black relationship, especially when the presence of blacks in the North is not accompanied by a proportionate rate of violence among the whites. It is also interesting that whites in South Africa, who also experienced frontier conditions and a subordinate nonwhite population, have a homicide-suicide ratio almost identical to the ratio for the American North but quite different from that of the Southern whites.

Subservience, rather than dominance, may be the condition that underlies a pattern of low SHRs. Frantz Fanon, in his controversial book, *The Wretched of the Earth,* suggests that the oppressed status of a colonial people produced a pattern of aggressiveness directed against fellow colonials and a need to achieve manhood through violence. That task of revolutionaries is to mobilize the aggressive drives, provide them a sustaining ideology, and direct them against the oppressors.[38] The South's defeat in the Civil War and its position as an economic dependency of the industrial Northeast qualifies it for consideration as a violent colonial region. In addition to the difficulty of separating the effects of subserviency from the effects of sheer underdevelopment, the problem with this line of reasoning is that the heroic myths created about the "Lost Cause" and the relatively early return of home rule after the Civil War may have mitigated the trauma of defeat and social dislocation. It would be difficult to maintain that the South's historical experience as a region is the equivalent of the sort of cultural conflict that leads to the loss of self-esteem, disrupts the processes of socialization, and initiates the cycle of self-crippling behavior within the subordinate group.[39] Furthermore, American Indians have responded to their experience of defeat and repression with higher rates of suicide and other intrapunitive behavior rather than with aggression against others. Similarly, while industrialization was transforming and disrupting its established folk culture, Harlan County, Ky., had the highest homicide rates in the country, but a study of community growth in New England finds suicide and depressive disorders highly correlated with the disruptive impact of geographic mobility.[40]

Though the social sciences offer no clear authenticated hypothesis that predicts the relationship in different populations between homicide and suicide rates,[41] there are some potentially illuminating investigations currently in progress. Assuming that depressed mental patients are people who have turned anger inward through the mechanism of introjection and guilt when under chronic stress, while paranoid patients are those who have turned anger outward through the mechanism of denial and projection, one study has found an interesting association between the pattern of intrafamily communication and the direction taken by mental pathology when it occurred. Depressed patients in this study came from families in which the children were forced to try by themselves to attain the desired forms of behavior through positive, "ought" channels. Children in the families of paranoid patients were forced into acceptable modes of behavior by negative "ought not" procedures.

> In families of *depressed* patients the child comes to view his environment as non-threatening to him physically. It is something to be manipulated by him in order to bring about the desired effects that will win approval. There is directionality here, and it is *from* the child *toward* his environment. On the other hand, in families of *paranoid* patients the child comes to view his environment as having potentially harmful properties that he cannot control and that must be avoided in some way. Here the directionality is *from* the environment *toward* the child.[42]

The hypothesis is that a manipulative attitude toward the environment will be associated with intrapunitive behavior and that a passive attitude toward the environment, with the absence of the internalization of a feeling of responsibility for the self, will be correlated with a greater use of projection in ego-defense.

There are firm indications that cultural patterning as well as child-rearing techniques will affect the perception of the environment and the orientation of the personality on the paranoia-depression continuum. In Burma, a hierarchical and age-graded society, the social and physical environment is typically perceived as potentially harmful, and Burma has one of the highest homicide rates in the world.[43] There is also the possibility of a connection between the high rates of violence among Afro-Americans and the recent diagnosis that the black psyche has been rendered paranoic by the hostile American environment.[44]

Testing the hypothesis that a paranoid perception of the environment is the root cause of the pattern of violence in the white South is a problem for future scholarship. The most immediately useful technique would be an opinion survey of attitudes toward violence, perceptions of the environment, feelings of personal efficacy, and other measures of alienation. There may be regional differentials in these categories as well as class, age, and sexual differentials. A rigorous comparison of rates of violence in perhaps a Kentucky county and an Ohio county at comparable stages of settlement is also a promising approach. The records of the county court, the reports of the state attorney general, and newspaper surveys might produce useful data on individual as well as collective violence. Some effort must be made to determine when the South became violent. The timing may reveal much about the relationship of slavery to violence. The possible effects of Scotch-Irish immigration, population density, temperature, and religious fundamentalism should be investigated with quantitative methods. Even though the SHRs of Australia and Canada fit the European mold, some insight may derive from pursuing such comparative cases in a detailed manner. There is much that can be done.

Meanwhile, in the search for a valid explanation of Southern violence the most fruitful avenue will probably be one that seeks to identify and trace the development of a Southern world view that defines the social, political, and physical environment as hostile and casts the white Southerner in the role of the passive victim of malevolent forces. When scholars locate the values that make up this world view and the process by which it was created and is transmitted, the history of the South will undoubtedly prove to have played a major role. The un-American experiences of guilt, defeat, and poverty will be major constituents of the relevant version of that history,[45] but perhaps they will not loom so large as the sense of grievance that is at the heart of the Southern identity.

The South was created by the need to protect a peculiar institution from threats originating outside the region. Consequently, the Southern identity has been linked from the first to a siege mentality. Though Southerners have many other identities, they are likely to be most conscious of being Southerners when they are defending their region against attack from outside forces: abolitionists, the Union Army, carpetbaggers, Wall Street and Pittsburgh, civil rights agitators, the federal government, feminism, socialism, trade unionism, Darwinism, communism, atheism, daylight saving time, and other byproducts of modernity. This has made for an extreme sensitivity to criticism from outsiders and a tendency to excuse local faults as the products of forces beyond human control or beyond local control. If the South was poor, it was because the Yankees stole all the family silver and devastated the region in other ways after the Civil War. If industrialization seemed inordinately slow in the South, it was because of a conspiracy of Northern capitalists to maintain the South as an economic colony. Added to this experience with perceived threats has been the fact that almost every significant change in the life of the South has been initiated by external powers. This is even true of industrialization. Though there was a fervent native movement to sponsor industrialization, absentee ownership has been characteristic. Furthermore, the real qualitative change in the Southern pattern of low value-added industry came as a result of the Second World War and the activities of the federal government.

Being Southern, then, inevitably involves a feeling of persecution at times and a sense of being a passive, insignificant object of alien or impersonal forces. Such a historical experience has fostered a world view that supports the denial of responsibility and locates threats to the region outside the region and threats to the person outside the self. From the Southern past arises the symbiosis of profuse hospitality toward strangers and the paradox that the Southern heritage is at the same time one of grace and violence.

NOTES

1. For example, see Charles O. Lerche, Jr., *The Uncertain South: Its Changing Patterns of Politics in Foreign Policy* (Chicago, 1964), 48-49. Representative comments can be found in: John Richard Alden, *The South in the Revolution, 1763-1789* (Baton Rouge, 1957), 34-35, and 41; Clement Eaton, *A History of the Old South* (New York, 1966), 260, 395, 404, 407, and 415; John Hope Franklin, *The Militant South, 1800-1861* (Cambridge, Mass., 1956); David Bertelson, *The Lazy South* (New York, 1967), 101-113, and 241; and H. V. Redfield, *Homicide, North and South: Being a Comparative View of Crime Against the Person in Several Parts of the United States* (Philadelphia, 1880).

2. A stimulating essay on this theme is Frank Vandiver, "The Southerner as Extremist," in Frank Vandiver, ed., *The Idea of the South* (Chicago, 1964), 43-56. A lighter treatment of the same subject is Erskine Caldwell, "The Deep South's Other Venerable Tradition," New York *Times Magazine* (July 11, 1965).

3. "The Pattern of Violence," in W. T. Couch, ed., *Culture in the South* (Chapel Hill, 1934), 678-692; and *Homicide in the United States* (Chapel Hill, 1932).

4. Stuart Lottier, "Distribution of Criminal Offenses in Sectional Regions," *Journal of Criminal Law and Criminology,* 29 (Sept.-Oct. 1938): 329-344.

5. Lyle Shannon, "The Spatial Distribution of Criminal Offenses by States," *Journal of Criminal Law and Criminology,* 45 (Sept.-Oct. 1954): 264-273.

6. Louis I. Dublin and Bessie Bunzel, *To Be or Not To Be: A Study of Suicide* (New York, 1933), 80 and 413.

7. Austin Porterfield, "Indices of Suicide and Homicide by States and Cities: Some Southern-Non-Southern Contrasts with Implications for Research," *American Sociological Review,* 14 (Aug. 1949): 481-490.

8. Ibid., 485.

9. Austin Porterfield, "A Decade of Serious Crimes in the United States," *American Sociological Review,* 13 (Feb. 1948): 44-54. See also James E. McKeown, "Poverty, Race, and Crime," *Journal of Criminal Law and Criminology,* 39 (Nov.-Dec. 1948): 480-483.

10. Norval D. Glenn, "Occupational Benefits to Whites From the Subordination of Negroes," *American Sociological Review,* 28 (June 1963): 443-448. See particularly Table 1.

11. *Southern Regions of the United States* (Chapel Hill, 1936), 208.

12. Edwin H. Sutherland and Donald R. Cressey, *Principles of Criminology* (New York, 1960), 92 and 146-149.

13. Van B. Shaw, "The Relationship Between Crime Rates and Certain Population Characteristics in Minnesota Counties," *Journal of Criminal Law and Criminology,* 40 (May-June 1949): 43-49.

14. Simple intercorrelations were run between the indices of homicide and suicide and measures of social and economic activity using data from: Bruce M. Russett et. al., eds., *World Handbook of Political and Social Indicators* (New Haven, 1964); and Statistical Office of the United Nations Department of Economic and Social Affairs, *Demographic Yearbook, 1963* (New York, 1964), Table 25, 592-611.

15. Richard S. Weinert, "Violence in Pre-Modern Societies: Rural Columbia," *American Political Science Review,* 60 (June 1966): 340-347; Harry Eckstein, ed., *Internal War* (New York, 1964); E. J. Hobsbawm, *Primitive Rebels* (New York, 1959). An important synthesis and statement of theory is Ted Gurr, "Psychological Factors in Civil Violence," *World Politics,* 20 (Jan. 1968): 245-278.

16. Herbert McCloskey and John H. Schaar, "Psychological Dimensions of Anomy," *American Sociological Review,* 30 (Feb. 1965): 14-40.

17. David Abrahamsen, *The Psychology of Crime* (New York, 1960): 18-21 and 177-183. These relationships are greatly illuminated by the discussion in David M. Potter, *People of Plenty: Economic Abundance and the American Character* (Chicago, 1954).

18. William H. Taylor, *Cavalier and Yankee: The Old South and American National Character* (Garden City, N.Y., 1963); C. Vann Woodward, "A Southern Critique for the Gilded Age," *The Burden of Southern History* (Baton Rouge, 1960), 109-140.

19. Jack P. Gibbs and Walter T. Martin, *Status Integration and Suicide: A Sociological Study* (Eugene, Ore., 1964), particularly Table 6, 54.

20. Lewis A. Coser, *The Functions of Social Conflict* (New York, 1956), 57, 62, and 71; Albert Pepitone and George Reichling, "Group Cohesiveness and Expression of Hostility," in Neil J. Smelser and William T. Smelser, *Personality and Social Systems* (New York, 1963), 117-124.

21. Coser, *The Functions of Social Conflict,* 72.

22. John Dollard, Neil E. Miller, Leonard W. Doob, O. H. Mowrer, and Robert R. Sears, *Frustration and Aggression* (New Haven, 1939); Leonard Berkowitz, *Aggression: A Social Psychological Analysis* (New York, 1962); Audrey Yates, *Frustration and Conflict* (New York, 1962).

23. Karl Menninger, *Man Against Himself* (New York, 1938), 23. The assumption that homicide and suicide are simply aggressions manifested in different directions is the basis of the concept of the suicide-homicide ratio.

24. Herbert Hendin, *Suicide and Scandinavia: A Psychoanalytic Study of Culture and Character* (Garden City, N. Y., 1965), Ch. 5.

25. *Suicide and Homicide: Some Economic, Sociological, and Psychological Aspects of Aggression* (Glencoe, Ill., 1954).

26. Porterfield. "Indices of Suicide and Homicide by States and Cities," 488.

27. Henry and Short, *Suicide and Homicide,* 119.

28. Martin Gold, "Suicide, Homicide, and the Socialization of Aggression," *American Journal of Sociology,* 63 (May 1958): 651-661. Gold organized the SHR, which he called the suicide murder ratio.

29. Ibid.

30. Melvin L. Kohn, "Social Class and the Exercise of Parental Authority," in Smelser and Smelser, *Personality and Social Systems,* 297-314; Martha Sturm White, "Social Class, Child Rearing Practices, and Child Behavior," Ibid., 286-296; Bernard C. Rosen and Roy D'Andrade. "The Psychosocial Origins of Achievement Motivation," *Sociometry,* 22 (1959): 185-215, cited in Marshall B. Clinard, ed., *Anomic and Deviant Behavior: A Discussion and Critique* (New York, 1964), 260-261. Bernard Berelson and Gary A. Steiner, *Human Behavior: An Inventory of Scientific Findings* (New York, 1964), 479-481.

31. William McCord and Joan McCord, *Origins of Crime: A New Evaluation of the Camridge-Somerville Youth Study* (New York, 1959), 172 and 198.

32. New York *Times,* July 25, 1968.

33. Carl Bakal, *The Right to Bear Arms* (New York, 1966), 346-353.

34. Thomas F. Pettigrew and Rosalind Barclay Spier, "The Ecological Stucture of Negro Homicide," *American Journal of Sociology,* 47 (May 1962): 621-629.

35. Wilbur J. Cash, *The Mind of the South* (New York, 1940, Vintage edition, 1960), 32-34, 44-52, 76, 115-123, 161, 220, 424.

36. Marvin E. Wolfgang, *Patterns in Criminal Homicide* (Philadelphia, 1958), 222-236.

37. John Dollard, *Caste and Class in a Southern Town* (Garden City, N.Y., 1949), Ch. 13.

38. Frantz Fanon, *The Wretched of the Earth* (New York, 1963).

39. Thomas Stone, Dorthea C. Leighton, and Alexander H. Leighton, "Poverty and the Individual," in Leo Fishman, ed., *Poverty and Affluence* (New Haven, 1966), 72-96.

40. Paul Frederick Cressey, "Social Disorganization and Reorganization in Harlan County, Kentucky," *American Sociological Review,* 14 (June 1949): 389-394; Henry Wechsler, "Community Growth, Depressive Disorders, and Suicide," *American Journal of Sociology,* 67 (July 1961): 9-16.

41. Jack O. Douglas, *The Social Meanings of Suicide* (Princeton, 1967), 3-160.

42. Hazel M. Hitson and Daniel H. Funkenstein, "Family Patterns and Paranoidal Personality Structure in Boston and Burma," *International Journal of Social Psychiatry,* 5 (winter 1959).

43. Ibid.

44. William H. Grier and Price M. Cobbs, *Black Rage* (New York, 1968).

45. C. Vann Woodward, "The Search for Southern Identity," *The Burden of Southern History,* 3-26.

Part 5

Processes of Rebellion
and Adjustment

INTRODUCTION

George Santayana's famous dictum that those who do not understand history are condemned to repeat it needs an important qualification. We do not "understand" history merely by careful study of a particular era or event. The circumstances and the motives and actions of people involved in one particular episode of violent conflict, for example, always differ in some ways from other episodes. It is only when different conflicts are compared that we can begin to detect the common patterns and processes that make real historical understanding possible. The three chapters which follow offer parallel case studies and interpretations of the processes and conditions which lead toward, or away from, violent conflict. Some skepticism is in order when reading these chapters because, while they are plausible and provocative, their interpretations are not and perhaps cannot be proven to be uniquely correct. Since general explanations require simplification, some alternative interpretations may be slighted and some evidence overlooked or distorted. The test for the reader should be how well they fit the evidence, not only the historical evidence available in this book and elsewhere, but the evidence provided by the unfolding of contemporary events in America.

Two conventional "explanations" of rebellion and revolution have been used popularly to explain the militancy and violence of some black Americans in the 1960s. One is that people rebel when they are suddenly awakened, perhaps by "agitators" or "promises," to their dismal status in life. The other is that people are especially prone to violence "when things are getting better," either because the taste of progress generates exponentially increasing expectations for more progress or because they intensely resent the few remaining barriers they face. James C. Davies suggests a different and more general pattern of change preceding rebellion, one illustrated by his case studies of the American Civil War, the Nazi revolution, and the uprisings of black Americans in the 1960s. In all these cases, Davies observes, revolt was preceded by a long period of improvement in conditions followed by a more or less sharp decline. The dynamic is that rising socioeconomic or political satisfactions generate in people expectations that improvements will continue. If such expectations are substantially frustrated for many people, popular uprisings are likely to occur.

This J-curve pattern of rising and then declining satisfactions can be detected in the changing political and economic status of Southerners vis-à-vis the North before the Civil War and in the conditions of black Americans after 1940. The economic condition of blacks, compared to white Americans, increased substantially toward equality after 1940 and their legal status began to improve in the 1950s, but by the mid-1960s the obdurate resistance of some white Americans to the continued expansion of black rights and opportunities, especially in the South, seemed to demonstrate that further progress was blocked. In Davies's view the behavior of black Americans would have been less explicable had they not reacted as they did to a intensely frustrating situation that paralleled the situations of rebellious people of other times and places.

The J-curve theory has been criticized on grounds that it does not specify the circumstances in which a J-curving pattern of change will or will not lead to rebellion. The discerning analyst is almost always able to find a rise and decline in some kind of satisfactions before the outbreak of violent conflict, while other J-curve patterns of change can be found which are not followed by rebellion.[1] This does not mean that the theory is necessarily wrong, only that it is incomplete. After all it is more concerned with the psychology of potential rebels than with their social or political situation, or with the different kinds of responses they meet from other groups, government above all. These situational factors are the focus of the chapters by Libman-Rubenstein and Siegel.

Violent conflict in America has erupted repeatedly out of efforts by social groups to improve their position in the system. Libman-Rubenstein's argument to this effect in Chapter 17 demolishes the myth of peaceful progress for out-groups in America and is amply reinforced by other evidence in this book. The reason, he proposes, is to be found in the nature of group structure, demands, and response in the American political system. Most out-groups have made limited demands on behalf of limited groups. Particularly common has been the demand for autonomy, for greater control over the group's political and economic fate. Protest and rebellion therefore have tended to be localized and segmental. Even when violence began, demands usually remained limited and could be dealt with by bargaining. Thus it has been possible for government and dominant social groups to deal effectively with out-groups using a mix of moderate reform and selective coercion. These kinds of group demands and responses did not threaten to transform the social system or displace the ruling elite.

But can this historical pattern of limited demands and limited response be expected to continue? At this point Libman-Rubenstein applies a Marxist analysis. The power of government and monopoly capitalism have never been threatened in America, he argues, because a whole class has never been mobilized against the system. At the present stage of American capitalism, however, both blue- and white-collar workers are increasingly homogenized. If boundaries among ethnic and occupational groups continue to blur, and if economic crisis persists—both of which Libman-Rubenstein thinks are likely—then large class-based groups are increasingly likely to challenge the capitalist system at its center.[2] By implication, the issues are likely to be revolutionary ones, not reformist.

This kind of speculation about the future course of conflict in America cannot be tested directly except by waiting and watching the march of contemporary events. If the argument also applies to other advanced capitalist societies, however, its plausibility can be tested by studying the emergence and consequences of class conflict in the countries of Western Europe. Class lines have long been more sharply drawn in Britain, France, Italy, and Sweden, for example, than they are in the United States. But the consequences have not been revolutionary in the Marxist sense. Instead, the political demands of the working class have been met by incremental changes: better welfare services, state ownership of a few industries. Indeed, most European elites have dealt with class-based challenges in ways similar to the response of American elites to the demands of more fragmented groups: selective coercion and moderate but cumulative reforms.

It is important to understand that not all group protest in America has been disruptive, and not all violence has resulted from attempts by groups to improve their situation. Some major groups, such as white Southerners, Northern immigrants, and American Indians, have resorted to defensive or retaliatory violence when external threat or deprivation has threatened their cultural integrity. When the threatened group is relatively powerless, however, quite a different response can occur: its members may attempt to establish and preserve their cultural identity by nonviolent defensive techniques. Anthropologist Bernard J. Siegel describes the nature of these defensive adaptations in Chapter 18. In the American context, examples of groups that have adapted defensively include Pueblo Indians of New Mexico, the Black Muslims, and religious bodies like the Amish, Hutterites, and Mormons. All such groups have certain characteristics in common: in response to perceived stress they develop and enforce detailed and rigorous codes for the regulation of their members' behavior, they increase cultural integration by emphasizing and elaborating a few key cultural values, and they intensify communication within the group while minimizing communication with outsiders. The two most general questions raised by the study of defensive groups for the contemporary problems of the United States are these: What effects do they have on the disposition to individual and collective violence? and, What are their consequences for the attainment of the American ideal of a culturally and socially integrated national society? The anthropological analysis implies that they minimize the former but at the cost of raising serious barriers to the latter.

NOTES

1. Representative of conceptual critiques of the J-curve theory are Peter A. Lupsha, "Explanation of Political Violence: Some Psychological Theories versus Indignation," *Politics and Society,* 2 (fall 1971): 89-104; and A.S. Cohan, *Theories of Revolution: An Introduction* (New York: John Wiley/Halstead Press, 1975), 193-99. The theory has stimulated much empirical work, for example, Raymond Tanter and Manus Midlarsky, "A Theory of Revolution," *Journal of Conflict Resolution,* 11 (September 1967): 264-80; and Abraham H. Miller et al., "The J-Curve Theory and the Black Urban Riots: An Empirical Test of Progressive Relative Deprivation Theory," *American Poltical Science Review,* 71 (September 1977): 964-82.

2. A somewhat different view is advanced by Seymour Martin Lipset, to the effect that class-based socialist revolution has never been likely in the United States because American

values already incorporate the highest aspirations of socialism. See his *Socialism: It's Conspicuous Absence in American Politics* (New Brunswick, N.J.: Transaction Books, 1977).

Chapter 16
The J-Curve of Rising and Declining Satisfactions as a Cause of Revolution and Rebellion

JAMES CHOWNING DAVIES

The J-curve is this: revolution is most likely to take place when a prolonged period of rising expectations and rising gratifications is followed by a short period of sharp reversal, during which the gap between expectations and gratifications quickly widens and becomes intolerable. The frustration that develops, when it is intense and widespread in the society, seeks outlets in violent action. When the frustration becomes focused on the government, the violence becomes coherent and directional. If the frustration is sufficiently widespread, intense, and focused on government, the violence will become a revolution that displaces irrevocably the ruling government and changes markedly the power structure of the society. Or the violence will be contained within the system, which it modifies but does not displace. This latter case is rebellion. Figure 16.1 shows what happens as a society heads toward revolution.[1]

This is an assertion about the state of mind of individual people in a society who are likely to revolt. It says their state of mind, their mood, is one of high tension and rather generalized hostility, derived from the widening of the gap between what they want and what they get. They fear not just that things will no longer continue to get better but—even more crucially—that ground will be lost that they have already gained. The mood of rather generalized hostility, directed generally outward, begins to turn toward government. People so frustrated not only fight with other members of their families and their neighbors. They also jostle one another in crowds and increased their aggressiveness as pedestrians and bus passengers and drivers of cars. When events and news media and writers and speakers encourage the direction of hostilities toward the government, the dispersed and mutual hostility becomes focused on a common target. The hostility among individuals diminishes. The dissonant energy becomes a resonant, very powerful force that heads like a great tidal wave or forest fire toward the established government, which it may then engulf.

This phenomenon of synergic unification of a public when frustration becomes widespread and deep is awesome in its tendency to erase hostility between people. It

---

AUTHOR'S NOTE: *James Chowning Davies is professor of political science at the University of Oregon. He is the author of* Human Nature in Politics *(John Wiley, 1963); editor of* When Men Revolt and Why *(Free Press, 1971); and has written a number of influential articles on the psychological foundations of social and political behavior.*

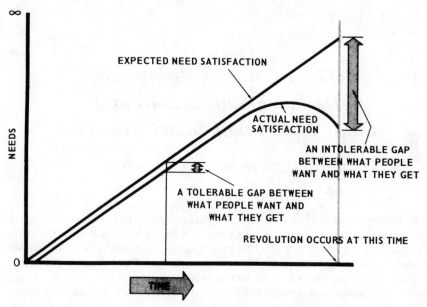

Figure 16.1: Need satisfaction and revolution

is akin to the feeling that develops in a quarrelsome household at times. A fighting family may just barely manage to hold together. The father may be unemployed and frequently drunk, the mother worn to a frazzle, the children quarrelsome as they displace the tensions generated by poverty and the frustrations of their fighting parents. The father, no longer able to provide for his family, may lose his authority within the family and strike out at those nearest to him. But when the landlord knocks on the door and announces that the rent must be paid by 10 o'clock tomorrow morning on pain of eviction, the family suddenly stops its own fighting, beats up the landlord, and throws him out on the street.

Such tension within the family is a microcosm of the tension within the national community; that is, among the individual members of the political society and among its conflicting regional, religious, racial, and socioeconomic groups. When the various segments of a deeply divided society suddenly sense that they all have the same enemy, the government, they can spontaneously unite for long enough to overthrow it.

CAUSES OF REVOLUTION AND REBELLION, PSYCHOLOGICALLY CONSIDERED

Revolutions and rebellions differ in result but have like origins. And the differences in origin are less ones of kind than of degree. Revolutions involve more segments of the population than do rebellions. The intensity of feeling in revolutions is probably greater and has taken a longer time to develop than in rebellions. The violent phase of a revolution is longer and more savage. The bitterness that lingers after the violence is likely to endure for decades or centuries after a revolution. The difference is not in causes and the violent action or even in the long-range consequences so much as it is in the immediate result. Rebellions do not remove the established government but instead are contained, partly as the consequence of the use of violent force in large enough amounts to override the rebels' anger at the government. The rebels may choose to live with their frustrations rather than endure the blows of police and the army and the dull, sick anguish of imprisonment. But rebellions also are contained within the established system to the extent that the government pays heed to the grievances that led to the rebellion. If the only response to extralegal violence is legal violence, then hatred of oppression becomes deeply imprinted in the minds of the momentarily silenced rebels. The hatred lingers and deepens like embers in dry tinder after firefighters have tried to beat to death a small fire.

As the American Declaration of Independence said in 1776, people do not for "light and transient causes" make a rebellion or revolution. What then are the grave and enduring conditions that produce the revolutionary state of mind?

The common condition appears to be the denial of satisfaction of those needs that are basic to all human beings. Not all needs (as for a new automobile) are basic, and not all basic needs are of equal revolutionary potential. Abraham Maslow has argued that man's basic needs are arranged in sequence, from the most to the least powerful. The most potent are the physical needs, which must continuously be satisfied for all people during their entire life. But when a person gains their satisfaction—as an infant, a child, and an adult—he does not then, animal-like, remain content with satisfying just these bodily needs. Soon after birth he demands affection and, if he gets it, he reciprocates affection toward others. But his physical needs persist, and if he is forced to choose, he will first satisfy his need for food and then his need for affection.

In early childhood the individual who has been regularly gratified in his physical and affectional needs does not then rest content with this mental state of affairs. He begins, usually no later than when he is eight or ten years old, to demand recognition as an individual who is worthy of his own regard for himself and of others' regard for him. In early childhood people begin to demand that others accord them respect. The respect of others is necessary if people are to acquire self-respect.

It is this kind of demand that lies so close to the surface of the Declaration of Independence, in the statement that all men are created equal and in the specific indictments of British rule—for example, in the great indignation expressed at the quartering of troops in private homes without the consent of the homeowners, and the removal of trials at law from the colonies to England. This demand is evident in the Declaration's "decent respect to the opinions of mankind," whose approval the American rebels sought.

And once these successive needs—the physical, the social-affectional, and the equal esteem or dignity needs—are sufficiently gratified, humans are not even then content: they then begin to look for that kind of activity that is particularly suited to them as unique individuals. Whether their competence is to be a ditchdigger, a powershovel operator, a construction foreman, a civil engineer or a building contractor, an architect, a mother, a writer, or a politician—they must do these things when they have become rather sure in the gratification of their even more basic physical, social, and esteem needs.

The crucial point is this: no human being so long as he lives is ever completely gratified in the satisfaction of his needs. Up to the moment of his death, he must eat and sleep; he must be with people; he has to be acknowledged as a distinct person; and he must realize his individual potential. When he ceases to do these things, he ceases to live. All of these needs of his have got to be gratified; they ultimately can be denied only by natural or by violent death. Armies and police forces can quash these natural and irrepressible human needs only by reducing human beings to animals and then killing them. The logic of this was stated in fictional form by George Orwell, in describing what was necessary for the perpetuation of dictatorship: "a boot, stamping in a human face, forever."

The Maslow need hierarchy is a necessary part of a psychological explanation of the causes of revolution. Marx to the contrary, revolutions are made not only by economically depressed classes and their leaders but by the joint effort of large numbers of those people in all social groups who are experiencing frustration of different basic needs. People deprived of career opportunities may join in revolt with people who have suffered indignities at the hands of employers, landlords, police, or military troops. They may also join with people who have suffered no indignities but are for the moment simply hungry.

The common characteristic of potential revolutionaries is that each of them individually senses the frustration of one or more basic needs and each is able to focus his frustration on the government. After this need frustration is generated, people begin to share their discontents and to work together. But preceding this joint action, there is no more conspiracy than there is among trees when they burst into flame during a forest fire.

THE J-CURVE AND PARTICULAR REVOLUTIONS

On the level of general theory, one can say precisely the same thing—in abstract terms—about each revolution and rebellion. But in some ways each revolution is unlike every other revolution. And from the practical research standpoint, directly comparable data are not available for all revolutions, particularly when they took place decades or centuries ago. In many nations now, the seeds of revolution are sprouting. But established governments in these nations are not likely to welcome social scientists in search of data by conducting public opinion surveys inquiring about attitudes toward the government.

In the interest of arriving at some conclusions and of arriving at the understanding that they are tentative, we can profitably consider particular revolutions. Two very different instances are the American Civil War and the Nazi revolution in Germany.[2]

The American Civil War of 1861

The difference between the terms "revolution," "rebellion," and "civil war" may be nothing more than this: revolution succeeds, rebellion fails, and civil war leaves the question open. All involve violence. In the Gettysburg Address of 1863, Lincoln referred to the ongoing conflict as "a great civil war"; at other times he called it rebellion and he never acknowledged the sovereign independence of the eleven Southern states that asserted it. It is not quite clear even a hundred years later that it was a rebellion or that it failed, but it is clear that the American Civil War did not end in Southern independence. It remains hard to characterize this most savage conflict. In proportion to the population of the time, this civil war produced the most catastrophic loss of life and property that America has ever suffered. The awesome depth of the conflict makes it important to explain.

The American Civil War is in some ways like the French Revolution of 1789, and in others like the Nazi revolution of 1933 examined in the next section. As in the French Revolution, the middle-class, entrepreneurial, and industrializing part of the nation was arrayed in battle against the landed aristocracy. Southern plantations fought a change in social institutions that would make them more suitable to the profound changes which captialism and industrialization brought with them. But the American Civil War lacked joint action by both American bourgeoisie and landlords against the national government. If Southern landlords and Northern industrialists had combined against the government, it is quite possible the civil war would have resembled the Nazi revolution. It could have established an oligarchical dictatorship of the urban upper-middle-class and rural landlords, as in many twentieth-century developing nations.

The American conflict does resemble the Nazi revolution in that it was initiated by conservative segments of society that were restive with the pace and direction of change. In both America before the Civil War and Germany before nazism, an agrarian economy was being rapidly replaced by industry, and the hegemony of landed aristocrats was threatened by the growing political power of merchants and industrialists. Industrialization was about as recent in both countries—about two generations, though its growth rate in Germany was greater. But the principal difference between America in 1861 and Germany in 1933 was in the orientation of the two revolutions: the latter was more progressive in its orientation in that there was a strong and real appeal in nazism to those people who felt they had been denied equal opportunity to acquire education and technical skills. In America the South denied the desirability of education and anything other than agricultural technology.

The gradual rise and rapid decline in gratifications in pre-Civil War America occur in two cycles, one contained within the other. There had been a very long cyclical rise in expectations of Americans generally, from the beginnings of colonization, through independence, and down to the great growth of wealth in the early nineteeth century. There also was a shorter term cycle in Southern expectations, which rose from about 1789, when the national government was established, and began to decline in the mid-1850s. That is, there was a roughly 200-year cycle and within it a 70-year cycle of rising and falling gratifications. The latter cycle is set forth in Figure 16.2.

The colonization of America in the seventeeth and eighteenth centuries provided a steady rise in expectations and gratifications until the 1750s and 1760s. But a common pattern of growth in the various colonies and a common determination on independence concealed some growing differences. In the Northern colonies, from New England down to Pennsylvania, the dominant settlers were religious dissenters, radically modern in their individualism and anticorporatism. The democratic New England town meetings emerged from the institution of theoretical democracy in the

New England church congregations.This democracy was an antithesis of the hierarchy in church and government that were so typical of England. This style of rule appeared also in Pennsylvania, dominated as it was by Quakers and their radically democratic ideology.

In Maryland, Virginia, the Carolinas, and Georgia, fewer of the settlers were democratically and individualistically oriented dissenters. Indeed there was a substantial influx of both Roman Catholics and their institutional cousins, Episcopalians. They were more accustomed to hierarchy and order established from above and they carried with them the nondissenting, establishment orientation of their English ancestors. There were, in addition, influxes of poor people with more individualistic and less establishment-oriented religious views, but they rarely were a major influence in the South, politically or socially, at any time before the Civil War, and they shared with the establishment-oriented plantationer class a dedication to the rectitude of slavery and to the virtues of the rural life.

Differences in institutions and values if anything became greater with the passage of time. Big cities of commerce and industry grew in the North and, with the exception of the great port city of New Orleans, never developed in the South. Agrarian development in the North was typified by family-sized farms. With their highly individualistic outlook, farmers had appreciable political power in the Northern state governments from the beginning of national independence. Agrarian development in the South was on the surface of things like growth in the North. There were far more family-sized farms in the South than there were plantations, but the plantationers dominated Southern politics, using the issue of black inferiority to all white men very effectively in maintaining acquiescence by poor whites in the rule of the large landholders and slaveowners.

Inevitably, as industrialization and commerce developed in the North it began to urbanize rapidly. This process included not just a division of labor between farmers and city dwellers, but also a rapid growth in population. Correlatively and inevitably, an agrarian society like that in the South experienced a slower growth in population. The growth toward political equalitarianism in the North became more and more fundamentally opposed to the oligarchical domination of politics by the plantationers. And so began—more exactly, continued—the widening of the gulf between economic and social values and ways of life between North and South.

In national politics, the question of who should rule echoed continuously across the ever-eroding canyon between South and North. The Virginia dynasty was not a legend but a reality for a generation after independence. Excepting the brief and not very portentous administrations of John Adams (1791-1801) and his son John Quincy Adams (1825-29), there was an unbroken line of Southern Presidents of the United States, from Washington through Jefferson, Madison, Monroe, and Jackson. John Calhoun of South Carolina served as Vice President during J. Q. Adams' administration and the first term of Jackson's. From 1789 to 1837 the presidency was almost continuously Southern.

This Southern domination became increasingly more romantic. The Southerners who became Presidents acted nationally, not sectionally. In Congress, the Missouri Compromise settled and unsettled (in 1820) the conflict over sectional representation. By this compromise the South won the votes in Congress of the border state of

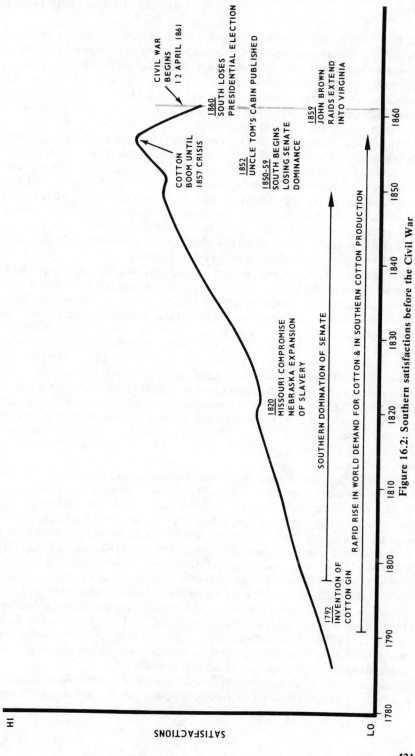

Figure 16.2: Southern satisfactions before the Civil War

Missouri, which was to be admitted as a slave state, and lost the free opportunity to expand its political power westward. The South did continue to dominate the Senate for another generation, judging at least by the 1854 Kansas-Nebraska Act, which, repudiating the Missouri Compromise, allowed slaves to come into these territories. Indeed the Senate was not just the last retreat of the South but also the only part of the government that did not reflect the ever growing social and economic dominance of the North.

The regional growth comparisons are awesome. In one decade, from 1850-1860, the population of the South grew greatly—about 23 percent; in the same decade the non-Southern population increased a fantastic 43 percent. Although adequate economic trend data over time are hard to come by, in 1860 the North was producing over 90 percent by value of all manufactured goods. The proportion produced by the North had apparently been increasing rapidly as the war approached. The North was even exporting food (grains and livestock) to the agricultural South. And free farmers were saying politically that they did not want to compete, economically or socially, with plantationers whose fieldhands worked without pay.

These developments suggest, at least in hindsight, that the South was mad to suppose that it could win a war against the growing industrial and commercial Yankee giant. But the South itself was enjoying, early in the 1850s, unprecedented prosperity. There was an almost insatiable world demand for cotton, of which the South had close to a world monopoly in production. The average annual production during the 1840-1850 decade was 2.2 million bales; it increased to 3.4 million in the next decade. At the same time the average annual price during 1840-1850 was about 8 cents per pound, rising more than 30 percent, to 10.6 cents, in the final prewar decade. Along with this—and an improvement in profit from tobacco and sugarcane production—came an increase in the price of prime field hands, the most commonly valuable category of slaves. Their price doubled during the 1850-1860 decade, reaching as high as $1,500 per head, and the demand was enormous. It was not easy for Southerners to concede the rightness or the efficiency of an economy based on free labor.

But the little-diversified agrarian Southern economy was fragile. A particular weakness was the plantationers' custom of buying on credit advanced before the sale of their crops. Even before the 1775 War of Independence, it was common for Southern planters to be thus in long-range debt to English merchants. After 1783 there was one change: the creditors were now Northern merchants, mainly in New York. The South quite simply remained money-poor up to 1861 (and beyond). On a sellers' market, which the South enjoyed with some ups and downs until 1857, the system of credit worked well enough for Southern planters. And it worked even better for Northern creditors. To protect themselves from market uncertainties—and from individuals who were poor credit risks—Northern dealers would charge Southern buyers higher than normal prices. Southern buyers, when they were paid by credit paper at harvest time, would sell the paper at a discount to pay their bills. So they paid twice at least: in the form of higher prices for the goods they bought, and lower prices for the credit paper they sold to pay off their annual debt.

This chronic low-intensity economic crisis, in the face of seemingly endless prosperity, is akin to the situation that produced the looting and burning of white-owned stores by blacks in the 1960s—more than a century later: the Southern plantationers developed no affection for the big Yankee houses that had the goods and sold them at a price higher than a Yankee would have to pay. They were unable to set fire to the New York stores and say "burn, baby, burn." But they did try to destroy the Union.

Near the end of this cycle of rising and then declining political gratifications was the more immediate and very threatening economic crisis of 1857. It was an epitome of the Southern dependence on the North, of the dependence of any raw-material-producing colony on the financial and other economic circumstances of the diversified "mother country." In 1857 the South was hit by a panic in the New York commodity exchange market. For a time money exchange with England virtually ceased, and so did the effective demand for cotton in England. Although the Liverpool price was 18 or 19 cents a pound for cotton, in contrast to 10 cents a pound in New York, Southerners for the most part had to sell in New York. Many of them had already committed their crop to New York buyers and so were stuck; many who had not committed their crop needed money badly and were in virtually the same bind as those who had already sold their crops for future delivery. A Southern Senator in Washington saw the situation with a clear intelligence and passed his judgment: a cotton crop that could have sold for $100 million went for $65 million. To save irresponsible and selfish Northern speculators—who perhaps blamed the system for producing the money crisis—the South lost $35 million.

This was the final critical downturn in the gratifications of Southerners. They had lost political power that they had exercised so successfully in nearly a half century of Southern but Nation-minded presidents of the United States. They had neared the final loss of their dominant power in the Senate, where so often they held a veto over laws demanded by Northerners. And now, in a process that so starkly showed their economic thralldom to the North, they had to save their economic masters to the tune of a loss of a third of the value of their major crop—and the nation's major export.

The growing and now enormous tensions found release in secession. The eventual outcome of the 1854 Kansas-Nebraska Act, which in 1854 still offered some hope of restoring the balance of sectional power in the Senate, soon became clear. An honest referendum on the slavery issue indicated an eight-to-one majority in Kansas in favor of entering the Union as a free state. After liberating a few slaves in Kansas, that madman and self-styled liberator, John Brown, in 1859 made a raid in search of arms of the U.S. arsenal at Harpers Ferry. But Harpers Ferry was not in Kansas; it was in Virginia. And it was clear where John Brown now proposed to commence the liberation of slaves.

So the South began to secede. South Carolina was the first to take the step, on December 20, 1860. And South Carolina fired the first shot, on the federal Fort Sumter in Charleston Harbor, on April 12, 1861. The Civil War had begun as the ever-romantic South came to the end of its neofeudal dream. Its expectations of freedom to continue to expand its wealth and way of life were shattered by the events of the late 1850s, in Congress and in the mercantile houses of New York.

The Nazi Revolution of 1933

The Nazi revolution was a German and a world catastrophe. It led to the partial destruction and the partition of a population that had been growing in unity, civilization, and recognition since the Protestant Reformation that Luther led, since the tremendous spurt in industrialization in the late nineteenth century, and since the surge of nationalism that took the form of empire building and then, in 1914, of war.

Germany was the first to experience a successful reformation, that major advance toward establishing the equalization and individuation of men. For whatever reasons, it was the last major European nation to undergo that profoundest of modernizers: industrialization. In one sense the first modern popular revolution took place in Germany in the sixteenth century, before industrialization had developed anything like its modern factory system anywhere. In another sense Germany never had a postindustrial revolution comparable to the French Revolution. The German Reformation was universalist in its equalitarian principles and so was the French Revolution. There was a messianic quality to the equalitarian beliefs of the German Reformation of the sixteenth century, the French Revolution of the eighteenth , and the Russian of the twentieth. These revolutions spawned and nurtured many popular movements in the world. But the Nazi revolution—the nearest counterpart to the postindustrial French Revolution—was not universalist. It was particularistic, intensely nationalistic, and imperialistic, proposing to subject and exploit both Slavic and Gallic peoples to the control and enrichment of the Germanic. It was a kind of revenge for the world recognition that came to France and Russia after their universalist revolutions, renown that had stifled Germany between two peoples that felt their own superiority to Germans.

The growth in vitality of German society and culture was relatively steady and continuous, perhaps for centuries up to 1918. Surely it was continuous since the tariff union (developing from 1819-1844) that intensified the trend, under Prussian domination, toward economic unity. With the growth of an enormous iron and steel industry, the basis was laid for building warships, artillery, and rifles. Construction of these commodities made war and expansion a euphoric dream that called for realization. In 1870, in battle, Germany defeated the France that had been the terror of Europe just two generations before. Within months, in January 1871, came the siege and subsequent surrender of Paris. Within days after the surrender of Paris came the formal inauguration of the unified German empire, when the Prussian king was crowned Emperor William I. The curves of rising expectations and gratifications were steadily rising, for Germans as individuals and as a nation.

In such a short analysis it is not possible to specify steps in the progress of Germany upward to its dismaying and unacknowledged defeat in world war in November 1918. It is clear enough that the long-range trend, accelerating rapidly after the tariff union and the 1871 unification, was upward. It is clear that the 1918 defeat came as a profound shock. It was sufficiently stunning and ambiguous to be regarded as only a temporary setback by those elitist individuals who believed in an imperial destiny and by those ordinary Germans who had a deep pride in their country. All these had entrusted basic decisions to the government. Under two emperors and such gifted paternalistic rulers as Bismarck and the Krupp family, the government had given them economic prosperity, social security, and world prestige.

Again, as in the analysis of the American Civil War, there was a centuries-long J-curve and a decades-short one. For present purposes, we can commence the analysis of the final rise and decline with the ambiguous 1918 defeat, recalling only that the advances up to 1918 had been real and enormous and remained in the memories of perhaps most Germans.

Both the French and the German Nazi revolutions were preceded by military defeat. But the former nation could not so easily turn the blame outward as could the latter. In the French case, the Seven Year's War, ending in 1763, was a virtually total defeat by England in North America. The vicarious French victory over England at Yorktown in 1781 produced independence for the United States and near-bankruptcy for France. The military action was far from France. England did not make demands intimately affecting Frenchmen in France in 1763 and the government's financial crisis in 1781 could hardly be blamed by Frenchmen on the defeated British.

With Germany after the 1918 armistice it was different. The Allies blockaded German ports and then occupied just enough German territory to hurt pride and business badly. German Communists, exalted by the Russian example, threatened their countrymen with total destruction of the established system, already shaken by the loss of the emperor. Germans therefore could readily displace blame and thereby dissociate the glories of an ever-greater German nation from the trickeries of external and internal enemies who sought only their own aggrandizement and German degradation. This hope for restoration of recently and meanly lost greatness was a very central part of the mental outlook of perhaps most Germans in the 1920s.

The continuation of hope and of pride in being German formed a cement that kept the nation from the disintegration that France experienced in the late eighteenth century. There was not quite the war of all against all that characterized prerevolutionary French society. Internal hostility was less personal and the enemies were more symbolic. The Allies, the French, the Communists, the Jews, the capitalists were the enemies rather than one's neighboring peasants, one's landlord, one's boss in the shoe factory, or the arriviste wealthy bourgeois who bought one's estate.

The impersonal contacts with enemies in Germany were such as to reinforce displacement of the internal tensions of an economy that had suffered the consequence of vast military expenditure, in an all-out war from 1914 to 1918. It was easier to forget the sanctions (government and industrial) against industrial strife than the more comfortable fact of punitive and unrealistic reparations. It was the government that initiated currency inflation. But the effect of the inflation on the internal economy could be overshadowed in people's minds by its effect on the French enemy, especially since the inflation was an effort to defeat the French and Belgian military occupation of the Ruhr Basin, starting in January 1923, by watering down the high price of reparations. German workers, who did strike in large numbers in this period, often regarded the French and Belgian occupying forces (and their attendant business experts who took over management control of the big enterprises) as the enemy. And then they could also blame those German capitalists, many of them Jews, who skillfully made fortunes out of the inflation. Because their customs made them stand out—particularly in the abstract—the Jewish capitalists were easier to blame that the German ones. And middle-class Germans could blame the Communists as agitators of the proletariat. In many such plausible ways, blame for Germany's ills could be projected outward. These plausible and sufficiently genuine external and internal enemies limited the tendency, which was never notably strong, of Germans to blame themselves for their problems, which in the 1920s indeed became severe.

The underlying optimism (a continuing heritage from the imperial and Reformation eras) and the surface displacement of responsibility for contemporary problems probably combined to encourage an irrepressible optimism in the mid-1920s. The inflation was a trauma. It began in August 1922 and ran wild for more than a year, until November 1923 when efforts at drastic monetary reform were undertaken. But the 1920s nevertheless were times of hope and progress in Germany. If the inflation wiped out private savings and insurance policies, it also wiped out internal public debt, and in April 1924 the Dawes plan promised a large influx of external capital for reconstruction. Though there were peaks of unemployment (1.5 million in January 1923, 2 million in February 1926, and 1.4 million in January 1928), the trend in jobs was generally upward. Taking the prewar year 1907 as a base of 100, by 1925 the number of gainfully employed had increased to about 127, and by 1933 had increased to 128. Again taking 1907 national population as a base of 100, by 1925 it had increased only to 102 and by 1933 to 106. In short, the proportion of the population that had jobs, roughly a decade after the world war ended, was a fourth larger than a decade before the war ended.

Up to 1929, economic conditions in Germany generally improved. And then, starting in July 1929, there was a steady, unremitting increase in unemployment until some time in the first quarter of 1933—that is, until after Hitler came to power on January 30, 1933. At the peak of unemployment, sometime in 1932, between 5.6 million and 7.3 million were unemployed. This was about three times the previous peak of about 2 million in February 1926 and ten times as high as the 560,000 people who were out of work in July 1928.

The depression hit hard in other ways. Germans, who as we noted had lost all their savings in the inflation, had begun to save again. Savings had increased by about half between 1928 and 1930. In the next year, 1931, the amount of money in savings accounts declined about 6 percent. This hurt many kinds of people, perhaps most seriously the lower middle class. And the shortage of work, statistically a cold figure, became a chilling reality, particularly for the working class. Germans on the average in 1928 worked 7.7 hours per day. By 1932, the hours worked per day had declined to 6.9—roughly by 10 percent.

What this adds up to, in summary, is that fewer people were working; those who worked were working fewer hours. And more money had to be drawn out of savings than could be put in. The sense that work and thrift would pay off, as Germany and Germans rose out of the defeat in war and the disgrace in postwar inflation and occupation, was rapidly replaced with despair. The gap between expectations and gratifications yawned wide, for perhaps a large majority of Germans. The gap was filled first with Nazi words and then with deeds as the economy was revived and geared toward war.

We have become so sensitive to the impact of ideology—perhaps as a consequence of the enormous amount of it generated and broadcast throughout the world since the 1917 Russian Revolution—that we tend to explain the success of the Nazis in terms of the racist, irrational rhetoric that stems from *Mein Kampf*. However nicely it fit the German mood in the late 1920s, the words would have found few ears if there had not been recurrent and at last catastrophic economic crisis. Figure 16.3 shows the series of crises.

The physical needs of millions of people were deeply denied. The standard diet of the unemployed consisted largely of potatoes and margarine. Working-class people might have been a force to oppose the racist or at least antiproletarian appeals of the Nazis. But unemployed people, particularly when they have suffered for several years, are more inclined toward apathy than activity. Those whose physical survival was not so directly endangered—those who had enough to eat—were threatened in virtually all walks of life with a regression to the economic level of 1919-1923.

Interclass conflict took different form in pre-1933 Germany from that in pre-1789 France. In the German instance, intergroup conflict seems to have been less pronounced, at least on anything approaching the personal level of hostility that prevailed in France in the late eighteenth century. Nevertheless various segments of the society did show hostility toward others, however vague its form and ill defined its object. There was a high degree of symbolic hostility between labor and capital in Germany, but the number and intensity of strikes declined greatly from 1925 on. At first this decline was probably due to the rather general prosperity of the mid-1920s. Later (1930-1932) it was probably due to the acuteness of unemployment, which led men to fear a strike because they would then be faced with a diet of potatoes and margarine. The conflict between labor and capital was thus more abstract and ideological than real, and took place more in politics than outside factory gates. As such it was inevitably attenuated. Its savagery diminished to a rather generalized hostility, perhaps on both sides.

The petty bourgeoisie, the *Kleinbürgertum,* is now almost fabled as the hard core of anti-Semitism. Indeed it may be that from this social group came those who formed the mobs that quite concretely smashed Jewish shops. In any case, the frustrated expectations of the petty bourgeoisie must have been compounded of the loss of their savings along with the fear that they would retrogress into the mass of pitiably poor people, whence they thought they had emerged by a combination of thrift and hard work.

One major segment of German society that saw its expectations frustrated were those who hoped for a resurgence of the nation that had fought so valiantly in the world war. This segment consisted principally of two groups—the military elite, those who were indeed Junkers or who styled themselves as such; and the returned veterans who after the war were met not with victory parades but often with contempt and derision. Even more crucially, veterans were often faced with unemployment or unemployability—the latter including many of those for whom military life had been their first successful occupation. They had no GI bill to train or retrain them for useful work. Thinking themselves heroes returned, they often found themselves drifters and bums. From this subgroup came many of the early Nazi rank and file. From the other subgroup, the officer caste, came those who first supported more

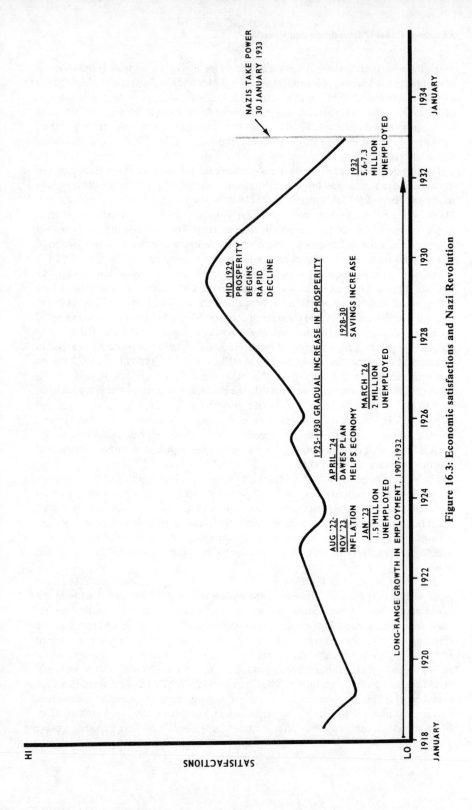

Figure 16.3: Economic satisfactions and Nazi Revolution

traditionally nationalist political parties than the Nazis, who then stood by and observed the arrant Nazis with mingled contempt and envy, and who at last became the willing instruments of the Nazis when the glorious war clouds gathered again.

The pervasive German attitude in the late 1920s seems to have been one of bafflement rather than of active support for the Nazi movement or widespread intergroup hostility. Labor was inhibited by fear of loss of jobs. Many of the middle class were disconcerted by their recurrent failure to better themselves. Members of the upper middle class could not believe that things were getting as bad for so many people as clearly was the case. And the old aristocracy remembered only the glories of feudalism and war or of the sheltered academic life.

It is this stunned state of mind that produced a high measure of political apathy or of active contempt for the inadequate efforts of the republican, parliamentary government to govern. The Nazi revolution was not just a coup d'état: it had broad popular support. But it did depend for its rise to power on the growing political irresoluteness of people who had hitherto been politically more self-confident (labor and upper middle class). And it depended on a high degree of involvement and participation on the part of those whose frustrations—whether military or economic —coincided with the medley of themes played by the Nazis. The Nazi revolution depended on the support of people whose desperation and consequent dissociation from reality led them to ignore, tolerate, and even take part in violence they would otherwise have abhorred.

The Black Rebellion of the 1960s

The black uprisings in America in the 1960s clearly amounted to a rebellion, but they were not in any precise sense a revolution like those of France in 1789 or Russia in 1905 and 1917. However, the differences between these revolutions and the black rebellion are largely quantitative. The latter involved a widespread joint commitment to rather fundamental change among all segments of black society: change in the political power structure of the country in all political units—cities, counties, states, and nation. And these changes, involving all blacks and all parts of the political community, were accompanied by the violence that is a universal element of revolution.

The differences between revolution and the black rebellion derive from several facts: blacks constitute only about 11 percent of the national population and therefore are numerically incapable of enforcing changes to the same degree as in a nation where a substantial majority is frustrated by the established government. The constitutions and laws of the national and most state governments have not contained many restrictions that discriminate against people on racial grounds—quite the contrary.

So there has been no basic change in principles. The Constitution and law of the land have been used or developed in ways that make them instruments to achieve changes in the nonlegal social practices and customs of discrimination. And there has been a sufficiently developed sense of commitment to equality as a major social value to make the equalizing of opportunities for black people a process against which most whites could not readily fight. They could not readily deny the applicability of their principles to those who had recently demanded equality. And that portion of the nation which frankly accepted the principle of racial inequality lost the savage Civil War. The very slow struggle for racial equality and human dignity for blacks commenced with Lincoln's 1863 Emancipation Proclamation and the military defeat of the South two years later.

What is striking, in a comparison of this (and other) contained rebellions with the great revolutions, is that the black rebellion appears to have been preceded by the same J-curve of expectations that are at first gratified and then frustrated. The same reaction patterns of this level of analysis appear to have developed in the minds of American blacks as have developed in the minds of those who have become revolutionaries in previous eras and other countries.

The difficulty in seeing this likeness relates to the vast gap between what whites and blacks have gotten in America. This gap has made it hard to see just what advances blacks have made and when. Those who as blacks and whites believe in equality have emphasized the vast and continuing inequalities. Black or white, they do not see what advances have been made. In the 1960s, when conditions were better than in the 1860s or than in the 1930s, the expressions of discontent were at their maximum. The new words and deeds of discontent can be understood only if one appreciates that profoundly deprived people are often incapable of expressing their discontent. In short, to understand why the black rebellion occurred, it is necessary to see how black people had already developed.

At the end of the Civil War, blacks were perhaps as near to minimal survival in the psychological sense, as human beings, as they had been since their initial transportation from Africa. They had lost the security of provision for food, clothing, shelter, and physical safety that had been fairly well assured them as long as they docilely accepted their position as slaves. They could no longer be sure that the master would provide for them. They had, often, to forage for themselves, like war refugees everywhere when crops have been destroyed and normal patterns of collaboration in productive work have been shattered. Overjoyed at their emancipation, they could use their freedom no more effectively than could concentration camp inmates in Germany when the doors at last swung open in early 1945. They could concern themselves really with only the satisfaction of their physical needs, which freedom is not and equality and dignity are not.

Those who must concentrate only on survival usually do not revolt: they are too hungry. This preoccupation with simply staying alive if anything strengthened in the late decades of the nineteenth century as the practice of lynching—the killing by mobs rather than by lawfully or other systematically employed force—continued. Between 1882, when records of lynchings were first kept, down to 1941, lynchings averaged 78 per year. The constant fear that one might be arbitrarily killed, maimed, or injured was one of the day-to-day facts of life for most blacks, particularly until the early 1920s. Lynching and physical injury could be said to have declined to a relatively minor worry—comparable perhaps to the level of worry about automobile accidents in the 1960s—in the late 1930s and the 1940s: the average for 1937-1942 was five per year and for 1943-1948 less than three per year. But the level of general health remained low and so did life expectancy.

The process of moving up off the even, flat plane of survival itself was of course continuous. But it was so slow that it seems best to date the first major upturn, from concern for mere survival for most blacks, as the beginning of the Second World War. Responding to the threat of a large demonstration, a repetition of something akin to the 1932 veterans' march on Washington, Franklin Roosevelt in 1941 issued an executive order prohibiting discriminatory hiring practices in all defense industries, and establishing the Fair Employment Practices Commission (FEPC) to administer the order. Though it worked unevenly and in many cases not at all, it nevertheless was a major basis for advance above subsistence for black Americans. By war's end, some two million blacks were employed in war industry, and the FEPC reported that 1,300,000 of these had gotten jobs in consequence of its efforts.

What could have been a cataclysmic frustration of rising expectations for blacks at war's end turned out not to be. The successful efforts to avoid a postwar recession, which would have witnessed the old (and still common) practice of discharging blacks first, benefitted blacks as well as whites. There was no widespread and sudden drop in black employment. Instead, the pace of rising economic opportunity continued. In 1946 the CIO and AFL trade-union organizations undertook a drive to organize black workers in the South and to integrate them into existing unions. By 1948, FEPC legislation had been passed in six states, taking up some of the slack when the ending of war contracts removed the protection of the wartime FEPC. Symbolically, and a bit more, the first black man was admitted in 1947 to major league baseball, Jackie Robinson; there were 14 major league black players in 1951; by 1954 all but three of the 16 major league teams were integrated. Racially integrated low-cost public housing after the war began the breakdown of discrimination in this basic concern of life. In 1956 all public housing in Washington, D.C., was desegregated. In 1962 President Kennedy issued an order prohibiting discrimination in any housing that was either financed or had mortgage insurance under a government program. It was estimated that this affected a fourth of all future housing construction in the nation.

These advances relate to jobs and housing and therefore to the physical needs, but they also—notably in the case of sports participation—have overtones of equal dignity. Advances that more directly related to this profound, nonphysical need for equality included the following:

The admission of blacks into the category of commissioned officer: 500 black officers in the Army in 1943, 7,500 by war's end; and 28 officers in the Navy in 1944, 50 by war's end;

The integration of 90 percent of all black army personnel into unsegregated units by 1953 and complete integration a year later;

The first desegregation of interstate buses in 1946, of railway dining cars in 1950, and of railway passenger cars in 1952;

The long series of steps designed to desegregate education, commencing with the court order to the University of Oklahoma in 1948 to admit on a segregated basis a graduate student who was black, to the University of Texas in 1950 to admit on a nonsegregated basis a black to the law school, down to and beyond the landmark 1954 case which ordered the integration of public secondary and primary schools "with all deliberate speed";

The similarly long series of steps to end discrimination in the voting process, starting with the court invalidation in 1944 of the white primary closed to blacks and continuing with the 1954, 1964, and later civil rights acts, which increasingly protected and enforced the right of blacks to register and vote in all elections.

The range and number of national and state legislative and judicial and administrative efforts to see that black people were accorded equal dignity is very large indeed. Repeatedly in the 1940s, 1950s, and early 1960s it gave evidence to blacks that progress was being made. Their expectations inevitably rose from the near-ground level before the Second World War to what proved increasingly to be excessively optimistic. Acts of legislatures, courts, and administrative agencies—and of private groups and citizens—to equalize life opportunities for black epople have never quite fulfilled their initial purpose. This brings us to the matter of promise and performance, to assessment of the gap between the expectations aroused by legislation, executive order, and court decision, on the one hand, and realization of equality, on the other.

The killing by lynch mobs dwindled to one case in 1947 and two in 1948. A new kind of killing of blacks began and at times something like the old lynch mob operated again. In 1952 a top state NAACP official in Florida who organized a campaign to secure the indictment of a sheriff charged with killing a black prisoner was killed by a bomb. After the 1954 commencement of public school integration, there were some 530 cases of violence (burning, bombing, and intimidation of children and their parents) in the first four years of integration. Schools, churches, and the homes of black leaders were bombed and many people were killed in these bombings. Federal troops were brought into Little Rock in September 1957 to integrate the high school; during the following school year (1958-1959), public schools were closed in Little Rock.

In short—starting in the mid-1950s and increasing more or less steadily into the early 1960s—white violence grew against the now lawful and protected efforts of blacks to gain integration. And so did direct action and later violence undertaken by blacks, in a reciprocal process that moved into the substantial violence of 1965-1968. That four-year period was the peak of the violence that constituted the black rebellion. It was violence mostly against white property and black people. It merits reemphasis that during this era of increased hostility, progress continued to be made. Indeed, the occurrence of some progress intensified both the white reaction to it and the black counteraction to the reaction, because every time a reaction impeded the progress, the apparent gap widened between expectations and gratifications.

Direct (but not violent) action by blacks began in late 1956 with the bus boycott in Montgomery, Alabama, which endured for over a year and succeeded. It was precipitated when a black woman got on a city bus, sat down in a front seat, was ordered to give up her seat to a white man, and refused. The bus boycott soon came under the leadership of Dr. Martin Luther King, Jr., whose belief in nonviolent resistance—and the mild temper of blacks in Montgomery at the time—succeeded in keeping the action relatively peaceful.

Direct violent action began in April 1963 in Birmingham, Alabama, in what may be called the first full-scale concerted violent encounter of blacks and whites in recent years. Seeking integration of such facilities as lunch counters, parks, and swimming pools, the blacks in Birmingham, most of them young, were met with water hoses, police dogs, and violent acts of police and white people. The number of demonstrators increased to some 3,000 and there were 1,000 arrests. The repressiveness of the police united a hitherto-divided black community in Birmingham. And it produced perhaps the first major case since the Second World War in which Southern blacks threw rocks and bottles at police. From this time on, violence deepened and spread among blacks. The Birmingham riots immediately touched off a response in other cities—according to one estimate, 758 demonstrations in the ten weeks following the Birmingham violence. And in six weeks of that 1963 summer, blacks (in Birmingham and elsewhere) succeeded in getting some 200 lunch counters and other public facilities desegrated.

The combined effect of substantial, though slow, progress in employment, housing, education, and voting did not have the effect of quieting blacks or stopping the rebellion of the 1960s. The full-fledged riots of Los Angeles in 1965 and Newark and Detroit in 1967 have been amply studied, at least from the descriptive viewpoint. But there is a tendency to see these events in isolation. It is recognized that riots in one place will touch off riots in another or—more likely—in several others, but the social-contagion theory (including the contagion of seeing African nations liberated after the Second World War) by no means gets to the roots of the rebellion. And neither does the notion that blacks are frustrated and are striking out rather blindly at the centuries of repression. If 300 years of repression have been too much, why were 200 or 280 not enough to produce rebellion?

What is striking is the time sequence of events. As in major historic revolutions, the events relating to the 1960s rebellion consist of a rather long period of rising expectations followed by a relatively brief period of frustration that struck deep into the psyches of black people. And I suggest that from the seventeenth to the early twentieth century there had been very little development beyond mere physical survival for virtually all black people in America (and in Africa). It is significant to note that in the prosperous 1960s, there was no sharp or sudden rise in unemployment of blacks. There was no marked deprivation of material goods to which blacks had become accustomed. But there was, starting notably in 1963, not the first instance of violence against blacks but a sudden increase in it. This resurgence of violence came after, and interrupted, the slow but steady progress since 1940. It quickly frustrated rising expectations.

This increase in violence, commencing so to speak with the firehoses and police dogs in May 1963 in Birmingham, affronted not only the physical safety of the demonstrators, thereby reactivating anxiety and fear of bodily harm itself—the most basic of human concerns. This increase in violence also affronted the dignity of black people as human beings. Black people sensed that their various and continuously rising expectations, now confronted with violence, were to rise no more.

In addition to this violence between whites against blacks and of blacks against whites, there was an explosive growth of private acts of violence of blacks against blacks. This activated the fear for physical safety itself. And the ever-growing congestion in the slums worsened housing conditions.

White people who fail to understand their own past and their own ever-rising expectations (if we have one car, we must have two; if we finished four years of college, our son must become a doctor or a lawyer) are puzzled at the dissatisfaction of blacks who have made such considerable progress since the Second World War. But what would be odd about blacks, and indicate that they indeed had some special nature, would be for them to be satisfied in present circumstances. The very rapidity of their advance makes them expect to continue its pace. The very low point from which they started makes them expect to reach equality with a few years or at the very most a few decades. Their mental processes are operating in an altogether normal manner. They would be less than human if they acted otherwise. The gap formed from the increased incidence of violence on the part of police and white citizens provided the quantum of energy necessary to raise black frustrations to the point of rebellion. Figure 16.4 shows the developments.

Two ways are possible of resolving the problem that arises when the expectations-gratifications gap develops—and perhaps there are others. One way to close the growing gap is to attempt to deprive blacks in America of all the gains that they have made since at least the beginning of the Second World War. These gains have been mostly in the satisfaction of their physical needs (in jobs and housing); their social and their dignity needs are beginning to gain prominence. In George Orwell's phrase, we may call this the technique of the boot stamping in a human face forever. If white people were to attempt and even succeed in so reducing black people to a life that consisted of trying to stay alive—the life they lived under slavery and, most of them, for two to four generations after emancipation—black rebelliousness could be contained. In the process white people would be reduced to the same animal-like behavior that they themselves were imposing on blacks, just as concentration camp guards and concentration camp inmates came to resemble each other in appearance and behavior.

A second way to resolve the problem is to recognize and help black people satisfy their expectations, which fundamentally are the expectations which degraded white people in decades and centuries long past have themselves achieved—notably the recognition of their equal dignity and worth. It is not to be supposed or hoped that black people then will at last become satisfied, any more than white people who achieve dignity become satisfied. But at least those blacks who have achieved dignity will then be that much closer to becoming fulfilled human beings, able at last to realize themselves in the climate of self-respect that is necessary for people to grow.

SOME TENTATIVE CONCLUSIONS

We have seen that the J-curve is a necessary though not sufficient part of the explanation of a civil war, a revolution, and a contained rebellion. This J-curve is a psychological, not a sociological explanation. The units of analysis are individual human beings. They may fall into visible categories (like blacks or students or working men or peasants), but their mental processes that relate to frustration and aggression are fundamentally the same. That is, we are positing that anyone deprived of food—whether this normal circumstances include the simple diet of poor people or the elaborate one of rich people—will suddenly become inclined to break any social convention to get food. We are also supposing that anyone who is physically secure in the provision of food, clothing, health, and physical safety will seek to establish

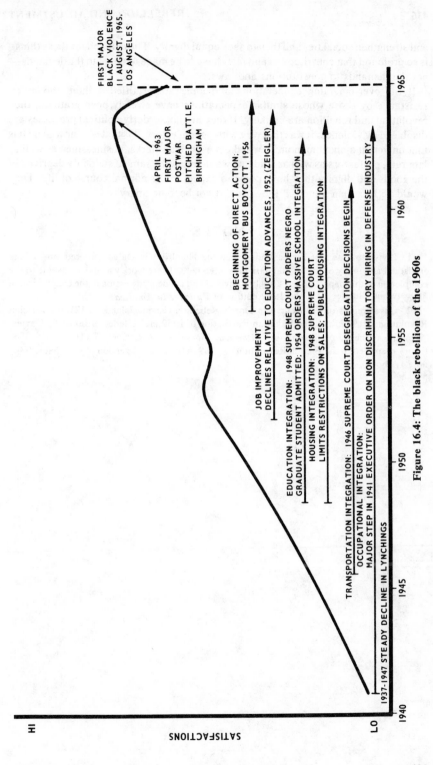

Figure 16.4: The black rebellion of the 1960s

SATISFACTIONS — HI / LO

1940 — 1945 — 1950 — 1955 — 1960 — 1965

1937-1947 STEADY DECLINE IN LYNCHINGS

TRANSPORTATION INTEGRATION: 1946 SUPREME COURT DESEGREGATION DECISIONS BEGIN

OCCUPATIONAL INTEGRATION:
MAJOR STEP IN 1941 EXECUTIVE ORDER ON NON DISCRIMINATORY HIRING IN DEFENSE INDUSTRY

EDUCATION INTEGRATION: 1948 SUPREME COURT ORDERS NEGRO
GRADUATE STUDENT ADMITTED; 1954 ORDERS MASSIVE SCHOOL INTEGRATION

HOUSING INTEGRATION: 1948 SUPREME COURT
LIMITS RESTRICTIONS ON SALES; PUBLIC HOUSING INTEGRATION

JOB IMPROVEMENT
DECLINES RELATIVE TO EDUCATION ADVANCES, 1952 (ZEIGLER)

BEGINNING OF DIRECT ACTION:
MONTGOMERY BUS BOYCOTT, 1956

APRIL 1963
FIRST MAJOR
POSTWAR
PITCHED BATTLE.
BIRMINGHAM

FIRST MAJOR
BLACK VIOLENCE
11 AUGUST. 1965.
LOS ANGELES

435

and strengthen social ties and then to seek equal dignity. The demand for these things is so profound that constitutions and laws have to be made to adapt to the demands— not the demands to constitutions and laws.

If the ever-emerging expectations of people are gratified without too much resistance by those whose similar expectations have already been gratified, then revolution and rebellion are unlikely. If they are not, orderly political processes are displaced by violence. It was that way with our ancestors; it is that way now. And it is that universal a phenomenon. Lawmakers as well as clerks, businessmen as well as laborers, professors as well as students would react the same if suddenly deprived of the goods and dignity they have come to expect in the normal course of life. They would be less than human if they too did not become angry.

NOTES

1. I wish to note that Janice Rademaker and Hendrik van Dalen gathered most of the statistical and many of the factual data presented here. There work was indispensable to the completion of this paper. This is a slightly revised and condensed version of the chapter which appeared as Chapter 19 in the 1969 edition of *Violence in America*.

2. Case studies of the J-curve in Dorr's Rebellion (Rhode Island, 1842), the Russian Revolution to 1917, and The Egyptian Revolution of 1952 are included in James C. Davies, "Toward a Theory of Revolution," *American Sociological Review*, 27 (162): 5-18. The theory is applied to the French Revolution of 1789 in the original version of this chapter (see note 1, above).

Chapter 17
Group Violence in America
Its Structure and Limitations

RICHARD E. LIBMAN-RUBENSTEIN

The tumultuous decade which began with the assassination of President Kennedy and ended with the resignation of President Nixon took most Americans by surprise. Students of American history and society were, on the whole, as unprepared as any other group for the racial uprisings, student revolts, volatile antiwar demonstrations and state violence of the period. Social scientists—not ordinarily a reticent group— were rendered temporarily speechless by events which seemed to contradict fundamental, widely held and cherished assumptions about the nature of American society. In 1968, the year of the Martin Luther King and Robert Kennedy assassinations, the Chicago and Washington racial uprisings, and the Democratic National Convention rioting, Clifford Geertz confessed that American social scientists did not understand the causes of domestic political violence. "Domestic disorder," he wrote, "is a product of a long sequence of particular events whose interconnections our received categories of self-understanding are not only inadequate to reveal but are designed to conceal."[1]

CONSENSUS SCHOLARSHIP AND HISTORICAL AMNESIA

Geertz's dismay reflected the failure of consensus scholarship, the dominant school of American social thought in the postwar period, to predict or explain the disorders of the sixties. For years, leading scholars had insisted that the United States was a "pluralistic" society characterized by shared social and political values and a "genius" for compromise.[2] American society, they held, was blessed by a blurring of divisions between a multiplicity of economic, social, political, and ethnic groups. For one reason or another—either because the land was fertile and the people hard-working, or because no true aristocracy or proletariat ever developed on

AUTHOR'S NOTE: *Richard E. Libman-Rubenstein is associate professor of political science at Roosevelt University, Chicago. He was an advisory consultant to the National Commission on the Causes and Prevention of Violence. His publications include* Rebels in Eden: Mass Political Violence in the United States *(Little, Brown, 1970);* Left Turn: Origins of the Next American Revolution *(Little, Brown, 1973); and the forthcoming* Terrorism and Politics.

American soil, because the United States was a nation of immigrant groups, or because the two-party system worked so well—any sizeable domestic group could gain its share of power, prosperity, and respectability merely by playing the game according to the rules.[3] In the process, the group itself would gradually lose coherence and be incorporated into the great middle class. The result, the scholars said, was a pattern of economic, social, and political mobility unique in world history. In America, rising domestic groups had not been compelled to be revolutionary, nor had the "ins" generally resorted to excessive force to keep them "out." The conclusion drawn by many was that the United States, having mastered the art of peaceful change, could in good conscience presume to lead the world.[4]

Surprisingly, the political explosions of the Kennedy, Johnson, and Nixon years failed to demolish the myth of peaceful progress. ("It seems," Geertz remarked, "that we do not want to learn too much about ourselves too quickly.")[5] The prevailing view in scholarly as well as popular circles is that, the period of disorder having ended, a "normal" state of consensus has been restored. Once again, it is considered realistic to assume that American society lacks the potential for serious internal conflict involving mass violence. The persistence of belief in the normality of consensus and the aberrational quality of political violence is an example of what some call *historical amnesia*. Psychologists and biologists have taught us much about amnesia, the individual capacity to "forget" painful experiences.[6] Social scientists might add, by analogy, that large groups—even whole societies—can alter or obliterate disturbing memories of violence and social disorder.[7] American society, which has endured frequent outbursts of mass political violence, seems to have a high propensity for historical amnesia. Particularly when levels of group conflict have declined, stormier eras fade in the imagination; we are easily led to believe that the lull which surrounds us is the norm, and lightening flashes of violence the rare exception. Thus, in the late 1970s, the dramatic disorders of the recent past already seem frozen in time, stock footage for a television documentary on "The Swinging Sixties." Selective memory sanctifies the nonviolent Martin Luther King, Jr., but "forgets" the martyrdom of more threatening figures. Who now celebrates the birthday of Malcolm X, or remembers that there ever was such a man as Fred Hampton of Illinois.[8]

A variation on this theme is the tendency to remember only the most recent episodes of political violence—for example, the disorders of the 1960s. Since these have ended, one can then assume that the period of conflict was exceptional, and that a normal state of social peace has been restored. Similarly, in order to account for episodes of political violence without abandoning belief in a norm of peaceful progress, rebellious groups and individuals may be described as exceptions to the rule, that is, as deviant social formations and personalities. During the period of racial disorders, for example, conservatives attributed political violence involving blacks to peculiar mental or moral characteristics of that group, while liberals discussed the uniqueness of black history, the heritage of slavery, and the prevalence of racial discrimination.[9] In *Beyond The Melting Pot*, a study of racial and ethnic groups in New York City published an embarrassingly short time before the outbreak of ghetto rioting, Nathan Glazer and Daniel Patrick Moynihan argued that urban blacks were basically similar to white ethnic groups which had risen from the social depths without resorting to intense or prolonged group violence or radical, antisystem politics. Following the occurrence of such violence and such politics, they reissued the book with a lengthy introduction explaining that their miscalculation was based on an understandable failure to predict that blacks would *choose* to act in a deviant manner, for example, by following irresponsible "militants" rather than more realistic traditional leaders.[10] Such reasoning, in essence, attributes serious social disorder to characteristics of the group rather than the social and political system. Like historical amnesia, it refuses to recognize that political violence in the United States has been frequent and widespread—as American, as H. Rap Brown put it, as cherry pie.

THE SCORESHEET OF DOMESTIC POLITICAL VIOLENCE

Whether in academia or in the streets, reactions to modern outbreaks of political violence testify to a widely held belief that such episodes are "un-American"—rare occurrences in American life bearing little significant relationship to the way domestic groups have succeeded in gaining political power, property, or prestige. The authorities frequently attribute such outbreaks to a few evil schemers (in the late President Johnson's words, "Mean and willful men") or to a lawless, anarchic mob run amok (the interpretation of the Watts uprising by the California Governor's Commission). Not surprisingly, those most vociferous in denouncing the violent few are often those who believe that *their* ethnic, economic, or occupational groups "made it" in America without resorting to violent revolt. This assumption is open to objection on two counts. First, if "making it" means owning capital and wielding significant political power, most domestic groups have not yet "made it" despite their occasional participation in violent rebellions.[11] Second, historical study reveals that American society has experienced regular episodes of serious mass violence directly related to the social, political, and economic objectives of numerous groups. A partial list of major groups which have been involved in violent rebellion[12] makes this clear.

(1) Beginning in the seventeenth century, American Indians engaged in a series of revolts aimed at securing their land and liberty against invasion by white settlers. Generally, the settlers were supported by colonial governments; where such support was not forthcoming, they sometimes participated in insurrections like Bacon's Rebellion in Virginia (1675). Despite continuous military reverses and the success of the U.S. government's successive "removal" and "reservation" policies, Indian uprisings were not finally crushed until early in the twentieth century. (Even then, Indian militancy showed a capacity to revive; in 1974, gunfire between Indians and federal agents was again exchanged at Wounded Knee, South Dakota, site of an infamous massacre of Native Americans by the United States Army.) Calling these conflicts "wars" against Indian "nations" does not alter their character. They were armed insurrections by domestic groups which the United States had determined to deny the privileges of citizenship as well as the perquisites of nationhood.[13]

(2) Farmers living in the western regions of the Eastern seaboard colonies participated in civil disorder from the 1740s, when Massachusetts farmers marched

on Boston in support of a land bank law, until the 1790s, when farmers and mountain men fomented the Whiskey and Fries Rebellions in Pennsylvania. The series of revolts now known as the Wars of the Regulators, the War of the New Hampshire Grants, Shays' Rebellion, and the Whiskey Rebellion were the principal actions engaged in by debtor farmers protesting half a century of economic exploitation, political exclusion, and social discrimination by East Coast merchants, shippers, and planters. Although individual insurgencies were defeated or dispersed by superior force, the series of revolts did not end until Jefferson's accession to the presidency in 1801 provided access to the political system and new land created fresh economic opportunity for the Scotch-Irish, German, Swedish, and other farmer-immigrant groups on the frontier. Where the "system" was especially rigid, as in New York's Hudson Valley, agitation and sporadic violence continued well into the nineteenth century.[14]

(3) American colonists, as we know, gained their independence from Britain after a decade of civil strife and six years of revolutionary war. What is now becoming clearer is the extent to which the struggle pitted Americans against Americans, with the insurgents resorting to modes of political violence and the authorities to modes of repression which were repeated in later "independence" revolts. During the decade of disorder, which began with passage of the Stamp Act (1765), the Sons of Liberty and similar militants organized campaigns against British colonial legislation, directing economic and physical terror against Tories, merchants tied to British interests, and other collaborators. With the outbreak of open warfare, civil strife increased in intensity and scope, spreading into rural areas where roving guerrilla bands fought bitterly. Blacks and Indians were pawns in a struggle whose excesses would not be confined to the period of formal hostilities; the massive Loyalist emigration which began in the last years of the war indicates how deeply revolutionary and counterrevolutionary passions ran.[15]

(4) From its inception, the slave system created an obvious potential for bloody revolt, fears of black retribution becoming rampant among white Southerners after the Haitian slaves rebelled in 1795. Although most domestic slave revolts were betrayed to the slaveowners or quickly quelled, the danger, dramatized by insurrections like that of Nat Turner in Virginia, militarized the white South. In the years between 1820 and 1860, white Southerners became, in Jesse T. Carpenter's words, "a conscious minority." How they moved from abortive civil disobedience during the Nullification controversy to outright secession is well-documented. So is the parallel movement of antislavery Northerners, who began with disobedience of the Fugitive Slave laws, later fielded a settler army in Kansas, supported John Brown's raid on Harper's Ferry in 1859 and (in coalition with former Whigs) elected a president committed to the preservation of the Union by force. Recent studies make it clear that the Civil War, although a massive military struggle, was much more than a series of formal battles between clearly defined sides. For example, while Northern agents attempted to provoke uprisings of slaves in the South, the New York Irish, rioting against Lincoln's conscription policy, destroyed large sections of New York and butchered dozens of blacks during the Draft Riot of 1863.[16]

(5) Less well publicized than the Civil War itself is the guerrilla war waged after the surrender at Appomattox by Southern terrorist groups like the Ku Klux Klan,

supported by large numbers of white Southerners. G. David Garson describes this struggle in detail elsewhere in this book. Its purposes—to prevent blacks from voting or participating in politics, to restore the substance of the prewar Southern social system, and to drive "carpetbagger" officials and their "scalawag" supporters out of the South—were substantially realized by 1871, when Congress first legislated against the Klan, and entirely realized in 1877, when President Hayes withdrew the last of the Northern occupying troops. This was not the end of Southern terrorism, however; continued racial domination and defense of the "Southern way of life" were maintained by lynching some 3,000 blacks, driving dissenting whites out of the territory, and meting out to "outside agitators" the kind of punishment inflicted on Viola Liuzzo, Colonel Lemuel Penn, and Martin Luther King, Jr.[17]

(6) During the nineteenth and early twentieth centuries, as immigrants poured into the developing nation, white, Anglo-Saxon, Protestant Americans (WASPS) engaged in a long series of riots, lynchings, mob actions, and abuses of power in order to protect their political influence, property values, and life styles against the immigrant onslaught. WASPS organized politically as "Native Americans" tore apart the Irish section of Philadelphia in 1844, and similar pogroms occurred in New York, Baltimore, Boston, and other port cities. On the West Coast, Chinese and Japanese immigrants, despite their relatively small numbers, were victims of both riots and discrimination; competition for jobs as well as prejudice as an important nativist motivation. Italians were lynched in New Orleans and Jews assaulted in New York, but the fiercest "patriotic" violence as directed against German Americans during the First World War (riots, intimidation, economic boycotts, and legal harassment) and against Japanese during the Second World War (internment in concentration camps, confiscation of property, etc.).[18]

(7) For their part, later immigrant groups often responded in kind; gang warfare for control of urban neighborhoods became part of the big-city way of life. More often, ethnic group hostility was directed socially downward, towards the blacks and newer-arrived immigrants, who were frequently used as strikebreakers in labor disputes. During the New York Draft Riot, the Irish burned draft offices and Yankee homes, killed the chief of police, and went on a rampage against that city's blacks. Following the Civil War, massacres of blacks in border state cities became frequent; and when, in the present century, race "wars" struck Northern cities like Chicago, white ethnic groups fearful of the black "invasion" were in the forefront of the battle. One is hard put to discover an American ethnic group which did *not* participate either in antiauthority revolt, intergroup rioting, or both.[19]

(8) From the 1870s until the 1930s, working men and women attempting to organize and defend trade unions fought with employers, their private armies, strikebreakers, police, and state or federal troops. The story is recounted in some detail by Philip Taft and Philip Ross in their contribution to this volume. In terms of lives lost and property destroyed, labor-management violence in America was for half a century unmatched in any other industrialized nation. Legislative reforms enacted by the New Deal and the great economic boom of 1940-1965 terminated this period of struggle. Nevertheless, violence accompanying hard-fought strikes continues in many industries, and labor's capacity for collective revolt (for example, in

the event of a serious decline in living standards) remains a question mark. We will have more to say on this subject later in this essay.[20]

(9) The long, bitter history of racial strife in the United States is described elsewhere in this volume. During the 1960s, black Americans living in urban ghetto areas participated in a series of spontaneous uprisings directed not so much against white persons as against white-owned stores and real property and those representing an oppressive legal order (especially the police). Smaller groups advocating either armed insurrection or armed self-defense of the black community against the authorities were decimated by legal repression, internecine warfare, and state violence. Although this period of disorder is generally considered to be ended, episodes of ghetto rioting continue, the most recent being the disorders experienced during the New York City power failure of 1976. Whether more conscious and selective forms of racial violence (e.g., "terrorism") are on the agenda for the future is a question still debated among analysts of American society.[21]

(10) Clearly the most violent group in United States history has been the minority which holds a near-monopoly of the means of violence—the American ruling class. Although discussion of state violence is postponed until later in this essay, it is important to note here that "official violence" has not been merely a response to group revolt, but a cause of it. Few of the riots or rebellions mentioned above lacked provocation in the form of persistent, often illegal violence by state agencies against groups and individuals considered to be "uppity," troublesome, or dangerous. Recent revelations concerning the activities of American intelligence agencies intended to "neutralize or disrupt" the Black Power and antiwar movements of 1963-1973 are reminders that provocation has long been a favorite weapon in the arsenal of state violence; time and again, state provocateurs fomented disorder in order to provide an excuse for intensified state violence against targeted groups and group leaders. Abuses of power by those in authority are a constant in American politics, although state violence seems to intensify domestically as an adjunct to interstate violence or war. Thus, in the twentieth century, the most serious abuses of power are identified with the First World War (persecution of German Americans and antiwar groups, the postwar "Red Scare" and the Palmer Raids), the Second World War (incarceration of Japanese Americans, prosecution of labor leaders under the Smith Act), the Cold War (the "loyalty-security" hysteria triggered by President Truman and continued by Senator McCarthy of Wisconsin), and the Indochina War (government action against numerous domestic "enemies," culminating in the Watergate debacle).[22]

VIOLENCE AND PROGRESS

Although incomplete, the list above provides a background against which one may test the most important implication of the myth of peaceful progress: the idea that mass violence in the United States has generally been both unnecessary and useless. It shows, for example, that the proposition, "Domestic violence is unnecessary," is fallacious no matter how one interprets it. It is false if it means that the established machinery for political and economic advancement has permitted all major "out-groups" to move nonviolently up the sociopolitical ladder. On the contrary, our institutions seem far better designed to facilitate the advancement of talented individuals than oppressed groups. Most groups which have engaged in mass violence have done so only after a long period of fruitless, relatively nonviolent struggle in which established procedures were tried and found unavailing. Similarly, the proposition is false if it means that the established order is self-transforming, or that groups in positions of power will share that power with outsiders without being threatened by actual or potential violence. The Appalachian farmer revolts, as well as violent urban demonstrations in sympathy with the French Revolution, were used by Jeffersonians to create a two-party system over the horrified protests of the Federalists. Northern violence ended the Southern slave empire, and Southern terrorism terminated Radical Reconstruction. Federal recognition of labor unions was granted in the midst of a depression, during a wave of violent strikes which provoked widespread fear of revolution. And urban blacks made their greatest legislative gains during the racial strife of the 1960s.

It is important, of course, not to misuse this information by asserting that violence always "works," or that it is always necessary. This would be to create a new myth— a myth of violent progress—which could easily be refuted by citing examples of violence without progress, like the American Indian revolts, and progress with little violence, like enactment of federal farm legislation by the New Deal. The examples listed above suggest that typical episodes of domestic rebellion may generate political *reform*, but they also raise a negative inference: mass political violence in America has seldom been *revolutionary* in effect, although it has often seemed so to contemporary observers. Indeed, for reasons we will explore, typical forms of domestic violence share many of the characteristics associated with what Eric Hobsbawm calls "primitive rebellion." While demanding changes in the distribution of goods, opportunities, or local power, domestic revolts do not generally threaten to transform the social system or to displace a ruling class. On the contrary, in studying these outbreaks one becomes conscious of a peculiar sort of correspondence between the forms of power wielded by America's rulers and the forms of rebellion resorted to by aggrieved groups seeking inclusion in the national "consensus." The correspondence is symbolized, perhaps, by the chant of the antiwar demonstrators at the Democratic Convention of 1968 in Chicago: "The whole world is watching!" Like the Democratic party leaders meeting in convention to nominate Hubert Humphrey for president, those involved in what the Walker investigative commission termed a "police riot" addressed themselves to the television audience, aiming not to overthrow the government but to expose it as violent in order to persuade a nation of passive onlookers of the necessity for reform.[23] (Compare the student rebellion of May 1968 in Paris, which was coordinated with strikes and aimed at persuading workers to join in an effort to overthrow the government of de Gaulle.)[24]

Discarding the myth of peaceful progress, then, one sees that violent politics have played a significant role in American political history. It is equally true, however, that much of this violence has been consistent, both in form and content, with established structures of national power. The "norm," in American politics, has not been peaceful progress but reformism, both nonviolent and violent. Perhaps this is why episodes of political disorder—even serious, long-lasting periods of strife—fade so quickly in the memory (the primary exception is the American Civil War, a domestic rebellion which *did* have revolutionary implications and consequences).[25] When a violent era ends, scholars tend to celebrate both the reforms generated during the period and the restoration of consensus. The impression given is not that violent reformism is an American political tradition, but that the violence was secondary— historically insubstantial, so to speak, and ultimately unnecessary.

Thus, the resignation of President Nixon, the prosecution of his confederates, and the accession of Vice-President Ford to the presidency in 1974 were widely held to vindicate the norm of peaceful progress. It would have been more accurate, however, to describe the Watergate episode as representative of a tradition of *factional violence* involving abuses of state power by cliques of politicians and businessmen. Since this sort of violence is seldom revolutionary either in intention or effect, one easily forgets or ignores its normality, and remembers only that it was suppressed and the political system was "vindicated." But what an odd form of vindication! It is the equivalent of asserting that the tenth or twentieth conviction of an habitual criminal vindicates the norm of legality. This reasoning effectively distracts attention not only from the quantity of domestic political violence but from its persistence and regularity (its significance as an aspect of the political norm). Even now, many consider the Watergate debacle an anomaly in the context of American history, when what was most unusual about this use of public power for private ends was not its occurrence but its exposure.[26] Moreover, focusing attention on "successful" system-responses to violence disables one from predicting its reoccurrence or anticipating the development of new forms of disorder. This may be one reason for our perennial astonishment at new outbreaks of group violence; consensus theory leads us to assume that the latest rebellion or abuse of power was the last, and that the current consensus is permanent.

Another example may make this clearer. For most labor historians, working-class violence in America is chiefly of antiquarian interest; far greater significance is attributed to the settlement of labor-management conflict engineered by the New Deal, which pacified the labor unions and provided a political basis for the current economic "consensus."[27] As this is written, however, the longest strike in the history of the coal industry is in progress, and truckloads of armed strikers are attempting to shut down nonunion mines in Appalachia and the South. To some observers, at least, it is becoming clear that the New Deal-Fair Deal settlement was effective during the great economic boom period 1940-1965, and that the end of the boom raises serious questions as to its continued viability. Whether or not the American working class has been "pacified" is once again a live issue.[28] Assuming that conflict in the coal industry in the winter of 1977-1978 lacked immediate revolutionary (or counter-revolutionary) potential, two things still seem clear: first, a fairly high degree of labor-management violence is consistent with existing norms. Second, an escalation of violence which could compel alteration of these norms is quite possible. By contrast, to assume the existence of a permanent settlement in the field of labor-management relations is to obscure both the persistence of class-based violence in the United States and its potential to intensify. (A parallel assumption, equally unwarranted, is that a racial and ethnic "consensus" now exists in urban areas.) Once again, the helplessness of consensus theory to understand or predict new outbreaks of domestic violence compels us to reexamine the tradition of violent politics in America.

THE STRUCTURE OF LOCALIZED REBELLION

Considering the sheer volume of political violence in American history, one of the most striking characteristics of out-group rebellion has been its predominant localism. Rarely, if ever, have domestic groups in revolt attacked the powers-that-be at their source. Appalachian farmers mounted no Tet Offensive against Eastern cities; they merely shut down local courts and drove tax collectors out of their territory. Southern terrorists did not attempt to overthrow the government at Washington (the 1868 Constitution of the Ku Klux Klan declared KKK allegiance to the United States Government). They murdered, silenced, or expelled their enemies from the South, and reasserted by force their dominion over native blacks. Labor violence was usually aimed at strikebreakers and Pinkertons, company property and local police; although class conflict tended to spread from locality to locality and from industry to industry, violent confrontations remained localized and uncoordinated. Similarly, urban immigrant groups fighting each other or the cops, or looting the "outsider's" store, did not dream of establishing a Paris Commune in America. To establish control over their territories seemed utopian enough. This pattern persisted throughout the violent 1960s. Although authorities feared a "nationalization" of black and student rebellion, ghetto and campus uprisings remained both internally and externally uncoordinated. Those resorting to more systematic and planned antisystem violence were a small minority, easily crushed by superior government force, while mass violence was characteristically riotous, tending to "burn itself out" at the level of local protest rather than sparking a more general conflagration.[29]

This does not mean that episodes of group violence have been evenly or randomly distributed over the course of American history. On the contrary, they seem to cluster during periods of disorder like the 1790s, 1850s, 1890s, and 1930s—periods which coincide with the breakup of one national governing coalition and the formation of another.[30] Nevertheless, the rarity of coordinated group revolts suggests that much domestic violence is an expression of specific group interests and emotions rather than a more general interest (for example, class interest) in system change. Indeed, rebellious groups in America often conceive of themselves as nations-within-the-nation—cultural entities struggling for some form of self-determination, rather than economic entities linked organically to some larger national or international group. Thus, the immediate causes of many domestic revolts are acts carried out by agents of central authority on an out-group's "territory." Mass violence, in such cases, is a spontaneous response to such "invasion" intended to expel the representatives of authority and their local collaborators from the territory. Similarly, the typical rebel leadership aims at replacing locally dominant outsiders with indigenous leaders, a goal which leads more logically to decentralization (or, in extreme cases, secession) than to a revolutionary struggle for power at the center.

For this reason, the ideology of domestic rebels seldom includes plans for a transformation of politics or the economy at a national level. The usual function of such ideology is to intensify group consciousness, and to describe those changes necessary to maximize group dignity and power within the existing national framework. Moreover, ideological explanations and prescriptions generally follow rather than precede violent revolts; an illustration is the ideology of Black Power, created *after* the uprisings of 1964-1967 had occurred in Northern ghettos. While employing the revolutionary rhetoric of "liberation," Black Power thinking was directed towards increasing black group consciousness and augmenting that group's power with the minimum amount of systemwide change necessary.[31] This style of political thinking, which attempts to mobilize a group's violent potential for essentially reformist ends, may become revolutionary in effect when diverse out-groups coalesce; in American history, this is illustrated by the secessionist movements of the 1770s and 1860s. Nevertheless, ideologies which intensify ethnic, racial, or occupational group consciousness militate naturally against the formation of coalitions based on ties of class. The Patriot and Southern coalitions were cross-class coalitions led by businessmen and united by group nationalism. Both movements may be described as politically revolutionary but socially conservative —as macrocosms, therefore, of group revolt in America.

The traditional weapons of domestic revolt are similarly directed to the end of maximizing group dignity and autonomy without destroying the national social fabric. Looting, arson, beating up or intimidation of persons, threats and whisper campaigns (ostracism), and use of arms are generally directed at ridding the territory of group enemies and silencing collaborators. Intimidation has always been a favorite tactic of domestic insurgents. A man ridden out of town on a rail will usually not return. Neither will a merchant burned out of the ghetto, nor a "nigger-lover" hounded out of the South. Moreover, since central authority is seldom attacked directly, the use of such weapons sometimes forces the authorities to respond by "invading" the group's territory, thereby solidifying resistence and escalating the level of violence. The authorities often prefer a strategy of containment, attempting to seal off rebellion, and to isolate rebellious groups, in order to prevent the spread of disorder. Where this strategy is not practicable, however, and an occupation of rebel territory occurs, the level of violence rises sharply; the presence of an occupying army is an invitation to more selective and aggressive acts of violence (i.e., terrorism).

Many domestic revolts have been conceived, to begin with, as defensive responses to outside aggression and have retained their localistic, reformist, autonomy-oriented character even after serious escalation has taken place. Two prerequisites for this type of revolt seem to be a high level of group coherence, usually based on a shared cultural heritage, and a definable territory which can be claimed for the group and protected against "invasion." This sheds some light, perhaps, on the unusual history of the American labor movement, which remained for the most part nonrevolutionary despite participation in a long series of bloody battles with the authorities. Constantly replenished (and undermined) by waves of foreign immigration and domestic migration, the American working class lacked both cultural homogeneity and a claimable territory (weaknesses consciously exploited by employers to keep the movement weak and divided). On the other hand, in the "Irish" anthracite fields of Pennsylvania, or in isolated timber and mining camps, where workers of diverse nationality lived together with their families, a stronger sense of group identity could emerge, and there was territory which could be defended against scab and police "invasion." Here, in the years before the Great Depression, labor militancy was at its most intense, although, characteristically, leaders like William Haywood of the Western Federation of Miners leaned towards anarcho-syndicalism rather than socialism.[32] Increasing sociocultural homogeneity among modern American workers has raised their potential for class-conscious revolt, but the persistence of racism among some white workers recalls earlier splits within the working class based on competing culture-group loyalties.

In any case, once a local revolt has begun, the common question is whether state violence or reform, or some combination of force and reform, will end it. Military suppression has ended some rebellions like those of the Indian peoples; capitulation to the insurgents, as in the case of the Reconstruction Klan has ended others; others have been terminated by military force. Ordinarily, however, authorities confronted by violent uprisings have responded more ambiguously, alternating the carrot of moderate reform with the stick of suppression. During the ghetto uprisings of the 1960s, police and troops called in to suppress disorders often used excessive violence, as in Newark and Detroit (1967), but did not commit massacres—for example, by machine-gunning looters. On the other hand, they showed no hesitation in involving activists with revolutionary intentions (for example, leaders of the Black Panther party) in shootouts, frameups by agents provocateurs, and even assassinations.[33] With few exceptions, this has been the recurrent pattern of state action against domestic rebels: frequent excesses of official violence stopping short of mass murder. Moreover, the characteristic response to continued group violence includes offers of moderate reform. Our previous analysis suggests that a combination of selective coercion and moderate reform has been effective in ending many domestic revolts because much domestic violence is reformist *ab initio*—that is, structured in such a way as to permit political bargaining to continue. This is clearly the case when group revolt is aimed at securing local power rather than at overturning the established order nationally. The Black Panther party's demand for "black control of the black community," for example, many have seemed revolutionary in the 1960s, but provided a rationale for traditional electoral activity in the 1970s, when blacks became mayors in cities like Newark, Cleveland, Detroit, and Los Angeles.[34]

In retrospect, it seems clear why so many domestic revolts were directed toward maximization of local group prestige and power. The control of territory was one way to break out of the cycle of dependence and group fragmentation afflicting those drawn into the vortex of American industrialism. Like infant industries established behind tariff walls, American culture groups attempted to develop behind ghetto walls the pride, abilities, and resources needed to compete with more powerful outsiders. Control over territory permitted some group members to accumulate capital by providing services to each other, to establish their culture as part of the national mosaic, to train and elect politicians representing group interests, to reconnect the group with the larger national community. In an era in which economic and political institutions were relatively decentralized, local control seemed the sine qua non for group survival as well as a springboard for group leaders seeking inclusion in local and national decision-making elites. Thus, even as late as the

1960s, black and student militants demanded that their respective communities be considered political units, that they police themselves, that outside authority recognize new local leaders more responsive to group needs and desires, and that their cultures be accorded respect as well. As Stokeley Carmichael and Charles Hamilton pointed out, such demands were not inconsistent with a desire for integration of the community into the American "interest group" system; one plays the game of coalition politics only when one has something to play with.[35] Among domestic rebels, the distinction between "integrationists" and "nationalists" is generally superficial, since group nationalism (or even separatism) is usually a metaphor. In modern usage, the secessionist "Don't tread on me" becomes "Get off our backs!", a demand for authoritative recognition of a group's right to control its own affairs on its own territory—a demand, ultimately, for its inclusion in the national consensus.

The difficulty, of course, is that American institutions are no longer decentralized. In an era in which "social integration" has come to mean the subordination of all interests to those of concentrated capital, the demand for community control seems hopelessly utopian. Nevertheless, this political direction is dictated not so much by conscious ideological choice as by the social structure of American culture groups. We have noted that rebellious domestic groups resemble small nations within the larger nation, each with its own hierarchy of classes, and each led by a stratum of businessmen, professionals, and politicians mirroring (although often in distorted form) the class structure of outside society. The traditional route to power for local elites has been to accumulate capital, prestige, and political influence on the local territory, using the group of origin, so to speak, as a springboard from which to acquire regional and national influence.[36] When local opportunities are blocked—for example, because the group as a whole is trapped at a low socioeconomic level or unable to defend its "turf" against outside penetration—local leaders may become angry and "radical." Nevertheless, their demands are frequently satisfied by recognizing the group's communal existence and integrating "responsible spokesmen" into local power structures.

Thus, the history of domestic violence in America reveals a clear connection between the particularism of many group rebellions and their successful suppression. Alliances entered into by such groups are essentially temporary expedients, although ideologues may attempt to give them a coloration of permanence. The New Left's "Maoism," to take a recent example, was a tortured attempt to establish a basis for an alliance between students, domestic minorities, and Third World peasants, excluding the massive American working class (which was considered to have been hopelessly corrupted by capitalism). Such alliances are easily shattered by exploiting cultural and material differences separating rebellious groups, as well as class differences existing within each group. The end of the Vietnam War and of conscription therefore extinguished the student movement, notwithstanding that the problems of the students' erstwhile black allies continued to worsen in the early 1970s. Meanwhile, while diehard black militants were eliminated as a political force, "responsible" black leaders were permitted to enter the universe of political bargaining and office-holding. Particularistic culture groups in America are particularly vulnerable to this combination of repression and cooptation, which offers group leaders a place in the sun provided that they represent group rather than class interests, and they they renounce antisystem goals and practices.

Our analysis suggests, then, that the group revolts of the 1960s did not represent a qualitative break with past patterns of domestic rebellion. Structurally, they were "independence" rebellions, seeking for each culture group concerned a local power base which would permit participation by group leaders in American life. The "youth vanguardism" of the New Left was a valuable clue that, notwithstanding the Maoist, Guevarist, anarchist, or "utopian socialist" language of its leaders, their most fundamental demands were for dignity (recognition of the group and its culture), local power (political influence in the universities and in university communities), and reform (ending the war in Indochina).[37] Indeed, the absorption of much of this leadership by the Democratic party after 1972 makes clear the reformist implications of rebellion based upon culture group consciousness rather than class consciousness. Advanced industrial societies like the United States are not transformed by discontented ethnic, racial, generational, or sexual groups seeking influence within the larger community. Only a class-based mobilization has the potential to alter a monopoly capitalist system at its center.

THE FUTURE OF DOMESTIC REVOLT

Will there be further group rebellions in the United States—and, if so, will they conform to the structural pattern described earlier in this essay? There are several reasons for believing that "independence" revolts will occur less frequently in the future, and that domestic rebellion will assume other forms. First, the termination of major movements of immigration and in-migration (except for the current wave of immigration from Mexico) has largely cut off the supply of new culture groups. The ethnic groups founded upon the immigration waves of 1880-1920 have lost both territoriality and coherence. If, in some respects, they remain "unmeltable," as Michael Novak suggests,[38] it is nevertheless clear that social integration of these groups is proceeding very rapidly, and that, as separate culture groups, their potential for rebellion has declined with equal rapidity. The influx of Mexican and other Spanish-speaking immigrants in recent years is the most significant source of potential culture-group rebellion, along with the persistence of racial communities in urban areas.[39] Urban blacks remain a ghettoized group, and whites living on or near the borders of the ghetto still defend their territories against "invasion"; now, however, their actions are based more upon "white consciousness" than a more specific ethnic group consciousness. In a sense, racial conflict represents the last form of culture-group conflict possible in a rapidly homogenizing society, although it remains a potent source of future political violence.

Second, even racial group identities are undermined, over time, by the integrative force of monopoly capitalism. Black workers still suffer abnormally high rates of unemployment, and are "superexploited" relative to whites; nevertheless, the percentage of black workers in industrial occupations has risen very rapidly, as has black participation in the labor movement.[40] This integration of blacks (and rural whites, Spanish-speakers, and others) into the working class is paralleled by the proletarianization of formerly middle-class groups, in particular, government employees, teachers, failed small businessmen, and the clerical or "white-collar" proletariat.[41] Formerly considered by many sociologists a separate class (or at least a separate status group), the white-collar group has clearly become "industrialized," and knows it; for this reason, the most rapid growth of American labor unions in recent decades has taken place among clerical and service employees. The tendency of monopoly capitalism to eliminate the petty bourgeoisie and to subject all employment to industrial norms increases both the size and the homogeneity of the working class. When the economic system appears healthy, homogenizing tendencies militate against mass violence, limiting rebellion to especially oppressed culture groups. But in times of long-term economic crisis, this relationship may be reversed; working-class homogeneity generates class-conscious rebellion, while culture groups are mobilized in support of the existing system.

The persistence of economic crisis in the United States suggests that future episodes of domestic violence will have more in common with the labor-management conflicts of the 1930s than with past episodes of culture-group rebellion. During the Great Depression, major outbreaks of violence and threats of potential disorder emanated not so much from specific culture groups as from the industrial proletariat as a whole, led for a time by class-conscious militants. (The three major strikes of 1934, of West Coast longshoremen, Minneapolis teamsters, and Toledo auto workers, were led, respectively, by Communist party members, Trotskyists, and members of A.J. Muste's American Workers Party.)[42] The New Deal's labor legislation was a direct response to the threat of continued class struggle, but the period of struggle was not ended by enactment of reforms; it was ended by mobilization for the Second World War, which generated an industrial boom and drove much of the American left into alliance with the American state.[43] Assuming (a) that the current economic crisis is profound, and based on intensification of competition worldwide, and (b) that world war is not a viable short-term option for the American ruling class, one can predict a revival of class-based violence in the United States. By the same token, attempts to divide American workers along culture-group and other lines are also predictable, although their effectiveness may be limited by the homogenizing trends noted earlier.

We began this essay by noting that outbreaks of group violence in America, including the outbreaks of the 1960s, caught most scholars by surprise. Our studies have not advanced far enough to make accurate interpretation of contemporary events and accurate predictions based on those interpretations possible. Nevertheless, an awareness of past patterns of domestic revolt makes it possible to compare the conditions which produced these revolts with conditions prevailing at present, and to draw tentative conclusions. Contemporary America has clearly not mastered the art of peaceful change. My conclusion is that continued political violence is likely, and it will take two (possibly competitive) forms: culture-group conflict based on race (or, in the case of Spanish-speakers, ethnicity), and class conflict based on intensified struggle between workers in and owners of monopoly enterprises. In the immediate future, the latter form of conflict is likely to be the most significant, particularly since the structural constraints on culture-group rebellion, described earlier in this essay, do *not* necessarily function to limit class-based violence. The coal strike of 1977-1978 could be the Watts Rebellion of the new era.

NOTES

1. Clifford Geertz, "Is America By Nature A Violent Society?" New York *Times Magazine*, April 21, 1968, p. 25.

2. Daniel Boorstin, *The Genius of American Politics* (Chicago: University of Chicago Press, 1953).

3. See Louis Hartz, *The Liberal Tradition in America* (New York: Harcourt, Brace, 1955); Lewis Coser, *The Functions of Social Conflict* (Glencoe: Free Press, 1956); Daniel Bell, *The End Of Ideology* (Glencoe: Free Press, 1960); Seymour Martin Lipset, *Political Man: The Social Basis of Politics* (Garden City, N.J.: Doubleday, 1963); Oscar Handlin, *Immigration As A Factor In American History* (Englewood Cliffs, N.J.: Prentice-Hall, 1959); Robert Dahl, *Pluralist Democracy In The United States: Conflict and Consent* (Chicago: Rand-McNally, 1967).

4. The foreign policy implications of consensus theory are made explicit in the work of modernization theorists, see, e.g., Samuel F. Huntington, *Political Order in Changing Societies* (New Haven: Yale University Press, 1968). A useful antidote is *American Power And The New Mandarins,* by Noam Chomsky (New York: Vintage, 1969).

5. Geertz, op. cit.

6. See, e.g., Sigmund Freud, *General Psychological Theory: Papers on Metapsychology* (New York: Collier, 1963).

7. According to numerous reports, official attitudes in modern West Germany have facilitated efforts to "forget" the Nazi period.

8. Fred Hampton, leader of the Black Panther Party of Illinois, and Mark Clark, another Illinois Black Panther, were shot and killed by Cook County Sheriff's Police in 1969 at Hampton's apartment on the West Side of Chicago. The incident was described as a "shootout" by police, although subsequent investigation failed to establish that any shots had been fired by the residents of the apartment, and suggested instead that Hampton had been killed while asleep in his bed. The Cook County Grand Jury failed to return an indictment of murder against State's Attorney Edward Hanrahan, but a civil suit against Hanrahan and others by families of the slain Panthers was still pending in 1978.

9. The conservative view is represented by Edward Banfield, *The Unheavenly City* (Boston: Little, Brown, 1968), and the liberal view by the *Report of the National Advisory Commission On Civil Disorders* (The Kerner Report, Washington, D.C.: Government Printing Office, 1967). Chapter 9 of the Kerner Report compares urban blacks with European immigrants to the cities, but does not recognize that domestic groups other than blacks resorted to mass violence as a method of group advancement.

10. Nathan Glazer and Daniel P. Moynihan, *Beyond The Melting Pot,* 2nd ed. (Cambridge, Mass.: MIT Press, 1970), pp. xiii et seq.

11. See Gabriel Kolko, *Wealth and Power in America* (New York: Praeger, 1963); G. William Domhoff, *Who Rules America?* (Englewood Cliffs, N.J.: Prentice-Hall, 1967); Richard H. Hamilton, *Class and Politics in the United States* (New York: John Wiley, 1972); Edwards, Reich, and Weisskopf, eds., *The Capitalist System: A Radical Analysis of American Society* (Englewood Cliffs, N.J.: Prentice-Hall, 1972).

12. The following list focuses on rebellions against authority and conflict between "outgroups." It is not intended to imply that "outs" are in any way more violent than "ins" or that the violence of the authorities is simply defensive. See paragraph (10), infra.

13. Roy Harvey Pearce, *The Savages of America* (Baltimore: The Johns Hopkins Press, rev. ed. 1965); John Tebbel, *The Compact History of the Indian Wars* (New York: Hawthorn, 1966); Dee Brown, *Bury My Heart At Wounded Knee: An Indian History of the American West* (New York: Holt, Rinehart, 1971).

14. Richard Maxwell Brown, *The South Carolina Regulators* (Cambridge, Mass.: Harvard University Press, 1963); Marion L. Starkey, *A Little Rebellion* (New York: Knopf, 1955); W.W.H. David, *The Fries Rebellion, 1798-1799* (1899, reprinted by Arno/New York *Times*, 1969); H.M. Breckenridge, *History of the Insurrection in Western Pennsylvania* (1859, reprinted by Arno/New York *Times*, 1969); Edward Bellamy, *The Duke of Stockbridge: A Romance of Shays' Rebellion* (1900, reprinted by Arno/New York *Times*, 1969).

15. Jackson Turner Main, *The Social Structure of Revolutionary America* (Princeton, N.J.: Princeton University Press, 1965); Edmund S. Morgan and Helen M. Morgan, *The Stamp Act Crisis: Prologue to Revolution* (Chapel Hill: University of North Carolina Press, 1953); Richard B. Morris, *The American Revolution Reconsidered* (New York: Knopf, 1967). See also Barrington Moore, Jr., *Social Origins of Dictatorship and Democracy: Lord and Peasant in the Making of the Modern World* (Boston: Beacon, 1966), Ch. 2.

16. Jesse T. Carpenter, *The South As A Conscious Minority, 1789-1861* (New York: New York University Press, 1930); Louis Filler, *The Crusade Against Slavery, 1830-1860* (New York: Harper and Row, 1960); Herbert Aptheker, *American Negro Slave Revolts* (New York: International Publishers, rev. ed. 1969); James McCague, *The Second Rebellion: The Story of the New York City Draft Riots of 1863* (New York: Dial, 1968); James M. McPherson, *The Struggle for Equality: Abolitionists and the Negro in the Civil War and Reconstruction* (Princeton, N.J.: Princeton University Press, 1964).

17. Arthur F. Raper, *The Tragedy of Lynching* (Chapel Hill: University of North Carolina Press, 1933); Stanley F. Horn, *Invisible Empire: The Story of the Ku Klux Klan, 1866-1871* (Boston: Houghton Mifflin, 1939); David M. Chalmers, *Hooded Americanism* (Garden City, N.J.: Doubleday, 1965); Allen W. Trelease, *White Terror: The Ku Klux Klan Conspiracy and Southern Reconstruction* (New York: Harper and Row, 1971).

18. John Higham, *Strangers In The Land: Patterns of American Nativism, 1860-1925* (New Brunswick, N.J.: Rutgers University Press, 1955); Richard Hofstadter, *The Paranoid Style in American Politics, and Other Essays* (New York: Knopf, 1966); Alan Wolfe, *Repression in America: The Seamy Side of Democracy* (New York: McKay, 1973).

19. On racial violence, see Chicago Commission Race Relation, *The Negro In Chicago: A Study of Race Relations and a Race Riot* (Chicago: University of Chicago Press, 1922): C. Vann Woodward, *The Strange Career of Jim Crow* (New York: Oxford University Press, rev. ed. 1957); Elliott M. Rudwick, *Race Riot at East St. Louis* (Carbondale, Ill.: Southern Illinois University Press, 1964); *Arthur I. Waskow, From Race Riot To Sit-In: 1919 and the 1960s* (Garden City: Doubleday, 1966). On the overlap between racial and labor violence, see Richard E. Rubenstein, *Rebels in Eden: Mass Political Violence in the United States,* 76 et seq. (Boston: Little, Brown, 1970).

20. See Louis Adamic, *Dynamite! The Story of Class Violence in America* (1937; Gloucester, Mass. Peter Smith, rev. ed. 1963); Samuel Yellen, *American Labor Struggles* (New York: Harcourt, Brace, 1936 reprinted 1956); Robert V. Bruce, *1877: Year of Violence* (Indianapolis, Ind.: Bobbs-Merrill, 1959); Robert J. Hunter, *Violence and the Labor Movement* (1914; Arno/New York *Times*, reprinted 1969); Farrell Dobbs, *Teamster Rebellion* (New York: Monad Press, 1972); Richard E. Rubenstein, *Left Turn: Origins of the Next American Revolution* (Boston: Little, Brown, 1973).

21. Robert Conot, *Rivers of Blood, Years of Darkness* (New York: Bantam, 1967); Thomas Hayden, *Rebellion In Newark: Official Violence and Ghetto Response* (New York: Vintage, 1967); *Report of the National Advisory Commission on Civil Disorders* (New York: Bantam, 1968); Joe R. Feagin and Harlan Hahn, *Ghetto Revolts: The Politics of Violence in American Cities* (New York: Macmillan, 1973). And see also the article in this volume by Morris Janowitz.

22. Alan Wolfe, op. cit.; William Preston, Jr., *Aliens and Dissenters: Federal Suppression of Radicals, 1903-1933* (New York: Harper and Row, 1963); Alan R. Bosworth, *America's Concentration Camps* (New York: Norton, 1967).

23. Daniel Walker, *Rights in Conflict*, Report of the Chicago Study Team of the National Commission of the Causes and Prevention of Violence (Washington, D.C.: U.S. Government Printing Office, 1968).

24. See, e.g., George Singer, *Prelude to Revolution: France in May 1968* (New York: Hill and Wang, 1970).

25. See Barrington Moore, Jr., op. cit., Ch. 3; Eugene Genovese, *The Political Economy of Slavery* (New York: Pantheon, 1965).

26. See Lacey L. Berg, et al., *Corruption in the American Political System* (Morristown: N.J.: General Learning Press, 1976).

27. An important theoretical defense of the view that labor has been integrated into the Democratic Party is J. David Greenstone, *Labor in American Politics* (Chicago: University of Chicago Press, 1977).

28. This issue was raised prior to the coal strike by Stanley Aronowitz, *False Promises* (New York: McGraw-Hill, 1973); Rubenstein, *Left Turn*; James Weinstein, *Ambiguous Legacy* (New York: New Viewpoints, 1975); and others.

29. Jerome H. Skolnick, *The Politics of Protest* (New York: Ballentine, 1969). See also Roy Wilkins and Ramsay Clark, chairmen, *Search and Destroy: A Report by the Commission of Inquiry into the Black Panthers and the Police* (New York: Metropolitan Applied Research Center, 1973); Harold Jacobs, *Weatherman* (Berkeley: Ramparts Press, 1971); Kirkpatrick Sale, *SDS* (New York: Random House, 1973).

30. The correlation between domestic violence and the life-cycle of national governing coalitions is suggested in Rubenstein, *Left Turn*; Part One.

31. A good example of reformism dressed in revolutionary clothing is Charles V. Hamilton and Stokeley Carmichael, *Black Power* (New York: Vintage, 1967).

32. William D. Haywood, *Bill Haywood's Book: The Autobiography of William D. Haywood* (New York: International Publishers, 1929). See also Marc Karson, *American Labor Unions and Politics, 1900-1918* (Carbondale, Ill.: Southern Illinois University Press, 1958).

33. See note 8, *supra*, as well as Paul Chevigny, *Cops and Rebels: A Study of Provocation* (New York: Pantheon, 1972) and Wilkins and Clark, op. cit.

34. This was anticipated by Chuck Stone in *Black Political Power in America* (New York: Delta, 1970). In 1976, former Black Panther Party leader Bobby Seale ran for mayor of Oakland, California, on the Democratic Party ticket.

35. Hamilton and Carmichael, op. cit.

36. See Oscar Handlin, *Immigration as a Factor in American History* (Englewood Cliffs, N.J.: Prentice-Hall, 1959); Stephan Thernstrom, *Poverty and Progress: Social Mobility in a Nineteenth Century City* (Cambridge, Mass.: Harvard University Press, 1964). Daniel Bell's discussion of ethnic groups and crime is apposite; see his *The End of Ideology* (New York: Free Press, 1962), 127 et seq.

37. Christopher Lasch recognized this early in *The Agony of the American Left* (New York: Knopf, 1969) and in his introduction to Norman Miller and Roderick Aya, eds., *The New American Revolution* (New York: Free Press, 1970). See also James Weinstein, *Ambiguous Legacy: The Left in American Politics* (New York: New Viewpoints, 1975).

38. Michael Novak, *The Rise of the Unmeltable Ethnics: Politics and Culture in the Seventies* (New York: Macmillan, 1972).

39. See, e.g., Armando Redon, *Chicano Manifesto* (New York: Macmillan, 1971).

40. William B. Gould, *Black Workers in White Unions: Job Discrimination in the United States* (New York: Cornell University Press, 1977); William Julius Wilson, *The Declining Significance of Race* (Chicago: University of Chicago Press, 1978).

41. See Richard Parker, *The Myth of the Middle Class: Notes on Affluence and Equality* (New York: Liveright, 1972); and Andre Gorz, *Strategy for Labor* (Boston: Beacon, 1967).

42. Art Preis, *Labor's Giant Step* (New York: Monad Press, 1964); Farrell Dobbs, op. cit.; Sidney Lens, *The Crisis of American Labor* (Cranbury, N.J.: A.S. Barnes, 1961).

43. Weinstein, op. cit., Ch. 3; William E. Leuchtenburg, *Franklin D. Roosevelt and the New Deal, 1932-1940* (New York: Harper and Row, 1963).

Chapter 18
Defensive Cultural Adaptation

BERNARD J. SIEGEL

In this chapter I explore the essential features of a class of societies whose members attempt to establish and preserve a cultural identity in the face of what they perceive to be threats to that identity from the environment. The study considers groups under stress, but departs from the general theme of this anthology in that it deals with a strategy of coping with stress that is basically nonviolent in nature. Such groups are of interest in the present context because they demonstrate that violence is only one among several strategies of social response to environmental threat. Members of all the defensive societies with which I am familiar see their surrounding environment as hostile, and the people in it as prepared to engage at any time in destructive or depriving actions against them. Such groups have been difficult for the disinterested investigator to penetrate as an observer. Willing informants are few in number and are often subject to reprisal and disciplinary action; individuals in defensive societies who do not readily submit to authority figures are likely to lose their membership in the group and to be physically rejected.

This analysis is mainly paradigmatic, in that it is primarily concerned with specifying the structure of defensive adaptation, its elements, and their relationship. This is an inductive task, though its aim is to generate some casual explanations about a variety of questions. What dimensions of stress and prior conditions of the group are likely to have a defensive or some other outcome? Will groups that have adopted a defensive strategy in relation to the larger society have, because of their very nature, less likelihood of responding violently than those that have not? At present no definitive answers can be given to these kinds of questions, but it is possible to provide some informed speculation.[1]

For purposes of exemplification I have confined myself to certain groups in the United States that appear to exhibit this pattern. Investigations at Taos and Picuris

AUTHOR'S NOTE: *Bernard Siegel is professor of anthropology at Stanford University. Some of his extensive fieldwork and theoretical analysis of group adaptations to stress are summarized in his study, written with Alan R. Beals, of* Divisiveness and Social Conflict: An Anthropological Approach *(Stanford University Press, 1966). Among his many articles are* "Cultural Integration and High Anxiety Levels: Notes on a Psycho-Cultural Hypothesis," Social Forces, *1955, and* "Conflict and Factionalist Dispute," *Journal of the Royal Anthropological Institute, 1960.*

Indian pueblos of eastern New Mexico first provided insights into the nature of the phenomenon; further confirmation was provided by studies of religious and ethnic enclaves like the Amish, Hutterites, and Mormons, and of the Black Muslims. The roster of societies for which the defensive paradigm in relevant includes many other historically unrelated groups: viz, Jews who lived, prior to the Second World War, in compact villages called "shtetls" in Eastern Europe; certain villages of Japan and Southeastern Asia; the Egyptian Copts; and village communites in the Alpine region of Europe.

THE STRUCTURE OF DEFENSIVENESS

Behavioral Controls and Training for Self-Restraint

Defensive groups have few and carefully controlled avenues for self-expression appropriate to the life situations usually encountered by their members. Rules of conduct tend to be very explicit, so that the individual must exercise great restraint over his own behavior, which in turn is closely supervised by an authoritative elite. The controls, therefore, are twofold, consisting of (1) the nurturance of self-discipline in the individual beginning very early (usually by the end of the second year), and (2) the allocation of authority or power at the broadest level to a small number of designated persons. The legitimation of political control is circular; it is derived from the imputed wisdom of the elite in interpreting cultural values; the values are, in turn, often elevated to sacred status, thus conferring additional authority upon the leaders.

One manifestation of control is the maintenance of a high level of anxiety, sometimes evidenced in a low incidence of heavy drinking or the use of strong disapproval and swift application of sanctions against offending individuals. As Hallowell put it, we find

> a conscious strict control or even rejection of available anxiety-reducing patterns and concomitant elaboration of in-group symbols of identification.[. . . certain anxieties may be inculcated in individuals as part of the socialization process] in order to motivate them in the performance of patterns of behavior that are socially approved.[2]

In such groups there are many occasions for intensive interaction among all members in communal ceremonials and other collective enterprises. As part of their approved repertoire for coping with others, they also sanction various kinds of malevolent accusations—witchcraft or other forms of denunciation—that wax and wane in frequency of expression.

In the past we have loosely and commonly assumed that, in the absence of other outlets, both these types of institutionalized behaviors—i.e., intensive interaction and displacement—tended to give comfort to individuals, to relieve tensions or to dispel them temporarily. Actually there is no real evidence for this assertion. Stated in this way, the assumption is very difficult to prove or disprove. Are the real and supposed dangers of individuals removed, at least in part, by the comfort of common participation in group-centered activities? Is their tension (however we may propose to measure it) relieved by displacement of aggression upon others? To the extent that studies of authoritarianism and relevant psychoanalytic theory made sense to the student of behavior, he tended to accept such statements rather uncritically. The most we can say in the present context is that these behaviors are prominent and that they coexist with other structural features of defensiveness.

In the defensive group there thus appears to be a conscious attempt to maintain comparatively intense anxiety states among members by requiring constant exercise of control over behavior potentially destructive to the group in relation to external threats. Real and perceived threats to continued existence require continual emphasis upon and renewal of social cohesion; laten conflict or cleavage demands both internal and external controls. I would propose that, in comparison with nondefensive societies, brawling, overt domestic quarreling, and excesses in aggressive behaviors that disrupt ongoing activities or call attention to dissension within the group occur infrequently and endure briefly in defensive groups before they are suppressed. Although the evidence at present is meager, I would also hypothesize that the suicides that do occur are of the kind that Durkheim spoke of as "suicide altruists," for the reasons that he maintains.[3] For the individual, the gains of adaptive behavior are measured in a high degree of security (in the form of continual support and approval from all others, and his confident knowledge of norms). The corresponding losses are the comparatively great effort he must make in self-discipline as well as the submission he must always display over much of his adult life in the face of authoritative decision-makers.

To provide examples, among pueblo Indians the early training for control of impulses, and particularly of direct forms of aggression, is almost proverbial. It is interesting to note the same emphasis among Black Muslims, in view of a popular image by nonmembers that portrays them as advocates of violence.[4] In the ideology of the movement, the black man is of vastly different metal from the white man and therefore must live in a way that is appropriate to that superiority, throwing off the vices taught his people by the malicious white man: tobacco, alcohol, gambling, gluttony, jealousy, father-absent families, several foods associated with the diet of the Southern blacks, and the like. In other words, he must cast aside the entire stereotype of the "so-called Negro" and lead a new life of strict morality and devotion to the welfare and development of his people and of the institutions of the Nation of Islam. To remain a member in good standing, he must conform essentially to a puritanical moral code.

The temples of Islam carry out active recruiting programs in the black slums of a large number of American cities, but they try to be selective by retaining only those who are likely to respond positively to the rigid retraining process. The initial step seems to be the isolation of the individual from his former identity and his identification with a new role. Isolation from white men is particularly imperative in view of their corrupting influence. Ties with members of the non-Muslim black community obviously cannot be cut in all cases, nor is it always desirable that they should be. However, one's family and friends must recognize the change, or they too are liable to be cast aside, with however much regret. Training for submission to authority is continuous, and takes place in many domains of behavior simultaneously. Resocialization takes place over a long period of time, in the form of lessons. The aim is a transformation so sweeping that it affects every part of a man's life and of his self-conception, reinforced in every conceivable way.

Cultural Integration

A central characteristics of defensive adaptation is the presence of a few key values. This lends a keen sense of cultural integrity to the group, in the sense of being complete or whole. As commonly used, the term "cultural integration" refers essentially to the degree of interrelatedness, interdependence, or linkage to be found among the elements of a culture.[5] In turn, these linkages seem to reflect the operation of values or underlying principles common to more than one activity. A tightly integrated system is characterized by a strong centralization of values; that is, the tendency for broad sectors of custom to be related to a few key values.[6] Under these circumstances a person who might otherwise favor a given innovation will often discard the idea because he knows that substitution for one custom that he no longer values will mean the loss of others which he does value.[7]

A central value of all defensive groups appears to be subordination of the individual to the welfare of the group. This is reflected in the generalization of cooperative effort in many in-group activities, the settlement of disputes by knowledgeable authorities before they become unregulated, and the emphasis upon steady goal-oriented work habits.

Symbols and Identity

However varied the content of these values, they are reflected in supporting symbols. By means of these symbols a given aggregate of individuals develops an intensive sense of group identification. They state, in effect: "I am a Taos," "I am a shtetl member," and so forth, and this identification is supported by a few badges which members are emotionally reluctant to discard. The latter commonly include language and special colloquialisms (ordinary discourse among members is carried on in one language, another being employed in conversations with nonmembers). They may also include special customs of deference, punctilious observance of particular rituals, and, when encountered in the form of natural communities, selection of marriage partners from within the group and a particular territory.[8] Acceptance of and conformity to behavior consonant with these symbols is not open to discussion; alternative means of coping with social situations are either prevented from coming to the attention of the groups, or, if individuals learn about them and propose them for adoption, they are carefully screened.

Insofar as supporting symbols assume the significance we impute to them, one would except as a corollary that identity problems that currently preoccupy so many students of personality development in our own society would be largely absent in groups with tightly integrated cultures. If such identity is originally weak, ambiguous, largely absent, or in a formative state, it will, under stress and as a group, become increasingly defensive, be invented and buttressed with available symbols from the past or present. In the process of emerging from the multimillion aggregate of American blacks, the Black Muslims very deliberately developed a social identity by means of certain symbols to which they assigned special meanings. To gain and retain membership, for example, Black Muslims are expected to assume a Mohammedan name. They are exhorted to dress in a manner that will not betray lower-class origins and to eat certain foods and to avoid others. They, of course, attend distinctive temples and learn a ritual language associated with a special version of the Koran.[9]

Members of defensive societies tend to interact with nonmembers in conventional ways. When interrogated on issues they consider sensitive—and they are usually many and pervasive—members will respond with ready-made answers which are meant to deceive. Potential innovations, as we have seen, are carefully screened by legitimate authorities. A special humor contains allusions deliberately confined to insiders. In general, social intercourse with nonmembers is of limited duration. Where enduring relations do occur (viz, between friends or godparents, between a patron or merchant and client or customer), they tend to be specific and established only with individuals who are known to be discrete and with whom there exists some implicit agreement to avoid all sensitive matters in conversation.[10]

Communication and Interaction Patterns

The net effect of such controlled intercourse and communication between members and nonmembers is to make the nonmember often want membership but to be kept at a distance, and to lead the member to reinforce emotionally the beliefs and behaviors which symbolize continuity of the group. To maintain this kind of solidarity requires continuous surveillance and some culturally available techniques that facilitate rapid communication and mobilization of public opinion. Most commonly these conditions are met by a dense or nucleated settlement pattern in which dwellings are located very close to, sometimes literally on top of, one another (as in pueblo societies and ghetto communities). Some numerically large and broadly dispersed groups that exhibit defensive structuring, like the Egyptian Copts, the Mormons, or the Black Muslims, have solved this problem by combining strong centralized authoritarian control at the top with the allocation of decision-making power in most daily affairs to highly autonomous neighborhood temples, church schools, and missions.[11] In the case of the latter, modern transport and communication techniques make possible continual links of the local groups to national leadership.

The Black Muslim group (the Nation of Islam) was founded in Detroit in the summer of 1930 by W.D. Fard Muhammad. At first, Fard simply went from house to house bringing people his message. As followers accumulated he secured a temple and instituted formal meetings. An organization was established to administer the cult both in ritual and in the recruitment of members. The group subsequently founded a parochial elementary and secondary school (the University of Islam); a minister, trained personally by the founder and assisted by junior ministers, was appointed to run the organization. In the early days all of these activities took place within a restricted district of Detroit. Headquarters were subsequently transferred to Chicago; the movement flourished and diffused to other cities where ministers, always subject to the overriding word of Elijah Muhammad, the patriarch, were appointed to the local temples.

Perhaps because the central feature of any meeting is the sermon (or more precisely, the exhortation), there is a great deal of exchange preaching done between temples, and Elijah Muhammad himself traveled all over the country to speak at gatherings. The establishment of a new tradition and the development of an orthodox commitment to it owe their success in large measure to mutually reinforcing communication networks: the acquaintance and interchange of ministers from diverse regions and the education of teachers on the school staffs at a single training center.[12]

Elites and Centralization of Authority

This pattern of shared understandings could not persist without the regular provision of strong centralized authorities for the group. Training individuals so that they will exert a considerable measure of control over their own behavior is characteristic of all defensive societies, but it does not work at all times. When cultural survival is thought to be at stake, the matter of regulation cannot be left exclusively to self-control. It is buttressed formally by a relatively small number of authoritarian powerholders. What is more, the legitimation of centralized authority stems from the urgent and apprehensive need for solutions to daily problems; the resource that confers power upon these offices is special knowledge. In most cases, therefore, the men who make decisions act in a sacred or quasi-sacred capacity. In some groups, they may inherit their offices, but in all cases they must constantly validate their right to exercise the functions associated with them.

Thus the Catholic priests of Quebec villages and Coptic priests of Egypt, respectively, control ritual performances of the church and church-related education which, in each case, is primarily a manifestation of group autonomy.[13] In the case of Hutterites or Mormons, clergy are elected from among all male members in good standing. The priesthood or its equivalent is therefore very broadly based. The highest authority, however, is vested in a few individuals, whose qualifications involve the ability to interpret the basic and traditional experiences and sacred texts of the group into living doctrine. The Hutterites santify their own history, using it as a sacred record for the interpretation of present problems and the presentation of appropriate solutions within the Hutterite tradition.[14] The Mormons similarly use the *Doctrine and Covenants*, which consists of instructions to the early church and the establishment of precedents for church administration. Throughout the period of his leadership of the movement, Joseph Smith continued to receive divine guidance in times of difficulty, and the instructions given him at those times are regarded as valid for present difficulties as well. Mormon doctrine indeed awards the president of the church the power to receive additional revelation in order to supplement the recorded guidance of the past.[15]

A significant attribute of many defensive groups is the implementing role of women. It appears that in all such communities, at least, women provide a basis for cultural maintenance but are essentially ignorant of the symbolism that expresses the particular goals of the group in a particular way. They learn that certain symbolic behaviors or places are important to defend, but they may not know connotations that such behaviors, things, or places actually have in the ideology of the group. Being in this sense nonrationally committed to cultural values, they may seek, even more stringently and less discriminately than men, to prevent strangers from having access to knowledge about them. By the same token, males also tend to screen the kind of communication available to females within the group. Therefore, however much special knowledge of the outside world the former may acquire, traditional defensive attitudes will be transmitted anew to each generation by virtue of the important role of women in early cultural transmission and socialization.

EXTERNAL PRESSURES AND GROUP STRUCTURE

Groups develop the properties we outlined above in response to external pressures or stress that, at a certain point, are felt to be a threat to continued existence. The stresses most commonly identified in the anthropological literature are encounters with alien people who interfere with the conventional modes of utilization of the environment. Alien contact may render ambiguous or useless some of the customary rules for regulating human relations and satisfying emergent wants, or they may call into question the viability of the group's universal values, upon which its very continuity depends. To more narrowly defined acculturation studies we should add a variety of other environmental transformations: urbanization, industrialization, urban-rural interaction, and the like.

Taos and Picuris Pueblos: A Controlled Comparison

Defensive adaptation, then, is a response to environmental pressures and changes, and more particularly to certain dimensions or variables of these pressures. As a prototype of this interaction between group and environment, we consider briefly the experiences of Taos pueblo and compare then with the experiences of a close neighbor, the pueblo of Picuris. The two societies are especially valuable for our purpose because they share a long history of settlement and tradition in the area out of a common past.[16]

Archeological evidence suggests that, prior to contact with agents of Western society, the ancestors of these people defended themselves against the encroachments of other Indian tribes that invaded their territories. In the past 400 years they engaged, first, in a number of hostile encounters with Spanish colonists and, later, in their relations with Anglos, had to compromise in many ways over land rights. When Coronado first visited them shortly after 1540, he estimated that they had roughly comparable populations. His estimate was around 3,000 inhabitants for each. Recent investigations at Picuris indicate this community (and Taos by implication) in fact had around 2,000 inhabitants. From his description and from more systematic investigation, we have every reason to believe that they shared a very similar social structure and culture. For reasons that are not entirely clear, both suffered dramatic population decreases at least through the middle of the 18th century, probably in part through the introduction of new diseases and in part through defections to the Spanish settlements. The census for 1890 lists, in round numbers, 400 and 300 persons for Taos and Picuris, respectively. From that time onward there was a steady increase in the former and a slight reduction in the latter, both suffering from the influenza epidemic after the First World War. Today, however, Picuris has barely 100 persons, while Taos has over 1,200. As we shall see, these figures are closely related to the corresponding differences in cultural vigor.

At this point—the turn of the century—environmental stresses on the two communities begin to diverge in what turn out to be important ways. Consider certail salient events at Taos during the periods of Mexican and Anglo political control: Boundaries were fixed (a process that has been in adjudication until very recently), thus stabilizing the ratio of people to resources among a traditionally agricultural people. A new community, part Spanish-American and increasingly Anglo in composition, was located only a mile from the Indian pueblo. Over the past 50 years it has attracted a variety of settlers and visitors, notably merchants, traders, teachers, builders, service persons, artists, and tourists. Pressure on the land was thus accompanied by the opening of new alternatives for employment—catering to the tourist trade, jobs as domestics, hotel aids and dancers, service station attendants and skilled workers.

This entire configuration of events was seen as a problem, or better perhaps as a set of problems. People continued to think of Taos citizenship as a good thing, but continuation of that entity is bound up with an agrarian adaptation, a supporting belief system about man's relation to nature, and related ceremonial activities. Increasing numbers of uncontrolled nonmembers in their midst, new jobs, and a conflicting set of rules regulating work habits may and do interfere unpredictably with pueblo expectations and demands. To render services and participate in activities of central concern to the village, one must leave work in which he is engaged elsewhere. Farming, by contrast, has traditionally been articulated with such demands. We can think of the new situation as a complication in patterns of communication. The settlement has become, as it were, encircled, and Taos leadership confronted with the problem of cultural survival. If we add (1) the presence of the United Pueblo Agency in Albuquerque and constantly changing, imperfectly understood policies toward Indians orginating in Washington; and (2) modern transport that enables dissident individuals to leave the village for urban employment, often some distance away, the return to it in an indeterminant manner, we can see how complex the environment must now appear to the great majority of the group that is committed to continuity of its cultural system.[17]

During the same period many of the stresses observed at Taos have confronted Picurenses, but in a different way. Children attend Indian schools on and off the reservation (boarding school at Sante Fe) where the curriculum is established and teaching done by aliens. Picuris is a few miles removed from the main highway that passes hard by Taos and is within walking distance only to a Spanish-American village that provides no regular job opportunities. To opt for employment off the pueblo means residing in towns and cities, the closest of which is 24 miles away (Taos). Individuals who do so much rely almost exclusively upon secondary languages, English and Spanish, and forego many of the emotional gratifications associated with the use of the native language (especially participation in pueblo-centered activities like the ceremonial calendar and houshold rituals, which make use of intensive social interaction to which Picurenses are socialized very early in life).

Elsewhere I have summarized the contrasting nature of pressures and outcomes in the two communities as follows:

Perhaps the single most important factor that distinguishes the recent history of Picuris and Taos is the different impact of stress created by environment changes. The proliferation of alternatives created in the immediate vicinity of Taos challenged the conventional power system, but in so doing strengthened it. The community as a whole began to take the shape of a nativistic movement. We might say that what happened in the process of this confrontation was the development of a keen sense of urgency in adapting to a perceive threat to cultural survival. In Picuris, by contrast, it is just this sense of urgency that is lacking. Being removed from the centers of development there is, so to speak, leisure in the contemplation of alternatives, perhaps too much leisure to confirm themselves in their beliefs. Disassociation from the pueblo, on the other hand, has seldom been a possible alternative except for those who have been incompletely socialized. The net result has been a classic example of pervasive anomie in the generation of young adult males (ages 16-38), partial integration in the next older generation (ages 40-58), and an integrated generation of elders (age 60).[18]

Dimensions of Perceived Stress

Examination of certain classes of historical events at Taos and Picuris will facilitate analysis of environment pressures as people see them. From these cases perceived stress appears to vary according to its direction, intensity, complexity, ambiguity, control, and effect on group image. Until approximately the end of the nineteenth century, members of both groups might well have perceived the alteration of their environment by the intrusion of others in very similar ways on all of these dimensions. Clearly this stress-inducing intrusion was of long duration; each group had to contend increasingly with agents of Spanish and Anglo tradition for over 350 years. It was unambiguous (the "others" are clearly different and threatening), controlling over their actions, and depreciating to themselves, as was explicit in the colonizing, missionizing, and politically defining efforts of first one of the dominant groups and then the other. If we think of intensity in terms of frequency of interaction, their experiences probably differed little in this regard as well.

After 1900, however, some of these features began to vary in magnitude. Duration, control, and effect on group image remained roughly the same. The construction of a new road and motor transport, on the other hand, left Picuris relatively isolated but generated a very pronounced increase in rate of interaction between Taosenos and nonmembers. Not only were there many new occasions for rubbing shoulders at Taos—curious or interested outsiders and artists, new enterprises, amusements, and the like—but they confronted the pueblo dweller almost continuously in everday life. Individuals and the group as a whole were faced with the problem of how to cope with these interactions. As one alternative, individuals might have been left free to make their own decisions at will: to remain traditionally occupied within the pueblo, communicating to a very limited degree with outsiders; to divide their time between both worlds; or physically to detach themselves from the group, either permanently by emigration or by leaving for indefinite periods and returning when emotionally or otherwise disposed to do so.

The strategy actually employed was to reinforce the value of group membership by selectively emphasizing traditional symbols. In the process Taosenos simplified the environmental context of their earlier life by redefining its complexity simply as threat, and they controlled the level of intensity of intercultural interaction by specifying the kinds, frequency, and content of relations that were permitted. The result was an affirmative defensive adaption that had revealed all the properties of this phenomenon described above.

At Picuris the aspects, but not the magnitudes, of environmental change were very similar to those at Taos. No such increase in stress intensity occurred; the environment to Picurenses remained very complex in terms of models and ambiguous concerning the messages they received. We observe, also, no such monolithic interpretation of such pressures. Some defined the situation as threat and emphasized a traditional solution; others, as new opportunities and new wants. An increasing majority, however, came to be confused by multiple choices of both valued goals and means of achieving them, to the point of immobilization of any effort and normlessness.

Interaction Between Group and Environment

It should be clear from this discussion that we must assume a continuing interaction between environmental pressures (as interpreted by an outside observer, or as perceived by members of some social entity) and the structure of groups in order to predict subsequent responses that the latter will make to environmental transformations.[19] Some previous tendency in the direction of centralized socio-political organization is probably necessary, in order to mobilize efforts of individuals to cope collectively with urgently felt needs for a more or less satisfying way of life in the face of forces that are perceived to be opposed to such an effort. The necessity for controlling the use of water in irrigation-based agriculture, it has been suggested, very possibly led to centralized community leadership among the eastern pueblos well before the Spanish contact period.[20] Another pattern sometimes occurs in a mass or aggregate of individuals with minimal organization structure. A social appeal to a felt need for value-oriented identity may attract a segment of such a population to a new, centralized structure. The Black Muslims are an outcome of such appeals among the Northern urban blacks of the United States.

By the same token, if the group-environment interaction process in the past had stabilized in a structure that was ill equipped to cope with new and traumatic perceived stress, we might predict an outcome other than defensive adaptation, no matter how closely the stress values approximated those described for Taos pueblo. I am not familiar personally with such a case from the annals of American history, but they are encountered in the anthropological literature.[21] I would hypothesize that a successful defensive reaction requires either a centralized prior structure or a loose one—viz, the earlier urban black ghetto community in its initial phase.

DISCUSSION AND IMPLICATIONS

Defensive Adaptation and Theories of Social Movements

The theory of defensive adaptation builds upon certain important lines of cultural theory and work on the problem of social movements. Several ethnic enclaves in the

United States had their origins in social movements: the Menonnites, Amish, and Hutterites, for example, began as sectarian movements in Europe and the Mormons in America.

Smelser makes a distinction between a norm-oriented movement and a value-oriented movement.[22] The NAACP is an example of the former. In its attempt to advance desegration in the United States, the NAACP is critical of certain practices in society but not of its fundamental democratic values. It proposes reforms as a more adequate realization of those values but does not advocate a far-reaching cultural transformation. A value-oriented movement, on the other hand, criticizes values; the Black Muslim movement is said to be value oriented and to advocate change at the core of society. "God is Black," their leaders assert, and thereby challenge the assumption that "God is White" with all that it connotes. In a very large sense, however, setting forth this dogma is simply a dramatic way of establishing a symbolic basis for identity and consensual commitment among individuals drawn from a distinctive but relatively unorganized social aggregate. Actually, in its efforts to socialize new members, the Black Muslims clearly stress central values of middle-class whites. The challenge to values of the larger society lies in the further assertion that the means by which this can be achieved is by complete segregation and new nationhood rather than by desegregation and increased meaningful interaction. The contrast with the NAACP in this respect is in means and not in goals. There is nevertheless a real difference in strategy; one is defensive, the other is not.[23]

Many defensive societies bear a close resemblance to a certain stage in the development of what Wallace, in a stimulating paper, has termed "revitalization movements," which are efforts to create a more satisfying culture from cumulative dissatisfactions.[24] Such movements emerge well along in the defensive process, after adherents have overcome hostility from the dominant community and a new cultural state, if suitably stress reducing, has become routinized and expressed through a new organization.

By far the most impressive scholarly contribution to the study of social movements is Aberle's analysis of the Peyote religion among the Navaho.[25] In this work Aberle has succeeded specifically in making an exhaustive and convincing evaluation of all the factors that differentiate those who are attracted and committed in varying degrees to the Peyote cult from those who are opposed to it. After examining all internal variables of Navaho society—viz, age, sex, education, livelihood, health, education, church membership, kin relations, participation in the tribal council, and degree of acculturation—he was forced to conclude that the only factor that was significantly associated with cult membership was the livestock reduction program initiated in 1933 by the national government, in an effort to control progressive erosion. This process he invites us to think of in terms of relative deprivation. Individuals who became members of the cult were not necessarily poorer than those who did not, but relative to others they lost a significantly greater amount of wealth.[26]

In a subsequent chapter[27] the author attempts to place the Peyote cult in the wider context of a theory of social movements that is full of useful insights. He arrives at some four types of such movements:

(1) Transformative movements that aim at total social-cultural change (comparable to Smelser's value-oriented movements and including millenarian movements and revolutions).

(2) Reformative movements that aim at a partial social-cultural change (comparable to Smelser's norm-oriented movements and including fluoridation movements, child-labor-law movements, and peasant rebellions).

(3) Redemptive movements that aim at a total change in individuals (the Peyote cult falls in this class, as would probably Jewish ghetto and shtetl communities, early Christianity, Mormonism, and the Black Muslims).

(4) Alternative movements that aim at a partial change in individuals (birth control movements).

He then proceeds to identify constant and variable features of each and to indicate the significance of relative deprivation, references groups, and environmental contexts in relation to choice of one or another type of movement. Aberle's observations are broad ranging and repay careful reading, although he makes no effort to construct an exhaustive theory of the phenomenon. By concentrating on process, this analysis understandably fails to indicate common structural characteristics of defensive adaptation that cut across several types of movements. Among the possible alternative reactions to status deprivation, however, the author does include a "defensive insistence on the rightness of its behavior in the face of known, or imagined, opposition." And, in discussing the context of social movements, he hypothesizes that "transformative goals are most likely when a deprived group is segregated spatially or socially and when its involvement with the larger social order is either slight or decreasing or both" [as when confronted with a superior technology or physical enclosure].[28] He would, I suspect, put Taos pueblo in this category. One might as well or better argue, on the other hand, that Taos leadership has mobilized its efforts to prevent transformation or even redemption through changed behavior, by a process of involution or turning in upon itself.

In brief, theories of social movements share, as elements in their analysis, a number of behavioral and environmental characteristics with a paradigm of defensive adaptation. Not all instances of the latter, however, are subsets of the former. In particular, defensive adaptations never take the form of revolution by violent means.

Defensive Adaptation and Culture

Defensive coping in the first place is a response to stress and perceived threat to continuities of, or barriers to, a meaningful way of life. It is a strategy that occurs when protagonists have limited resources for direct and possibly violent confrontation with the source(s) of frustration. Nevertheless, there are many instances of aggressive collective confrontation in the face of limited resources. Activist and so-called militant groups in America today are cases in point. This suggests that it is necessary to take into account something more than either of these factors in order to predict a defensive outcome.

An understanding of defensive adaptation ultimately is derived from the single most fundamental attribute of culture. This can be stated simply: culture is (symbolic) communication. People who respond positively but defensively to perceived threat from whatever exogenous source—subjugation, exploitation, urbanization, industrialization, urban-rural interaction, and the like—must either have a tradition or, out of a felt need, succeed in creating one. In either case, sharing at least core values over the long haul requires the means for sustaining regular and frequent communication. Minority ethnic enclaves, whether composed of immigrant groups or small-scale societies that came to be surrounded by dominant others in the course of settlement in American history, meet this requirement. In addition to groups specifically mentioned in this essay, we should include the Spanish-Americans in the Southwest and Mexican Americans in the West, Chinese, Italians, Irish, and so forth.

Not all of these groups perceived a danger to their cultural integrity, hence made a defensive adaptation. An interesting example of cognitive change in an altered social context is described in a sociology dissertation. The data for this study involved aspects of adjustment patterns of a small minority of Catholics in relation to a preponderantly Mormon majority (about 93 percent of the total) in a small Idaho city (total population about 8,000). The Catholic enclave, instead of losing elements of value identification in their relations with the Mormons, which they would according to a theory of social marginality, actually exhibited considerably more cohesion and support of communal values than did Mormons. In this situation the church authorities exercised greater control over the individual's behavior than was true in comparable urban parishes from which immigrants came. For example, the Irish Catholic element, comprising about 30 percent of the total within this group, revealed almost none of the traditional pattern of drinking, which in this community came to be severely frowned upon. Family-centered internalized control in other areas of overt behavior was similarly reinforced by the same external authorities. These conditions obtained despite amiable relations between Catholics and Mormons generally. Leaders of the Catholic enclave perceived danger of group extinction as a distinctive entity. They were also able to communicate the reality of this threat to members and to enforce latent control over individual behavior to emphasize collective goals.[29]

The Jews, with such a long historical tradition, are a special case. It would be possible and useful to investigate response patterns at various peaks periods of stress in the trajectory of their experiences from classical to modern times. More directly relevant, perhaps, it would also be instructive to study comparatively the immigrant population of eastern European shtetl Jews in relation to second- and third-generation American-born Jews. Both orthodox Jewish and Mormon traditions stress the value of formal learning. In so doing they embrace a paradox within the context of the larger society; namely, the alienation of the young who are exposed to important conflicts between school and home and church by virtue of the content of what is learned and to what purpose. The paradox is only partly resolved by the establishment of parochial schools. It would be interesting to study Jewish university leadership roles in the Students for a Democratic Society, and to compare this phenomenon with their goal-oriented activism of a generation ago (in Trotskyite and Stalinist movements) in relation to cultural commitment.

Shared value commitment need not restrict itself to societies in the conventional sense of the word. To pull together and to hold members in some kind of long-range organization with a sense of shared urgency, however, require rapid communication that approximates face-to-face interaction. These are precisely the conditions that, in contemporary America, make possible the creation of viable defense groups, like the Black Muslims, from broadly distributed sectors of society.

In a personal communication, Dr. William S. Madsen, then engaged in a field study of Alcoholics Anonymous in the San Francisco Bay area, informed me that this group—and probably all Anonymous groups, like Heroins Anonymous and Gamblers Anonymous—pinpoints precisely the structural elements we have identified with defensive adaptations (including the stress values, derived in this instance from the preception of hostile norms of nonalcholics of the established society). Alcoholics Anonymous, of course, is not an enclave and does not recruit members from married group members. However, it does have rather explicit criteria for "citizenship" in the sense of minimal conformance with a set of standards of behavior. Nonconformists are rigidly excluded, leaving a residual group strongly committed to these standards and to the authoritative controls of a small elite.

People who participate in defensive organizations are, in a sociological sense, minorities in that they feel deprived in relation to dominant institutions. They exist at the sufferance of others who have the means, should they wish to employ them, to suppress completely their efforts at independent cultural identity. Dependency behavior and subordination of decision-making to powerful centralized leadership develops out of a necessity to cope rapidly with day-to-day situations with which the group may be confronted. So, too, training for impulse control has strategic value in these groups because they possess limited resources and in the long run cannot hope to succeed by violent means.[30] They might, of course, attempt to do so by coopting large numbers of the dominant society to their cause, but in this way they run the risk of losing or weakening their identity. The early Christians, themselves a defensive society, succeeded admirably in missionary efforts, but ultimately gave rise to a rash of schisms and sectarian movements. I would invite more knowledgeable students about the subject than I to speculate in this vein about the defensive nature of the trade-union movement at the time of its early florescence under Samuel Gompers, and perhaps even in the early phase of the CIO. Most of the violence associated with some strike activities in the 1930s was, after all, initiated by suppressive elements of the dominant society. The coopting of powerful members of the latter through the political process led to successful efforts at achieving the cultural goals of the labor movement—and in the end to its transformation and integration with the establishment. It is instructive to observe the conservative tendency of labor unionism today and the loss of the ideological persuasion that attended its earlier phases.

A final note. By inference, people who are organized defensively are less likely than members of weakly organized groups or persons who participate in temporary collectivities (viz, ad hoc confrontations) to engage in violence. This is so because they have come to share a sense of cultural purpose that, in the social context in which they find themselves, can only be maintained by discipline and subordination of the individual to the larger entity. Crowds and assemblages are hard to discipline, given the nature of the communication process and unfiltered selection of participants. When defensive adaptation does occur, it always displays the same structure. Perhaps it is replicated in its essential features because for any group, category, or aggregate of people, it is the most economical and efficient means of coping with the problem of perceived severe stress applied over a long period of time. Some of the remarks in this concluding section are more firmly wedded to the central analysis than others. I have engaged in a certain amount of speculation about selected problems of relevance to the nature of violence in America that clearly demand detailed, expert investigation. All of the comments, however, are shaped by a general paradigmatic theory of defensive adaptation.

NOTES

1. Detailed historical analysis of the emergence of defensive societies—a history of the Mormons, of the Jews, at least from the nineteenth-century ghetto period through second-generation American Jewry, of Taos and other Indian pueblos, and of the Black Muslims— would provide some of the best evidence for the solution of these kinds of problems. Systematic comparison of culturally related groups, which vary only with respect to specific dimensions of environmental changes, is another method of predicting alternative strategies of adaptation. For want of space both of these methods can be applied only in a limited way in this essay.

2. A.I. Hallowell, "The Social Psychology of Acculturation," in Ralph Linton, ed., *The Science of Man in the World Crisis* (New York: Columbia University Press, 1945). See also Barnard J. Siegel, "High Anxiety Levels and Cultural Integration: Notes on a Psychocultural Hypothesis," *Social Forces* (Oct. 1955). Concerning drinking behavior in these contexts, see Charles R. Synder, *Alcohol and the Jews: A cultural study of drinking sobriety* (Glencoe, Ill.: Free Press, 1958); Lincoln, 1961 (see n. 4); Peter B. Field, "A new cross-cultural study of drunkenness," in D.J. Pittman and C.R. Synder, eds., *Society, Culture and Drinking Patterns* (New York: Wiley, 1962); and Edwin M. Lemert, "Alcohol, Values, and Social Control," ibid.

3. Emile Durkheim, *Le Suicide* (Paris: Ancienne Librairie Germer Bailliere, 1897), Chs. II and III. See also Jack P. Gibbs and W.T. Martin, "A Theory of Status Integration and its Relationship to Suicide," *American Sociological Review*, 23 (1958): 140-47; Jerrold E. Levy, "Navaho Suicide," *Human Organization*, 24 (1965): 301-18; and E.G. Palola, T.L. Dorpat, and W.R. Larson, "Alcoholism and Suicidal Behavior," in Pittman and Synder, op. cit.

4. Observation about the Black Muslims are derived from two sources: C. Eric Lincoln, *The Black Muslims in America* (Boston: Beacon Press, 1961); and E.U. Essien-Udom, *Black Nationalism* (New York: Dell, 1962).

5. Or, as Ward Goodenough has expressed it, the "limiting effect [of each custom] on the forms that other customs can conveniently take." *Cooperation in Change* (New York: Russell Sage Foundation, 1963): 68. Hence, where there is a high degree of integration in this sense we would expect a continual scrutiny of inconsistencies and ambiguities among beliefs.

6. It is perhaps not accidental that the holistic approach to the concept of culture, an emphasis upon the functional interdependence of custom and belief, came early to dominate the thinking of anthropologists, as a consequence until recently of their almost exclusive concern with the study of small-scale, relatively isolated and discrete primitive societies. The communication network of defensive societies tends to approximate that of primitive isolated groups, and is indeed intended to foster isolation in the complex environments of the modern world.

7. Not all so-called tribal and peasant societies exhibit this reluctance to accept innovations and proliferate alternatives, a view once commonly assumed by Western advocates of technological innovation who encountered so many negative experiences. Quite

the contrary, as many postwar studies vividly reveal. This characterization, an artifact of oversimplifed classification of human groups by many anthropologists, often masked their variability in this respect. The error was compounded by failing to consider as part of social theory the continuous interaction of group and environment. See, for example, Raymond Firth, *Elements of Social Organization* (London: Watts, 1951): 109.

8. The high degree of endogamy among orthodox Pueblo Indians, Jews, and Mormons is well documented. Among Black Muslins marriage with a white is emphatically prohibited. Less well known is the fact that, in comparison with blacks as a whole, marriage is strongly preferential within the group. When a member does marry a non-Muslim, great pressure is put on non-Muslin spouses to join the nation.

9. See Essien-Udom, op. cit., 199.

10. To the investigator this wall of seclusion is both frustrating and challenging. The gates seldom open wide, and then for short intervals, always attended by vigilant gatekeepers—to use Kurt Lewin's graphic simile. This is why some of the best ethnographies are the products of members or former members who have become behavioral scientists and retain an entree into the group.

11. See Edward Wakin, *A Lonely Minority: The Modern Story of Egypt's Copts* (New York: Morrow, 1963): 141 and 147 ff.; also Lincoln, op. cit. 15 ff and 199. For many years the Copts had a strong central political organization. Its influence over the past few years had progressively weakened as they identified their own welfare in Egyptian colonial days with dominant European Christians. With the virtual elimination of other non-Moslem minority groups during the Nasser regime (Jews and non-Coptic Christian groups), they once more lived in a world in which they perceived the threat of being absorbed into the general population and of economic and social deprivation. It is interesting to note, as they recall with increasing alarm the belligerence of the Moslem Brotherhood and Egyptian nationalism, unmistakable evidence of increased Coptic nationalism.

12. Other dispersed defensive societies, like Mormons and shtetl Jews, similarly evolved mechanisms for frequent communication of active members both with and between communities.

13. Wakin, ibid.; Walter A. Riddle, "The Rise of Ecclesiastical Control in Quebec," doctoral dissertation, Faculty of Political Science, Columbia University, 1916, 94 ff; Everett Cherrington Hughes, *French Canada in Transition* (Chicago: University of Chicago Press, 1962): 9.

14. Lee Emerson Deets, "The Hutterites: A Study in Social Cohesion," doctoral dissertation, Faculty of Political Science, Columbia University, 1939: 17. For more recent studies, see: John W. Bennett, *Hutterian Brethren: The Agricultural Economy and Social Organization of a Communal People* (Stanford: Stanford University Press, 1967); John A. Hostetler and G.E. Huntington, *The Hutterites in North America* (New York: Holt, Rinehart, and Winston, 1967); and Victor Peters, *All Things Common: The Hutterian Way of Life* (Minneapolis: University of Minnesota Press, 1965).

15. Thomas F. O'Dea, *The Mormons* (Chicago: University of Chicago Press, 1957): 49, 130, and 143. See also Gaylon L. Caldwell, "Mormon Conceptions of Individual Rights and Political Organization," doctoral dissertation, Department of Political Science, Stanford University, 1952: 234. Both the Hutterites and Mormons initiate virtually all adolescent males into the church's esoteric matters and responsibilities. From late adolescence on, they constitute a reservoir of potential members of the priesthood.

16. See, e.g., Fred Eggan, *Social Organization of the Western Pueblos* (Chicago: University of Chicago Press, 1950): 291-324.

17. For a more detailed analysis of stress and social process in Taos pueblo, see Alan R. Beals and Bernard J. Siegel, *Divisiveness and Social Conflict: An Anthropological Approach* (Stanford: Stanford University Press, 1965): Chs. 3 and 4.

18. Bernard J. Siegel, "Social Disorganization in Picuris Pueblo," *International Journal of Comparative Sociology*, 6 (1965): 205.

19. This point of view, and indeed most anthropological conceptions of society and culture, however inductively arrived at, is consistent with modern systems theory. In the interest of clarity, I have tried to avoid the introduction of unnecessary jargon. For an introduction to a systems outlook, the reader is referred to Walter Buckley, ed., *Modern Systems Reserach for the Behavioral Scientist* (Chicago: Aldine, 1968).

20. See Esther S. Goldfrank, "Irrigation Agriculture and Navaho Community Leadership: Case Material on Environment and Culture," *American Anthropologist*, 47, 2(1945): 262-277. Although she deals principally with the Navaho, Dr. Goldfrank considers also data relating to the pueblos.

21. See, for example, the excellent analysis of such a case among Yiryiront, a society of Australian Aboriginese, as recounted by Lauriston Sharp, "Steel Axes for Stone Age Australians," in E.H. Spicer, ed., *Human Problems in Technological Change* (New York: Russell Sage, 1952): 69-90. The evidence that Sharp provides suggests, among other things, that sporadic stress encounters, however traumatic, will not lead to social change either in the direction of defense structuring, other than disorganization, or in any other direction away from the status quo ante.

22. Neil J. Smelser, *Theory of Collective Behavior* (New York: Free Press, 1963).

23. It is interesting in this regard to note the general detachment of American Indians from active involvement in and support of the civil rights movement. What the blacks are struggling for, they feel they already have and are not about to jeopardize their cultural vitality by participation in a larger incorporative organization.

24. A.F.C. Wallace, "Revitalization Movement," *American Anthropologist*, 58, 2 (1956): 264-281.

25. David F. Aberle, *The Peyote Religion Among the Navaho* (New York: Wenner-Gren Foundation for Anthropological Research, 1966).

26. This is a gross simplification of a much more sophisticated argument.

27. Aberle, op. cit., Ch. 19.

28. Ibid., 327, 330.

29. See Jack Homer Curtis, "Group Marginality and Adherence to Religious Doctrine in an American Community," doctoral dissertation, Department of Sociology, Stanford University, 1954.

30. If we were to inquire further, we would probably see that dispersed defensive associations tend to attract and to hold within the central core persons characterized by strong dependency needs, however varied their social and cultural backgrounds (substantial number of dissidents are sloughed off or removed in one way or another), and then to weld them into a novel organization.

Part 6
Violence in America
Some Conclusions

The two chapters which follow offer the editors' conclusion about the sources of violence in American society, past and present, some of its consequences, and its implications for our future as a democratic society.

Chapter 19
The Paradox of
American Violence

HUGH DAVIS GRAHAM

The historical coexistence of violence and institutional stability—this is the paradox of American violence, the curious puzzle that this chapter addresses. What was puzzling was not the stability, the historic continuity of America's vital public institutions. Indeed, this was the staple of our civics texts, the hallmark of our uniqueness. What was puzzling was the even longer tradition of collective domestic violence, not only that of the tumultous 1960s, but also its newly rediscovered antecedents, both of which surprised us. What follows is, first, an assessment of the "consensus" view of American society that was widely shared by American scholars on the eve of the 1960s, and that therefore conditioned our surprise. Then we turn to a brief empirical and comparative demonstration of the paradoxical dimensions of the coexistence of violence and stability in America. The third section probes the origins of our nonmilitary domestic violence, largely in terms of those broad historical experiences—e.g., immigration, the frontier, Lockean-Jeffersonian liberalism, and economic abundance—that formed our national character (and that consensus scholars had celebrated as the origin of our uniqueness), and the fourth section seeks in the same experiences an explanation as to why the violence they generated was defected from our vital institutions. The final section surveys the theoretical disagreements and empirical research that have been produced in the decade since the original publication of *Violence in America* in 1969, and suggests some conclusions in relation to the paradox of violence and stability, conflict and consensus with which we began.

HISTORICAL ROOTS OF THE AMERICAN CONSENSUS

The eruption of violence in the 1960s appeared paradoxical to a generation of Americans who witnessed the emergence from depression to unparalleled affluence of a nation they regarded as the world's moral leader in defense of freedom. Only a

AUTHOR'S NOTE: *Hugh Davis Graham is professor of history at the University of Maryland Baltimore County. His books include (with Numan V. Bartley)* Southern Politics and the Second Reconstruction *(Johns Hopkins University Press, 1975), which won the Chastain Award of the Southern Political Science Association as the best book on Southern politics in 1975, and* Violence *(Johns Hopkins University Press, 1971).*

generation ago America's historians and behavioral scientists were celebrating the emergence of a unique society, one sustained by a burgeoning prosperity and solidly grounded in a broad consensus. The "consensus" school of American scholars, and particularly of its historians,[2] was reacting against an older "progressive" view that had pictured America as a crucible of conflict—colonials against the British, Jeffersonians against Federalists, Jacksonians against the banks, North against South, East against West, capital against labor, Republican against Democrat. While regarded as morally as well as materially superior to Europe, America in this older discordant view nonetheless functioned according to a common Western dynamic of class and ideological warfare.

Not so, said the consensus scholars of the 1950s, who focused their reinterpretation on the unifying agent of culture rather than the divisive agent of class. Rather, America had evolved as a truly unique society in which class, party and sectional divisions only served superficially to blind us to a far greater and distinctive cultural commonality. We were told—and the implications were reassuring—that our uniqueness was derived from a progression of fundamental historical experiences which, mutually reinforcing one another, had joined to propel us toward a mainfestly benevolent destiny.

We were, first, a nation of immigrants, culturally enriched by the variety of mankind. From America's melting pot would emerge a new and superior synthesis of mankind—what Hector St. John de Crèvecoeur called "the American, this new man." It is hard, from the more cynical perspective of the latter quarter of the twentieth century, to recapture the grandeur of this noble dream—as did Emma Lazarus, writing a century earlier in "The New Colossus":

> Give me your tired, your poor,
> Your huddled masses yearning to breathe free,
> The wretched refuse of your teeming shore,
> Send these, the homeless, tempest-tossed, to me:
> I lift my lamp beside the golden door.

In the introduction to this Pulitzer Prize-winning book on American immigrants, *The Uprooted*, Oscar Handlin wrote: "Once I thought to write a history of the immigrants in America. Then I discovered that the immigrants *were* American history."

What did these millions of immigrants encounter upon their arrival in the New World? They found a vast and rich continent, thinly populated by native "Indians," who were themselves Asian immigrants from millenia past. In the extraordinary three-century process of exploring and settling this fertile wilderness, the American immigrants and their progeny were themselves transformed into the unique American democrat. The frontier, in the view of its most celebrated historian, Frederick Jackson Turner, lured the discontended and the dispossessed, the restive and the ambitious. This second formative influence encouraged ingenuity, demanded self-reliance, broke down class distinctions, nurtured opposition to governmental coercion, reinforced the sanctity of private property and contract, and fostered political individualism. Though many were illiterate, America's immigrants insisted upon universal education as a prerequisite for an informed and productive citizenry.

Universal education profoundly shaped the American character, thus contributing to America's uniqueness, power, and creative enterprise.

These distinctive traits, the American democratic ethos, were probably more reflected in than molded by a third historical source of our unique commonality: the American Revolution. We were told by the consensus historians that our revolution was essentially a *conservative* revolution, in that it achieved independence, through a surgical separation from Britain, for a "nation" that had already evolved its liberal ethos and lacked only the acute self-awareness that anticolonial revolution inevitably brings.

Hence the new federal Constitution and government forged by the founding fathers rested squarely upon a common ideology of Lockean-Jeffersonian liberalism, our fourth historic wellspring of American uniqueness. This liberal creed was shared by virtually all Americans, whether self-consciously or not—whether Federalist, Whig, Democrat, or Republican—for a revealing *negative* reason: America lacked a feudal past. In the Old World, encumbered as it was by an ancient feudal tradition, the fires of social revolution raged in societies deeply cleft by divisions of class and ideology. Hence, in Europe, the ideological spectrum would remain broad, and legions on the far left and the far right would make socialism and communism and fascism possible. But in pragmatic and nonfeudal America, ideological loyalties remained tightly clustered around the liberal center and extremist politics could find no sizeable constituency.

This celebration of the American liberal consensus must be qualified historically by acknowledging the prominent exception of the "reactionary enlightenment" of the Southern slavocracy. But every schoolchild knows that this near-fatal flaw was purged by the Civil War, and that this cancerous contradiction between the Declaration of Independence and the Constitution was at last resolved in favor of the former by the addition to the latter of the Thirteenth, Fourteenth, and Fifteenth Amendments. During Reconstruction the South also was committed to provide free public education to all citizens, thereby belatedly embracing the crucial American doctrine that democracy depends upon a literate and informed as well as free electorate.

Hence, when the next major historical transformation swept America, the urban-industrial revolution, America accomplished it with turbulence but without Marx. Whereas labor in Europe, given the Old World's feudal legacy of acute class consciousness, had automatically gone socialist, American workers virtually ignored socialism and produced instead the solidly capitalist American Federation of Labor and the Council of Industrial Organizations. Given "Americanism," who needed socialism—or any other "ism?" American workers did not hate Andrew Carnegie; they wanted to *become* an Andrew Carnegie. And, uniquely in rags-to-riches America, that seemed possible, for America was clearly destined to become the richest nation in the world.

Affluence, then, was perhaps the climactic historical source of American uniqueness. According to the foremost historian of the American national character, David M. Potter, Americans have been most characteristically a "people of plenty." American abundance was perhaps the keystone of the unique American arch. It made viable the pressure-relieving, rags-to-riches dream of upward mobility. It made the two-party system stable and workable by guaranteeing that transitions in power—between two parties that did not differ ideologically very much anyway—would also make relatively small difference in the distribution of property. (Abundance thereby afforded America the luxury of apathetic voters.) Indeed, abundance probably made democracy itself possible, by cushioning the abrasions inherent in an aggressive society bent on maximizing both the exercise of rights and the accumulation of property.The system was admittedly imperfect, for liberal, pluralistic societies inherently tolerate a measure of inequity as the price extracted by equality of opportunity. But the established system had produced in the aggregate a democratic nation unmatched in longevity of Constitution and currency, two-party stability, exercise of civil liberties, and standard of living.

It was a just and proud legacy, one which seemed to make sense in the relatively tranquil 1950s. America could still vividly remember then that even when the Great Depression had devastated the Western world and so much of Europe had turned in desperation to extreme ideologies of the left and right, America had simply once again switched leaders and parties. Turning her back, as ever, on red flags and brown shirts, she had shored up her rickety capitalism by reforming it through the New Deal. Changes were wrought which legitimized the power of government to shape economic forces in the interests of the general welfare, reduced the power of the capitalist elite, and broadened the popular base of participation in the economic system. Concurrently, America muddled through until the Second World War brought both recovery and—characteristically for America—victory. Indeed, the consensus view of the American past seemed ideally constructed to ratify the present: locked in a Cold War with totalitarian communism, the United States represented not only the powerful and self-acknowledged leader of the Free World, but also a politically stable and democratic model society that the rest of the world might seek to emulate.

THE DIMENSIONS OF PARADOX

But with the 1960s came shock and frustration. It was a decade against itself: the students of affluence were marching in the streets; the nation that had never lost a war to any power was mired in a seemingly endless, unpopular, and unwinnable land war in Asia; the national consciousness was shocked by savage assassinations; and black Americans were responding to ostensible victories in civil rights and to their collectively (and relatively) unprecedented prosperity with a paradoxical venting of outrage. It seemed as if America, so long especially blessed by the fates, had suddenly been cheated. Emerging victorious from the world war against fascism, she faced not a century of Pax Americana (as her British counterparts had faced a century of Pax Britannica after defeating Napoleon) but instead, frustrating cold and hot war abroad and turmoil at home. It was against this background of national and international strife, and especially in response to the assassinations of Martin Luther King and Robert Kennedy and the associated urban rioting in the spring of 1968, that President Johnson appointed the National Commission on the Causes and Prevention of Violence. The following year the report of the commission's Comparative and

Historical Task Force, of which I was codirector with Ted Robert Gurr, was published as *Violence in America: Comparative and Historical Perspectives.*
The research design for *Violence in America* was based upon the assumption that most could be learned by juxtaposing historical analysis and cross-national comparison. Hence our report not only delved into the various historical categories of American violence—i.e., frontier and vigilante, labor, racial and ethnic, violent crime, antiwar protest; it also contained cross-national comparisons that, while lacking in historical depth, were particularly revealing of the paradoxical relationship between the high incidence of American violence in comparison with other nations and, at the same time, the relative stability of institutions that has mitigated the severity of our violence.
One cross-national study of data on political violence in the previous 20 years concluded that, when greatest weight was given to the frequency of violent events, the United States ranked fourteenth among 84 nations. Yet when the major criterion was the severity of all manifestations of political instability, violent or not, the United States stood below the midpoint, forty-sixth among the 84. A more detailed comparison of the characteristics of civil strife in 114 nations and colonies in the 1960s concluded that in total magnitude of strife the United States ranked first among 17 Western democracies and twenty-fourth in the overall sample.[3] Yet, again reflecting the relative stability of the American social structure, most demonstrators and rioters in the United States were protesting rather than rebelling or engaging in organized violence. As a consequence, even though about 220 Americans died in violent civil strife in the five years before mid-1968, the rate of 1.1 deaths per million population was exceedingly low compared with the average for all nations and colonies of 238 deaths per million.
Richard Hofstadter, in his introductory essay to the excellent documentary collection *American Violence*, aptly posed the paradox as follows:

> Most of the countries we regard as acutely violent we also regard as suffering from chronic upheaval and political instability. But not in the United States, which has long shown a political stability that compares favorably with, say, that of England or the bland polities of Scandinavia, and yet has a level of civil violence that rather resembles some Latin American republics or the volatile new states of Asia and Africa.[4]

Our original report documented this paradoxical relationship and catalogued a tumultous history that most Americans' selective recollection had previously obscured. But it failed adequately to explain why our high levels of collective violence have largely been deflected from our vital institutions, thereby permitting the exceptional degree of continuity in the American civic culture that most of Europe and the rest of the world have historically enjoyed to a considerably lesser extent.

THE GENERATION OF AMERICAN VIOLENCE

Much more is known about why violence occurs than why it fades. Theoretical explanations of the origins of collective violence tend to be generalized rather than culture-specific, and modern social scientific inquiry has tended to reject earlier explanations that were based primarily on assessments of national character—and for two good reasons. First, such explanations are often stereotypical and prejudicial (e.g., Nazism triumphed in Germany because the German personality is authoritarian; Mussolini's armies fought poorly because the Italians are happy-go-lucky). Second, such explanations seem inherently tautological (e.g., certain behavior is typically American because it is characteristic of Americans to behave that way). But different national experiences indubitably produce differing national cultures that condition our perceptions, and if we are careful not to press our generalizations too far, much can be explained by reference to our unique and culturally shared historical experiences—otherwise historical ignorance, like amnesia, cripples our self-understanding.

Consider the influence on the generation of American violence of four broad historic circumstances: (1) the federal, capitalistic structure; (2) racial and ethnic heterogeneity; (3) affluence; and (4) the American creed as reflective of our national character. In a society as thoroughly capitalistic as ours has been, private hands have been endowed with great power to bestow rewards or mete out punishment; in the absence of a powerful state equipped with physical controls sufficient to punish aggression quickly and effectively, private sources of economic power became lightning rods to attract protest. And what generated the lightning? In large part, class, ethnic, and racial competition for the promised abundance. As a pluralistic society, probably the most pluralistic major society in the world, America has been especially vulnerable to the frustration of disappointed expectations, because historically we have employed the pluralistic political process of generating demands through pressure groups as a means of leverage to bring about change and progress. But the very success of this process has generated new demands on the part of newly emergent groups, and renewed resistance on the part of groups defending earlier achievements.

Given these self-reinforcing engines of aggression, and given ready access to such instruments of aggression as firearms, American society has been poorly equipped historically to cope with the violence it has generated. At the root of our national character has been an obdurate commitment to the notion of equality—more specifically, as de Tocqueville perceived it, to equality of opportunity. David M. Potter has seen as "the most pronounced of all the concrete expressions of American beliefs in equality" the rejection of authority, a pervasive taboo that has led to an extraordinarily strong emphasis on permissiveness.[5] This taboo on authority has, in turn, been shaped and reinforced by a frontier individualism and a sympathy for the underdog that has endowed with the mystique of Robin Hood such spectacular agents of violence as the James brothers, Billy the Kid, Pretty Boy Floyd, John Dillinger, and Bonnie and Clyde. Add to this the Higher Law doctrine that was embodied in the Revolution, the abolitionist crusade, the trials at Nuremberg, and the civil disobedience associated with the modern civil rights and antiwar movements, and it is not difficult to fathom why America, despite official rhetoric to the contrary, has never been a very law-abiding nation.

Within the last half century there have been four large-scale situations wherein major public sympathy in America was with the lawbreakers: (1) with Germans who rejected Nazi law, and particularly with those who attempted to assassinate Hitler; (2) with Americans who refused to obey racial segregation laws in the South; (3) with protesters who violated law in their demonstrations against the Vietnam War; and (4) with whites who refused to obey decrees to integrate their schools, especially through such devices as cross-neighborhood busing. There has even been some sympathy for looters who are trapped in poverty, and for lawbreaking students who regard school authorities as contemptuous of their consent. The sword of the Higher Law is, of course, two-edged: one strikes for equality; the other for liberty—a basic contradiction that has been generally unappreciated by generations of Americans who have thoughtlessly equated liberty and equality, and who have consequently misread the powerful ambiguities in American life and have remained oblivious to the violence in our past and puzzled by the violence in our midst.

In the conclusion to our original report, we noted the abiding confict that is inherent in a dual commitment to liberty and equality, although we did not elaborate upon it. But it may be that American violence is rooted in American values. Alexis de Tocqueville observed long ago in *Democracy in America* (1835) that the materialistic Americans exploited their political liberty in an insatiable quest for equality of opportunity. Their democratic individualism led them to reject the sanctions of tradition, family, church, and state; and this unique freedom from external, institutional restraints required a self-restraint that imposed an enormous psychic burden upon the individual, in the unending quest for material equality. Persistently faced with a social reality that denied such equality, the frustrated American democrat became peculiarly vulnerable to seizures of violent aggression. Given a remarkably fluid society, a boom-and-bust economy, minimal state sanctions, and an unparalleled racial and ethnic heterogeneity, private targets for violent aggression, whether displaced or direct, have been plentiful and inviting.

THE DEFLECTION OF AMERICAN VIOLENCE

Consider, on the other hand, how these same four national experiences have historically contributed not only to the generation of American violence but also to deflecting its lethal thrust away from our vital public institutions. One plausible, albeit only partial reason why violence has not been directed against public institutions in the United States to the degree that it has in so many other nations may be (at least until the recent period) that, given America's federal, capitalistic structure, public institutions historically have been less important than private institutions or than public institutions in other societies. Capitalism pitted labor against industry, farmers against the railroad or an impersonal market system. Consider our long and turbulent history of frontier and agrarian discontent: the Paxton boys; the New Jersey land rioters; the New York antirent movement; the North Carolina Regulators; the New Mexico White Caps; the Shays, Whiskey, and Fries rebellions; the Western Claims Clubs; the Kentucky tobacco cooperatives; the Grangers, Greenbackers, Alliancemen, Populists; the Green Corn Rebellion; Oklahoma socialists; the Farmers' Holiday Association—the list stretches from Nathaniel Bacon in 1676 (excluding the American Indians) to Cesar Chavez in 1976. Yet most frontier and agrarian violence was not directed against central government, and when it infrequently was, it was quickly and usually easily put down. Our labor history is of more recent vintage, but also more bloody. It is true that the state frequently lent its militia and National Guard and occasionally federal troops to the support of the industrialists, and that police and sheriffs as agents of the state were also rarely neutral. But the carnage associated with the Molly Maguires, Homestead, Coeur d'Alene, the Black Hole of Ludlow, and Gastonia had little to do with the national government. It was a local industrialist and magistrate, Judge Gary, not President Cleveland, whom the embattled and enraged steelworkers alleged had never seen a blast furnace until the day he died.

There are, of course, notable exceptions. To the Indians, the state was devastatingly important, much as it was to slaves and, to a much lesser extent, the Mormons. But the Indian wars were remote from public institutions, slave rebellions were few and abortive, and the Mormons perforce modified one of *their* peculiar institutions to fit the preconditions of the monogamous state. The crowning exceptions were, of course, the Revolution and the Civil War. But their circumstances were so unusual that, crucially important as they were, they skew the picture of workaday violence in America—and, in any event, the state and its dominant institutions, with the crucial exception of chattel slavery, emerged greatly fortified from both conflagrations.

A second reason why the thrust of American violence has been largely directed away from the nation's vital institutions is our unparalleled racial and ethnic pluralism. Consider how much of our collective violence has been intergroup, how frequently group frustrations have generated displaced aggression against racial and ethnic scapegoats: the Know-Nothings and the American Protective Association; the antiabolitionist mobs; the Irish rampage against blacks in New York in 1863; the terror of the first and third Ku Klux Klans, and the chastisements of the second Klan; the lynching of blacks; the Westerners' attacks upon Orientals; the massive white urban rioting against blacks in the pre-Harlem (1943) pattern of race riots, and the destruction of symbolic private property and attacks upon police in the post-Harlem pattern. Perhaps those New York Irishmen in 1863 should logically have confined their protest against an inequitable conscription law to attacks upon the federal government which imposed it, rather than upon city officials, the mansions of the wealthy, and especially the virtually helpless and blameless blacks. But while local scapegoats were handy, the federal presence was remote—and, once the troops returned from Gettysburgh, far too powerful. Until very recently, no single racial or ethnic group has been numerous or strategically enough located to venture serious frontal aggression against the state. This, of course, does not apply to the historically dominant Anglo-Americans, but the behavior of the state far less often militated against their interests.

Yet a third reason has been American affluence. Too much could be made of this, for we know that abundance has been unequally distributed and that such economic inequities may generate violent protest. And we also know that societies characterized by abject poverty and minimal expectations are unlikely to spawn revolutions. But students of the American franchise have concluded that the increase in national wealth has been paralleled by a general decline of voter participation, to such an extent that only rarely have as many as two-thirds of qualified twentieth-century

Americans bothered to vote even in presidential contests. Contrast this to the high percentage of voting that characterizes most Latin American nations, where the relationship to those in power is so crucial to people's livelihood and where violence and political instability are endemic. Apparently, prosperity as well as poverty can generate apathy. By implication, those tens of millions of Americans who have been insufficiently concerned with public policy to bother casting their votes (this, of course, excludes those disfranchised) are unlikely candidates for attacks on the government.

A fourth reason is closely linked to the economic performance discussed above. The rewarding payoff of American material progress reinforced faith in the legitimacy of the system and sanctified the dominant institutions of the state. It has been a faith of astonishing tenacity, deeply rooted in the wisdom of the Founders; the American Dream of a New Jerusalem, of a City on a Hill; the fetish of constitution worship; the rags-to-riches, log cabin-to-White House mythos; the iron, conservative grip of the liberal consensus. To appreciate the ubiquity of this nationalistic faith, to acknowledge its awesome power, is not necessarily to celebrate it after the fashion of Boorstin and the more conservative consensus historians. From the perspective of our more cynical era, it is astonishing to contemplate its historic grip upon millions of black Americans, whose everyday lives for centuries cruelly mocked and belied it.

The European state, lacking the broad sanction of such a secular faith, encumbered by a feudal past, generally endowed with greater and more centralized power, its population less divided by ethnic and racial heterogeneity, perforce was more vulnerably to violent conflict and to totalitarian self-defense. Recall that in Chapter 3, Charles Tilly has traced the evolution of three basic European forms of collective violence. The first, "primitive" violence, was characterized by diffuse and unpolitical objectives and was based upon communal forms of organization that produced apolitical village brawls and guild clashes, the mutual attacks of hostile religious groups, and the peasant *Jacquerie*. In America, the rioting in colonial seaports, the slave rebellions, the celebrated family feuds, town and gown clashes, the frontier lynching mobs, and wars between sheepmen and cattlemen partook of this primitive, communal character. But lacking a feudal past— to the exclusion of the South's abortive "Reactionary Enlightenment"—America's primitive violence has a more truncated history and has been far less pervasive than that of Europe.

Tilly's second category is "reactionary" violence.

Reactionary disturbances are also usually small in scale, but they pit either communal groups or loosely organized members of the general population against representatives of those who hold power, and tend to include a critique of the way power is being wielded. The forcible occupations of fields and forests by the landless, the revolt against the tax collector, the anti-conscription rebellion, the food riot, and the attack on machines were Western Europe's most frequent forms of reactionary collective violence. The somewhat risky term "reactionary" applies to these forms of collective violence because their participants were commonly reacting to some change that they regarded as depriving them of rights they had once enjoyed; they were backward-looking.[6]

It is at this level that differences between American and European violence are most striking, for the "representatives of those who hold power" in Europe were far more often representatives of the national state and its public institutions than has been the case in America. We have had our Whiskey rebellions, to be sure, but far more predominant in America has been the racial, ethnic, and economic violence of the extrapolitical and intergroup nature that has been discussed above.

THE PARADOX CONFRONTED: EVIDENCE FROM RECENT SCHOLARSHIP

But was this cause for self-congratulation? The more conservative consensus scholars tended to think so, but not their more liberal colleagues, whose sensitivity to the suffering of the poor and the exploited underclass in America inclined them to ask whether the intergroup pattern that was so characteristic of American violence was not a scapegoat phenomenon that played into the hands of conservatives elites. In his probing introduction to *American Violence: A Documentary History*, Richard Hofstadter acknowledged that the United States had a history but not a *tradition* of violence, not only because we had been inclined until quite recently not to remember it, but more importantly because our violence lacked both an ideological and geographical center. So various, diffuse, and spontaneous were our patterns of violence that they lacked the cohesion necessary to forge a tradition of "single, sustained, inveterate hatred shared by entire social classes."[7] Hofstadter saluted the paradoxical dimensions of our violence, conceding its basically noninsurrectionary nature, arguing that its incubation was more urban than frontier, and observing that it was rooted more deeply in ethnic, religious, and racial than in class divisions. He acknowledged that these antagonisms were exacerbated by such national circumstances as weak government, localism, diffusion of authority and power, rapid urbanindustrial growth, massive migrations, and widespread access to guns. But Hofstadter was especially struck by the conservative bias that seemed to characterize so much of America's intergroup violence, unleashing it against "abolitionists, Catholics, radicals, workers and labor organizers, Negroes, Orientals, and other ethnic or racial or ideological minorities," and using it to protect "the American, the Southern, the white Protestant, or simply the established middle-class way of life and morals."[8] So much of it seemed to come from top and middle dogs against the bottom, and this surely helped to explain why so little of it had been directed against state authority and also why it had been so easily and indulgently forgotten.

It remained for Hofstadter's junior editor in the collection, Michael Wallace, to sharpen the indictment that was implicit in his mentor's speculations about the conservative bias of America's intergroup violence. In a cogent essay published in 1971, Wallace rightly complained that American historical scholarship had suffered from lack of participation in the debate being pressed by such students of European collective violence as George Rudé, E.J. Hobsbawm, E.P. Thompson, and Charles Tilly, who argued that it was less irrational than purposive and expressive, a normal and political technique of protest, a claim to social justice, and a demand for change.[9] America had experienced much instrumental turmoil, to be sure, but it was characterized chiefly by its relative scarcity, low level, and lack of challenge to the legitimacy of the state. Surveying patterns of racial, economic, and ethnic violence, Wallace concluded that "American violence has been characteristically repressive,"[10] waged between groups in conflicts that have repeatedly skidded out of the normal political process, the great bulk of it used by dominant groups defending their own positions of privilege. And when state power was occasionally drawn into the fray, it was rarely neutral, and almost always aided dominant elites.

But what could account for this relative lack of revolutionary violence in the United States? Wallace acknowledged that much of the explanation seemed obvious: the liberal American consensus minimized fundamental objections to the bourgeois-capitalist order, and intergroup conflict deflected violence from the weak and fragmented American state, as did widespread white male integration into the political process, and the overlapping quality of American group pluralism. But Wallace saw at the root of our violence a "peculiar" American distinctiveness: "our dominant groups have been, for the most part, *majorities*," and he conceded in an almost crotchety fashion that "American history has been a great success story (in purely material terms) for a large portion of the population."[11] This prompted him to conclude that the repressive ethos of American violence was a prime example of Tocqueville's dictum: it was "but the ultimate form of the tyranny of the majority."

In Chapter 17, Richard Libman-Rubenstein seems to share Wallace's attitude of radical disapproval of the way American material success has blunted class consciousness and focused cultural-group conflict into a fragmented, Balkanized contest for inclusion in the national consensus. In 1970 Libman-Rubenstein (then writing as Richard E. Rubenstein) had argued in *Rebels in Eden* that America's long history of violent episodes constituted wars of group liberation against repressive capitalist elites.[12] Rubenstein was right on target in attacking the self-serving American myth of peaceful progress, but *Rebels in Eden* was grounded in a colonial metaphor that ran afoul of its own evidence, which clearly suggested, as Chapter 17 in this volume even more forthrightly acknowledges, that these were less Third World-type revolts for anticolonial independence than reformist, often defensive assertations of territorial autonomy and group localism. Like Wallace, Libman-Rubenstein acknowledges the iron grip of the liberal consensus while deploring its inequity and its ability so consistently to subordinate class consciousness to culture-group consciousness.

America's out-groups, then, sought not independence but reformist inclusion in the power brokerage of the polity, and if this long and turbulent quest was inconsistent with the myth of peaceful progress, its decidedly nonrevolutionary character was also inconsistent with the radical vision. Both historian Wallace and political scientist Libman-Rubenstein had employed historical analysis within a generalized and implicit theoretical framework that emphasized the primacy of economic or class interests as opposed to cultural or racial/ethnic/local interests, but if their historical depth was admirable, their selection of evidence was less systematic than modern canons of social scientific inquiry demand. Until quite recently there had been no body of American historical research that was comparable to the European work on collective violence of Rudé, Hobsbawm, Thompson, and the Tillys[13]—analysis that was at once historically deep, theoretically explicit, and empirically rigorous. Not until, that is, the publication of William Gamson's *The*

Strategy of Social Protest in 1975,[14] which merits more than cursory summary and comment.

Gamson is a sociologist who shares with Charles Tilly, an historical sociologist, a preference for testing his analysis with historical data, and a theory that is neo-Marxist in its basic assumptions about ruling elite groups and their hammerlock on the polity.[15] In *The Strategy of Social Protest* he is primarily concerned with testing and refuting liberal pluralist theory, as exemplified by Robert Dahl's *Who Governs* and *Pluralist Democracy in the United States*,[16] which emphasizes procedural consensus on the rules of the game, cross-cutting solidarities in overlapping groups, open access to the intermediating group basis of pluralist politics, and therefore multiple centers of power. Gamson sees pluralist theory as the other side of the coin of collective behavior or mass society theory, in that the former emphasizes practical, centrist bargaining and mutual backscratching, while the latter emphasizes the symbolic, abstract and irrational politics of extremist outsiders whose pathological behavior is best understood by social psychologists. Like the Tillys, Gamson rejects the dualism of rational insiders and irrational outsiders and directs his research design toward testing the question of access to the polity, of its permeability.

To do this he focuses historically on the fate of "challenging groups" in the United States between 1800 and 1945 (he excludes contemporary groups because their challenges tend still to be in process, and groups whose constituency is confined to a single state), groups whose chief attributes are that (1) they are seeking to mobilize an unmobilized constituency, and (2) their antagonist lies outside of their constituency. Gamson and his colleagues searched the standard historical and bibliographical literature to generate a universe of 500 to 600 challenging groups, then took an 11 percent equal probability sample that ultimately produced the 53 groups he analyzes. They range from the staid American Association of University Professors to the violence-prone Tobacco Night Riders of Kentucky and Tennessee, and were divided into four broad constituencies: (1) occupational groups, such as blue-collar unions, craftsmen, farm and teacher organizations (20 groups or 38 percent of the sample); (2) reform groups, such as antislavery, peace, civil rights, and third parties (17 or 32 percent); (3) socialist groups (10 or 19 percent); and (4) right wing or nativist groups (6 or 11 percent). Gamson's primary concern was not with violence per se but with the outcomes of such challenges, which were classified along two dimensions of *acceptance* and *new advantages*, which became his dependent variables in a simple percentage analysis (rather than a multivariate regression) to identify the correlates of success and failure.[17]

Gamson's most striking findings is that "unruly groups"—i.e., those using violence, strikes, and other disruptive tactics—were unusually successful in securing acceptance and new advantages. Conversely, groups that were the recipients of violence were very unsuccessful. That is, initiating violence is seen not as a product of frustration, weakness, and desperation, an act of last resort whether by authorities or challengers, but as a symptom of impatience born of confidence and rising efficiency, a relatively safe and productive strategy reflective not of the weakness of the user but of his vulnerable target, a symptom rather than a cause of success. Also positively related to success are such organizational attributes as large size, bureaucracy, centralization of power, and absence of factionalism, and also the pursuit of goals which were single-issue and did not require displacing other groups from power. Clearly, it was more strategically blessed to give than to receive, and the disastrous record of the recipients of violence prompts Gamson to comment that "the restraint which pluralist theory claims for political actors does not cross the boundaries of the polity. One uses only limited means against members, but challengers are fair game for a whole gamut of social control techniques."[18]

Yet Gamson concedes that violence was the exception, that both challengers and authorities normally avoided it, and that when it occurred it was rarely used as a primary tactic. Furthermore, his appended data reveal that *only 28 percent* of his aggrieved challengers became involved with it, and that those split about evenly between success and failure (although the correlation of user with success and recipient with failure was powerful). Moreover, while the majority of all four types of groups avoided violence, the correspondence of group *type* with success or failure seems more revealing (because the total sample involved far more groups and people) than similar correlations of the minority in each category who got involved in violence. For the occupational groups, 60 percent ultimately achieved a full response or successful combination of both acceptance and new advantages. For the reform groups the record is somewhat more uneven, with 41 percent achieving full response, 23 percent preemption, none (somewhat oddly) being coopted, and 35 percent collapsing. But for socialist and right wing/nativist groups the results represent unmitigated disaster, with 90 percent of the former and 83 percent of the latter suffering collapse.

Breaking down such a small sample into such smaller cells yields percentages based on tiny numbers of cases, of course, and the equal probability sample's luck-of-the-draw excluded, for instance, such large instruments of violent social control as the Ku Klux Klan(s) or the White Cap movement. Also, the organizational focus of the study excludes much individual and localized violence, such as violent crime, clan feuds, urban race riots, and the more spontaneous outbursts of lynching and vigilantism. Moreover, compressing historically disparate phenomena into a four-cell paradigm of outcome categories inevitably irritates the historian's sense of uniqueness and evidential subtlety. But even taking Gamson's analysis on its own terms, the relative rarity of violence and the more typical nonviolent collapse of radical groups on both the right and the left in American history could be interpreted as supporting consensus and pluralist notions about broad agreement on the rules of the game and a centrist disapproval of ideological radicalism. The overall picture we get is one wherein 72 percent of the groups in the sample worked out their challenges in nonviolent ways, and when we assess their outcomes by group type, the occupational groups (which tended to be much the largest) did splendidly, and the reformers did fairly well, but the socialist and right wing/nativist groups almost invariably failed. Might not such a portrait thrill Daniel Boorstin, and even Robert Dahl?

Even sociologist Roberta Ash, who shares with Gamson and Tilly a strong disapproval of pluralism, in *Social Movements in America*, her more impressionistic interpretation of the fate of social movements in American history, acknowledged the weakness of the radical right, bemoans the failure of the radical left, and concedes the pervasiveness of American political legitimacy and its tendency to integrate both radical and reform groups into central institutions.[19] Hers is less a disagreement with the liberal consensus uniqueness of American history (she acknowledges her reliance on Louis Hartz) than a denunciation of its effectiveness and its subservience to elites in the cooptation of the radical and reform impulse—as opposed, for instance, to the European experience as exemplified by France,

> Where radicals have repeatedly breached the legitimacy of political institutions . . . because the very power of the center has reduced the number of possible local and peripheral targets for movement activity, forcing it into radical attacks on the center itself; thus almost paradoxically, the power of the center has contributed to the repeated downfalls of central elites.[20]

So we are returned to paradox again, where in America the Lockean-liberal consensus has uniquely combined with Madisonian decentralization, physical isolation, geographic and economic abundance, and frequent invitations to intergroup scapegoating. This combination has produced high levels of violence that nevertheless have been largely deflected from our most vital public institutions, violence that has been more private than state-repressive, as in the European sense, where the Tillys call attention to the opposite paradox.[21] To say that American violence has been paradoxical is to imply that there is something contradictory about the coexistence of violence and relatively stable democratic institutions. But if violence has been a normal concomitant of America's civic culture, then the paradox is more apparent than real, and we have instead what appears to be an almost symbiotic relationship, one that is dynamic but never in equilibrium, one in which democratic institutions invite collective mobilization and protest along a broad spectrum of activity that includes violence but consists primarily of nonviolent action. Violence has been normal, but it has not been the norm. As Gamson says, it has been the spice, not the meat and potatoes.

Since comparison is the essence of social science, it is regrettable that at present we lack a study similar to Gamson's which embraces both Europe and America, and perhaps even other societies as well, in a systematic and historical comparison based on a unified research design (this volume in its rich variety accomplishes much more than that, but it also thereby accomplishes less). But such a study would be an enormous and exceedingly complex undertaking. In its absence, the evidence and analysis that we have suggest, for historical reasons this essay has explored, that when compared historically with violence in other societies, the American pattern has been generally less lethal in lives lost and vital institutions destroyed, and less based on economic than sociocultural conflict. Violence has been more peripheral to the political process, and more reflective of the abrasions of competitive pluralism than desperate combat for survival. We have had our long nightmare of slavery, Indian eradication, brutal lynching, our shameful and still-thriving legacy of citizen gunslinging, to be sure. If our violence has had a conservative bias, it has weighed against radicals of the right as well as the left (although not equally so). But our high levels of violence have surged around and not against our vital institutions, and perhaps have left more long-run hope for short-run losers.

This board historical judgment, which is implicitly comparative and emphasizes some of the more desirable attributes (given the general undesirability of its topic) of American uniqueness or at least difference, must also be mindful of a rapid convergence since World War II between the United States and Western Europe, one which also encompasses Canada, Australia, New Zealand, and to some degree Japan. This convergence has been mutual, based on growing economic interdependence and shared concerns for defense, and reinforced by the accelerated interchange of people, ideas, and popular culture. One could even make a case for the emergence of a shared bourgeois-liberal ideology and two-party equilibrium, coupled with acceptance of a large, quasi-socialist state. This convergence has been mutual in the sense that America has lost her innocence, her splendid and arrogant isolation, her omnipotence and sense of manifest destiny, while other industrial democracies have come to share America's materialism and stability of democratic institutions. The darker side of this convergence is a shared, often imitative pattern (with pronounced local variations) of widespread and disruptive protest, high levels of violent crime, and frequent episodes of terrorism—patterns documented in Chapters 2, 12, and 13. The larger paradox is that everywhere in the West the heightened level of violence seems not to threaten institutional stability. Democracies in the West have devised ways of coping with disorder which protect their core institutions without abandoning democratic processes.

NOTES

1. This chapter incorporates elements of three of the author's previous essays: "The Paradox of American Violence: A Historical Commentary." *Annals of the American Academy of Political and Social Science*, 391 (September 1970): 74-82; the "Conclusion," coauthored with Ted Robert Gurr, to the first edition of *Violence in America* (1969); and *To Establish Justice, To Insure Domestic Tranquility: Final Report of the National Commission on the Causes and Prevention of Violence* (Washington, D.C.: U.S. Government Printing Office, 1969), Ch. 1, 1-16.

2. Preeminent among the consensus analyses have been Daniel Boorstin, *The Genius of American Politics* (Chicago: University of Chicago Press, 1953); David M. Potter, *People of Plenty Liberal Tradition in America* (New York: Harcourt, Brace and World, 1955); Richard Hofstadter, *The American Political Tradition and the Men Who Made It* (New York: Knopf, 1954); and Clinton Rossiter, *Parties and Politics in America* (Ithaca: Cornell University Press, 1960). A useful historiographical critique of the literature of conflict and consensus, which distinguishes between the uni-ideological interpretation of Hartz and the nonideological interpretation of Boorstin, is Bernard Sternsher, *Consensus, Conflict, and American Historians* (Bloomington: Indiana University Press, 1975)—see especially Chapter 5, "The Belated Recognition of Violence in Our Past."

3. Ivo K. Feierabend, Rosalind L. Feierabend, and Betty Nesvold, "Social Change and Political Violence: Cross-National Patterns," in *Violence in America*, 2 (Washington, D.C.: U.S. Government Printing Office, 1969): 497-542; Ted Robert Gurr, "A Comparative Study of Civil Strife," in *Violence in America*, 2, 443-496.

4. Richard Hofstadter and Michael Wallace, eds., *American Violence: A Documentary History* (New York: Knopf, 1970): 11.

5. David M. Potter, "The Quest for the National Character," in John Higham, ed., *The Reconstruction of American History* (New York: Harper and Brothers, 1962): 216. See also David M. Potter, *Freedom and Its Limitations in American Life* (Stanford: Stanford University Press, 1976).

6. Tilly's third category, "modern violence, is based upon a broad associational base that is conducive to large-scale activities which are not intrinsically violent, such as the strike or

demonstration, and that provide leaders with a greater measure of control in striking for rights considered due them, but not yet enjoyed. The modern American labor and civil rights movements are obvious examples. More recently, Tilly has employed a model that distinguishes between competitive, reactive, and proactive forms of collective action that vary in the probability that they will lead to violence. See Charles Tilly, Chapter 3.

7. Hofstadter, op. cit., 3.

8. Ibid., 11.

9. Michael Wallace, "The Uses of Violence in American History," *The American Scholar*, 41 (winter, 1970-1971: 81-102.

10. Ibid., 99.

11. Ibid., 100.

12. Richard E. Rubenstein, *Rebels in Eden: Mass Political Violence in the United States* (Boston: Little, Brown, 1970).

13. The more recent research has been dominated by the Tillys: Charles Tilly, "Revolutions and Collective Violence," in Fred I. Greenstein and Nelson W. Polbsy, eds., *Macropolitical Theory* (Reading, Mass.: Addison-Wesley, 1975): 483-555; Charles Tilly, Louise Tilly, and Richard Tilly, *The Rebellious Century 1830-1930* (Cambridge: Harvard University Press, 1975); and Charles Tilly, *From Mobilization to Revolution* (Reading, Mass.: Addison-Wesley, 1978).

14. William A. Gamson, *The Strategy of Social Protest* (Homewood, Ill.: Dorsey, 1975).

15. The theoretical debate over the causes and meaning of collective violence is intense and generally involves a polarization between proponents of Marxist or solidarity theories, especially the socioeconomics of resource mobilization (RM) on the one hand, and on the other pluralist theories and especially the social psychology of relative deprivation (RD). A useful critique of both bodies of theory is David Snyder, "Collective Violence: A Research Agenda and Some Strategic Considerations," *Journal of Conflict Resolution* (September 1978); and a revealing exchange is Elliott Curie and Jerome H. Skolnick, "A Critical Note on Conceptions of Collective Behavior"; and Neil J. Smelser, "Two Critics in Search of A Bias: A Response to Currie and Skolnick," in James F. Short, Jr. and Marvin E. Wolfgang, eds., *Collective Violence: The Annals of the American Academy of Political and Social Science*, 391 (September 1970): 34-55.

16. Robert Dahl, *Who Governs?* (New Haven, Conn.: Yale University Press, 1961), and *Pluralist Democracy in the United States: Conflict and Consent* (Chicago: Rand-McNally, 1967).

17. Gamson relied heavily on the judgment of professional historians in "interviewing " documents and secondary books with his elaborate questionnaire, which contains 103 items, and is conveniently included in the appendix together a brief description of the 53 groups, a discussion of sampling procedures, the basic codes and raw score data, and a brief discussion of some negative results. His four-cell paradigm for assessing outcomes of resolved challenges is as follows: Full response and collapse represent relatively unambiguous success and failure, cooptation means acceptance without new advantages, and preemption means new advantages without acceptance.

18. Gamson, op. cit., 141-142.

19. Roberta Ash, *Social Movements in America* (Chicago: Markham, 1972).

20. Ibid., 231.

21. Tillys, *Rebellious Century*, 257, et seq.

Chapter 20
Alternatives to Violence in a Democratic Society

TED ROBERT GURR

The belief that democratic societies are insulated by their political values and institutions from violent conflict is historically a myth. Events of the 1960s laid it to rest in the United States and most European societies. The paradoxical character of violence in democracy, analyzed by Hugh Davis Graham in the preceding chapter, is on its way to being recognized as a truism: disruptive conflict is as common in democracies as elsewhere but ordinarily it focuses on limited issues and rarely threatens dominant political and economic institutions. Or so it seems. Since Western democracies have fallen before the onslaught of revolutionaries, for example in Germany in the early 1930s and Czechoslovakia in 1948, even this generalization has limited applicability: democracies are resistant to revolutionary challenge but not wholly immune to it.

Meanwhile citizens and officials in democratic societies, the United States in particular, must deal with hard questions about how to cope with the recurring fact of violent conflict. Group violence has a private face and a public face: it is used by those out of power and those in power. So there are two sets of questions. First, when are private groups warranted in the use of violence in a society that professes democratic procedures, and what consequences should they expect? On the public side of the equation of conflict are questions about whether and when it is legitimate for those in power in a democratic society to respond violently to the opposition of private citizens, and what practical alternatives they have to meeting force with force.

The answers to these questions in the United States are constrained by constitutional theory. The United States is not a pure, majoritarian democracy. Its constitution guarantees a "republican form of government," and hence its political institutions were designed not only to ensure the majority a decisive voice in most political decisions, but also to protect the rights of minorities against potential abuse by majorities. The constitutional concern for minority rights constrains the use of

AUTHOR'S NOTE: *The author is Payson S. Wild Professor of political science at Northwestern University. His many books and monographs include* Why Men Rebel, *which won the Woodrow Wilson Prize as the best book in political science in 1970, and* Rogues, Rebels, and Reformers: A Political History of Urban Crime and Conflict *(Sage Publications, 1976).*

force by majorities against minorities, even if the majority wills it, and by implication it gives minorities an ultimate right of self-defense against an abusive majority.

The realities of political power also limit answers to questions about responses to violence. A government in power is always tempted to tilt its policies to favor its own interests and those of its supporters. There are privileged minorities as well as disadvantaged ones, and the ever-present risk is that when conflict comes to a violent head, especially empowered minorities will be better served than other groups. Constitutional prescription and institutional checks-and-balances limit but do not eliminate the possibility of favoritism; the ultimate redress is the electoral success of a majority in opposition. So it must be recognized at the outset that, constitutional democracy being imperfect in practice, public responses to private challenges will often be less than even-handed.

From the viewpoint of both constitutional theory and democratic practice, responses and alternatives to violence can be judged only by reference to the issues and groups involved. Neither justice nor public order are served if the same public response is meted out to a large aggrieved minority demanding reform and a band of revolutionaries using armed violence against the state. The analysis begins by categorizing some historical examples of group demands which have given rise to violence in the United States. The second part of the essay identifies several basic strategies of public response to group demands. This foundation of historical fact provides a basis for speculation about the strategies most likely to enhance civil peace.

ORIGINS OF GROUP VIOLENCE

The disorderly skein of violent conflict in American history is more understandable if we concentrate on three of its major themes. Some groups have organized for the purpose of defending a threatened status quo, others have sought limited or "reformist" ends within the existing system, while still others have declared themselves in open rebellion against it. All these objectives can be pursued without leading inevitably to violent conflict; conflict turns violent when a group pursuing one of these objectives encounters the resistance of another, public or private group. The potential for violence and the prospects for reducing or avoiding it depend most fundamentally on who is seeking what from whom.

Defensive Groups

Defense of the status quo has been the most common source of group violence in American history. A central theme of the growth of the American Republic has been flight from external oppression and resistance to its reappearance in the New World. Thus colonial settlers in America resisted British, French, or Spanish imperialism, settlers on the Appalachian frontier opposed seaboard authorities, and enthusiasts of local or states rights fought against metropolitan or national encroachment—as in New England during the late eighteenth century, in Texas in the 1840s, and in the South during the Civil War era. Among the episodes reviewed by Brown in Chapter 1 are Shays' Rebellion in Massachusetts, 1786-1787; Fries' Rebellion in eastern

Pennsylvania, 1798-1799; some of the activities of the Grangers, Greenbackers, and Farmers' Alliance after the Civil War; and the "Green Corn Rebellion" of Oklahoma farmers during the First World War. Most of these frontier rebellions and rural uprisings were centered on the hinterland's opposition to change in the form of onerous political restrictions or economic centralization and its attendant disloca- tions. The reformist rhetoric of the yeomen and the agrarian liberalism of the populist should not be discounted as disingenuous or paranoid, for their suffering was genuine and their rebellions heartfelt. But neither should it obscure the common theme of their defense of local conditions against disruptive changes that were externally imposed, whether by governmental policy or mysterious economic forces. The farmers' march on Washington in spring 1978 and their threat of withholding cropland from production was one recent manifestation of collective rural resistance to threatening external conditions.

For more than two centuries America's aboriginal settlers, the Indians, resisted the encroachment of white settlers in a series of raids, wars, and "disturbances," sketched briefly by Jeanne Guillemin in Chapter 11. From King Philip's War in colonial Massachusetts, 1675-1676, to the last rising of the Sioux in South Dakota in 1890-1891, it is well-nigh impossible to find a major episode of conflict in which the Indians sought anything more than preservation of their territory and way of life. Whites too saw themselves in a defensive role, defending the outposts of expanding civilization against the depredations of "savages," whose very right to existence they were prepared to deny.

The Indian wars contributed to a strain of aggressive vigilantism that has been a recurrent response of white middle- and working-class Americans toward outsiders or lesser classes who seemed to threaten their status, security, or cultural integrity. The most celebrated examples come from the expanding frontiers, where more than 350 vigilante movements existed between the 1760s and 1900. They were found in almost every state and territory outside the Northeast and claimed the lives of more than 700 men. All were organized by private citizens who concluded that they had no other effective way of establishing and preserving law and order. Not all vigilantes operated on the Western frontiers, either. Brown has traced in Chapter 6 the course of such vigilante groups as the "Regulators" of pre-Revolutionary South Carolina and the Bald Knobbers of the Missouri Ozarks in the late nineteenth century, and the largest vigilante movement of them all, which dominated San Francisco in the middle 1850s.

The frontier vigilantes are distinguishable more in style than substance from the Ku Klux Klan, which rode three times in less than 100 years. Each time the Klan sought to defend a way of life that was threatened, not by crime but by social change. The first Klan was founded in 1867 in resistance to Reconstruction. It used political pressure, coercion, threats, and widespread violence in a ten-year campaign, which ended only when blacks were resubjugated and their Northern Republican sympa- thizers relinquished control of Southern state governments, as described by Garson and O'Brien in Chapter 8. The second Klan flourished in the 1920s. Its strength was nationwide in the East, Midwest, and Pacific states, as well as the South. Most of its victims were not the blacks, Catholics, or Jews railed against in Klan propaganda, but white Protestants who failed to abide by the Victorian moral code of small-town middle America. The third Klan arose in the 1950s among working class Southerners who feared the effects of civil rights for black Americans on their own precarious position.

The spirit of vigilantism is far from dead in contemporary America. Racial tensions in the 1960s spurred the rise of neo-vigilante organizations among urban Americans, both black and white. At the same time there was sporadic harassment of "hippie" communes in rural and small-town America. These brief flashes of violent resistance to social change were followed by vigilante-style opposition to court-ordered school busing and midnight raiding on behalf of environmental causes. Most of these were isolated, local episodes and seldom had the deadly consequences of nineteenth-century vigilantism, but they shared much of its style and spirit of group defense.

All these defensive movements were based on deeply felt grievances. But some of the movements were long-lived and intensely violent, while others were short-lived. There were two crucial differences among them: their extent of support and the responses of political authorities. Responses are considred in a later section; here we need only point out the importance of popular support. Vigilantes usually had the support of the "better sort" of citizens in the territories where they operated, and they were numerous and effective as a result. The purposes if not the tactics of the first Ku Klux Klan were enthusiastically endorsed by almost all white Southerners and its purposes were achieved, though the Klan itself was discredited by the very tactics that helped put an end to Reconstruction policies. The third Klan, by contrast, could win little public support for campaigns of violence against civil rights workers; its cause is lost and its organization a faint shadow of its predecessors. The essential point is that violence arising from defensive movements is likely to be a serious and persistent occurrence to the extent that it is based on grievances that are deeply and widely felt, and go unremedied.

Reformist Groups

The demand for reform has been the second most common source of violent conflict in American history. Whereas defensive violence originates among groups that have mobilized to resist change, reformist violence arises from the organized advocacy of change. Obviously defensive and reformist violence may be two different names for the same phenomena, the clash of those seeking change with those resisting it. Our focus here is on the kinds of groups that have mobilized in hopes of achieving change.

American history is studded with ethnic violence but rarely before the 1960s did it arise out of the organized demands of ethnic minorities. It is true that American society has been especially vulnerable to the frustrations of rising but disappointed expectations, for Americans proclaimed their country the "land of opportunity" and invited millions of destitute immigrants to partake of its fulfillment. Many sought and achieved individual mobility, others failed. But rarely did those who felt excluded organize and press their demands collectively to the point of violence. Anti-Irish and anti-Italian riots of the nineteenth century and race riots before the Second World War were initiated by groups further up the socioeconomic ladder who felt threatened by the prospects of Catholics or blacks getting "too big" and "too close." Janowitz describes the character of early twentieth-century race riots in Chapter 9. The first large-scale mobilization of an ethnic group for collective action occurred among blacks in the 1950s, in the form of the civil rights movement. It has since inspired many emulators among other ethnic and segmental groups, including Hispanos, Indians, women, and even some traditional white ethnic groups like the Italian-Americans. Some Americans may not know that the current hostilities in Northern Ireland began in 1969 with a peaceful civil rights movement among Irish Catholics that was directly modeled on the American civil rights movement. Almost all organized advocates of minority and woman's rights in the United States have advocated peaceful dissent, and their activists have seldom initiated violence. The civil rights marchers, for example, were frequent targets of violence but never its agents. When massive violence did erupt, in the ghetto riots and rebellions of 1964 to 1970, it was the unorganized who rioted, not the organized. Even during these years, civil rights demonstrators outnumbered rioters and looters by a large margin, as documented in Chapter 2, Table 2.2.

The history of American labor conflict between the 1870s and 1930s illustrates more clearly the path from group mobilization on behalf of reform, to confrontation between organized forces for change and organized resistance. Each decade saw hundreds of bloody clashes between workers and employers. They often claimed dozens of lives a year, 200 of them between 1902 and 1904 alone. The 1913-1914 labor war in the Colorado coal fields was the single most violent incident in American labor conflict. It involved pitched battles between union men and the National Guard, and ended only after 74 men, women, and children had been killed. As Taft and Ross show in Chapter 7, violence in these labor-management conflicts was seldom a deliberate tactic of working-class organizations. Usually it was the result of forceful employer resistance to workers' efforts to organize and the use of nonviolent but then-illegitimate tactics, like the strike and picket line. Companies repeatedly resorted to coercive and sometimes terroristic activities against union organizers and used violent tactics to break strikes. Violence by employers often provided both model and impetus to retaliation in kind by workers, leading in many situations to an escalating spiral of violent conflict to the point of military intervention or mutual exhaustion. The National Guard and federal troops repeatedly were ordered to intervene; they did so on at least 160 occasions. In many industries, including railroads, urban transportation, coal, and steel, violent strikes occurred time and time again. Neither side "won" permanent victories and neither side conceded permanent defeat.

Another source of violence on behalf of reform has been opposition to war, reviewed by Brooks in Chapter 10. In the War of 1812, the pacifist citizens of Plymouth, Massachusetts, seized their prowar congressman and kicked him down the main street of town. During the Civil War, Southerners violently resisted the draft in half a dozen states. In New York City, antidraft mobs of 50,000 fought police and troops for five days in July 1863 at a cost estimated as high as 1,300 lives. Pacifists were more often violated than violent, though. During the First World War pacifist meetings and marches were attacked time and again by "patriots." In Collinsville, Illinois, a young German was lynched and his killers were acquitted after their attorneys called the act a "patriotic murder." Some other pacifists and socialists were killed, many were beaten or jailed. In the 1960s an estimated three million Americans took part in hundreds of demonstrations against the United States' involvement in the Vietnam War. Almost all the 1,600 people injured in these demonstrations were activists who were attacked by angry supporters of the war and, occasionally, by police. By 1969, though, some war resisters had soured on peaceful dissent and resorted with growing frequency to the violence of firebombs and high explosives, culminating in the campaign of the Weather Underground described by Bell and Gurr in Chapter 12.

The pattern which emerges when we look at reformist movements is that their members are more often victims than attackers. This is not to say that American reform movements have been genteel! Strikes, walk-outs, sit-ins, building occupations, and massive demonstrations may not be violent but they are disruptive. And reformers have seldom turned the other cheek when attacked. They have been more inclined to drop their placards and use their fists. But the seriousness of violence arising out of reformist movements does not depend directly on how deeply and widely felt the reformers' grievances are. It depends largely on how violently the reformers are oppposed, and by whom. Reformist protest on behalf of widely supported causes is not likely to cease until some change has been achieved. Reformist violence is minimized when those who oppose the reformers use nonviolent means.

It is not difficult to understand why reformers are usually less violent than those who defend the status quo. Most reformers in the United States have thought they had more to lose and less to gain from violence. This is one of the ironies of democracy as practiced in America: reformers have been hopeful enough of success to try to avoid violently antagonizing the Establishment, while the Establishment has often felt so threatened by the reformers' chances of success that coercion was necessary.

Rebellion

The essence of rebellion is complete rejection of superior political authority in favor of a new political system. The two deadliest conflicts in American history illustrate the two paths rebellion may take: depending on the rebels' circumstances and strategy, they seek revolution or autonomy. In the Revolutionary War the colonists seized power from British officials, in the Civil War the South attempted to secede from the Union. Neither conflict need necessarily have been violent: the British crown might have let the colonials go without a fight, and the Republican administration in Washington in 1861 might have been equally benign toward the South. But those in power rarely cede it without a struggle.

With the exception of the Revolutionary and Civil Wars, serious separatism and revolutionary movements have been remarkably rare in American history. I suggest above that the Shay, Whiskey, and other "rebellions" were defensive movements with limited objectives, not full-fleged attempts to secede from the Union. Much the same can be said of two briefly successful "revolutions" at the state level: Dorr's Rebellion in Rhode Island (1842) and the White League's armed seizure of power in New Orleans (1874). But the historical landscape contains no serious attempts to carry out a populist or socialist revolution in the United States, despite the precedents provided by France in 1789 and again in 1848 and 1871, or by Russia in 1917, or China in 1949. Nor have the South or the West or New England or even Hawaii talked seriously of seceding from the Union, not since the 1860s.

Revolution in the United States during the past century has fascinated groups such as the Industrial Workers of the World, the Socialist Worker's Party, and the Communist Party, but only a few tiny bands of activists ever tried to implement a revolutionary strategy by relying on what anarchists called "propaganda of the deed"—terrorism, to use the contemporary term. Here lies a source of confusion, because the *tactics* of terrorism, including bombings and assassinations, have been fairly common in the United States both historically and at present (see Chapter 12 by Bell and Gurr). But with rare exceptions the tactics have been used by defensive groups like the Ku Klux Klan, not by revolutionaries.

Some political terror in the 1970s has had revolutionary objectives, just as it did for a handful of radical labor organizers at the turn of the century. Police in black ghettos were attacked in a short-lived campaign of the Black Liberation Army because they were symbols and agents of a white Establishment. Public buildings, banks, and corporate offices were bombed by young revolutionaries in a more sustained but equally ineffectual campaign to overthrow rather than reform the same Establishment. And a small band of Puerto Rican nationalists continue a sporadic 30-year campaign of symbolic violence on behalf of a cause supported by less than a tenth of natives of the island. In none of these campaigns have the terrorists received significant support from the group for whom they claim to act, no more than did labor terrorists three generations ago. Most of their potential supporters have been too apolitical or too deeply committed to reformist movements to be attracted by revolutionary martyrdom.

On the Outcome of Group Violence

The outcomes of private resorts to violence are problematic. The most visible mark of success is the capitulation of government in the face of rebels, but this is not the only or necessarily the best criterion of "success." In a recent study of the fates of a sample of protest groups in American history, William Gamson defines their success according to whether they secured acceptance and new advantages.[2] A still more precise criterion is the extent to which the grievances which give rise to collective protest and violence are resolved. Even revolutionary victories do not necessarily lead to complete success in these terms. The American Revolution placed effective political control to the hands of the colonists, but eventually led to an expansion of state and federal authority that diminished local autonomy to the point that uprising broke out in frontier areas over essentially the same kinds of issues that had caused the revolution. The Bolshevik revolution of 1917 ended Russia's participation in the First World War, which was perhaps the greatest immediate grievance of the Russian people, and in the long run it brought great economic and social benefits; but the costs of the 1918-1920 civil war, famine, and totalitarian political control were enormous.

If revolutionary victory is unlikely in modern democracies, and uncertain of resolving the grievances that give rise to revolutionary movements, are there any circumstances in which less intensive private violence is successful? In Gamson's study, cited above, he found that American groups which initiated violence, including strikes and other disruptive tactics, were more likely than others to win acceptance and advantages. But violence was rarely a primary tactic of the groups he studied, which leaves open the question of whether and when disruptive tactics of themselves are likely to be successful. I suggest that private violence can succeed when both the tactics and objectives of violence are widely regarded as legitimate. The vigilante movements of the American frontier had widespread public support as a means of establishing order in the absence of adequate law-enforcement agencies, and were generally successful. The Ku Klux Klan and similar organizations of the Reconstruction era similarly had the sympathy of most white Southerners and were instrumental in reestablishing and maintaining the prewar social and political status quo. Both movements occurred in regions whose inhabitants were acclimatized to violence. Southerners had just fought a much bloodier Civil War to defend privileges they now sought through interracial and anti-Republican violence, while probably the majority of Western vigilantes were veterans of the Mexican-American, Civil, or Indian wars.

The chronicles of American labor violence, however, suggest that violence was almost always ineffective for the workers involved because their objectives usually were not widely supported. In a very few instances there was popular and state governmental support for the grievances that had led to violent confrontations with employers, and in several of these cases state authority was used to impose solutions that favored the workers. But in the great majority of cases the public and officials did not accept the legitimacy of labor demands, and the more violent the conflict, the more disastrous the consequences for the workers who took part. Union organizations involved in violent conflict seldom gained recognition, their supporters were harassed and often lost their jobs, and tens of thousands of workers and their families were forcibly deported from their homes and communities.

A similar principle applies, with two qualifications, to peaceful protest. If demonstrations are regarded as a legitimate way to express grievances, and if the grievances themselves are widely held to be justified, protest is likely to have positive effects. One qualification is that if public opinion is neutral on an issue, protest demonstrations can have favorable effects. This appears to have been an initial consequence of Southern Freedom Rides and civil rights demonstration of the early 1960s on opinion in the North. If public opinion is negative, however, demonstrations are likely to exacerbate popular hostility. In the ante-bellum North, for example, abolitionist demonstrations frequently were broken up by mobs, and in 1860 none of the four presidential candidates embraced the unpopular abolitionist cause. During the First World War, pacifist demonstrations were attacked, with widespread public approval and sometimes official sanction. Contemporary civil rights demonstrations and activities in the South and in many Northern cities have attracted similar responses.

The second qualification is that when violence occurs during protest activities, it is rather likely to alienate groups that are not fundamentally in sympathy with the protesters. I mentioned above the unfavorable consequences of labor violence for unions and their members, despite the fact that violence was more often initiated by employers than by workers. In the long run, federally enforced recognition and bargaining procedures were established, but this occurred only after labor violence had passed its climacteric, and moreover in circumstances in which no union leaders advocated violence.

The evidence supports one basic principle: force and violence can be successful techniques of social control and persuasion when used for purposes which have extensive popular support. If such support is lacking, their advocacy and use are ultimately self-destructive, either as techniques of governmeth or of opposition. The historical and contemporary evidence of the United States suggests that popular opinion tends to sanction violence in support of the status quo: the use of official violence to maintain public order, the use of private violence to maintain popular conceptions of social order when government cannot or will not. If these assertions are true—and not much evidence contradicts them—the prolonged use of force or violence to advance the interests of any segmental group may impede and quite possibly preclude reform. This principle is a fundamental trait of the American character, one which is ignored by advocates of any political orientation at the risk of broken hopes, institutions, and lives.

ALTERNATIVE RESPONSES TO POLITICAL VIOLENCE

Different types of political violence call for different types of public response. The first question is just what an ideal "democratic response" might be. Presumably it is the set of policies that restores civil peace with the least pain, and the most gain, for society at large. In the United States the major constitutional constraint on this principle is that minority rights are to be respected in the process, which means that majorities may sometimes be required to accept a modicum of discomfort in order to ensure equity to minorities. The practical political constraint is that majorities, and privileged minorities, will seldom surrender significant advantages without putting up a fight themselves. So there is no one ideal strategy. That which restores civil peace in one circumstance may foment civil war in another. Three basic kinds of strategy have been used historically by American officials in response to political violence: acquiescence, control, and reform.

Acquiescence

The easiest response to political violence is sometimes to do nothing. Federal and state officials seldom interfered with vigilantes; the vigilantes were often doing state and territorial governments a favor, even if outside the limits of the law. During the same era that Westerners were violently ridding their new towns of undersirables, Southern lynching parties were disposing of some 2,000 blacks who had transgressed the white social code. The lynchings rarely attracted any more governmental attention than did vigilantism, perhaps less. The reasons may have been different but the situation was the same: private citizens were allowed to use murderous violence against other private citizens with impunity. In neither circumstance did officials think that their or the public interest was seriously threatened.

Passivity in the face of violence may have been practicable in nineteenth-century America; it can be decisively rejected in the late twentieth century. Public and private interests both oppose such a policy. First, contemporary society is less tolerant of private violence than it once was and is more likely to learn of the occurrence of serious incidents via the mass media. Public demands for the restoration of order thus can be expected to be more insistent than they were on the frontier or in the South after the Civil War. Second, the United States is a much more thoroughly governed and policed society now than in the nineteenth century. Officials even more than the public are committed to maintaining public order, and they have most of the necessary means of control at their disposal. It is still possible for instances of violent, unregulated conflict to be ignored by local officials; elected peace officers are not likely to have searched diligently for the strikers responsible for sporadic violence in the 1977-1978 coal strike, for example. But such situations are increasingly rare, especially as state and federal agencies are watchfully ready to step in when local control falters.

Control: The Official Uses of Force

The more common official response in America has been to suppress outbreaks of violence, not to ignore it. The more threat violence has posed to the nation's political and economic institutions, the more likely it is that authorities will attempt to contain it. But there are two quite different strategies of control, as well as intermediate strategies that combine elements of both.

Events at Kent State University, Ohio, in the spring of 1970 were typical of a strategy of control that has been employed hundreds of times over the past century. The clash began with the actions of a disruptive, sporadically violent group of protesters. Outside forces were called in to restore order. The inevitable confrontations occurred and finally fatal shots were fired. The most unusual thing about events at Kent State was that they occurred on a campus; traditionally they were more likely to take place in city slums or outside factory gates. The aftermath again was typical. Investigations were conducted, commissions of inquiry met, grand jury indictments were returned, but no clear and binding determination of guilt or innocence has ever been made. And the residue of bitterness was the source of recurring confrontations as recently as 1978. Kent State was typical of *reactive control* and distinct from a strategy of *preemptive control*.

Preemptive control of political violence involves two governmental tactics. One is the use of intelligence activities to anticipate violent confrontations, the other is preventive force to keep those situations cool. The details of these tactics became quite familiar in the 1960s and early 1970s. They included surveillance of potential "trouble-makers," infiltration of activist groups by informers and agents provocateurs, the harassment and arrest of influential activists, and saturation police tactics during demonstrations and incipient riots. Historically there are few American examples of intensive surveillance because only in the last few decades have law enforcement agencies developed effective means of surveillance and exchange of information. But the use of spies, harassment of activists, and massive preventive force have ample American precedents, especially in labor-management conflicts.

Neither reactive nor preemptive responses to group violence may satisfy liberal ideals about how democratic governments should deal with dissent, but force is widely believed to be effective. The revolutionaries who inherited the doctrines of Frantz Fanon and Che Guevara tell us that if those who use it are dedicated and presistent enough, revolution can always be accomplished. The vehement advocates of "law and order" hold essentially the same faith: the sufficient use of official violence will always deter private violence. This fundamental agreement of radicals and conservatives on the effectiveness of force for modifying others' behavior is striking. But to what extent is it supported by theory and by the historical evidence reviewed in this book?

The two most fundamental human responses to the use of force are to flee or to fight. This assertion rests on rather good psychological and ethological evidence about human (and animal) aggression. Force threatens and angers people, especially if they believe it to be illegitimate or unjust. Threatened, they will defend themselves if they can, flee if they cannot. Angered, they have an innate disposition to retaliate in kind. Thus people who fear assault attempt to arm themselves. Americans fearing a crime wave are infected by a rage to punish; according to public opinion surveys, two-thirds or more of white Americans in 1967 thought that black looters and arsonists should be shot. Governments facing violent protest often regard compromise as evidence of weakness and devote additional treasure to counterforce. Yet if a government responds to the threat or use of violence with greater force, its effects may be identical to the effects that dictated its actions: its opponents will resort to greater force.

There are only two inherent limitations on such an escalating spiral of violence and counterviolence: the exhaustion of one side's resources, or the attainment by one of the capacity for genocidal victory. There are societal and psychological limitations as well, but they require tacit bonds between opponents: one's acceptance of the ultimate authority of the other, arbitration of the conflict by neutral authority, recognition of mutual interest that makes bargaining possible, or the perception that acquiescence to a powerful opponent will have less harmful consequences than resisting certain death. In the absence of such bases for cooperation, regimes and their opponents are likely to engage in violent conflict to the limit of their respective abilities.[3]

To the extent that this argument is accurate, it suggests one more kind of circumstance in which violence succeeds: that in which one group so overpowers its opponents that they have no choice short of death but to desist. This was the point to which American Indians had been pushed a century ago. As with the eternal peace Rome brought to once-troublesome Carthage, history records many instances of successful uses of overpowering force. Not surprisingly, the list of successful official violence against opponents is much longer than the list of dissident successes against government, because most governments have much greater capacities for violence, provided they keep the loyality of their generals and soldiers. Some dissident successes discussed in this volume include the American Revolution, and white Southerners' successful resistance to the first Reconstruction. Among the many governmental successes in the United States are the North's victory in the Civil War and the quelling of riots of the 1960s.

Official violence is likely to be successful in quelling specific outbreaks of private violence except in those rare circumstances when the balance of force favors its opponents, or the military defects. But the historical evidence also suggests that governmental violence often succeeds only in the short run. The government of imperial Russia quelled the revolution of 1905, but in doing so it intensified the hostilities of its opponents, who mounted a successful revolution twelve years later, after the government was weakened by a protracted and unsuccessful war. The North "won" the Civil War, but in its very triumph created hostilities that contributed to one of the greatest and most successful waves of private violence in our history. The 17,000 Klansmen of the South in the 1960s were neither peaceable nor content with the outcome of the "War of Northern Aggression." State or federal troops were repeatedly dispatched to quell violent or near-violent labor conflict and were immediately successful in almost every case, yet did not deter subsequent labor violence.

The long-range effectiveness of public force in maintaining civil peace seems to depend on three conditions: public belief that governmental use of force is legitimate, consistent use of that force, and remedial action for the grievances that give rise to dissidence.

Remedial Strategies

Remedial strategies are those that are directed at the cause rather than the symptoms of political violence. There is some debate about whether "conspiracy" or "alien ideologies" are causes of political violence. Of course they can be causes, but only contingent ones: they contribute to political violence only when they operate on prior grievances. The remedial strategies are directed at the grievances, and are of three distinguishable types.

The *paternalistic strategy* is to attack the immediate symptoms of grievance. If people are unemployed, as millions were during the Depression of the 1930s, the paternalistic approach is to put them on the dole or public assistance. It also is represented by the welfare approach to the problems of the poor. It makes individuals lives more bearable in the short run but of itself provides no long-run solution.

The *accommodation strategy* is to increase opportunities within the existing system for discontented individuals. The accommodation approach to unemployment is to create new jobs, directly by work projects, indirectly by "pump-priming" and job training. It is essentially the approach taken by the federal government to black Americans' demands for improvement in their economic status. By giving blacks (and Hispanos and women) equal access to occupational training and higher education, and by assuring them fair treatment on the job market—using quotas if necessary—the strategy of accommodation gives potential dissidents an individual stake in existing institutions.

The strategy of accommodation may lead to gradual but ultimately very substantial changes in the distribution of economic and political power. Those who have wealth, power, and status in American society today are far more heterogeneous in ethnic background then they were 100 or even 50 years ago. But this is the result of individual mobility. The *radical reform strategy* requires a direct adjustment in the structure of political and economic power by improving the status of collectivities as such. The collectivities may be communities, associational groups, people with a common ethnic origin, classes, or even biologically defined groups—women, the elderly, the handicapped. The crux of the radical reform approach is that groups acquire some of the means necessary to resolve their grievances themselves. Just what those necessary means are depends on the collectivity and its needs. They may include rights: to organize, to be represented in decision-making, to raise and spend funds. They may also include more tangible benefits: government grants, group-administered service programs.

The radical approach has the sanction of American political tradition. It was colonial Americans' solution to their painful dependence on Britain: by seizing power they improved their capacity to help themselves. The principle was institutionalized when they established the decentralized structure of American government. Each state and settlement retained a significant measure of authority to manage its own affairs and resolve its own problems—though in this century the federal government has steadily encroached upon state and local autonomy. The principle was extended only grudgingly from political communities to associational groups. The struggle of the labor movement to obtain recognition and rights was the great breakthrough, and demonstrates aptly how radical reform can resolve some kinds of conflict.

Violent conflict between labor and management has abated in the past 50 years partly because of growing prosperity, but more fundamentally because employers now have almost universally recognized unions and will negotiate wage issues and other grievances with them rather than retaliate against them. The movement toward recognition and negotiation was strongly reinforced when workers in most occupations were guaranteed the right to organize and bargain collectively by the National Labor Relations Act of 1935. The act has been effective not just because it established procedures, but because of the concerted effort to enforce them by the National Labor Relations Board and the willingness of both employers and unions to recognize the board's authority. Their willingness is a testimony also to their own and public dismay at the destructiveness of earlier conflicts. It is worth emphasizing that in this situation the long-range consequence of radical reform was a decrease not increase in violent conflict. In fact, violence was chronic so long as union recognition was denied. The outcome suggests the inadequacy of arguments that concessions inevitably breed greater violence.

There are other, more recent applications of the same kind of principle. Black Americans have sought recognition as a collectivity since the 1950s and in the give-and-take of politics they have been acknowledged as such—as many ethnic groups were before them. They have had less success in efforts to develop effective community organizations or to obtain greater control of community affairs at the neighborhood level. The flight of middle-class whites to the suburbs provides an unintended solution in some cities: where black urban majorities elect black municipal administrations, they have achieved a measure of community control. Another kind of example is provided by the changed status of college and university students on most campuses. Part of their political quiescence in the late 1970s can be credited not only to the end of the draft or a renewed concern with "making it," but also to the great increase in social and political rights won by student organizations from university administrations during the 1960s. Tribal Indians did not have to struggle, like blacks and students, to win recognition as collectivities; the federal government has treated them as such from the beginning. But in the past they were treated as wards of the state, while the 1970s they have gained much more control over social services, education, and use of their land and natural resources.

The principle of conferring rights and resources on quasi-autonomous groups has its limits as a means of conflict resolution. The stronger and more self-assertive each newly empowered group, the more likely it is to collide with the individual and collective rights of outsiders. If the principle is applied too widely and well, the likely consequence is an increase in intergroup conflict. But the social costs of such routinized conflict between more or less equal collectivities are probably less than the persistence of festering pockets of poverty and powerlessness.

OPTIMUM STRATEGIES FOR CIVIL PEACE

Each strategy of response to group violence has disadvantages that must be weighed against its historical successes. If one asks which is most desirable for democracy as planned and practiced in America, again there is no single, unambiguous answer. The most appropriate strategies depend on the social basis of violence. It is necessary to consider the underlying cause—revolutionary, reformist, or defensive—and how much popular support it commands.

Terrorism on behalf of revolutionary causes arouses great public concern but if it serves only the interests of little clusters of militants, it is potentially easy to deal with. It must be recognized at the outset that the grievances of political revolutionaries can seldom be satisfied by nonrevolutionary means. If they are incompetent or isolated, they deserve little attention. When they threaten public safety or confidence, though, preemptive control is likely to be both necessary and sufficient. This strategy presents problems for democracy only when police agencies exercise too must zeal and too little discrimination. It is particularly important that police, prosecutors, and judges dealing with revolutionaries and other dissidents follow due process and respect democratic liberties. To the extent that they violate democratic norms in the quest for order, they lend support to the revolutionaries' claims.

What if revolutionaries have potential large-scale support? They may give voice to widely shared grievances of people who otherwise disavow the tactics of violence and would prefer the slow certainties of reform to the disruption and uncertain outcome of revolutionary conflict. This has been the situation of much of the black community and many students in times recently past: they have sought radical reform but rejected violent, revolutionary means to achieve it. In this circumstance preventive control can work only if remedial strategies are also followed. Revolutionary terrorists believe that the Establishment will prove them right by using force rather than reform. If an Establishment does use all force and no reform, revolution is indeed one step closer.

The solutions to violence in defense of the status quo depend on who is violating the status quo. If it is government itself, the alternatives are only to back off, or to persist. If some larger justice demands persistence—which it does for civil rights, for example—then preventive control over violence is needed first of all. Second to that is remedial action to compensate for the pain of change. It requires only a little social insight to see that poor Southern whites or urban blue-collar workers would be less opposed to racial equalization if their own life prospects were better.

Reformist movements are the other common stimulus to status quo violence. In this case reformist and status quo violence are two sides of the same coin: a democratic solution to one must embody a solution to the other. This situation is always the most difficult because whatever mix of strategies is used, some substantial group is likely to get hurt. Doing nothing can be quickly ruled out as a response because it means that the contending groups will go on fighting until one wins—which may be never. Even if victory comes early, the social costs are not democratically tolerable. The federal government tolerated them in the South after the Civil War, at the cost of renewed subjugation of freed slaves. But "good" democracies do not tolerate the oppression of one group by another.

The same thing must be said about the contemporary demands of white Southerners, black activists in the inner cities, and millions of other Americans for community control and relief from government interference—demands made in the name of democratic values. It is not a "radical reform" for the democratic Establishment to give over full responsibility for local affairs to those who will use it as a license for oppression. Communities' petitions for democratic decentralization are valid only insofar as they practice democratic tolerance of local minorities and dissidents. Higher levels of government are obliged to retain sufficient authority that democratic liberties can be protected at the local level.

When the status quo and reformist movements meet head on in violent conflict, the optimum response must be a mix of control and remedial strategies. If control alone is used, both groups will likely be at one another's throats whenever control is relaxed. This was for many decades the official American response to violent industrial disputes: to send in the National Guard. But time and again the Guard's departure saw the resumption of conflict. And the controlling forces may find themselves under attack from both sides as well, which was the unhappy circumstance of the British army in Nothern Ireland throughout the 1970s.

If remedial strategies are used alone, the contending groups are likely to go on fighting, which makes reform more difficult if not impossible. Reforms cannot be introduced if order is wholly lacking, and reforms will not be made if those who have the means to make them are constantly in jeopardy. The immediate cost of continued fighting is human loss. The further cost is uncompromising hatred, which will veto any future solution.

In summary, democratic leaders who are charged with responsibility for outbreaks or threats of group violence can respond in two ways. They can forcefully tighten up social control, or they can exert public effort and encourage private efforts to resolve the issues that give rise to violence. Increased control is usually necessary to reestablish peace. Remedial strategies must be followed simultaneously if enduring civil peace is sought—with the specific strategies depending on the groups and issues at conflict. One common and potent contemporary strategy is "radical reform" in the guise of granting more rights, power, and resources to disadvantaged groups, in the expectation that they can work out solutions themselves. One can be skeptical about the prospects for radical reform if it requires officials and those they represent to give up some of their own powers and privileges. In this circumstance the radical critic expects dissent to be met with force and nothing else. Yet the historical record does not warrant such pessimism. Grudgingly and with much tumult, the dominant groups in American society have moved over enough to give immigrants, workers, and women better—not the best—seats at the American feast of freedom and plenty. Many of them think the feast is bounteous enough for dissatisfied students, Indians, blacks, and the Hispanos. Whether there is a place for young militants who think the feast has gone rotten, no historical or comparative evidence we know of can answer, because absolute, revolutionary alienation from society has been very rare in the American past and no less rare in other prosperous democracies.

NOTES

1. This chapter synthesizes and extends arguments previously made by Hugh Davis Graham and the author in the conclusion to the 1969 edition of *Violence in America,* and by the author in "A Historical Perspective" in *The Response to Political Violence through Democratic Means,* proceedings of a National Institute cosponsored by Catholic University Law School and The American Jewish Committee (New York: American Jewish Committee, Institute of Human Relations, October 1972).

2. William A. Gamson, *The Strategy of Social Protest* (Homewood, Ill.: Dorsey, 1975). The findings are summarized by Hugh Davis Graham in Ch. 19.

3. This discussion is drawn from arguments and evidence in Ted Robert Gurr, *Why Men Rebel* (Princeton: Princeton University Press, 1970), Ch. 8. The survey results are from Hazel Erskine, "The Polls: Demonstrations and Race Riots," *Public Opinion Quarterly,* 31 (winter 1967-68): 655-77.

INDEX

Reuther, Walter, 234
revolution,
    demands for in U.S., 323-324, 485, 498-499
    global frequency of, 49
    ideology of, 501
    J-curve theory of, 282-283, 411-412, 415-436
    as motive for conflict, 69-71
    and terrorism, 330-345
    in Western countries, 72, 85-86
    See also American Revolution; France,
        Revolution of 1789; rebellion; Russian
        Revolution
revolutionaries:
    government responses to, 504
    in U.S. labor movement, 188-189
Richard, L. L., 46n
Richardson, James F., 44n, 320, 326n
Riddle, Walter A., 470n
Riley, James Whitcomb, 140
riots, stages in, 266-269
    See also collective violence; interracial
        riots in U.S.
Rister, Carl Coke, 181n
Ritchie, Thomas, Jr., 24
Robbins, Terry, 335
Robinson, Jacke, 431
Rockwell, George Lincoln, 26
Rodgers, William Warren, 237n
Roe, E. P., 137
Rogers, Henrietta G., 180n
Ronfeld, David, 346n
Roosevelt, Pres. Franklin D., 431
Roosevelt, Pres. Theodore, 32, 174, 205, 219
Rose, James A., 179n, 181n
Rose, Thomas, 41n, 185n
Rosebault, Charles J., 184n
Rosen, Bernard C., 409n
Rosenbaum, H. J., 185n
Rosenbaum, Ron, 347n
Rosenberg, Charles E., 42n
Ross, Philip, 15, 48n, 147, 187, 441, 495
Rossiter, Clinton, 489n
Rothert, Otto, A., 44n
Rothstein, Arnold, 28
Rothstein, David A., 42n
Rubenstein, Richard, see Libman-Rubenstein, Richard
Rudé, George, 116, 117n, 320, 484, 485
Rudolph, Lloyd I., 46n

Rudwick, Elliot M., 284n, 452n
Russel, Robert B., 436n
Russell, Charles A., 347n
Russett, Bruce M., 116n 408n
Russian Revolution (1971), 427, 497, 502
Ruthenberg, C. E., 238n
Ruttenberg, Charles, 74n

Sabean, David, 117n
Sale, Kirkpatrick, 453n
Salem, Mass., history of crime, 360
San Francisco Labor Council, 222
San Francisco State rebellion (1968), 57 317
San Francisco Vigilance Committee (1856) 31-32, 147, 154, 156, 161, 164, 172 174-175, 177, 178n
San Jose State College, 317
Sanders, Wilbur Fisk, 164, 174
Santayana, George, 411
Satten, Joseph, 43n
Savitz, Leonard, 45n
Scandinavia, crime rates, 363-365
Schaar, John H. 408n
Scharf, J. Thomas, 324n
Scherer, A. B., 182n
Schiff, Jacob H., 184n
Schlesinger, Andrew Bancroft, 46n
Schneider, John C., 36, 46n
Schwab, Charles, 230
Schwartz, David C., 74n
Schwartz, Michael, 117
Scott, Rev. William Anderson, 177, 185n
Seale, Bobby, 453n
Sears, David O., 76n, 285n
Sears, Robert R., 409n
Second World War, 478
    dissent against, 314-315
Sederberg, Peter C., 185n
Sedition Act (1918), 314
Sefton, James F., 259n
Seidman, David, 372n
Sellers, Charles G., 310, 324n
separatism,
    in Western countries, 68, 111, 331-332
    in U.S., 448, 496-497
    See also Civil War
Settle, William A., 43n
Shalett, Sidney, 43n
Shalloo, J. P., 44n, 238n
Shannon, Fred, 291, 304n
Shannon, Lyle, 408n